Lighthouses & Coastal Attractions of

Northern New England

Lighthouses & Coastal Attractions of
Northern New England

Allan Wood

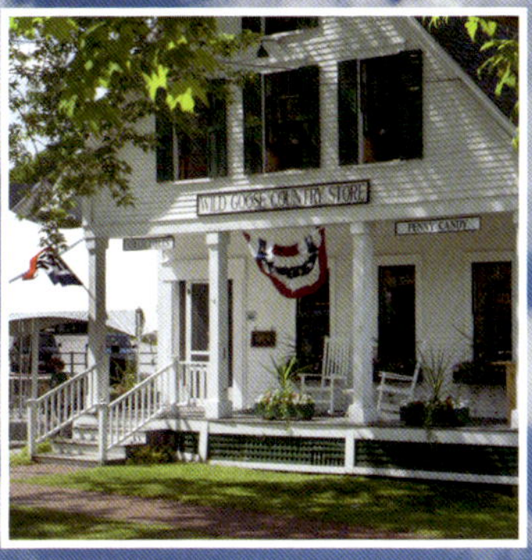
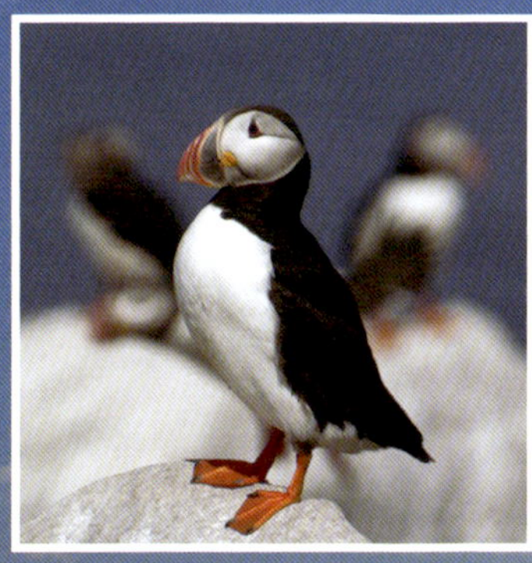
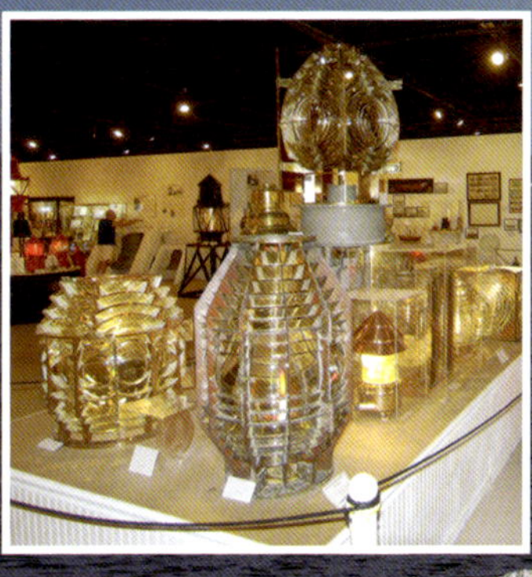
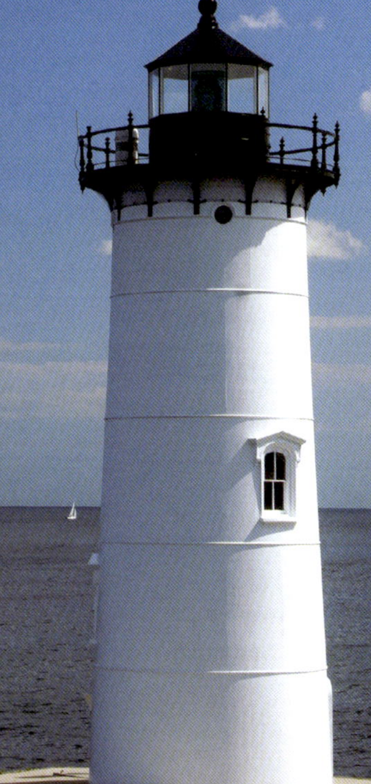
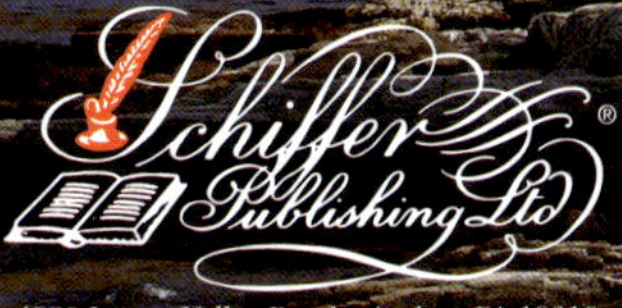

4880 Lower Valley Road • Atglen, PA 19310

New Hampshire | Maine | Vermont

Library of Congress Control Number: 2016954740

All images are by the author unless otherwise noted.

Designed by Matt Goodman
Cover design by John Cheek

Type set in Minon & Trade Gothic

ISBN: 978-0-7643-5235-5
Printed in China

Published by Schiffer Publishing, Ltd.
4880 Lower Valley Road
Atglen, PA 19310
Phone: (610) 593-1777; Fax: (610) 593-2002
E-mail: Info@schifferbooks.com
Web: www.schifferbooks.com

DEDICATION

This book is dedicated in memory to my parents, who recently passed, for their constant support in any endeavor or project I chose in life. My dad, Larry Wood, always loved to take the back roads, away from the highways to explore the communities around him. His "short cuts" usually took a lot longer than planned, but the views and new attractions were worth the ride. He also won the battle against alcoholism, and spent the last thirty-nine years of his sobriety helping others battle this disease. My mom, Kay Wood, always taught me to be committed, never give up, and take on any challenges with a sense of humor. This book is also dedicated to those service members and local individuals in their community where they live in or serve, past and present, who risked their lives to help those in peril, because it was their duty, or because they felt it was the right thing to do. Thank you.

CONTENTS

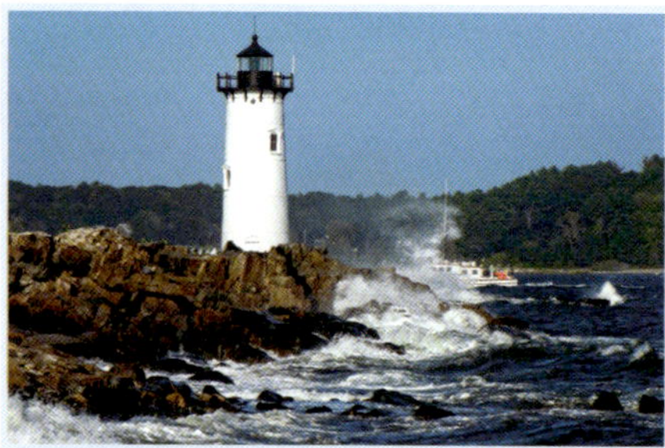

Fishing boat heads home past Portsmouth Harbor Lighthouse through rough surf.

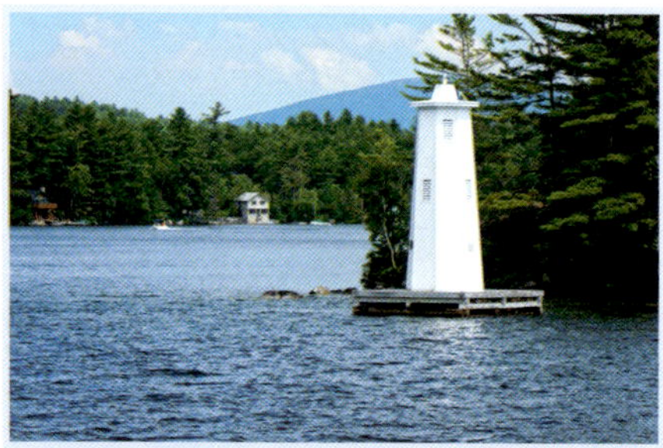

Herrick Cove Lighthouse on Lake Sunapee, New Hampshire.

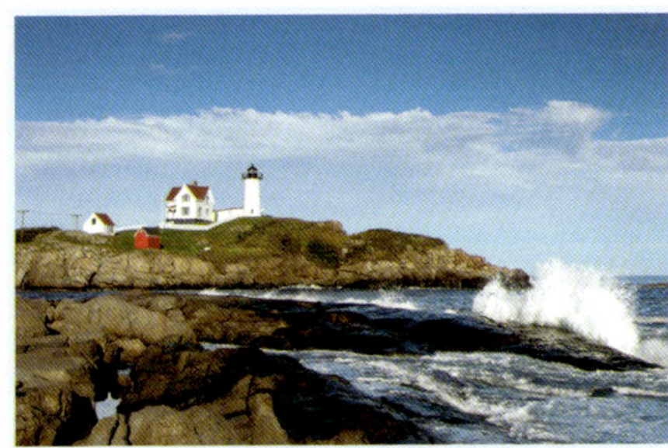

Waves crashing at Cape Neddick (Nubble) Light.

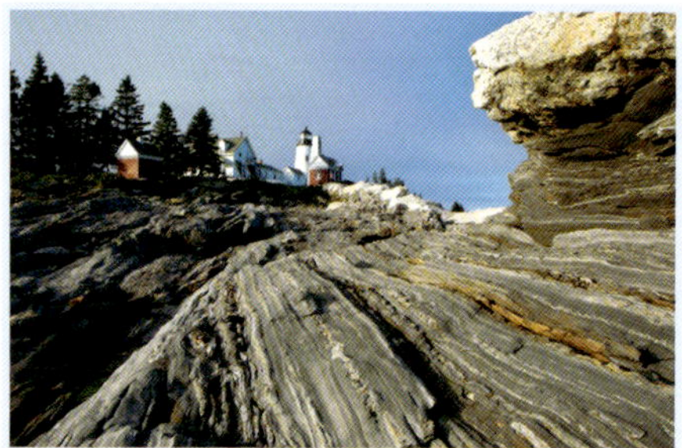

Rock formations lead to Pemaquid Point Lighthouse.

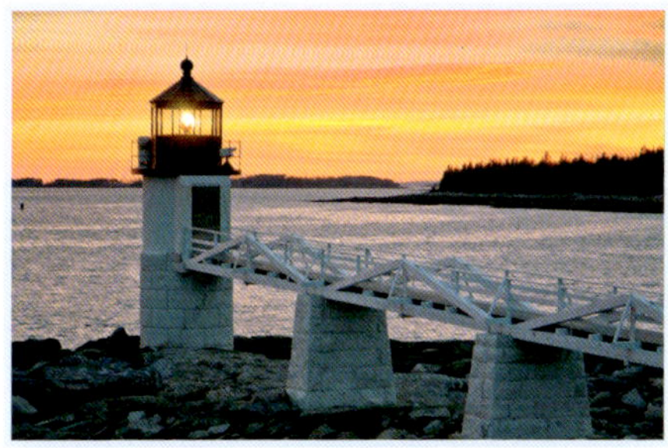

Sunset at Marshall Point Lighthouse.

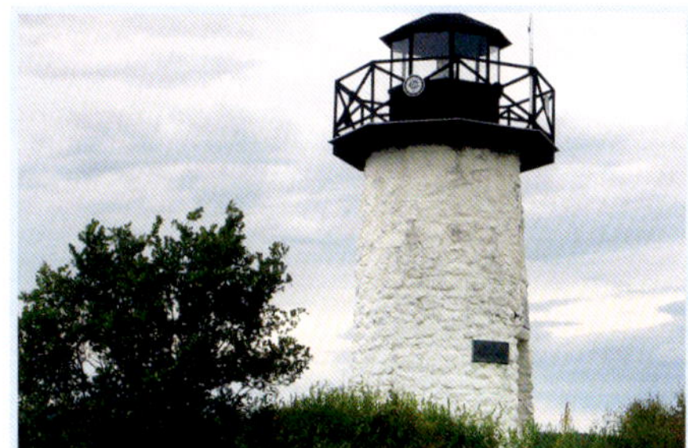

Cobbossee (Ladies Delight) Lighthouse is Maine's only inland lighthouse.

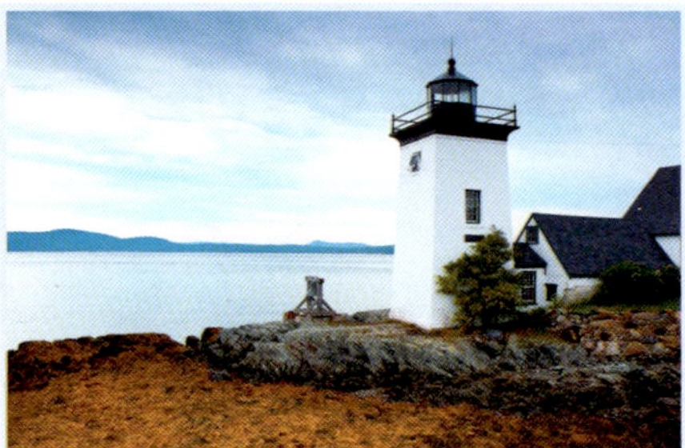

Grindle Point Lighthouse on Islesboro Island.

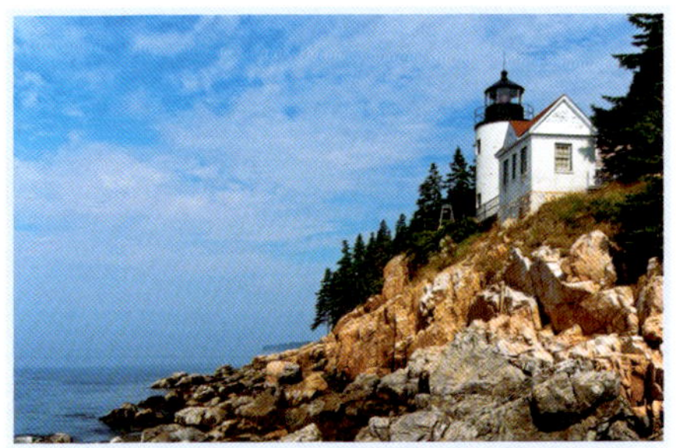

Bass Harbor Lighthouse is one of the most photographed beacons in New England.

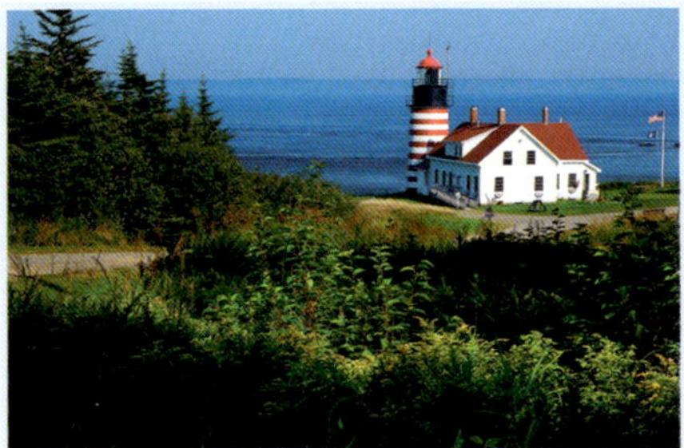

West Quoddy Head Lighthouse lies in the easternmost corner of the United States.

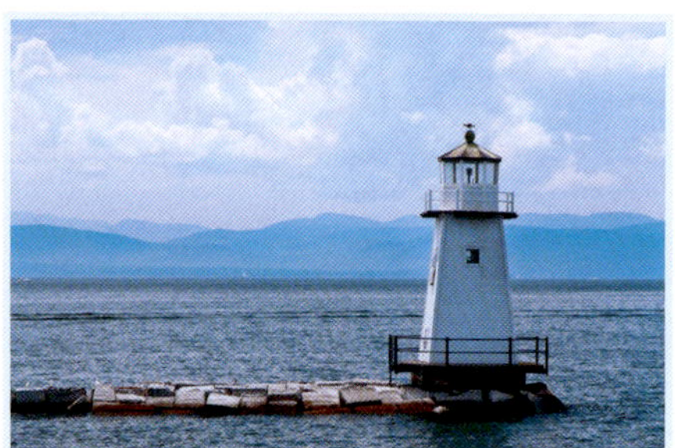

Burlington North Breakwater on Lake Champlain.

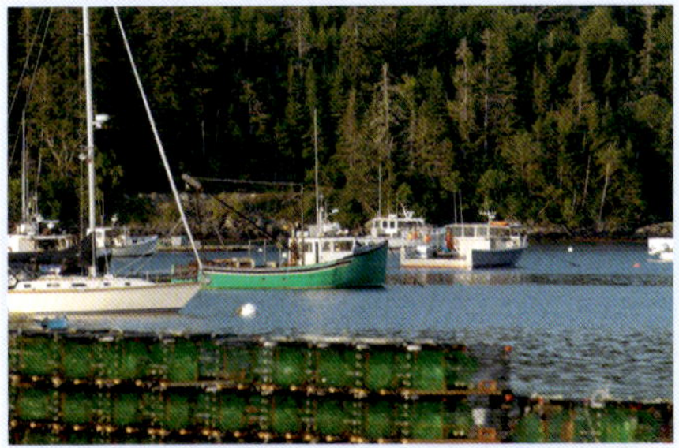

Sailing and lobster boats in Cutler Harbor in northern Maine.

Acknowledgments

Thank you to the following people and organizations for their contributions:

The folks at Schiffer Publishing for their support and belief in this book.

The US Coast Guard for their public domain vintage images.

I also want to thank my parents for allowing me to follow the path less traveled, my wife Chris for her constant support in any endeavor or special project that comes my way, and my two boys for their constant humor that keeps me grounded.

Introduction

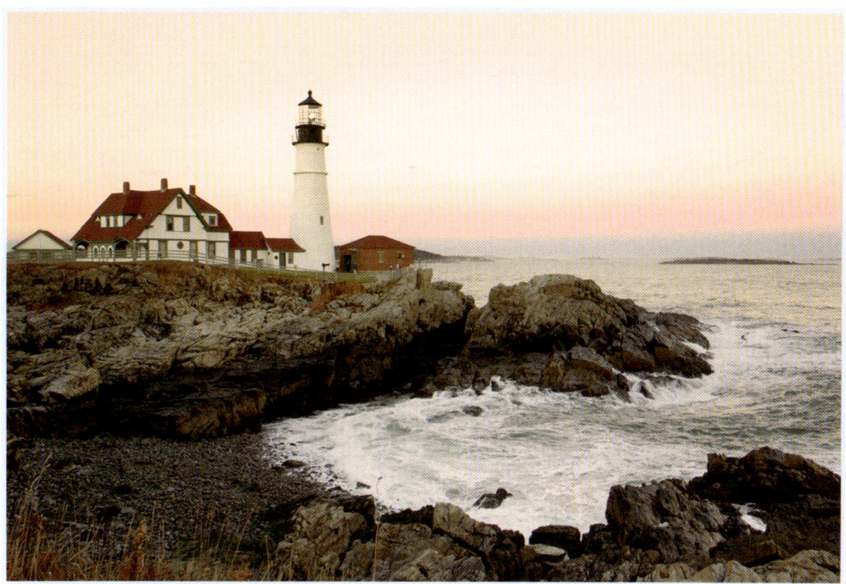

Dusk descends on Portland Head Lighthouse in Maine.

Lighthouses signify endurance and strength. They have acted as guides for mariners, fishermen, tourists, and immigrants alike. They not only beckon us to come and learn about their history, but also to explore their surrounding coastal communities. As one of the many "lighthouse hunters" who enjoys researching and photographing New England's lighthouses and scenery, I often found myself trying unsuccessfully to find information on nearby attractions, and I wanted to read about the lighthouse human interest stories. I decided to write this book to educate, share stories about the lighthouses, and offer current information on local culture, thereby establishing a connection between these beacons and the communities they protected. Welcome to your Northern New England lighthouse travel guide!

This book contains my own photographs of Northern New England's seventy-six lighthouses, along with vintage lighthouse images courtesy of the Coast Guard. It also includes human-interest stories of events that took place at each lighthouse, and lots of resource information for each beacon. Included are hiking and driving directions to marinas, town landings, and harbor docks, along with boat cruises to lighthouses in each region. Illustrative maps show the locations of groups of lighthouses, and there is contact information for organizations involved in the care and maintenance of these beacons in each state.

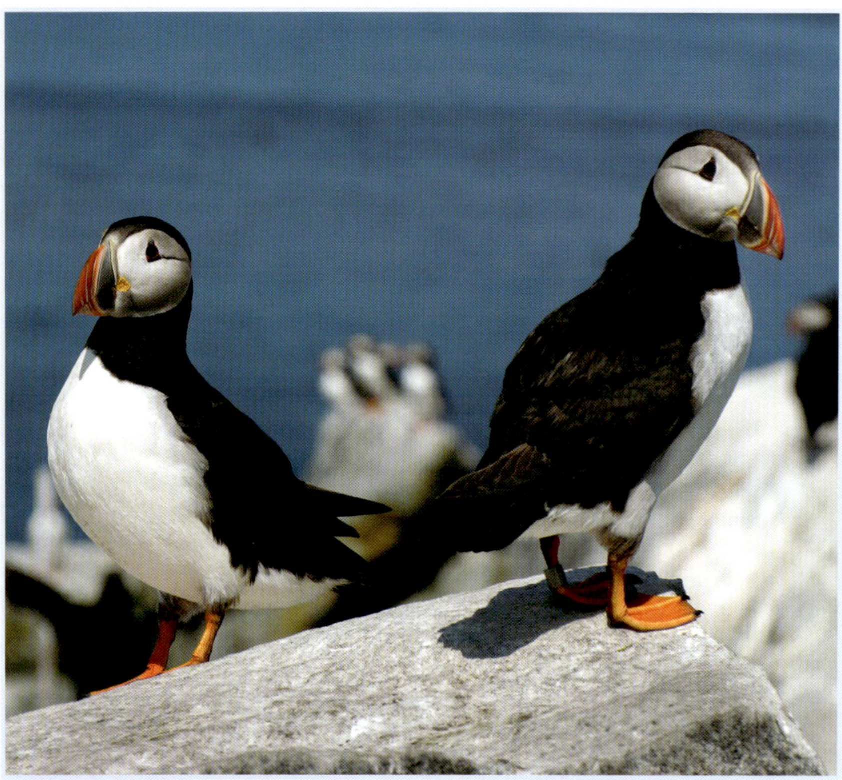

Puffins on one of Maine's protected coastal islands.

You'll also find descriptive information on coastal attractions near the lighthouses. These may include parks, museums, and special out-of-the-way attractions, so you can explore not only the historical aspects of each lighthouse, but also their surrounding communities. Contact information is also provided for attractions in each region.

In the appendix are additional resources, such as a brief glossary of mariner terms and contact information for companies that offer cruises on windjammers, tall ships, and other types of vessels. There is also a compilation of haunted Northern New England lighthouses and their stories, as well as lighthouses that provide overnight accommodations.

Lighthouse History

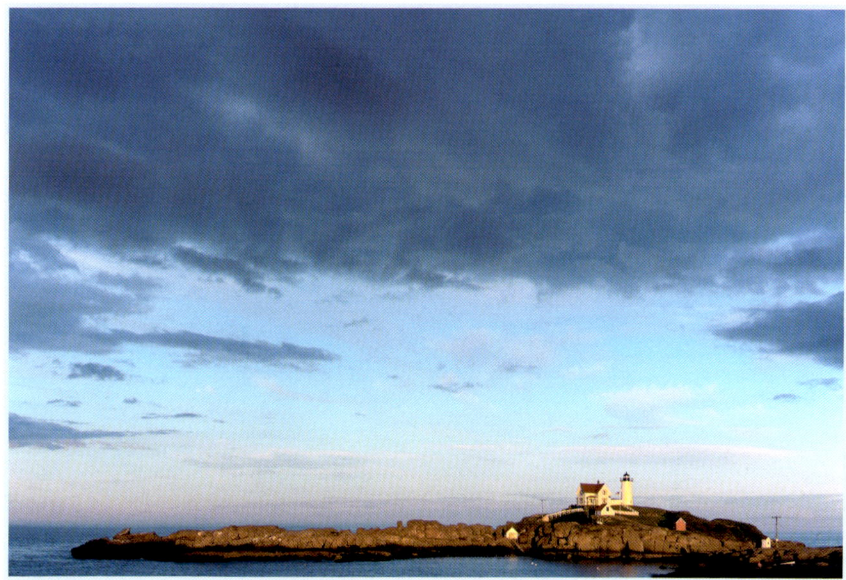

Cape Neddick (Nubble) Lighthouse as storm approaches at sunset in Maine.

New England has arguably the most dangerous populated coastline in the world. As the population along the coast dramatically increased in the early eighteenth century, this in turn created many shipping ports to accommodate the advance of shipping, fishing, and whaling trades coming into the region, and commercial products being exported. With New England's many surprising and violent storms, many shipwrecks occurred on the many ledges, reefs, shoals, and sandbars that populated the New England coastline. As these incidents increased in the seventeenth and eighteenth centuries, petitions were filed requesting a warning fire or reflective device to keep mariners from getting stranded. During the early period, locals would post lanterns from a house, hang an enclosed fire on a pole, or light a fire inside a tar-filled barrel. They would also place food and survival supplies on ledges or islands for stranded shipwreck victims.

The first lighthouse, Boston Harbor Lighthouse, in Massachusetts, was built in 1716. By the time the Constitution had created the Lighthouse Establishment Act, which became the law of the land in 1789 under federal control, twelve lighthouses were already built in the United States. It was at this time that lighthouse control passed from the states to the federal government's Treasury Department as the US Lighthouse Service.

During the eighteenth and nineteenth centuries, with the continued increase of commerce and immigration, lighthouses were built all along the East Coast to warn mariners of dangerous natural formations and guide traffic into busy ports and harbors. Due to congressional budget constraints, these early lighthouses were usually contracted to the lowest bidder. Their often cheap and shabby construction

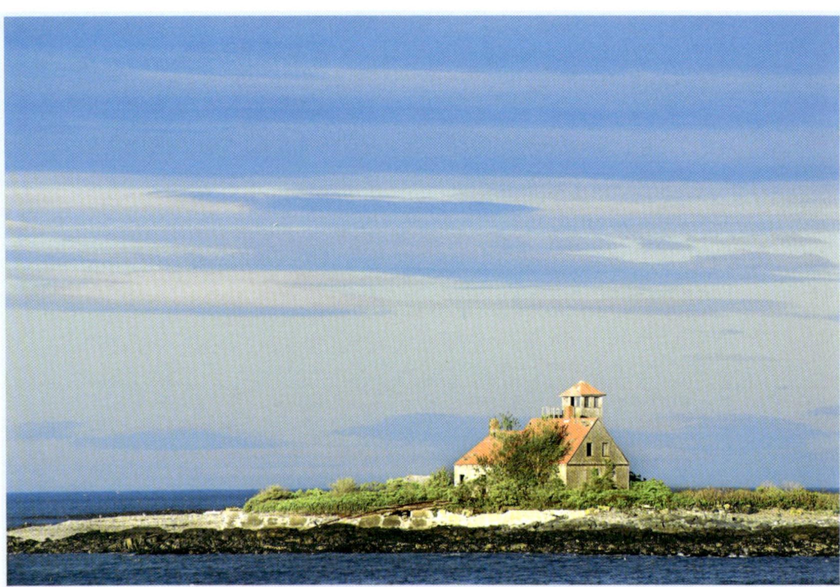

Wood Island Lifesaving Station, on the New Hampshire and Maine border across the Piscataqua River.

deteriorated rapidly, causing the beacons and surrounding buildings to be replaced after a decade or so of operation. Many keepers and their families had to bear the constant dampness, mold, and dangerous conditions. Many got sick, and some died, from exposure to these elements.

After receiving many petitions, in 1852 Congress created the United States Lighthouse Board to improve its beacons. This board of experts would oversee the construction of high-quality lighthouses that provided consistent illumination. They introduced the expensive but accurate Fresnel lens and recruited responsible keepers. The board also established a qualified inspector for each of the nation's twelve districts. These inspectors and their appointed assistants were responsible for maintaining the lighthouses and ensuring that the keepers upheld the highest standards. Published guidelines, rules, and procedures were developed for lighthouse staff, along with a *Light List* publication for mariners describing each region's navigational aids.

Keepers and their assistants were to maintain the lights at all costs. Their daily tasks involved tending the wicks, fueling the tanks, polishing the brass, cleaning the soot off the lenses and prisms, and maintaining the tower and surrounding buildings. They would also participate in nearby rescues. Their rescue equipment consisted of a rowboat or lifeboat, and lines and life preservers for hauling survivors into the boat. The light had to be kept burning, especially during a storm.

After the Civil War, with commerce and tourism continuing to expand along the coast, lifesaving stations were built within five to ten miles of lighthouses to service a broader area. This idea of having shore-based stations began with trained volunteers set up by the Massachusetts Humane Society and spread to other states. Congress established the US Life Saving Service in 1871. The units, also referred to as surf stations, consisted of a keeper, or captain, and trained crew of six to eight men, with the necessary buildings to house them and their equipment.

Massachusetts was also the first state to use range lights. To distinguish the entrance to the harbor in Newburyport during colonial times, mariners routinely set bonfires or erected poles that held torches on the northern end of Plum Island. In 1783, two "day beacons" were put up. The Marine Society of Newburyport, a predecessor to the US Lifesaving Service, hired men to raise the lanterns to the beacons each night. These twin lights at Plum Island are believed to be the first time range lights were employed. Over the years, range lighthouses were built. They appeared to mariners as two lights on the horizon; however, when they were lined up correctly, they would appear as one atop the other, or one behind the other. A mariner would then know that he was on the correct path into the channel. Range lights were helpful around constantly shifting sandbars and channels caused by New England's fierce storms, especially at the mouth of rivers emptying into the ocean. Today most range lights have been deactivated or removed, except in Maine, where range lights still guide mariners along a sharp bend on the Kennebec River.

Whereas lighthouse keepers and their assistants were only allowed to attempt rescues near the lighthouse, life saving stations could assist a larger number of distressed survivors on a wreck some distance from shore. The stations had a more mobile force that was specifically trained for rescue. These mostly volunteer crews were in service from fall until late spring when the New England weather was most dangerous. They were proudly called "soldiers of the surf" or "storm warriors." They completed many successful rescues because of the nearly daily drills and provided shore patrols within five miles on either side of the station. Many surf men risked their lives to save shipwrecked victims, and some received lifesaving medals from the federal government or the humane society.

Lightships were used in the late 1800s as mobile floating lighthouses at dangerous locations, or in busy shipping channels where it was not possible to build a lighthouse. Both the lighthouses and lifesaving branches were programs of the US Lighthouse Service.

The Revenue Cutter Service was initially involved in rescue efforts on open waters, and later coordinated its efforts with the Lighthouse and Lifesaving Services. In 1915, the US Lifesaving Service, US Lighthouse Service, and Revenue Cutter Service merged into what we now know as the Coast Guard

Fresnel Lenses

Lighthouses in the early 1800s were constructed with the same solid, steady lights of the same white color. These early beacons made it difficult to distinguish one lighthouse from another, often causing confusion and dangerous conditions for passing ships, and for mariners caught in New England's surprise storms and fog banks.

A French physicist named Augustin Jean Fresnel introduced a prism glass lens that revolutionized lighthouse optics in 1822 and made waterways safer for mariners around the world. The use of prisms allowed rays of light that would normally scatter in all directions to be concentrated and magnified as a single beam. The

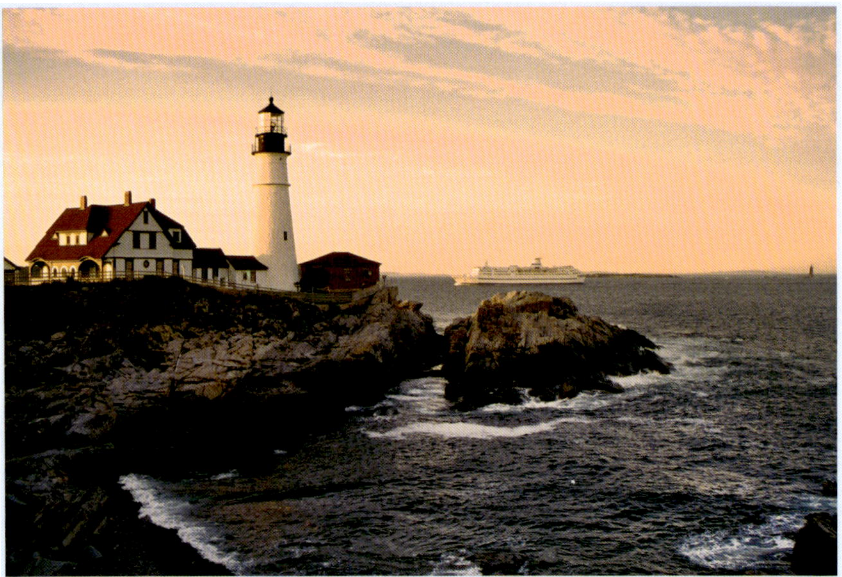

Fresnel lenses displayed at the Rockland Lighthouse Museum in Maine.

development of this type of lens also had the ability to produce individual light patterns called characteristics. This provided for an almost unlimited combination of light beams and flashes, depending on the number of flash panels and the speed at which the lens revolved. Originally, a clockwork-type mechanism was used to rotate the Fresnel lens around the lamp to produce a flash. Later, with individual flash patterns, lighthouses along the coast were easily differentiated and recognized. Although most lights still flashed a white beam, some were set up as flashing red or green lights, or combinations of the two, to further distinguish one beacon from another.

Fresnel lenses were divided into different sizes, called orders. The first-order lens was the largest and most powerful, standing at twelve feet in height and more than six feet in diameter. It was used primarily as a seacoast light to warn of approaching dangerous headlands or indicate the most prominent points for mariners to navigate around or toward. These giant lenses had a concentrated beam visible over twenty miles out to sea. Other orders were used depending on the strength of the light beam needed. The second-order lens was installed on lighthouses marking the mouths of large rivers and harbors, or dangerous shoals surrounded by shallows. The third-order lens was used to protect mariners at the mouths of rivers and to mark entrances to roadsteads and vessel anchorages around harbors and inlets. Fourth-order and fifth-order lenses marked the entrance to smaller ports or harbors, or the direction of a strait, or a river's current. The sixth-order lens is the smallest lens, about one foot wide, and is used in small harbors and channels.

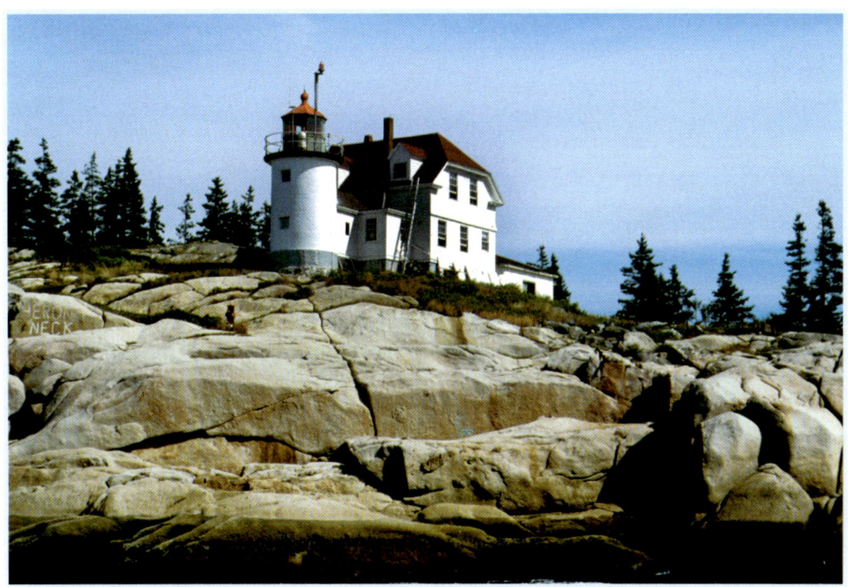

Heron Neck Lighthouse undergoing repairs, which started the Lighthouse Preservation Act.

Lighthouse Preservation

Maine has been at the forefront on conservation efforts of not only its lands and wildlife, but its lighthouses as well. As lighthouses became automated in the middle to late 1900s and government budget cuts became more frequent, lighthouses fell into disrepair and became vandalism targets. Almost a century later, organizations began forming to preserve lighthouses across the country. In 1992, Maine-based *Lighthouse Digest* magazine was created to champion lighthouse history and preservation. In 1994, the American Lighthouse Foundation was established, also in Maine, to preserve lighthouses nationally.

A project called Heron Neck led to the development of the Maine Lights Program in 1996. In the early 1990s, the Island Institute of Rockland asked the Coast Guard if it could acquire the Heron Neck Lighthouse on Vinalhaven Island. The lightkeeper's house there was in need of restoration after a fire badly damaged it. The Coast Guard had intended to demolish the structure and possibly the beacon, which outraged Vinalhaven residents who viewed the light as a dependable beacon for mariners and part of the scenic landscape.

Conceived by Peter Ralston of the Island Institute, and backed by Senators George Mitchell and Olympia Snowe, the Maine Lights program allows the transfer of lighthouse properties to private stewardship agencies, with the Coast Guard retaining responsibility only for the lights themselves. Twenty-eight light stations in Maine were transferred to nonprofit organizations as the Coast Guard relinquished ownership. Stewardship of these beacons was awarded by a competition based on the organizations' plans for maintaining and providing public access to the lighthouses. The stewards would also raise funds for restoration.

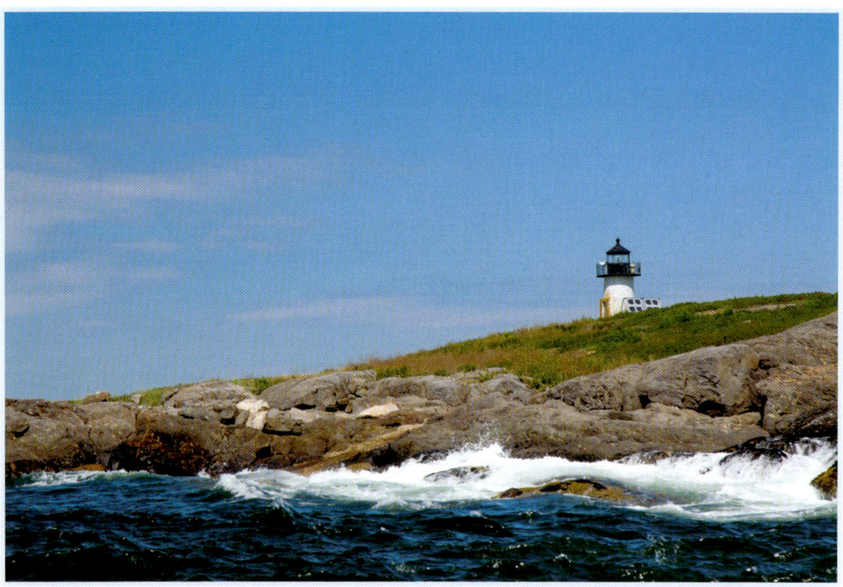

Pond Island Light sits on one of the protected islands in Maine's wildlife refuge complex.

In 2000, Congress passed the Lighthouse Preservation Act, creating a similar program on a national scale supervised by the National Park Service. These modern keepers protect the coastal beacons from vandals and souvenir hunters and have transformed some of them into tourist attractions and living history centers. In addition, Congress recently declared August 7 as National Lighthouse and Lighthouse Preservation Day to raise awareness of their critical role in US history.

Today the American Lighthouse Foundation (ALF), headquartered at Owls Head Light in Rockland, sponsors events at lighthouses and has many nonprofit organizations, or chapters, especially in New England, that provide assistance to beacons in need. Their growing army of volunteers contributes over 25,000 hours of service annually to lighthouse preservation. The ALF also provides educational and public access programs, and help with reusing historic sites throughout the nation.

September 14 is known as Maine Lighthouse Day, sponsored by the United States Coast Guard, the Maine Office of Tourism, and the American Lighthouse Foundation. The public is offered the rare opportunity to climb and learn about over two dozen historic Maine beacons. The Mid-Coast Maine Lighthouse Challenge is another event where visitors can take a cruise and view up to seven lighthouses.

The Maine Coastal Islands National Wildlife Refuge Complex protects Maine's many species of nesting birds and animals. It encompasses over forty-seven offshore islands and three coastal parcels totaling more than 7,400 acres and several lighthouses. The complex spans more than 150 miles of Maine's coastline, including its five national wildlife refuges: Petit Manan and Cross Island in Down East Maine, Seal Island in Rockland, and Franklin Island and Pond Island in the Boothbay area.

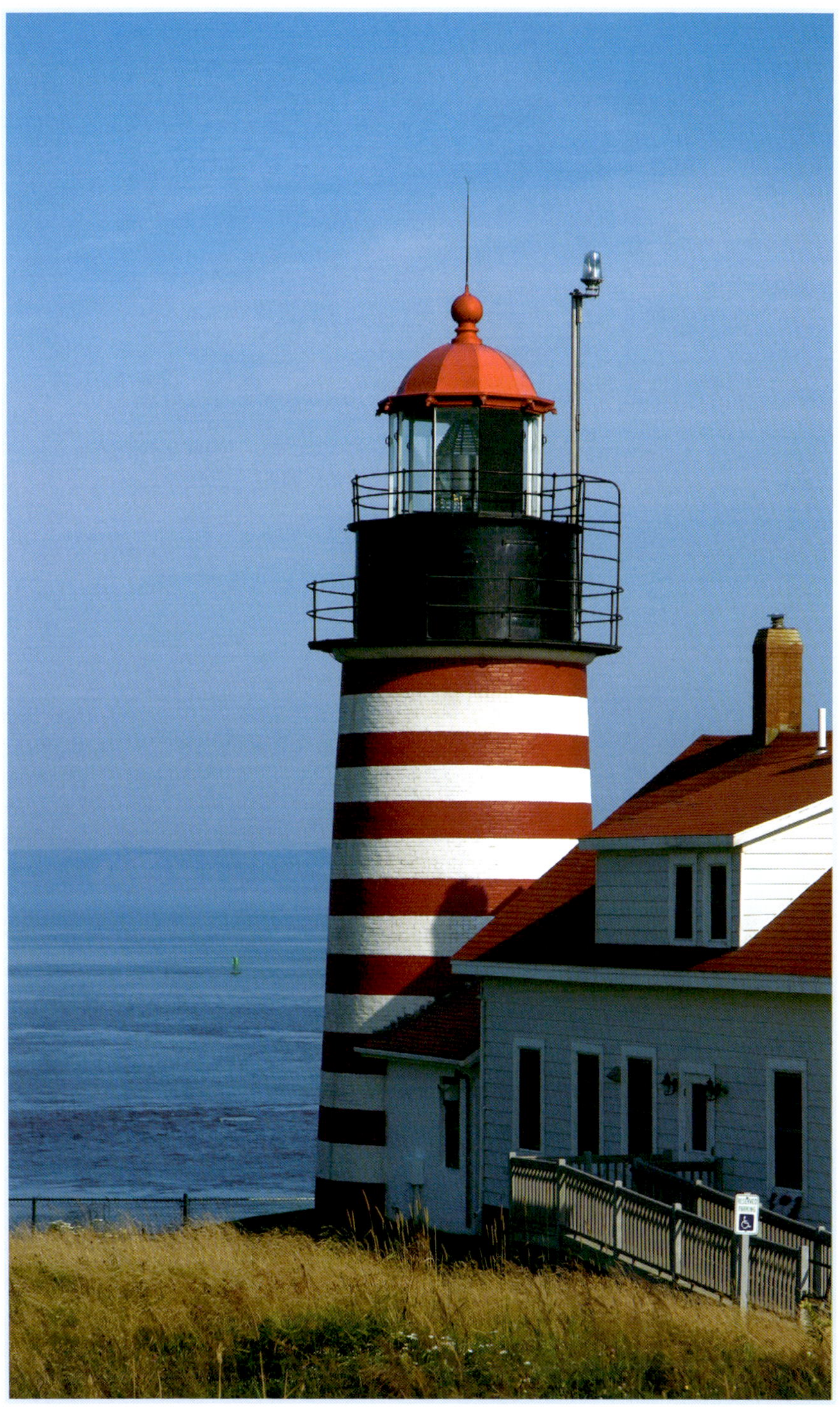

Quoddy State Park with its lighthouse has miles of nature trails.

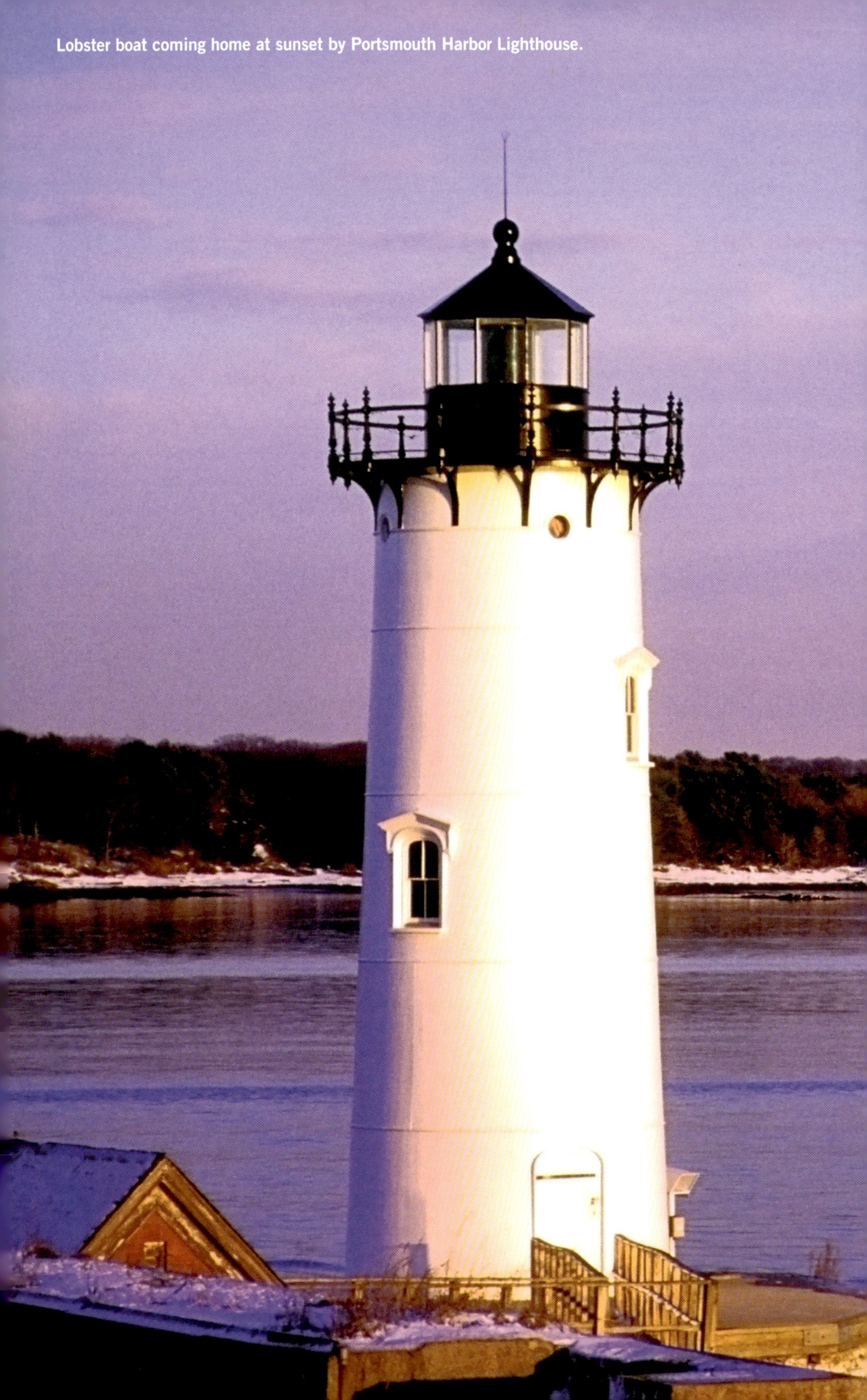
Lobster boat coming home at sunset by Portsmouth Harbor Lighthouse.

New Hampshire Lighthouses

There are five active lighthouses in New Hampshire. Portsmouth Harbor Lighthouse and White Island Lighthouse are on the seacoast, while Loon Island Lighthouse, Burkehaven Lighthouse, and Herrick Cove Lighthouse were built on the western side of New Hampshire on Lake Sunapee, about two hours from the coast. These three beacons guided tourists who took steamboats to destinations along this ten-mile-long rural lake surrounded by Mount Sunapee.

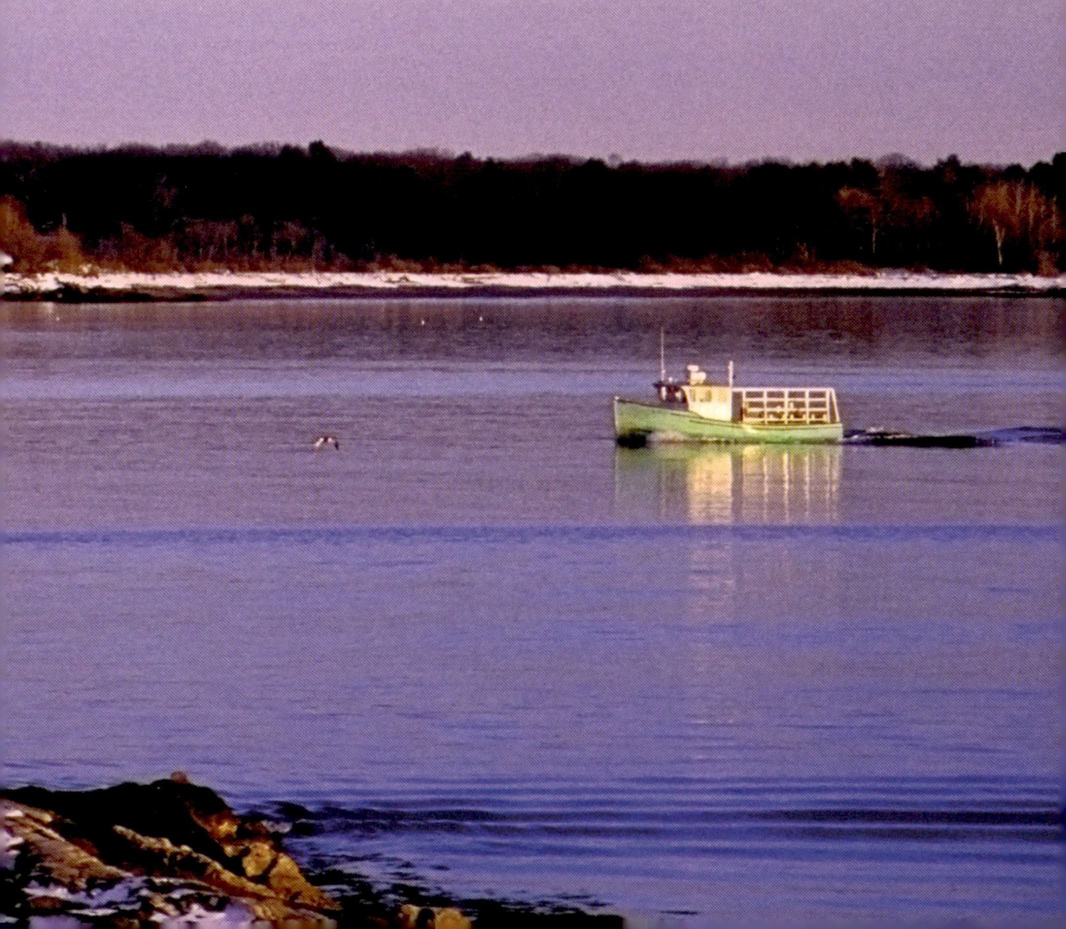

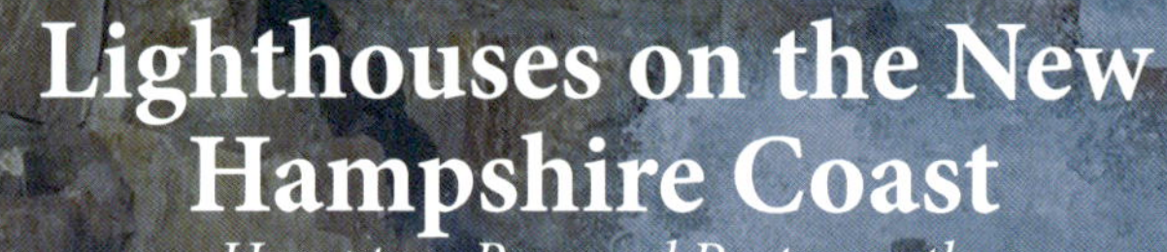

Lighthouses on the New Hampshire Coast

Hampton, Rye, and Portsmouth

There are only two lighthouses on New Hampshire's eighteen miles of coastline. The first, Portsmouth Harbor Lighthouse, marks the entrance to Portsmouth Harbor on the Piscataqua River. The British built it inside a military fortification, the site of one of the first acts by the colonists against the British that started the Revolutionary War. Portsmouth was and still is an important shipping and trade port, and Portsmouth Harbor Light still guides mariners, shipping vessels, and tourists through the treacherous currents of the Piscataqua River into Portsmouth. The second New Hampshire seacoast lighthouse, White Island Lighthouse, also referred to as the Isles of Shoals Lighthouse, is about six miles from the mainland. This lighthouse was built among nine rocky islands called the Isles of Shoals, which are split between New Hampshire and Maine.

Fishing boat heads home past Portsmouth Harbor Lighthouse through rough surf.

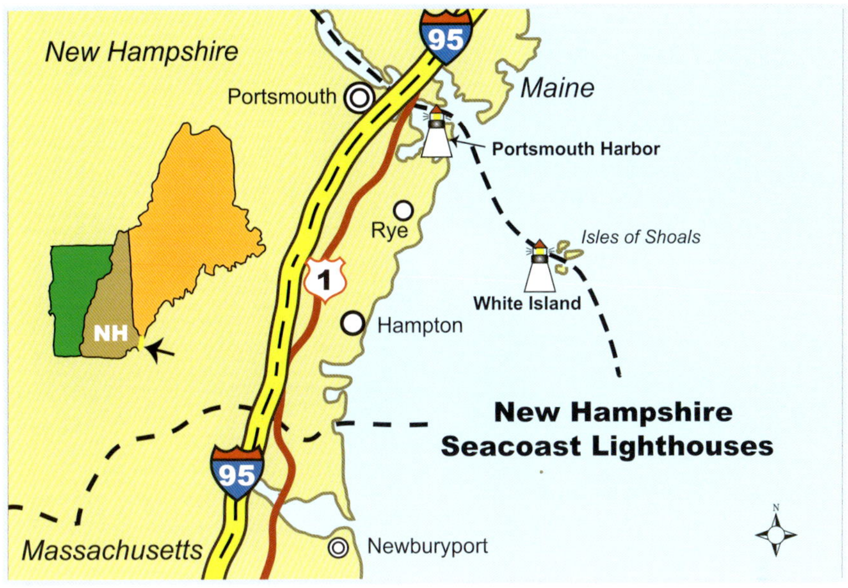

Coastal map of lighthouses on New Hampshire's Seacoast.

White Island (Isles of Shoals) Lighthouse

Rye (1821) • Latitude: 42° 58' 02" N • Longitude: 70° 37' 24" W

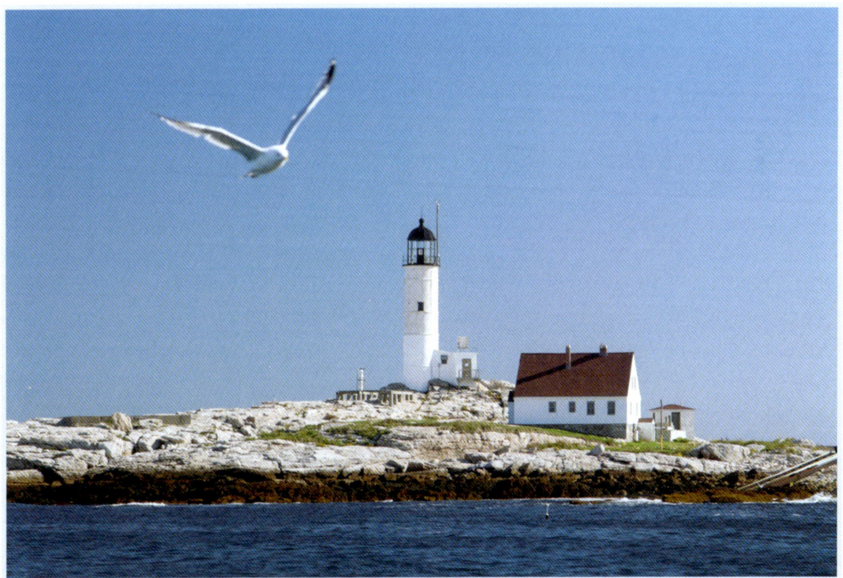

White Island (Isles of Shoals) Lighthouse is six miles from the mainland.

The first lighthouse in the Isles of Shoals was established on White Island in 1821 as a stone tower, and was later encased with wood to brave the constant storms that

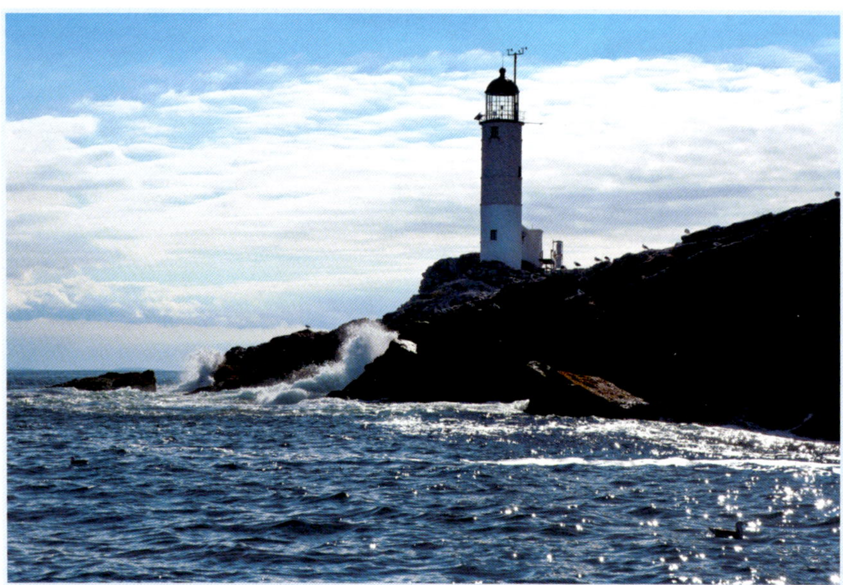

Cliffs by White Island (Isles of Shoals) Lighthouse.

washed over the island. In 1839, Thomas Leighton became keeper at White Island Light. Sometimes he was forced to bring his cow into the kitchen for protection from storms. His daughter, Celia, later gained widespread fame as Celia Thaxter, poet and author. During a severe gale in 1839, the vessel *Pocahontas* was wrecked on a nearby sandbar and all aboard perished. The memory of this incident inspired Celia Thaxter's poem, "The Wreck of the Pocahontas." She also wrote extensively about the islands' gardens, murders, and ghosts, which attracted tourism. In 1873, one of the islands, Smuttynose, received media attention when two young women were found brutally murdered with an ax. The culprit was caught and hanged in public. It was also believed to be the site of Blackbeard's buried treasure, though none has ever been found. Today the Isles of Shoals remain a major tourist attraction. Apparitions have been observed and documented over the centuries. One of these, on White Island, is believed to be Blackbeard's wife, who was sworn to oath to stay with the treasure. The apparition appears as a tall woman wrapped in a dark sea cloak, with long-flowing blonde hair. She has been seen on the rocks gazing out into the waters as if looking for her husband. Screeching, human-like sounds have also been heard coming from White Island, but many believe it is from the snowy white owls that frequent the area.

Acting Lighthouse Keeper Becomes Hero. In March of 1855, the new keeper to White Island (Isles of Shoals) Light, Captain Richard Haley, was making preparations to move his family from the mainland to the lighthouse. He asked a local island "shoaler," John Bragg Downs, who had assisted previous keepers, to act as its temporary keeper until he returned. Downs, who would always help anyone in need, accepted the task, and also brought a friend to help. Five days into his position, a major blizzard descended and a Russian brig headed for Salem, Massachusetts, got

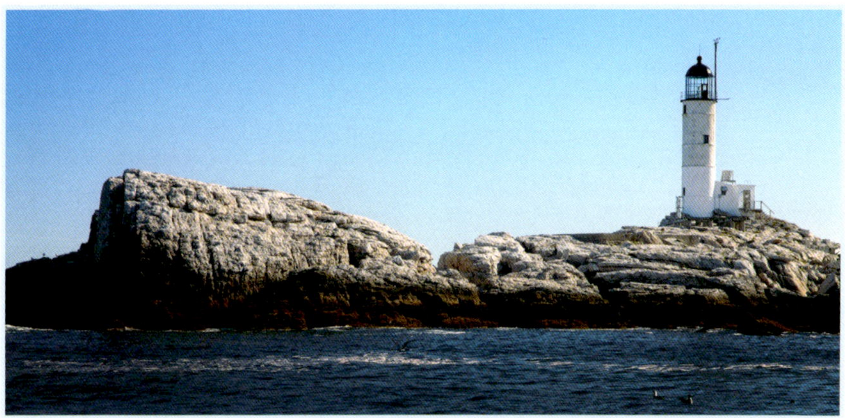

White Island Lighthouse protects mariners around the rocky Isles of Shoals islands.

caught in the storm. The captain was unable to see the lighthouse in the blinding snow and believed he was many miles away from the mainland. He wrecked on the shore by the lighthouse. Just after midnight there was a calm in the storm, and the captain saw the bright beam of the lighthouse very close to their position.

This was a lucky but very dangerous situation. He knew the vessel was going to break apart from the pounding waves and that all would perish if they could not could get help. One of the sailors, a large, burly man, volunteered to get help. He was lowered over the bow, lit only by the beam of the lighthouse. As he climbed over barnacle-covered rocks, huge waves washed over him, dragging him over the jagged edges. He finally reached a ledge above the waves and scrambled over the rocks toward the lighthouse. Bruised and bloody, he made haste for the keeper's house, where he could see a light inside.

Downs had been watching for vessels most of the day and night, but could not see anything in the blinding snowstorm. He was preparing something to eat while his friend was catching a nap after midnight, when a loud rap on the door startled the men. Downs quickly lit his lantern and opened the door. There stood the large Russian sailor, covered in blood like some ghastly figure in the night. The sailor cried in broken English, "Brig ashore, sir! Right near the lighthouse tower!" Downs and his assistant quickly gave him warm garments and tended to his worst cuts.

The three men grabbed a line and other equipment and headed over the icy rocks to the shoreline, where they found the wreck still intact. Downs ventured out on a ledge, throwing a line to the crew on the vessel. The line was caught and secured on the ship. However, there was no place to fasten the line on his end. Using his own body as an anchor, he climbed into a crevice and secured the line around his waist. He told the Russian sailor and his friend to hold him fast on the line. One by one, the fourteen men climbed over the line to safety and were cared for by Downs and his friend.

As the storm continued for days, the food supply was desperately low. Finally the storm subsided and keeper Haley was able to bring provisions. When he arrived, he cooked them a hearty meal and the fourteen grateful crew members were transported to the mainland. As he was not a government-appointed keeper, John Bragg

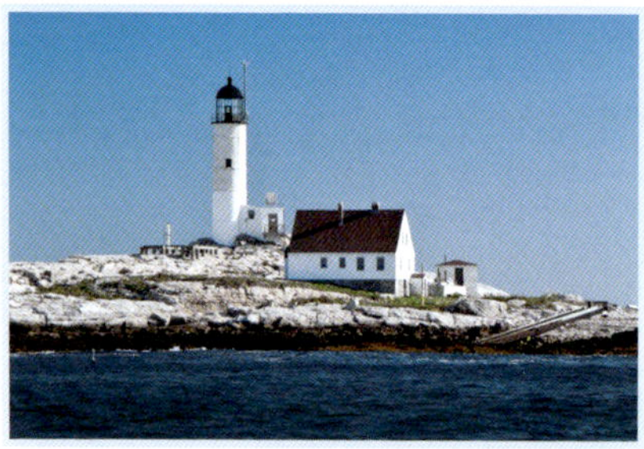
Lighthouse Kids raised money to fix the tower base.

Downs never received a medal for risking his life that night, but he was praised throughout the New Hampshire and Maine seacoast region, and by peers nationwide as news spread. For many years afterward, Downs would venture to the rocky shore by the lighthouse to the location of the crevice where he risked his life to save the men of the shipwrecked brig.

"Lighthouse Kids" Save White Island Light. Many years of constant storms had taken a toll on the lighthouse. In 1991, New England experienced two of its worst storms in many years. Hurricane Bob and the ferocious "perfect storm" of October 1991 washed away the old fog signal tower and the walkway from the tower to the house. Over the years, the lighthouse tower developed major cracks in its lower exterior and was at risk of falling into the ocean. This inspired a group of seventh-grade students calling themselves the "Lighthouse Kids" in North Hampton, New Hampshire, to raise money to save the lighthouse. Each year the class raised more funds, and in 2005, they presented Governor John Lynch with a check for $110,000 toward its restoration. This amount was added to matching federal funds acquired by Senator Judd Gregg in 2003, and most of the restorative work was completed during the summer of 2005.

Two years later, another storm in the spring of 2007 destroyed the walkway and solar panels, but the tower remains in good condition and "the kids" are still raising funds. The founder of the lighthouse kids, teacher Sue Reynolds, is now retired but is still active in raising funds. She operates Island Cruises from Rye Marina to the Isles of Shoals each summer on board the *Uncle Oscar*. The boat makes stopovers on nearby Star Island and passes by White Island Lighthouse. Check out their website at www.lighthousekids.com.

Portsmouth Harbor Lighthouse

New Castle (1791) • Latitude: 42° 39" 43" N • Longitude: 70° 40' 52" W

Portsmouth Harbor Light, as it is known today, was built on a historical site once occupied by the British inside Fort William and Mary. In 1771, a wooden lighthouse was established at the fort on what is now the island of New Castle outside Portsmouth Harbor, near the mouth of the Piscataqua River. It was the first light station established at a military installation of the British colonies. The site is also famous as one of the catalysts of the American Revolution when, in December 1774, Paul Revere rode to Portsmouth from Boston to warn the colonists of British plans to reinforce Fort William and Mary. The colonists raided the fort and made off with ammunition and supplies, which were used against the British at the Battle of Bunker Hill, one of the early battles in the Revolutionary War. When Americans gained control of the fort after the revolution, its name was changed to Fort Con-

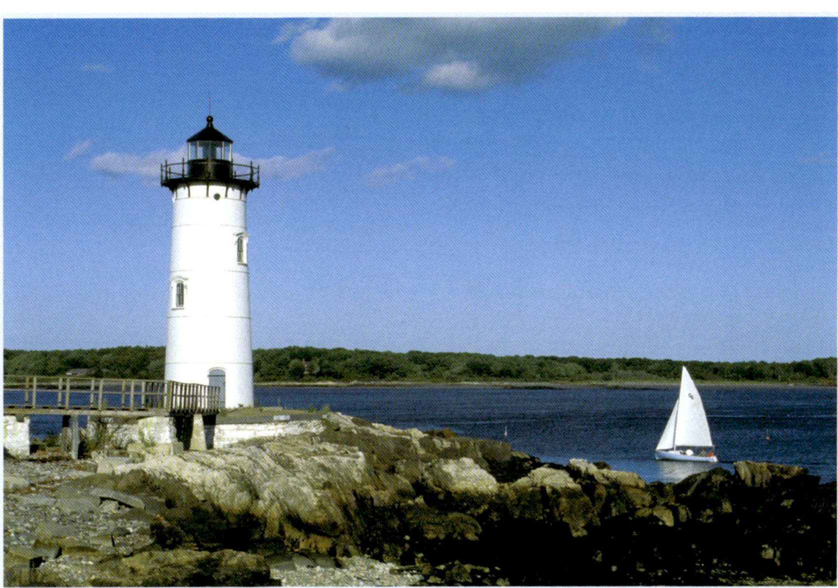

Sailboat glides past Portsmouth Lighthouse at low tide.

stitution. The lighthouse was owned by the new federal government in 1791, and in 1793 President George Washington ordered that the light be maintained at all times, with a keeper living on site. Since then, the lighthouse has been moved a number of times within the area; it has been at its present position within the walls of Fort Constitution since 1906.

In 1878, a new cast iron tower was built inside the old tower, which was then removed. Cast iron was a rare type of construction at this time. The lighthouse was painted a reddish-brown color, which brought complaints from mariners who claimed it was difficult to see during storms. In 1902, the lighthouse was painted the current white. In spite of the lighthouse, many ships on the rocky coastline outside the harbor, got caught in the Piscataqua River tidal current, or were stranded a few miles out in the Isles of Shoals. The fort and lighthouse provided a safe place to bring both rescued sailors in need of attention and those who perished, and there have been many ghost sightings over the years.

Portsmouth's Famous Lighthouse Keeper. In 1874, Joshua Card, former keeper at the desolate Boon Island Lighthouse, accepted the keeper position at Portsmouth Harbor Light. He loved life around the fort and lighthouse, and enjoyed entertaining his neighbors in New Castle and Portsmouth.

Keeper Card maintained the light for years without taking a single day off. With his thirty-five-year tenure, he became the seacoast's oldest lighthouse keeper. It is reported that in that span, from 1874 to 1909, he failed to light the lamp only eleven times. He died in 1911. One newspaper writer wrote that Card had high intelligence, was punctual to the minute, and possessed a kindly humor.

Joshua Card still seems to be involved in many of the ghost stories of the area as well. Although he retired after having an apparent stroke, some people believe he retired

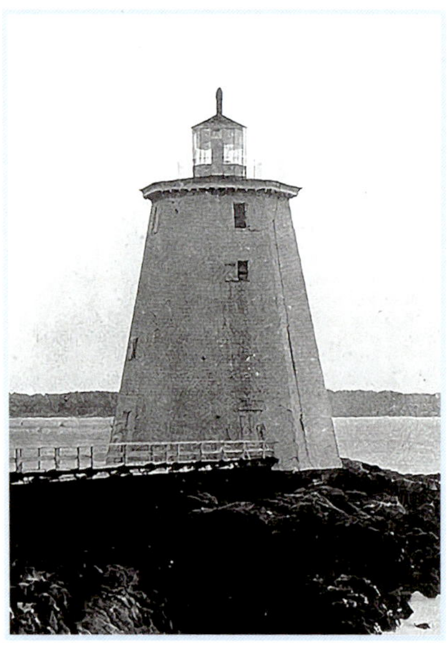

Vintage image shows 1804 construction. *Courtesy US Coast Guard.*

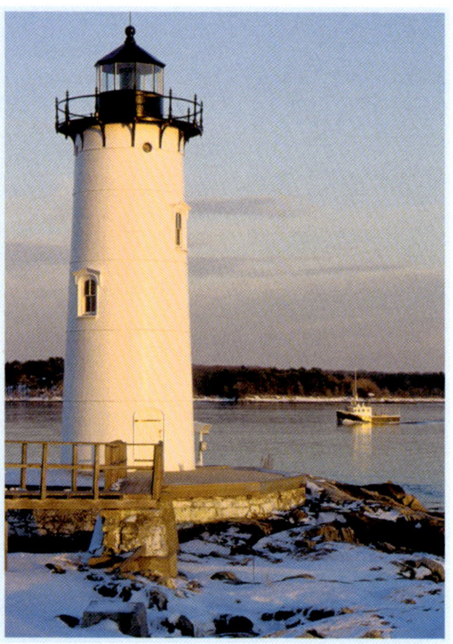

Portsmouth Harbor Lighthouse guides a lobster boat home.

against his will at age eighty-six, and his ghost has been seen and heard over the years.

Rescue of the Oliver Dyer. On November 25, 1888, the schooner *Oliver Dyer* was heading to her home port of Weehawken, New Jersey, with a load of coal from Saco, Maine. As the winds picked up, the captain dropped anchor near the entrance to Portsmouth Harbor about a half mile from Jerry's Point Lifesaving Station near Portsmouth Harbor Lighthouse. By 1:15 the next morning, huge waves had begun dragging the schooner toward the rocky ledges.

In the poor visibility, surfman Ernest Robinson did not see the stranded vessel until just before daybreak. By that time, the *Oliver Dyer* lay stranded on the ledges a few hundred yards offshore. Robinson ran to the station to notify keeper Silas H. Harding, who sounded the alarm and called all hands. Then the men ran down to the rocks to assess the danger. The vessel had lodged itself about seventy-five feet from a large, flat rock covered in ice, which was breached continuously by the vicious surf. Harding had no choice but to launch the rescue from the rock.

As Harding and his crew reached the rock, they saw one man had already jumped from the schooner and was struggling in the icy waters. Surfman Ephraim S. Hall jumped into the waves and grabbed the man. The rest of Harding's crew began dragging both of them toward the ice-covered ledge. Just as they reached it, a huge wave knocked both men and their rescuers into the water. Luckily, they were on the shoreline side of the ledge, and when the waves receded the men regained their footing. Surfman George W. Randall grabbed Harding and held tightly until he could reach the rock. All the men were bleeding from being bashed against the rocks, with Surfman Hall receiving the worst wounds. Harding's crew managed to climb back on the rock, and Surfman Hall and the survivor were brought to safety.

The frightened crew remaining on the *Oliver Dyer* could see that soon the wreck

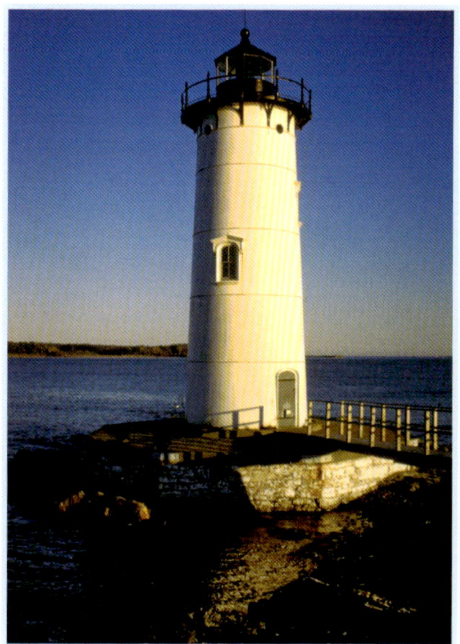

Portsmouth Lighthouse at sunset.

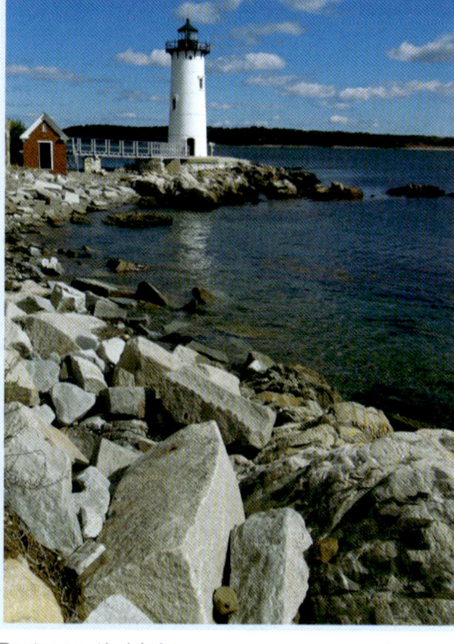

Portsmouth Light on a warm, sunny day.

would be breaking up. As they witnessed the rescue of one of their comrades, the cook jumped overboard and was rescued from the undertow by Surfman Randall.

Keeper Harding used a heaving stick and line to rescue the two remaining crew members. They tied the lines around their bodies and under their arms, and Harding persuaded them to jump into the freezing waters. The men were then carefully dragged onto the rock to safety.

Harding's exhausted crew and the survivors were cared for at the station for two days. Harding's men had saved all crew members except for one who was washed overboard before they reached the wreck. The incident made Harding and his crew local heroes, and each received a Gold Life Saving Medal. The other recipients included surfmen John Smith, Winslow A. Amazeen, and Selden F. Wells.

Exploring the grounds. The lighthouse is on the corner of New Castle Island, marking the entrance to Portsmouth Harbor on the edge of the Piscataqua River. Fort Constitution is worth exploring, and the grounds are open to the public until 4 p.m. They offer a close view of the lighthouse just outside the fort walls. Friends of Portsmouth Lighthouse gives tower tours on select weekends during the summer.

Directions. From I-95 in Portsmouth, take exit 5 and go south on Route 1 bypass for a little over two miles. Turn left on Elwyn Road, and continue for about a mile and a half until the road ends. Turn left on Sagamore and then right on Wentworth Road, which is Route 1B. After about two miles, look for signs directing you to turn right to the Coast Guard Station, Portsmouth Harbor, and Fort Constitution. During daylight hours, park in the Fort Constitution parking lot and walk inside the fort.

Coastal Attractions in New Hampshire

Hampton, Rye, and Portsmouth

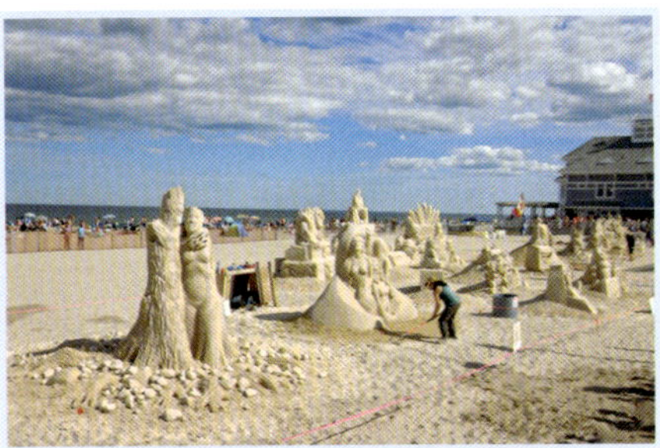

Sand sculpture event at Hampton Beach draws artists from all over the word.

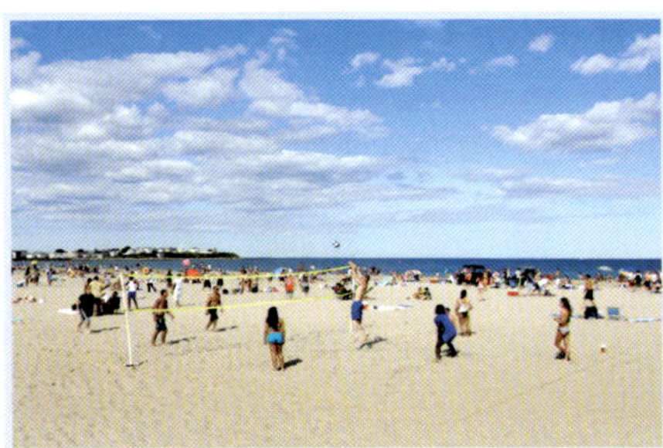

Hampton Beach has plenty of room for volleyball and other activities.

Although New Hampshire's seacoast is only eighteen miles long, there are plenty of parks, beaches, and tours for visitors to enjoy. Crossing from Massachusetts into New Hampshire, you'll find the town of Seabrook and Seabrook Beach. **Eastman's Fishing Fleet** offers deep-sea fishing and whale watching.

Hampton Beach is New Hampshire's longest and most popular beach, with top-notch concerts at the **Hampton Casino Ballroom.** You'll also find festivals, fireworks displays, attractions, and restaurants, along with an amphitheater for local shows and concerts. A world-class sand sculpture event takes place mid-June, and an annual seafood festival is held in mid-September.

Al Gauron offers deep-sea fishing, whale-watching, and pirate cruises out of Hampton. For a smaller boat experience, try **Sunrise Adventure Tours** offering fishing and lighthouse tours to Portsmouth Harbor and Isles of Shoals. For whale-watching tours, and deep sea fishing out of Hampton, check out **Yellowbird Deep Sea Fishing** or **Smith & Gilmore Deep Sea Fishing**.

As you travel along the winding Route 1A, you'll enjoy picturesque views of the rocky coastline and Victorian and twentieth-century mansions. Jenness Beach, North Beach, and Wallis Sands offer smaller, quiet beaches along the way. Stop in at **Fuller Gardens**, a massive, turn-of-the-century botanical garden.

The Rye Harbor State Marina offers fishing and lobstering, and there are whale watch expeditions and deep-sea fishing from **Granite State Whale Watch** and **Atlantic Whale Watch**. For a more private charter, try **South End Charters** out of Rye, which offers deep-sea fishing excursions. **Sail NH** has narrative historic sailing charters out to the Isles of Shoals and around Portsmouth Harbor, where you may also view the lighthouses.

The Isles of Shoals are nine islands located six miles off the New Hampshire coast. They have been a popular destination for tourists, writers, and artists alike for centuries, especially the largest, Star Island. White Island Lighthouse can be easily viewed from Star Island. **Island Cruses**, the mail boat to the island out of Rye Harbor, offers daily stopovers at **Star Island** for a few hours or the day. Eat lunch or stay overnight at the Victorian Era Oceanic Hotel and explore the island and its timely stone cottages and church, built to withstand

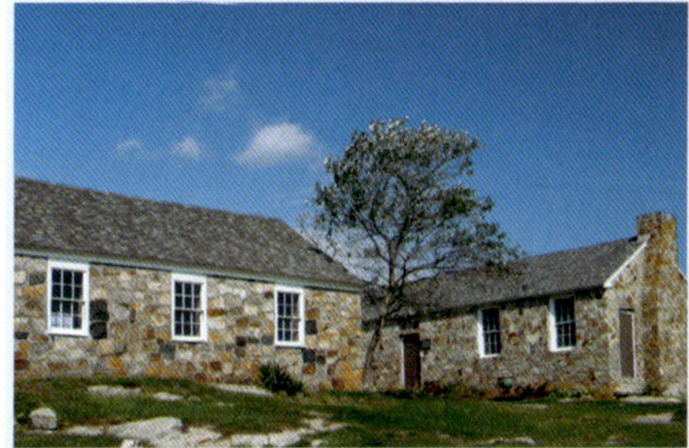

Stone cottages on Star Island were built to withstand harsh nor'easters.

the harsh weather. Other boats out of Portsmouth Harbor provide tours to Star Island as well. For the adventurous, **Atlantic Aquasport** offers diving expeditions off White Island near the lighthouse.

Quick stop! Reverend John Tucke (1702–1773) was a wealthy minister, judge, educator, and physician. His obelisk gravestone is on Star Island, and is the **tallest gravestone in New Hampshire**.

The **Seacoast Science Center** offers extensive programs and exhibits in marine education. It is on **Odiorne Point State Park**, with beaches, a rocky shore with tide pools, and extensive wooded trails nearby. The park is the largest undeveloped stretch of shoreline in New Hampshire.

New Castle Island lies just outside Portsmouth, separated by narrow waterways and connected by Route 1B. Dine or spend the night at the renovated Wentworth by the Sea Hotel, where kings, queens, and presidents stayed in the 1800s. For boaters, the marina is just across the street. One of the most beautiful oceanside parks in the region is **Great Island Common**, within walking distance of Portsmouth Harbor Lighthouse. It offers beaches, recreation, rocks to climb, and views of Whaleback Lighthouse across the river in Kittery, Maine. This is probably the only place on the East Coast where you can get close views of lighthouses in different states. As the park is at the mouth of

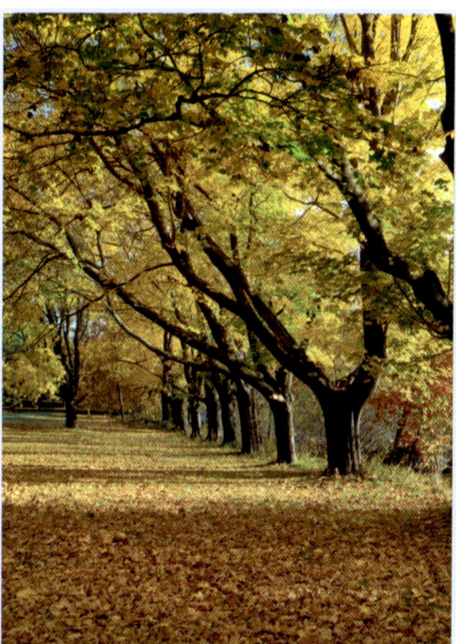

Walking trails along the wooded sections of Ordiorne State Park in autumn.

the Piscataqua River, you may be treated to views of tugboats escorting shipping traffic to and from Portsmouth, or lobster boats and fishing boats going off to work. Walk around the grounds of Fort Constitution nearby and get close views of Portsmouth Harbor Lighthouse.

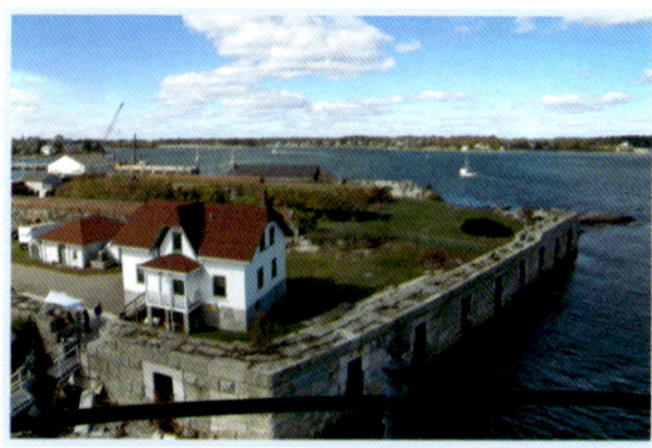

View of Fort Constitution with keeper's quarters from Portsmouth Lighthouse tower.

Many boat tours pass close to Portsmouth Harbor Light, and Whaleback Light on the Maine side (see New Hampshire Lighthouse Cruises). **Friends of Portsmouth Harbor Lighthouses (FPHL)** provides tours inside the lighthouse during the summer months on weekends and coordinates haunted and pirate tours. Noted lighthouse historian and FPHL founder Jeremy D'Entremont offers daily lighthouse tours, driving visitors up Maine's coast and stopping at lighthouses along the way. He also coordinates tours of Portsmouth Harbor Lighthouse.

Historic Portsmouth offers many cultural events, specialty shops, and restaurants. It's the kind of small waterfront city where you can walk to almost everything, including to the dock where tugboats wait to bring ships along the Piscataqua River. The **Seacoast Trolley Company** provides narrated tours of Portsmouth Harbor and Whaleback Lighthouses, along with tours of the city.

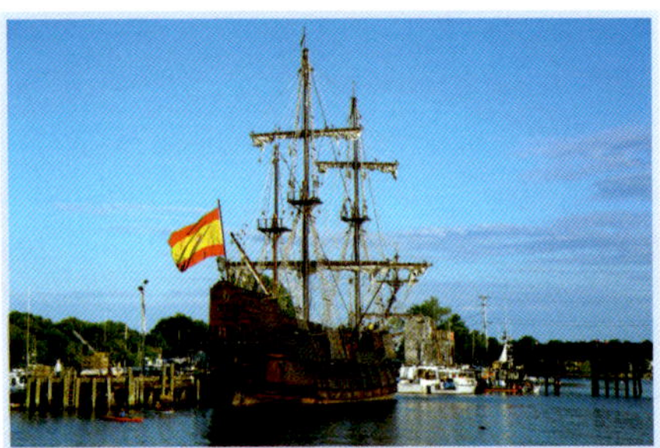

A Spanish galleon replica at the fishing dock across from the Prescott Park.

During the summer in Portsmouth, enjoy the beautiful gardens, music, and arts festivals of **Prescott Park,** along with other indoor theaters in the area, like the **Seacoast Repertory Theatre**. An outdoor theater production at Prescott Park entertains visitors each week during the summer, and sometimes tugboats bring ships directly past the park. There are all kinds of events happening around the park. Across the street, Strawberry Banke offers an outdoor museum of architecture and demonstrations of how people lived from the late seventeenth century to the twentieth century. For a unique experience, the nonprofit **Gundalow Company** provides sailing tours around the harbor on the *Piscataqua*, a traditional reproduction of the flat-bottom gundalow barge that carried heavy cargo along local waterways. Visitors can also walk over a short bridge from the park to Pierce Island and watch fishing boats coming in to unload their goods.

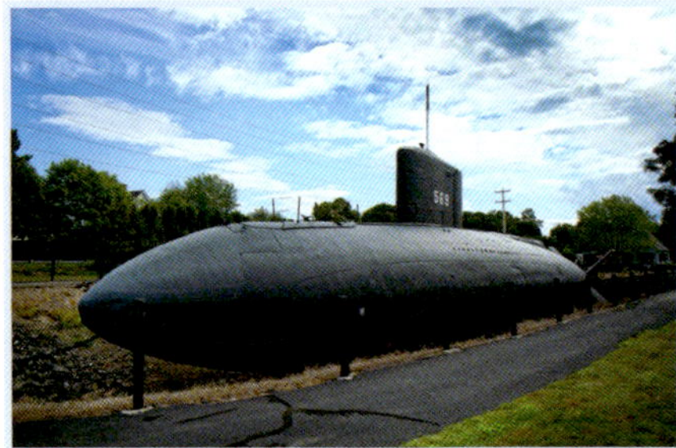

Albacore submarine museum.

The **Music Hall**, built in the late 1800s, hosts acclaimed film, music, theater, and dance performances year-round. For family fun, you'll find **Water Country** off Route 1 in Portsmouth. The **Albacore Submarine Museum** invites visitors to explore the inside of the USS *Albacore* submarine, the prototype for modern submarines.

The **Great Bay National Estuarine Research Reserve** encourages visitors to hike and learn about the Native American cultures that thrived in the area.

A few miles inland, stop at Dover's **Children's Museum** and the **Woodman Institute Museum,** which contains New England's largest collection of animals, minerals, Native American and prehistoric artifacts, and wartime artifacts, including the saddle President Lincoln used while reviewing his troops on horseback, and a four-legged chicken.

Contacts for Coastal Attractions in New Hampshire

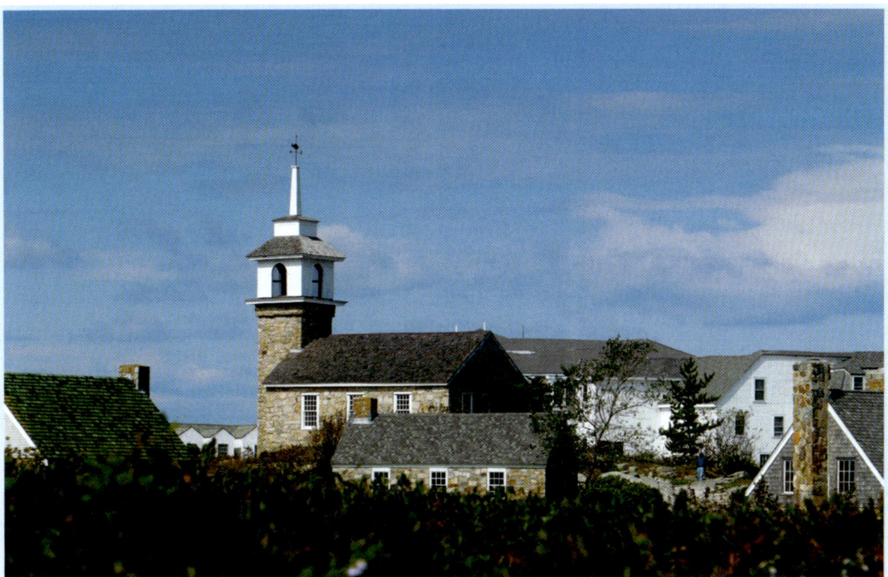

Star Island on the Isles of Shoals with its unique cottages and church.

Eastman's Fishing Fleet, Seabrook
(603) 474-3461
eastmansdocks.com

Hampton Beach
(603) 926-3784
hamptonbeach.org

Al Gauron Whale Watching, Hampton
(800) 905-7820
algauron.com

Sunrise Adventure, Hampton
(603) 435-4946
sunriseadventurecharters.com

Yellowbird Deep Sea Fishing, Hampton
(603) 929-1995
yellowbirdfishing.com

Smith & Gilmore Fishing, Hampton
(603) 926-3503
smithandgilmore.com

Fuller Gardens, North Hampton
(603) 964-5414
fullergardens.org

Star Island, Rye
(603) 430-6272
starisland.org

Island Cruses, Rye
(603) 964-6446
uncleoscar.com

Atlantic Whale Watch, Rye
(603) 964-5220
atlanticwhalewatch.com

Granite State Whale Watch, Rye
(800) 964-5545
granitestatewhalewatch.com

Seacoast Science Center, Rye
(603) 436-8043
seacoastsciencecenter.org

South End Charters, Rye
(603) 205-1806
southendcharters.com

Sail NH, Rye
(603) 380-3804
sailnh.com

Odiorne Point Park, Rye
(603) 436-6507
nhstateparks.com/odiorne.html

Seacoast Trolley, Portsmouth
(603) 431-6975
seacoasttrolley.com

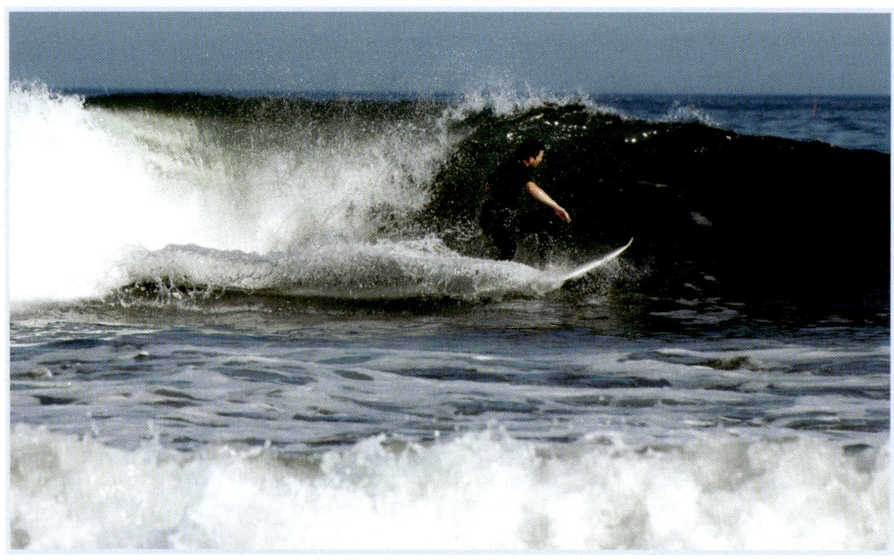

Surfer enjoys riding waves at high tide.

Atlantis Aquasport, Portsmouth
(603) 436-4443
atlanticaquasport.com

Lighthouse Tours, Portsmouth
(603) 431-9155
newenglandlighthouses.net

FPHL Tours, Portsmouth
(603) 534-0537
portsmouthharborlighthouse.org

Gundalow Sailing, Portsmouth
(603) 433-9505
gundalow.org

Portsmouth Music Hall
(603) 436-2400
themusichall.org

Water Country, Portsmouth
(603) 427-1111
watercountry.com

Strawberry Banke Museum, Portsmouth
(603) 433-1100
strawberrybanke.org

Prescott Park Arts Festivals, Portsmouth
(603) 436-2848
prescottpark.org

Seacoast Repertory Theatre, Portsmouth
(603) 433-4793
seacoastrep.org

Great Island Common Park, New Castle
(603) 436-1992
newcastlenh.org

Albacore Submarine Museum, Portsmouth
(603) 436-3680
ussalbacore.org

Great Bay Estuarine Reserve, Greenland
(603) 778-0015
greatbay.org

Woodman Institute, Dover
(603) 742-1038
woodmaninstitutemuseum.org

Children's Museum, Dover
(603) 742-2002
childrens-museum.org

Lighthouse Cruises on the New Hampshire Coast

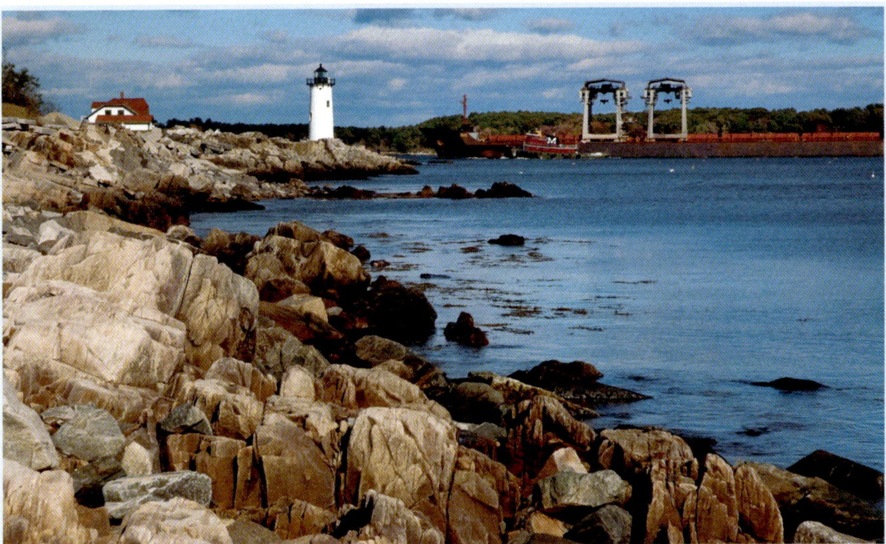

Tanker passes rocky shoreline at Portsmouth Harbor Lighthouse.

Isles of Shoals Steamship Co.

Narrated tours of Portsmouth Harbor and Isles of Shoals with close-up views of lighthouses. Lots of dinner and nightlife cruises.

- 315 Market Street, PO Box 31, Portsmouth
- (603) 431-5500 or (800) 44-4620
- islesofshoals.com
- **Lighthouses:** Portsmouth Harbor, White Island (Isles of Shoals), and Whaleback.

Portsmouth Harbor Cruises

Narrated Portsmouth Harbor cruise provides a tour of nearly 400 years of the area's history. The Isles of Shoals Cruise covers all nine islands and provides close views of White Island Light.

- 64 Ceres Street, Portsmouth
- (603) 436-8084 or (800) 776-0915
- portsmouthharbor.com
- **Lighthouses:** Portsmouth Harbor, White Island (Isles of Shoals), and Whaleback

Sail NH

Sailboat charters to the Isles of Shoals and Portsmouth from Rye Harbor.

- Captain Rick Philbrick, Malagar Group LLC
- 188 Bunker Hill Ave., Stratham
- (603) 778-1372
- sailnh.com
- **Lighthouses:** Portsmouth Harbor, White Island (Isles of Shoals), and Whaleback

Sunrise Adventure Charters

Two-hour Portsmouth Harbor tour and Isles of Shoals cruises with close views of the lighthouses. Offers deep-sea fishing excursions aboard a twenty-five-foot Sport Cabin boat.

- 55 Harbor Road, Hampton
- (603) 345-4946 or (603) 424-4946
- sunriseadventurecharters.com
- **Lighthouses:** Portsmouth Harbor, White Island (Isles of Shoals), and Whaleback

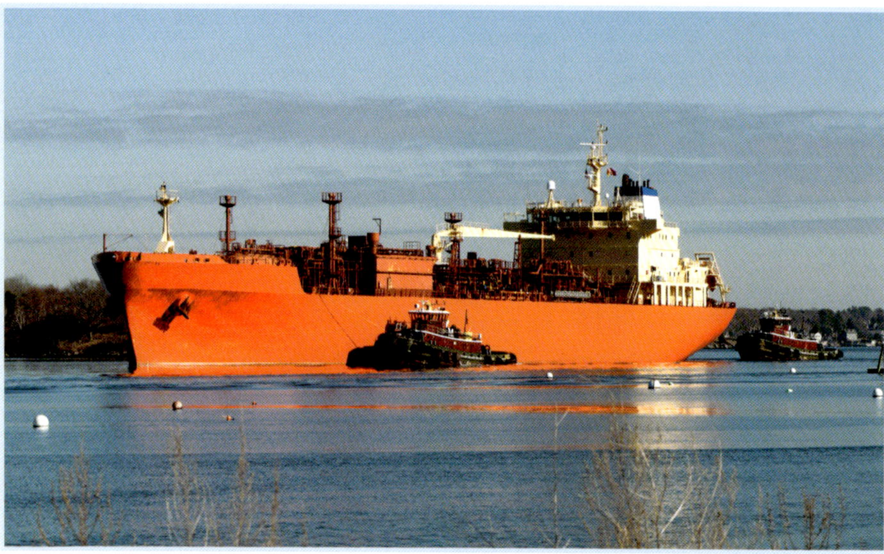

Tugboats guide ship along the Piscataqua River toward Portsmouth harbor.

Granite State Whale Watch

Besides daily whale-watching tours, they have a narrated tour of all nine islands of the Isles of Shoals.

- PO Box 768, Rye
- (800)-964-5545 or (603) 964-5545
- granitestatewhalewatch.com
- **Lighthouse:** White Island (Isles of Shoals)

Island Cruises, Inc.

Tours to the islands along the Isles of Shoals, including a stopover on Star Island where you can eat at the Oceanic Hotel and enjoy a nice view of White Island (Isles of Shoals) Light. Sue Reynolds, founder of the "Lighthouse Kids" who raised funds to help restore the lighthouse, owns the boat.

- Rye Harbor State Marina
- Route 1A, Ocean Boulevard, Rye
- (603) 964-6446
- uncleoscar.com
- **Lighthouse:** White Island (Isles of Shoals)

Sunrise Adventure Charters

Deep-sea fishing and whale-watching charters on a private twenty-five-foot vessel, as well as a two-hour lighthouse tour to the Isles of Shoals and a Portsmouth Harbor tour.

- 47 Meetinghouse Road, Merrimack
- (603) 345-4946
- sunriseadventurecharters.com
- **Lighthouses:** Portsmouth Harbor, White Island (Isles of Shoals)

Waterfront Directions

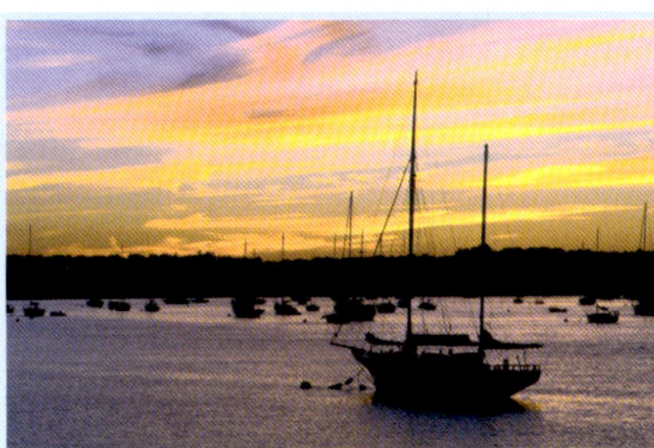

Sunset over Wentworth by the Sea Marina in New Castle.

Seabrook Waterfront

Take I-95 north, and then take exit 60 (Route 286). Go straight through the first set of lights, left at second set onto Route 286, and follow to the end. Take a left at the light on Route 1A north, then left again at the lights, (before Hampton Bridge) on River Street.

Hampton State Pier

From the north, take I-95 south to the Hampton tollbooth. Take exit 2 and Route 101 east until you reach the beach. Turn right and continue one mile until just before the Hampton-Seabrook Bridge. The State Pier is on the right. From the south, take I-95 north to just over the New Hampshire state line. Take exit 60. At the second set of lights, take a left onto Route 286 and follow all the way to the beach. Turn left and continue for about a mile and a half. Just past the Hampton River Bridge on the left you'll see the State Pier.

Rye Harbor Marina

Take I-95 north, then take exit 2 (at the Hampton toll booths). When you come out of the remote tollbooth, take the left fork on Route 101 east (formerly Route 51) and continue for about a half mile. Take the exit for Route 27, and then turn right onto Route 27 east. Stay on Route 27 until it ends at the ocean (about three and half miles). You are now at Route 1A. Turn left on Route 1A north for five miles until you come to Rye Harbor on the right.

Portsmouth Docks

From Route I-95 north, take exit 5 to the Portsmouth traffic circle. From I-95 south, take NH exit 7, then left at the light. At the traffic circle, take your second right onto the Route 1 Bypass North (Maine). Take the second exit on Maplewood Avenue and turn right at the end of the ramp. Proceed to first set of lights and take a left onto Deer Street. Follow Deer Street to the end, take a left at the stop sign. The Isles of Shoals Steamship Company dock is on the right, just after the salt pile, across from the Sheraton Harbor. For Portsmouth Harbor Cruises, just past the Sheraton Hotel on your right, you will see a small alley on your left marked "Private Way" and the "Olde Harbour District." This is Ceres Street, where you'll find the dock. There is an inexpensive parking garage a few streets away from the waterfront on Hanover Street.

Wentworth by the Sea Marina (New Castle)

From Route 1A north, follow past Rye and take a right onto Route 1B. Follow it a few miles and you'll see Wentworth by the Sea Hotel. The marina is across the street.

From I-95 in Portsmouth, take exit 5 and go south on Route 1 bypass for a little over two miles. Turn left on Elwyn Road, and continue for about a mile and a half until the road ends. Turn left onto Sagamore and then right onto Wentworth Road, which is Route 1B. Follow this for a few miles until you see Wentworth by the Sea Hotel.

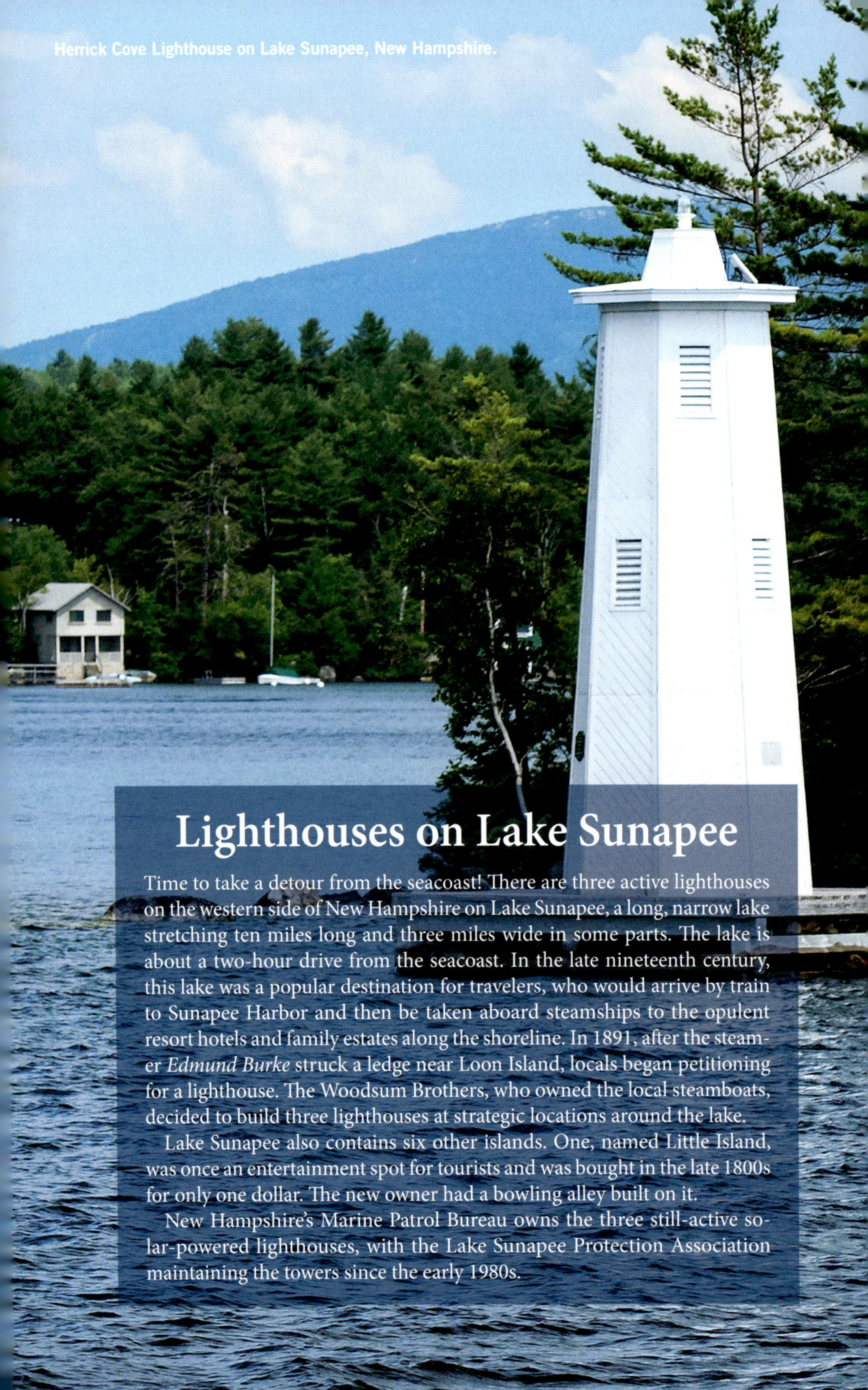

Herrick Cove Lighthouse on Lake Sunapee, New Hampshire.

Lighthouses on Lake Sunapee

Time to take a detour from the seacoast! There are three active lighthouses on the western side of New Hampshire on Lake Sunapee, a long, narrow lake stretching ten miles long and three miles wide in some parts. The lake is about a two-hour drive from the seacoast. In the late nineteenth century, this lake was a popular destination for travelers, who would arrive by train to Sunapee Harbor and then be taken aboard steamships to the opulent resort hotels and family estates along the shoreline. In 1891, after the steamer *Edmund Burke* struck a ledge near Loon Island, locals began petitioning for a lighthouse. The Woodsum Brothers, who owned the local steamboats, decided to build three lighthouses at strategic locations around the lake.

Lake Sunapee also contains six other islands. One, named Little Island, was once an entertainment spot for tourists and was bought in the late 1800s for only one dollar. The new owner had a bowling alley built on it.

New Hampshire's Marine Patrol Bureau owns the three still-active solar-powered lighthouses, with the Lake Sunapee Protection Association maintaining the towers since the early 1980s.

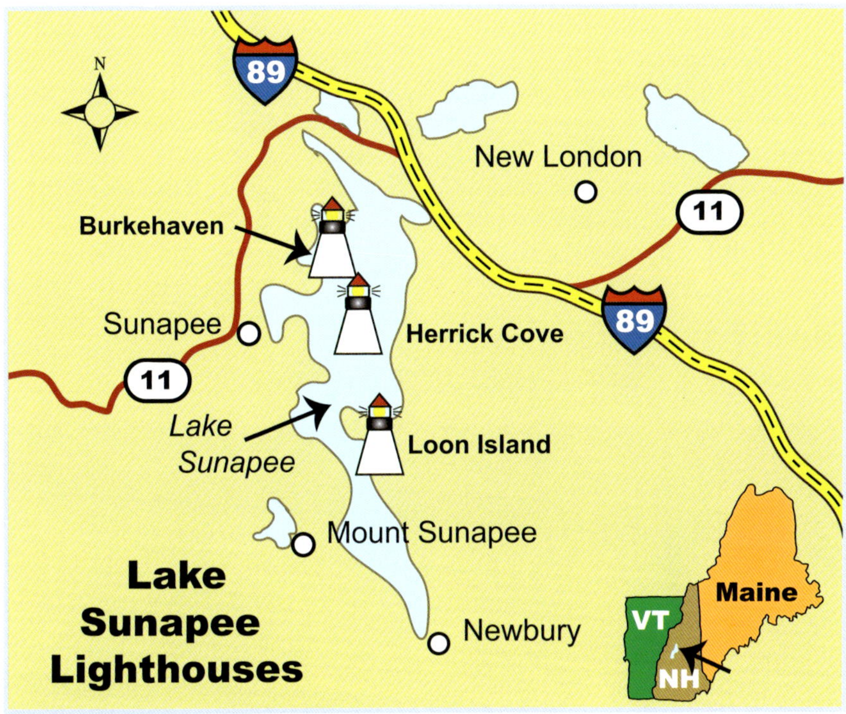

Map of lighthouses on New Hampshire's Lake Sunapee.

Loon Island Lighthouse

Sunapee (1893) • Latitude: 43° 23' 31" N • Longitude: 72° 03' 36" W

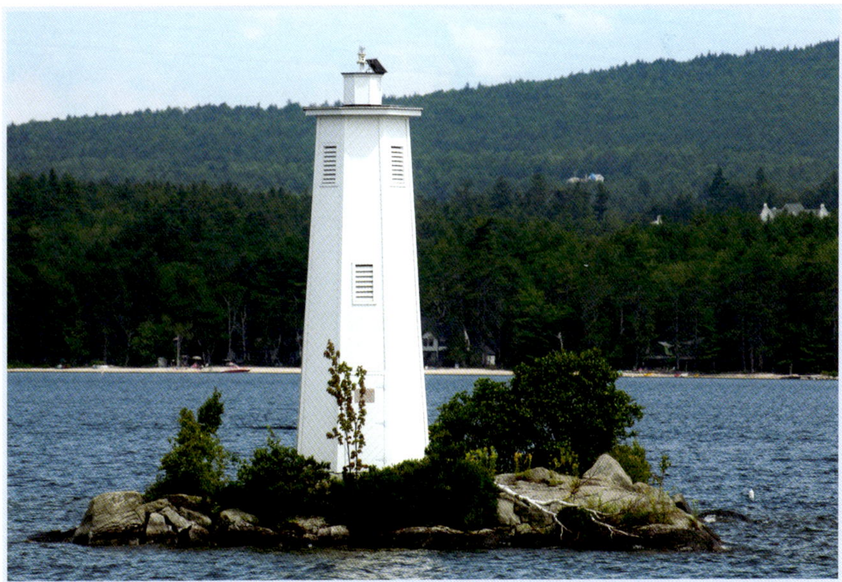

Loon Island Lighthouse guides boaters away from ledges.

Loon Island is a small, rocky island in the middle of Lake Sunapee, with shallow waters and ledges around it.

A wooden tower named Loon Island Light was built in 1893. In 1896, the local fire department was repairing the lighthouse when it caught fire. The firemen had one bucket and put out the fire with the lake water.

The tower was struck by lightning in 1960 and burned down. It was rebuilt in the same year, after a fund drive for private contributions. In the 1980s, solar panels were installed in the lighthouse.

Burkehaven Lighthouse

Sunapee (1893) • Latitude: 43° 22' 18" N • Longitude: 72° 03' 57" W

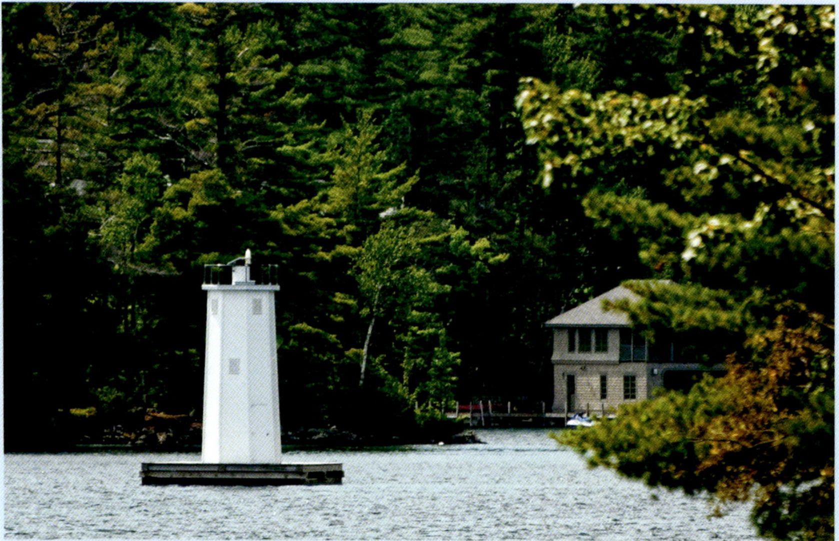

Burkehaven Lighthouse is south of Sunapee Harbor.

Burkehaven Lighthouse is just offshore on a rock near the tip of Burkehaven Isle in Lake Sunapee, south of Sunapee Harbor. In the 1930s, the Great Depression led to the abrupt demise of steamship travel and tourism in the area. In 1935, Burkehaven Light was destroyed by ice and began to deteriorate. In 1983, the Lake Sunapee Protective Association raised funds and rebuilt the lighthouse. By 1994, the base had again been badly damaged by ice and was rebuilt.

Herrick Cove Lighthouse

Sunapee (1893) • Latitude: 43° 24' 40" N • Longitude: 72° 02' 30" W

When the "grand era" came to a close during the Great Depression, Herrick Cove Lighthouse was left to the weather and deteriorated rapidly until it was finally rebuilt in 1960.

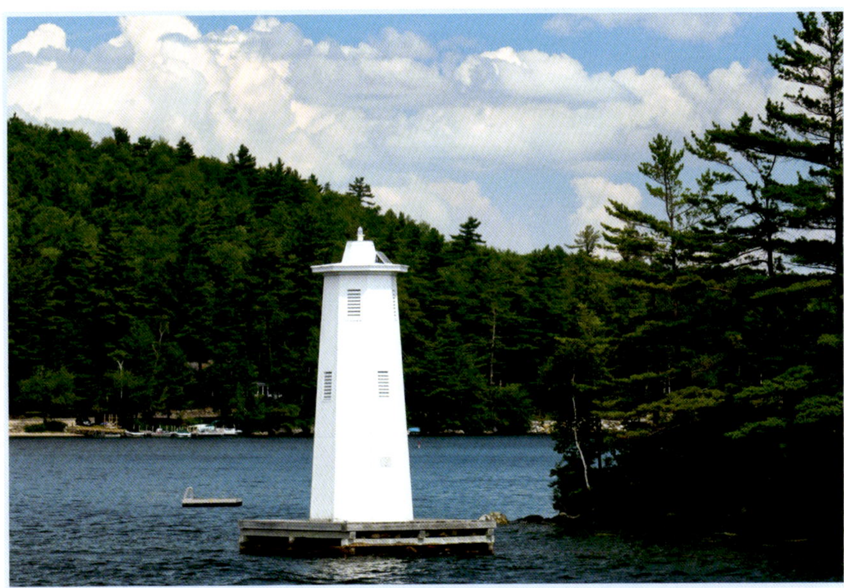

Herrick Cove Lighthouse is the oldest of the three Lake Sunapee beacons.

In 1983, the lighthouse was damaged by ice from a fierce winter and was again repaired using donations and public funds. In 1996, extensive repairs were needed, and much of the funding was donated by the local Cross family. Court Cross was chair of the Lake Sunapee Protective Association's lighthouse committee. His daughter, Ginger, had perished in an avalanche in 1996 while skiing in Wyoming, and many donations were given to the LSPA in her honor. A plaque in her memory was placed on the restored lighthouse.

In September 2003, the lighthouse's foundation was in desperate need of repairs, so a helicopter was brought in to lift the lighthouse ashore. The lighthouse weight was underestimated and the helicopter struggled to get it airborne, causing the tower to be dunked in the lake for a brief time before finally being lifted out. Luckily, the tower did not suffer any significant damage from the water. The structure and foundation were repaired and a solar light was installed. It was flown back to its restored base in 2004 and relit.

Attractions around Lake Sunapee

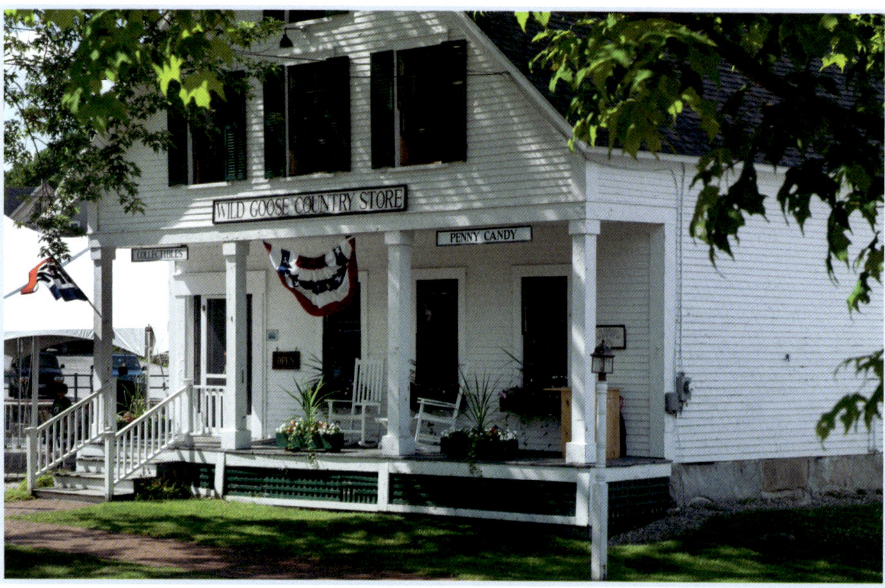

Wild Goose General Store overlooks Sunapee Harbor.

Lake Sunapee is a scenic, two-hour detour from the seacoast, and a favorite destination for those who want a quiet, rustic vacation.

The Lake Sunapee region is named for the lake and the mountain that rises from its southern shore. Nearly ten miles long and three miles wide, Lake Sunapee's rocky shore with its three working lighthouses contains many private and public beaches, like the public beach at **Mount Sunapee State Park**. You'll also find lots of art galleries and nineteenth-century architecture. Sunapee Harbor seems stuck in time. The Sunapee Riverwalk is a half-mile trail along the Sugar River behind Marzelli's Cafe at Sunapee Harbor. The **Wild Goose Country Store**, which sells a variety of products made by local artists and vendors, provides a great view of the harbor. Next to it, Flander's Stage offers live music in the summer. Speaking of music, Aerosmith's Steven Tyler and Joe Perry grew up in Sunapee.

Stop by the gardens of The Fells /John Hay National Wildlife Refuge surrounding the historic **Fells colonial estate** in Newbury. In the neighboring towns of Cornish, Newport, Meriden, Bradford, and Warner, you'll find a large collection of covered bridges. Only two out of an original thirteen Concord & Claremont Railway Company covered railroad bridges still exist in Newport, just west of Sunapee. These remaining bridges—the Wright's Bridge and the Pier Bridge (also referred to as Chandler Station Bridge)—are on Chandlers Mills Road. They cross the Sugar River and are part of the nearly ten-mile Sugar River Rail Trail. At nearly 217 feet long, the Pier Bridge, built in 1871, is the longest covered "railroad bridge" in the world. The Cornish-Windsor

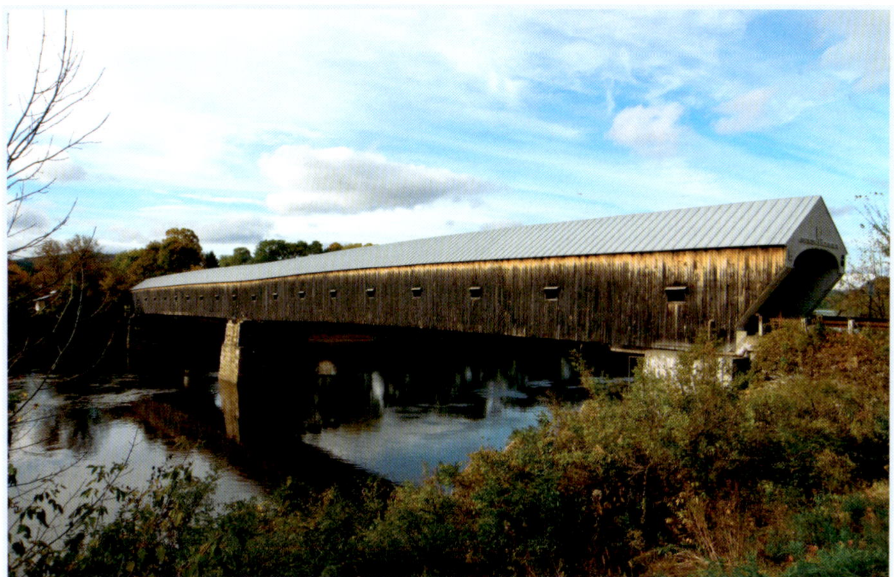

The Cornish-Windsor Bridge is the longest covered bridge in the US.

Bridge, the longest covered bridge in the United States at 449 feet, 5 inches, is a short distance west of Sunapee. It connects New Hampshire and Vermont across the Connecticut River.

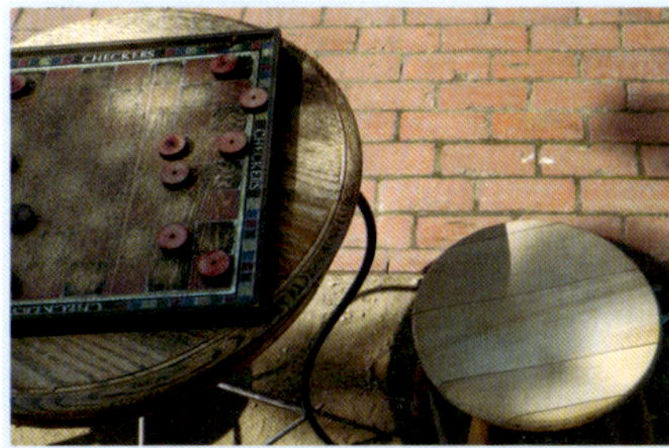

Old checkerboard beckons players.

Behind Lake Sunapee is Mount Sunapee, which offers hiking and skiing. Mount Sunapee is a five-mile-long mountain ridge spanning Newbury and Goshen in western New Hampshire. The state park's extensive trail system is used in all seasons for hiking and in winter for snowshoeing. Each August the Mount Sunapee State Park hosts the nation's oldest crafts event, the **League of New Hampshire Craftsmen's Fair**. Lake Solitude sits near the top of Mount Sunapee, about a mile's hike from the summit lodge. This small, isolated lake is in the crater of an ancient volcano. There are three trails leading from the base to the summit of Mount Sunapee.

Take in a play or musical at the **New London Barn Playhouse**, or explore the 200-year-old **Ruggles Mine** in Grafton with its giant rock tunnels.

If you enjoy antiques, the granddaddy of them all is the spacious **Prospect Hill Antiques** and Home Furnishings store in Georges Mills. For a glimpse into the Shaker culture, visit the **Enfield Shaker Museum** in Enfield. The **Hood Museum of Art** at Dartmouth College displays art from ancient cultures, the Americas, Africa, and Europe, and is one of the oldest and largest college museums in the country. **Mount Kearsage Indian Museum** covers Native American cultures, and the **Old Fort at No. 4** is a living history museum in Charlestown.

Contacts for Attractions around Lake Sunapee

Sunapee, Newbury, Enfield, and Georges Mills

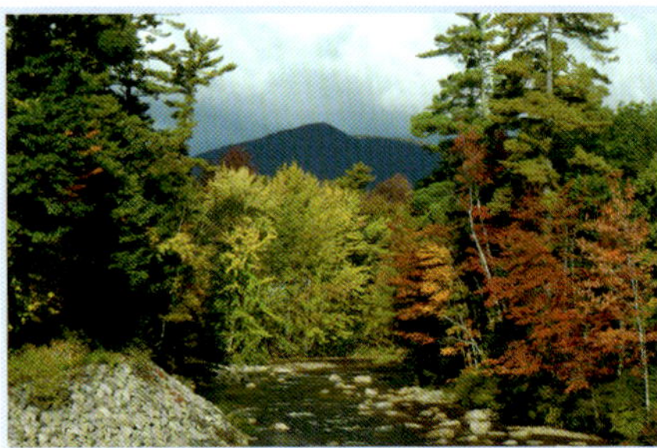

Autumn in the Lake Sunapee region.

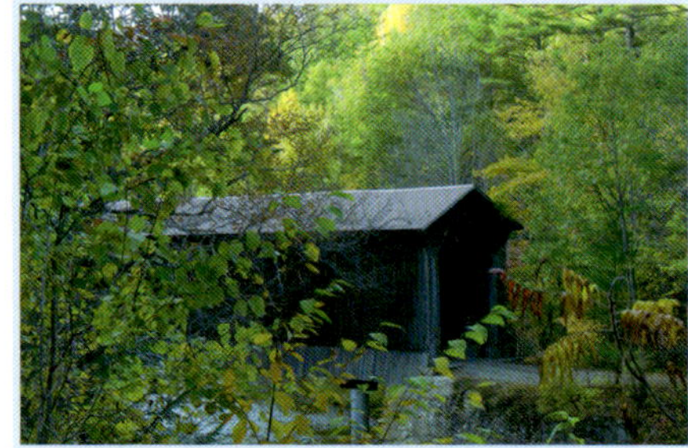

Pier Bridge is the longest covered "railroad bridge" in the world.

Wild Goose Country Store, Sunapee
(603) 763-5516

Mount Sunapee State Park, Newbury
(603) 763-5561
nhstateparks.com/sunapee.html

Mount Kearsage Indian Museum, Warner
(603) 456-2600
indianmuseum.org

Old Fort at No. 4, Charlestown
(603) 826-5700
fortat4.org

Hood Museum of Art, Hanover
(603) 646-2808
hoodmuseum.dartmouth.edu

League of New Hampshire Craftsmen Fair, Newbury
(603) 224-3375
nhcrafts.org

New London Barn Playhouse, New London
(603) 526-6710
nlbarn.org

Ruggles Mine, Grafton
(603) 523-4275
rugglesmine.com

The Fells Estate and Gardens, Newbury
(603) 763-4789
thefells.org

Prospect Hill Antiques, Georges Mills
(603) 763-9676
prospecthillantiques.com

Enfield Shaker Museum, Enfield
(603) 632-4346
shakermuseum.org

Lighthouse Cruise on Lake Sunapee

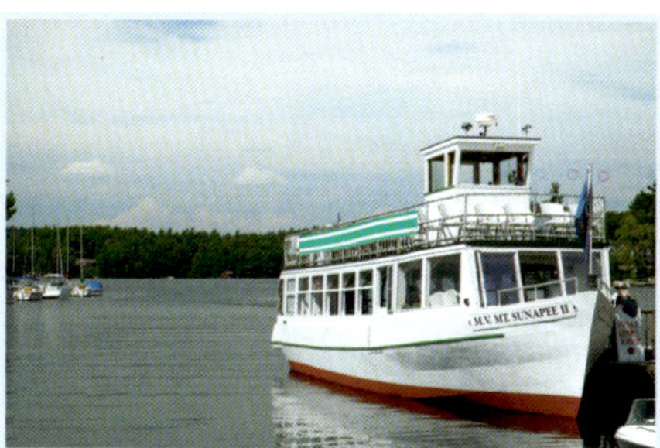

The *M.V. Mount Sunapee II* provides daily lighthouse and nature tours on the lake.

Sunapee Cruises

The *M. V. Kearsarge* runs various tours and dinner cruises that go past the lighthouses. The *M.V. Mount Sunapee II* runs a lighthouse and nature tour every day in the summer.

Sunapee Harbor, Lake Sunapee

(603) 763-4030

sunapeecruises.com

Waterfront Directions

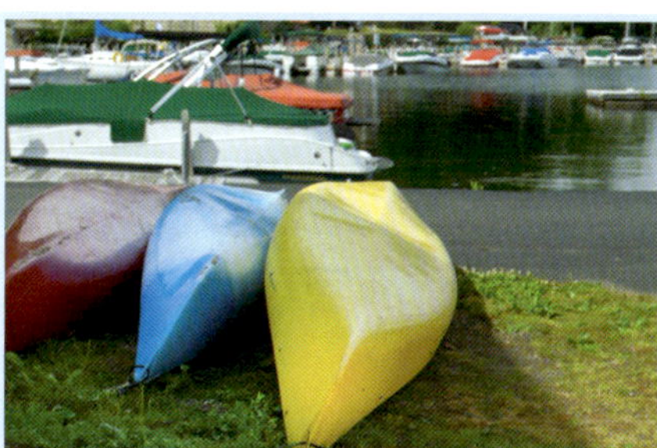
Kayaks at the dock in Sunapee Harbor.

Sunapee Harbor

All three lighthouses on Lake Sunapee are best viewed by boat. Coming from the south, take Route 89 to exit 12A, and then take a left at the end of the exit ramp. Coming from the north, take Route 89 to exit 12A, and then take a right at the end of the exit ramp. At the first light turn right onto Route 11 and follow for three miles. Take a left at the blinking light and go up and over the hill. For more parking, turn right on Burkehaven Hill Road, where there are more spaces next to the bandstand.

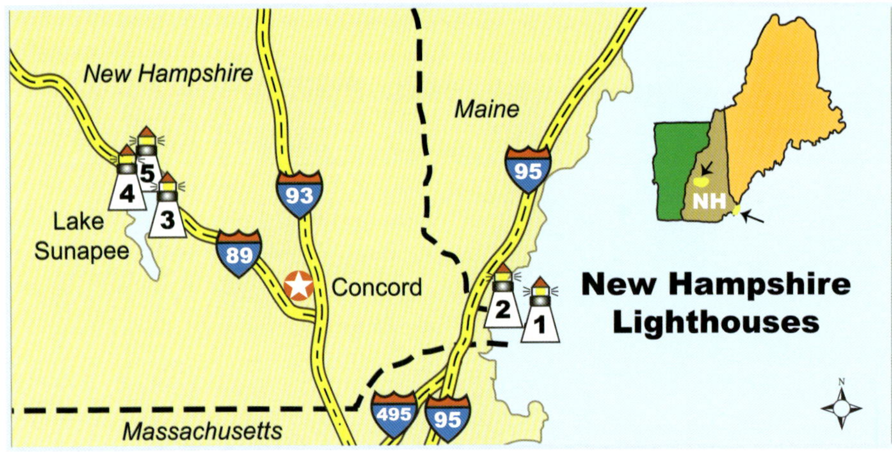

Map of New Hampshire's lighthouses. (1) White Island (Isles of Shoals), **(2)** Portsmouth Harbor, **(3)** Loon Island, **(4)** Herrick Cove, **(5)** Burkehaven.

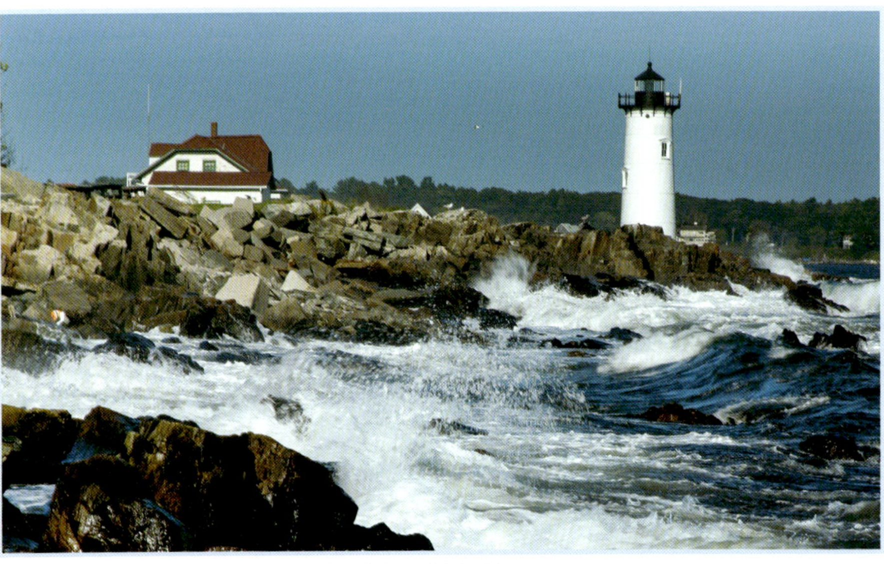

Waves crash around Portsmouth Harbor light at high tide.

Lighthouse Organizations in New Hampshire

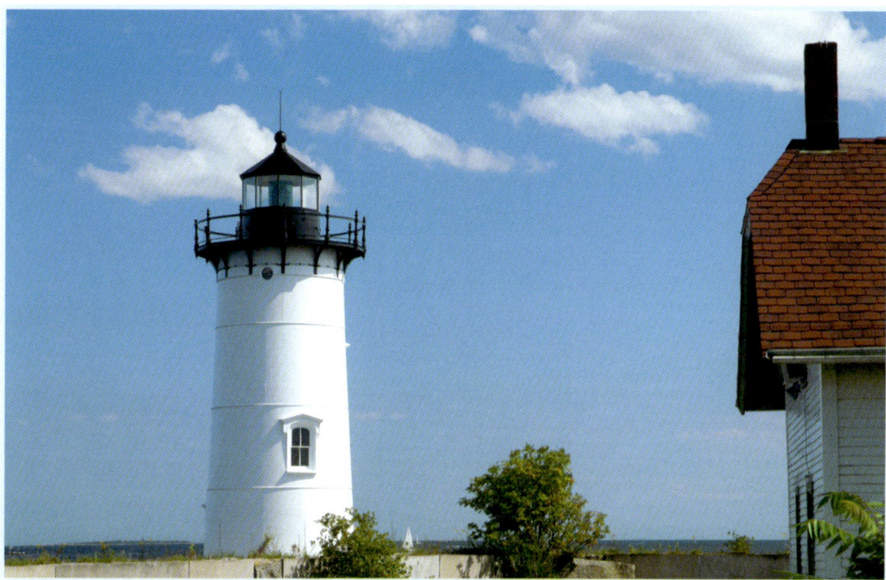

Portsmouth Lighthouse's "Friends" organization gives summer tours.

Burkehaven, Sunapee
Lake Sunapee Protection Association
(603) 763-2210

Herrick Cove, Sunapee
Lake Sunapee Protection Association
(603) 763-2210

Loon Island, Sunapee
Lake Sunapee Protection Association
(603) 763-2210

Portsmouth Harbor, Portsmouth
Friends of Portsmouth Harbor Lighthouse
(603) 431-9155

White Island (Isles of Shoals), Rye
NH Parks and Recreation
(603) 271-3556

White Island, Rye
Lighthouse Kids Incorporated / Sue Reynolds
(603) 978-2097

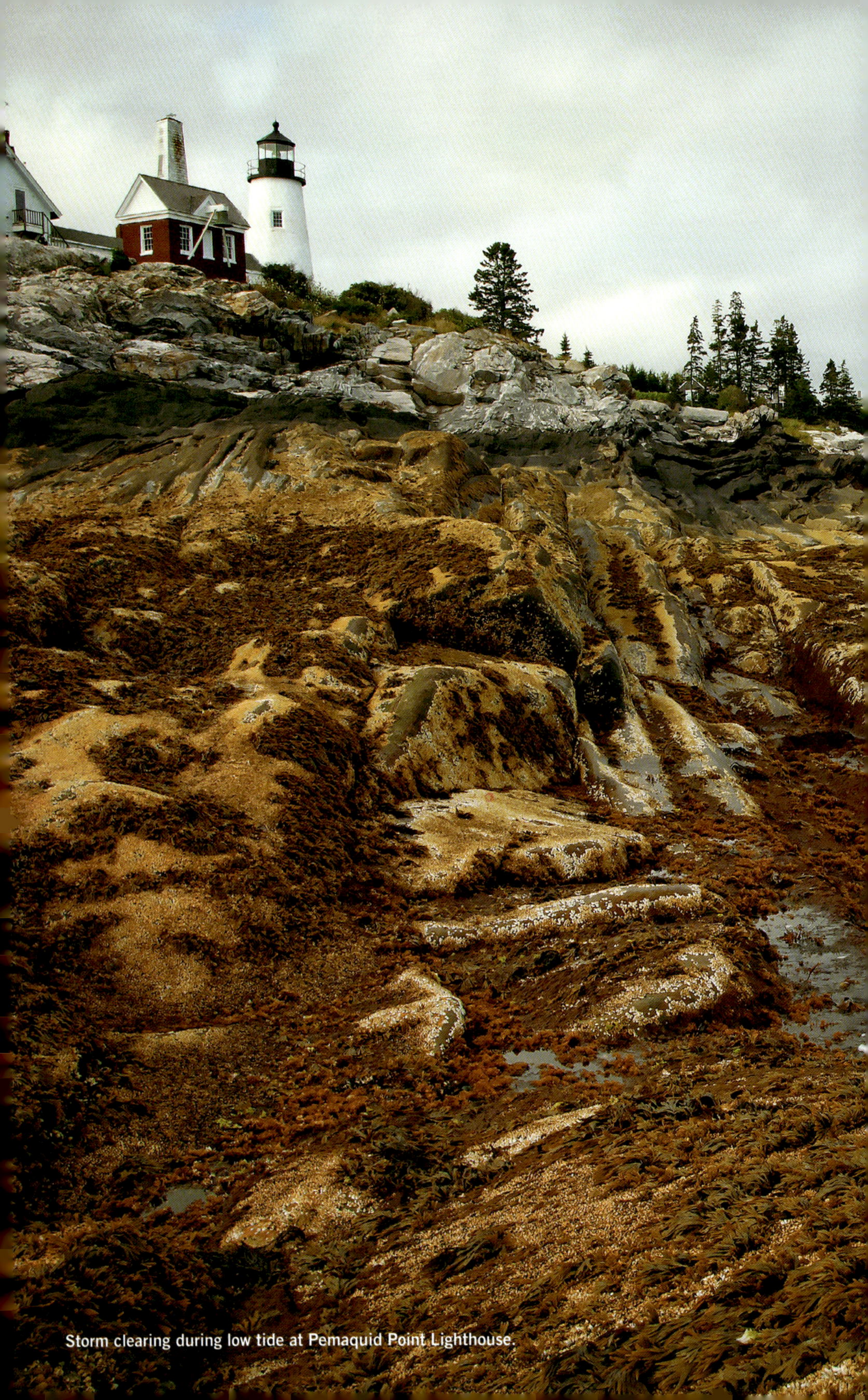

Storm clearing during low tide at Pemaquid Point Lighthouse.

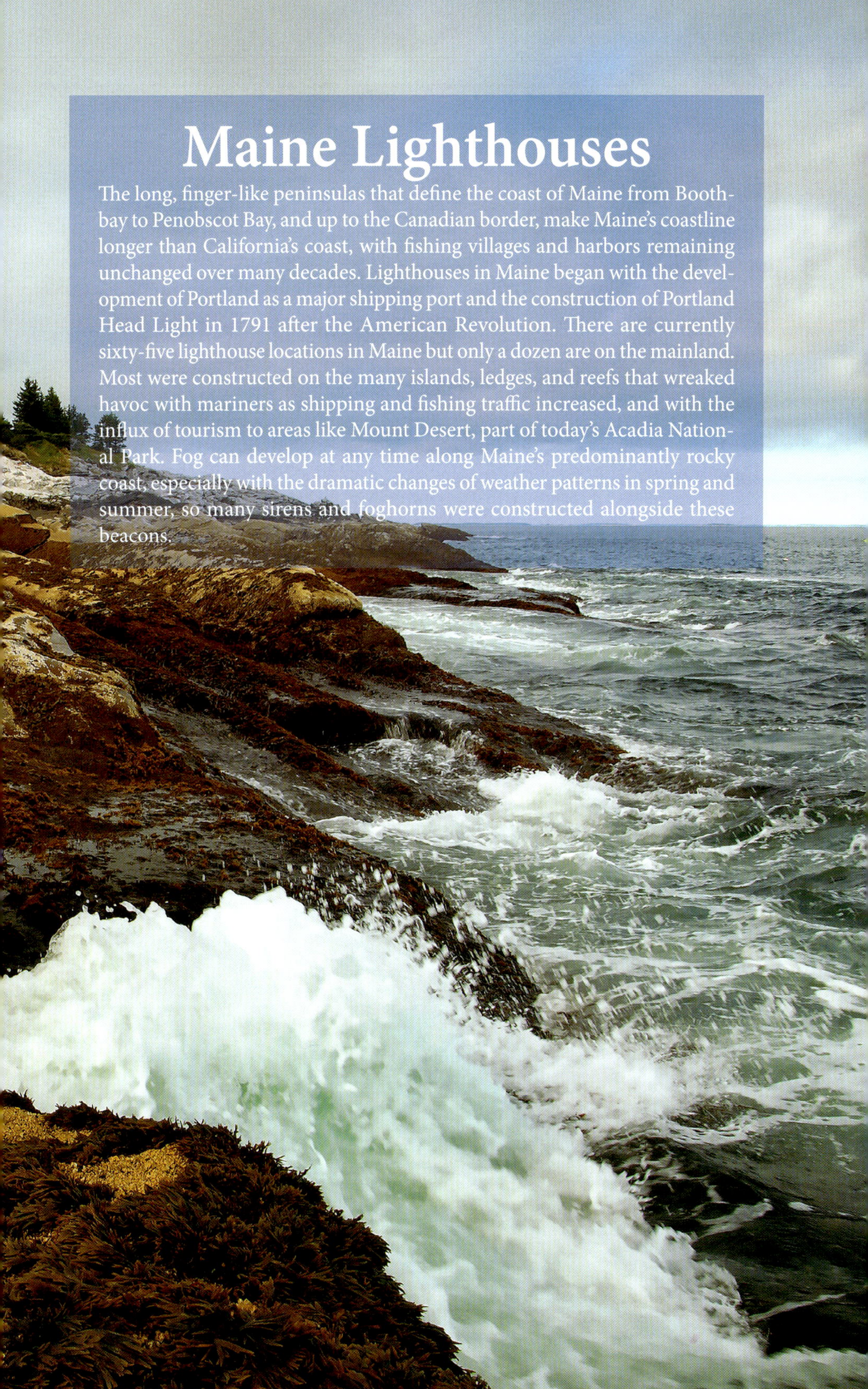

Maine Lighthouses

The long, finger-like peninsulas that define the coast of Maine from Boothbay to Penobscot Bay, and up to the Canadian border, make Maine's coastline longer than California's coast, with fishing villages and harbors remaining unchanged over many decades. Lighthouses in Maine began with the development of Portland as a major shipping port and the construction of Portland Head Light in 1791 after the American Revolution. There are currently sixty-five lighthouse locations in Maine but only a dozen are on the mainland. Most were constructed on the many islands, ledges, and reefs that wreaked havoc with mariners as shipping and fishing traffic increased, and with the influx of tourism to areas like Mount Desert, part of today's Acadia National Park. Fog can develop at any time along Maine's predominantly rocky coast, especially with the dramatic changes of weather patterns in spring and summer, so many sirens and foghorns were constructed alongside these beacons.

Southern Maine Lighthouses

Kittery, York, Kennebunk, Cape Elizabeth, and Portland

Lighthouses along southern Maine's coastline helped to guide shipping traffic into Kittery, York, Kennebunk, and Portland harbors, as well as the many lobstermen and fishermen earning their living. Portland Head Light is the oldest lighthouse in Maine, and the second oldest in the US after Boston Harbor Light in Massachusetts. Along with Cape Elizabeth, Spring Point, and Portland Breakwater lighthouses, these beacons guided mariners along Casco Bay into the shipping port of Portland, and away from treacherous ledges and shoals such as Whaleback, Boon Island, Ram Island, and Halfway Rock. Goat Island, Cape Neddick, and Wood Island Lighthouses guided mariners into nearby harbors.

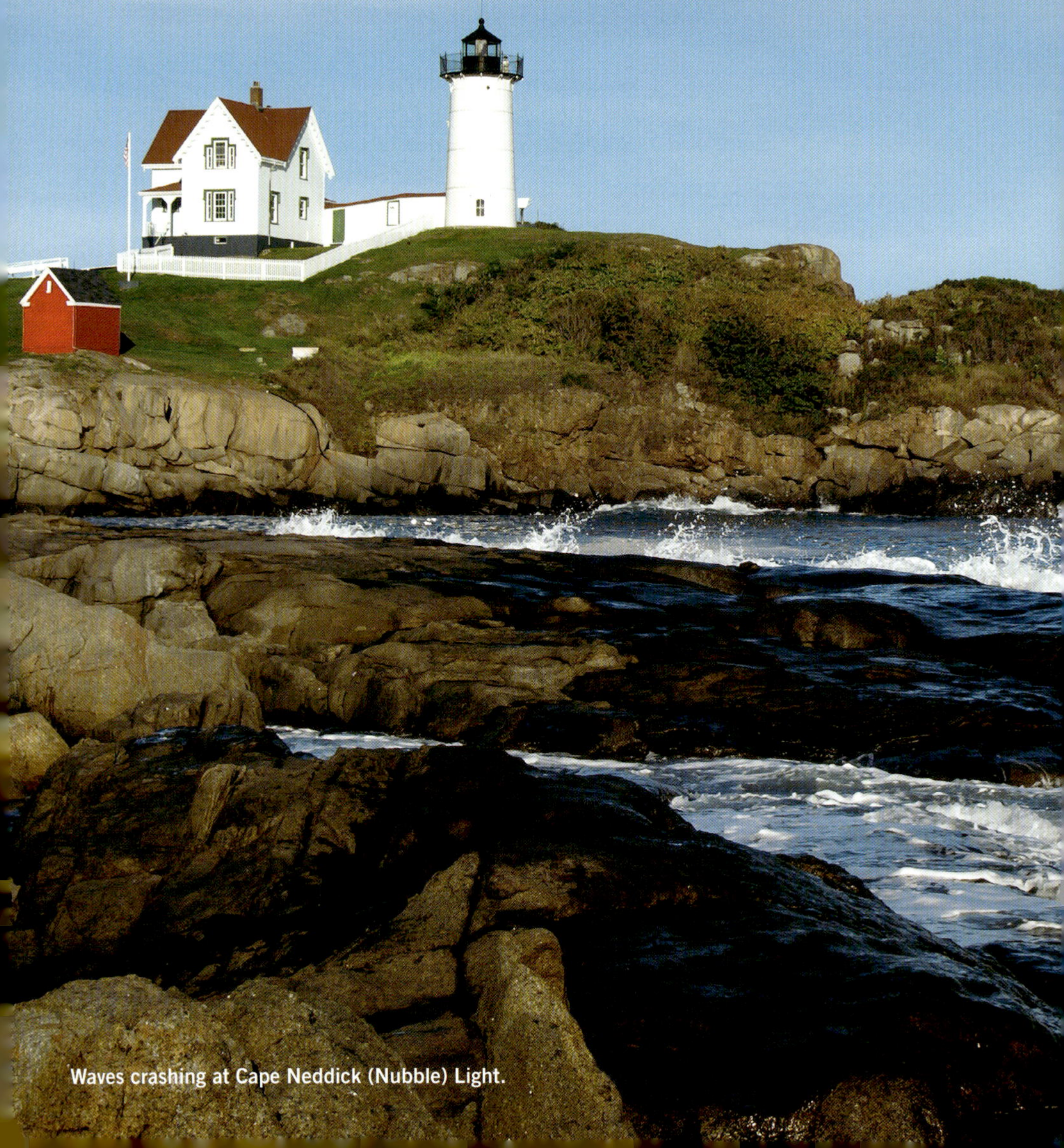

Waves crashing at Cape Neddick (Nubble) Light.

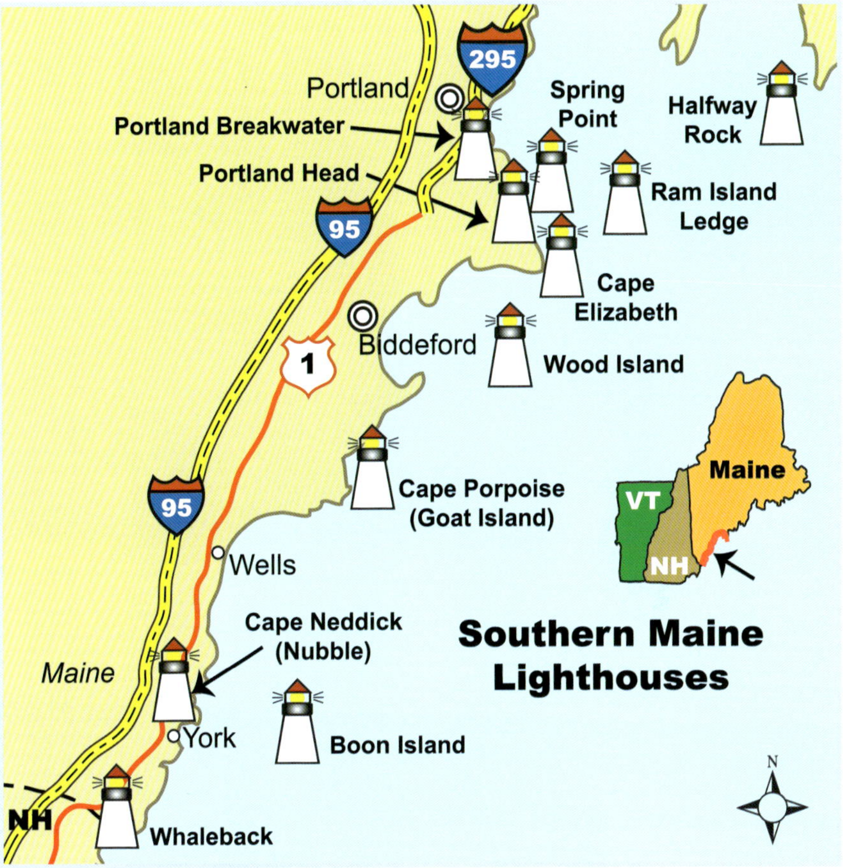

Map of southern Maine lighthouses.

Whaleback Lighthouse

Kittery (1830) • Latitude: 43° 03' 31" N • Longitude: 70° 41' 48" W

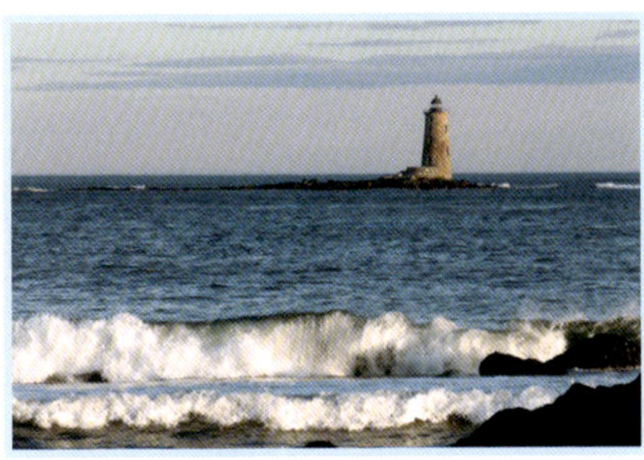

Whaleback Lighthouse during high tide.

At the mouth of the Piscataqua River, guarding the entrance to Portsmouth Harbor in New Hampshire and Kittery Harbor in Maine, Whaleback Lighthouse protected shipping traffic from the menacing Whaleback ledge, which is usually underwater at high tide. The lighthouse was rebuilt several times due to initially poor construction, its proximity to the water, and the constant bashing of New England storms.

In March 1871, keeper Ferdinand Barr, a Civil War veteran, went out in heavy seas to tend his lobster traps. Hours went by, and his three children sent out a dis-

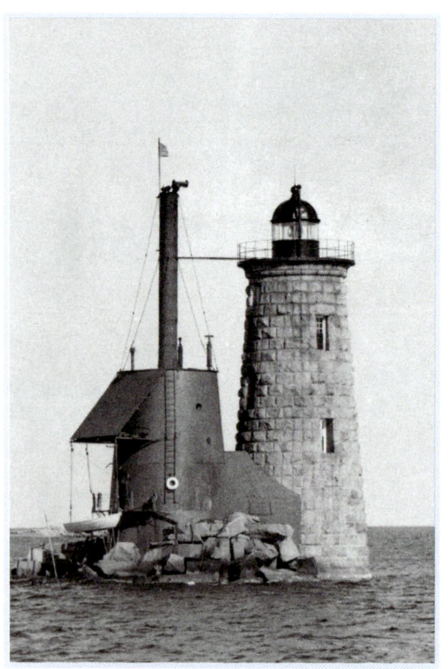

Vintage image of attached foghorn and boathouse. *Courtesy US Coast Guard.*

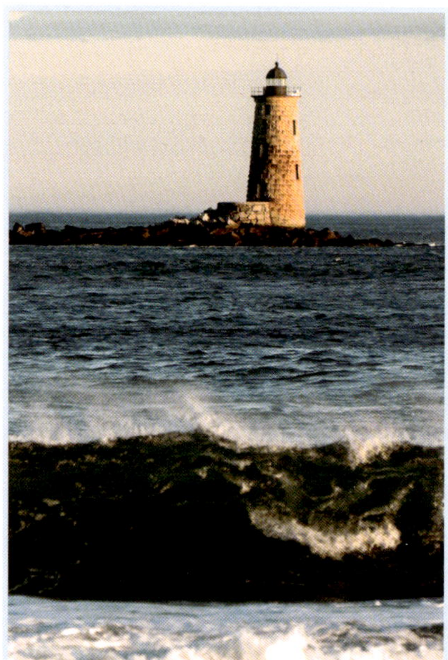

Whaleback Light in strong surf.

tress signal. The keeper's wife was in the city on errands. The watchman on nearby Wood Island lifesaving station and a local fisherman went out to locate the keeper, but they came back empty-handed; his body was never found.

Storms in 1869 caused cracks in the tower and foundation, and funds were allocated for a new tower to be constructed of granite, in the same design as Minot's Ledge Light in Massachusetts in 1870. The original tower remained standing while the new one was being built. The process was slow, as work could only be done at low tide. It was finally completed in 1872, although the old tower remained for a few more years. In 1877, it briefly served as a fog signal house.

During a fierce storm on February 15, 1863, the British Schooner *Rouser*, on its way to Boston from St. John, New Brunswick, crashed against the rocks near the lighthouse. The men pleaded with the keeper to throw them a line, but he was unable to bring the line to a safe spot. He watched in agony as all seven crew members perished.

In 1882, assistant keeper John Lewis was painting the fog signal tower when he slipped and fell to the rocks below. He later died from his injuries.

A violent storm in 1886 sent huge waves smashing against the lighthouse that flooded the living quarters of keeper Leander White, nearly drowning him. Luckily, Kittery residents Walter S. Amee and Samuel Blake rescued him after spotting his distress signal—a blanket hung from the tower.

In December 1948, historian Edward Rowe Snow, known to lighthouse keepers as the "Flying Santa," dropped a bundle of Christmas gifts from a plane, including his book *Storms and Shipwrecks of New England*. The drop was too far away for the Whaleback keepers to retrieve it, and it was carried out to sea. Three weeks later,

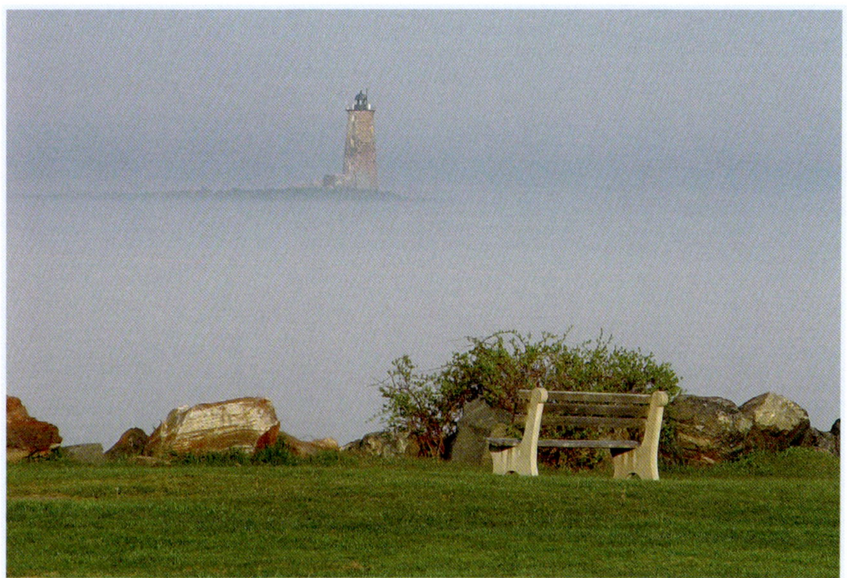

Whaleback Light encased in fog.

Eugene S. Clark was walking on a beach in Sandwich, Massachusetts, on Cape Cod and found the package, ninety miles from where it had been dropped.

Father-Daughter Rescue. The Piscataqua River has a strong current, and rogue waves are common in the area. Keeper Jedediah Rand of nearby Rye, New Hampshire, stayed at the lighthouse from 1849 to 1853, and learned firsthand the dangers of the river.

In September 1849, his fifteen-year-old daughter, Elizabeth Jane, spent three weeks at the lighthouse with her father. On the morning of September 25, Rand launched the station's rather small boat to take his daughter to New Castle Island across the river, but the craft was suddenly overturned by a large wave. The boat spilled both occupants into the water and the keeper swam to his daughter to keep her near the boat. Rand tried unsuccessfully to right the boat, and his exhausted daughter slipped into unconsciousness.

Luckily, a passing schooner heard keeper Rand's cries for help and quickly dispatched a boat to bring them across the river to New Castle. The rescuers were able to revive the girl just before they reached land. She spent only a short time in medical care on the island, returning to the lighthouse with her father that day.

 **Directions.** To get a close view of the lighthouse from Fort Foster in Kittery, from I-95 north in Portsmouth, take exit 2 and follow it to Route 236. At the traffic circle, take the third exit onto Route 236 (Rogers Road). Continue to follow Route 236 for about a mile, then bear left on Route 103. Turn right at Chauncey Creek Road and take another right at Gerrish Island Lane, which becomes Pocahontas Road. Park at the gate and walk about three-quarters of a mile to the shoreline inside Fort Foster where you can walk the pier and view the lighthouse a few hundred feet away.

On the New Hampshire side, you can see both Whaleback and Portsmouth Harbor lighthouses from Great Island Common on Route 1B, on New Castle Island.

Boon Island Lighthouse

York (1811) • Latitude: 43° 07' 18" N • Longitude: 70° 28' 36" W

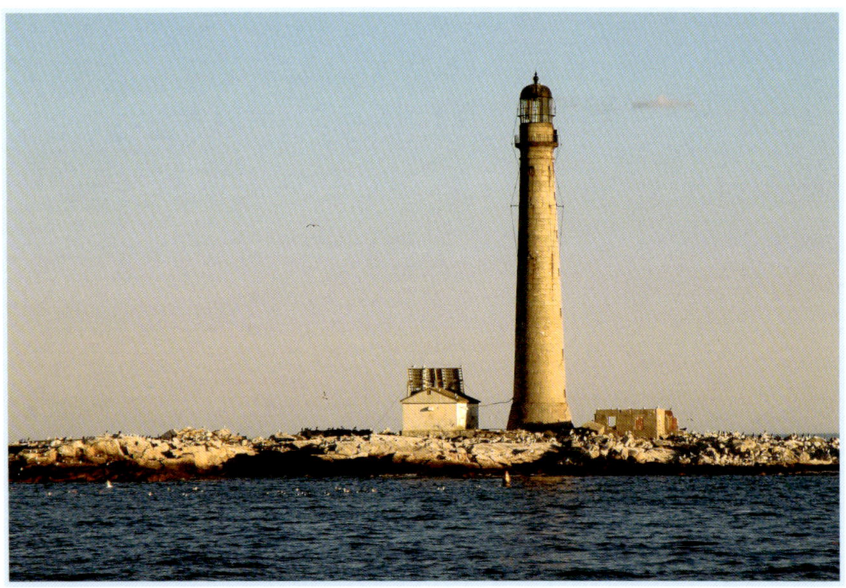

Boon Island Light at sunset.

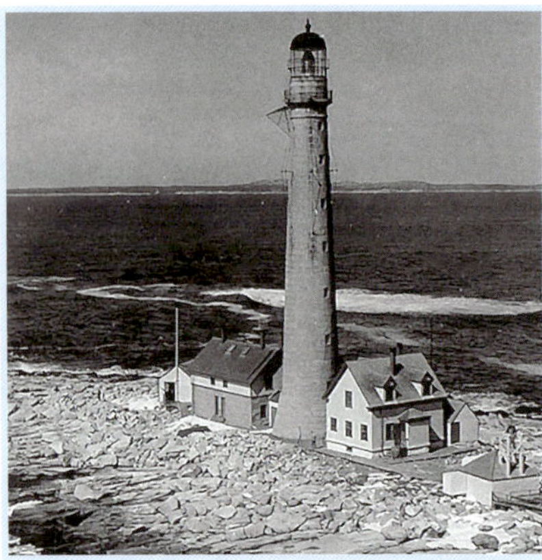

Vintage image with keeper's quarters. *Courtesy US Coast Guard.*

Boon Island lies about six miles from the York coastline and can only be viewed by boat. The rocky island is just 700 feet by 300 feet and stands only fourteen feet above sea level at its highest point.

Many shipwreck stories originated on Boon Island. In the winter of 1710, survivors of the wrecked *Nottingham Galley* survived for three weeks on the rock by resorting to cannibalism. In fact, the name "boon" came after that incident, when fishermen began placing packed food and clothing, called boon, for mariners stranded on the island. Recently, cannons found nearby in about twenty-five feet of water were believed to have been on board the *Nottingham Galley*.

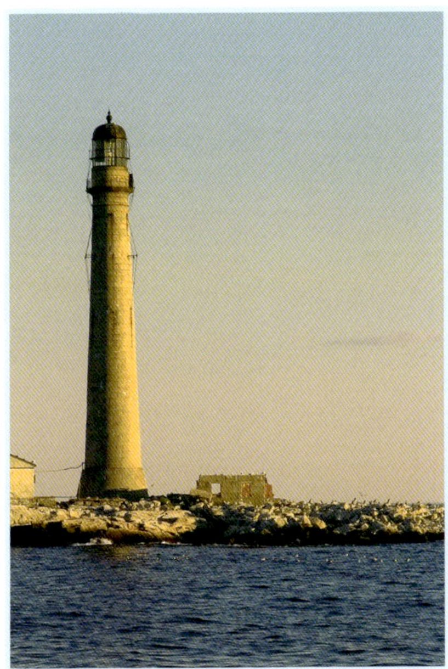

Boon Island is the tallest lighthouse tower in New England.

The lighthouse's lonely desolation and the constant pounding of waves caused the first two keepers to resign within weeks. Eliphalet Grover, the fourth keeper who started in 1816, managed to stay for twenty-two years.

Keepers had to climb the tower's 175 steps several times each night to trim and fill the lamps, often toting heavy containers of lamp oil.

In 1846, the schooner *Caroline* shipwrecked on the island during a storm and keeper Nathaniel Baker saved the entire crew. Even so, he was dismissed in 1849 for speaking out against the government, a common treatment of federal employees in those times.

During the great blizzard of 1978, three Coast Guard keepers clung to the spiral staircase inside the tower, which was swaying in the storm. They were rescued by helicopter the following the day during a lull in the blizzard and were the last keepers to staff the tower. The storm destroyed the buildings, and the Coast Guard burned the remnants to the ground in the 1980s. Only the automated tower remains today. The original second-order Fresnel lens is on permanent display at the Kittery Historical and Naval Museum.

At 133 feet, Boon Island Light is the tallest lighthouse in New England.

Keeper's Wife Goes Mad. In the mid 1800s, assistant keeper Lucas Bright arrived at Boon Island Lighthouse with his new bride, Katherine. A few months after they arrived, a December nor'easter blew in, sending huge waves over the tiny island.

Lucus Bright was feeling ill, but needed to make sure the lantern was lit in the tower. He tied a rope to his waist and went out into the biting winds and spray. Waves were breaking all around him, coating the rocks in ice as he tried to secure a bolt to the tower door. All of a sudden a rogue wave swept over the rocks and he lost his grasp, slipped into the freezing waters, and drowned.

Katherine, watching in horror, managed to grab onto the rope and pull her husband's body ashore, leaving it at the foot of the lighthouse tower.

The storm continued for five days, as Katherine, stricken with grief, took over the lighthouse duties. She ate what little food was left and slept little.

On the sixth day, when the storms had passed, the exhausted Katherine let the light go out. Fishermen from York went to investigate. The tower's temperature had fallen to ten degrees below zero. There they found Katherine, freezing from exposure and driven mad by grief and exhaustion. She was sitting at the bottom of the stairs holding the hand of her frozen husband. The fishermen brought Katherine and her husband's corpse ashore, but by then she'd completely lost her mind. She died a short time later. Over the years many keepers and mariners have reported seeing the ghost of a distraught woman on the rocks.

Cape Neddick (Nubble) Lighthouse

York (1876) • Latitude: 43° 09' 54" N • Longitude: 70° 35' 30" W

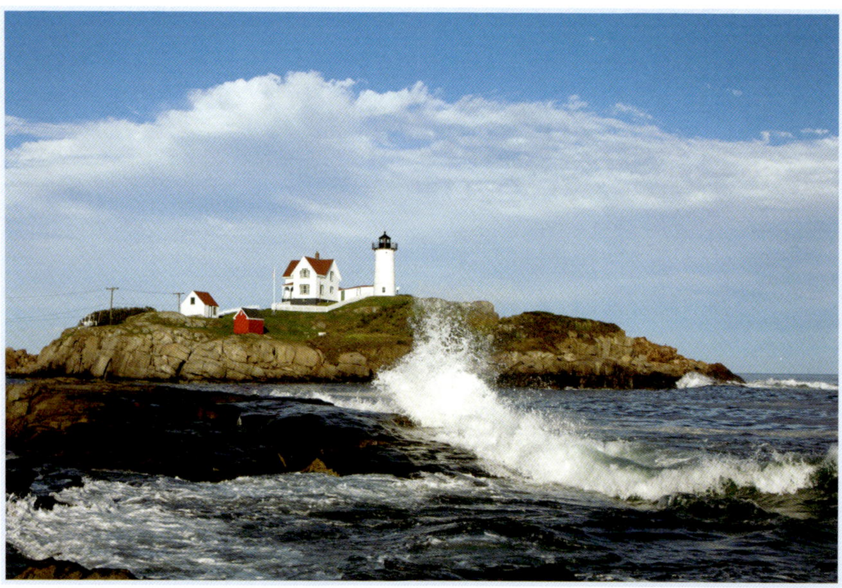

Cape Neddick Lighthouse is one of the most popular beacons in the US.

Cape Neddick Lighthouse is on a small, rocky island called Nubble Rock, sometimes referred to as Nubble Island. The first keeper was Nathaniel Otterson, followed by Brackett Lewis, who stayed for nineteen years. His daughter Hattie had a baby at the station. The first lighthouse was painted a reddish-brown, and then changed to the current white in 1902, after mariners complained that it was hard to see.

Nubble Rock is only a few hundred feet from the mainland shore, making the lighthouse a popular tourist attraction. During very low tide, people could walk to the lighthouse (although this was prohibited). Lighthouse staff used a special bucket to move supplies to and from the mainland. The second keeper, William Brooks, was fired when he was found charging visitors to be ferried to the lighthouse.

Keeper Eugene Colman's nineteen-pound cat named Mr. T, left behind from a previous keeper, used to swim the tiny channel several times a day to catch rodents along the rocky shore, making him a tourist attraction.

In the late 1960s, Coast Guard keeper David Winchester put his two children in the bucket each morning to send them on their way to school. When the district commander discovered it, he prohibited families with school-age children from being stationed at the light.

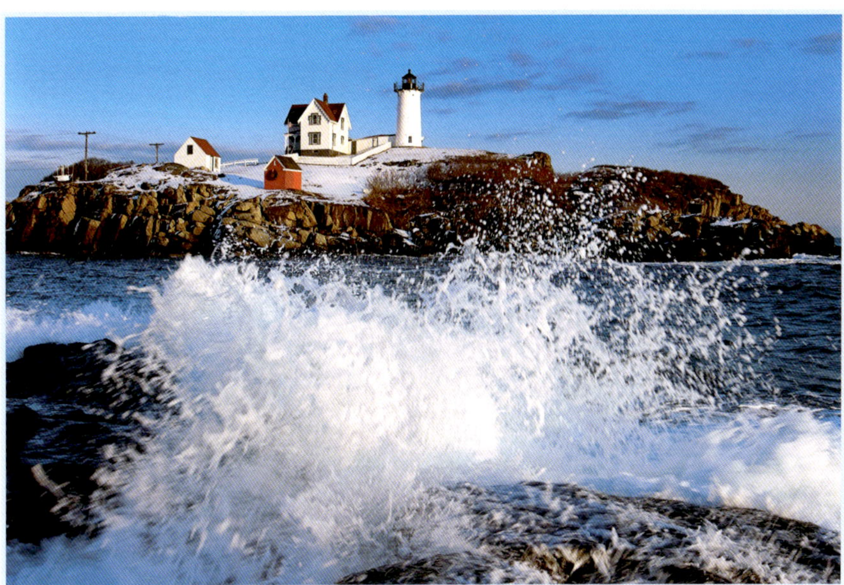

Waves crash around the rocks near Cape Neddick (Nubble) Light.

The Wreck of the Isadore. The story of the *Isadore* tragedy in 1842 begins a couple of nights before it set sail with a load of cargo from Kennebunkport, Maine. One of the crewmen, Thomas King, dreamed about the wreckage of a ship resembling the *Isadore* and its crew washed up on shore as seven coffins. He told the dream to the captain, Leander Foss, and begged to be left ashore, but the captain threatened that he had better be on board when the ship left or face serious consequences. Another crewman had the same dream and was given the same ultimatum when he confronted the captain.

On Thanksgiving night, the call went out for all crew to make ready for sail. King decided to desert his post and hid in town. The *Isadore* sailed out of Kennebunkport with a load of lumber, bound for New Orleans. As it was leaving port, the wind picked up out of the northeast and snow began to fall, and soon the storm intensified to gale-force winds. Twenty-foot waves tossed the vessel toward Cape Neddeck Island in blinding snow, where it crashed on the rocks and sank.

The wreckage was discovered the next morning. The bodies of seven crewmen, out of fourteen aboard, washed ashore. One of the bodies was the other crewman who had also dreamed about the coffins but was too frightened of the captain's wrath to remain ashore. Captain Ross's body was never found. The incident generated many petitions for a lighthouse on Nubble Rock.

Exploring the grounds. The lighthouse is one of the most photographed in the US, and is on a small "nubble" island near the entrance to the York River, a few hundred feet from Sohier Park, off Nubble Road from York Beach. If you carefully wander onto the rocks of the park during high tide, you can get great photos of waves crashing in front of the lighthouse. There is a restaurant just before the parking lot, and a few hundred feet up the road is an ice cream shack.

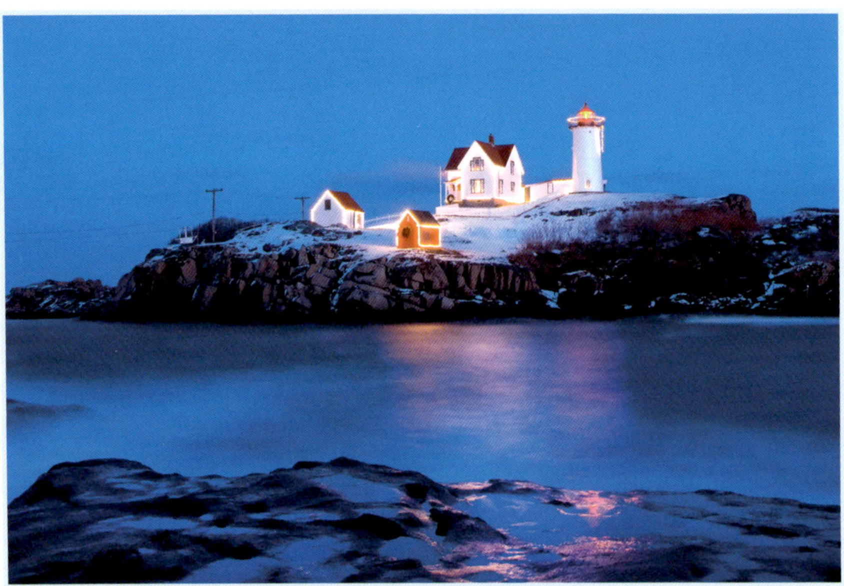

Cape Neddick (Nubble) Light is decorated and lit during the holiday season.

The lighthouse is decorated and lit during the holiday season and the annual Christmas in July event.

 **Directions.** Take Route 1 in York, to Route 1A, following it to York Beach (called Long Sands Beach). At the north end of the beach, take Nubble Road to Sohier Park Road to the parking lot.

Goat Island (Cape Porpoise) Lighthouse

Kennebunkport (1835) • Latitude: 43° 21' 30" N • Longitude: 70° 25' 30" W

Goat Island Light marks the entrance to Cape Porpoise Harbor on Goat Island. It was built to guide mariners into Cape Porpoise Harbor, which had become a busy fishing center. There were treacherous rocks and ledges near and around Goat Island, which continued to claim vessels, even with the lighthouse nearby—forty-six boats between 1865 and 1920.

Fortunately there were no deaths from these accidents, thanks to the heroism of the keepers at Goat Island. Coast Guardsman Joseph Bakken and his family were on Goat Island during a 1947 gale that sent waves crashing across the island, causing damage to the walkway and boat slip. During the storm, the family forgot about their dog and her newborn puppies. The mother and her litter were later found safe and sound in a box floating in several feet of water in the flooded basement. In 1990, Goat Island Light became the last lighthouse in Maine to be automated; the community had been determined to keep it manned to avoid vandalism.

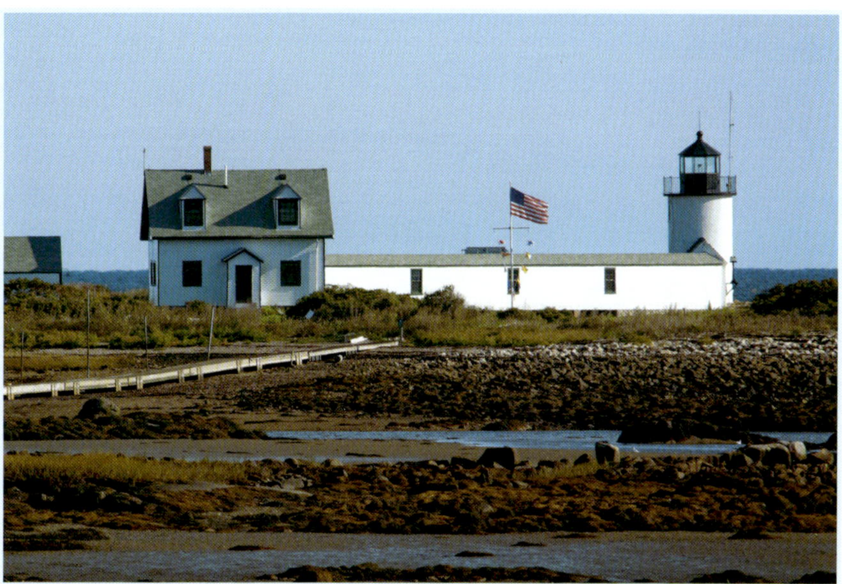

Goat Island (Cape Porpoise) Lighthouse with new walkway construction.

During the George H. W. Bush presidency, Secret Service agents lived at Goat Island to keep a watchful eye when the president visited his home in Kennebunkport a short distance away along the shore.

In 1992, the station was leased to the Kennebunkport Conservation Trust, and in 1998, with the establishment of the Maine Lights Program, the station was turned over to the trust for maintenance, restoration, and preservation under the new guidelines. In 2009, the trust started restoring the station to what it would have looked like in the 1950s. In 2011, the fog bell and walkway were reconstructed.

 **Directions for distant view.** From Route 1, take Highway 9E through Kennebunkport. Bear right at the fork by the Cape Porpoise Post Office, onto Pier Road to the fishing pier, where you can view the lighthouse from a distance.

Wood Island Lighthouse

Biddeford (1808) • Latitude: 43° 27' 25" N • Longitude: 70° 19' 45" W

Maine's second oldest lighthouse marks the entrance to the Saco River. Benjamin Cole was its first keeper, and it was plagued with problems because of the poor construction. The island was full of trees until 1869, when they were destroyed by a fierce winter gale and then by fire later that year. The lighthouse was rebuilt in 1858 and has been the source of legends, rescues, and ghost stories over the years.

Keeper's Heroism Appreciated by the Canadian Government. Eben Emerson was keeper during the Civil War years. In March of 1865, thick fog rolled into the region accompanied by heavy surf from an offshore storm. The keeper was awakened by

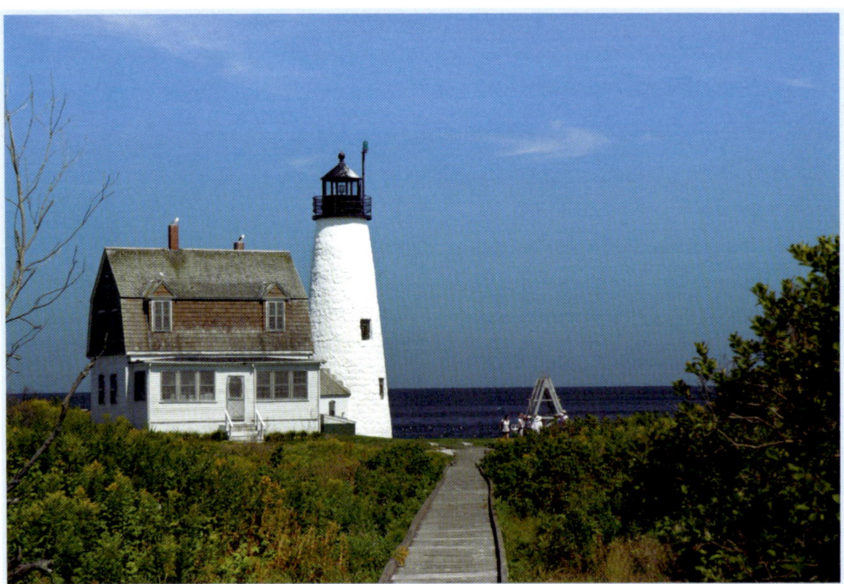

Wood Island Lighthouse in Biddeford, Maine.

screams coming from the brig *Edyth Ann* from Nova Scotia. The vessel had wrecked onto nearby Washburn Ledge. Emerson found a resident fisherman to help him in the rescue, and the two men launched the light station's small rowboat into the heavy seas. They found the crewmen clinging to the rigging, and Emerson climbed onto the brig, where he found one lifeboat still safely hanging. The keeper convinced the frightened crew to climb onto the lifeboat, and then he quickly returned to his rowboat. He waited patiently for a large wave to come near the lifeboat, and yelled, "Cut loose!" The boat dropped onto the wave and the crew rode the wave to safety away from the vessel. The wreck started to break apart as they looked on.

The Canadian government would later award a plaque and a special pair of binoculars to Emerson for his extraordinary heroism. After Emerson retired from his duties as lighthouse keeper, he became Biddeford's deputy marshal.

Famous Dog "Sailor" at Wood Island Light. Keeper Thomas Henry Orcutt tended Wood Island lighthouse from 1886 to 1905. Around 1894, he acquired an eight-week-old puppy named Sailor, who became a constant companion and an eager learner as he watched his master work.

In foggy weather, the bell sounded two strikes to identify the lighthouse station. In fair weather, it was also customary for passing ships to salute the lighthouse keeper with three whistle blasts, to which the keeper would respond by ringing the fog bell. After months of training, whenever coastal fog blanketed the area, or when he heard a ship's whistle blowing, Sailor would eagerly run out of the lighthouse quarters to the fog bell, grab the rope in his mouth, and ring the requisite number of tolls.

Sailor became quite famous to the local mariners over the years as the "Wood Island Dog." The ships would ring their bells or blow their whistles as they passed

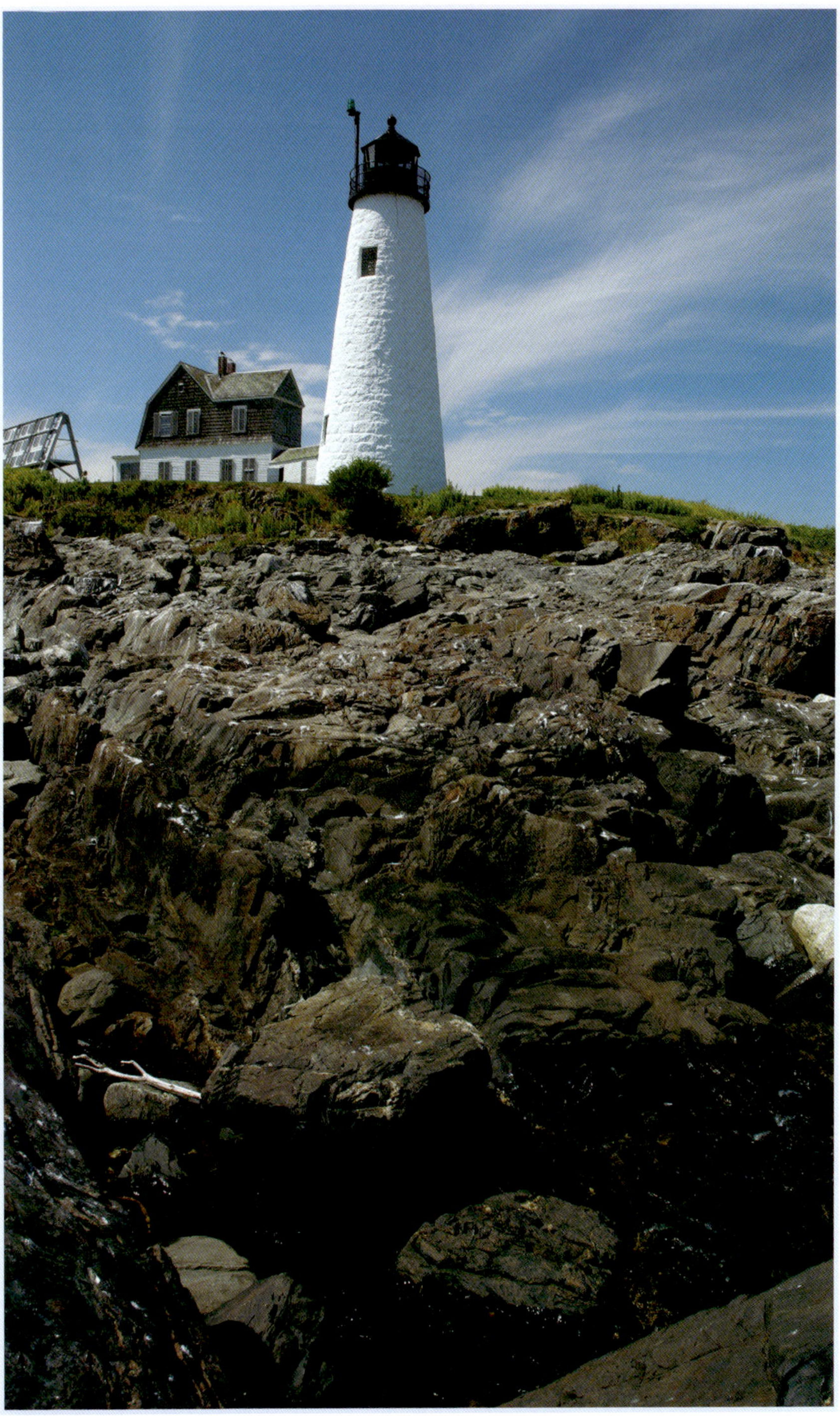

The Wood Island Lighthouse protected mariners from the rocky shoreline.

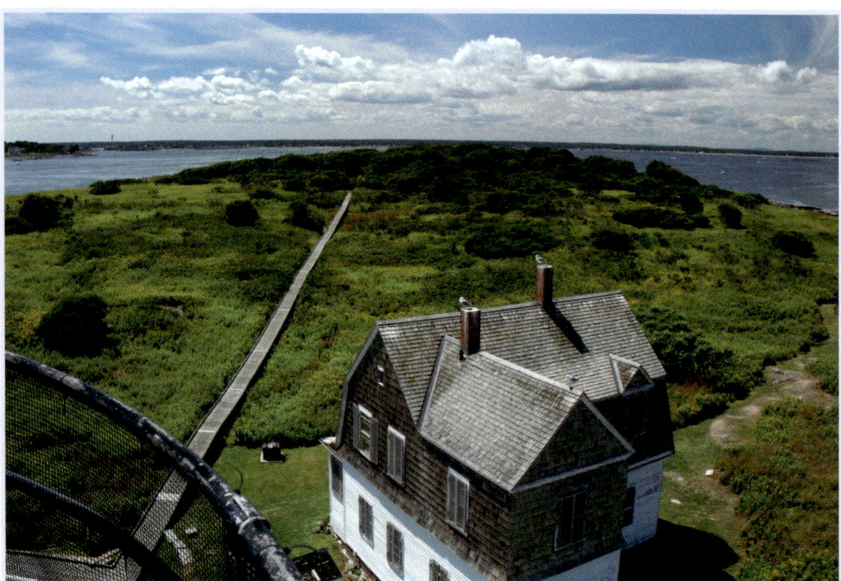

View of Wood Island from the lighthouse tower.

by the lighthouse, and then watch as the dog would run over to the bell and ring it in response. Sailor was perfectly content to stay alongside the keeper while he performed his duties, and was always excited when the opportunity arose to ring the bell.

Sailor died of old age in keeper Orcutt's arms in 1905. A few months later, Orcutt, deeply depressed at the loss of his companion and getting along in years himself, resigned his post and passed away shortly afterward.

Lobsterman Shoots Local Sheriff. One of the best-known Maine lighthouse legends involves a murder-suicide from an altercation between a lobster fisherman, who was also a local sheriff peacefully living on the island, and a drunken resident who shot the sheriff, then shot himself.

Frederick Milliken was a lobster fisherman and part-time sheriff at Biddeford Pool near Biddeford in Maine. He lived on Wood Island with his wife and three children and was a rather large, peaceful man in his thirties, known as the town's gentle giant. Two drifters who were part-time fishermen, Howard Hobbs and William Moses, persuaded Milliken to rent them his empty chicken coop shack. Both men had a drinking problem and fell behind in their rent.

One day in June 1896, Hobbs and Moses returned to the island from a session of heavy drinking on the mainland. Sheriff Milliken asked them to meet him at his house to discus the overdue rent. Hobbs, carrying a rifle, started arguing with Milliken. Milliken tried to persuade Hobbs to hand over the weapon. Hobbs claimed that his gun was not loaded as he waved it around, but as Milliken reached for it, the gun fired into Milliken's abdomen. Milliken's wife, who had witnessed the event, helped carry her wounded husband to his house. Hobbs followed, apologizing, still holding the gun.

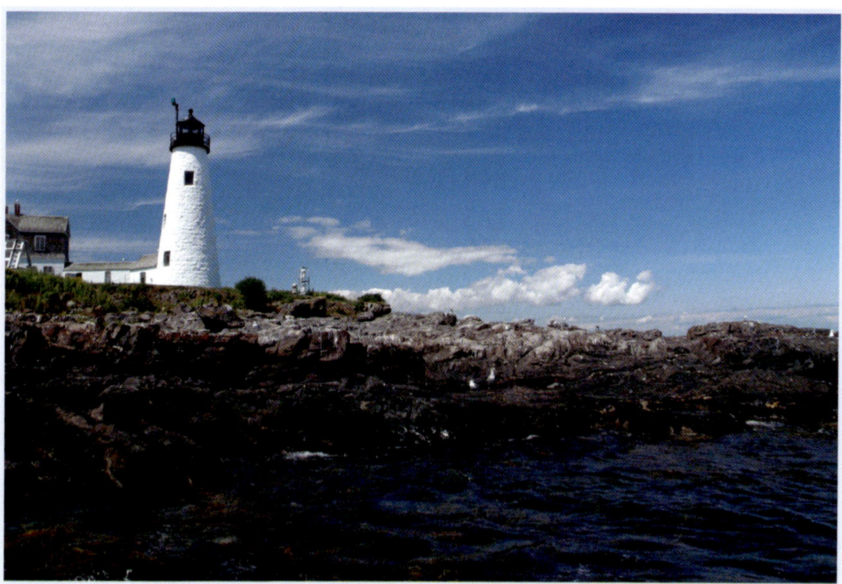

Wood Island Lighthouse and the rocky shoreline.

Still in a drunken daze, Hobbs ran off to the nearby lighthouse keeper's dwelling to get help from keeper Orcutt. Milliken died less than an hour later, and keeper Orcutt advised Hobbs to give himself up to the authorities. Instead, Hobbs ran off to his shack and shot himself in the head.

Many believe the ghosts of Hobbs and Milliken haunt Wood Island Lighthouse. People have reported hearing moans coming from the shack, seeing shadows and a woman in white (believed to be Milliken's wife), and locked doors that have been mysteriously opened at the lighthouse.

Rescue of the Keeper's Daughter. Laurier Burnham was the Coast Guard keeper at Wood Island Lighthouse with his wife Lily and two children from 1959 to 1963. On November 29, 1960, a near-tragedy occurred when his two-year-old daughter, Tammy, became seriously ill and needed to get to the mainland for immediate medical attention. The seas were rough as a storm approached in the late afternoon. Burnham signaled the Coast Guard station at Biddeford Pool that he needed help. They sent a thirty-foot boat towing a small skiff with a four-man crew. Manned by two seamen, Ed Syvinski and Raymond Bill, the skiff was sent to the island boat ramp to pick up the sick child and transport her back to the main boat.

Keeper Burnham handed over his daughter to the seamen. As they set out for the main boat, a thick fog rolled in and a rogue wave capsized the small skiff, tossing the little girl and the two seamen into the water. In the darkening skies and thick fog, neither Burnham nor the anchored Coast Guard boat knew that the three were struggling in the cold waters. Seaman Raymond Bill took off swimming toward the Coast Guard boat to get help. Chief John F. Kennedy and engineman Kenneth Rouleau spotted seaman Bill with their searchlight and got him to safety.

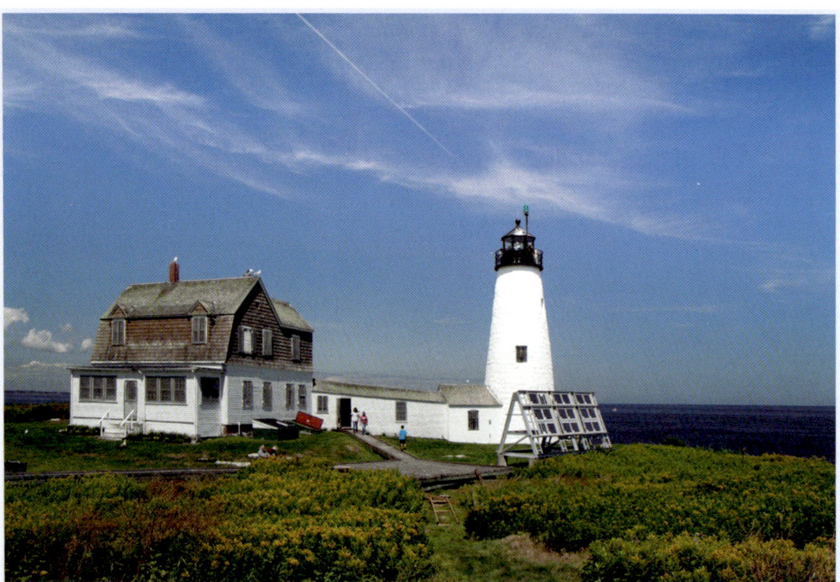

Lighthouse tours are offered in the summer.

Seaman Syvinski still hung onto little Tammy even though he sank below the chilling waves several times. He finally made it to nearby Negro Ledge Island and held her in waist deep water, while waiting for help.

An hour had gone by when keeper Burnham got a call from Fletcher's Neck Station, stating they found seaman Bill but believed Syvinski and the keeper's daughter had drowned. Against orders to stay at his post in the storm, Burnham set out to find the pair in his peapod boat. He knew the area quite well, and his initial hunch was to check nearby Negro Island, where he luckily found them. After she was pulled into the boat, Tammy slipped into unconsciousness, and the keeper quickly headed toward the dim light from the Coast Guard boat. Chief Kennedy spotted him with his searchlight and radioed the Fletcher's Neck Light Station that they had the survivors.

Keeper Burnham was ordered back to the lighthouse, but the Coast Guard vessel became disoriented in the heavy fog of the storm. Preston Alley, a local lobsterman who had been navigating the harbor for over thirty years, heard the calls on his two-way radio and set out to help. He found the Coast Guard boat near a ledge and persuaded the reluctant crew to give the girl to him. Alley made haste for the shore as the Coast Guard boat followed. Chief Kennedy radioed the hospital and told his family to bring blankets to the dock. When he and Alley arrived at Biddeford Pool, Kennedy's family members were waiting on the dock with warm blankets, along with Tammy's grandparents.

When Tammy arrived at Notre Dame Hospital, her body temperature had plummeted to a dangerous eighty-two degrees. As the night wore on, miraculously her temperature increased. Within five days she was released from the hospital and became known locally as the "little lighthouse child." Thanks to the brave efforts of seamen Ed Syvinski and Raymond Bill, chief Kennedy, engineman Rouleau, keeper Burnham, and lobsterman Preston Alley, Tammy made a full recovery.

Exploring the grounds. The lighthouse is on Wood Island, east of the mouth of the Saco River about a mile from the mainland. The lighthouse and grounds are operated by the Friends of Wood Island Light (FOWL). FOWL provides daily water shuttle tours to Wood Island during the summer months, and will guide visitors to the other side of the island where the lighthouse is. The lighthouse tower and keeper's house have been restored close to their original state. Ghost-hunting and other special tours are also being offered to raise funds for the continuing restoration.

Bob Orcutt was awarded the Friends of Wood Island Lighthouse Len Hadley Volunteer of the Year award in 2012 as one of the three Light Runner Captains who provide access to the island. He carries on a long tradition of service as the great-grandson of famous Wood Island Lighthouse keeper Thomas Henry Orcutt.

Directions to Wood Island Shuttle. From Route 9, turn off and follow Route 208 (Bridge Avenue) to Biddeford Pool. At the end of Bridge Avenue, turn left on Mile Stretch Road and head toward the fire station. When you pass Hattie's Restaurant, the road bears right. Mile Stretch Road meets L. B. Orcutt Boulevard at the top of the rise. Turn left on L. B. Orcutt, and then go over the rise and straight down the hill a couple of hundred yards. Vine's Landing is behind the Red Geranium Store, where you can park on the road using the parking signs.

Cape Elizabeth Lighthouse

Cape Elizabeth (1829) • Latitude: 43° 33' 56" N • Longitude: 70° 12' 00" W

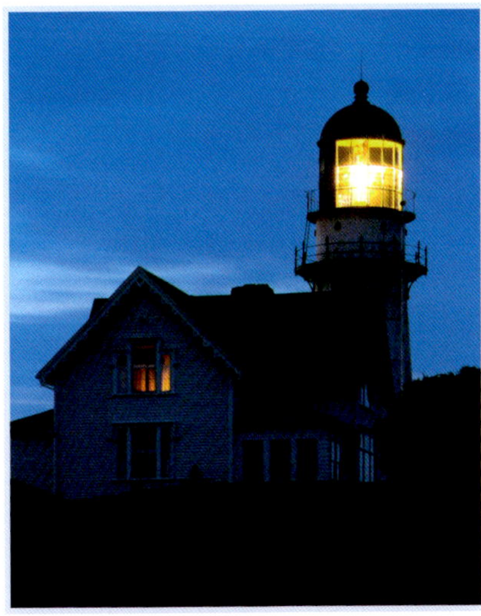

Cape Elizabeth Lighthouse is one of the most powerful beacons in New England.

Built as two rubble stone towers 300 yards apart, this station was originally called Two Lights. The east or Front Range tower had a fixed light, and the west tower or Rear Range light had a revolving light. This combination was set up so the station would not be confused with Portland Head Light or Wood Island Light. Elisha Jordan was the first keeper, one of eighteen applicants. Steam-driven warning whistles were installed in the twin towers in 1869, the first used in North America. Both lights were rebuilt in 1874. In 1924, the government had the west tower dismantled. American painter Edward Hopper painted several views of Cape Elizabeth's Two Lights in 1927 and 1929. His oil painting, *The*

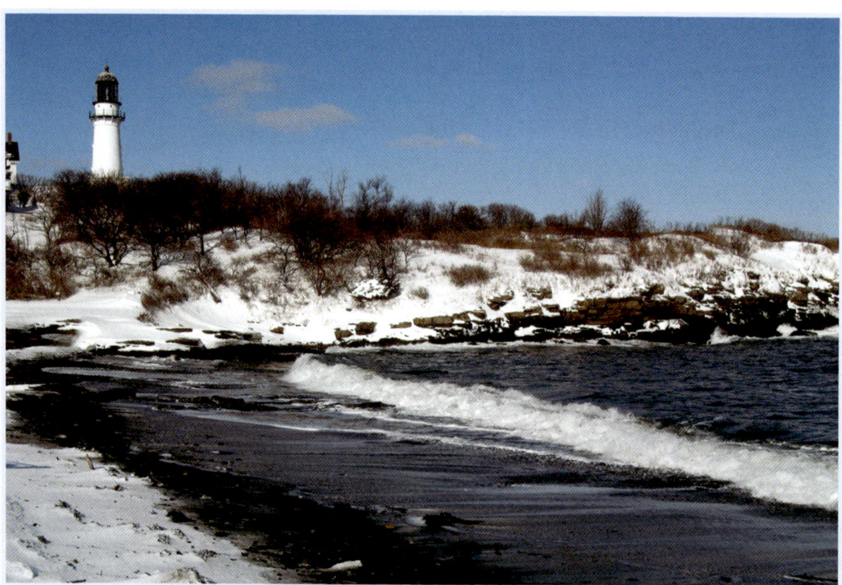

Lighthouse atop a rocky shoreline.

Lighthouse at Two Lights, became his best-known lighthouse painting after it was featured on a US postage stamp in 1970 commemorating Maine's statehood. The paintings are occasionally displayed at the Metropolitan Museum of Art.

In January 1934, sixty-five-year-old keeper Joseph H. Upton went to fix an auxiliary light, as the main light had suddenly failed at the east tower. Hours later, when he failed to return, his wife discovered him unconscious with a fractured skull. He had fallen down the stairs to the base of the tower and later passed away. Some claim to have seen his uniformed ghost near the tower.

On March 3, 1947, the *Oakley L. Alexander* broke up in a fierce gale eight miles out. Luckily, all thirty-two crew members were on the rear half of the vessel when it broke away. They were miraculously carried to the rocks at Two Lights, where keeper Earle Drinkwater, his crew, and local fishermen were able to rescue all aboard.

During World War II, the west tower became an observation point after its lantern was removed. In 1971, actor Gary Merrill, ex-husband of Bette Davis, purchased the west tower for $28,000, and later resold it. Today the Cape Elizabeth Light is one of the most powerful lights on the New England Coast, visible for twenty-seven miles.

The Wreck of the Bohemian. On February 4, 1864, the 295-foot steamer *Bohemian* was leaving Liverpool, England, for Portland, Maine. It carried about 219 passengers consisting of 200 Irish immigrants and nineteen cabin-class passengers. The *Bohemian* was only a couple of miles from the rocky shoreline of Cape Elizabeth and was proceeding dangerously close to Alden's Rock, marked only by a silent buoy, when Captain Borland miscalculated the distance in the fog. At 8:00 p.m., the *Bohemian* struck the ledge, ripping a gash in the hull that sent water pouring into the engine room. Most of the boats launched in the hysteria were not full and con-

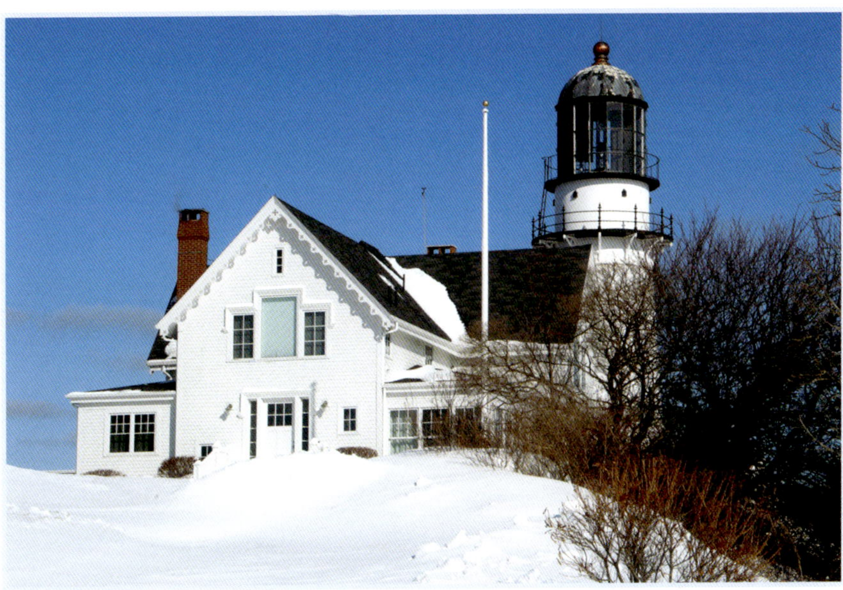

Cape Elizabeth Light (front east tower) after winter storm.

tained mostly men. The frightened passengers and crew aboard the lifeboats refused to return to the sinking ship to pick up those stranded on the deck, for fear of capsizing. Some jumped into the icy waters in hopes of being hauled into the boats, but many drowned.

An hour and a half later, the *Bohemian* sank. Two crew members and forty passengers, all Irish immigrants from the lower steerage class, perished. Cape Elizabeth residents opened their homes to the exhausted survivors, and city hall provided a temporary shelter area as survivors tried to notify their families in England and Ireland. The Portland Board of Trade collected money for clothing.

The jury concluded that Captain Borland was responsible for the disaster and that his crew did not act professionally. After public outcry, the Portland Board of Trade had bell buoy markers placed, including at Alden's Rock. Portland Head Lighthouse's visibility was also improved by raising the tower twenty feet in 1865. A second-order Fresnel lens was also installed to generate a more powerful light.

Most Dramatic Lighthouse Rescue. One of the most dramatic rescues in lighthouse history involved keeper Marcus Hannah. In 1885, a January blizzard kept keeper Hannah up all night sounding the fog whistle. He had an extremely bad cold, and after sunrise, the exhausted keeper trudged through huge snowdrifts from the fog house to the keeper's house to try to get a few hours of sleep. Early in the morning, he was awakened by his wife, who told him that the *Australia* had shipwrecked on Dyers Ledge at Two Lights.

Hannah ran down to the shoreline and had his assistant keeper, Hiram Staples, get help nearby. The ship's captain had been washed overboard and the other pair of crew members were frozen to the ice-covered rigging, barely alive.

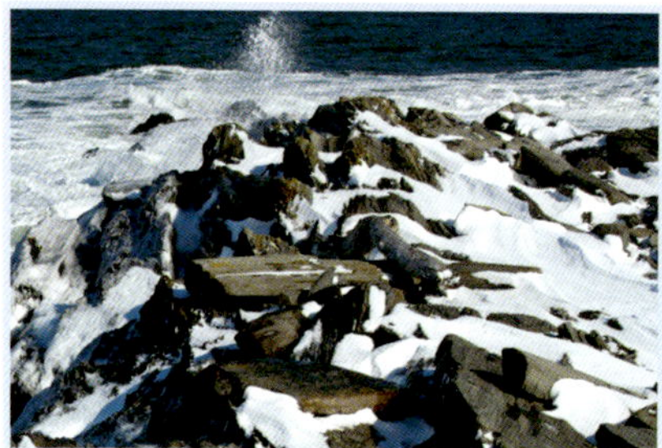

Ice-covered rocks along the shoreline.

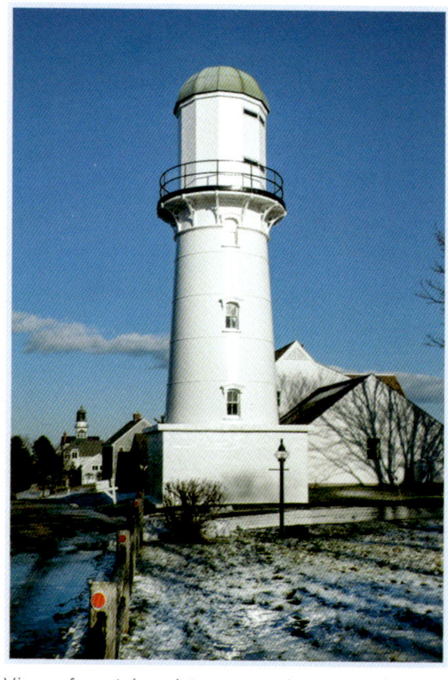

View of east (rear) tower, no longer active, with main beacon in background.

After a number of ill-fated attempts to throw a line from the shore, and his limbs practically frozen, Hannah waded waist-deep into the ocean. This time he was able to get a line to the vessel, and the crewman, Irving Pierce, managed to tie the line around himself and was pulled to shore.

Hannah then threw a line to the second crewman, William Kellar. With his own strength failing from exhaustion and exposure to the cold, Hannah struggled to pull Kellar toward the shore. Luckily, Staples arrived just in time, and with help from two other neighbors, the four men brought Kellar safely ashore.

After two days of round-the-clock attention from Hannah, his wife, and Staples, the crewmen were able to make the trip to Portland Hospital by sled, where they recovered. Marcus Hanna received a gold lifesaving medal six months later for "heroism involving great peril to his life."

Exploring the grounds. The lighthouses overlook Casco Bay and are off Route 77 at the end of Two Lights Road near Twin Lights Park. The park is a great place to picnic. The lighthouses are both private residences, so be mindful of their privacy. The main, active front lighthouse is easily viewed from the tiny beach at the end of the road. Next to the parking lot you can grab a bite to eat at the Lobster Shack Restaurant or relax at the beach.

Directions. From US Route 1 north, take Route 207 south (Black Point Road) in Scarborough and follow to Route 77 north toward Cape Elizabeth (about five and a half miles). Take a right onto Two Lights Road, and if you bear right you will find Two Lights State Park. If you bear left and continue straight for about a mile, you will come to a parking lot at the end of the road by a tiny beach. The lighthouses are to the left of the lot in a residential area.

Portland Head Lighthouse

Cape Elizabeth (1791) • Latitude: 43° 37' 24" N • Longitude: 70° 12' 30" W

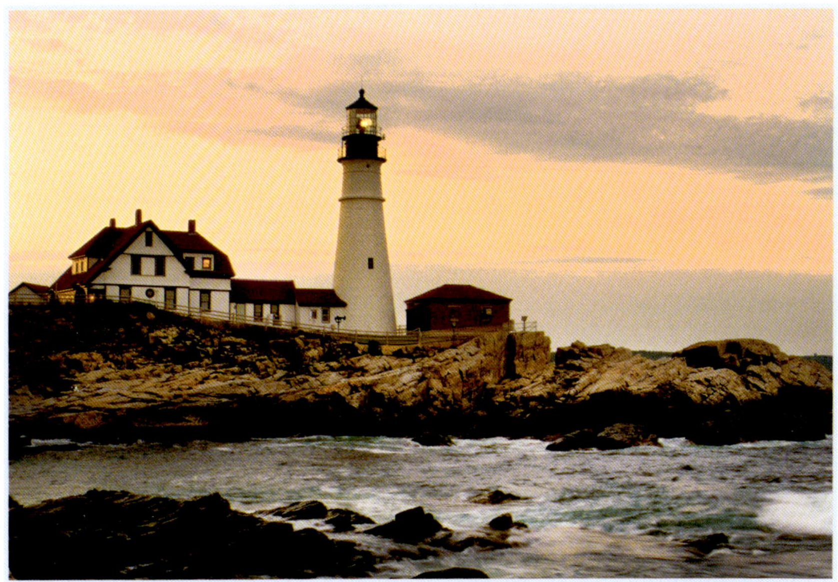

Sunset over Portland Head Light.

Maine's oldest lighthouse was erected during George Washington's administration, after many petitions following the deaths of two shipwrecked locals in 1787. Its location atop a rocky cliff marks the picturesque entrance to Maine's Portland Harbor in Casco Bay. Four shipwrecks occurred in the vicinity of the lighthouse, three a short distance from the lighthouse, and one a few miles south near Cape Elizabeth Lighthouse (the *Bohemian*—see Cape Elizabeth). After the *Bohemian* tragedy, the Portland Head Lighthouse tower was raised. Four generations of the Strout family famously served this lighthouse, dedicating over 100 years of combined service.

Four Generations of the Strout Family. In the 1820s, Joshuas Strout's mother, Jane, worked as the teenage housekeeper at Portland Head Lighthouse for an earlier keeper, Captain Joshua Freeman. She was so inspired by the joyful keeper that when she married years later, she named her son Joshua Freeman Strout. Joshua Strout went to sea at the age of eleven, and by the time he was eighteen, he became a cook on a tugboat. He was captain of the brig *Scotland* in 1854, transporting cargo around South America. He captained other vessels and enjoyed sailing all around the world, dealing in foreign trade.

Sometimes deep-water sailors like Strout were retired to respectful positions on shore. A severe fall from the mast of his ship, *Andres*, forced Strout to retire from sailing, and in 1869, he was made keeper of the Portland Head Lighthouse, assisted by his mother. His wife, Mary, served as assistant keeper for ten years until 1877,

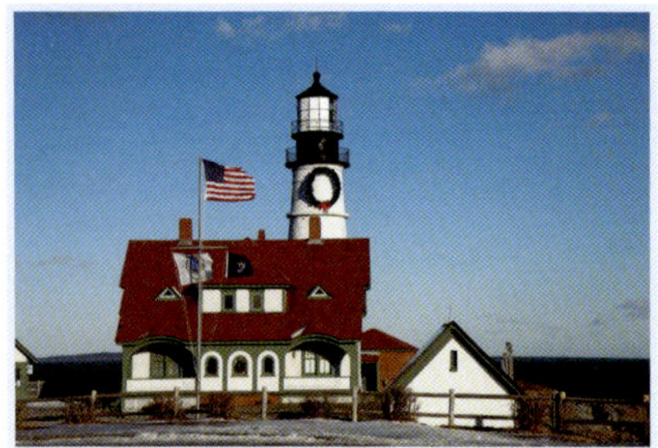

Portland Lighthouse decorated for the holidays.

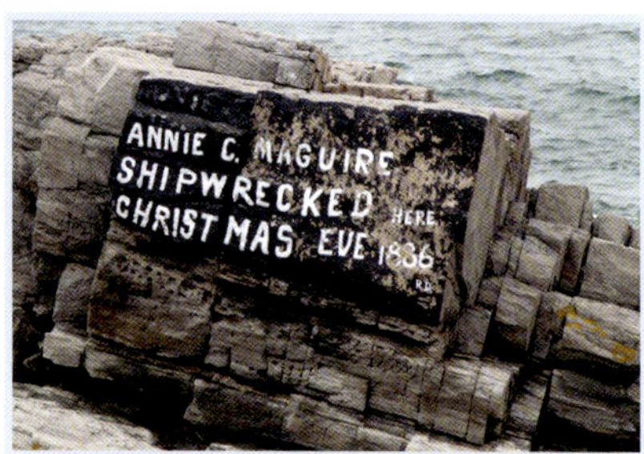

Inscription marking the shipwreck of *Annie C. Maguire.*

when their fourth son, Joseph, age twenty-one, took over as assistant keeper to his father.

The Strouts loved lighthouse life. Henry Wadsworth Longfellow, who lived nearby in Portland, would visit a day or two each week and the two men became close friends. Longfellow wrote "The Lighthouse" and other poems while relaxing at the site. Joshua served nearly seventeen years without taking any time off.

Joshua and Mary raised eleven children at the lighthouse, but lost three sons at sea. When Joshua retired as Maine's oldest lighthouse keeper in 1904 at age seventy-nine, his son Joseph took over. He had a joyful personality like his father and was affectionately called Cap'n Joe.

Joshua Strout passed away a few years later at the age of eighty-one. Father and son kept the Portland Head Lighthouse for a total of fifty-nine years from 1869–1928. In 1912, Joseph's twenty-one-year-old son John became the third-generation Strout to serve Portland Head Light.

After several years as assistant keeper, John worked at nearby Spring Point Light, and then at the Lighthouse Depot in Chelsea, Massachusetts. The Strout family had the rare distinction of serving 128 years as lighthouse tenders, with over 100 years of combined service at Portland Head, including Joshua's mother's tenure as housekeeper.

The Wreck of the Annie C. Maguire. On Christmas Eve 1886, the Strout family was preparing for bed around 11:30 when the *Annie C. Maguire* ran aground 100 feet from the lighthouse. Joshua and his son Joseph quickly ran out, followed by Joshua's wife, Mary, who carried torches to light the area. The men used an ordinary ladder as a gangplank, and one by one, the eighteen-member crew was helped to shore. Joshua had been asked to watch out for the vessel, as its creditors wanted to seize it. He sent word to the sheriff, who came to claim the vessel, and asked the Strouts to remove everything that could be salvaged for the creditors.

Because the ship was so beaten up, the creditors received only $177 at auction. The sheriff had searched the ship's sea chest for special papers and cash, but came up with nothing.

The crew was discharged a few days earlier and sent home by the British Vice Counsel. Years later it was discovered that the captain, with the help of his devious wife, had ransacked the chest and carried the cash, papers, and other items of value in her hatbox during the rescue.

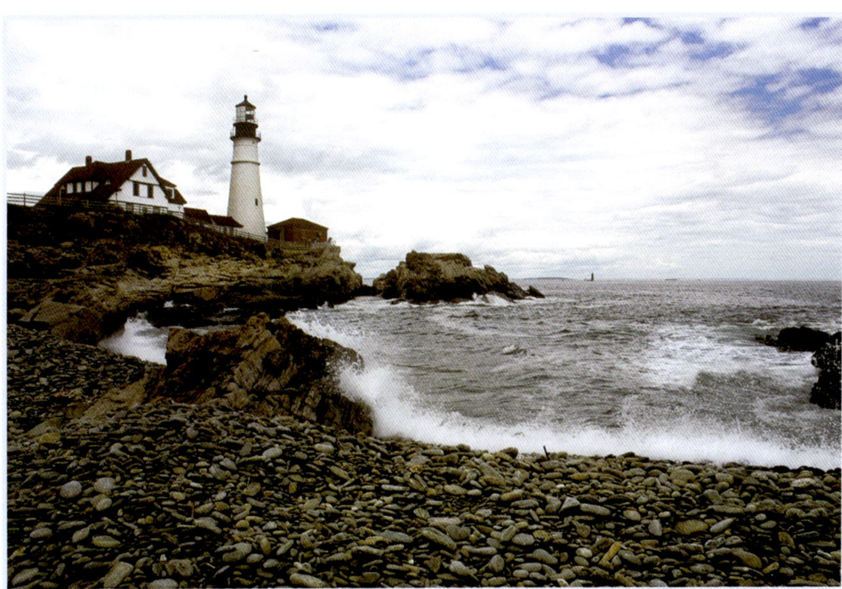

Storm clearing over Portland Head Light.

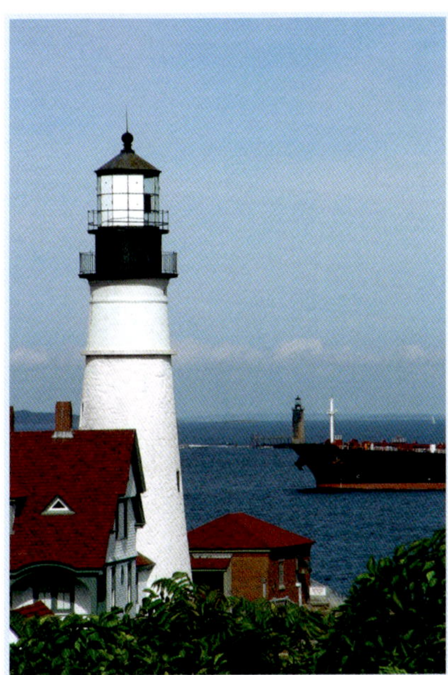

Ship passes between Portland Head Light and Ram Island Light in the background.

On his twenty-first birthday, John Strout painted an inscription on the rocks that read, "In Memory of the Ship Annie C. Maguire, Wrecked on this point Christmas Eve, 1886." It has been periodically repainted over the years, evolving into a simpler inscription reading, "Annie C Maguire, shipwrecked here, Christmas Eve 1886."

Less than a year after the *Annie C. Maguire* incident, the schooner *D. W. Hammond* crashed onto the rocks near the same location during a storm on November 30, 1887. Joseph and his brother Gilman were able to pull the captain and two crew members to safety before the vessel broke apart.

Many years later, on October 4, 1932, the seventy-two-foot schooner *Lochinvar,* carrying over twenty tons of fish, was caught in a heavy fog and crashed less than 100 feet from where the *Annie C. Maguire* had struck some forty-six years before. The cargo was destroyed, but the captain and crew survived.

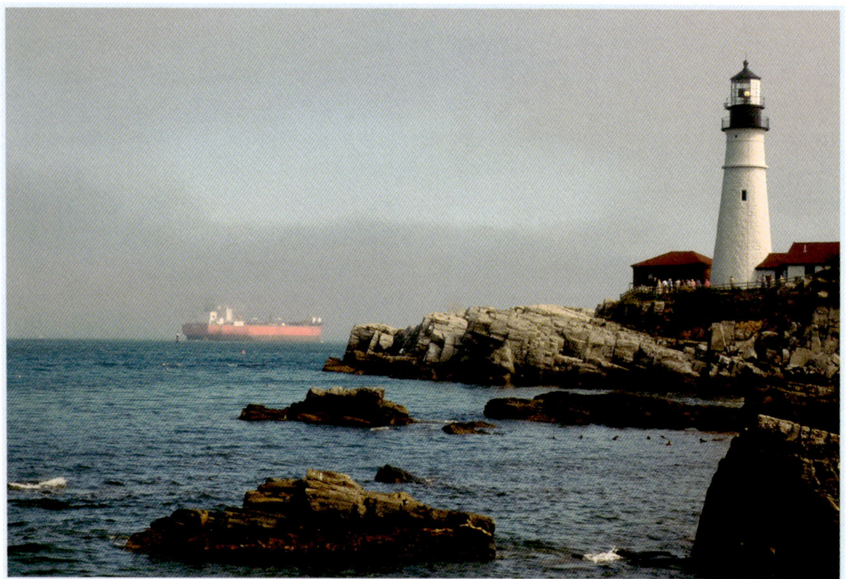

Tanker passes Portland Head Light in the fog.

Exploring the grounds. The lighthouse is inside the forty-one-acre Fort Williams Park. Visitors can hike along the cliffs, explore the old fort, and spend a day picnicking and kite flying. The tower is not open to the public, but visitors can explore the Museum at Portland Head Light at the keeper's house. Ram Island Ledge Light in Casco Bay is visible in the distance.

Directions. From Route 1 north outside Portland to 1A, take Route 77 south through South Portland until you reach Shore Road on the left. Follow Shore road to Fort Williams State Park on the left. You'll also see lighthouse signs along the way.

Ram Island Ledge Lighthouse

Cape Elizabeth (1905) • Latitude: 43° 37' 54" N • Longitude: 70° 11' 12" W

Ram Island Ledge is a large reef that lies underwater in high tide. On February 24, 1900, the 440-foot steamer *Californian* left Portland just before midnight bound for Liverpool, England, during a brief rainstorm. Captain John France had let his vessel drift slightly off course, and before he discovered his error, the ship hit the reef straight on, coming to rest on the island. Fortunately, the twenty-one passengers and crew were safely rescued and the ship's cargo was unloaded. Finally pulled free six weeks later, the hull was badly damaged, but after repairs in Boston, the steamer returned to service.

The incident prompted the need for a lighthouse, and in 1902, funds were appropriated for construction. During construction, on September 22, 1902, the British three-masted schooner *Glenrosa* wedged itself on the rocks after its captain misread

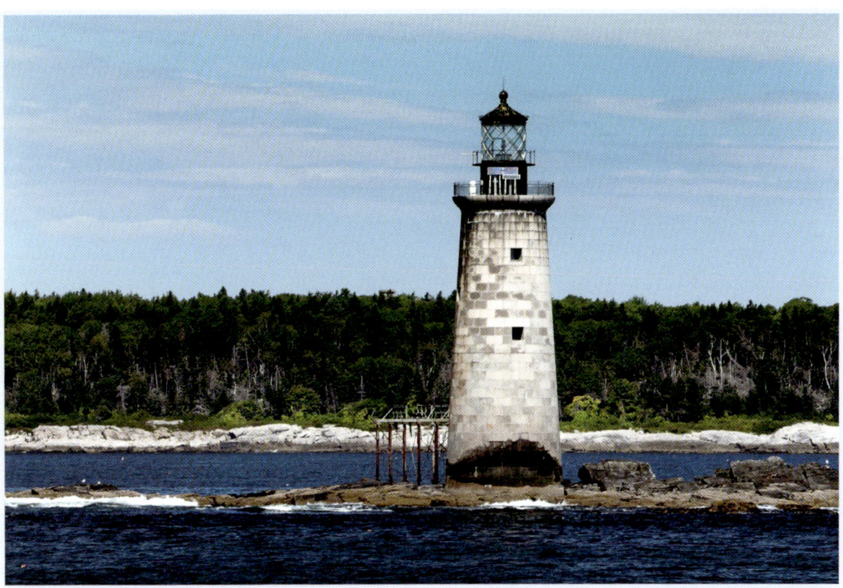

Ram Island Ledge Lighthouse in Casco Bay.

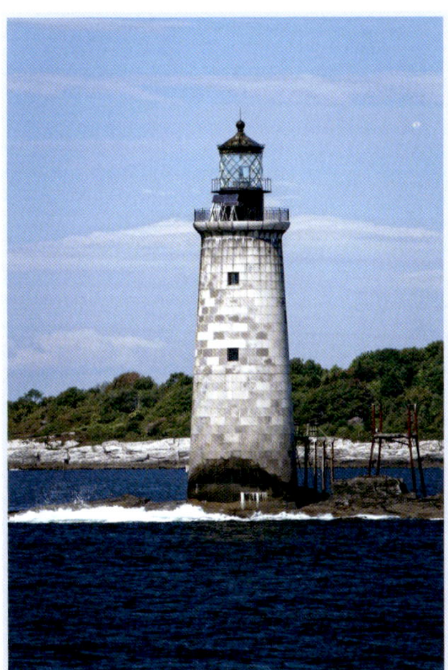

Ram Island Ledge Light stone tower.

Portland Light's foghorn and believed his ship was heading down the middle of the channel. The crew was able to stay on the island for the night and row to shore at daybreak, but the ship was a total loss. Less than three months later, the schooner *Cora & Lillian* suffered the same fate on the reef.

Ram Island Ledge lighthouse was not completed until 1905, as the ledge could only be worked on during low tide. Its construction was considered an engineering feat, and there has not been a major shipwreck since.

William C. Tapley was appointed the first head keeper of Ram Island Ledge Lighthouse and held the position until 1929. During the early years, local lobstermen complained that lighthouse keepers were using the advantage of their location to compete with the lobstermen. Tapley responded to an inspector that he had too much work to do at the lighthouse to get involved in lobstering, nor did he really want to make any additional income. The inspector found that the fishermen made much more money than the keepers and dismissed the complaints.

Three keepers were assigned to the station in twelve-hour shifts for two week intervals, followed by a week of shore leave and were confined to living in the lower part of the tower. With the station's remote location, keepers were often stranded for longer periods. Assistant keeper Johansen and another assistant once spent forty-five days at the lighthouse during rough weather and were reduced to eating oatmeal.

Spring Point Ledge Lighthouse

South Portland (1897) • Latitude: 43° 39' 07" N • Longitude: 70° 13' 26" W

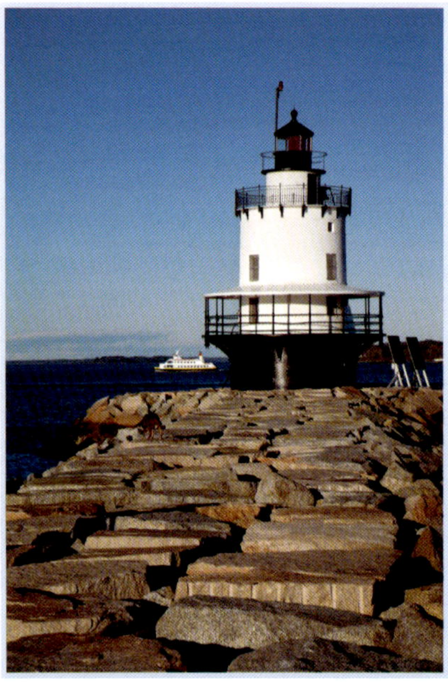

Spring Point Ledge Light sits at the end of a 900-foot breakwater.

Before Spring Point Lighthouse was built, many ships got stranded on the ledge that runs from Fort Preble out to the main ship channel. Some managed to free themselves at high tide, but others perished. On September 7, 1832, the *Nancy*, a lime coaster out of Rockland, hit the ledge and burst into an uncontrollable fire caused by the salt water combining with the lime. Public outcry resulted in a huge buoy being placed at the point, but accidents continued.

The most famous accident occurred when the nearly 400-ton vessel *Harriet S. Jackson* ran aground during a storm on March 21, 1876. Luckily, the crew survived. Spring Point Ledge Light sits a few hundred yards offshore. It marks the southern entrance to Portland Harbor, and was originally surrounded by water. In 1951, a 900-foot long breakwater consisting of 50,000 tons of granite was built leading to the lighthouse.

One of Spring Point's keepers, Aaron Wilson, who tended the beacon from 1918 to 1934, gained fame as a carver of wooden bird decoys. One of his creations went for $195,000 at an auction in 2005.

Most keepers tried to get exercise. It was once calculated that fifty-six laps around the tower's main deck equaled one mile. One keeper forgot to close the trap door before running his laps and fell through the opening. Luckily, a ladder broke his fall, as it was seventeen feet to the rocky ledge below.

 **Exploring the grounds.** The lighthouse is at the end of a nearly quarter-mile breakwater. Portland Harbor Museum (originally the Spring Point Museum) and Fort Preble Park at the lighthouse are open during tourist season. The long breakwater is a nice walk with opportunity for fishing off the rocks. There is also

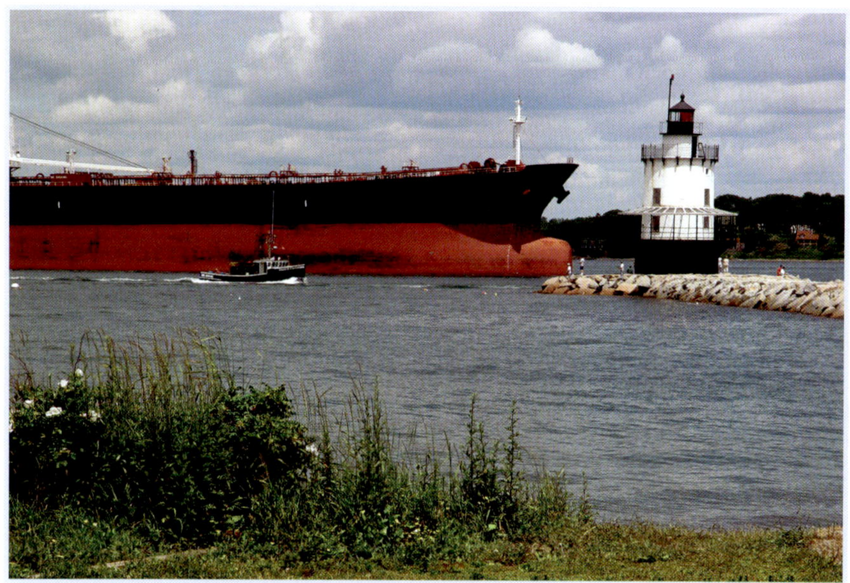

Tugboat guides tanker past Spring Point Light.

a tiny beach area from which to watch boat traffic in and out of Portland. There are a couple of snack shacks a short walk from the parking lot.

 **Directions.** From Route 1 take exit 6A and bear right onto Broadway Street in South Portland. Stay on Broadway to Pickett Street and turn right, then left onto Fort Road, which ends at Fort Preble. You can also follow Route 77 from Fort Williams State Park (Portland Head Light), and take a left onto Broadway to Pickett Street to the end, then left onto Fort Road. You'll find Spring Point Museum by the parking lot.

Portland Breakwater (Bug Light) Lighthouse

South Portland (1855) • Latitude: 43° 39' 20" N • Longitude: 70° 14' 06" W

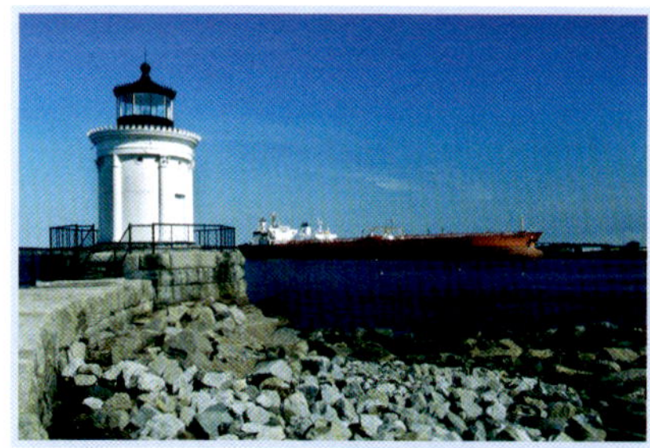

Tanker docked near the lighthouse.

The lighthouse was originally a wooden tower standing only two feet above high tide on a manmade breakwater. It was constantly being washed by salt water, making it a maintenance disaster. During storms, waves and spray inundated the breakwater, battering the lighthouse and often soaking the keeper. Before the keeper's house was built, keepers would have to crawl the 1,800 feet of uneven breakwater to the lighthouse. It took many years to complete the new lighthouse and breakwater and construction often stopped because of funding problems and

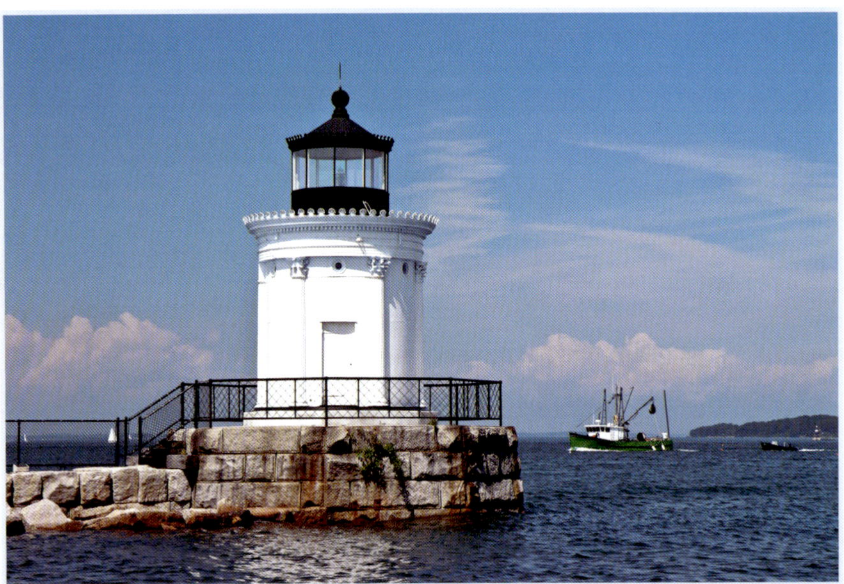

Fishing trawler heading past Portland Breakwater Light.

contractor issues. The lighthouse was rebuilt with a unique design of six fluted columns in 1875, modeled after Greek architecture from the fourth century BC. The original wooden tower was moved to nearby Little Diamond Island and became a lookout tower. In 1934, the beacon was electrified, and years later, during World War II, the area was filled in, with only 100 feet left of the breakwater. The beacon was discontinued in 1942. The most recent restoration and a new park, known as Bug Light Park, were completed in 2002.

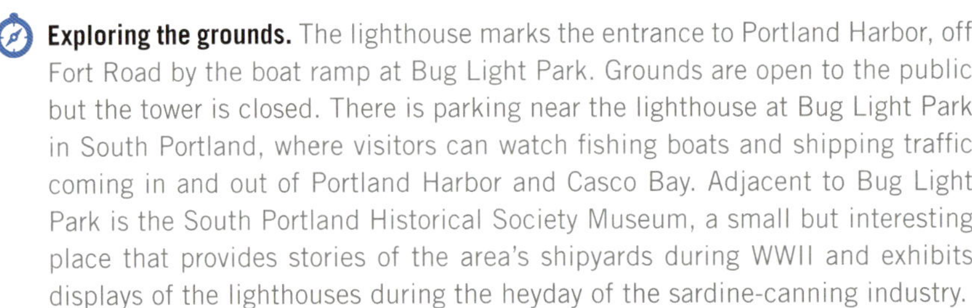

Exploring the grounds. The lighthouse marks the entrance to Portland Harbor, off Fort Road by the boat ramp at Bug Light Park. Grounds are open to the public but the tower is closed. There is parking near the lighthouse at Bug Light Park in South Portland, where visitors can watch fishing boats and shipping traffic coming in and out of Portland Harbor and Casco Bay. Adjacent to Bug Light Park is the South Portland Historical Society Museum, a small but interesting place that provides stories of the area's shipyards during WWII and exhibits displays of the lighthouses during the heyday of the sardine-canning industry.

Directions: From Route 1 north, take exit 6A and bear right onto Route 77 (Broadway Street) in South Portland. Stay on Broadway to Pickett Street and follow it to the end at Fort Road in front of the marina. Take a left onto Fort Road and follow signs to a boat ramp (quarter mile). You will see a parking lot to the boat ramp alongside a warehouse; the lighthouse will be on your right. This lighthouse is about half a mile from Spring Point Light.

Halfway Rock Lighthouse

Harpswell (1871) • Latitude: 43° 39' 21" N • Longitude: 70° 02' 12" W

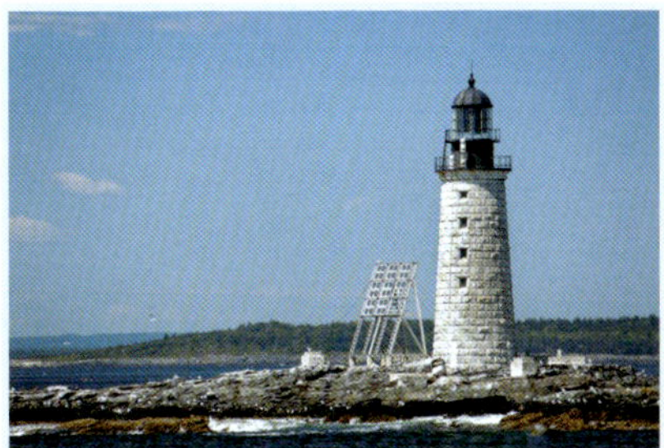

Halfway Rock Lighthouse lies about ten miles out in Casco Bay.

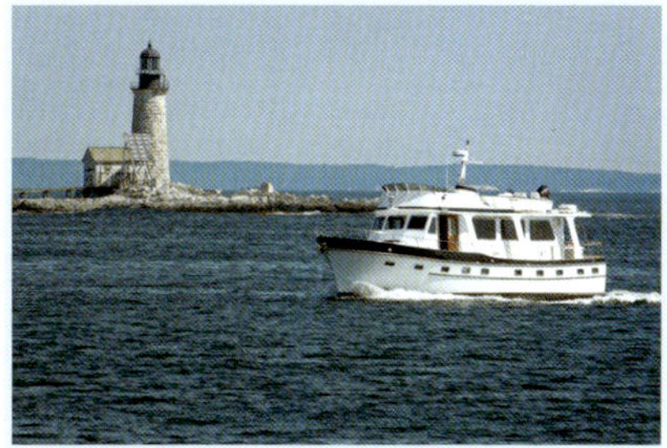

The beacon guides mariners away from the ledge.

Halfway Rock Light sits on a rocky ledge about ten miles out in Casco Bay. After many shipwrecks and lots of petitions beginning in the 1830s, construction funds were appropriated in 1869. Two major storms caused delays, and additional funds were needed. Tower construction resumed in 1871 and was completed in late summer. Its design was similar to Massachusetts' Minot's Ledge Light and Maine's Ram Island Ledge Light, with massive granite blocks cut out at specific angles to be dovetailed precisely together.

George A. Toothaker, from nearby Harpwsell, Maine, spent over twelve years at Halfway Rock as an assistant keeper and principal keeper between 1872 and 1885. The isolation bothered him, and he wrote that others who worked with him at the beacon were also affected physically and mentally. Keepers had to get creative to keep busy. One group created a chart of daily fly killings. Another keeper reported to the local newspaper that he picked up a basketball that had washed ashore and counted 2,448 pimples on it in one day!

Keepers had constant issues with the lighthouse's cramped quarters so many miles out in the ocean. Reaching the mainland for supplies required an eleven-mile row to Portland, often made difficult or impossible by rough seas or ice. In February 1934, the keepers reported that ice an inch thick extended all the way past Halfway Rock. Eventually, the Coast Guard sent a buoy tender vessel to deliver weekly supplies. Getting on and off the wave-swept ledge was always dangerous, and there were many stories of boats flipping over in the seas.

Arthur S. Strout, of the famous Strout family of Maine lighthouse keepers, spent seventeen years at Halfway Rock, beginning as a second assistant keeper in 1928. In 1939, when the Coast Guard took over management of lighthouses from the old civilian Lighthouse Service, Strout joined that branch of the service and became the first Coast Guard keeper at Halfway Rock.

Coastal Attractions in Southern Maine

York, Kennebunkport, Portland, and up to Brunswick

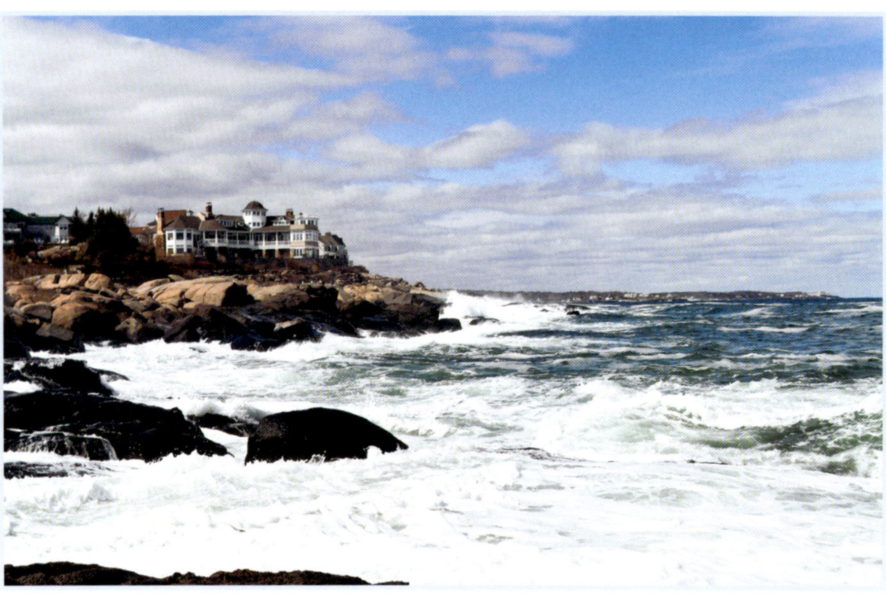

High surf coming in along Maine's rocky coast.

This is probably one of the most concentrated areas for tourist entertainment, whether it is shopping, boat cruises, enjoying the many beaches, or just exploring. Route 1 has lots of restaurants and commercial businesses, while side roads offer scenic coastal views and beach access. In fact, nearly ninety percent of Maine's sandy beaches are in southern Maine, nestled between sections of rocky coastline. Most of the lighthouses are accessible by car, and boat cruises offer great views from the water.

 **Quick stop!** The scenic harbor ride along Route 103 from Portsmouth over the Maine border into Kittery will lead you to **Chauncey Creek Lobster Pier** to enjoy lobsters in the rough, steamers, and chowders in a BYOB family outdoor picnic table atmosphere. This place is a favorite for kayakers and small boaters (no yachts). Great views. Just park when you see the line of cars on the side of the road.

The area is steeped in military history, as there are a series of forts on the New Hampshire and Maine side of the Piscataqua River. Heading across the border from Portsmouth into Kittery along Route 103, stop at the nineteenth-century military fort Fort McClary, which protected Portsmouth Harbor during various wars. Explore the tower and fort to enjoy distant views of Portsmouth Harbor Light and Whaleback Light.

Views of Whaleback Lighthouse from the Kittery, Maine, side can be seen from Fort Foster, with its trails, two beaches

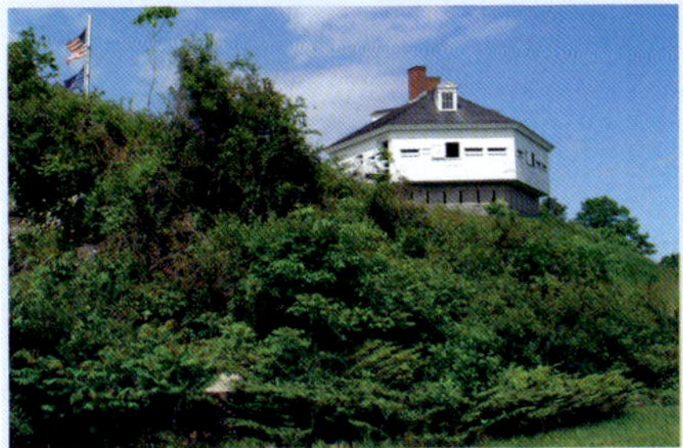

Fort McClary military defense tower in Kittery, Maine.

(Whaleback Beach and Rocky Beach), and long boardwalk. On the New Hampshire side, visit historic Portsmouth, Fort Constitution, Fort Stark, Great Island Common on the island of New Castle, and Odiorne Point, where you can see Whaleback Light.

Kittery, the oldest town in Maine, is a quiet seacoast community across the river from Portsmouth. Kittery's **Historical and Naval Museum** is loaded with historical lighthouse and naval artifacts, including local shipyard and submarine memorabilia. Many visitors enjoy the famous Kittery Outlets with over 120 stores along a one-mile stretch on Route 1. For the kid in all of us, visit **Take Flight Aerial Adventure**, Maine's largest high ropes challenge course with over sixty activities and challenges, including two zip line tours through the trees.

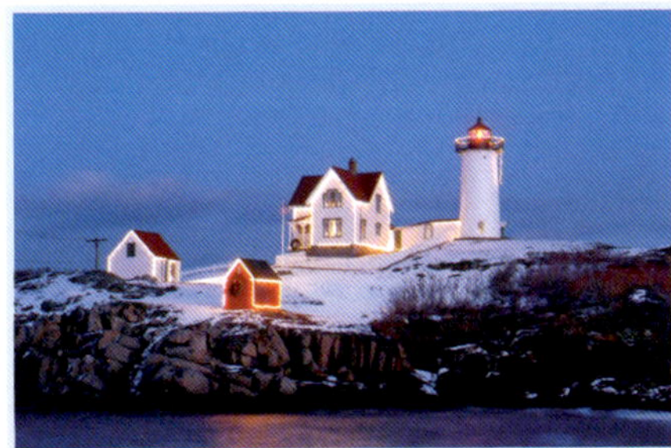

Cape Neddick (Nubble) lit up for the holidays.

York is an affluent community with beautiful Victorian homes and beaches and many year-round events. In the heart of York Village lies the **Museums of Old York** operated by the Old York Historical Society. The museums consist of nine historic buildings including the Old Jail (Gaol), the nation's oldest royal prison, where the jail keeper's family lived above the prisoners' dungeon. Other buildings include the 1834 Remick Barn, Jefferd's Tavern, dating to 1750, and an old schoolhouse. Mount Agamenticus nearby is an easy hike on which to enjoy mountaintop views and the occasional concerts that happen there during the summer. Just follow Mountain Road from Route 1.

Cape Neddick (Nubble) Light is one of the most photographed lighthouses on the East Coast. One of the most popular current events is the annual "Lighting of the Nubble" during the holiday season, and also during the "Christmas in July" event.

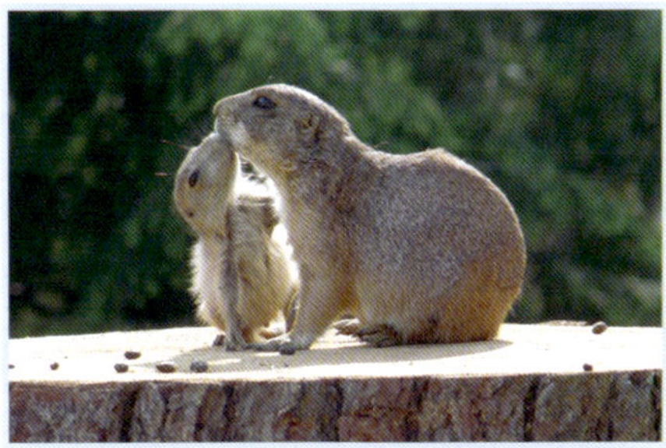

York's Wild Animal Kingdom has animals large and small.

There are two beaches near the Cape Neddick Light—the mile-and-a-half Long Sands Beach for true beach lovers, and Short Sands Beach between two rocky cliffs with lots of shops, amusements, and places to eat. You can also see saltwater taffy being made the old-fashioned way at the Goldenrod Restaurant. **York's Wild Animal Kingdom** near Short Sands Beach has an old-fashioned amusement park and zoo where you can ride an elephant, play miniature golf in the shade, or ride the Ferris wheel, among other amusements.

Heading north a few miles, you'll find the inviting tourist towns of Wells and Ogunquit, full of curio shops, clean beaches, and fine restaurants. The **Rachel Carson Wildlife Refuge** in Wells offers a paved one-mile walkway along coastal marshland for those interested in birding, and kayak launches for further wildlife observation. The **Wells Reserve at Laudholm** offers nearly seven miles of nature trails through a unique coastal estuarine and past historic farm buildings (great also for cross-country skiing in the winter). The **Wells Auto Museum** has over eighty antique and classic cars and an abundance of vintage motorcycles, music boxes, and games for the young at heart.

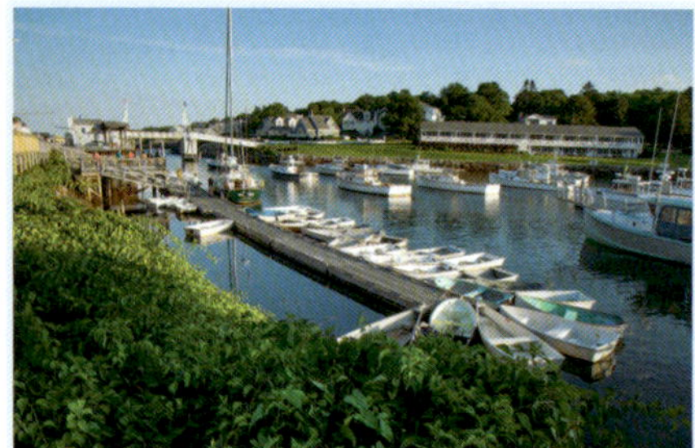

Perkins Cove in Ogunquit.

Ogunquit is a community of artists. Relax at the tiny harbor of picturesque Perkins Cove, or take a scenic walk along Marginal Way, which is probably the most popular one-mile walk in Maine, with dramatic views of rocky shoreline. Take a dip in the pristine, sandy, three-mile Ogunquit Beach, make reservations for deep sea fishing, sea kayaking, sailing, and whale watching excursions, learn from its museums, or take in a performance at the **Ogunquit Playhouse**, **Booth Theater** or the **Ogunquit Performing Arts**.

Finest Kind Cruises, in picturesque Perkins Cove, offers a special Nubble Lighthouse cruise, and also offers lobstering and sailing trips, a cocktail cruise, and a breakfast cruise. **Silverlining Sailing Cruises** will take you out in a wooden Maine sloop sailboat built in 1939, and **Cricket Sailing Cruises** offers sailing on a wooden boat designed in the style of the late 1800s boats used for coastal lobstering (no engine). For sailing on a larger and more luxurious vessel, **The Gift Sailing Cruises** offers cruises on a forty-foot world-class sailing yacht. For deep-sea fishing, try **Bunny Clark**.

If you don't feel like dealing with a car and parking, the **Shoreline Explorer Trolley Service** operates from York to Kennebunk to destinations like local beaches, downtown, etc. You can take this special service from a number of locations of arriving and departing Amtrak Downeaster stations. For those looking for nostalgia, the **Seashore Trolley Museum** in Kennebunkport is the oldest and largest museum of mass transit vehicles with over 250 vehicles. You can even step back in time with a trolley ride.

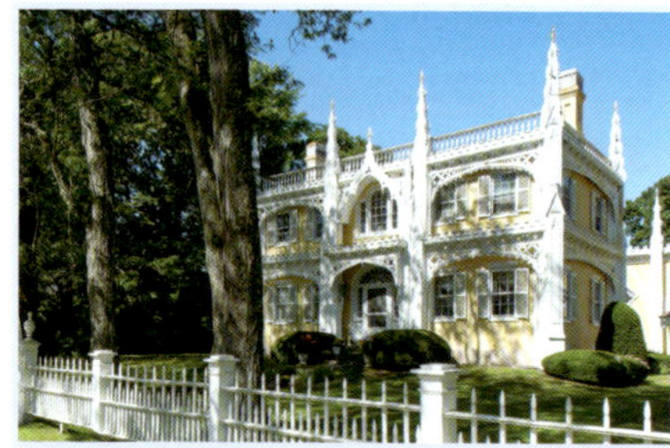

The Wedding Cake House in Kennebunkport.

Kennebunkport is an affluent community with its pristine, three-mile long Goose Rocks Beach, upscale restaurants, and many art galleries and shops. Most of the shops are concentrated in Dock Square, which outlines the Kennebec River. Near the center of town, take a tour of the much-photographed **Wedding Cake House**, part of the Maine Stay Inn.

A drive along Ocean Avenue (Route 9)

gives visitors a nice view of the Bush compound at Walker's Point, where you can sometimes catch glimpses of members of the famous Bush family on vacation. There are plenty of other mansions to enjoy as you drive along this scenic, winding road.

Pineapple Ketch Sailing offers a two-hour sail along the rugged southern Maine coast, including sunset excursions. To experience the bigger vessels, climb aboard the **schooner *Eleanor*** for a two-hour sail down the historic Kennebunk River.

Cape Porpoise, where Goat Island Light is located, is a small, quiet fishing and artist community where you can get fresh lobster right off the boats. If you're interested in whale watching or taking a scenic lobster cruise, look up **First Chance Whale Watch**. During the holiday season, visitors will find a huge outdoor holiday tree made of lobster traps and fishing gear next to the firehouse at the center of Cape Porpoise.

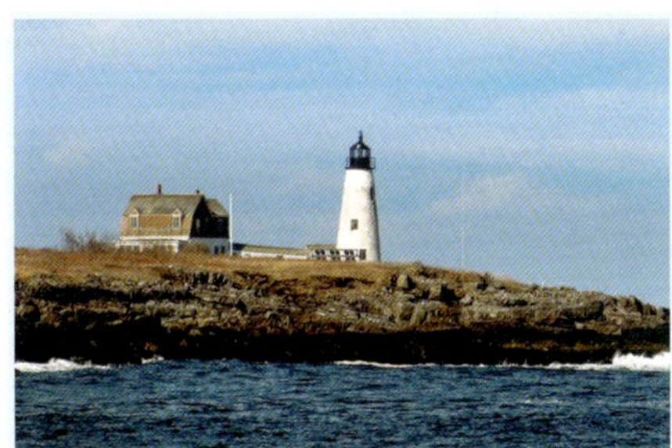

View of Wood Island Light from across the Saco River in Biddeford Pool.

Biddeford and neighboring Saco were busy textile mill and manufacturing towns in the nineteenth and twentieth centuries. Saco's **Funtown Splashtown** and **Aquaboggan Park** are popular tourist attractions for the whole family. Biddeford comprises an assortment of distinctive villages, such as Biddeford Pool, Hills Beach, and Fortune Rocks. Biddeford Pool is a small ocean village community where visitors can view Wood Island Light from a distance by taking the walking trail along the golf course owned by the East Point Audubon Sanctuary. You'll find this after bearing right after the firehouse. At the shoreline you can hike around the area, and if you happen to be there during blueberry season (July and August), the paths are filled with fresh blueberries. Friends of Wood Island Lighthouse offers a water shuttle and summer lighthouse tours.

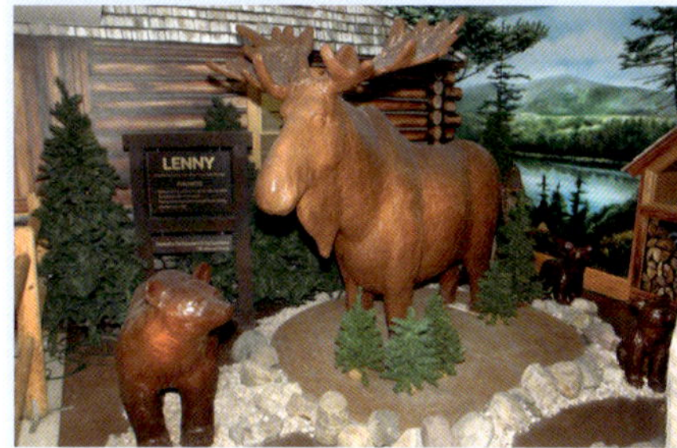

Lenny, the world's only life-size, 1,700-pound chocolate moose and friends.

Just a few miles north lies one of Maine's major tourist playgrounds, **Old Orchard Beach**, with its 500-foot pier, beaches, camping, shops, Palace Playland amusement park, and nightlife.

Looking for a candy shop for the true chocoholic? In Scarborough, on Route 1, you'll find **Len Libby Candy Shop**. In addition to candy made by their own chocolatiers, you'll also find Lenny, the **world's largest 1,700-pound life-size chocolate moose**, in true Maine tradition. You'll also find his friends, a 350-pound chocolate bear and a couple of her eighty-pound chocolate bear cubs. The store stays cool all year to keep the chocolate from melting.

Cape Elizabeth is a quiet town with well-preserved Victorian homes, clean parks, and beaches, including Crescent Beach. Two Lights State Park, sometimes referred to as Twin Lights State Park near the lighthouses, offers picnic tables, hiking trails, and ocean views. You can walk from the park to the Cape Elizabeth Lighthouses (Two Lights). Eat by the parking lot at the Lobster Shack Restaurant and enjoy great shoreline views.

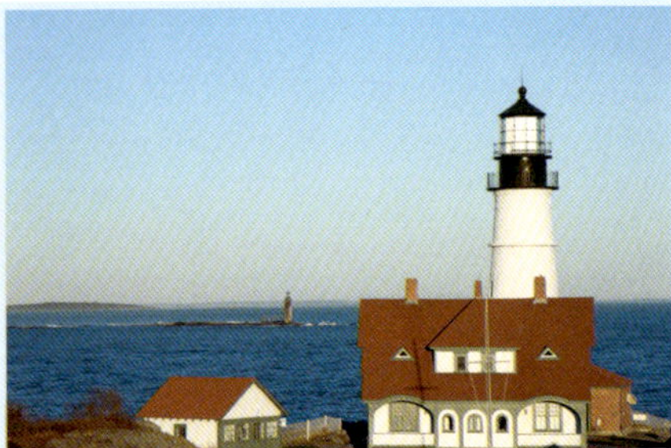

Portland Head Light is the second oldest lighthouse in the country.

In South Portland, visit the **Portland Harbor Museum**, formerly the Spring Point Museum, inside Fort Preble. Spring Point Light and its grounds are just outside the fort. About a half mile from the Spring Point Light, is Portland Breakwater Light at Bug Light Park in South Portland. The Harbor Walk Trail leads from Bug Light Park over the Casco Bay Bridge and around the Portland waterfront. A path also runs from Bug Light Park approximately six miles to Wainwright Field Athletic Complex at the western edge of South Portland.

Portland is one of the largest seaports in New England, Maine's largest and arguably most cultural city, offering lots of specialty restaurants and shops, artist galleries, and

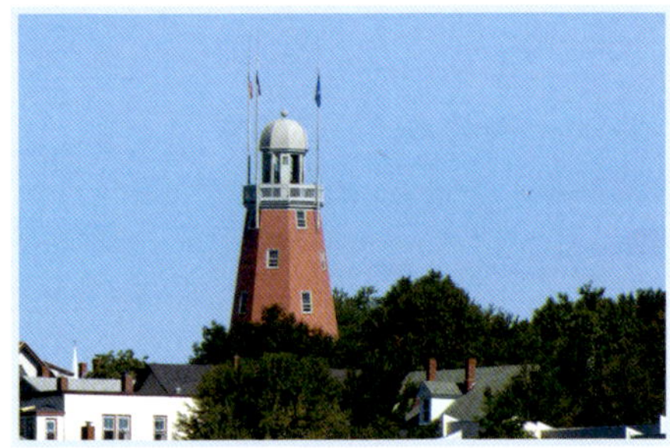

Portland Observatory is the last remaining signal tower in the country.

museums. Visit the historic Old Port district or follow Portland Trails through the city. The Eastern Promenade provides nearly seventy acres of water views and recreation.

For sports enthusiasts, take in a minor league baseball game at **Hadlock Field**, home to the Portland Sea Dogs of the Eastern League. If you visit during hockey season, grab tickets for the **Portland Pirates** minor hockey league, affiliate of the Florida Panthers, at the Cross Insurance Arena.

If you happen to look at Portland's skyline you may see what appears as a red lighthouse on a hill. The **Portland Observatory** is the only known remaining historic maritime signal tower in the United States. The **Victoria Mansion**, also known as the Morse-Libby House is a unique example of American residential architecture. Stop by the **Portland Museum of Art**, the largest and oldest public art institution in Maine, to appreciate American, European, and contemporary art, as well as iconic works from Maine.

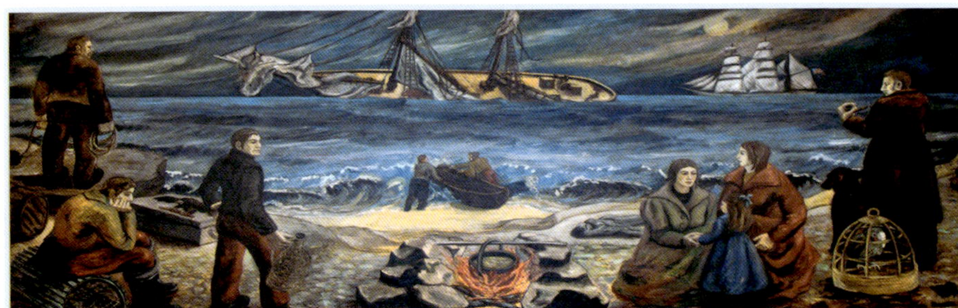

Wreck of the *Bohemian* mural in South Portland Post Office.

 **Quick stop!** For the lighthouse historians and enthusiasts, inside the lobby of the South Portland Post Office is a **mural painting of the wreck of the RMS *Bohemian***, which sank off Cape Elizabeth on February 22, 1864. It was Maine's worst disaster (see story in Cape Elizabeth Twin Lights). At least twelve of the forty-two lives that were lost are also remembered in a small monument in nearby Calvary Cemetery in South Portland.

Portland Discovery not only provides special lighthouse tours, but also trolley tours of the city. Try a narrated tour with Downeast Duck Tours aboard a duck boat. These are amphibious vehicles that ride through Portland and into the water past the Portland Breakwater Lighthouse and Spring Point Light. There are also many other boat tours leaving the Portland waterfront.

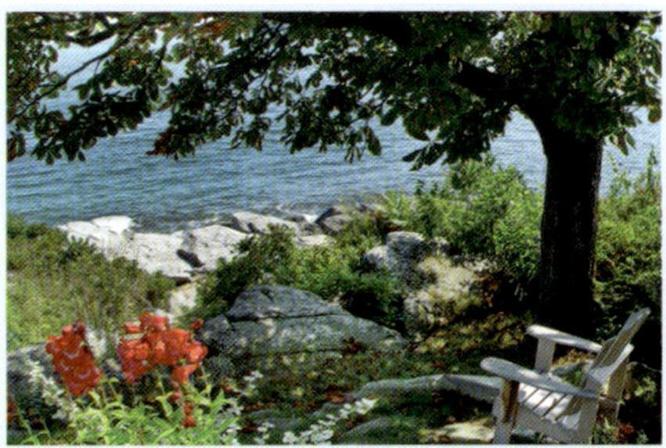

Decorative landscape along Peaks Island invites visitors to relax.

Casco Bay Cruise Lines gives visitors access to some of the popular islands in Casco Bay (there are over 200 islands in the region). You may find yourself renting a bike on Peaks Island (twenty-minute boat ride) to explore its artist community, hiking Long Island's huge conservation area, or simply walking along the quiet roads on Chebeaugue Island or Great Diamond Island. For those who want to learn about lobstering, **Lucky Catch Cruises** will haul up lobster traps for your enjoyment and passes by Portland Head Light. They also offer nature cruises and cruises to Fort Georges and Jewell Island in Casco Bay.

To experience authentic schooner sailing of the early 1900s, book a two-hour windjammer sail or overnight excursion on the *Wendameen* or *Bagheera* with the **Portland Schooner Company**. You can also sail the *Frances* with **Maine Sailing Adventures**. She is a replica of a working coastal pilot cutter that would have sailed New England waters between 1790 and 1812. The company provides sunset and wine sails to Peaks Island. **Odyssey Whale Watch** offers whale-watching and deep-sea fishing tours. You can also charter sailing tours aboard a classic thirty-six-foot Hinckley Yawl vessel.

North of Portland in Falmouth, Yarmouth, and Freeport, you'll find the largest boot sculpture in front of the LL Bean store, among 170 other name-brand retailers. A short distance away you can explore 200 acres of Wolfe's Neck Woods State Park, especially if you want to observe ospreys. The park rangers provide one-hour guided tours. **Capt. Lyman Stuart** offers tours of Casco Bay on his thirty-foot sloop, the *Marisa III*.

The **Desert of Maine**, created from rough farming in the late 1800s, exposed an ancient glacial sand deposit that overtook the farm and now covers over forty acres of land. Hike nature trails and visit the original Tuttle Barn, now a museum.

Check out **Eartha,** the world's largest revolving 3-D globe nearly forty-two feet in diameter at the DeLorme (Map) Headquarters in Yarmouth. It rotates as if seen from space.

Between Portland and Brunswick, visitors will find many roads leading from Route 1 out into the many peninsulas and islands that make up Maine's coastline. Bailey Island

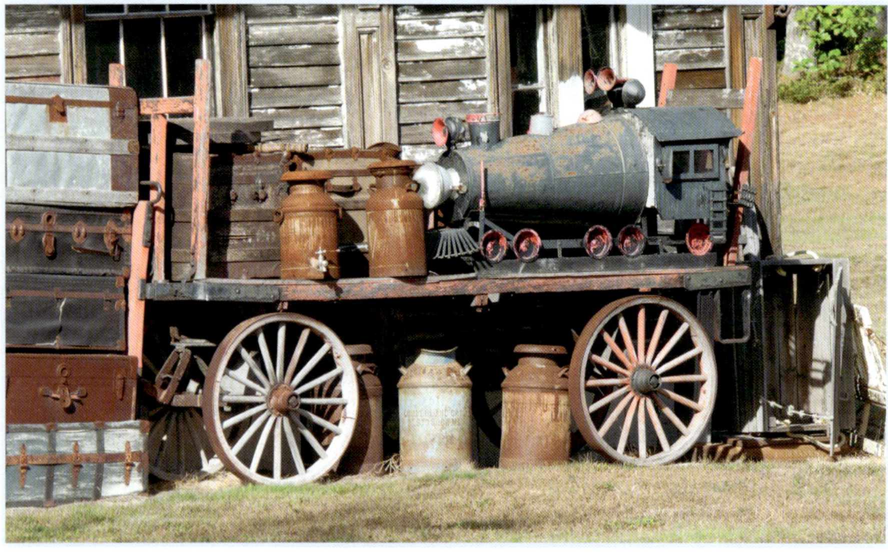

Antique shops and museums are found all along the Maine coast.

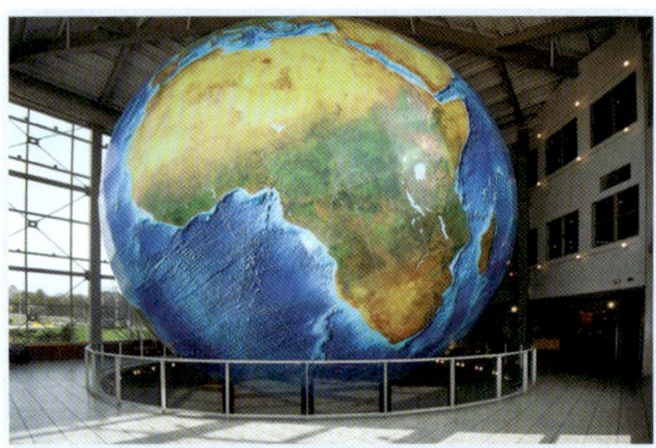

Eartha is the world's largest rotating globe.

and nearby Eagle Island are quiet, rustic places dotted with artists galleries, fishing boats, and local places to eat that seem stuck in time, and are accessible from boats like Casco Bay Cruises out of Portland.

Bailey Island, reached via Route 24 off Route 1 in Brunswick, offers bird watching, fishing, or simply exploring this one-mile-by-three-mile island. There are only a few roads, so it's hard to get lost. A small sandy cove called Cedar Beach off Robinhood Road is a good place to relax and watch the waves at high tide. Take a walk on Baily Island Bridge, a one-of-a-kind crib stone bridge. **Sea Escape Cottages and Charters** offers windjammer sailing around on the seventy-foot wooden tall ship *Schooner Alert*. They also provide private sailing charters on their vessel the *Tevake*, and trips to Eagle Island.

Eagle Island, accessible only by boat, has recently been designated a National Historic Site. A bird nesting sanctuary with plenty of hiking trails, it was home to the famed arctic explorer Admiral Peary. It is also a favorite kayak and boating destination and is maintained by the Friends of Peary's Eagle Island.

On the mainland, along Routes 123 or 24 in Harpswell, there are marked hiking trails to explore. In addition to good food, the **Dolphin Restaurant and Marina** (off Route 123) provides a twenty-minute boat shuttle to Eagle Island.

In Brunswick, visit the **Bowdoin College Museum of Art,** which houses the new **Peary-MacMillan Arctic Museum,** named after Admiral Peary, the first man to reach the North Pole. The **Brunswick Diner** offers great breakfasts, desserts, and lobster rolls since 1946 in an authentic 1950s interior.

Contacts for Coastal Attractions in Southern Maine

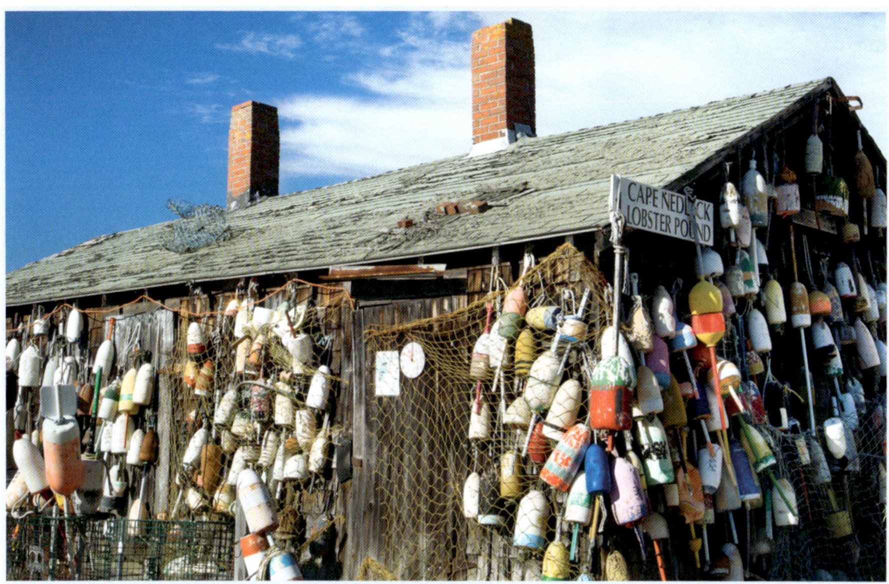

A lobster shack, one of many unique sights along the rugged shoreline.

Kittery Outlets, Kittery
(888) 548-8379)
thekitteryoutlets.com

Historical and Naval Museum, Kittery
(207) 439-3080
kitterymuseum.com

Chaucey Lobster Pier, Kittery
(207) 439-1030
chaunceycreek.com

Fort McClary, Kittery
(207) 490-4079
fortmcclary.org

Take Flight Aerial Adventure, Kittery
(207) 439-8838
takeflightadv.com

Museums of Old York, York
(207) 363-1756
oldyork.org

Ogunquit Attractions, Ogunquit
(207) 646-2939
ogunquit.org

Finest Kind Cruises, Ogunquit
(207) 646-5227
finestkindcruises.com

Silverlining Sailing Cruises, Ogunquit
(207) 646-9800
silverliningsailing.com

The Gift Sailing Cruises, Ogunquit
(207) 646-3758
sailthegift.com

Cricket Sailing Cruises, Ogunquit
(207) 646-5227
cricketsailing.com

Bunny Clark, Ogunquit
(207) 646-2214
bunnyclark.com

Lighting of the Nubble, York
(207) 363-1040
nubblelight.org

Mount Agamenticus, York
(207) 361-1102
agamenticus.org

York's Wild Kingdom, York
(207) 363-4911
yorkzoo.com

York Parks and Recreation, York
(207) 363-1040
parksandrec.yorkmaine.org

Wells Reserve at Laudholm, Wells
(207) 646-1555
wellsreserve.org

Wells Auto Museum, Wells
(207) 646-9064
wellsautomuseum.com

Rachel Carson Wildlife, Wells
(207) 646-9226
fws.gov/refuge/rachel_carson

Ogunquit Playhouse, Ogunquit
(207) 646-5511
ogunquitplayhouse.org

Booth Theater, Ogunquit
(207) 646-8142
boothproductions.com

Ogunquit Performing Arts, Ogunquit
(207) 646-6170
ogunquitperformingarts.org

First Chance Whale Watch, Kennebunk
(207) 967-5507
firstchancewhalewatch.com

Shoreline Explorer Trolley, York
(207) 459-2932
shorelineexplorer.com

Seashore Trolley Museum, Kennebunkport
(207) 967-2800
trolleymuseum.org

Wedding Cake House, Kennebunkport
(207) 967-2117
mainestayinn.com

Pineapple Ketch Sailing, Kennebunkport
(207) 468-7262
pineappleketch.com

Schooner Eleanor, Kennebunkport
(207) 967-8809
schoonereleanor.com

Aquaboggan Water Park, Saco
(207) 282-3112
aquabogganwaterpark.com

Funtown Splashtown, Saco
(207) 284-5139
funtownsplashtownusa.com

Wood Island Lighthouse, Biddeford Pool
(207) 200-4552
woodislandlighthouse.org

Old Orchard Beach, Old Orchard
(207) 394-2500
oldorchardbeachmaine.com

Largest Chocolate Moose, Scarborough
(207) 883-4897
lenlibby.com

Portland Head Light Museum, Cape Elizabeth
(207) 799-2661
portlandheadlight.com

Portland Harbor Museum, South Portland
(207) 799-6337
portlandharbormuseum.org

Casco Bay Cruise Lines, Portland
(207) 774-7871
cascobaylines.com

Portland Discovery, Portland
(207) 774-0808
portlanddiscovery.com

Downeast Duck Tours, Portland
(207) 774-DUCK (3825) or (888) 240-6656
downeastducktours.com

Portland Observatory, Portland
(207) 774-5561
portlandlandmarks.org/observatory

Portland Museum of Art, Portland
(207) 775-6148
portlandmuseum.org

Hadlock Field Baseball, Portland
(207) 874-9300

Portland Pirates Hockey, Portland
(207) PIRATES
portlandpirates.com/

Victoria Mansion, Portland
(207) 772-4841
victoriamansion.org

Portland Schooner Company, Portland
(207) 766-2500
portlandschooner.com

Maine Sailing Adventures, Portland
(207) 749-9169
mainesailingadventures.net

Odyssey Whale Watch, Portland
(207) 775-0727
odysseywhalewatch.com

Lucky Catch Cruises, Portland
(207) 761-0941
luckycatch.com

Desert of Maine, Freeport
(207) 865-6962
desertofmaine.com

Capt. Lyman Stuart Sailing, Yarmouth
(207) 615-6917
gosailingcascobay.com

Eartha at DeLorme Map, Yarmouth
(800) 561-5105
delorme.com

Bowdoin College Museum Art, Brunswick
(207) 725-3275
bowdoin.edu/art-museum

Lighthouse Cruises in Southern Maine

Isles of Shoals Steamship Co.

Portsmouth Harbor and Isles of Shoals tours. Nubble Light and Boon Island Light in Maine are included during its Fall Extravaganza lighthouse tour.

315 Market Street, PO Box 311 Portsmouth, NH 03801

(603) 431-5500 or (800) 441-4620

islesofshoals.com

Lighthouses: Portsmouth Harbor (NH), White Island (NH), Whaleback, Boon Island, Cape Neddick (Nubble)

Portsmouth Harbor Cruises

Narrated Portsmouth Harbor and Isles of Shoals tours

64 Ceres Street, Portsmouth, NH 03801

(603) 436-8084 or (800) 776-0915

portsmouthharbor.com

Lighthouses: Portsmouth Harbor (NH), White Island (NH), Whaleback

Finest Kind Scenic Cruises

Coastal and wildlife tours.

PO Box 1828, Ogunquit, ME 03907

(207) 646-5227

finestkindcruises.com

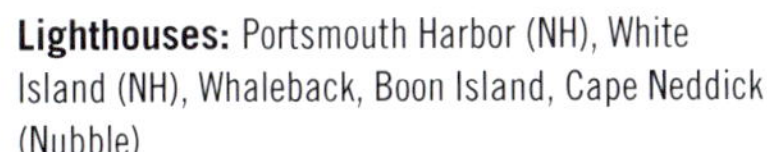

Lighthouses: Portsmouth Harbor (NH), White Island (NH), Whaleback, Boon Island, Cape Neddick (Nubble)

Friends of Wood Island Lighthouse

Shuttle service to and from Wood Island and narrated lighthouse tours during the summer months.

PO Box 26 Biddeford Pool, ME 04006

woodislandlighthouse.org

Lighthouse: Wood Island

Portland Duck Tours

Ride these amphibious vehicles through Portland and as they also pass by Portland Head and Portland Breakwater (Bug) Lighthouses as part of their tours.

177 Commercial Street, Portland, ME 04101

(207) 774-DUCK (3825)

downeastducktours.com

Lighthouses: Spring Point Ledge, Portland Breakwater, Portland Head

Portland Discovery

Offers a Sunset Lighthouse cruise, a ninety-minute Lighthouse Lovers cruise, and a Portland City and Lighthouse tour, including a trolley tour of Portland.

Long Wharf Portland, ME

(207) 774-0808

portlanddiscovery.com

Lighthouses: Portland Breakwater, Spring Point Ledge, Ram Island Ledge, Portland Head

Lucky Catch Cruises

Lobster boat cruises and custom excursions by request.

170 Commercial St., Portland, ME 04101

(207) 761-0941

luckycatch.com

Lighthouses: Portland Breakwater, Spring Point Ledge, Portland Head

Sea Escape Cottages and Charters

Fishing excursions and charters from Bailey Island. You can also take a windjammer cruise on the *Schooner Alert* or the sailboat *Tevake*.

PO Box 7, Bailey Island, ME 04003

(207) 833-5531

seaescapecottages.com

Lighthouse: Halfway Rock

Waterfront Directions

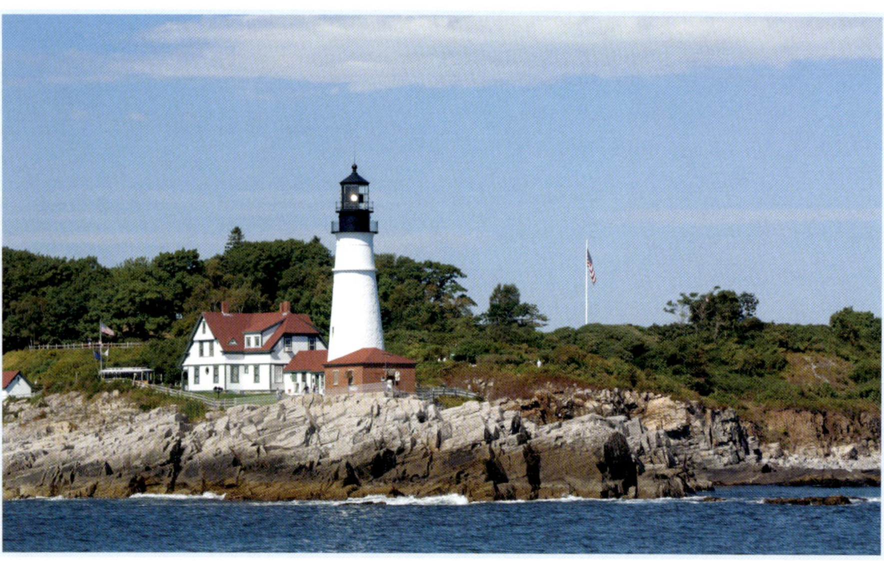

Most boat cruises out of Portland pass by Portland Head light.

Perkins Cove in Ogunquit

From I-95 north, take exit 19 for Wells and Sanford. At the stoplight, turn left on Route 109. At the end turn right on Route 1 south. In about five miles, turn left on Shore Road, then, after a mile, turn left on Perkins Cove.

Kennebunkport

Ocean Avenue will take you to your cruise destination. From I-95 north, take exit 19 and turn left on Route 9/109 to Wells/Sanford. Turn left on Route 1, and then turn right on Route 9 east. Turn right on Ocean Avenue.

Portland's Piers and Wharfs

Most of the waterfront in Portland can be accessed off Commercial Street. Coming from Cape Elizabeth Light or Portland Head Light, follow Route 77 across the river (Broadway Street) into Portland.

From I-95 north, keep right at the fork to continue on Route I-295 north and follow signs for Portland/Downtown Portland. Take exit 4 to Casco Bay/Portland Waterfront. Cross Veteran's Memorial Bridge onto Fore River Parkway. This will take you to Commercial Street, where you can find the wharf or pier for your cruise.

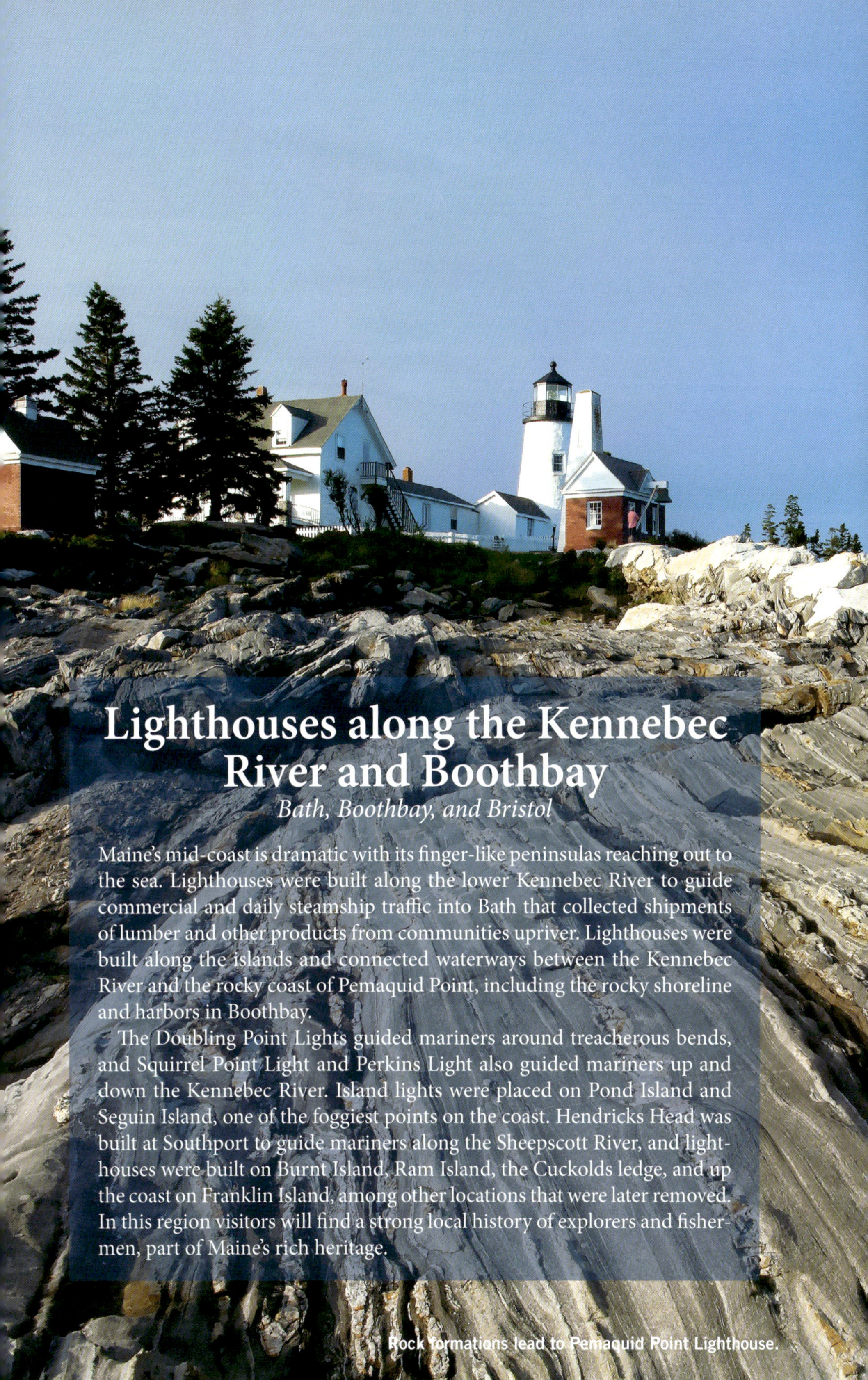

Lighthouses along the Kennebec River and Boothbay

Bath, Boothbay, and Bristol

Maine's mid-coast is dramatic with its finger-like peninsulas reaching out to the sea. Lighthouses were built along the lower Kennebec River to guide commercial and daily steamship traffic into Bath that collected shipments of lumber and other products from communities upriver. Lighthouses were built along the islands and connected waterways between the Kennebec River and the rocky coast of Pemaquid Point, including the rocky shoreline and harbors in Boothbay.

The Doubling Point Lights guided mariners around treacherous bends, and Squirrel Point Light and Perkins Light also guided mariners up and down the Kennebec River. Island lights were placed on Pond Island and Seguin Island, one of the foggiest points on the coast. Hendricks Head was built at Southport to guide mariners along the Sheepscott River, and lighthouses were built on Burnt Island, Ram Island, the Cuckolds ledge, and up the coast on Franklin Island, among other locations that were later removed. In this region visitors will find a strong local history of explorers and fishermen, part of Maine's rich heritage.

Rock formations lead to Pemaquid Point Lighthouse.

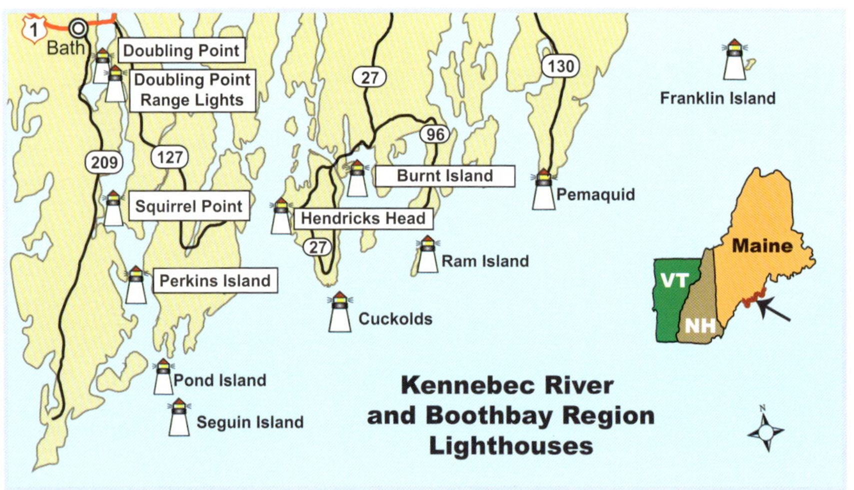

Map of Boothbay lighthouses.

Seguin Island Lighthouse

Georgetown (1795) • Latitude: 43° 42' 30" N • Longitude: 69° 45' 30" W

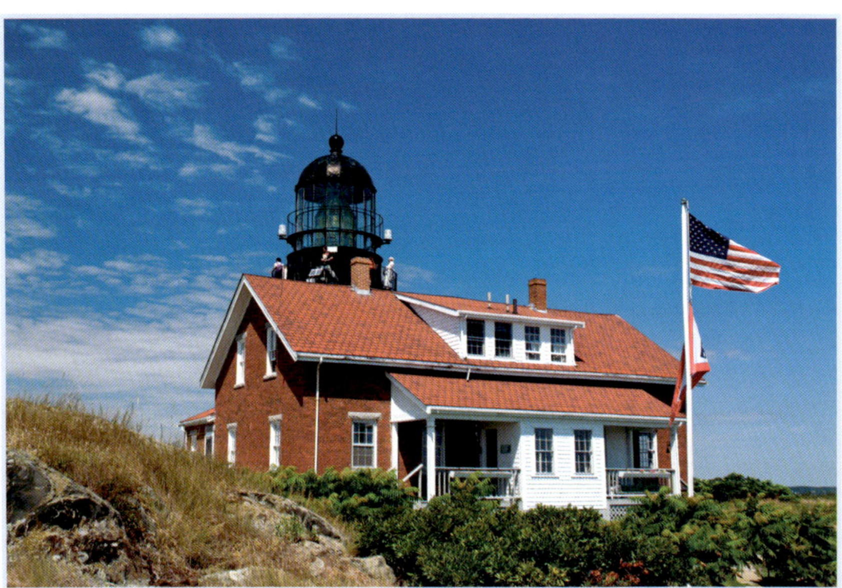

Seguin Island Light is the only beacon with its first-order Fresnel lens in the tower.

Seguin Island Lighthouse is Maine's second oldest lighthouse. It was originally illuminated by sixteen oil lamps with crude reflectors placed in a circle on a wooden bench. At 186 feet above sea level, it is also the highest lighthouse in the state. In 1857, the tower was rebuilt and a first-order Fresnel lens was installed in the lantern room. Shipping traffic was heavy, and the light had to extend out for many miles. The lighthouse also had one of the largest foghorns, since fog was present nearly

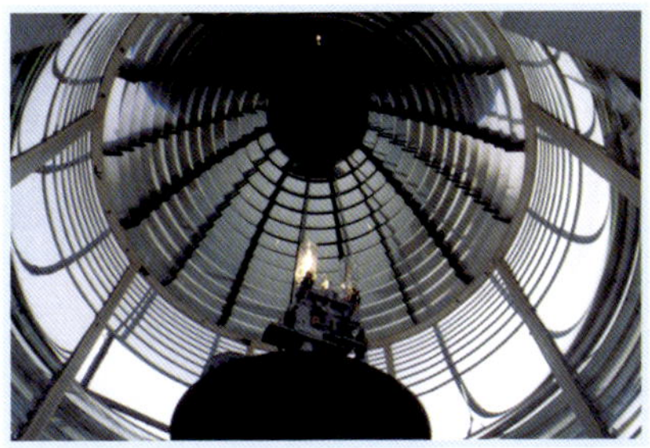

Inside view of the restored first-order lens, the most powerful lens in Maine.

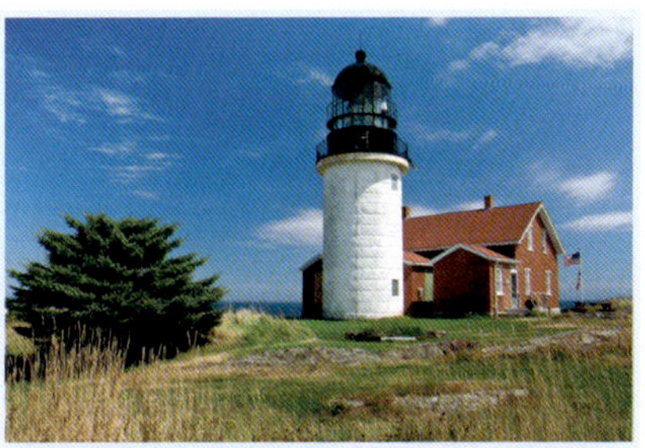

Seguin Island Lighthouse provides plenty of areas to hike.

one-third of the time. Gulls were observed being knocked down by the foghorn's powerful concussion (not the air blast).

Seguin Island Light's first keeper was Major (Count) John Polereczky. His meager salary was unfit for the hardship of living in the remote, exposed location. His brother-in-law, Christopher Pushard, served as his assistant for a few years. Pushard brought his wife for a brief period, and they had their first child, Jane, there. He soon moved his family back to the mainland, as relations between he and Polereczky were strained.

In the early 1900s, keeper Herbert Spinney created a "museum" of mounted birds, butterflies, and minerals, which filled most of the wall space at the lighthouse. This brought many tourists to the lighthouse, and he began charging a dime admission fee to keep the crowds manageable.

Because of the steep quarter-mile climb to the lighthouse, a tramway system was installed from the boathouse to the keeper's house. After a near-tragic accident on the tramway involving the keeper's wife and baby in the mid-1900s, passengers were not allowed on the structure.

In 1999 and 2000, the lighthouse was the subject of debate between preservationists and the Coast Guard, which wanted to extinguish the light and put up a solar-powered skeletal tower. In March 2000, under pressure from Congress and the public, the Coast Guard dropped its plans to deactivate the light. The first-order lens is still at the lighthouse and was restored in 2007, making it the only lighthouse in Maine with a first-order Fresnel lens.

Seguin Island Lighthouse is considered the most haunted lighthouse on the East Coast. Stories include sightings of a young girl running in the house, believed to be the daughter of one of the keepers who died at the lighthouse; piano music playing over the water; and furniture being moved around in the lighthouse by the "Old Captain."

Piano Playing Causes Keeper to Go Insane. Seguin Island Lighthouse is famous for its paranormal activity, perhaps because it is one of the most fogged-in lighthouses in New England. One story involved a former caretaker around the mid-1800s who was driven insane, murdered his wife, then took his own life.

According to legend, the keeper, newly married, brought his young wife with him to tend the light. She became increasingly bored and depressed, constantly complaining about not having anything to do. So the keeper ordered a piano to be brought to the island just before winter set in. After finally hauling the piano up the side of the rocky hillside, he proudly presented it to her.

The wife was delighted, but could not play without sheet music. Fortunately, one song had come with the piano, so she set to playing the simple Scott Joplin tune. By this time, the island was icebound; no other deliveries could come in. She played continually, the same song over and over again.

This eventually drove the keeper insane. Finally he'd had enough, took an axe, and chopped the piano to bits. Then he turned on her and chopped her up. Realizing what he had done, he also killed himself. It's said that on foggy nights on the Kennebec River, the ghostly tune can be heard floating out over the calm, quiet water.

 **Exploring the grounds.** Seguin Island is a little over two miles offshore from the mouth of the Kennebec River, near Fort Popham and Popham Beach State Park. The grounds and museum are open to the public, and lighthouse tours are provided during the summer months. The *Fish 'N Trips* boat, also called the Sequin Island Ferry, provides seasonal ferry service. It is a good hike to the lighthouse on top of the hill. Wear appropriate clothing, as you may have to jump out of the boat in knee-high water when launching and tying up.

Pond Island Lighthouse

Georgetown (1821) • Latitude: 43° 44' 24" N • Longitude: 69° 46' 12" W

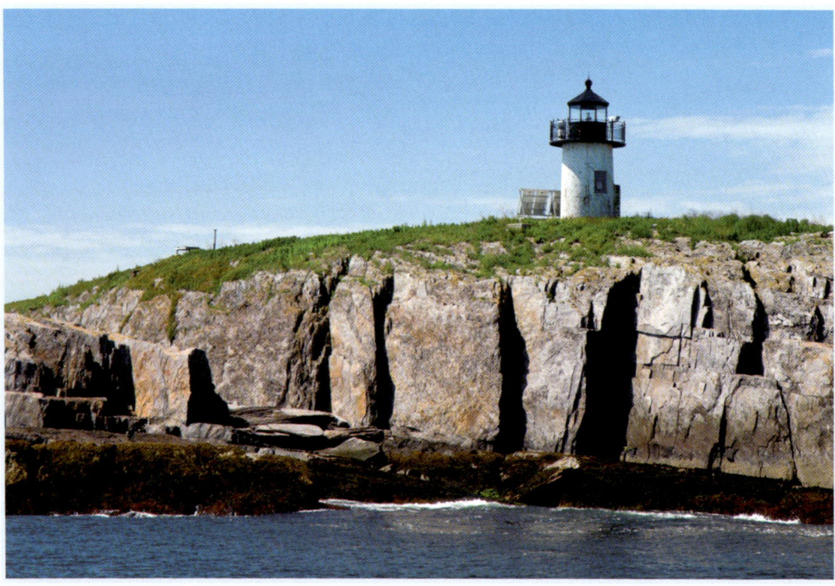

Pond Island Light marks a rocky shoreline.

As was the case with most early lighthouses, construction was awarded to the lowest bidder, who usually cut costs. Pond Island Lighthouse was no exception, and

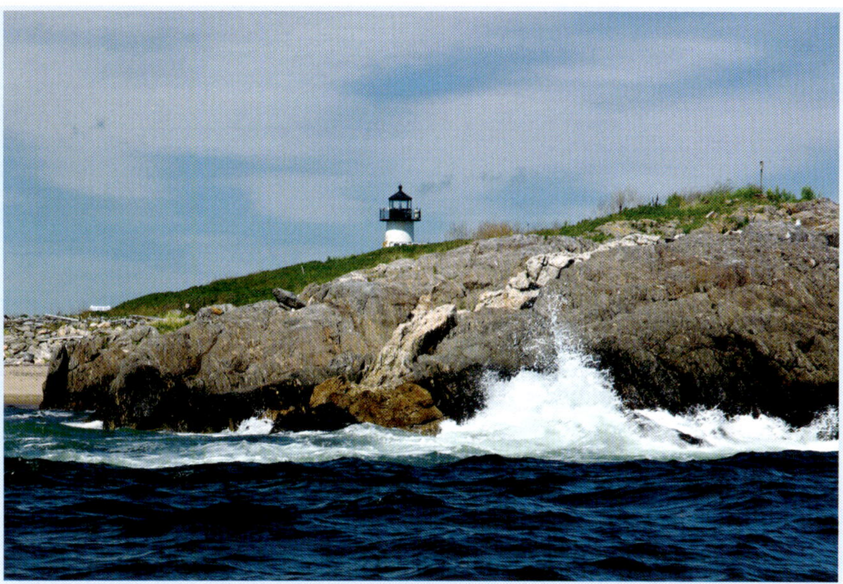

Pond Island Lighthouse is now part of a bird refuge.

the original beacon lasted only until 1835. After years of pleas from the keepers, a cistern was built to eliminate trips to the mainland for water during dry weather.

In November 1849, the *Hanover* was caught in a fierce storm near Pond Island Lighthouse. As the captain was trying to get around Pond Island to a safer spot inland along the Kennebec River, the ship ran into a bar off nearby Wood Island and sank with all twenty-four crewmen on board. Only a dog survived.

Another storm on September 8, 1869, caused widespread damage from Portland to Bath. The fog bell tower and the striking mechanism were destroyed, and the following year the bell was replaced with a new 1,200-pound bell.

Isaac Morrison, a well-known fiddler player, became keeper in 1889. One young resident who leaved nearby, Hiram Stevens, would row out to the lighthouse for weekly music lessons. Stevens later became a successful composer and had several pieces performed by John Philip Souza's band. Morrison was keeper until 1903, when he suffered a stroke and retired.

After four years at nearby Seguin Island Light, Napoleon Bonaparte Fickett became keeper in 1926. Fickett remained until 1948, when he fell ill and retired. He and his family weathered the great storm of March 3, 1947, when surf broke over the top of the lighthouse. Down the coast in the same storm, the *Oakey L. Alexander* ran aground near Cape Elizabeth Light.

Today, the island is a US Fish and Wildlife Service bird refuge for roseate terns, common terns, and eiders. Although best viewed by boat, visitors can view the lighthouse from Popham Beach at the end of Route 209. At low tide, it is often possible to walk to nearby Fox Island, climb up the rock hill, and get a closer view of the lighthouse.

Perkins Island Lighthouse

Georgetown (1898) • Latitude: 43° 47' 13" N • Longitude: 69° 47' 09" W

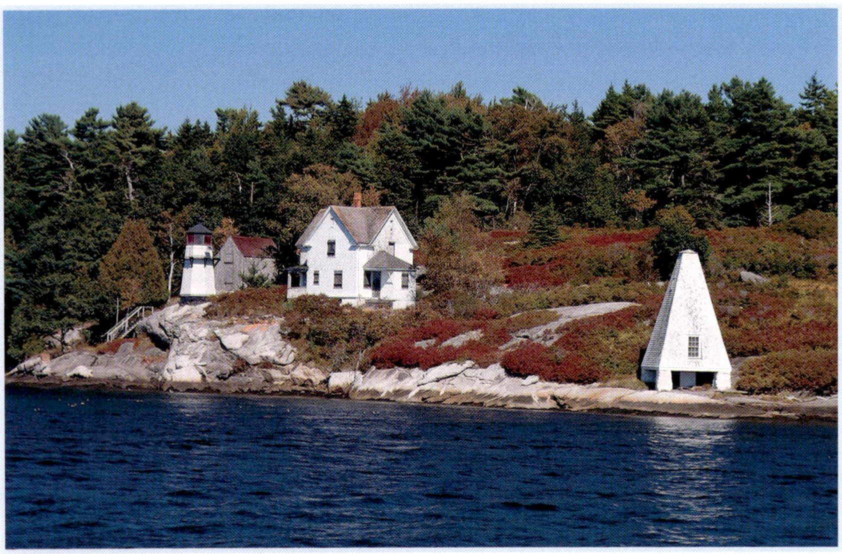

Perkins Island Lighthouse along the Kennebec River in autumn.

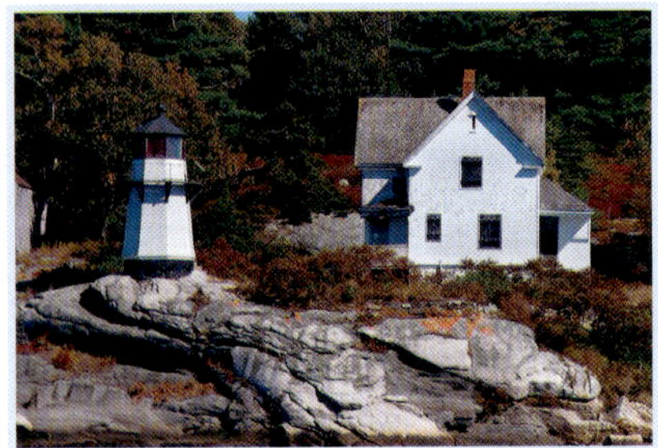

Perkins Island Light sits atop a rocky shore.

During the 1800s, navigational aids on the Kennebec River were maintained by the Kennebec Steamboat Company, using lanterns at turning points and other difficult sections of the river. However, during harsh weather or foggy nights, these small lights could barely be seen. In 1892 alone, 3,137 vessels were counted entering the river, excluding the large passenger steamships that traversed the river daily. The first lighthouse was finally built in 1898 after many petitions.

Life on Perkins Island was generally quiet, except for some occasional excitement. J. W. Haley, the keeper from 1911 to 1927, was praised in 1916 for having saved a man whose rowboat was swamped. The boat was filled with lumber, and Haley saved most of the cargo as well.

Keeper Eugene Osgood received a commendation from the secretary of commerce for his rescue efforts on June 16, 1931. As he was leaving the lighthouse to pick up his mail in Phippsburg, he saw a man struggling in the currents after a rogue wave overturned his rowboat. Osgood quickly launched his own boat and rescued the man.

Another time, Osgood heard a signal bell and cries of help during a fierce storm. Setting out in the station boat, he located a party of nineteen people whose boat had grounded in the storm. He managed to get them all back to the lighthouse, where his wife dried their clothes and fed them.

Squirrel Point Lighthouse

Arrowsic (1898) • Latitude: 43° 49' 00" N • Longitude: 69° 48' 11" W

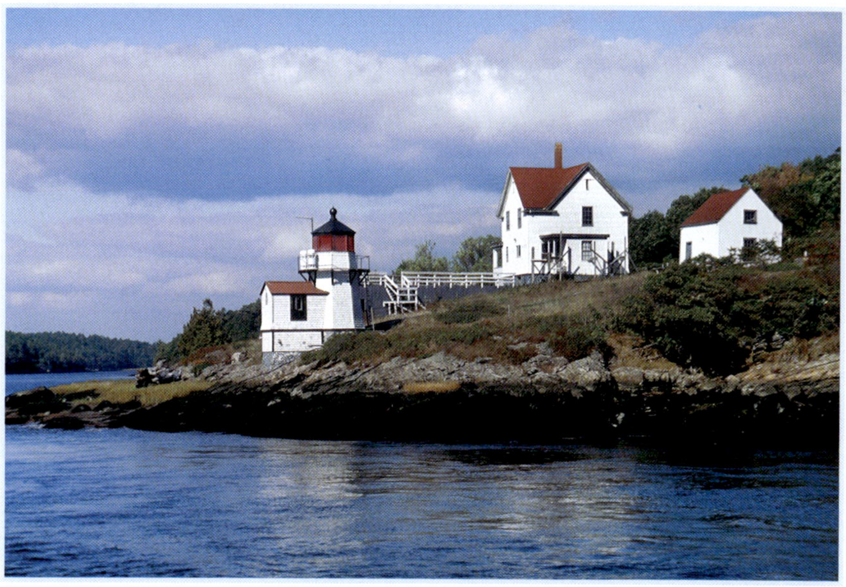

Squirrel Point Light marks a dangerous curve in the Kennebec River.

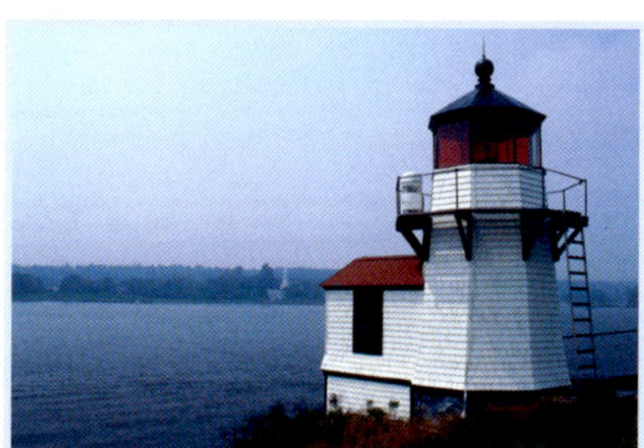

Squirrel Point Lighthouse along the Kennebec River.

Bath was an important shipbuilding center in the 1800s. As river traffic continued to grow, the Kennebec Steamship Company and towboat operators cooperated to provide spotty guidance with hanging lanterns, which were hard to see in bad weather. In 1895, President Grover Cleveland appropriated funds from Congress for construction of the Squirrel Point station, and at the same time for additional lights along the Kennebec River at Perkins Island and Doubling Point. All four stations were completed by 1898.

The keeper at the Kennebec River Range Light Station also tended the Squirrel Point Lighthouse until it was automated in 1979.

Over the years, as the buildings started to deteriorate, many lawsuits were filed regarding owner's rights and tenancy, education, and conservation. By 2005, all rights, title, and interest in Squirrel Point were put back in the federal government's hands. Finally, in 2008, a fifteen-year lease was granted to the Chewonki organization with the contingency that it would offer education and conservation programs.

Exploring the grounds. Squirrel Point's five acres are part of 640 acres of conservation land. The lighthouse is less than a mile's hike in the woods on relatively level ground and well-marked trails.

 **Driving and hiking directions.** From Route 1 over the Kennebec River in Bath, take Route 127 south to Steen Road on the right. When you come to a fork, stay to the right on the dirt road. Bear left on Bald Head Road and continue to the end. At a small dirt parking lot, take the first footpath on the right. Now you've got a three-quarter-mile or so hike in the woods (bring insect repellent). At a fork in the trail after crossing a wooden bridge; bear left by the tree with signs on it (turning right takes you to Fishing Point, which provides a nice overlook of the lighthouse). Stay on the main trail to the lighthouse. The views are worth the hike.

Doubling Point Lighthouse (Kennebec River Light)

Arrowsic (1898) • Latitude: 43° 52' 58" N • Longitude: 69° 48' 25" W

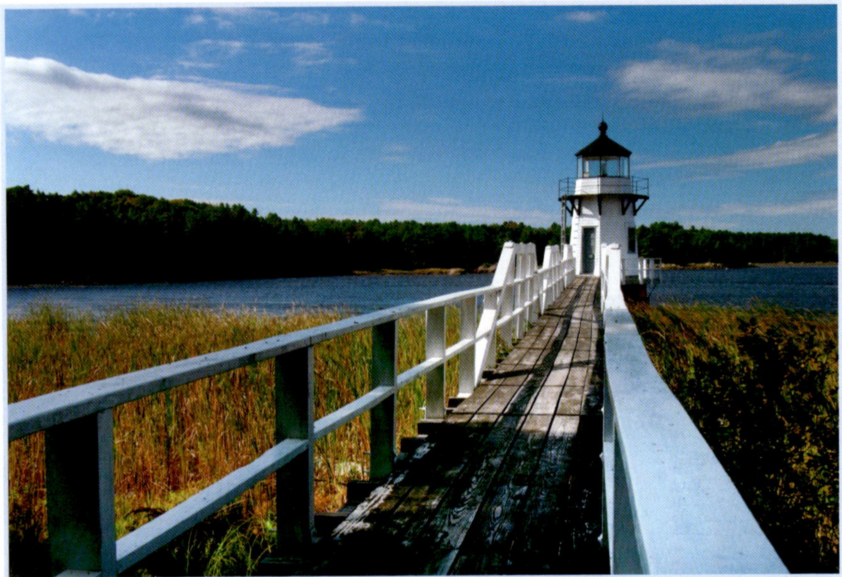

Doubling Point Light at the end of wooden walkway.

Doubling Point Light, a.k.a. Kennebec River Lighthouse, was built on a sharp double bend around Arrowsic Island, on the Kennebec River, near the shipbuilding harbor of Bath. It was one of four lights approved by Congress in 1895 to guide mariners around the Kennebec River's winding turns. The wooden, octagonal lighthouse tower was originally built on shore along with the keeper's house, shed, and bell tower. For better visibility, in 1899 the lighthouse was moved offshore to a stone pier connected to the island by a footbridge.

From 1898 to 1935, the station had only two keepers. The first was Merritt Pinkham, a former keeper at remote Seguin Light. He lived at the light until 1931, at the age of eighty-five. Charles W. Allen, who worked at Boon Island and Eagle Island lighthouses, became the station's second and last keeper until 1935.

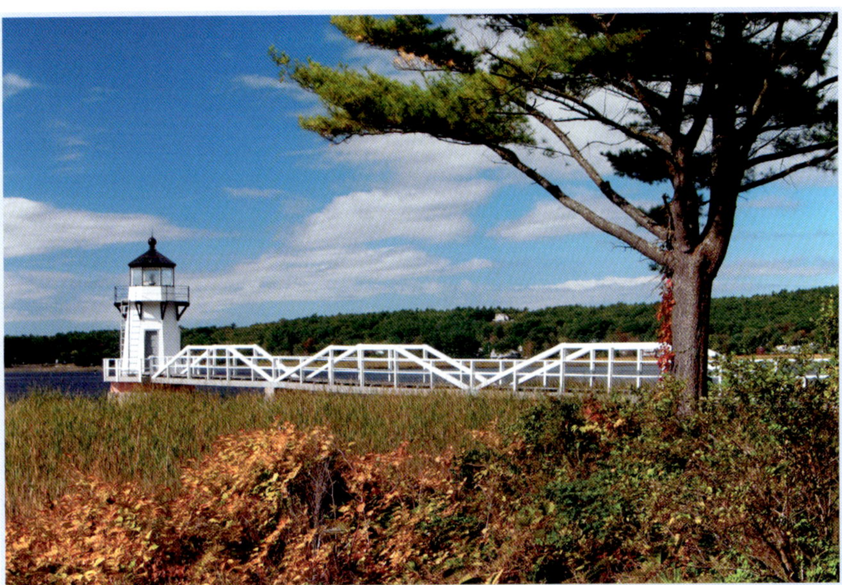

Doubling Point Lighthouse in autumn.

In 1935, the keeper's house was sold to a private owner and the Doubling Point Range Lights keeper became responsible for both stations. Then from 1981, one keeper was assigned to look after the Doubling Point Range Lights, Doubling Point Light, and Squirrel Point Light. Over the years, ice floes had washed down the Kennebec River each spring, crashing into the lighthouse's granite-block foundation. With the foundation in desperate need of repairs, the Friends of Doubling Point Light raised $25,000, which was matched by a grant from the Kurt Berliner Foundation of New York. This permitted the group to hire Reed and Reed, a local construction company out of Woolwich, to repair the foundation.

On December 10, 1999, in front of a crowd that had gathered to witness the event, the five-ton tower was lifted off its granite block foundation by a huge crane and placed on a barge to be moved upriver to the construction company's yard for temporary storage. Working in frigid conditions, the contractors inserted stainless steel rods in the granite block, reset each six-ton block into position, and filled the center with concrete. In January 2000, repairs were completed and the beacon was placed on the new foundation and reactivated.

Doubling Point Range Lights (Kennebec River Range Lights)

Arrowsic (1898) • Latitude: 43° 52' 58" N • Longitude: 69° 48' 25" W

The Kennebec River Range Lights, or Doubling Point Range Lights, were built on Arrowsic Island to mark an extreme double turn in the channel at Fiddler Reach. It is the only range light in Maine with two towers with identical lights. When the

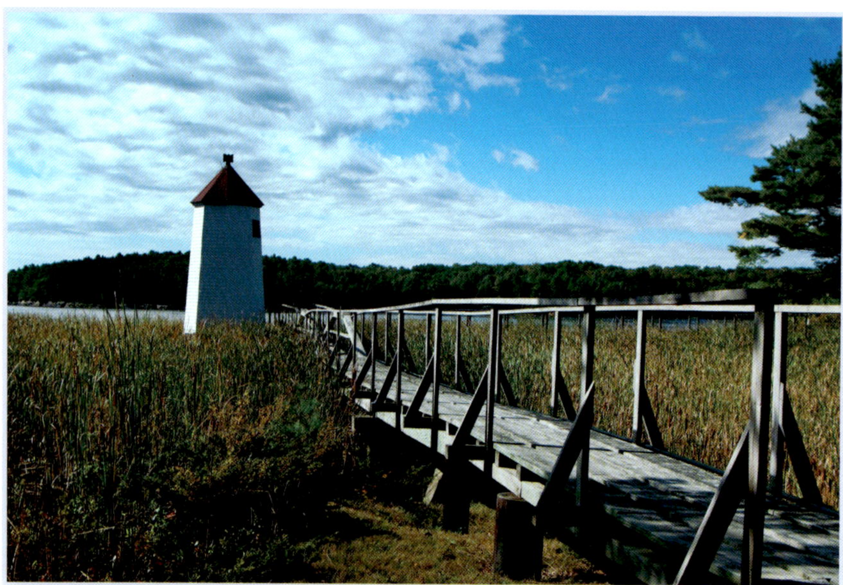

Doubling Point Front Range Light.

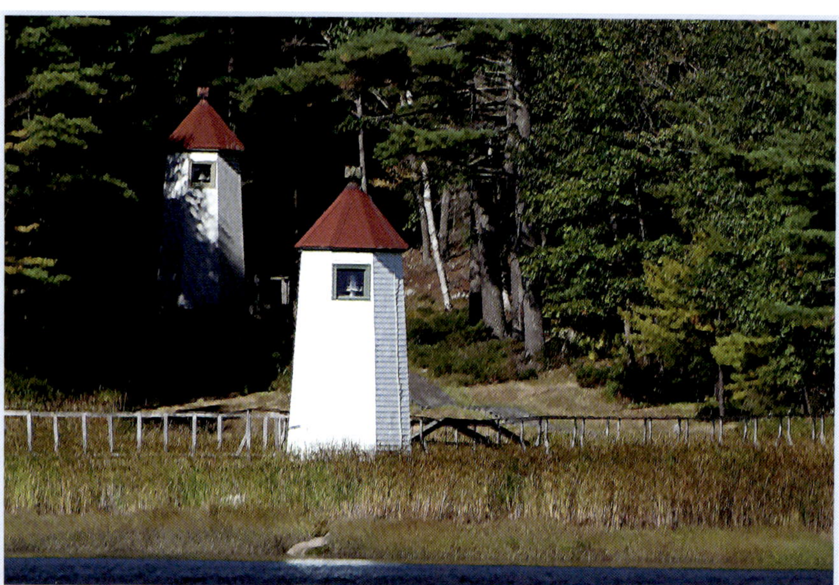

Doubling Point Range Lights view from river.

two light towers are aligned, captains know they are safely on course in the middle of the channel.

On December 28, 1928, keeper Captain Harry L. Nye made a rare rescue of four young men caught on a large ice floe that had broken away and was carrying them out to sea. In 1938, Lucy Mae Woodward, the young daughter of keeper William H. Woodward, fell in the river near the keeper's house and drowned, despite frantic attempts to revive her by the local police and neighbors. Many believed a slight heart attack caused her to fall.

In 1990, the range lights became one of the last light stations in the United States to be automated. They are still used as navigational aids at a private residence whose occupants also maintain Doubling Point Light and Squirrel Point Light.

Directions. The Doubling Point Lighthouse and the Doubling Point Range lights are close together in a residential area. The people who live at these places will probably allow you to take photographs if you ask permission. They were very gracious when I asked.

From Route 1, after you pass through Bath, cross the bridge over the Kennebec River. Take Route 127 south for nearly two miles until you come to a dirt road on the right with the sign that reads "Doubling Point Rd." Proceed down the dirt road and take a left at the mailboxes (you're still on Doubling Point Road), and then bear right at the fork to reach Doubling Point Light. If you bear left at the fork you will come upon the Doubling Point Range Lights.

Burnt Island Lighthouse

Boothbay Harbor (1821) • Latitude: 43° 49' 31" N • Longitude: 69° 38' 27" W

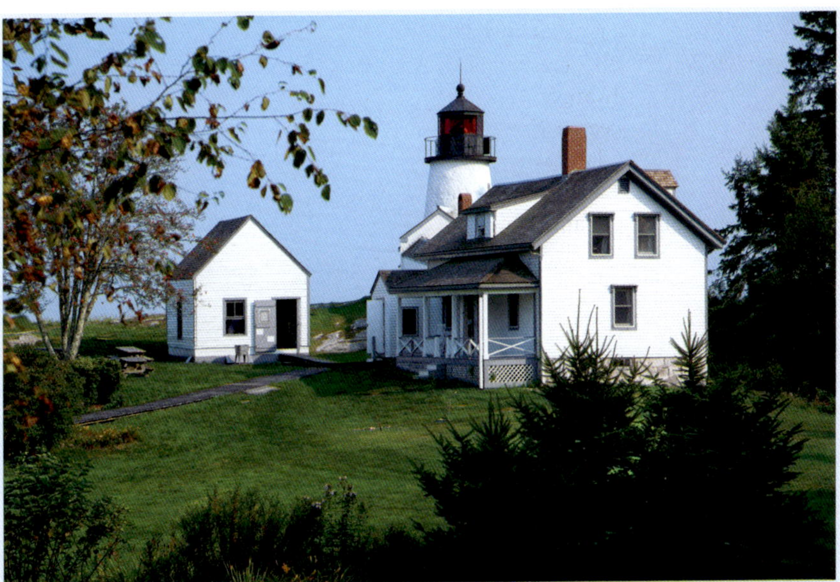

Burnt Island Lighthouse is on a beautiful five-acre island.

Burnt Island got its name from the practice of sheep farmers regularly setting the island afire to improve grazing. The lighthouse was one of the early ones in the area, built to accommodate increasing business at Boothbay Harbor's fishing port. Most keepers relished living on the island, only a mile from Boothbay Harbor. The beautiful, five-acre island provided plenty of room for a keeper's children to explore. The

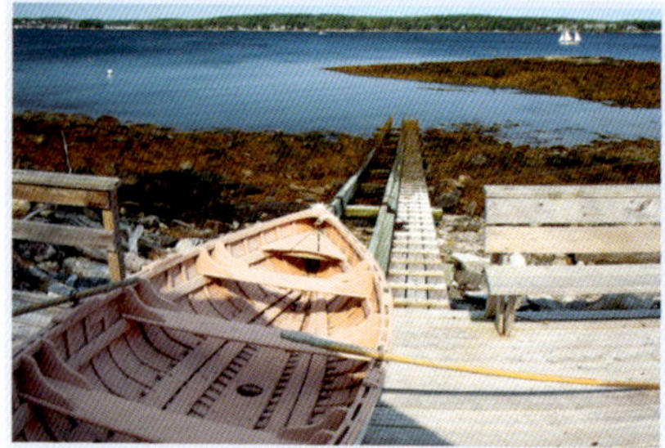

View from boathouse and ramp.

lighthouse has the oldest original tower in Maine, as Maine was part of Massachusetts until it became its own state in 1820, and the lighthouse was built in 1821, making it the first lighthouse in the new Maine state.

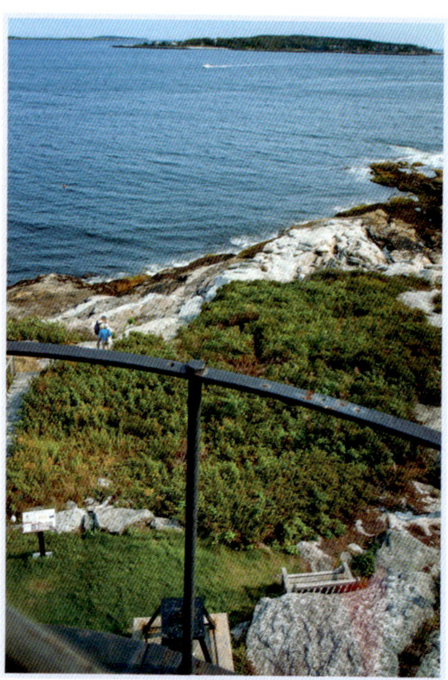

View from the lighthouse tower.

James A. McCobb was keeper from 1868 to 1880. He was a former sea captain who took the position at age fifty with his wife, Martha. After Martha died of cancer in 1879, McCobb's disposition changed, and he often complained about the many visitors. When he retired, due to failing health in 1880, Freeman Grover replaced him. Grover's descendants still operate Grover's Hardware Store in Boothbay Harbor.

Joseph Muise was keeper from 1936 to 1951. Originally from Nova Scotia, he, too, loved life on the island with his wife Anna and their children. He was a kind man who helped the local fishermen, who in turn provided his family with fresh lobster or fish. Muise's family was on the route of the "Flying Santa"—first Bill Wincapaw and then Edward Rowe Snow, who would fly over the island to drop Christmas presents.

In April 1962, Burnt Island Light became the last lighthouse in New England to be converted from kerosene to electricity, and was one of the last Maine lights to be automated in 1988. From 1821 to 1988, thirty keepers served at Burnt Island Light.

 **Exploring the grounds.** Balmy Days Cruises, Boothbay Harbor Cruises, and Tidal Transit Kayak Company offer tours to the island and lighthouse grounds. Balmy Days Cruises offers a three-hour tour twice a week in summer as part of the Living History program to show visitors the refurbished lighthouse and keeper's dwelling. The boat trip takes fifteen minutes out of Boothbay Harbor. Actors dressed in 1950s clothing portray John Muise's family and explain what life was like at the lighthouse in that era (no plumbing!). The keeper's dwelling is furnished from 1950 as well.

Hendricks Head Lighthouse

Southport (1829) • Latitude: 43° 49' 22" N • Longitude: 69° 41' 23" W

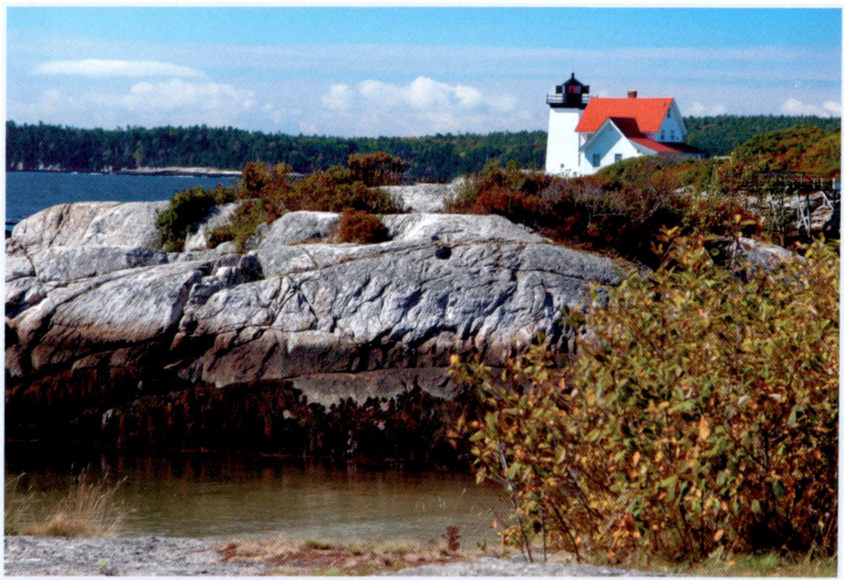

Hendricks Head Lighthouse guides mariners up the Sheepscot River.

Hendricks Head Lighthouse was erected on the western side of Southport Island to guide vessels up the Sheepscot River to the shipbuilding center at Wiscasset Harbor. It was rebuilt in 1875.

Jaruel Marr was appointed keeper in 1866, partly as compensation for injuries he sustained while fighting in the Civil War; these appointments were common. During the conflict, he was wounded and incarcerated in a Confederate prison in Virginia, where he was nursed back to health by a fellow prisoner and Union army doctor named Wolcott. To honor the doctor, Jaruel and his wife named their next child Wolcott. Wolcott became keeper at Cape Elizabeth and the Cuckolds Lighthouse, before returning to be keeper at Hendricks Head after his father's retirement. Coincidentally, Wolcott Marr was born, married, and passed away in the same room at the lighthouse.

Charles Knight became keeper after Wolcott passed away in 1912. On a stormy night in 1932, their dog Shep kept barking as if something was wrong. The keeper let the dog out and watched it run to the shoreline. Feeling something was wrong, he rang the fog bell to sound an alarm. Two powerboats responded and found a couple adrift in a rowboat, as they had lost their oars. The couple were rescued, and a few months later Shep was awarded a bronze medal by the Anti-Vivisection Society of New York for his heroic barking.

Hendricks Head Lighthouse is known for two sensational stories that occurred there. One involves a rescue of a baby girl by keeper Jaruel Marr, and the other a suicide attempt by a mysterious woman.

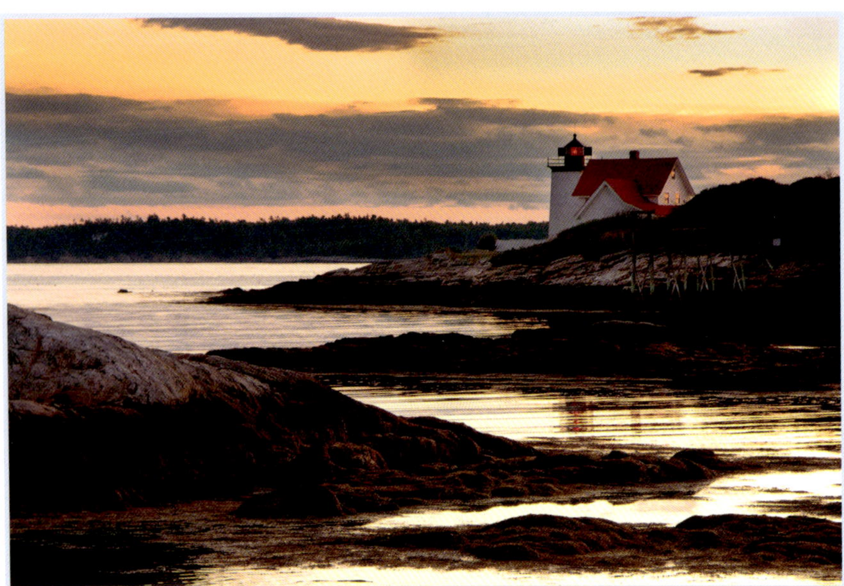

Sunset at Hendricks Head Light.

Miracle Baby Rescue. This story involves keeper Jaruel Marr, who was keeper at Hendricks Head Lighthouse near Boothbay Harbor in Maine from 1866 to 1895. During a March blizzard in 1875, blinding snow came up the Maine coastline. The captain of a small sailing vessel got caught in the rough seas as he was trying to make it ashore and could not see the lighthouse in the driving snow. The vessel ran aground on a rocky ledge about a half-mile from the lighthouse point.

Keeper Marr noticed the vessel lodged on the rocks. He could see the survivors clinging to the rigging and watched helplessly as the icy waves continued to wash over them. He anxiously debated whether he could launch his dory, but the ferocious high seas would have meant certain disaster for him.

As darkness fell, the wind began to subside, allowing keeper Marr and his wife to light a large bonfire for the victims as a signal that help was waiting, if they could miraculously find a way to the shore. About an hour later, as he was feeding the fire, Marr noticed a strange large bundle floating in the waves. He ran to the boathouse for a hook and line and asked his wife to help him hold the line as he waded into the freezing waters, secured the bundle, and brought it safely on shore. It contained two small feather beds tied together, and inside, a box with a crying baby girl. He ran to the house with the line still around his waist and placed the infant near the fire to warm her. His wife quickly wrapped the baby in warm blankets.

Keeper Marr rushed back to the shore to signal to the victims, but it was too late. The seas had smashed the vessel to pieces and there were no survivors. In the infant's bundle, the keeper found a locket and a message from the mother in the hopes that God would help her child. The baby girl, later named Seaborn, was believed to have been adopted by a doctor and his wife who were summer residents. This story has been disputed, and some believe it originated from a book published around 1900 called *Uncle Terry*. However, keeper Marr's ancestors claim that it is true.

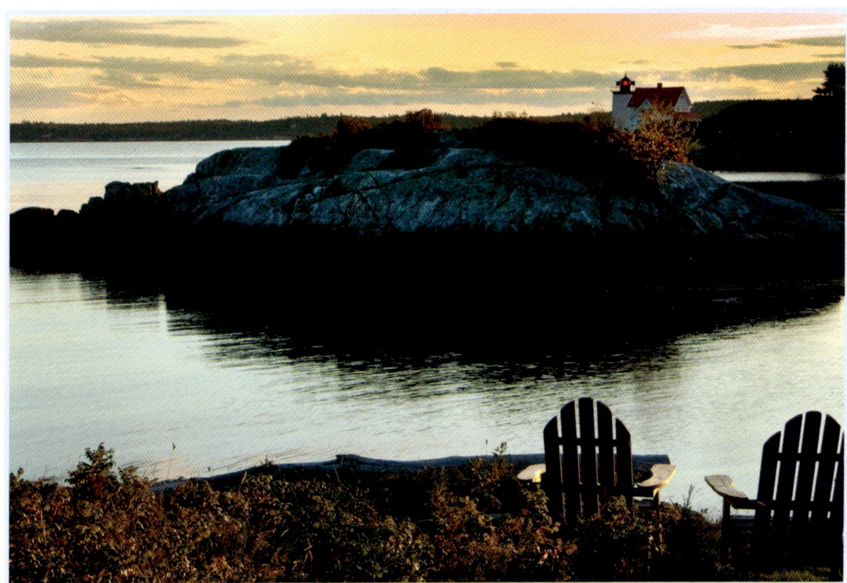

The lighthouse at sunset.

The Lady in Black. This lighthouse story is one of Maine's unsolved mysteries. On a cold early-December afternoon in 1931, a woman dressed in black, with the clothing and speech of someone in high society, stopped at Charlie Pinkham's post office store and asked his wife for directions to an open sweep of ocean. Mrs. Pinkham stated, "You're near Hendricks Head Lighthouse, but it might be dark before you get back, and it's lonesome." The woman seemed to know the area and thanked her. Mrs. Pinkham observed the woman walking toward Hendricks Head.

By late afternoon, cold winds continued to blow and the sun began to hide behind thickening clouds. By dusk, keeper Charles Knight arrived at the post office store, where Mrs. Pinkham asked him if he had met the woman on the road. He insisted he hadn't seen anyone. Worried for the woman's safety, Knight headed back toward Hendricks Head Lighthouse but found no one.

By the next day, many Southport residents had heard about the woman in black and started looking for her. In the sandy soil a short distance from the lighthouse, they found footsteps believed to be from a woman. Many feared she had waded into the icy water. Charlie Pinkham, who was also a volunteer firefighter, gathered a search party that found her body about a week later on Sunday, December 6, 1931. It had washed ashore on the ledge at the north end of the little beach near the lighthouse. A leather belt had been used to attach an electric iron to her wrist, presumably to weigh her down in the water. Detectives later discovered her bag was left at the Fullerton hotel, where she signed in as Louise Meade. Her description ran in papers throughout the nation.

Finally, on January 8, 1932, after weeks of investigation, and with no one to identify her or claim the body, the townspeople buried her in their old cemetery on the road to Hendricks Head.

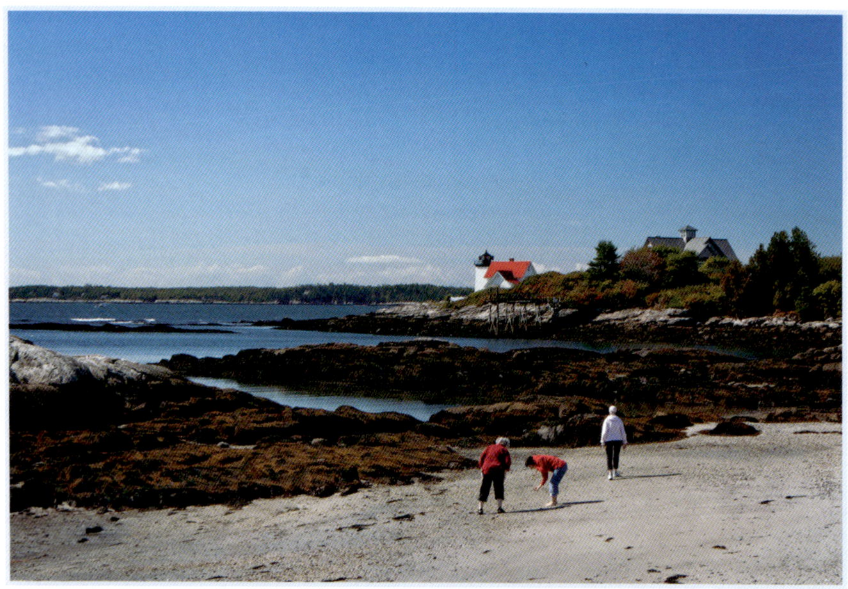

A small beach near the lighthouse.

Over the years, her ghost has been sited at twilight near the lighthouse, and she has become known as the "Lady of the Dusk."

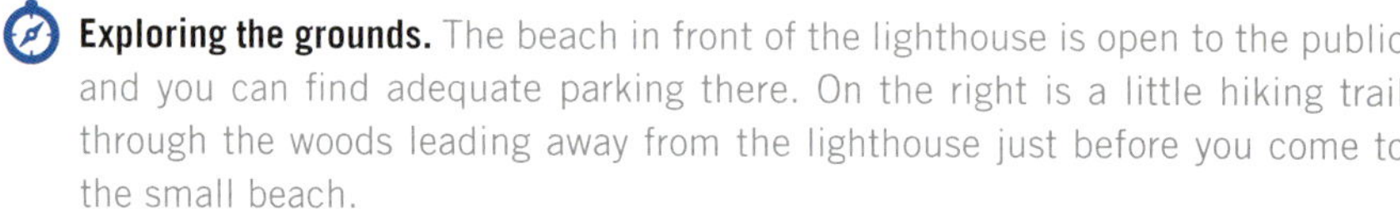

Exploring the grounds. The beach in front of the lighthouse is open to the public and you can find adequate parking there. On the right is a little hiking trail through the woods leading away from the lighthouse just before you come to the small beach.

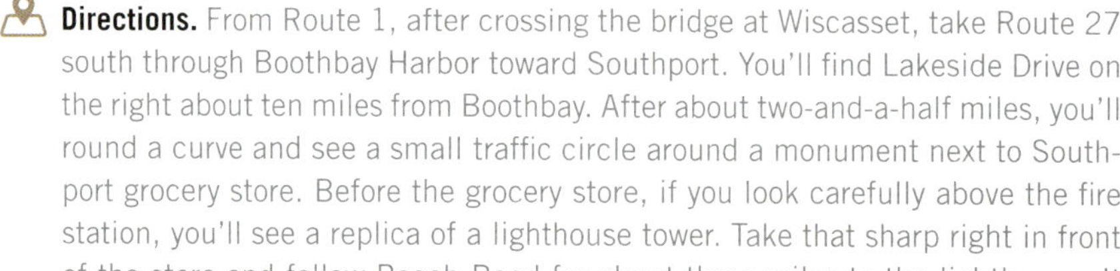

Directions. From Route 1, after crossing the bridge at Wiscasset, take Route 27 south through Boothbay Harbor toward Southport. You'll find Lakeside Drive on the right about ten miles from Boothbay. After about two-and-a-half miles, you'll round a curve and see a small traffic circle around a monument next to Southport grocery store. Before the grocery store, if you look carefully above the fire station, you'll see a replica of a lighthouse tower. Take that sharp right in front of the store and follow Beech Road for about three miles to the lighthouse. It is privately owned, but you can park near the beach and view the lighthouse.

Cuckolds Lighthouse

Newagen (1892) • Latitude: 43° 46' 8" N • Longitude: 69° 39' 00" W

The rocky island on which Cuckolds Lighthouse sits is a mile from Southport Island, and in the late 1800s it was a serious threat to the heavy shipping traffic in and out of Boothbay Harbor. The island's first 1892 navigational aid was a steam-driven fog signal house, but when shipwrecks continued to occur, mariners petitioned the government to install a lighthouse. In 1907, a light tower was added on top of the

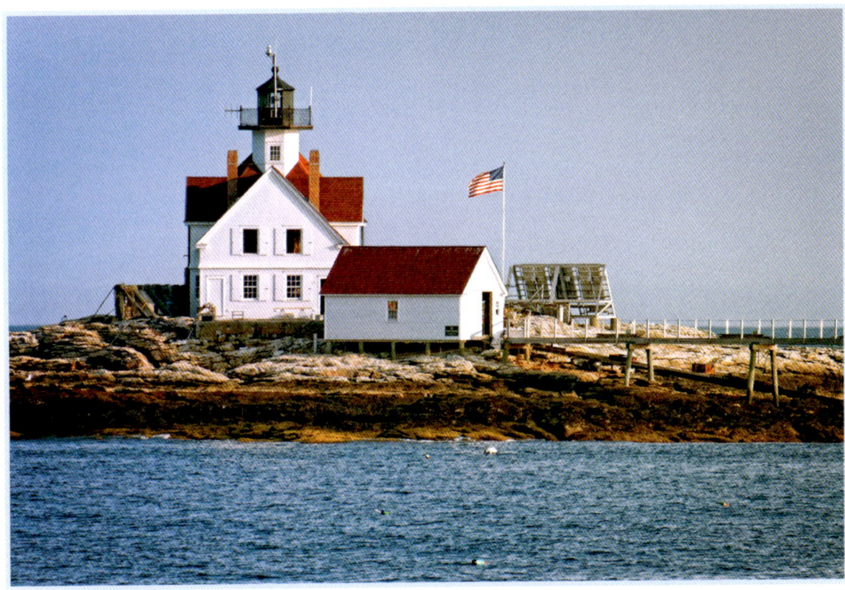

Cuckolds Lighthouse during restoration.

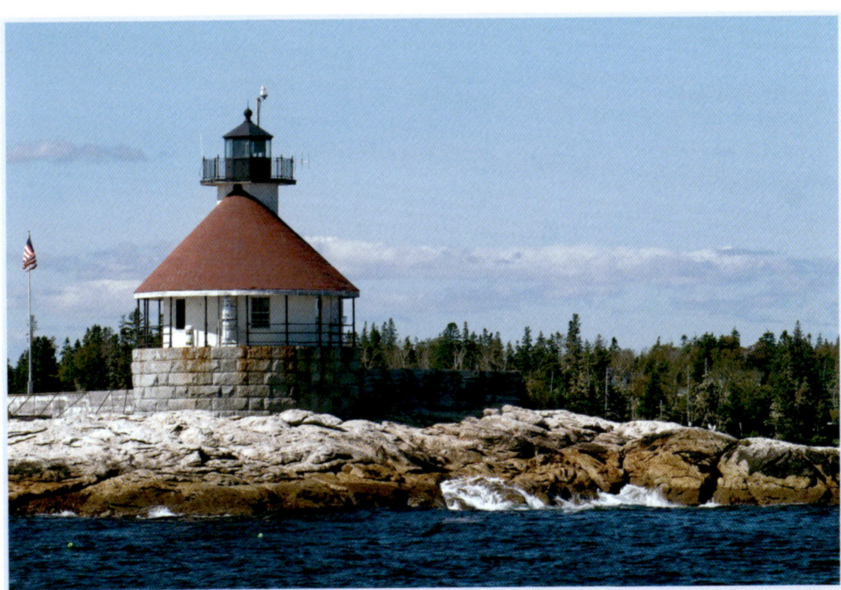

Original construction.

conical fog signal building, giving it the unique cylindrical shape. It was one of the last lighthouses to be built along the Maine coast.

On a bitterly cold night in January 1896, fog signal keepers Edward H. Pierce and Clarence Marr rescued six crewmen from the Canadian schooner *Aurora*, with help from two Cape Newagen lobstermen. The Canadian government rewarded them with silver watches; however, it took four years for Washington to follow suit.

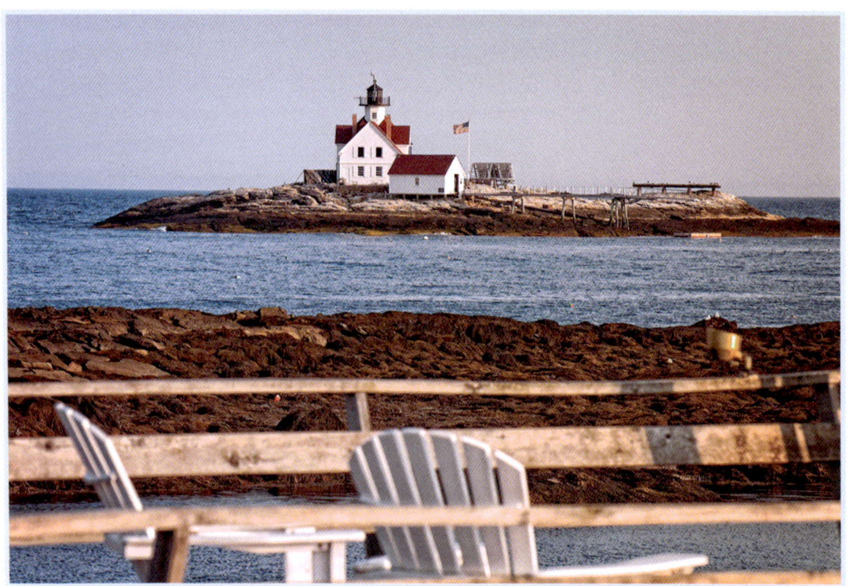

View of lighthouse from Newagen town landing in early summer evening.

Rogue waves constantly washed over the low-lying island. One keeper's wife was sewing in front of the second floor window when a huge wave poured through, drenching her and damaging some of the furniture.

Keepers were kept busy, sometimes rescuing distressed motorboats. In September of 1925, keeper Fred Robinson saved several people from a motorboat that had broken down and was drifting rapidly out to sea. In 1930, keeper E. D. Elliot towed a boat with seven people to safety after their motor failed.

On January 27 and 28, 1933, a mighty nor'easter known as the "Great Gale" swept over the island, destroying the radio and cutting communications with the mainland. The storm lasted over two days washing away the back porch, breaking most of the windows, smashing through the wall to the dining room, and flooding the rooms with seawater. Most of keeper Harold Seavey's belongings were destroyed. Luckily, he was reimbursed by the Department of Commerce.

In April 2006, the Cuckolds Island Fog Signal and Light Station organization was given the deed to the lighthouse under the provisions of the National Historic Lighthouse Preservation Act. To lower maintenance costs, the lighthouse has been rebuilt and the keeper's quarters remodeled to accommodate overnight guests, who can even rent the entire island if desired. The renovated keeper's dwelling is now called the Inn at Cuckolds Lighthouse.

Directions for a distant view. The Cuckolds Lighthouse is best viewed by boat, but you can get a distant view from Cape Newagen on Southport Island, south of Boothbay Harbor. From Boothbay, continue on Route 27 over the drawbridge and onto Southport Island. Turn left onto Route 238. Take Route 238 for about four miles, then turn left on Landing Road and continue to the end at Newagen. A sign for the town landing on the right directs you to the pier to view the light.

Ram Island Lighthouse

Boothbay Harbor (1883) • Latitude: 43° 48' 14" N • Longitude: 69° 35' 58" W

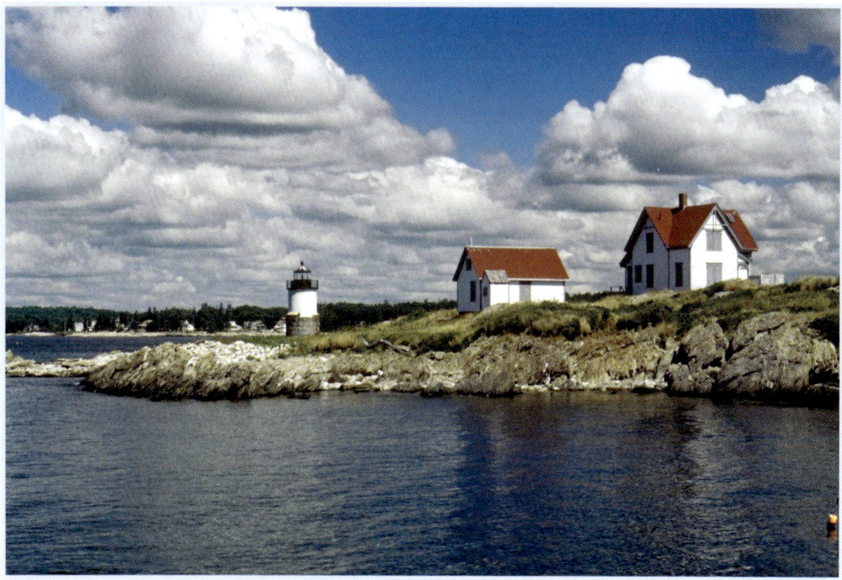

Ram Island Lighthouse in Boothbay Harbor.

In the years before the lighthouse was built, a lobsterman and three fisherman took it upon themselves to tend a series of homemade lanterns for mariners. When the fourth man stopped tending the lantern, there were many stories of ghosts being seen on the island for years afterwards. The form of a ghostly "white woman" is said to have saved many lives by appearing with a light to warn ships of danger. Some reported seeing her in a burning boat or on a nearby reef, and even accompanied by lightning. But all described her as a glowing form frantically waving them off the rocks in the area. One captain reported hearing a fog whistle that saved him during a blizzard, even though there was never such an aid on Ram Island.

In 1903 the schooner *Harriet W. Babson*, returning from Newfoundland with a load of salted herring, ran into the walkway leading to the lighthouse and destroyed it. It was rebuilt soon afterward.

During World War II in early 1945, when German U-boats were feared, new keeper Ralph Norwood was rowing to the mainland with his two sons when he was greeted by men on the shore armed with loaded shotguns. A nervous local had observed the rowboat and did not recognize the keeper and his sons, so she called the police and FBI to report that German spies were coming ashore.

The light was automated in 1965, but storms over the years destroyed the walkway again. In late 2002, the Ram Island Preservation Society restored the house and reconstructed the walkway from the shore to the lighthouse tower.

The One-Legged Keeper. Samuel John Cavanor was Ram Island Light's first keeper. Before that, he had served aboard the lighthouse tender *Iris*, and one day his leg

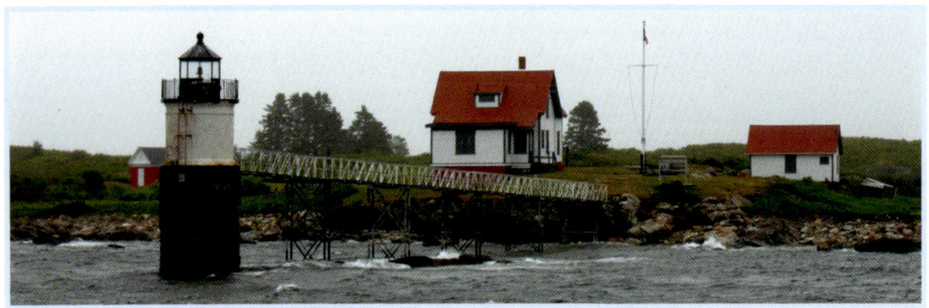

Ram Island Light during small storm

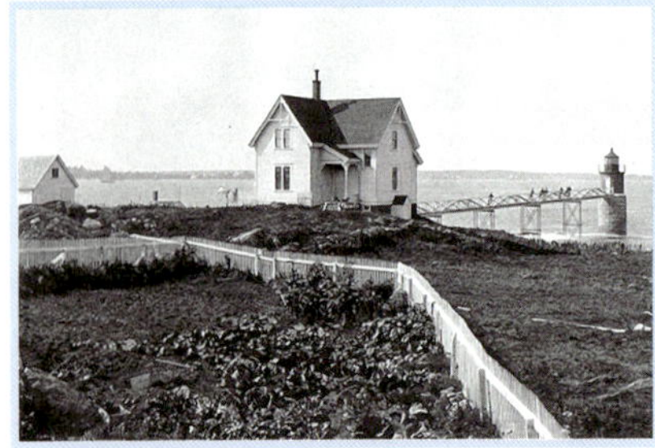

Vintage image. *Courtesy US Coast Guard.*

was crushed by a buoy being hauled aboard. Cavanor's leg had to be amputated, but his peg leg didn't slow him down. He was considered one of the most active keepers on the Maine coast. During his first winter storm, windows were shattered in the lantern room from hailstones that also broke the lantern glass, extinguishing the light. Cavanor spent the night in the lantern room, blocking the open windowpanes with newspapers, and making sure the light stayed illuminated.

 **Directions for a distant view.** You can reach Boothbay Harbor along Route 27 from Route 1. If you take a left on Route 96 from Route 27 in Boothbay and follow it for about ten miles to the end, you'll be treated to a special area referred to as Ocean Point, where surf meets rocks along the shoreline. You can see Ram Island Light about a mile offshore as well. There is no public access to the island.

Pemaquid Point Lighthouse

Bristol (1827) • Latitude: 43° 50' 12" N • Longitude: 69° 30' 21" W

Built in 1827 and rebuilt in 1857, Pemaquid Point Lighthouse sits atop a unique set of beautiful and particularly dangerous geological rock formations. Its first keeper was Isaac Dunham from Bath, Maine.

By the late 1800s, Pemaquid Point was a desirable location for many keepers and their families, as it was easily accessible by land and allowed keepers to raise animals and crops. Pemaquid Point was not, however, easy to reach by water because of the rock formations. Lighthouse tenders were forced to anchor offshore and ferry supplies over the rocks.

Keeper Joseph Lawler and his wife, Sophronia, welcomed a baby girl named Susie in 1868; Susie Lawler was the only child ever born at the lighthouse. Marcus A. Hanna, known for his courageous rescue at Cape Elizabeth Lighthouse, succeeded Lawler in 1869 and stayed at Pemaquid until 1873.

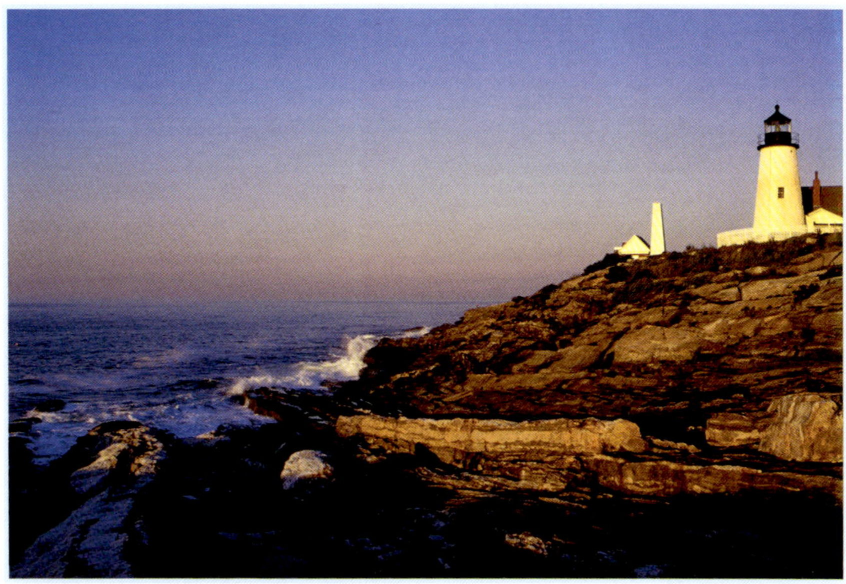

Pemaquid Point Lighthouse in the early morning.

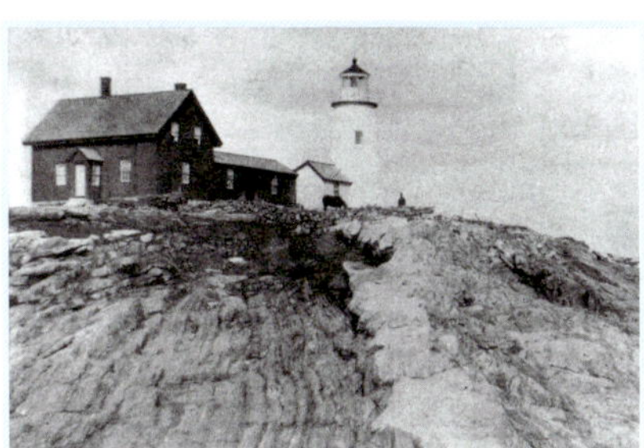

Vintage image from the 1850s. *Courtesy US Coast Guard.*

Shipwrecks would sometimes still occur on the dangerous rocks, such as the *Annie F. Collins* on May 4, 1891, and the *Alice P. Higgins* on September 18, 1893. The three-man crew aboard the *Annie F. Collins* was lost. Those aboard the *Alice P. Higgins* made it to shore by boat, landing at Pemaquid Light. Both vessels were carrying paving stone and were bound for New York.

On August 17, 1917, in heavy fog, the two-masted schooner *Willis and Guy* struck the rocks near Lighthouse Point. Her crew of three were saved, but a hurricane four days later destroyed the vessel, scattering her cargo of 216 tons of coal all over the rocks. The wreck proved a wonderful gift for the townspeople, who were able to salvage enough coal to heat their homes the following winter.

Keeper Leroy Elwell rescued three people from a capsized sailboat on August 6, 1930, and later received a commendation for his heroism. During Elwell's tenure, the lighthouse was one of the first in Maine to be automated in 1934.

The keeper's quarters were converted to the Fisherman's Museum in 1972 and is still open today. The current tower stands seventy-nine feet above mean sea level, and with its fourth-order Fresnel lens, the beacon is visible up to fourteen nautical miles in clear weather.

Pemaquid Point Lighthouse is on Maine's commemorative quarter, along with Maine's state tree, the white pine, and the three-masted schooner *Victory Chimes*,

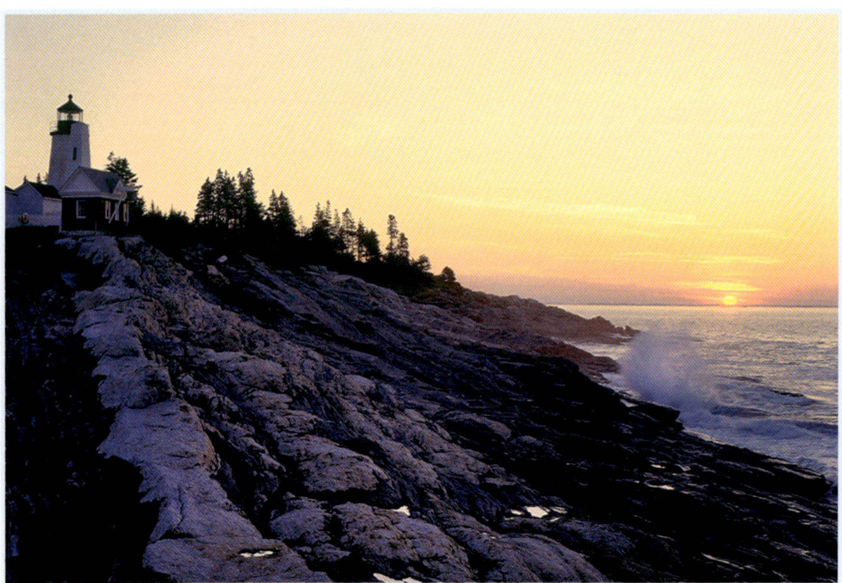

Sunrise at Pemaquid Point Lighthouse.

which visitors can still sail out of Rockport. It is the last of the three-masted schooners in the Maine windjammer fleet.

Two Wrecks during a Fierce Storm and a Strange Coincidence. On September 16, 1903, after a dense fog lifted, a violent storm hit the region. The small coasting schooner *Sadie and Lillie* was heading for Boston with its cargo and wrecked by the rocks near the lighthouse. Weston Curtis was near the lighthouse grounds, and was able to get a line to the vessel in the raging surf, and after a fierce struggle with the heaving waves, two of the crew were brought to safety. Captain Willard C. Harding remained on board to try to free the schooner, but realized it was a futile effort. Harding then tried to use the line and make it to the shore, but the line became entangled in the rocks and he perished in the raging waters.

In the same storm, the fishing schooner *George F. Edmunds*, loaded with mackerel, was attempting to round the point, but the winds were too strong for the sturdy vessel. Captain Willard G. Poole decided to try and make the little harbor in South Bristol, instead of hugging the coast and landing in Portland Harbor many miles away. He was the only person who had some knowledge of the Pemaquid area and headed for Lighthouse Point near the beacon. The vessel was within a mile from the point as the winds increased in fury, forcing the ship toward the rocks. The captain made a miscalculation in the drift of the schooner and the vessel ended up smashing against the rocks by Pemaquid. It started to break apart almost immediately.

The captain ordered the men to launch the dories, which were put over the side, only to be smashed to pieces on the rocks. Some of the crewmen tried to swim toward shore but the undertow carried them away, and they perished.

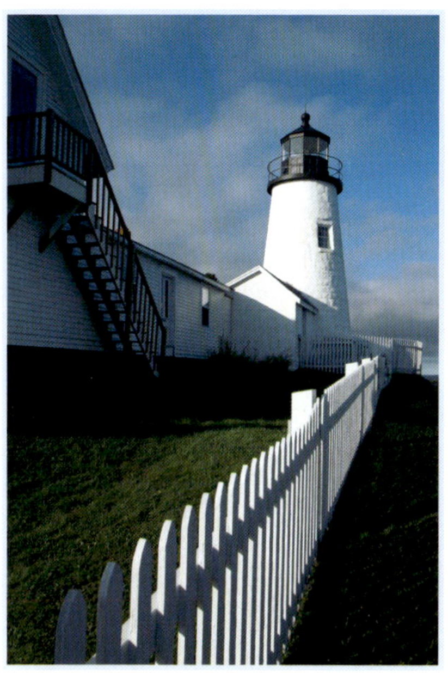

A picket fence surrounds the lighthouse.

One of the dories succeeded in avoiding the rocks and headed for shore with five crew members. Halfway there, a huge wave capsized the craft and only two of the men reached shore. Of the sixteen men aboard the *George F. Edmunds*, fourteen, including Captain Willard Poole, perished in the storm. The following day, when the storm subsided, all that remained of the *George F. Edmunds* and the *Sadie and Lillie* were splintered wood and twisted iron.

William P. Sawyer of Pemaquid Point interviewed the two survivors of the *George F. Edmunds* and wrote down their stories for the public. On September 17, 1945, almost exactly forty-two years later, Sawyer's body was found near the Pemaquid Lighthouse. His sudden passing remains a mystery.

 **Exploring the grounds.** The lighthouse guards the entrance to Muscongus Bay and John Bay at Pemaquid Point at the end of Route 130. The **Fisherman's Museum**, part of the original keeper's building, is open during the summer months providing historical marine documents, tools, and artifacts from the fishing community dating back to the 1800s. Visitors may be able to climb the lighthouse tower as well. There is a restaurant and gift shop (great pies!) with oceanside views just outside the parking lot. Pemaquid Point Lighthouse offers some of the most spectacular scenery in Maine, with its unique rocky shoreline and park for visitors to relax and explore. On the lighthouse grounds, you can climb all around the unique rock formations that jut out to the sea (be wary of high tide) or just enjoy the splendor. A one-bedroom upstairs apartment in the keeper's house is available for weekly vacation rentals.

 **Directions.** From the Route 1 business district in Damariscotta, turn south on Highway 129 and drive just under three miles to the intersection of Highways 129 and 130. Take Highway 130 south for about twelve miles to Pemaquid Point, where you will see the lighthouse by a large parking lot.

Franklin Island Lighthouse

Muscongus Bay (1807) • Latitude: 43° 53' 32" N • Longitude: 69° 22' 29" W

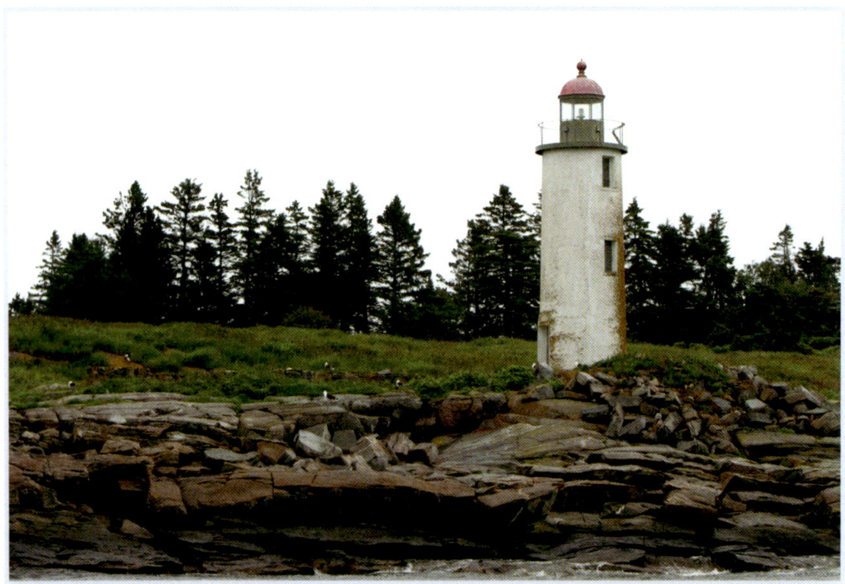

Franklin Island Lighthouse is the third-oldest lighthouse in Maine.

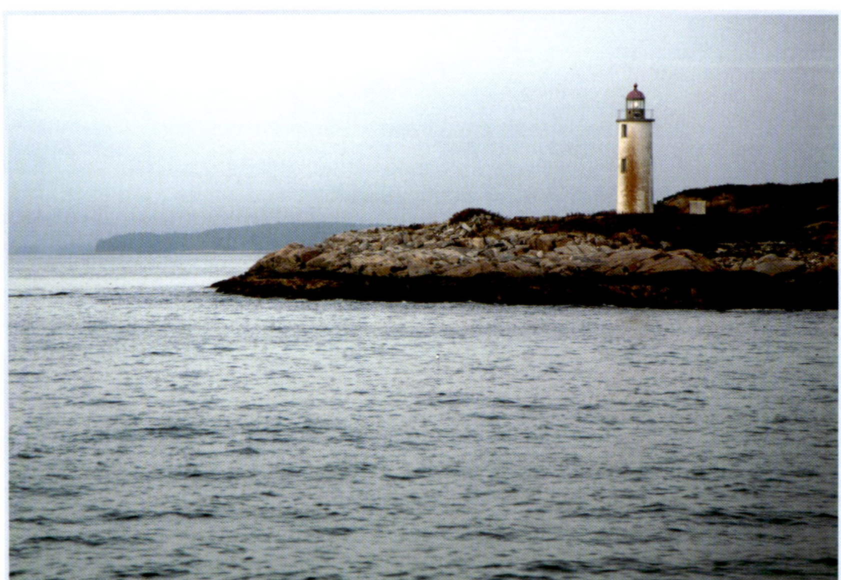

Franklin Island Lighthouse is five miles from the mainland.

Franklin Island Lighthouse was built to guide mariners in Muscongus Bay. It is the third oldest lighthouse station in Maine and is five miles from the mainland town of Friendship. John Lowell was the first keeper and remained at the station for

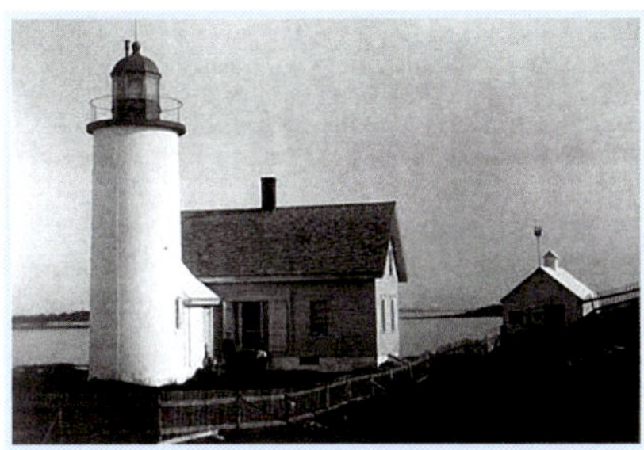
Vintage image. *Courtesy US Coast Guard.*

twenty-three years. In 1853, the inspector of the new lighthouse board deemed the beacon and its building "entirely worthless" and a health hazard to the keepers. Funds were appropriated for a new brick lighthouse and wooden keeper's house, which were completed in 1855.

Even though the lighthouse was five miles from shore, keepers were given only a tiny rowboat to use for transport. George E. Woodward served as keeper from 1924 to 1926. On January 9, 1925, Woodward, who was in poor health and could barely perform the basic lighthouse duties, heard a distress signal and went to the assistance of a fishing party marooned near the station. He brought the men back to the lighthouse, fed them, and loaned them his small boat so they could get ashore.

His son, Coleman George Woodward, was often called on to fill in for the keepers, who were given twenty-eight vacation days each year. As there were no telephones on the island, keepers who needed help would fly the American flag upside down from the top of the tower and hope passing ships would notice. Once, keeper Woodward had a bad case of the flu and flew the signal for nearly three days, but no one saw it. He got better a few days later.

Coastal Attractions along the Kennebec River and Boothbay

Bath, Boothbay, and Bristol

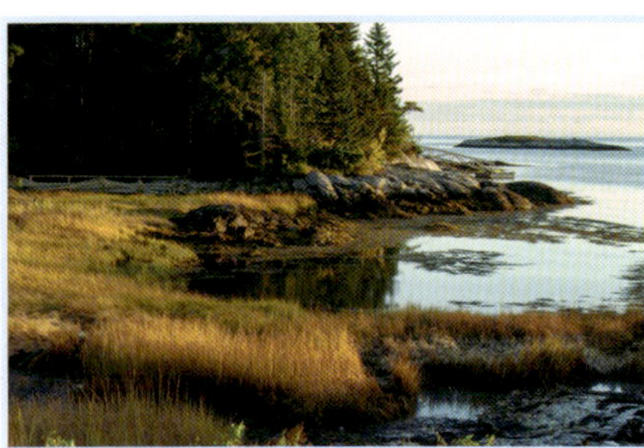

The Boothbay region offers miles of scenic shoreline drives.

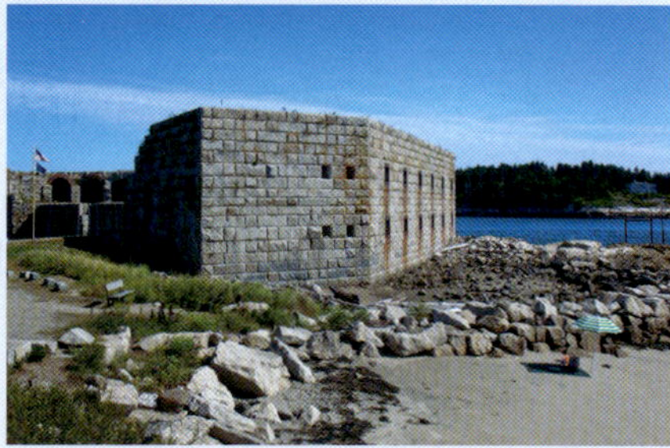

Fort Popham is the starting point for the miles-long Popham Beach.

Route 1 is the main highway up the coast, and the communities surrounding lighthouses can be accessed from the many roads off Route 1. A lot of these areas have rural fishing villages that haven't changed over the years. Bath is a major shipbuilding port, and the **Maine Maritime Museum** is worth a visit. **Maine's first ship**, the *Virginia*, was the first English ship built in North America over 400 years ago. Learn about shipbuilding by checking out a replica being built on Commercial Street in Bath. Bath's historic year-round waterfront is set along the banks of the Kennebec River amid nineteenth century buildings, artist galleries, specialty shops, and eateries. Stop by the **Chocolate Church Arts Center** for regional music and performance arts.

Following Route 209 south off Route 1, Phippsburg and Parker Village are quiet fishing communities along the Kennebec River. Continuing south about ten miles, you'll come to Popham State Beach Park, truly one of Maine's rare geologic landforms with a long, curved stretch of sand beach that goes for miles. From the beach at the village of Popham, you'll find close views of Pond Island Light, and if you happen to arrive at Popham Beach during low tide, you can actually walk out to nearby Fox Island, climb up the rock hill, and enjoy breathtaking views of Pond Island, with Sequin Island Lighthouse in the distance. Fort Popham State Historic Site is part of Popham Beach within the state park, where you can also explore Fort Popham and Fort Baldwin. Climb the tower at Fort Baldwin to get a full view of the coast.

Quick stop! Before going over the bridge at Wiscasset heading toward Boothbay, you'll find **Red's Eats** snack shack; just look for the line of people. Red's is best known for its tasty lobster rolls and fried clams. The building is a real lobster shack and has been a local attraction since 1938.

After crossing the huge Kennebec River Bridge in Bath, travel down Route 127 and you'll find a mile-long hike out through marked, wooded trails to Squirrel Point Lighthouse. You can also find Doubling Point Road and can ask permission to explore the Doubling Point Lighthouse and the Doubling Point Range Lights across the street. Stop at Reid State Park, Maine's first state-owned saltwater beaches, which stretch out over a mile. You'll also find large sand dunes, sweeping views of islands and lighthouses, and lots of nesting birds.

Wiscasset is on the way to the Boothbay Harbor region and is commonly known as Maine's prettiest village, with an abundance of antique shops, galleries, and museums. The **Musical Wonder House** exhibits a vast collection of antique mechanical musical instruments, and you can also explore the **Maine Art Gallery**. Check out the **Old 1812 Jail**, Maine's first prison built for notorious felons. Wiscasset is also home to the **Wiscasset, Waterville & Farmington Railway Museum**, a two-foot-gauge steam railroad in operation, and **Castle Tucker**, an unusual Regency mansion of the early 1800s. If you're looking for some thrills, explore **Monkey C Monkey Do**, Maine's high-flying family adventure park using zip lines!

 **Quick stop!** At the center of Boothbay Village you'll find **Bet's Fish Fry**, a local snack shack where the catch of the day is fried to perfection and piled multiple fillets high in a sandwich. Yum!

On Route 96, stop at the East Boothbay General Store for an authentic Maine experience. The Boothbay Harbor area offers quaint inlet harbors and small villages, like Southport, along with many B&Bs. Boothbay Harbor lives up to its reputation as a destination for all kinds of water excursions, from fishing and lobstering to whale watching. If you're into kayaking, some of the best views are out of Boothbay. Most tour boats leave out of Fisherman's Wharf in the harbor center.

Want to head out to an island for a traditional Maine clambake? **Cabbage Island Clambakes** provides tours out of Boothbay to five-acre Cabbage Island for this unique experience. To experience how lobsters are

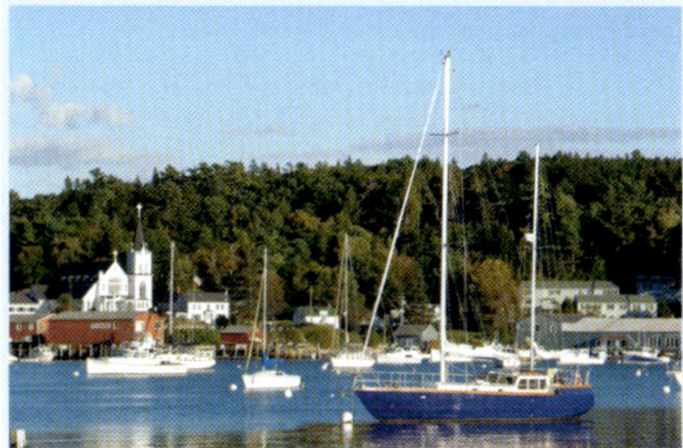

View of boats in Boothbay Harbor from tour boat.

caught, take a ride with **Go Lobstering!**, or try **Hay-Val Charters.** How about a sailing lobster boat? Book a spot on Maine's last sailing lobster boat with **Sail Muscongus**, on a restored friendship sloop named *Sarah Mead*.

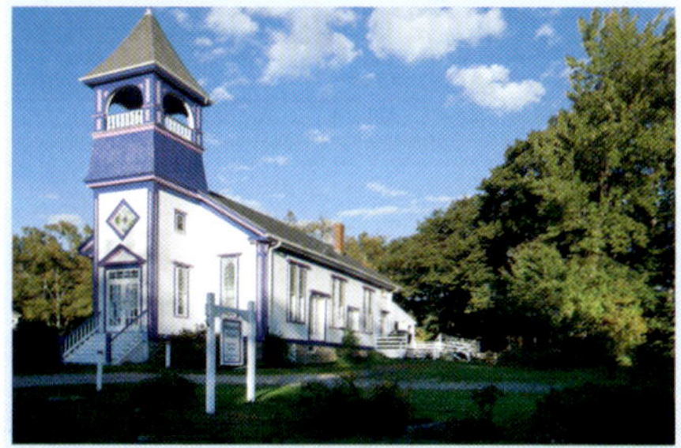

Boothbay has many unique attractions, like this purple church.

Carousel Music Theatre & Supper Club serves up a classic dinner theater experience. For celebrating the arts in traditional music, poetry, and artwork, try the **Lincoln Arts Festival**. The historic **Opera House in Boothbay Harbor** brings year-round live performances to the region.

Boothbay Railway Village showcases transportation from many eras, from horseless carriages to steam-powered vehicles, streamlined cars of the 1930s, and a Rolls Royce. The **Maine State Aquarium**, on the western side of Boothbay Harbor, has a variety of exhibits, including a twenty-foot-long touch tank, a twenty-three-pound live lobster, and rare blue lobsters. To explore Maine's flora, visit the 250-acre **Maine**

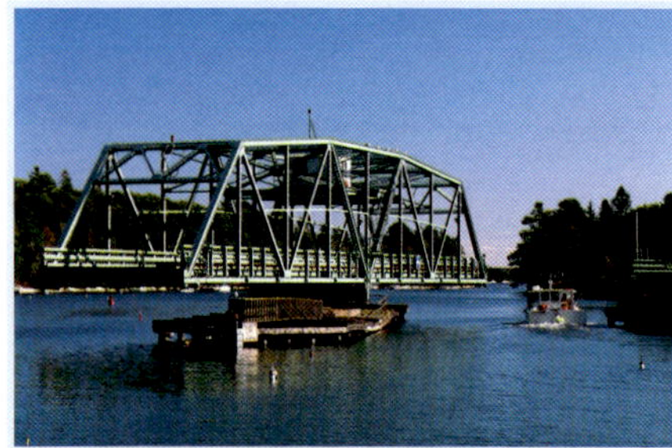

Drawbridge swings horizontally to allow boats to pass.

Coastal Botanical Gardens or the **Boothbay Region Land Trust**, with over thirty miles of hiking trails. At **Coastal Maine Botanical Gardens**, you can also take a **Sheepscot River Cruise** on board the first and only fully electric US Coast Guard vessel in Maine, the *Beagle*.

Driving along Route 27 or Route 96 over the island around Southport, you'll find one of Maine's two swinging truss bridges, which swing open sideways for boat crossings. The **Hendricks Hill Museum** features an 1810 house with eight rooms of antique furniture. At the **Southport Fire Station**, you'll find a replica of a small lighthouse tower on top.

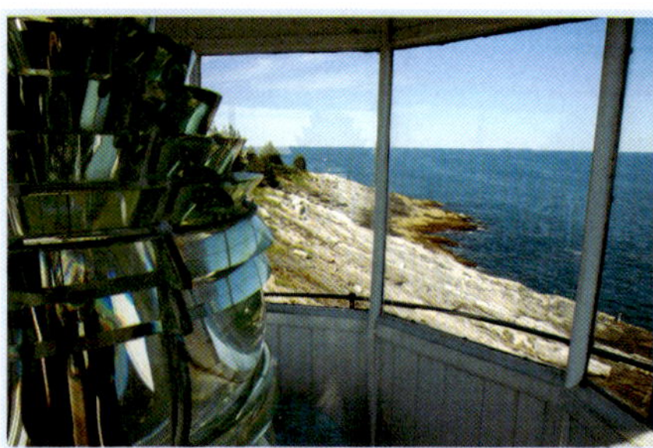

View from Pemaquid Lighthouse tower with Fresnel lens.

In Damariscotta and Newcastle, you'll find nineteenth-century storefronts, and restaurants and galleries. Head down Route 129 from Route 1, to Route 130, with more galleries along the way to Pemaquid Point Lighthouse in Bristol. Nearby is Pemaquid Beach, a quarter-mile jewel of white sand beach on the west shore of Pemaquid Neck in Bristol, with its famous geological rock formations jutting out to the sea. Other places to visit include **Colonial Pemaquid Historic Site**, where visitors will find Fort William Henry, once the largest fort in New England, built in the late 1600s, and the **Pemaquid Art Gallery**.

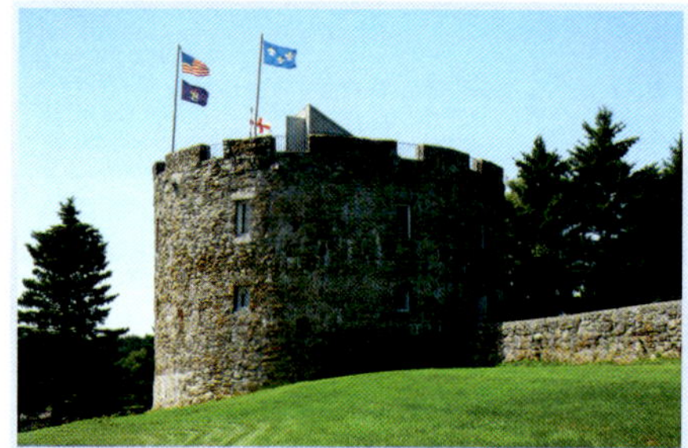

Fort William Henry in Pemaquid, built in the late 1600s.

Contacts for Coastal Attractions along the Kennebec River and Boothbay

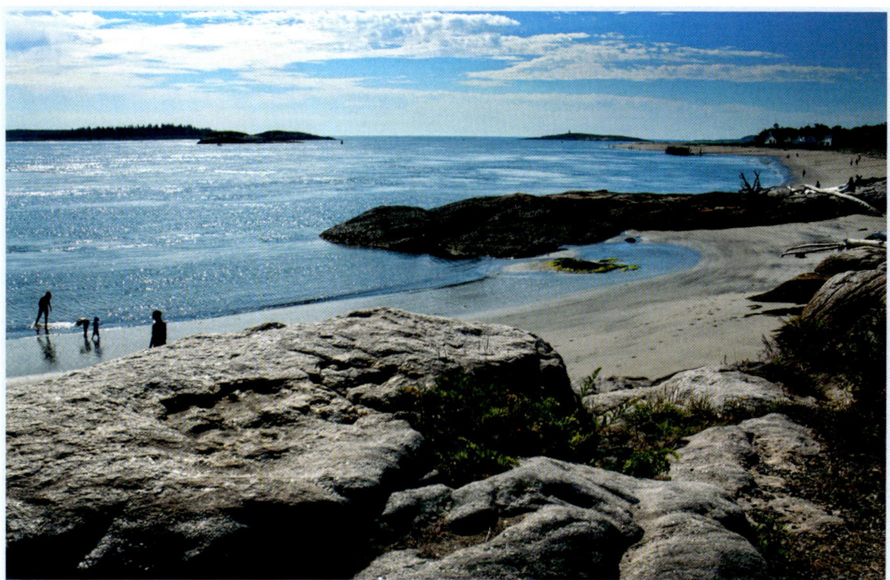

Popham Beach stretches for miles between rock formations.

Maine Maritime Museum, Bath
(207) 443-1316
mainemaritimemuseum.org

Chocolate Church Arts Center, Bath
(207) 442-8455
chocolatechurch.com

Maine's First Ship, Bath
(207) 443-4242
mfship.org

Musical Wonder House, Wiscasset
(207) 882-7163
musicalwonderhouse.com

Maine Art Gallery, Wiscasset
(207) 882-7511
maineartgallery.org

Old 1812 Jail, Wiscasset
(207) 882-6817
lincolncountyhistory.org

Wiscasset Railway Museum, Alna
(207) 882-4193
wwfry.org

Castle Tucker Mansion, Wiscasset
(207) 882-7169

Monkey C Monkey Do, Wiscasset
(207) 882-6861
monkeycmonkeydo.com

Boothbay Railway Village
(207) 633-4727
railwayvillage.org

Maine State Aquarium, Boothbay Harbor
(207) 633-9559

Maine's Coastal Botanical Gardens, Boothbay
(207) 633-4333
mainegardens.org

Boothbay Region Land Trust
(207) 633-4818
bbrlt.org

Carousel Music Theater, Boothbay
(207) 633-5297
carouselmusictheater.org

Lincoln Arts Festival, Boothbay
(207) 633-3913
lincolnartsfestival.net

Boothbay Opera House
(207) 633-5159
boothbayoperahouse.com

Sheepscot River Cruises, Boothbay
(207) 633-6598
sheepscotrivercruises.com

Cabbage Island Clambakes, Boothbay
(207) 633-7200
cabbageislandclambakes.com

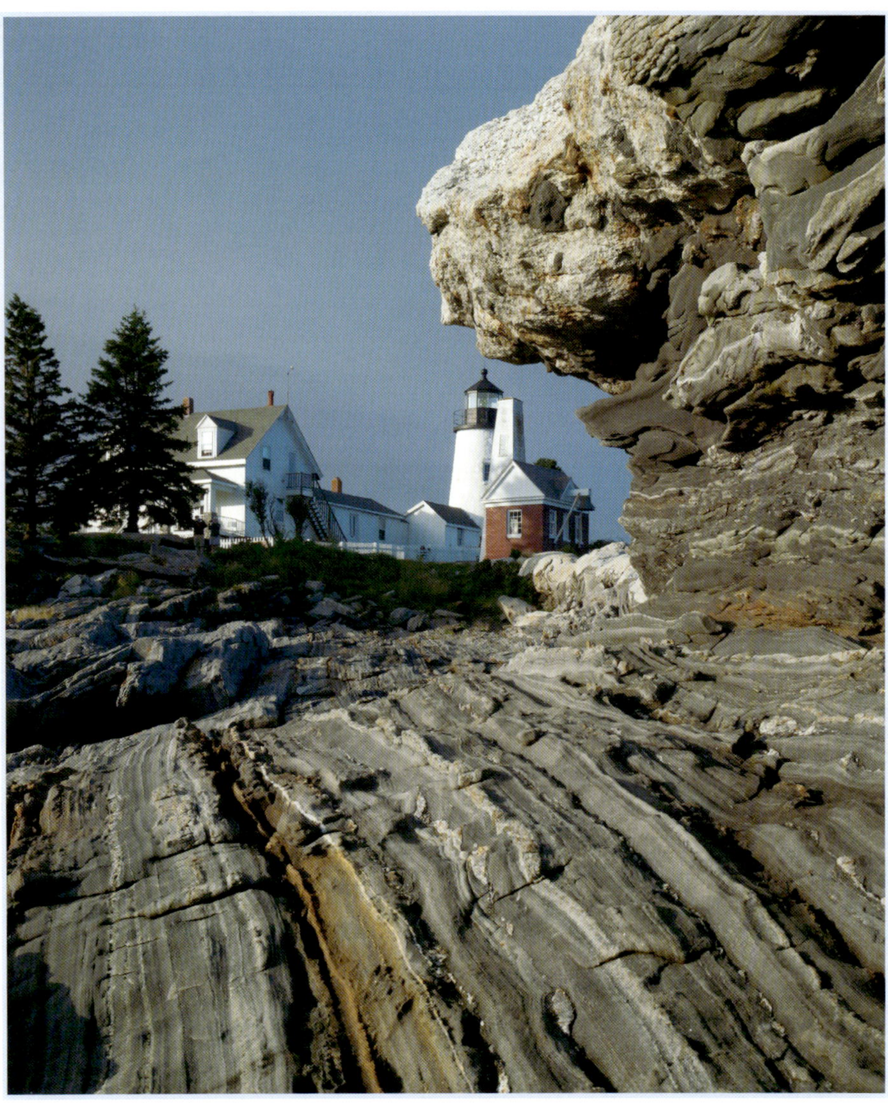

The most unique geological rock formations are found by Pemaquid light.

Go Lobstering!, Boothbay
(207) 380-7677
golobstering.com

Sail Muscongus, Boothbay
(207) 380-5460
sailmuscongus.com

Hendricks Hill Museum, Southport
(207) 633-1102
hendrickshill.org

Cuckolds Lighthouse, W Southport
(855) 212-5252
innatcuckoldslighthouse.com

Colonial Pemaquid, New Harbor
(207) 677-2423
friendsofcolonialpemaquid.org

Pemaquid Art Gallery, Bristol
(207) 677-2752
pemaquidartgallery.com

Fisherman's Museum, Bristol
(207) 677-2494
thefishermensmuseum.org

Lighthouse Cruises along the Kennebec River and Boothbay

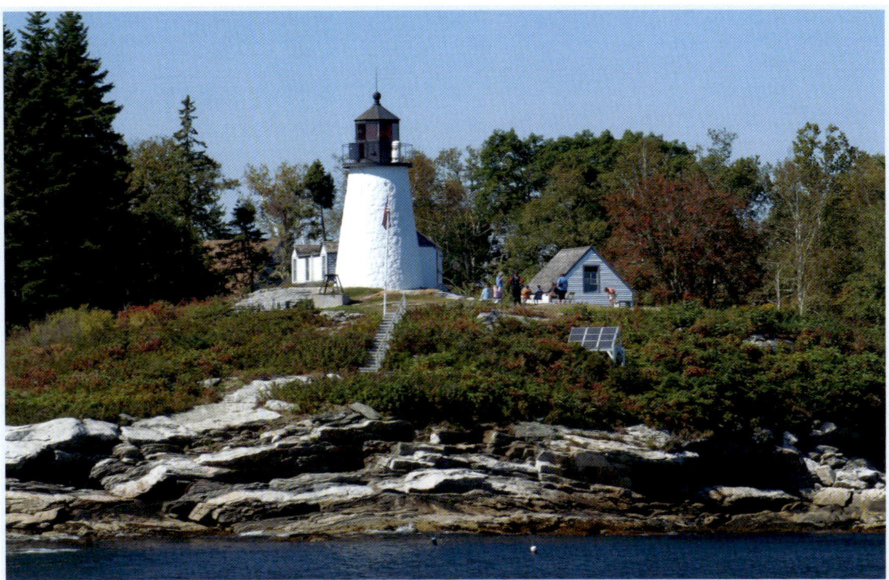

Boats leaving Boothbay Harbor usually pass Burnt Island Light.

Cap'n Fish's Whale Watch and Scenic Nature Cruises

During the summer season they offer daily excursions to lighthouses along coastal routes you can choose from. Other trips include whale watching, puffins, and fishing.

- Boothbay Harbor
- (207)-633-3244, (207)-633-2626,(800) 636-3244
- boothbayboattrips.com
- **Lighthouses:** Seguin Island, Perkins Island, Squirrel Point, Doubling Point, Doubling Point Range Lights (Kennebec Range Lights), Pond Island, Cuckolds, Ram Island, Burnt Island, Hendricks Head, Pemaquid Point

Fish 'N Trips / Sequin Island Ferry

Ferry service to Seguin Island almost daily, where you can hike up to Sequin Island Lighthouse. Also provides chartering for fishing.

- PO Box 150 Phippsburg
- (207) 841-7977
- fishntripsmaine/sequinislandferry.com
- **Lighthouse:** Seguin Island

Atlantic Seal Cruises

Two-hour tours to Sequin Island weekly in summer, plus seal cruise and cruises to Eagle Island.

- Freeport
- (207) 865-6112
- atlanticsealcruises.com
- **Lighthouse:** Seguin Island

Maine Maritime Museum

Lighthouse tours along the Kennebec River and Boothbay Harbor, along with wildlife tours.

- 243 Washington Street, Bath
- (207) 443-1316
- mainemaritimemuseum.org
- **Lighthouses:** Sequin Island, Perkins Island, Squirrel Point, Doubling Point, Doubling Point Range Lights, Pond Island, Cuckolds, Ram Island, Burnt Island, Hendricks Head

River Run Tours

Chartered pontoon boat offers a relaxing way to view lighthouses, natural formations, and wildlife.

- 28 Walnut Point, Woolwich
- (207) 504-BOAT (2628)
- riverruntours.com/
- **Lighthouses:** Perkins Island, Squirrel Point, Pond Island, Doubling Point, Doubling Point Range Lights, Burnt Island, Ram Island, Squirrel Island, Cuckolds, Hendricks Head

Balmy Days Cruises

Lighthouse excursions, plus fishing and whale-watching.

- Pier 8, 42 Commercial Street, Boothbay Harbor
- (207) 633-2284 or (800) 298-2284
- balmydayscruises.com
- **Lighthouses:** Burnt Island, Pemaquid Point, Monhegan Island, Squirrel Point

Hardy Boat Cruises

- PO Box 326, New Harbor
- (800) 2-PUFFIN or (207) 677-2026
- hardyboat.com
- **Lighthouses:** Pemaquid Point, Monhegan Island, Franklin Island

Tidal Transit Kayak Company

- 18 Granary Way, Boothbay Harbor
- (207) 633-7140
- kayakboothbay.com
- **Lighthouse:** Burnt Island

Hay-Val Charters

Lighthouse and lobster tours around Boothbay

- Southport, Maine
- (207) 633-2039 or (207) 319-8123
- hayvalcharters.com
- **Lighthouses:** The Cuckolds, Burnt Island, Hendricks Head, Ram Island, Pemaquid Point, Seguin Island

Schooner East Wind

Two-hour sailing excursions around Boothbay Harbor

- 20 Commercial Street, Boothbay Harbor
- (207) 633-6598
- schoonereastwind.com
- **Lighthouses:** The Cuckolds, Burnt Island, Ram Island, Pemaquid Point

Schooner Lazy Jack

Two-hour windjammer sails

- Pier 1, Boothbay Harbor
- (207)-633-3444 or (207)-975-2628
- schoonerlazyjackcruises.com
- **Lighthouse:** Burnt Island, Squirrel Island

Waterfront Directions

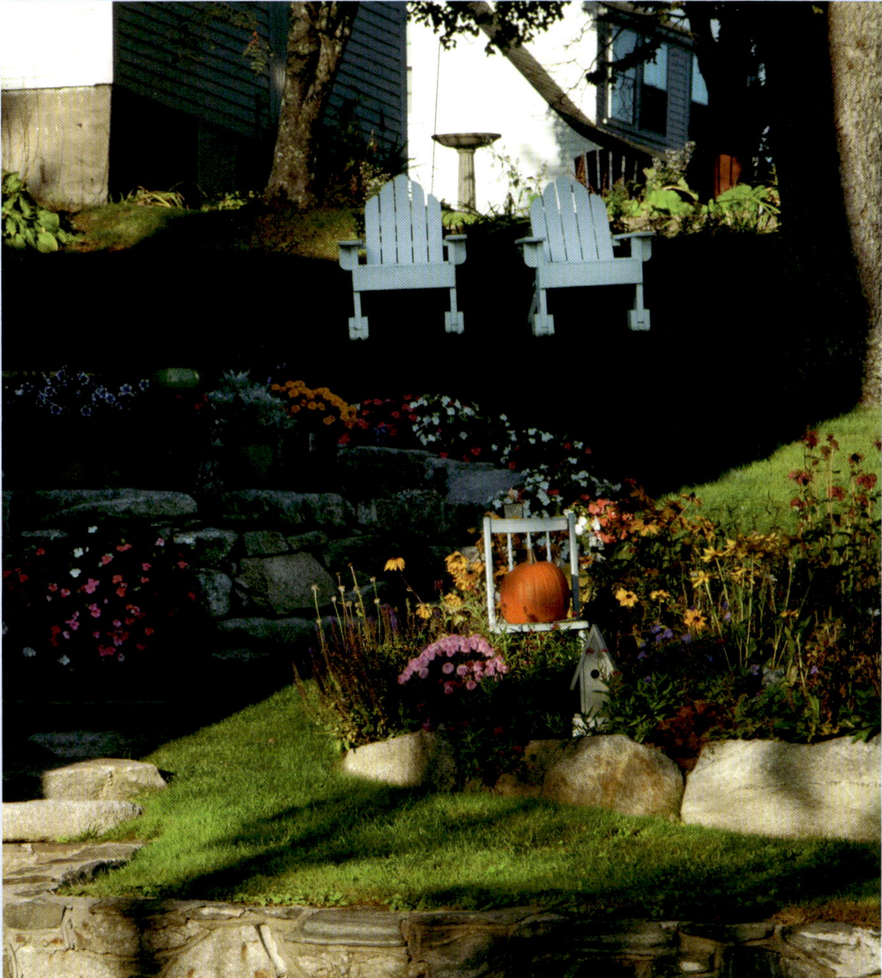

Boothbay Harbor is a great place for exploring.

Phippsburg Town Landing (Fort Popham)

From Route 1, take Route 209 South into Phippsburg. Follow signs to Popham Beach and Fort Popham.

Boothbay Harbor

From Route 1 north, take Route 27 south for about fifteen miles, arriving at downtown Boothbay Harbor by the docks.

New Harbor

From Route 1 north, turn right onto Business Route 1 (second right after Dodge/Jeep dealership). Follow it to downtown Damariscotta. Turn right after the First National Bank on Route 130 (Bristol Road). Continue for about twelve miles, and then turn left on Route 32.

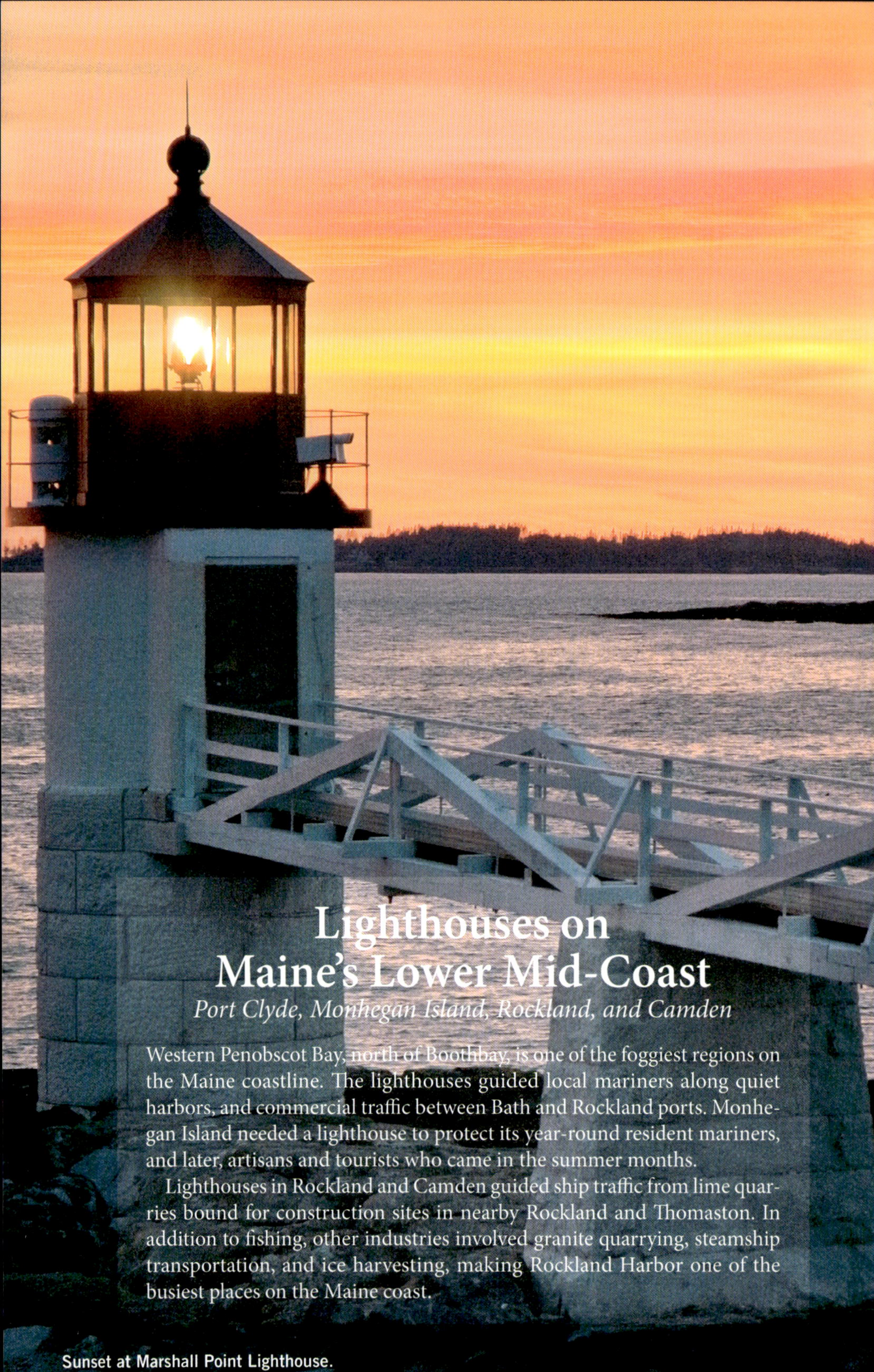

Lighthouses on Maine's Lower Mid-Coast

Port Clyde, Monhegan Island, Rockland, and Camden

Western Penobscot Bay, north of Boothbay, is one of the foggiest regions on the Maine coastline. The lighthouses guided local mariners along quiet harbors, and commercial traffic between Bath and Rockland ports. Monhegan Island needed a lighthouse to protect its year-round resident mariners, and later, artisans and tourists who came in the summer months.

Lighthouses in Rockland and Camden guided ship traffic from lime quarries bound for construction sites in nearby Rockland and Thomaston. In addition to fishing, other industries involved granite quarrying, steamship transportation, and ice harvesting, making Rockland Harbor one of the busiest places on the Maine coast.

Sunset at Marshall Point Lighthouse.

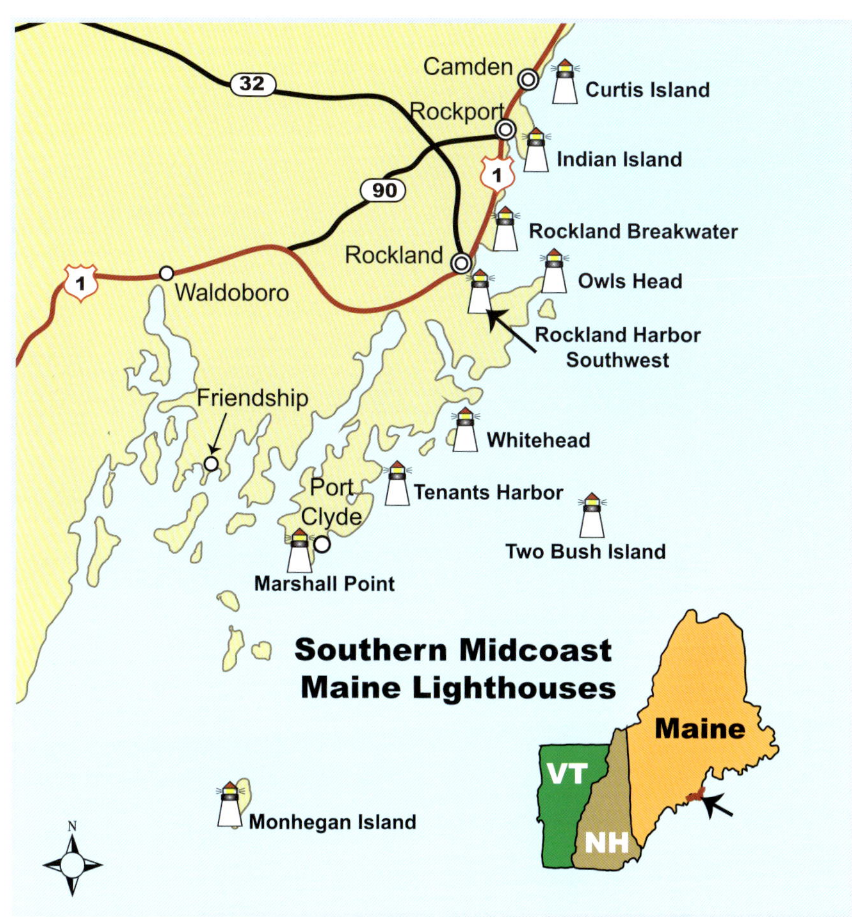

Map of lighthouses in Maine's lower mid-coast.

Marshall Point Lighthouse

Port Clyde (1832) • Latitude: 43° 55' 03" N • Longitude: 69° 15' 41" W

In the 1800s, Port Clyde became a busy shipping port for granite, timber, and fishing, and a haven for writers and artists, as it still is today. Marshall Point Lighthouse was constructed of rubble stone in 1832, and the tower was added in 1858. The first keeper was John Watts, a War of 1812 veteran. His son Joshua took over as keeper in 1835 and stayed until 1839.

The keeper who served the station for the longest period was Charles Clement Skinner, a Civil War veteran who worked at Marshall Point from 1874 to 1919. This was the longest tenure of any keeper at the same lighthouse in lighthouse service history. Of his six children, his two youngest daughters, Eula (1891–1993) and Marion (1895–1992) lived at or by the lighthouse during their entire, extraordinary long lives.

In the early morning hours of February 10, 1886, the steamer *Cambridge* wrecked on a ledge nearby, and luckily the passengers and crew all made it to safety on Allen

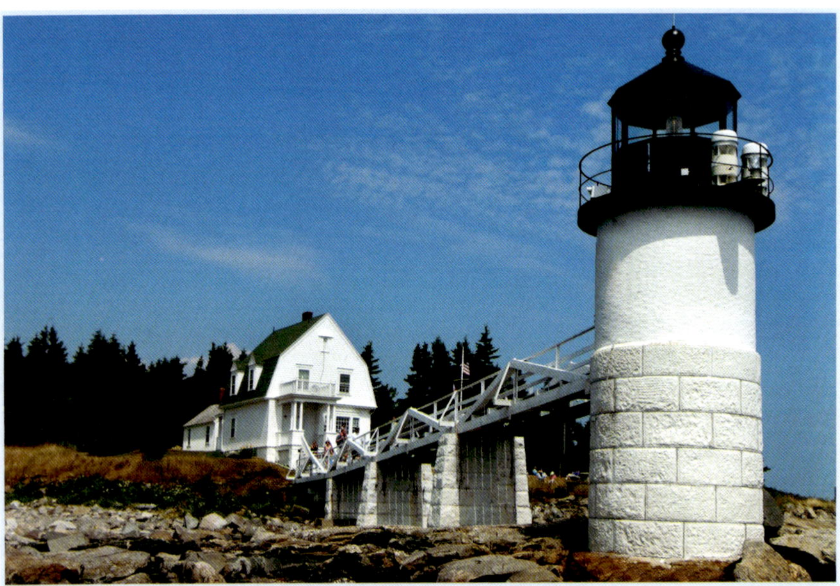

Marshall Point Lighthouse in Port Clyde.

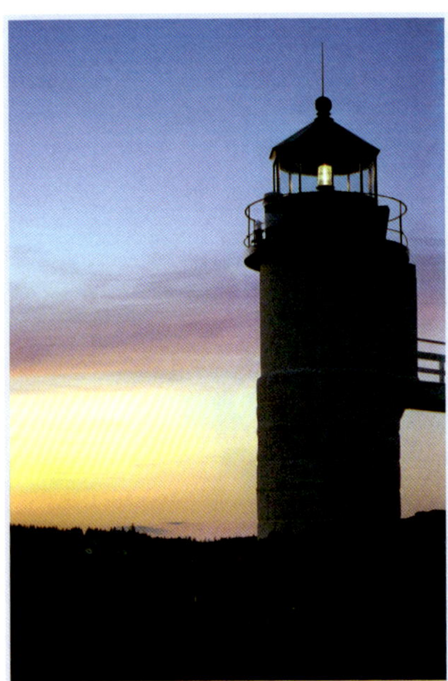

Dusk at Marshall Point Light.

Island. The steamer *Dallas* took them off the ledge in the afternoon and brought them to Rockland. As word got out that the vessel was in the process of breaking apart as a total loss, about forty schooners of local fishermen went out to salvage whatever cargo they could.

In 1895, the original lighthouse was destroyed by lightning and rebuilt in the same location.

In 1935, Marshall Point was converted to electricity. The lighthouse was automated in 1971, and the keeper's house became a LORAN (Long Range Navigation Station), which was used to send signals over a range of 14,000 square miles. In 1980, the outdated equipment was removed and the house was boarded up. In 1900, the keeper's house was restored and the first floor is used as the Marshall Point Lighthouse Museum.

The lighthouse gained worldwide notoriety when it appeared in the 1994 movie *Forrest Gump*. The walkway of the lighthouse is the end point in his cross-country journey, and he decides not to run anymore.

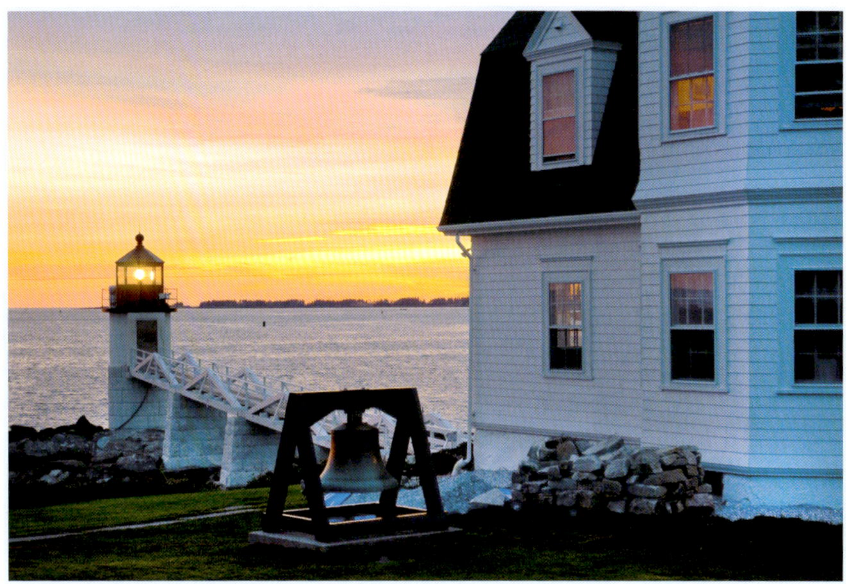

Marshall Point Light has many enjoyable sunsets.

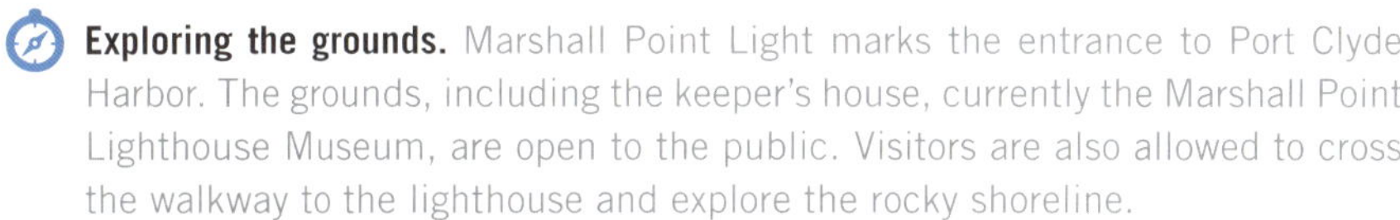

Exploring the grounds. Marshall Point Light marks the entrance to Port Clyde Harbor. The grounds, including the keeper's house, currently the Marshall Point Lighthouse Museum, are open to the public. Visitors are also allowed to cross the walkway to the lighthouse and explore the rocky shoreline.

Directions. From Route 1 in Thomaston, take Route 131 south to Port Clyde. At the main intersection turn left, then take a right immediately after a restaurant. The unmarked but paved Marshall Point Road will lead you a mile to a small parking lot at Marshall Point Light.

Monhegan Island Lighthouse

Monhegan Island (1824) • Latitude: 43° 45' 54" N • Longitude: 69° 18' 54" W

Before Europeans settled on Monhegan Island in 1619, making it the first permanent European settlement, it was long used by Native Indians who named it Mohegan, which means "island of the sea." As trade increased, a lighthouse was built at one of the island's highest elevations.

In 1861, keeper Joseph Humphrey was called to fight in the Civil War, along with his two sons. His wife, Betsy, was left with her other eight children to tend the light. Joseph Humphrey died in battle in 1861 and Betsy became the official keeper. One of her two sons was killed in the Civil War and the other returned home disabled. Betsy continued to tend the light until 1880.

The light was automated in 1959. The 1874 keeper's house was converted to a museum in 1968, focusing on the island's history and natural wildlife.

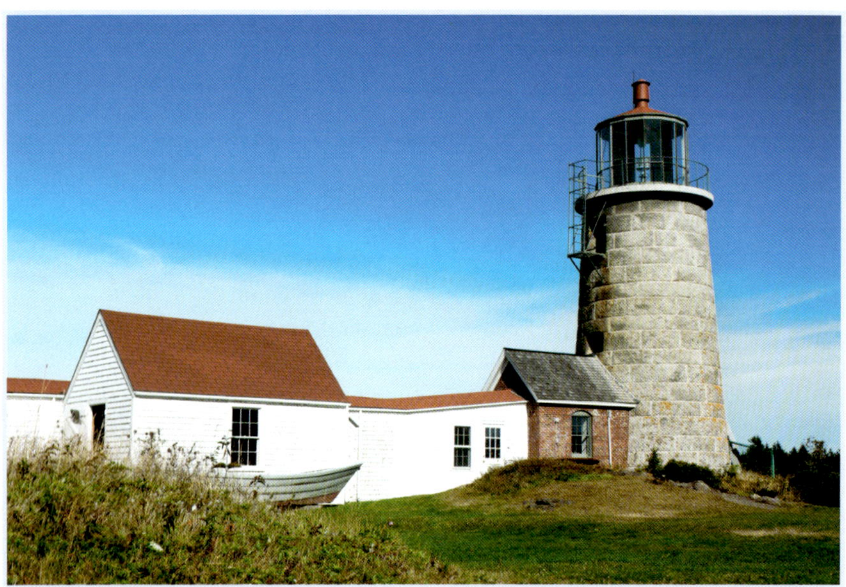

Monhegan Island Lighthouse.

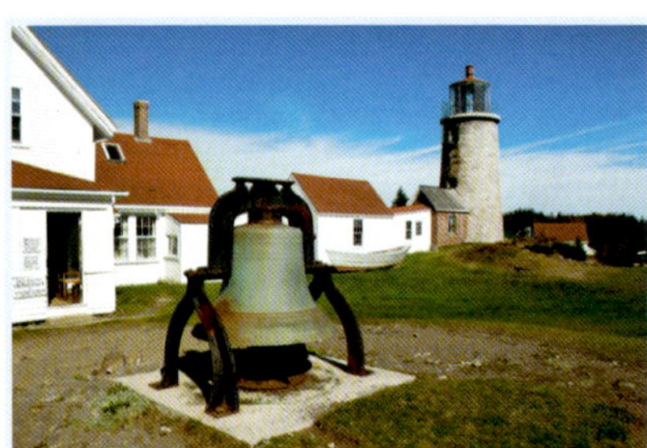

Fog bell at lighthouse grounds.

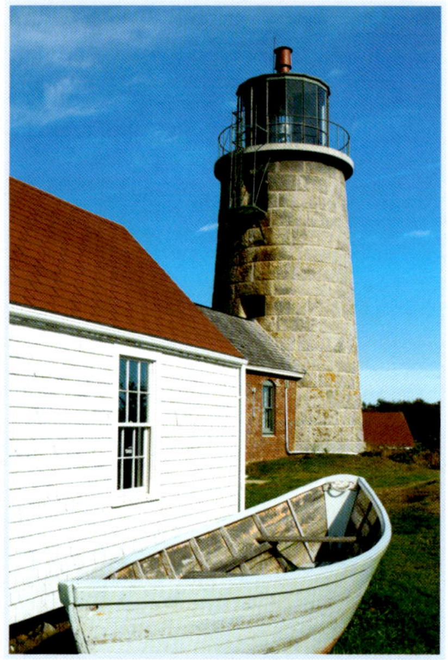

Years ago, artists placed this boat next to the lighthouse.

Keeper Paul Baptiste. In 1951, keeper Paul Baptiste and his wife Helen were looking to settle near a school for their growing family. He was assistant keeper at Bakers Island Lighthouse in Salem, Massachusetts, which had only part-time residents and did not have a schoolhouse. After a Monhegan Island keeper quit unexpectedly, Baptiste was offered the job at this remote location eleven miles from shore. The family packed up and headed up the quiet coastline, out to the end of one of Maine's tranquil peninsulas, then took a ferry to the island. When they arrived, they found that Monhegan Island was a rather large, beautiful, isolated place where the islanders stayed year-round. (The one-room schoolhouse still exists today.)

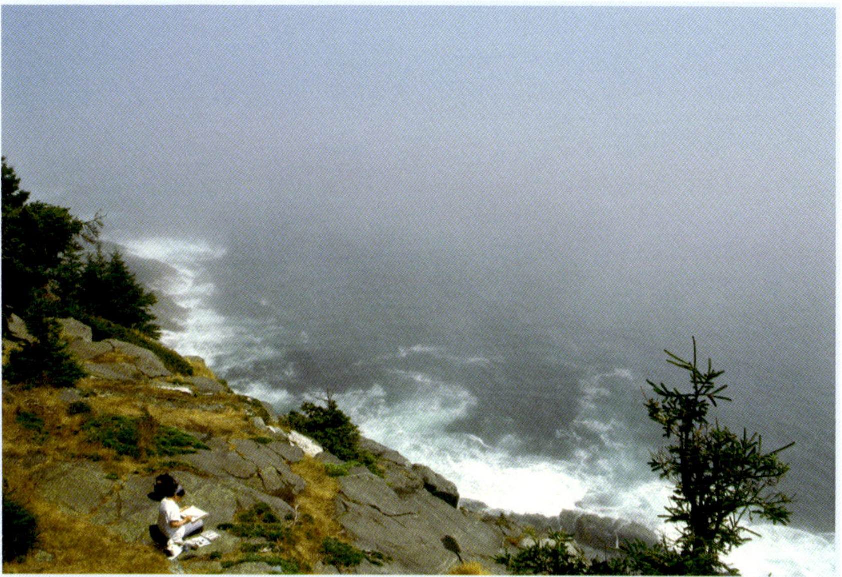

Artist painting surf on a foggy day.

The Baptiste family found the inhabitants resistant to change. One week, Baptiste was given orders to paint the lighthouse lantern room red and the rails green. After he finished the job, an elderly islander told him he couldn't paint the lighthouse lantern room any color but black. Baptiste said he was only following orders, but a few days later, his commander told him to paint the lantern and rails black. Apparently, the islander had some pull with the commander.

Water was scarce and used mainly for drinking, especially during the winter months. When the Baptiste family arrived, one of the lobstermen told them not to shower all winter. They obliged their neighbors and waited until spring to shower. When the weather improved, Paul would perform carpentry to make extra income. They became quite fond of their neighbors, and vice versa.

Their "Flying Santa" friend, Edward Rowe Snow, attempted to drop packages during the holiday season. But because of the lighthouse's tricky location, he often missed his mark, and the locals brought the presents to the Baptistes.

In the early 1950s, the entire island was using kerosene for illumination, as there was no electricity. Baptiste had a generator at the lighthouse that was only used to pump water to the building. He got permission to use the generator for electricity for the first floor of the keeper's house. In 1952, he bought the first TV on the island and installed an antenna on top of the roof, which annoyed some of his neighbors. By pointing the antennae out toward the sea, he could pick up stations from as far away as North Carolina. He became quite popular, as many locals stopped in to see what shows were playing on the new black box.

The Baptiste family stayed on Monehgan Island until 1954. Tourists would visit the island and lighthouse from Memorial Day until Columbus Day weekend. The locals called these people "day-trippers." Many years later one of the elder sons, now middle-aged, returned to visit the lighthouse. At a store, he overheard someone refer to him negatively as a “day-tripper” and decided to correct the elder lobsterman, commenting that he was one of keeper Paul Baptiste’s sons who had grown up in the lighthouse. He quickly received a hero’s welcome, with everyone in the building welcoming him home.

Exploring the grounds. The grounds and lighthouse museum are open to the public, and you can climb the tower on Thursdays in summer. Hiking trails around the island will take you to an old tugboat shipwreck and up along cliffs that reach about 130 feet above sea. Monhegan Island seems trapped in a time capsule, as most of it is undeveloped. You’ll also notice rock cairns scattered around the island. There are plenty of artists who invite visitors to stop by their small studios and observe their work. By the way, the boat set next to the lighthouse was put there by artists some years ago and was never used by keepers.

Tenants Harbor Lighthouse

St. George (1858) • Latitude: 43° 57' 43" N • Longitude: 69° 11' 18" W

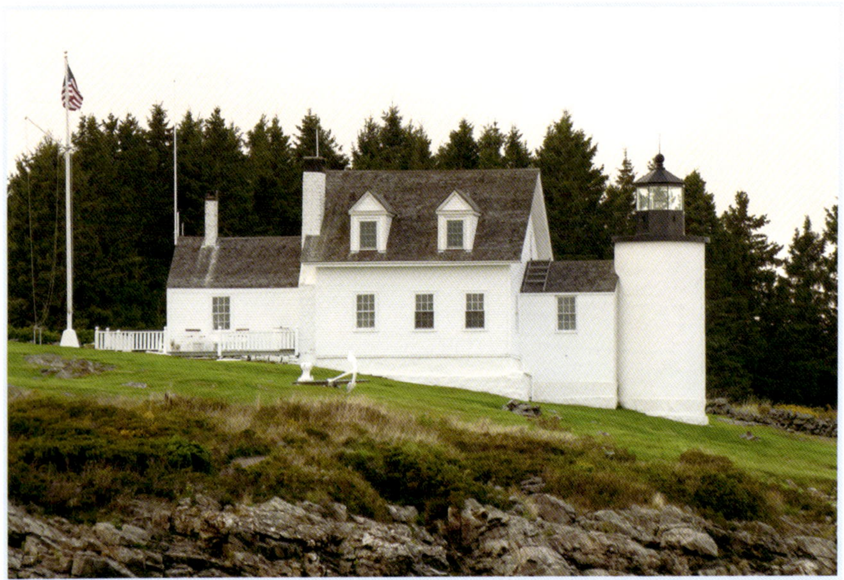

Tenants Harbor Lighthouse as fog lifts at sunset.

Tenants Harbor Lighthouse on Southern Island marks the entrance to Tenants Harbor. The keeper’s building was originally painted brown, the tower was painted white, and the lantern roof and ventilator ball were painted red. The station had a hand-operated fog bell that was later replaced with a wooden pyramid bell tower using automatic striking machinery. Levi Smalley, a local man, was the first keeper to live in the little red house. Smalley was followed in 1867 by a local blacksmith named John A. Farnham. Years later, Farnham was removed for neglecting his duties after an unannounced inspection.

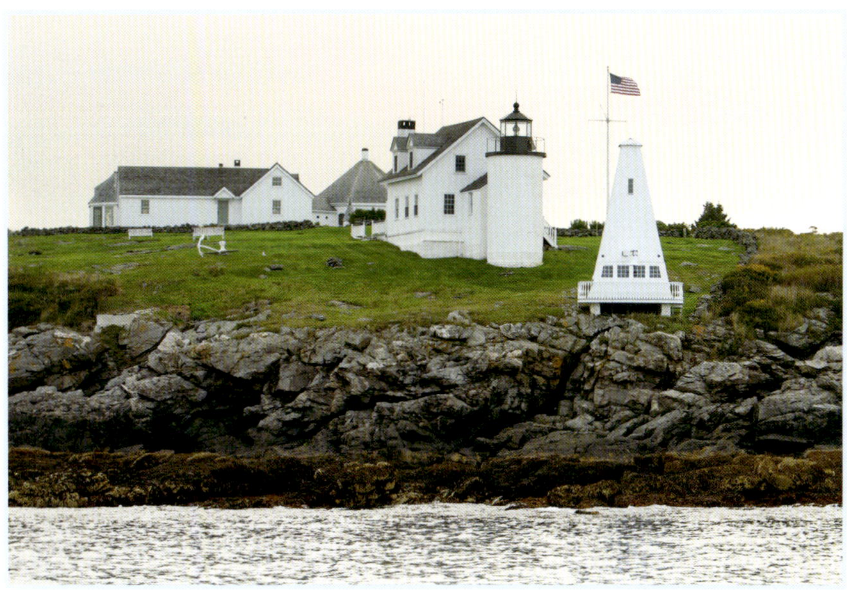

Tenants Harbor Lighthouse is owned by a family of artists.

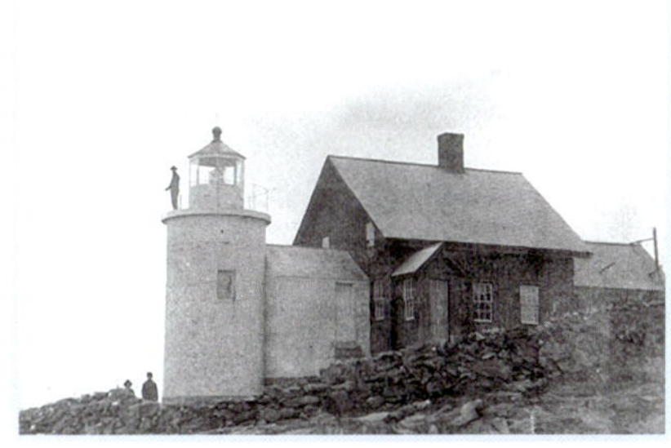

Vintage image. *Courtesy US Coast Guard.*

Keeper Joseph Jellison stayed the longest at the lighthouse, for twenty-two years. The government sold the lighthouse in 1934 and it had various owners. The late artist Andrew Wyeth and his wife, Betsy, purchased the lighthouse in 1978, and designed a studio in the base of the bell tower. Since 1990, Betsy has lived on the island with their son, artist Jamie Wyeth, and Jamie's wife, Phyllis. Andrew and Jamie's work is displayed in many art galleries in the area. Tenants Harbor Lighthouse is one of only eleven privately owned lighthouses in Maine.

Whitehead Lighthouse

St. George (1804) • Latitude: 43° 58' 47" N • Longitude: 69° 07' 30" W

Whitehead Island Lighthouse guided cargo and fishing vessels through Muscle Ridge Channel in Penobscot Bay. The first keeper, Ellis Dolph, was dismissed when he was found to be selling oil from the government's lighthouse supply to the locals around Thomaston.

Between the lifesaving station residents and the lighthouse keepers, there were lots of children on the island. Funds were appropriated to establish a tiny school district with a one-room schoolhouse and teacher.

Isaac Grant became keeper in 1875. His wife was Abbie Burgess Grant, who had gained fame as a teenage heroine (see Matinicus Rock Lighthouse). In 1881, Isaac

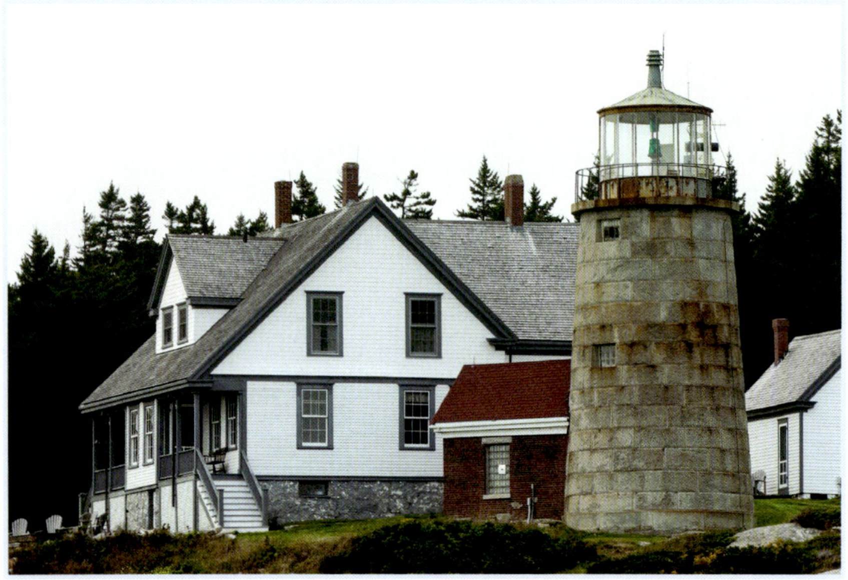

Whitehead Lighthouse as fog lifts at sunset.

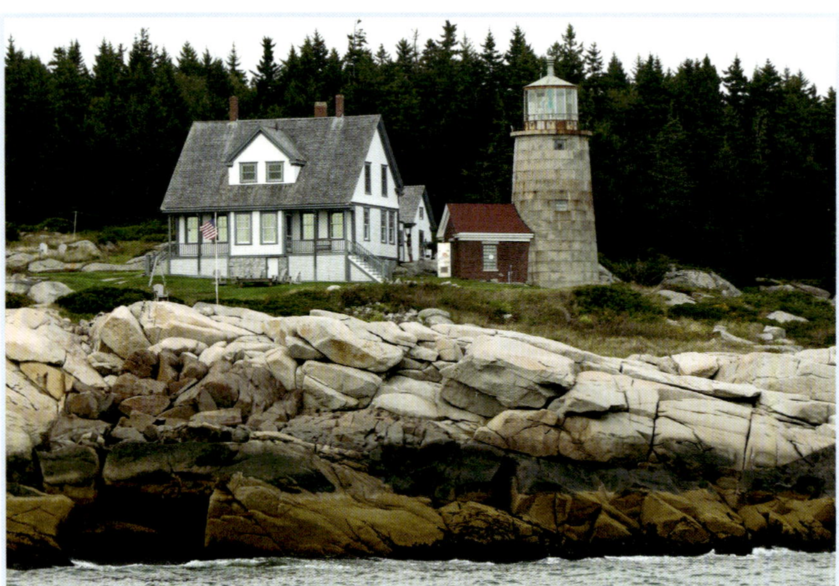

Adult education programs and overnight lodging are provided at Whitehead Lighthouse.

Grant rescued two men whose schooner capsized and was awarded a silver medal.

The island is fogged in about twenty-five percent of the time, and huge amounts of coal were needed to operate the steam-powered fog whistles. A donkey named Jack achieved fame on the island, brought from the mainland by keeper Hezekiah Long around 1885. It was adopted by Isaac and Abbie Burgess Grant, and then

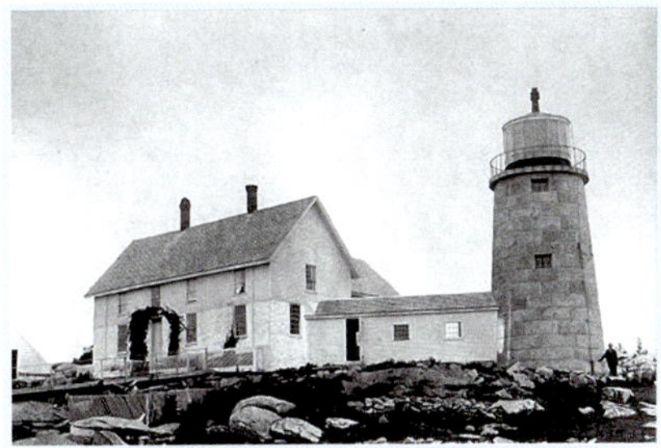

Vintage image. *Courtesy US Coast Guard.*

later by keeper Frank Jellison. In his nearly nineteen years of dedicated service to his caretakers by carrying coal, Jack enjoyed exploring the island, became a tourist attraction, and frequently visited the children at the one-room schoolhouse. At times they invited him inside.

A recent rescue occurred on a stormy December morning in 1980, when a lobster boat with two crew members started taking on water. Coast Guard keeper Ken D. Johnson launched his small boat in ten-foot seas and rescued the men.

The light was automated in 1982 and converted to solar power in 2001, and the keeper's house was restored in 2008. Adult education programs are provided in the summer months and visitors can rent the station rooms.

Two Bush Island Lighthouse

Spruce Head (1897) • Latitude: 43° 57' 51" N • Longitude: 69° 04' 26" W

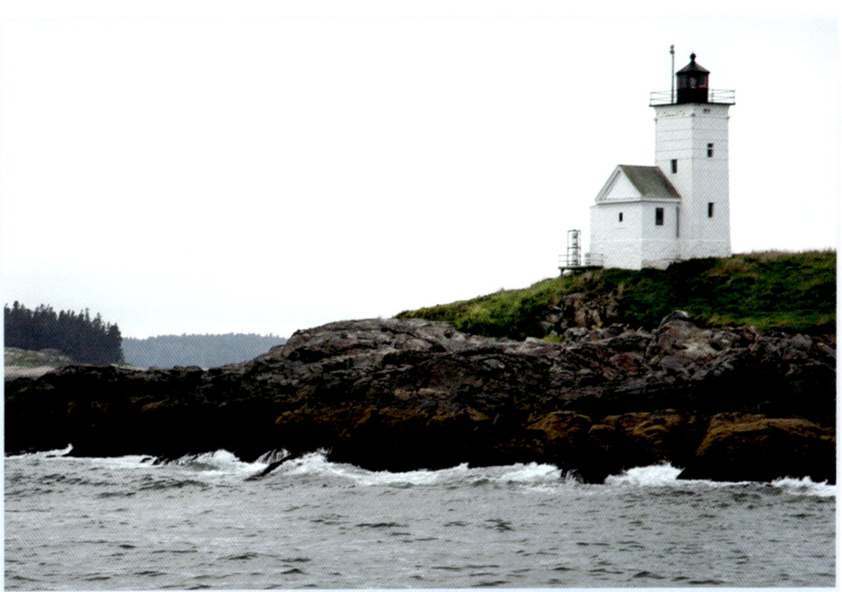

Two Bush Island was named for two lone trees that are now gone.

Bush Island was named for two lone bushes or trees, now gone, that served as day beacons before the lighthouse was built. Two Bush Island Light was one of the last lighthouses built on the Maine coast.

Winters could be treacherous at this island four miles from the mainland. Even if a keeper was able to make it ashore during calm seas using a round bottom "double-ender" boat, he still had to travel seven miles to Rockland for supplies.

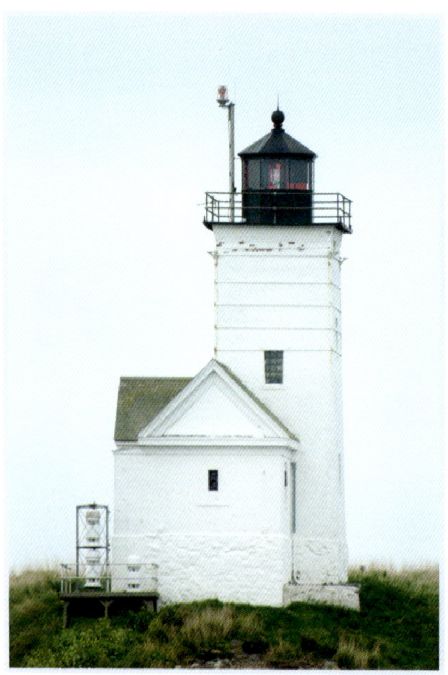

Two Bush Island Light had a famous dog named Smut that saved a fishing schooner.

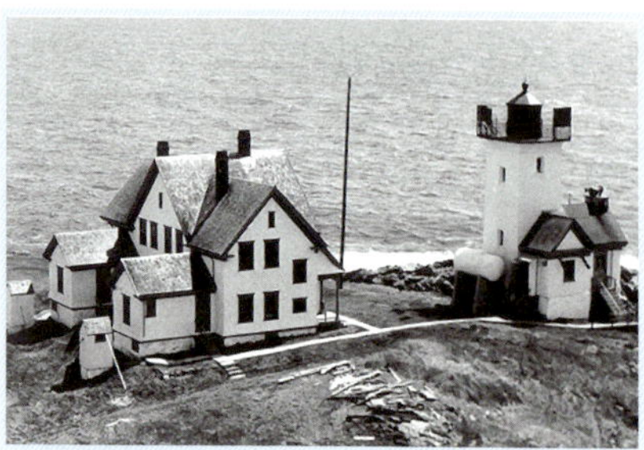

Vintage image. *Courtesy US Coast Guard.*

In 1923, when the bay had frozen over after nearly three weeks of freezing temperatures, the two keepers, with the help of local fishermen, tried to haul the boat over the ice to the mainland. At times their feet broke through the ice, and they had to hold onto the boat until they found firm footing.

In 1970, the Coast Guard allowed a group of Green Berets to blow up the keeper's house as a demolition exercise. Two Bush Island Light was automated in 1964 and converted to solar power in 2000. The Maine Coastal Wildlife Refuge currently maintains the lighthouse.

Keeper's Dog Saves Schooner Crew. The first keeper of Two Bush Island Light, Altiverd Norton, had a dog named Smut who became a hero during a storm in March 1902, when a fishing schooner, the *Clara Bella*, started taking on water. Keeper Norton and his family were asleep and any outside sounds were muted by the fierce winds. The dog, however, apparently heard the boat crash on the rocks and the men's cries for help. Sensing danger, he started barking and frantically scratching the door to be let out. The keeper let Smut outside and followed him down to the rocks, where in the distance he could see a small dory with two men aboard. The men were desperately trying to find a way to land on the island and Smut's barking guided them to the shoreline.

The dory overturned in a huge wave, but Norton threw a line to the men and hauled them to safety. Keeper Norton told the men how Smut heard their cries, and the grateful survivors hugged and thanked the dog. They wanted to purchase Smut, but the keeper could not let go of his favorite four-legged companion. He told them that Smut was priceless.

Rockland Harbor Southwest Lighthouse

Owls Head (1987) • Latitude: 44° 60' 00" N • Longitude: 69° 50' 00" W

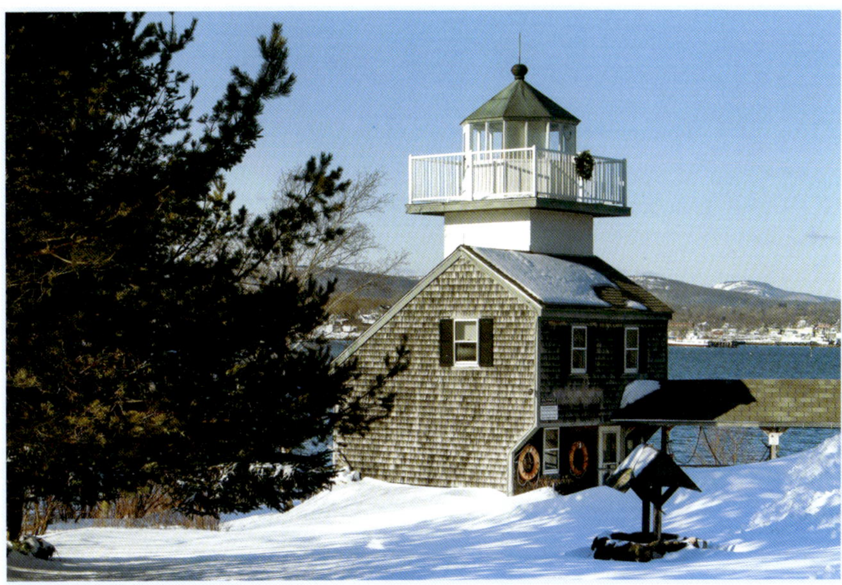

Rockland Harbor Southwest Light is the only privately built Coast Guard-certified lighthouse.

Bruce Woolet often spent the night at his adopted grandparents' house and enjoyed watching the flashing light of Rockland Breakwater in his bedroom at night. He became a lighthouse enthusiast and later built Rockland Harbor Southwest Light. He consulted with the Maine Lighthouse Museum (formerly the Shore Village Museum) in Rockland to ensure it was constructed to Coast Guard standards. Construction started in 1981 and finished in 1987, and the Coast Guard accepted the lighthouse as a privately maintained aid to navigation. It is one of the newest lighthouses added to the Maine Coast Guard list and the only lighthouse in New England that has been privately built. The lighthouse warns Seal Ledge mariners of shallow waters southwest of Rockland Inner Harbor. A fifth-order Fresnel lens used at the Doubling Point Range Lights was installed in 1998. It was sold in 1998 to the new owner, John Gazzola, who continued to renovate the building.

 **Directions.** The lighthouse can by viewed across a small cove, or, if you're discreet, from the lighthouse driveway, as it is a private residence. To view the lighthouse across the small cove, take Route 1 into Rockland, and then take a right on Route 73 (you can also see Owls Head Light along this route). Follow Everett Avenue on your left to the shoreline. To view the lighthouse near the residence, follow Route 73 until you see a sign for a dirt fire road labeled FR C230. If you've gone past Admiral's Attic, you've gone too far. Follow that road to the end, and then bear right at the sign describing the lighthouse.

Owls Head Lighthouse

Owls Head (1826) • Latitude: 44° 05' 33" N • Longitude: 69° 02' 39" W

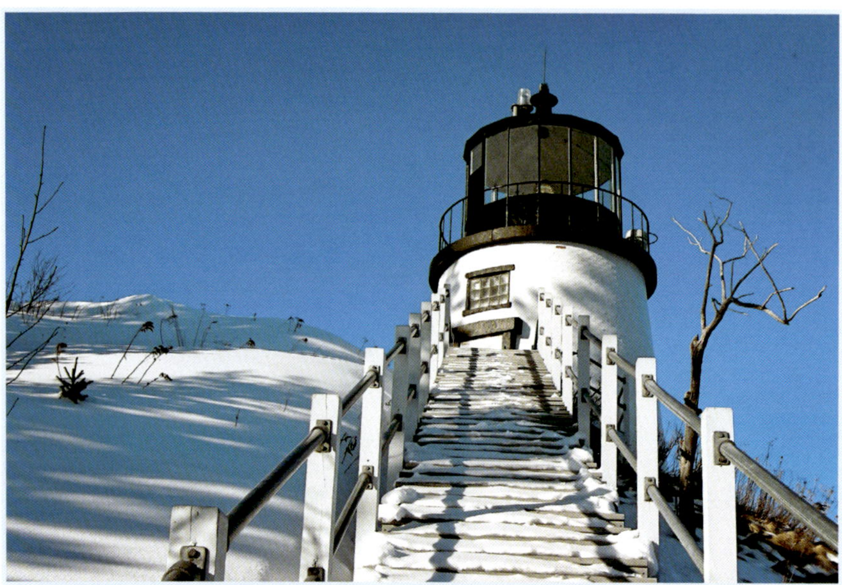

Owls Head Lighthouse sits on a 100-foot cliff overlooking Rockland Harbor.

The growing trade of lime mined in Rockland and nearby Thomaston led to the need for Owls Head Lighthouse, on the mainland overlooking the entrance to Rockland Harbor. Authorized by President John Quincy Adams, with Isaac Sterns as its first keeper, it has been the site of many shipwrecks. Its tower, though only twenty feet tall, is on a high cliff more than 100 feet above water, and frequent wind gusts made the climb to the tower a dangerous affair. Isaac Sterns's wife, Lucy, was heading over to the lighthouse one windy day to trim the wicks, climbing along the side of the hill. When she reached the top, a gust of wind blew her off her feet and she barely escaped falling off the cliff into the sea. It would take nearly fifty years before walkways and stairs were built from the keeper's house to the beacon.

Spot Saves the Mail Boat. In the 1930s, keeper Augustus Hamor had a dog named Spot whom the children taught to ring the fog bell by tugging on the rope with his teeth every time he heard a ship's whistle. Spot would spend the day watching for ships passing near the lighthouse and would ring the fog bell to warn them of the impending danger. When the captain of the boat returned the fog signal, Spot would run down to the water happily and bark until the boat was out of earshot.

Spot's favorite vessel was the daily mail boat. He knew its engine sound and when it was due to pass the lighthouse. The mail boat's captain, Stuart Ames, was also fond of the dog and its owners and brought treats when he visited the Hamor family. Each time the mail boat passed Owls Head Lighthouse, the skipper would give a toot for Spot, and the dog would answer by ringing the fog bell.

One wintry night a blizzard brought near whiteout conditions, covering the region

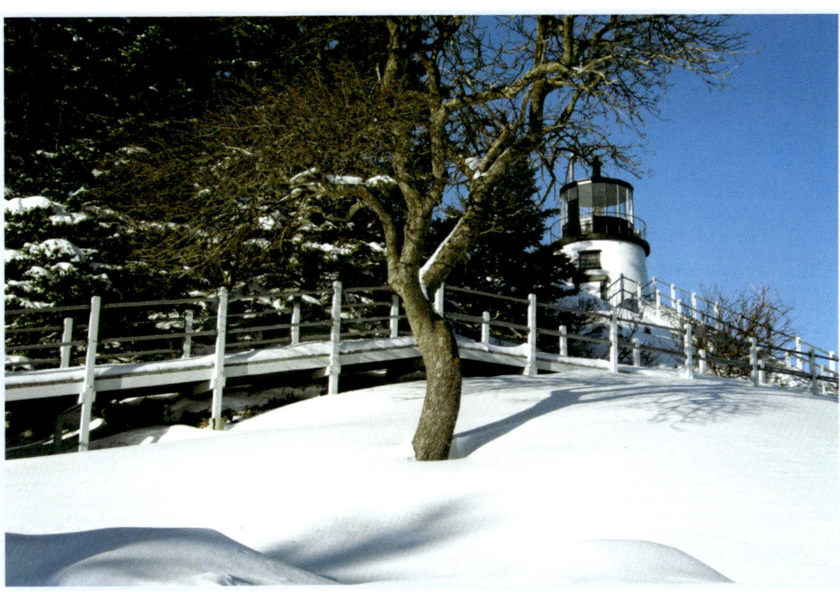

Owls Head Light after snowstorm.

in deep snow. As the following day wore on, fewer vessels passed by the lighthouse, as most had already found shelter in nearby harbors. As nightfall approached, Hamor felt it safe enough to leave the tower to quickly join his family for dinner.

As the Hamors were preparing to eat, the phone rang with a desperate call from Captain Ames's wife, who said her husband was over two hours late and asked if he had passed by the lighthouse. Knowing of Spot's keen ears, she asked the keeper to let Spot outside to see if he could hear her husband's whistle.

Spot didn't hear anything at first, but a short time later he jumped up and pawed at the door to be let out. Lunging over snowdrifts, Spot was unable to find the fog bell rope, so he ran to the edge of the cliff barking loudly. Keeper Hamor and his daughter Pauline got dressed and followed. They could hear the faint whistle of the mail boat. Captain Ames also heard Spot's barking and gave three blasts of the whistle to signal that he had heard the dog. Two hours later, Captain Ames' wife called to thank the family, and especially Spot, for helping her husband reach the harbor.

The Frozen Lovers. One of the most bizarre rescues in Maine's maritime history occurred at Owls Head Light on December 22, 1850. At Jameson's Point Wharf, near Rockland, a small coasting schooner from Massachusetts was anchored, ready to start for Boston the next morning. The captain had gone ashore for the night, leaving seaman Roger Elliott, mate Richard B. Ingraham, and passenger Lydia Dyer, Ingraham's fiancé, aboard the vessel.

Around midnight a storm blew in, snapping the anchor cables and blowing the boat across the harbor toward the rocks at Owls Head. Soon the schooner ran aground on an icy ledge just south of Owls Head Lighthouse. It was wedged so tightly that it did not sink as it filled with water, leaving the deck exposed. The three

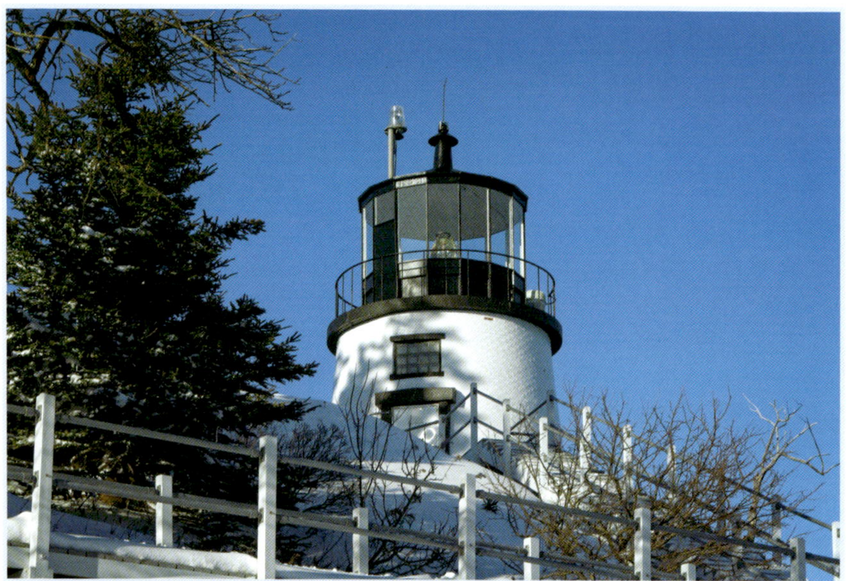

Snow-covered walkway to the lighthouse tower.

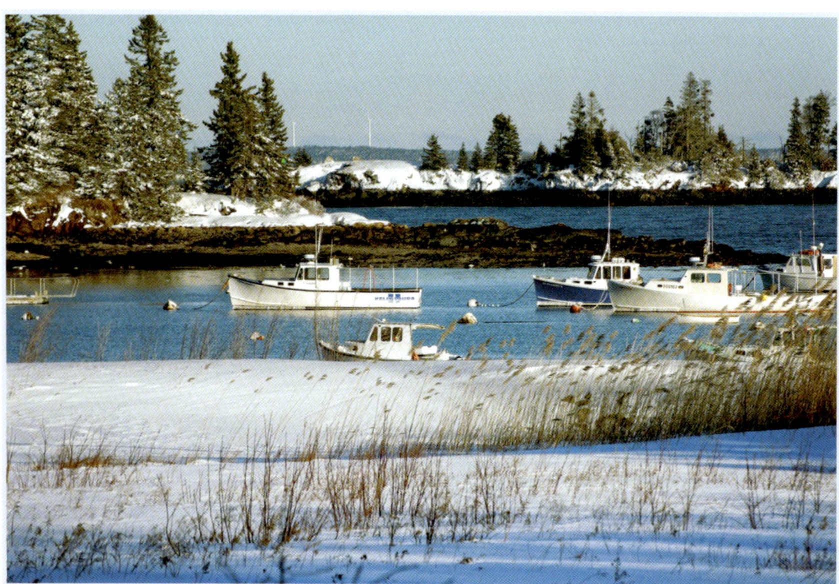

Lobster boats in Owls Head Harbor after snowstorm.

survivors wrapped themselves from head to foot in large woolen blankets creating a cocoon to try to fend off the icy spray and somehow stay dry.

The tide rose and the frigid waves continued to break over the deck, forming an icy coating on everything they touched. The hours passed, and the three could feel themselves weakening from exposure. Their woolen blankets were becoming an icy tomb inches thick and Ingraham and Dyer slipped into unconsciousness.

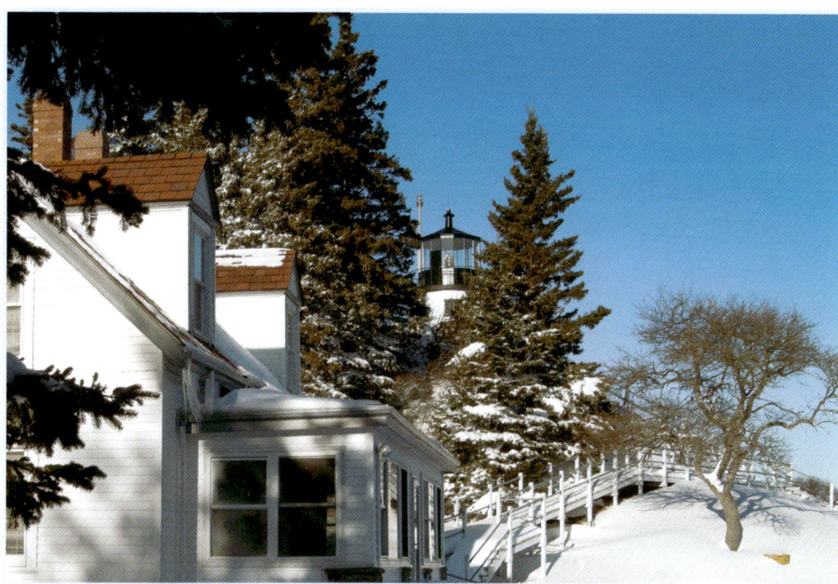

Keeper's house with Owls Head Light behind pine tress.

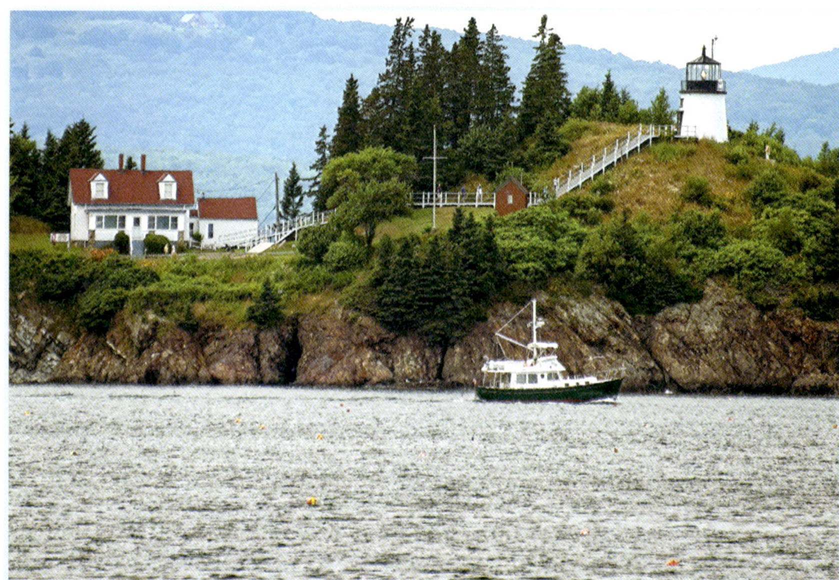

View of Owls Head from ferryboat.

As the schooner started to break apart near daylight, seaman Elliot hacked his way out of his ice-covered blanket with his sheath knife. He jumped into the frigid waters and fought his way over the icy rocks to the shoreline, then climbed through snowdrifts to the lighthouse. Luckily, keeper Henry Achorn happened to be riding by in his sleigh, on the lookout for shipwrecks, and brought Elliot inside. Overcome with hypothermia and barely able to speak, Elliott told the keeper about Richard

Ingraham and Lydia Dyer. Achorn quickly rounded up a group of neighbors and they headed to the shoreline, following Elliot's footprints in the snow.

The waves started to subside, allowing the keeper and his crew to eventually reach the wreck. There they found Ingraham and Dyer clinging together inside the blankets under the thick coating of ice. It looked like the couple had perished, but Achorn thought he could feel a faint pulse in each of them and was determined to try to save them.

Back in the keeper's warm kitchen, the rescuers removed the couple's clothing and the ice on their bodies, placing them in water just above freezing and slowly raising the water temperature to bring up their body temperature. The men took turns massaging the couple's limp arms and legs. After almost two hours, they were astonished to find Lydia showing signs of life. Another hour passed, and Ingraham miraculously opened his eyes and said, "What is all this? Where are we?"

The following day, the pair were able to eat a little, but it was several weeks before they could get up and walk around, and many months before they fully recovered. They married that following June and later had four children. Elliott never recovered from the exposure and never went back to sea. The captain of the ill-fated schooner was never found. Many speculated he had learned that he was going to be fired, or that he heard about the wreck and left town to avoid blame.

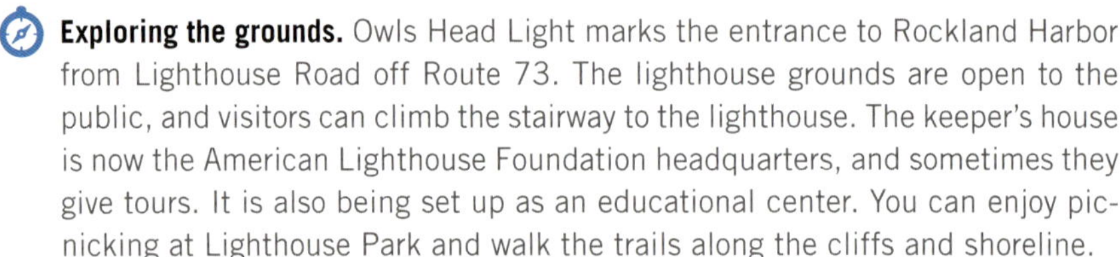

Exploring the grounds. Owls Head Light marks the entrance to Rockland Harbor from Lighthouse Road off Route 73. The lighthouse grounds are open to the public, and visitors can climb the stairway to the lighthouse. The keeper's house is now the American Lighthouse Foundation headquarters, and sometimes they give tours. It is also being set up as an educational center. You can enjoy picnicking at Lighthouse Park and walk the trails along the cliffs and shoreline.

Directions. From Route 1 in Rockland, take Route 73 to North Shore Drive and turn left. Keep going until you reach the Owls Head Post Office, turn left, and follow it to Lighthouse Road on the left. This will bring you to the parking lot of Lighthouse Park. A short walk along a dirt road from the parking lot will lead you to the lighthouse.

Rockland Breakwater Lighthouse

Rockland (1888) • Latitude: 44° 06' 15" N • Longitude: 69° 04' 39" W

During the year 1879, keepers at nearby Owls Head Light counted over 21,000 ships during the daytime and estimated that another 10,000 sailed by at night. This busy traffic prompted a lighthouse to be built at the entrance to Rockland Harbor. The original 1888 lighthouse stood at the end of a 1,600-foot breakwater. As more funds became available, the breakwater was extended in phases, and workers would erect a small beacon at the end of each new section. The final 1902 light and keeper's quarters stand at the end of the breakwater nearly a mile out into the harbor. The breakwater was made from nearly 700,000 tons of granite.

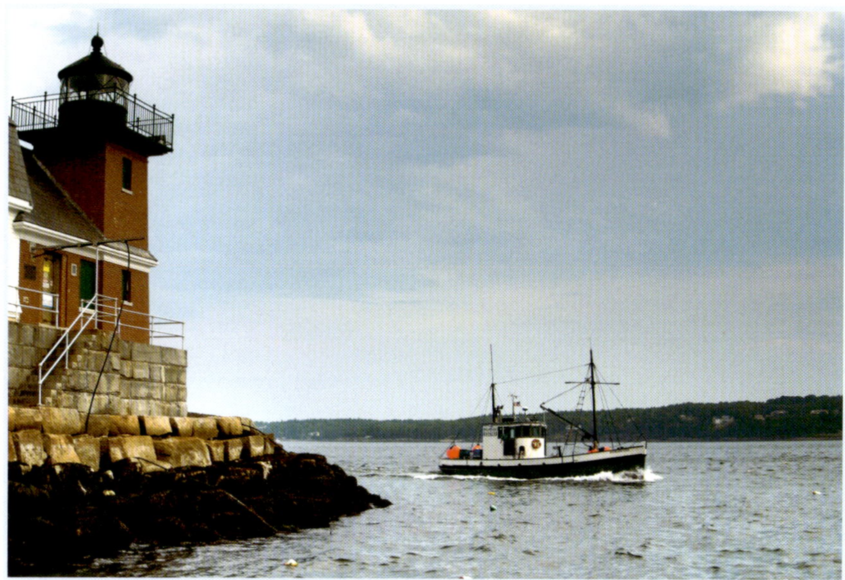

Rockland Breakwater Lighthouse guides fishing boat.

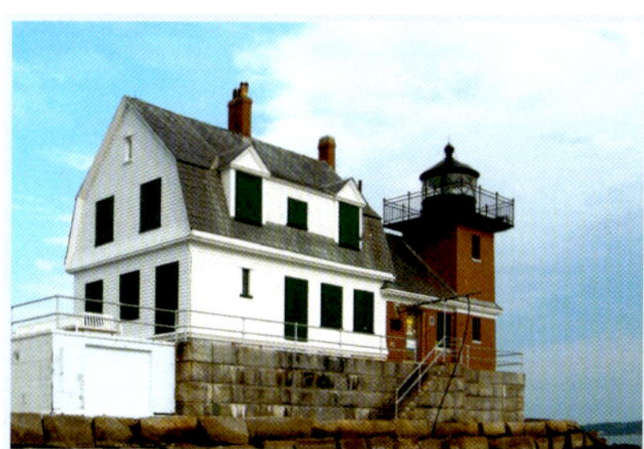

Rockland Breakwater Light.

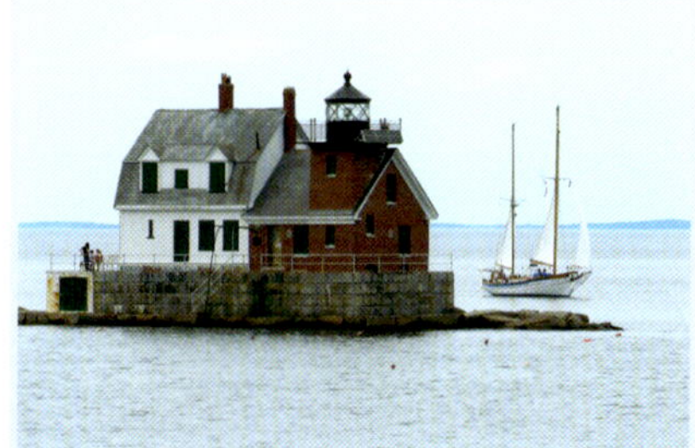

Sailboat passes Rockland Breakwater Light.

The first keeper was Howard P. Robbins, with his son Clifford as assistant keeper. Robbins served lighthouses for twenty-five years before his appointment. For nearly four winters in a row, from 1905–1909, the lighthouse was engulfed in thick ice and made life miserable for the father-and-son team. In 1909, they both resigned, with Harold saying he was fed up with lighthouse keeping.

In 1951, a former Coast Guardsman stationed at the lighthouse caught a twenty-seven-pound lobster off the breakwater. The Maine Lighthouse Selection Committee approved the transfer of Rockland Breakwater Light to the City of Rockland in 1998, and over the years made improvements to the beacon and surrounding area. The current lighthouse lantern stands nearly forty feet above water and is visible for seventeen miles.

The Flying Santa(s). Lighthouse keeping was a lonely and desolate life. Holidays were difficult, especially for those stationed off the mainland. Sometimes the keepers themselves needed an "emotional rescue."

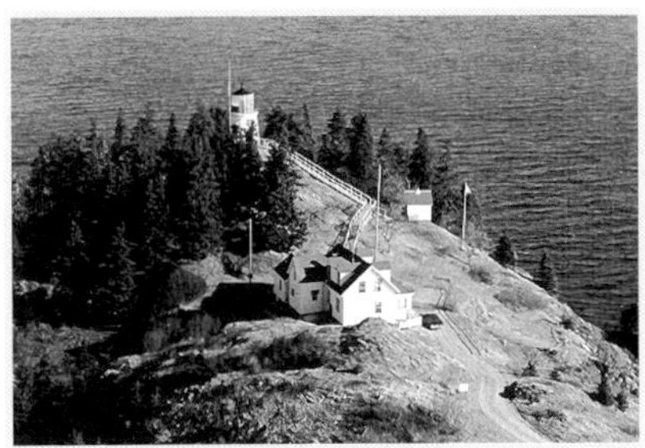
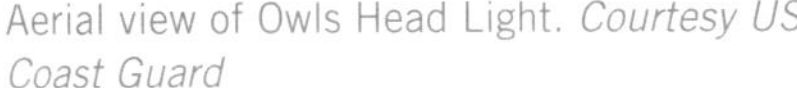

Aerial view of Owls Head Light. *Courtesy US Coast Guard*

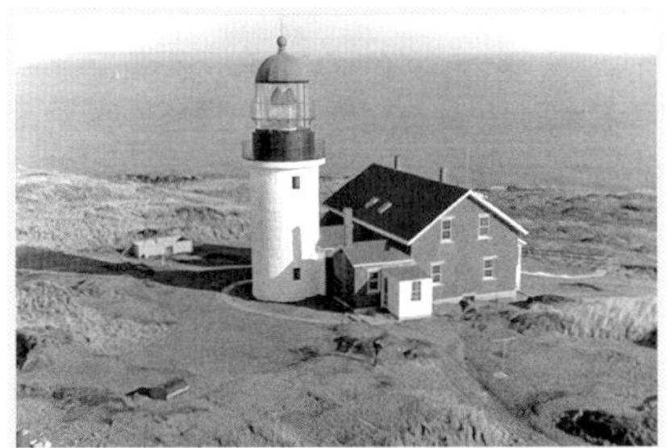

Aerial view of Seguin Island Light. *Courtesy US Coast Guard.*

In the late 1920s, Captain William Wincapaw from Friendship, Maine, thought up the concept of a "Flying Santa" who would bring gifts and supplies to lighthouse keepers and their families. He was an excellent pilot who helped save the lives of Penobscot Bay islanders and would transport the sick or injured even in inclement weather. He used lighthouse beacons to navigate all along the coastline and appreciated the keepers' dedication. When time and weather allowed, Captain Wincapaw would land his plane at various light stations and spend time with the keepers.

During a winter storm in 1929, Wincapaw got lost over the North Atlantic. His compass wasn't working and his plane was dangerously low on fuel. Finally, he was relieved to spot the beam of a lighthouse on Penobscot Bay, and then another, and followed the beacons to a safe landing. He decided to show his gratitude.

On Christmas morning, he loaded his plane with a dozen packages containing newspapers, magazines, coffee, candy, tobacco, soap and yarn, dropping them at stations in Rockland Harbor and Penobscot Bay. After finishing the Santa run, he spent the rest of the day with his family. He was so surprised at the outpouring of thanks that he decided to make the trip each year, increasing his range to additional stations along the northern New England coast, and dressing in costume.

By 1933, Wincapaw was delivering presents to ninety-one lighthouses and Coast Guard stations all along the New England coast. In 1934, his sixteen-year-old son, Bill Jr., became one of the youngest licensed pilots in Massachusetts, where the family had moved, and an excellent pilot under his father's direction. That Christmas he helped his father continue the tradition, and in 1935 flew solo to some of the stations.

In 1936, Bill Jr. introduced his father to Edward Rowe Snow, one of his teachers at Winthrop High School, and a lighthouse enthusiast and maritime historian. Captain Wincapaw immediately took a liking to Snow, who wanted to help in Wincapaw's efforts. He arranged to have Snow help his son deliver Christmas gifts to stations in southern New England.

When WWII broke out, Captain Wincapaw and his son were called to duty, as was Snow. In 1942, Snow was wounded during a bombing mission in Northern Africa and unable to continue the tradition that year as he lay in a foreign hospital bed. He was discharged in 1943 because of his wounds. With the unease along the coast that year, it was uncertain whether Snow would be able to deliver the gifts. But he was granted permission just before Christmas and again hired a pilot and delivered bundles to the grateful families.

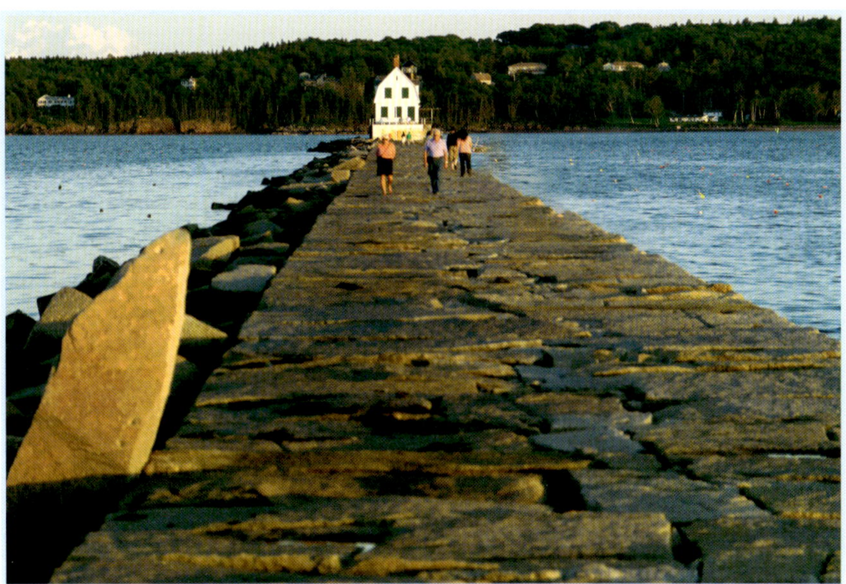

Rockland Breakwater Light is at the end of a nearly mile-long breakwater.

By 1945, with the end of the war, the tradition was back in full force and Snow's wife started to accompany him all along the New England coast. Wiggins Airways donated prop planes, helicopters, and additional pilots to expand the effort, and commercial sponsors donated gifts.

On July 16, 1947, as Captain Wincapaw was taking off from Rockland Harbor with a passenger, Robert Muckenhirn, he suffered a heart attack and the plane crashed in the ocean, killing both men. As the memorial service began on the afternoon of July 19, keepers sounded foghorns and bells heard across Penobscot Bay. That December, Snow would drop a memorial wreath in Rockland Harbor in honor of his close friend.

In 1947, Snow expanded the delivery to 176 lighthouses. Over the years, he often hired pilots out of his own pay. On April 12, 1982, Snow passed away at the age of seventy-nine. He had written over ninety books on maritime history and was Flying Santa for nearly forty-four years. In 2000, a granite memorial marker was placed at the visitors' pavilion on George's Island in Boston Harbor, Massachusetts. It reads "Author, Historian, and 'Flying Santa.'" His efforts and writings remain in the hearts of all who have been touched by his generosity. The tradition continues on a smaller scale with a helicopter that drops presents at select stations.

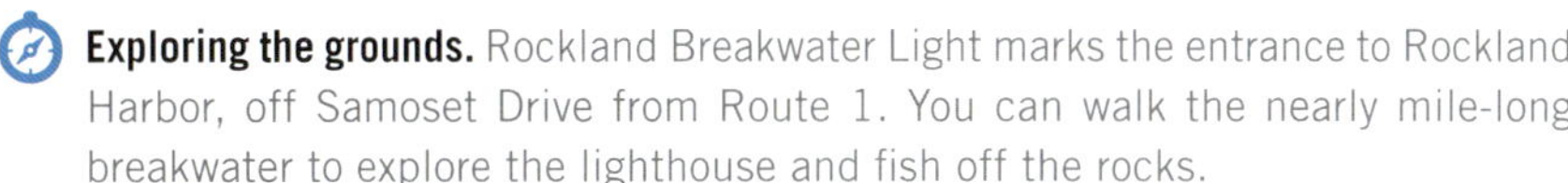

Exploring the grounds. Rockland Breakwater Light marks the entrance to Rockland Harbor, off Samoset Drive from Route 1. You can walk the nearly mile-long breakwater to explore the lighthouse and fish off the rocks.

Directions. From Route 1 north in Rockland, turn right onto Waldo Ave (across from the gas station on the left), and then turn right onto Samoset Drive, following it to a small parking lot at the end, or park along the left side of the road. Alternately, from Route 1 take Falls Street to the end for sunrise photos.

Indian Island Lighthouse

Rockport (1850) • Latitude: 44° 09' 57" N • Longitude: 69° 03' 38" W

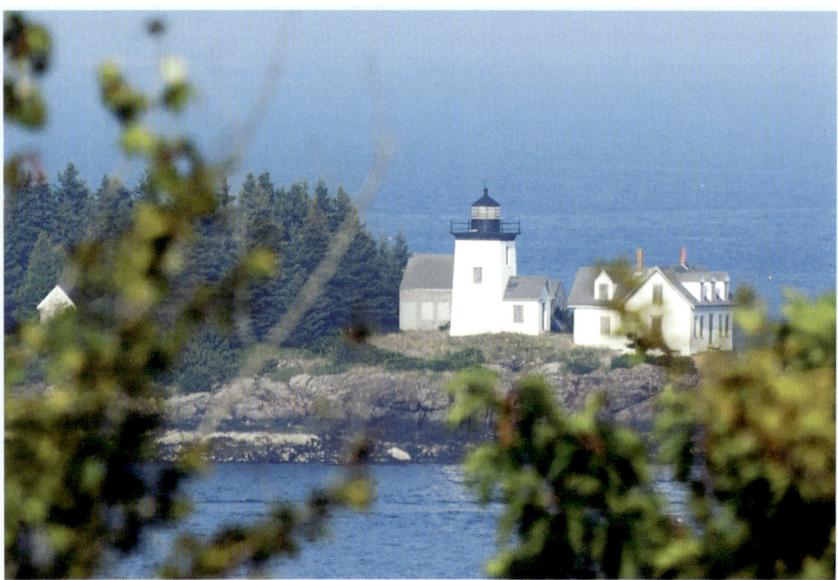

View of lighthouse from hilltop.

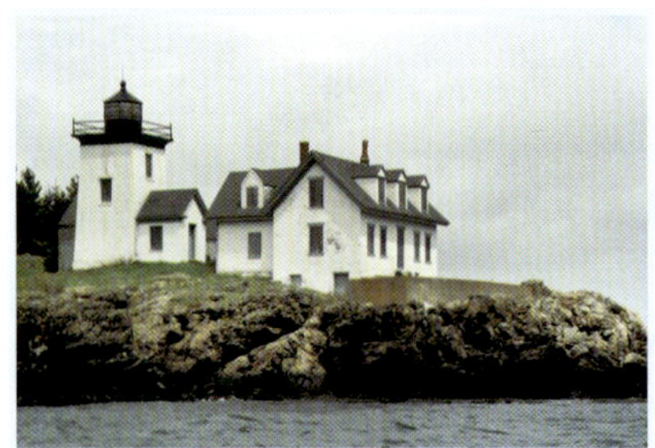

Indian Island Lighthouse was used from 1850–1859, deactivated, and then reactivated from 1875–1933.

During the French and Indian War, Native Indians took refuge on the island, which marked the eastern entrance to Rockport Harbor. It later became known as Indian Island.

As the lime trade brought more traffic into Rockport Harbor, Indian Island lighthouse was built with a lantern mounted on the roof of the keeper's house. A fourth-order Fresnel lens was installed in 1856. The first keeper of the original Indian Island Light was David Sargent, who served for only a month. Silas Piper replaced him and stayed for three years. The lighthouse was decommissioned a few years later in 1859, when shipping traffic into Rockport leveled off.

By 1874, shipping traffic had picked up again, and the lighthouse had fallen into disrepair. It was rebuilt in 1874 and relit in January 1875, with Joseph Small as its new keeper. The new tower was a square, white-and-black brick tower attached to the keeper's dwelling by a covered breezeway. Keeper Foster Reed stayed at the lighthouse from 1925 to 1933. His granddaughter, Barbara, would spend many weekends and vacations on the island. When Foster Reed retired from the Lighthouse Service in 1933, he and his wife, Celia, moved to Camden, Maine. Barbara graduated from Camden High School in 1940 and visited her ailing grandfather on graduation day. Foster Reed passed away that night, probably content that he had seen his granddaughter one last time and that she would do well in life.

The lighthouse was decommissioned again in 1932 and sold to a private owner in 1933.

 **Directions for a distant view.** The lighthouse marks the eastern entrance to Rockport Harbor. Grounds and lighthouse are closed to the public, as it is a private residence. Although best viewed by boat, you can get a decent shoreline view from Rockport Marine Park. From Route 1 North in Rockport, turn right on Main Street when you see Rocknacs Yacht Sales on your right. At the bridge, turn right, then follow the road until you see the sign for Rockport Marine Park on your left.

Curtis Island Lighthouse

Camden (1832) • Latitude: 44° 12' 06" N • Longitude: 69° 02' 54" W

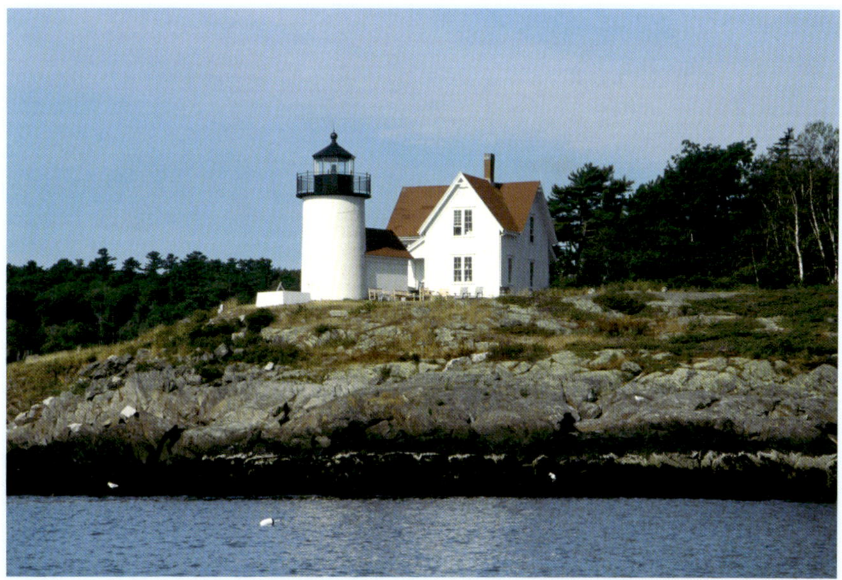

Curtis Island Lighthouse was a favorite station for keepers because it was close to Camden Harbor.

Curtis Island was originally called Negro Island. The story goes that James Richards, an early settler from New Hampshire, came to Camden Harbor in 1769 with an African cook aboard. The African said the white man could have the mainland, but he wanted to stay on the little island. The cook was granted his wish, and so it was called Negro Island. Years later, in 1934, when Cyrus Curtis, a Maine native who became famous as the publisher of the *Saturday Evening Post*, *Ladies Home Journal*, and other magazines, gave Camden waterfront land and a building (which became the Camden Yacht Club), the name was changed to Curtis Island.

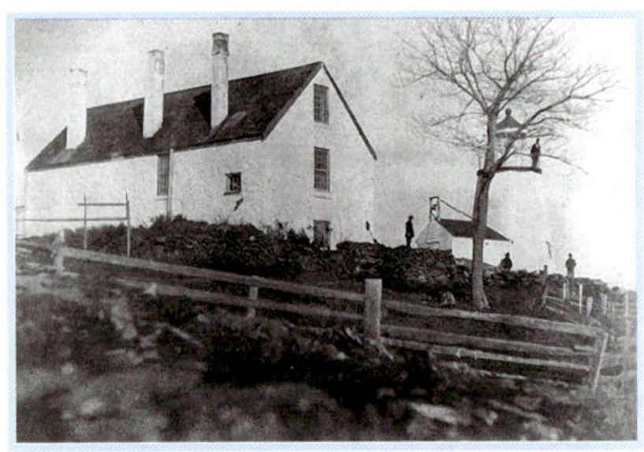
First light station. *Courtesy US Coast Guard.*

Camden's well-protected harbor helped the town develop into a major lime kiln and shipbuilding location. First built in 1832 under President Andrew Jackson, then rebuilt in 1896, the current lighthouse stands fifty-two feet above water guarding the entrance to Camden Harbor. The lighthouse's close proximity to Camden Harbor made it a popular station for keepers.

For many years the Boston-Bangor Steamships used the island as a signal station. The lighthouse keeper would raise a ball on a pole near the tower to indicate that a ship was on its way. A cry would go up, "The ball is up!" and interested villagers would start out for the wharf.

In 1993, a lighthouse caretaker found what she thought was a sick dolphin on the shoreline, which later died and was identified as a rare beaked whale. There has never been a confirmed sighting at sea of this species, and only sixteen beaked whales have been seen in North America, and six in Europe.

In November 1997, Camden voted to assume ownership of Curtis Island Light. In 1998, the lighthouse became the property of Camden under the Maine Lights Program.

 **Directions for a distant view.** The lighthouse area is a public park accessed by private boat, though the lighthouse is closed to the public. Although best viewed by boat, you can get a decent shoreline view. From US Route 1 before entering the center of Camden, take a right onto Chestnut Street past the post office, then turn left on Penobscot Avenue, then left again at the next stop sign. Bear left at the barricade and you'll see the lighthouse on the left. There is no easy place to park since you are in a residential area, but the neighbors won't mind if you snap a quick photo.

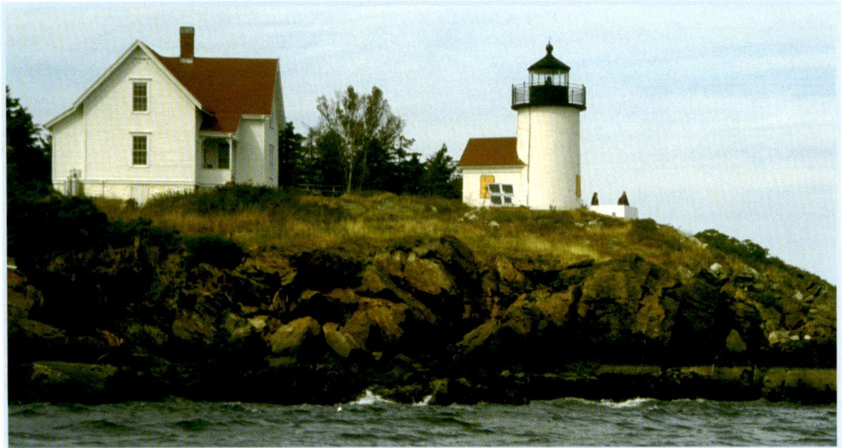
Curtis Island Light during restoration.

Attractions along Maine's Lower Mid-Coast

Port Clyde, Monhegan Island, Rockland, and Camden

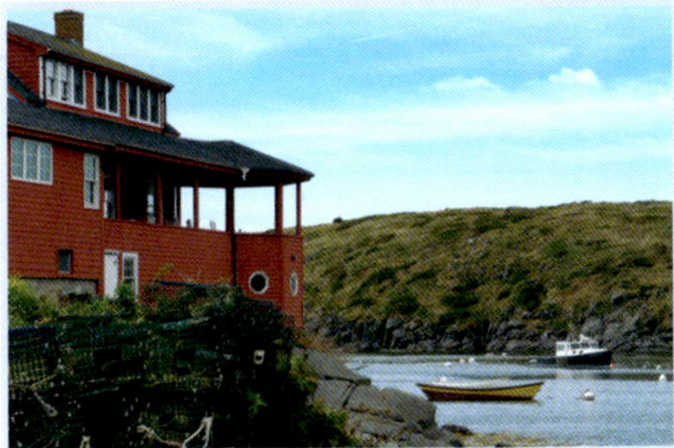

Monhegan Island residence overlooking the harbor.

Maine's many peninsulas off Route 1 provide opportunities to explore picturesque fishing villages and farmland. Off Route 1 in Waldoboro, you'll find the famous **Moody's Diner**, a favorite stop since 1927. Just north of the diner, **Fawcett's Antique Toy & Art Museum** has an extensive collection of antique toys and original comic art, including Mickey Mouse and friends as they were originally crafted in the 1930s. You'll also find a traditional antique shop and contemporary art by the owner.

Route 27 takes you to the beautiful coastal town of Friendship. This is where the original Flying Santa, Captain Bill Wincapaw, started the famous tradition of dropping presents to keepers and their families from his plane. **Friendship Museum**, formerly a one-room schoolhouse, has interesting model ships and other artifacts. You'll find unspoiled coastal views here as well.

Quick stop! Check out the hand-carved wood items, like model boats and furniture, at the **Maine State Prison Gift Shop**. This maximum-security prison housing 900 male inmates was built originally in Thomaston in 1824 and relocated to Warren in 2002. No online buying here, and they don't ship; it's the law. The original prison ruins are in back of the gift shop.

Port Clyde, Thomaston, and Tenants Harbor are still predominantly fishing villages where you'll also find artists galleries, beautiful sunsets overlooking the harbors, and true Maine spirit. Over twenty-five artists in St. George hold an annual Open Studio Tour each summer. Thomaston is an old seaport noted for its antique architecture. To view some of the local history of the Revolution, visit the **Henry Knox Museum**. A half-mile up Roaring Spout Road, off Harts Neck Road in Tenants Harbor, is an area called Roaring Spout, where there are exciting rock formations to hike around. Between Tenant's Harbor and Port Clyde, beachgoers will enjoy the Drift-In Beach.

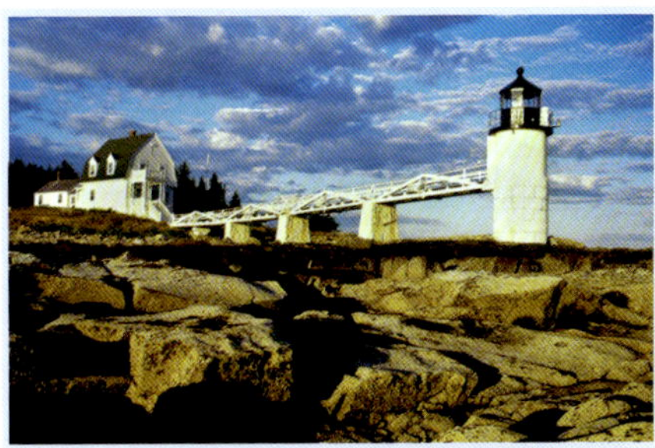

Clouds over Marshall Point Lighthouse.

Check out Maine's Lighthouse week on the third full week of June, which includes a parade of sailing schooners or windjammers, and a chance to sail on these graceful vessels out of Boothbay, Rockland, and Camden. The annual **Mid-Coast Maine Lighthouse Challenge**, usually in late June, run by the **American Lighthouse Associ-**

ation, offers tours to seven lighthouses and special cruises out of Port Clyde.

Monhegan Island, ten miles offshore from mid-coast Maine, is a picturesque fishing community and summer haven for artists and vacationers. The island is about two miles long by a mile wide, with hiking

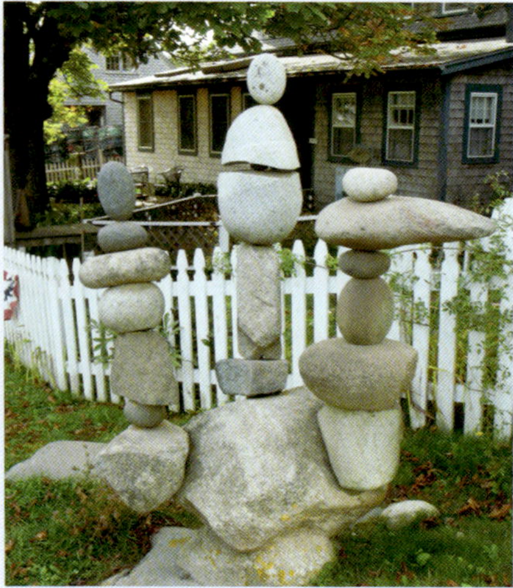

Unique rock sculptures are found all over Monhegan Island.

trails in wooded areas and along the shoreline that lead up to 130-foot cliffs over the sea. You'll find rock sculptures everywhere created by mystery artists. Stop by artists' galleries, enjoy fine cuisine in one of the island's few inns, and walk along the dirt roads, since the only vehicles are used by the inns. Monhegan Island has over 600

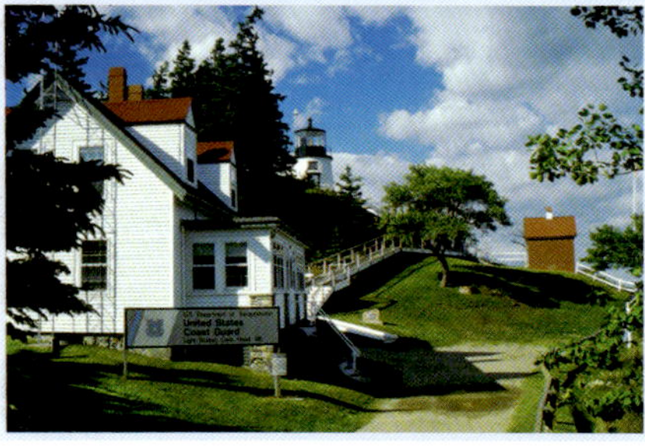

Owls Head keeper's quarters and lighthouse grounds.

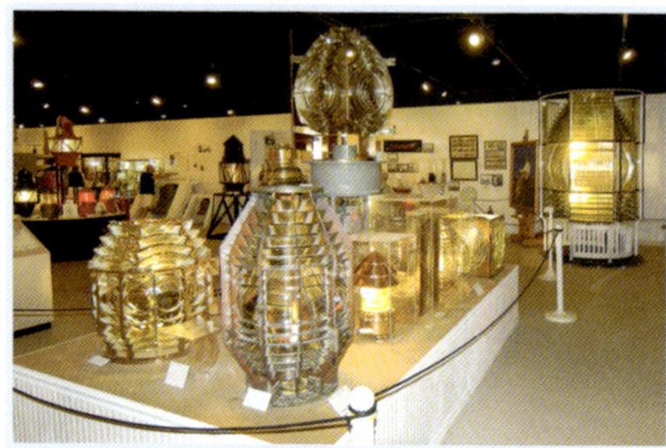

Fresnel lenses at Rockland's Maine Lighthouse Museum.

varieties of wildflowers and more than 200 species of birds. Look for the harbor seals on Duck Rocks near Pebble Beach.

In Rockland, the famous **Maine Lighthouse Museum** contains one of the largest collections of Fresnel lenses in the country. Near Rockland Breakwater Light is the Marie H. Reed Breakwater Park. The museum is part of the nearly six-mile Rockland Harbor Trail through the city and its open spaces.

The **Sail, Power, and Steam Museum** offers scale models of sailing vessels and steam engines, as well as folk music entertainment and exhibits on the art of boat building. Rockland is a major music destination, especially for those who love the blues. Each July, Rockland hosts the **North Atlantic Blues Festival**, and throughout the year top blues acts visit the **Strand Theater** or the **Time Out Pub**. **Arts in Rockland** is home to over twenty galleries and First Friday events.

During the first week of August each year, the **Maine Lobster Festival** in Rockland features the world's largest lobster pot, serving up tens of thousands of pounds of lobster.

The **Center for Maine Contemporary Art** (CMCA) exhibits work by 300-400 living artists each year and offers educational programs and professional development workshops. The Rockport Marine Park gives visitors a glimpse into the lime industry, with old kilns by the waterfront, a replica

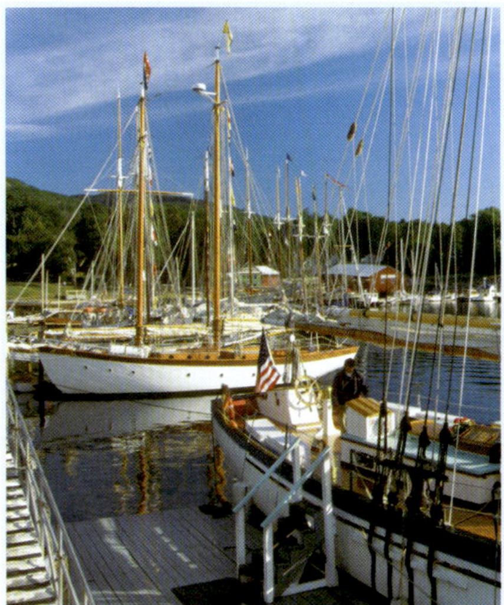

Early morning sailboats in Camden Harbor.

of a lime-transporting locomotive, and a memorial statue of Andre the Seal that was found and raised by a local fisherman.

Camden is a beautiful, affluent tourist town that calls itself the yacht capital of the world. Indeed, people from all over the world come here by land and sea. Explore the 5,000-acre **Camden Hills State Park** with over thirty miles of trails. Hike or drive to the top of Mount Battie for a spectacular view of Camden Harbor and Penobscot Bay, or hike along Mount Megunticook. Off Route 52, in Camden, you'll find a mile-long easy trail to Maiden Cliff, and great views of Megunticook Lake. A few miles inland, on 1,200-foot Ragged Mountain, part of the Georges River Land trust, the **Camden Snow Bowl** is a four-season destination. You can hike and bike this location, which in many places is quite steep, and during the winter you can ski, tube, or toboggan. Explore Maine's horticultural treasure, **Merryspring Gardens**, or take in a show at the **Camden Opera House**. Camden Harbor Park & Amphitheatre provide great views of this picturesque harbor, and you may be treated to concerts, festivals, and theater productions.

Penobscot Bay extends forty miles long and contains more than 200 islands. This natural, windy shelter offers a unique opportunity for sailing adventures and is why the ports of Rockland, Rockport, and Camden have the highest concentration of windjammers or tall ships in the country. Most of these ships are docked in Camden and are one of the major attractions. Some of these historic schooners use only their sails for power, as they did over a hundred years ago. These ships will take you out to neighboring islands, around the harbor, or cruise up and down Maine's coast. Some head south to warmer climates in the winter and visitors can book tours for these adventures as well. In this area you'll find lots of festivals involving windjammers, like Schooner Gam, Windjammer Days, the Great Schooner Race, Maine Windjammer Parade, and the Camden Windjammer Festival in September.

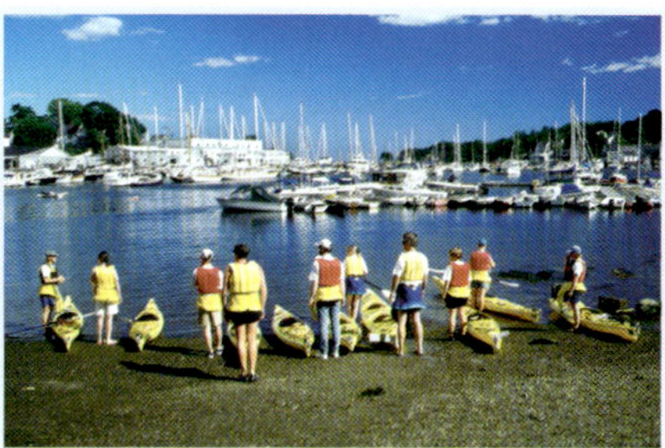

Kayakers prepare for late afternoon trip around Camden Harbor.

Liberation Charters provides private sailing charters aboard a thirty-five-foot sloop. **Camden Sailing Charters** offers daily sails in Penobscot Bay. For those who love sea kayaking, **Maine Sport Outfitters** offers equipment and rentals, a two-hour Camden Harbor tour, a four-hour tour between Rockport and Camden harbors, and a full day Muscle Ridge tour around remote islands.

Contacts for Attractions along Maine's Lower Mid-Coast

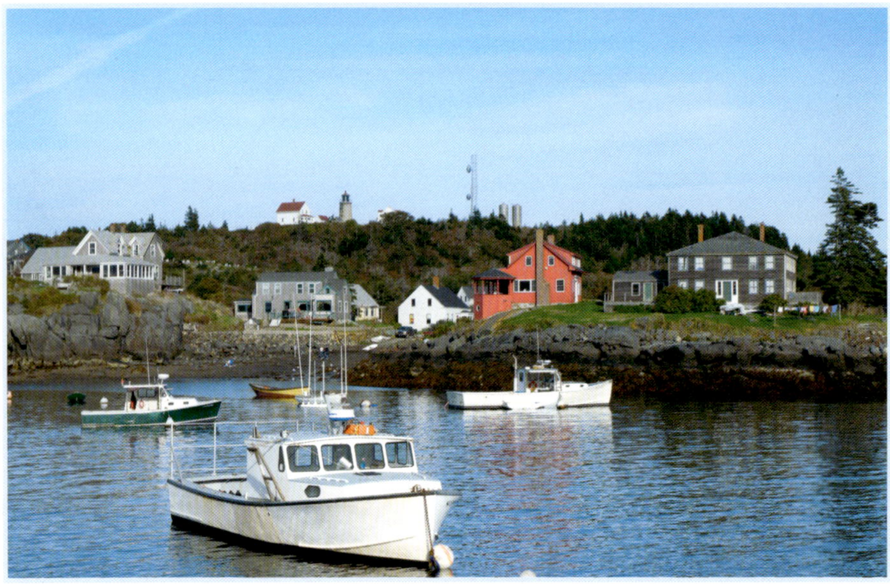

Water view of Monhegan Island with the lighthouse on the highest point.

Moody's Diner, Waldoboro
(207) 832-7785
moodysdiner.com

Fawcett's Antique Toys, Waldoboro
(207) 832-7398
home.gwi.net/~fawcetoy

Friendship Museum, Friendship
friendshipmuseum.org

Henry Knox Museum, Thomaston
(207) 354-0885
knoxmuseum.org

Prison Gift Shop, Thomaston
(207) 354-9237

Monhegan Island Light Museum, Monhegan
(207) 596-7003
monheganmuseum.org

Marshall Point Lighthouse Museum, Port Clyde
marshallpoint.org

Maine Lighthouse Challenge, Port Clyde
(207) 594-4174
lighthousefoundation.org

Port Clyde Kayak Tours, Port Clyde
(207) 372-8100
portclydekayaks.com

Whitehead Light Classes, St. George
(207) 200-7957
whiteheadlightstation.org

Owls Head Transportation Museum, Owls Head
(207) 594-4418
ohtm.org

Maine Lighthouse Museum, Rockland
(207) 594-3301
mainelighthousemuseum.org

Farnsworth Art Museum, Rockland
(207) 596-6457
farnsworthmuseum.org

Sail, Power, and Steam Museum, Rockland
sailpowersteammuseum.org

Captain Jack's Lobster Boat, Rockland
(207) 542-6852
captainjacklobstertours.com

Bufflehead Sailing Charters, Rockland
(207) 691-5407
sailrockland.com

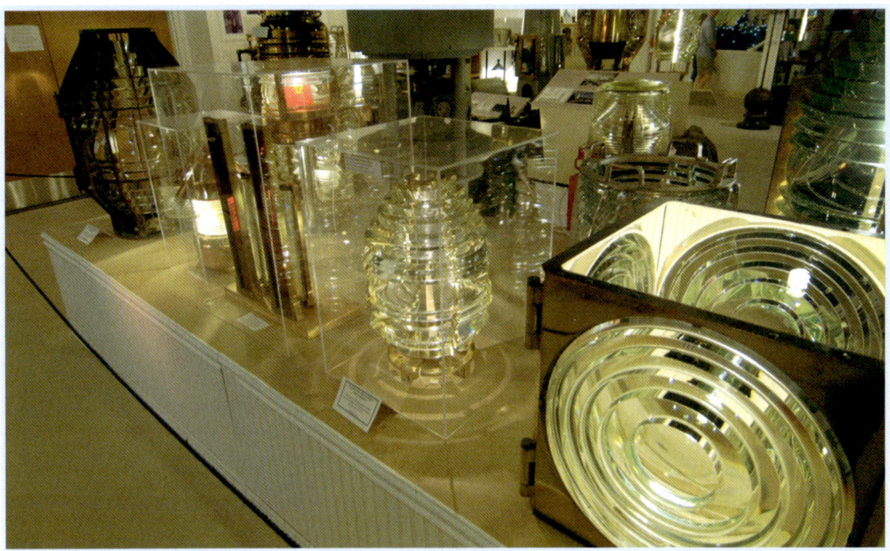

Maine Lighthouse Museum has the largest collection of Fresnel lenses.

Morning In Maine, Rockland
(207) 594-1844
amorninginmaine.com

Maine Lobster Festival, Rockland
(800) LOB-CLAW
mainelobsterfestival.com

American Lighthouse Foundation, Rockland
(207) 594-4174
lighthousefoundation.org

Strand Theater, Rockland
(207) 594-0070
rocklandstrand.com

Time Out Pub, Rockland
(207) 593-9336
northatlanticbluesfestival.com

Center for Maine Contemporary Art, Rockport
(207) 236-2875
cmcanow.org

Schooner Heron, Rockport
(207) 236-8605
sailheron.com

Rockport Charters, Rockport
(207) 691-1066
rockportcharters.com

Camden Snow Bowl, Camden
(207) 236-3438
camdensnowbowl.com

Maine Windjammer Assoc., Camden
(800) 807-WIND
sailmainecoast.com

Liberation Charters, Camden
(207) 542-1908
liberationcharters.com

Camden Sailing Charters, Camden
(207) 691-6541
camdensailingcharters.com

Camden Harbor Cruises, Camden
(207) 236-6672
camdenharborcruises.com

Merryspring Gardens, Camden
(207) 236-2239
merryspring.org

Camden Opera House, Camden
(207) 236-7963
camdenoperahouse.com

Camden Hills State Park, Camden
(207) 236-3109

Maine Sport Outfitters, Camden
(207) 230-1284
mainesport.com

Lighthouse Cruises and Ferry Service along Maine's Lower Mid-Coast

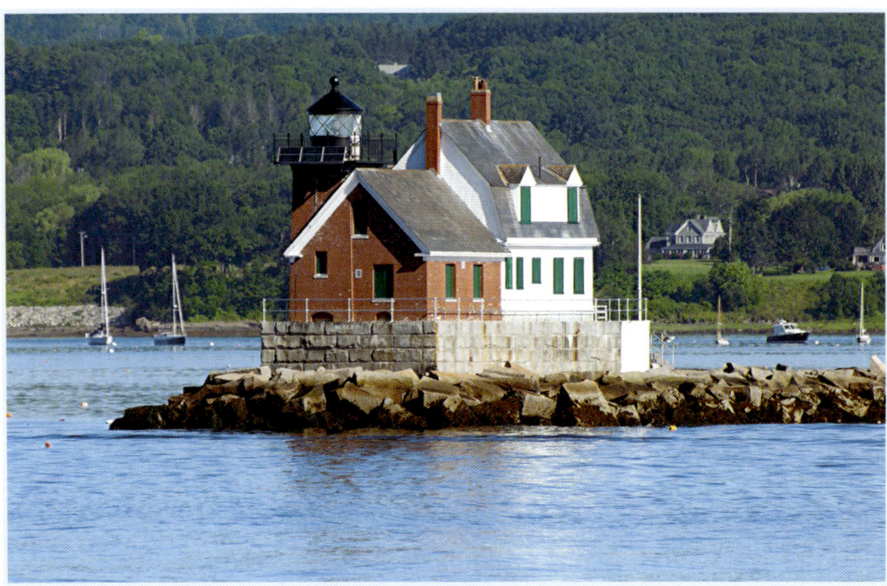

Rockland Breakwater Lighthouse water view from boat.

Balmy Days Cruises

Lighthouse tours, daily trips to Burnt Island.

- Pier 8 42 Commercial Street, Boothbay Harbor
- (207) 633-2284 or (800) 298-2284
- balmydayscruises.com
- **Lighthouses:** Burnt Island, Pemaquid Point, Monhegan Island, Squirrel Point

Hardy Boat Cruises

Special lighthouse cruises available.

- New Harbor
- 1-800-2-PUFFIN or (207) 677-2026
- hardyboat.com
- **Lighthouses:** Pemaquid Point, Monhegan Island

Monhegan Boat Line

Ferry leaves out of Port Clyde to Monhegan Island daily during the summer.

- Port Clyde
- (207) 372-8848
- monheganboat.com
- **Lighthouses:** Monhegan Island, Marshall Point, Whitehead, Two Bush Island, Tenants Harbor

Port Clyde Kayaks

Tours around Muscongus Bay.

- Port Clyde
- (207) 372-8100
- portclydekayaks.com
- **Lighthouses:** Marshall Point, Pemaquid

Maine State Ferry Service

Ferry to Matinicus Island, Vinalhaven, and Northhaven.

- 517A Main Street, Rockland
- (207) 596-2202 or 1-800-491-4883
- maine.gov/mdot/ferry/
- **Lighthouses:** Owl's Head, Rockland Breakwater. Access to islands mentioned above with lighthouses.

Captain Jack's Lobster Tours

Close-up views of Owls Head and Rockland Harbor Breakwater lighthouses on its lobstering tours.

- 1 Park Drive, Rockland
- (207) 542-6852
- captainjacklobstertours.com
- **Lighthouses:** Owl's Head, Rockland Breakwater.

Rockport Charters

Lobster boat cruises from Rockport Harbor to Camden Harbor, a bay cruise, island excursions, and lighthouse and island lobster bake cruises.

- 40 Pleasant Street, Rockport
- (207) 691-1066
- rockportcharters.com
- **Lighthouses:** Curtis Island, Indian Head, Grindle Point

Camden Harbor Cruises

One-hour lighthouse lobster tour and a three-hour Sunday lighthouse cruise aboard a classic wooden motor vessel, the *Lively Lady*.

- 16 Camden Public Landing, Camden
- (207) 236-6672
- camdenharborcruises.com
- **Lighthouses:** Curtis Island, Indian Head, Owl's Head, Browns Head, Rockland Breakwater

Waterfront Directions

Port Clyde Town Landing

From Route 1 north in Thomaston, take Route 131 south (just after Montpelier, the Knox Mansion). Continue for fourteen miles to Port Clyde.

Rockland, Rockport, and Camden Harbors

These harbors are right off Route 1 with easy access to wharfs and docks. Parking may be a challenge; just follow signs.

Scenic Flights

Penobscot Island Air

Charters a variety of lighthouse viewing flights.

- Knox County Regional Airport, Owls Head
- (207) 596-7500 or (207) 542-4944
- penobscotislandair.net

Windjammer Sailing Cruises out of Rockland, Rockport, and Camden

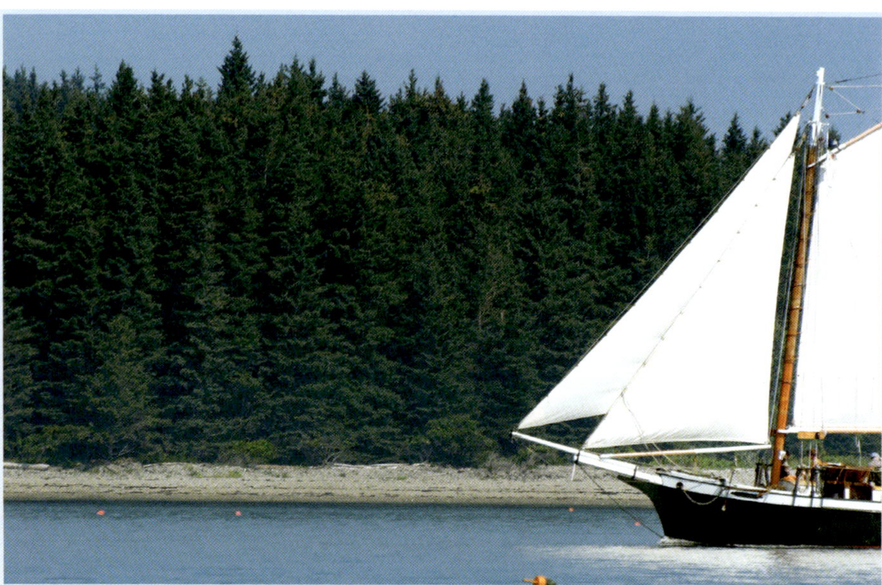

The Rockland to Camden region has the heaviest concentration of windjammer schooners.

Much of Maine's windjammer fleet is in this region, as Penobscot Bay has some of the best sailing conditions in the world. The following schooner windjammer sailing cruises offer many types of tours; many of them pass lighthouses.

Schooner Heron

This sixty-five-foot schooner sails out of Rockport Harbor three times a day.

111 Pascal Avenue, Rockport

(207) 236-8605

sailheron.com

Schooner Isaac H. Evans

Originally built in 1886, this ninety-nine-foot schooner offers day and night and themed cruises, like the week-long Old Salts and Maine Lighthouses Cruise. The schooner is a National Historic Landmark.

Rockland

(877) 238-1325

isaacevans.com

Schooner J. & E. Riggin

Built in 1927, this 120-foot, two-masted schooner has Kids, Knitting, Maine Food, and Music overnight cruises, as well as three- and four-day Lighthouses and Lobsters cruises.

136 Holmes Street, Rockland

(800) 869-0604

mainewindjammer.com

Schooner American Eagle

Cruises lasting from two to nine days.

11 Front Street, Rockland

(207) 594-8007 or (800) 648-4544

schooneramericaneagle.com

Schooner Stephen Taber and Schooner Bowditch

Classic 140-year old schooner offers a variety of multi-day cruises focused on themes such as photography, wine, music, and food.

- Windjammer Wharf, Rockland
- (207) 594-4723 or (800) 999-7352
- stephentaber.com

Maine Windjammer Cruises

Restored nineteenth-century schooners *Grace Bailey* and *Mercentile* carry up to twenty-nine passengers. The smaller *Mistress* offers a unique sail for up to six passengers. Weekly and weekend cruises along the Maine coast and Penobscot Bay.

- Camden
- (207) 236-2938 or (800) 736-7981 or Fax: (207) 236-3229
- mainewindjammercruises.com

Schooner Olad

The *Olad* is a restored, classic yacht built in 1927. Provides daily two-hour, half-day, full-day sails, and sunset sails, along with various event sails. Charters are available on the *Owl*.

- Camden
- (207) 236-2323
- maineschooners.com

Schooner Angelique

Schooner *Angelique* offers weekly wildlife, brews, wine, wellness, and photography cruises; lighthouse cruises in July and August; and has cruises that explore the Acadia region.

- Yankee Packet Company, Camden
- (800) 282-9989
- sailangelique.com

Schooner Mary Day

Tours include four-day lighthouse cruises, natural history, Maine coast beer, environmental education, and events cruises.

- 10 Atlantic Ave., Camden
- (800) 992-2218
- schoonermaryday.com

Schooner Surprise

This fifty-seven-foot racing schooner built in 1918 offers two-hour windjammer cruises around Camden Harbor and Penobscot Bay, including sunset sails, wine tasting, and full moon sails.

- (207) 236-4687
- camdenmainesailing.com

Schooner Lewis R. French

Built in 1871, this is the last remaining nineteenth-century Maine schooner. Three-, four- and six-day sailing vacations focus on themes such as fall foliage, music, lighthouses, and birding. The lighthouses tour includes tickets to the Maine Lighthouse Museum in Rockland. The schooner is a National Historic Landmark.

- Camden
- (800) 469-4635
- schoonerfrench.com

Schooner Appledore

This wooden eighty-six-foot schooner cruises Penobscot Bay at least three times a day, seven days a week.

- 3 Lily Pond Drive, Camden
- (207) 236-8353
- appledore2.com

Schooner Heritage

The 145-foot *Heritage* is the newest coasting schooner carrying passengers along the Maine coast. It offers three-day to six-day sails without a specific itinerary. Both captains are maritime historians.

- 5 Achorn Street, Rockland
- (207) 594-8007 or (800) 648-4544
- schoonerheritage.com

Schooner Victory Chimes

This vessel is the only original three-masted schooner in the famed Maine Windjammer fleet and was featured on the US minted quarter with Pemaquid Light. Three- and four-day sails including the Lighthouse Parade, Maine Humor, and Irish Music cruises.

- Rockland
- (800) 745-5651
- victorychimes.com

Maine's Inland Lighthouse

Time for another detour from the seacoast! Inland on Lake Cobbosseecontee, the lake has its share of rocky ledges and reefs, which became a challenge as tourism increased. There was also a passenger launch that would transport visitors around the northern area of the lake and would occasionally run aground on Ladies Delight Island and nearby islands in foggy or stormy weather before the lighthouse was constructed in 1908. The Lake Cobbosseecontee Yacht Club was established in 1904 as a result of this scenic region, and was directly involved in the construction of the Ladies Delight Lighthouse in 1908 out of the necessity in helping mariners navigate around the island and surrounding areas. It is the only inland lighthouse in Maine.

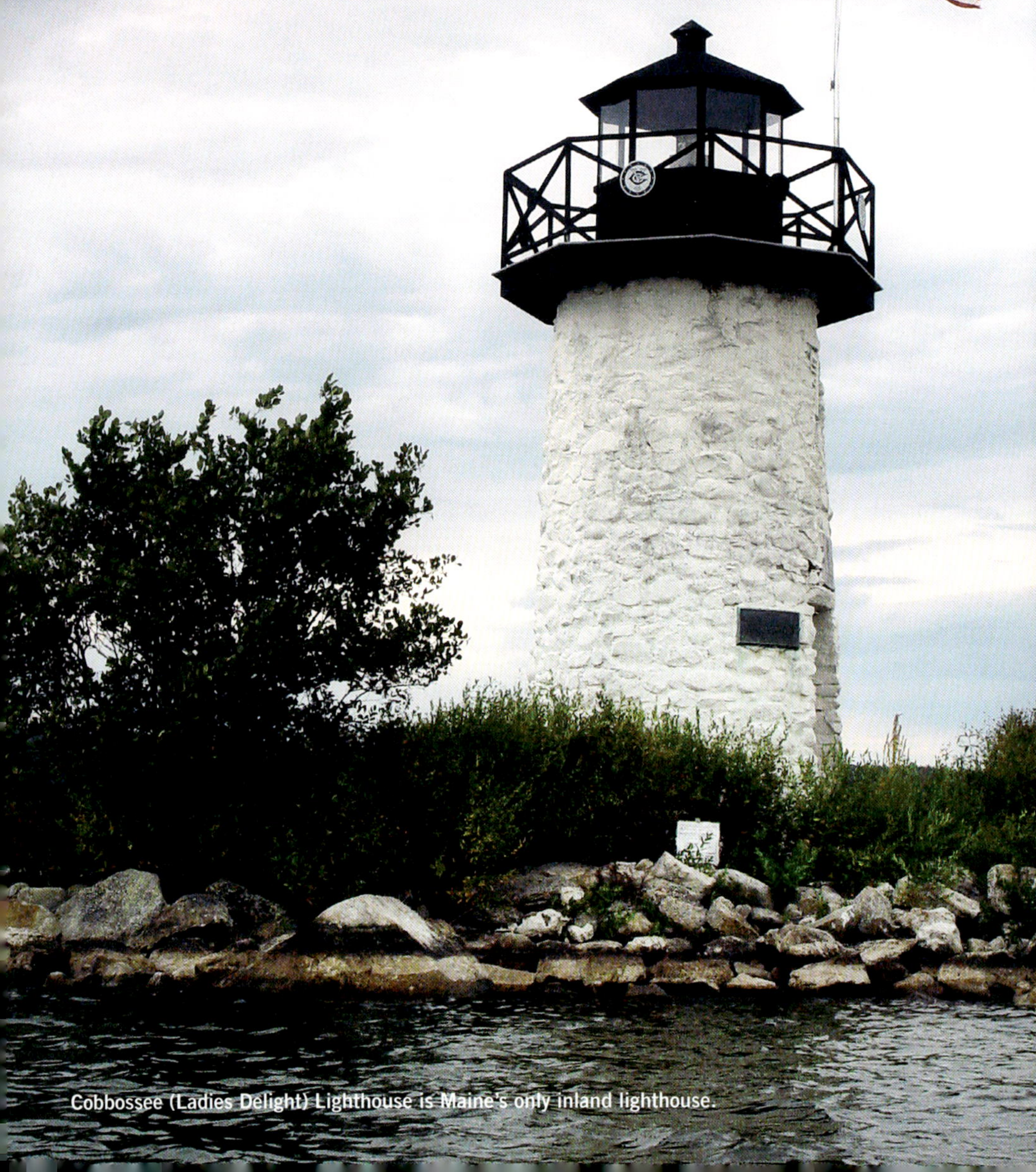

Cobbossee (Ladies Delight) Lighthouse is Maine's only inland lighthouse.

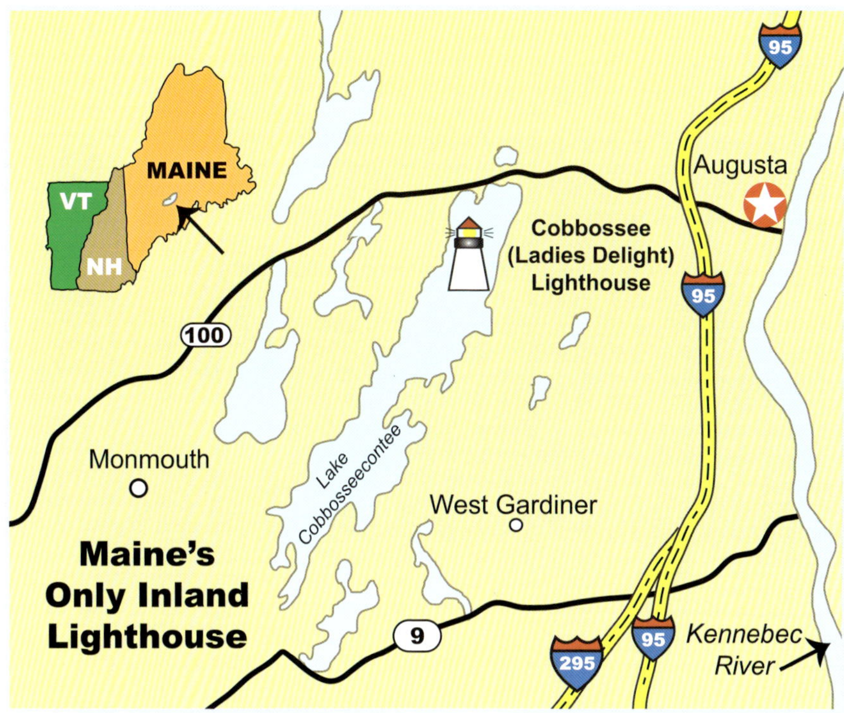

Map of Cobbossee (Ladies Delight) Lighthouse.

Cobbossee (Ladies Delight) Lighthouse

Winthrop (1908) • Latitude: 44° 18' 16" • Longitude: 69° 53' 48"

Lake Cobbosseecontee is one of the longest lakes in Maine (about nine miles) and became a major tourist attraction in the Augusta region in the nineteenth century. Filled with salmon and trout at the time, Lake Cobbosseecontee, which is Abenaki for a "place of many sturgeon," attracted fishermen, in particular, to the many sportsmen's camps along its shores. Steamboats provided transportation to vacation inns and cottages, and the area also became a social mecca for sailing regattas. The early 1900s song "On Moonlight Bay" by composer Percy Wenrich was thought to have been inspired by Lake Cobbosseecontee.

In addition to its beauty, the lake has its share of rocky ledges and reefs, which became a challenge as tourism increased. The Lake Cobbosseecontee Yacht Club, established in 1904, was involved in the construction of the lighthouse, which marks the northern edge of a jagged underwater reef that runs down the middle of the lake. The small islands and exposed ledges are the visible high points of that reef. Before the nearby Manchester dam was built, the lake's water level was about eight feet lower than it is today, exposing more of the dangerous rock formations. Two other lighthouses constructed during this period—Belle Island Light, and Crow Island Light—are now gone.

Two oxen were to be used in the construction, but only one at a time could fit on the barge. As the crew dropped off one ox on the tiny island and attempted to retrieve

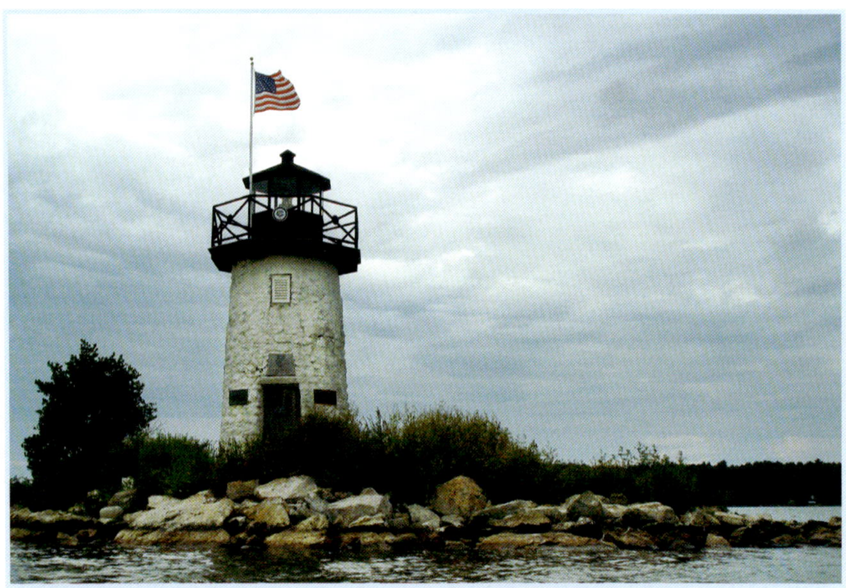

Cobbossee (Ladies Delight) Lighthouse on Lake Cobbosseecontee.

the other on the mainland, they found the first ox, probably bored and lonely for his buddy, attempting to swim back to the mainland.

In the early days, a volunteer keeper from the Cobbosseecontee Yacht Club maintained the lighthouse, and the club still maintains it today. It was renovated in 2005, in time for its 100th birthday in 2008. Cobbossee (Ladies Delight) Lighthouse is the only landlocked lighthouse in Maine. About a mile from shore, it is best viewed by boat.

Attractions around Lake Cobbosseecontee

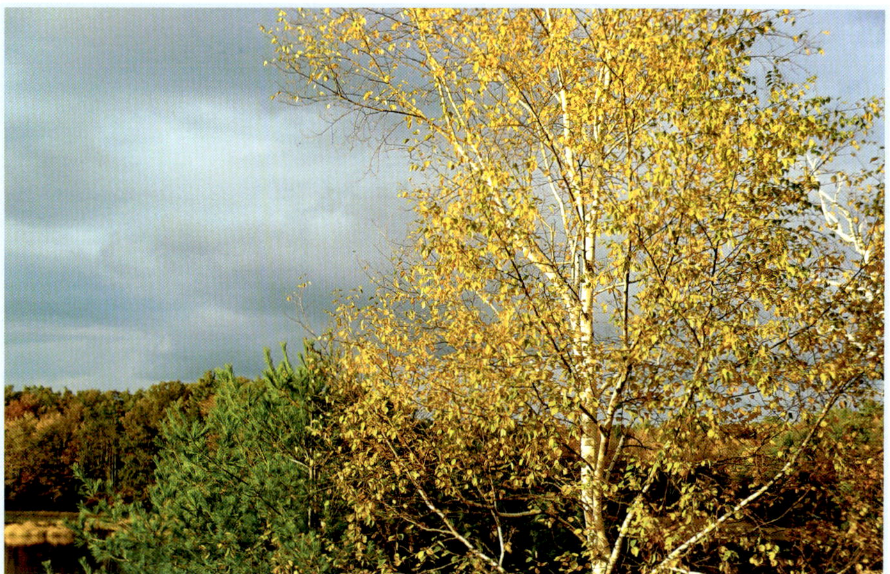

Autumn colors decorate the lakes and rivers.

The lake, just south of Augusta, has some of the best fishing in the region, predominantly bass and trout. The Cobbosseecontee Yacht Club offers cruises to the lighthouse by appointment during the summer. If you stay at the Lakeside Motel and Cabins, you can also rent a boat or kayak to get out to the lighthouse. On the fourth Saturday in July, visit the CYC Annual Concert in Horseshoe Cove, and on the first week of August, check out the Annual Lighthouse Regatta.

This rural area has lots of hiking trails along the shoreline of Lake Cobbosseecontee and surrounding lakes. On the Kennebec Land Trust, on Horseshoe Island, there is an undeveloped shoreline and a beautiful white pine and hemlock forest. Just look for the KLT sign. The easiest trails are in the Winthrop area. Cobbosseecontee Stream is an ideal spot for canoeing and kayaking.

If you enjoy outdoor museums, visit the **Monmouth Museum,** which houses eight buildings and exhibits from the nineteenth century. You can also take in a show at the **Theater at Monmouth**.

In nearby Augusta, Maine's capital city, you'll find museums, parks, nightlife, and other attractions. Explore the **Old Fort Western Museum**, the oldest fort in New England built in the mid-1700s The **Maine State Museum** and **Children's Discovery Museum** are also worth a visit. For architectural splendor, explore the **Blain House**, the governor's mansion. **Viles Arboretum** (also known as the Pine Tree State Arboretum) invites visitors to appreciate the many varieties of Maine's trees and flora.

Contacts for Attractions around Lake Cobbosseecontee

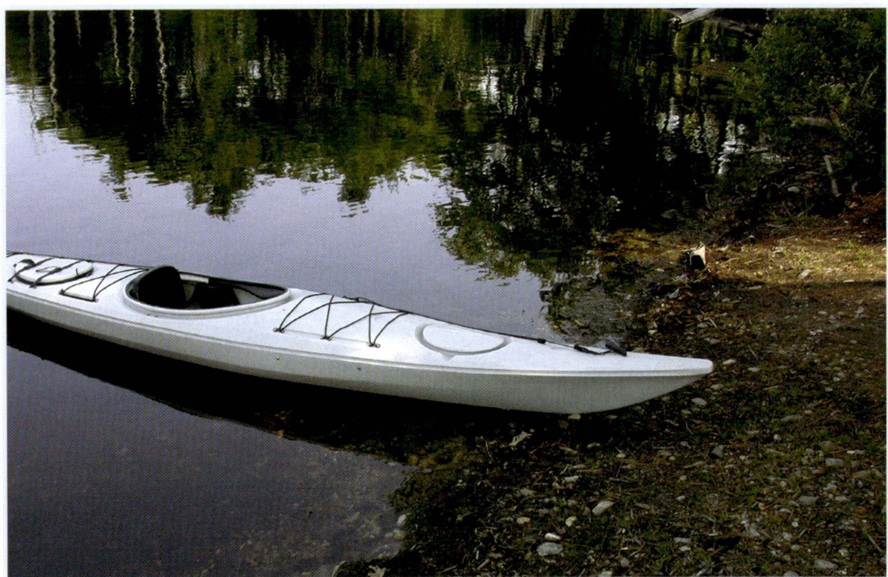

This region is a favorite of kayakers who enjoy wildlife.

Blaine House, Augusta
blainehouse.org

Children's Discovery Museum, Augusta
(207) 622-2209
childrensdiscoverymuseum.org

Maine State Museum, Augusta
(207) 287-2301
mainestatemuseum.org

Old Fort Western Museum, Augusta
(207) 626-2385
oldfortwestern.org

Monmouth Museum, Monmouth
(207) 933-2287
monmouthmuseuminc.org

Theater at Monmouth
(207) 933-9999
theateratmonmouth.org

Viles Aboretum, Augusta
(207) 626-7989
vilesarboretum.org

Lighthouse Cruise on Lake Cobbosseecontee

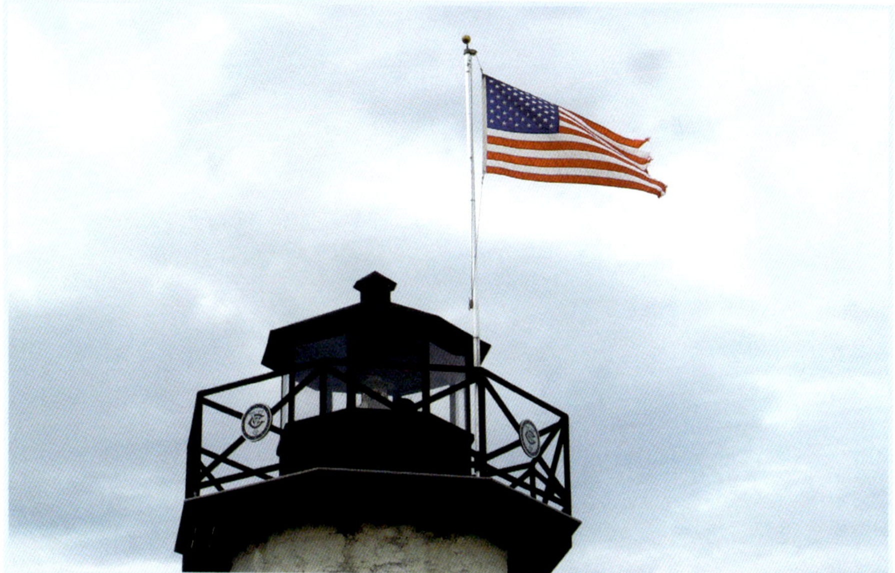

Cobbossee (Ladies Delight) Lighthouse maintained by the Cobbosseecontee Yacht Club.

Cobbosseecontee Yacht Club

The Cobbosseecontee Yacht Club, one of the oldest inland waters yacht clubs in America, offers cruises out to Ladies Delight Light, and sponsors an annual lighthouse regatta, "boat-ins," concerts, and many other events to educate, and raise funds for preservation efforts on the lake.

- ✉ Cobbosseecontee Yacht Club, Winthrop
- ☎ (207) 623-1123
- 🌐 cycmaine.org

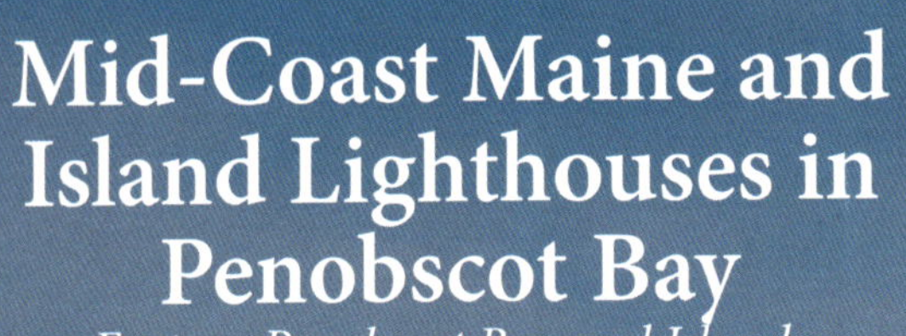

Mid-Coast Maine and Island Lighthouses in Penobscot Bay

Eastern Penobscot Bay and Islands

Penobscot Bay is Maine's largest coastal waterway, comprised of approximately 857 square miles and over 200 islands, including the major islands of Matinicus, Vinalhaven, North Haven, Islesboro, Deer Isle, and Isle au Haut. The islands provide protection from the open sea and make the bay a popular destination for sailing, pleasure boating, and sea kayaking. The lighthouses on these islands, and on dangerous ledges between them, made the foggy waterways safer for the booming lumber trade heading to Bangor, the shipping of potatoes from Maine's interior, and the export of granite quarried in Vinalhaven and other islands.

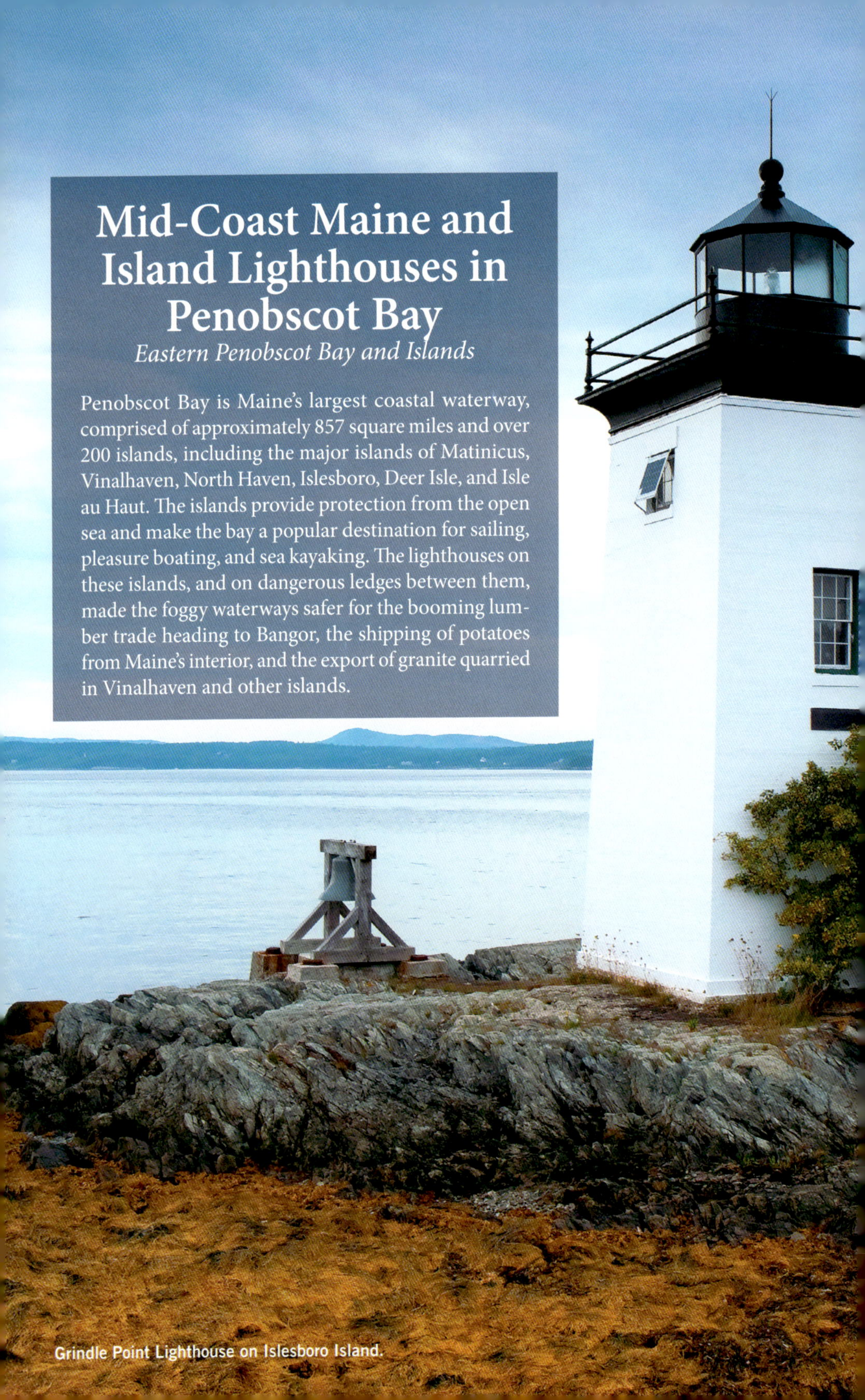

Grindle Point Lighthouse on Islesboro Island.

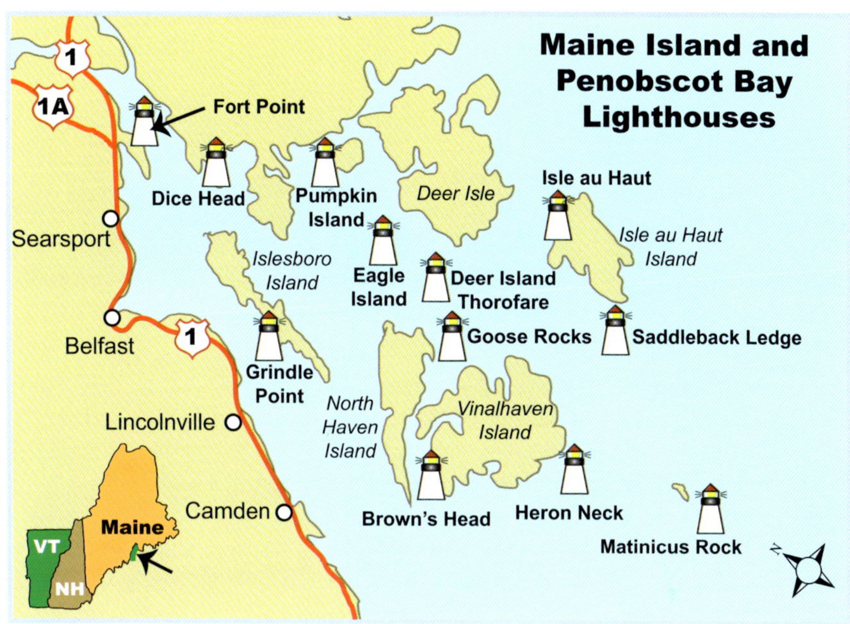

Map of Maine's island lighthouses in Penobscot Bay.

Matinicus Rock Lighthouse

Matinicus (1827) • Latitude: 44° 47' 00" N • Longitude: 68° 51' 18" W

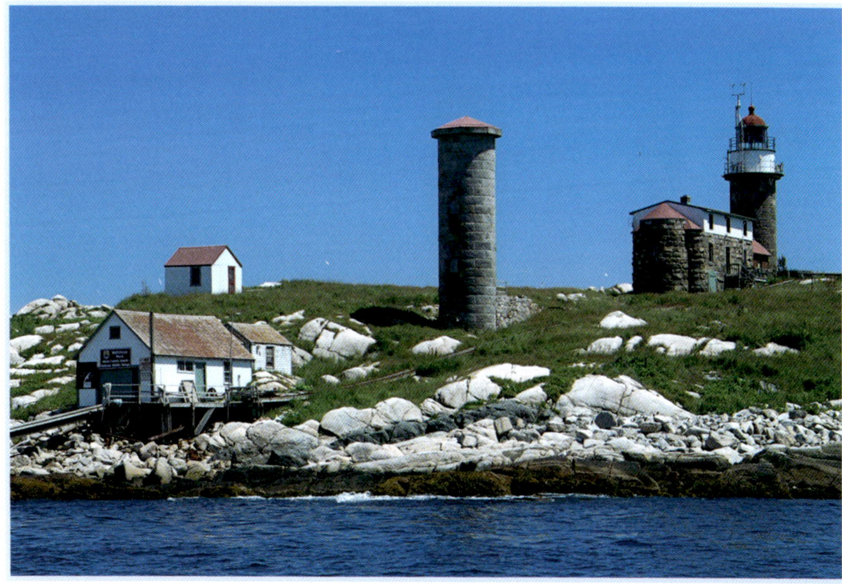

Matinicus Rock Lighthouse with both north (capped) and south towers.

Matinicus Rock Lighthouse lies about twenty-three miles from Rockland and five miles from the larger Matinicus Island. Originally built as two lighthouses, many

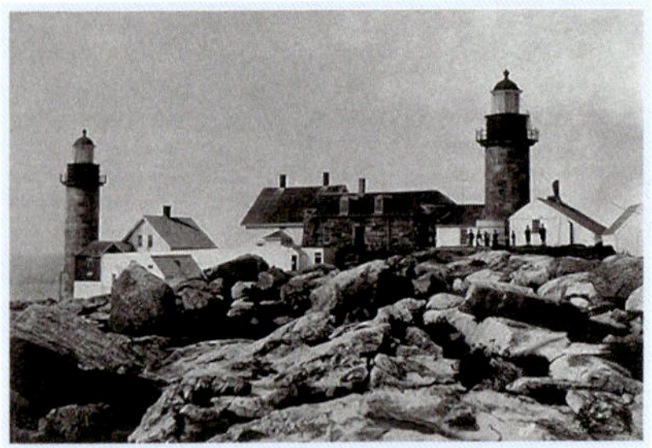

Both Matinicus towers with buildings. *Courtesy US Coast Guard.*

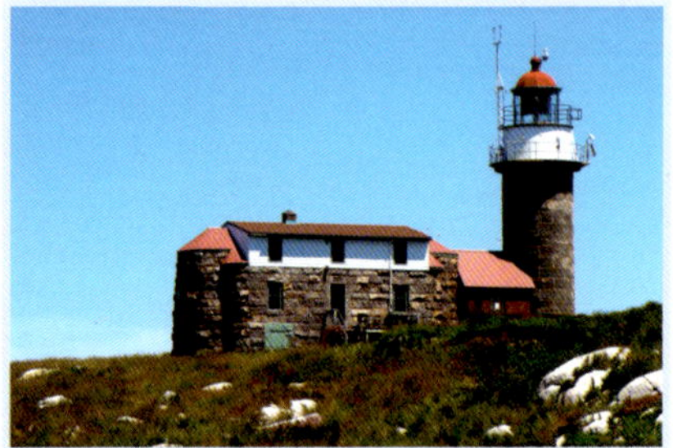

Matinicus Rock Lighthouse is Maine's most remote lighthouse.

of its keepers became ill, and some died, presumably from the constant cold, damp air. Samuel Burgess became keeper in 1853, bringing his invalid wife and several of their ten children to live at the light station. One daughter, Abbie, became a skilled keeper and later single-handedly kept her family safe during a storm.

The second north light was discontinued in 1923, leaving the one south light tower. In 1983, the south light was automated. The National Audubon Society researches and protects the island's seabird population, which includes puffins.

Abbie Burgess, Teenage Heroine. On January 16, 1856, keeper Burgess, fearing his family would be trapped over the winter without provisions, decided to make the trip to Rockland on the mainland. By late afternoon, a storm blew in, and by early evening, waves were crashing over the rocks and lighthouse structures on Matinicus Rock. The storm's ferocity continued for three days. Fearing the keeper's house might be weakened by the storm, Abbie moved her mother and sisters to the north lighthouse tower, believing it was the safest structure and location.

On the fourth day, on the morning of January 19, Matinicus Rock was practically underwater. Abbie waded knee deep in the freezing water to rescue her pet chickens from their coop. With the chickens safely by the tower, Abbie looked over at the old keeper's house where her mother had been staying. At that moment, a giant wave crashed over the dwelling, and not a stone was left in place.

For the next month, pounding storms made it impossible for anyone to land on the island. Seventeen-year-old Abbie kept the lights burning on both towers while caring for her mother and sisters. Some days, hurricane-force winds would batter the buildings with sleet and snow as Abbie made the long climb up the stairs to maintain the two lights. She would fill the lanterns, trim the wicks, and clean the many glass lenses. She stood watch for distressed vessels, taking short naps each day to keep her strength.

Abbie wrote, "The new dwelling was flooded and the windows had to be secured to prevent the violence of the spray from breaking them in. As the tide came, the sea rose higher and higher, till the only endurable places were the light-towers. If they stood we were saved, otherwise our fate was only too certain. But for some reason, I know not why, I had no misgivings, and went on with my work as usual. For four weeks, owing to rough weather, no landing could be affected on the Rock. During this time we were without the assistance of any male member of our family. Though at times greatly exhausted with my labors, not once did the lights fail.

Under God I was able to perform all my accustomed duties as well as my father's." About four weeks after he had left for the mainland, keeper Burgess finally made it back to Matinicus Rock, elated to find his family alive and well.

In 1857, she again proved her mettle when her father was away on the mainland. During a lull in a storm, her brother went looking for food in a small skiff. Neither her brother nor her father came back for the next twenty-one days, during which time the family was reduced to daily rations of one cup of corn meal mush and an egg. During this time, she tended both the family and the lighthouse. After three weeks, father and son returned with food and found Abbie exhausted from worry, fearing that both had drowned. Her tenacity won praise from locals on the mainland, who referred to her as the teenage heroine of Matinicus Rock Light.

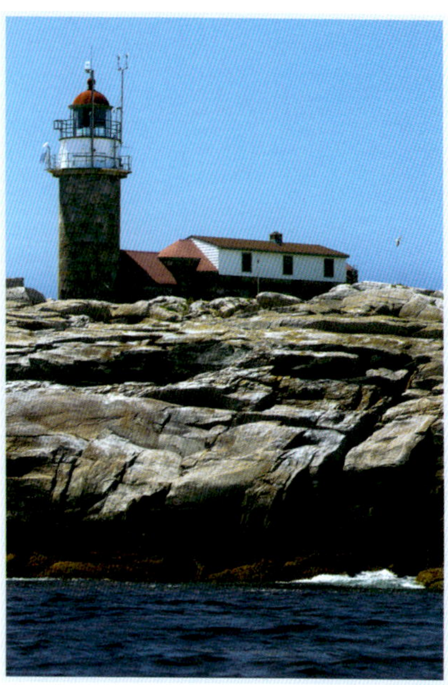

Active south tower and keeper's building on Matinicus Rock.

Years later, Abbie trained her father's replacement, Captain John Grant. She married his son Isaac and they had four children at Matinicus Rock. Abbie Burgess Grant is known as the most famous teenage heroine in Maine's history.

Heron Neck Lighthouse

Greens Island (1854) • Latitude: 44° 01' 30" N • Longitude: 68° 51' 44" W

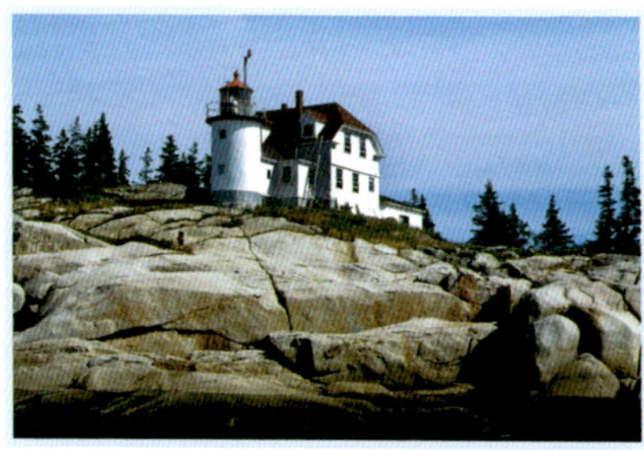

Heron Neck Light was the catalyst for the national Lighthouse Preservation Act.

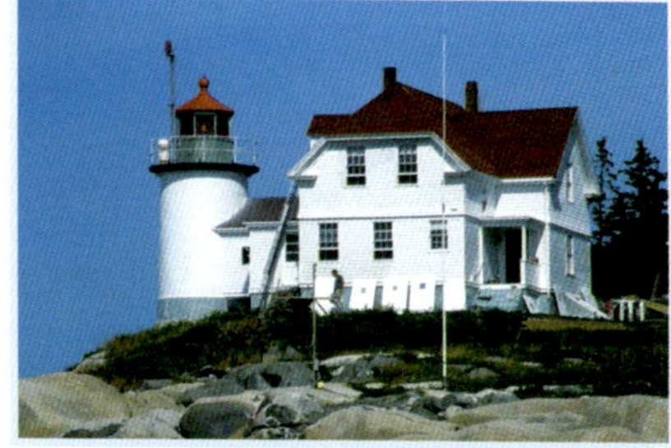

Restoration efforts on the keeper's building as part of Maine Lights Program.

Heron Neck Lighthouse on Green Island helped guide mariners into Carver's Harbor on Vinalhaven Island. The first keeper was James G. Smith from Vinalhaven. Poor construction contributed to dampness and mold, and unhealthy conditions were attributed to five deaths. It was torn down and rebuilt in 1895.

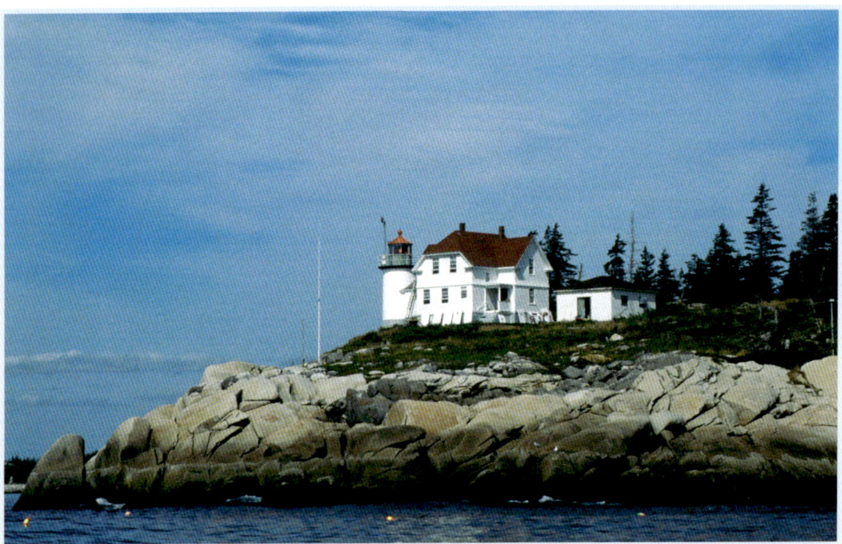
Heron Neck Lighthouse guides mariners around Vinalhaven Island.

In the early 1900s, Heron Neck Lighthouse had a famous dog named Nemo, a Newfoundland named after Jules Verne's *Captain Nemo*. Keeper Levi Farnham had trained him to run down to the shore and listen for ships' horns on foggy days, barking to warn them of the rocks. In fair weather, captains would steer their boats close to shore and throw Nemo treats to thank him for what they called "fog barks."

In the 1940s, local fishermen kept the light station's Coast Guardsmen supplied with lobsters and fish, especially during the winter months.

Lighthouse Preservation Act. Maine has been at the forefront on conservation efforts, not only of its lands and wildlife, but also its lighthouses. As lighthouse automation began in the middle to late 1900s, and as government budget cuts became more frequent, many lighthouses fell into disrepair and became vandalism and souvenir targets.

Organizations sprouted up to preserve lighthouses all over the country, including two in Maine. In 1992, *Lighthouse Digest* magazine was established, and the American Lighthouse Foundation was founded in 1994 to spearhead lighthouse preservation on a national scale. Heron Neck Light was automated in 1982. In 1989, a fire severely damaged the keeper's dwelling, sparing the tower. An investigation found that an electrical short in the kitchen area was the likely source. Lacking funds to restore the dwelling, the Coast Guard proposed demolishing it but faced strong public opposition. This started to spark a long discussion of alternative solutions. Peter Ralston, of the Rockland-based Island Institute, founded the Maine Lights Program to transfer lighthouse properties to local organizations with a vested interest in their survival, with the Coast Guard retaining responsibility only for the lights themselves. In 1993, Heron Neck Lighthouse was the first lighthouse to use this program when it was turned over to the Island Institute, which in turn leased the property to a private party to help restore the house.

This project inspired the Island Institute in Rockland to initiate the Maine Lights Program. By 1996, with help from Senator George Mitchell and Senator Olympia Snowe, the Maine Lights Program was passed into law. Twenty-eight light stations in Maine were transferred to various nonprofit organizations. These organizations competed for stewardship by submitting detailed plans for maintenance, public access, and restoration funding.

In 2000, Congress passed the Lighthouse Preservation Act, creating a similar program on a national scale under National Park Service supervision. These modern keepers have protected the coastal beacons from vandals and souvenir hunters and transformed some of them into tourist attractions and living history centers. They provide a national and international blueprint for modern-day lighthouse conservation. To further raise awareness, Congress declared August 7 National Lighthouse and Lighthouse Preservation Day.

Saddleback Ledge Lighthouse

Vinalhaven (1839) • Latitude: 44° 00' 54" N • Longitude: 68° 43' 36" W

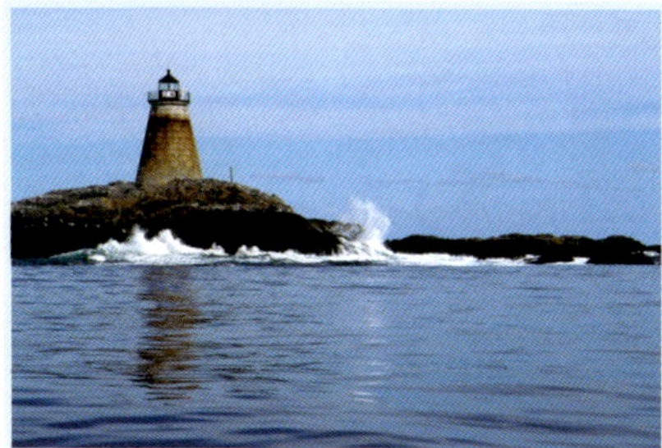

Saddleback Ledge Light is one of the most remote lighthouses in Maine.

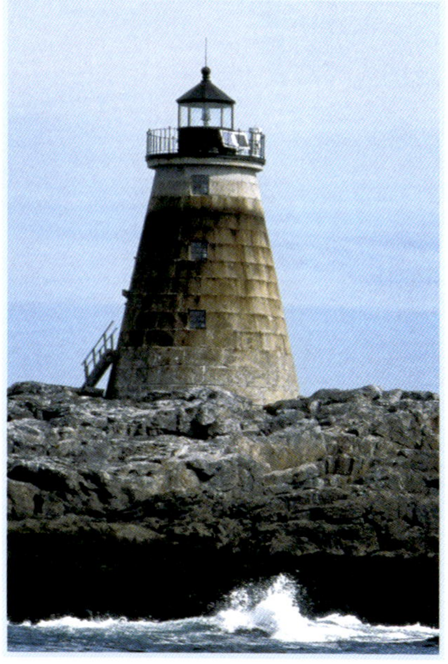

The tower is active, but the keeper's building was destroyed in a military exercise.

Saddleback Ledge Lighthouse is on a rocky ledge halfway between Vinalhaven Island and Isle au Haut. In 1836, *Royal Tar*, which was carrying a cargo of circus performers and animals, caught fire and sank near the ledge. This created a public outcry and petitions for a lighthouse to be built on the ledge.

Many lighthouse keepers have described Saddleback Lighthouse as one of Maine's most remote and barren lighthouse locations. The first keeper, Watson Hopkins, lived with nine family members on the second floor of the tower. In 1843, his wife, Abigail, gave birth to a baby girl and needed to be transferred to the mainland. On the way to the mainland, the baby was dropped briefly into the icy water, but was quickly pulled out before any harm was done.

In 1885 a derrick with a swinging arm and attached chair was added to help people get on and off the rocky ledge. In unrelated incidents, keepers have recorded unusually high numbers of dead birds piled up on the tiny ledge after crashing into the lighthouse tower.

Saddleback Ledge Light was automated in 1954 and the keeper's dwelling was blown up as a Green Beret military exercise in 1960 to reduce maintenance costs. The tower is still in operation.

Goose Rocks Lighthouse

Vinalhaven (1890) • Latitude: 44° 08' 08" N • Longitude: 68° 49' 50" W

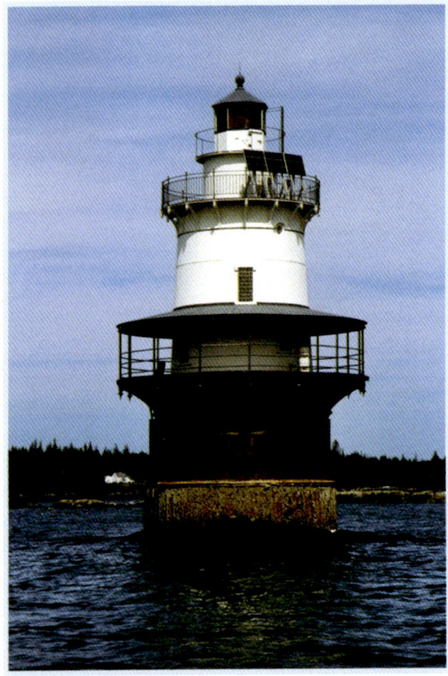

Goose Rocks Light is between Vinalhaven Island and North Haven Island.

Goose Rocks Lighthouse, known as a spark plug-type lighthouse, was built at the entrance to the Fox Islands Thorofare, a busy waterway between Vinalhaven Island and North Haven Island. The top of the caisson served as a storage area, while the lighthouse itself was divided into five levels. The three bottom levels served as cramped living quarters for the keepers. It was set up as a stag station, where the keeper's families would stay on the mainland in housing provided by the Lighthouse Service. Keepers would spend eight continuous days with their families each month. Myrick Morrison, from North Haven, was keeper from 1920 to 1938 and had more than his fair share of family tragedies. His wife Eva died in 1928. Harold, the youngest son, died in the sinking of a Japanese prison ship in WWII, and another son, Norman, drowned in a fishing accident. The light was automated in 1963. For a number of years after automation, locals, called "lamplighters," were hired to control the fog signal. The lighthouse was purchased by Jordan and Ted Northrop, who formed the Beacon Preservation, Inc. Goose Rocks Lighthouse has been carefully restored and is open for overnight visitors.

Browns Head Lighthouse

Vinalhaven Island (1832) • Latitude: 44° 06' 42" N • Longitude: 68° 54' 36" W

About thirteen miles from Rockland, Vinalhaven Island is part of the Fox Islands, named for the gray foxes that once lived there in abundance. Vinalhaven residents had always been fishermen, but in 1826, its reputation for granite began to grow.

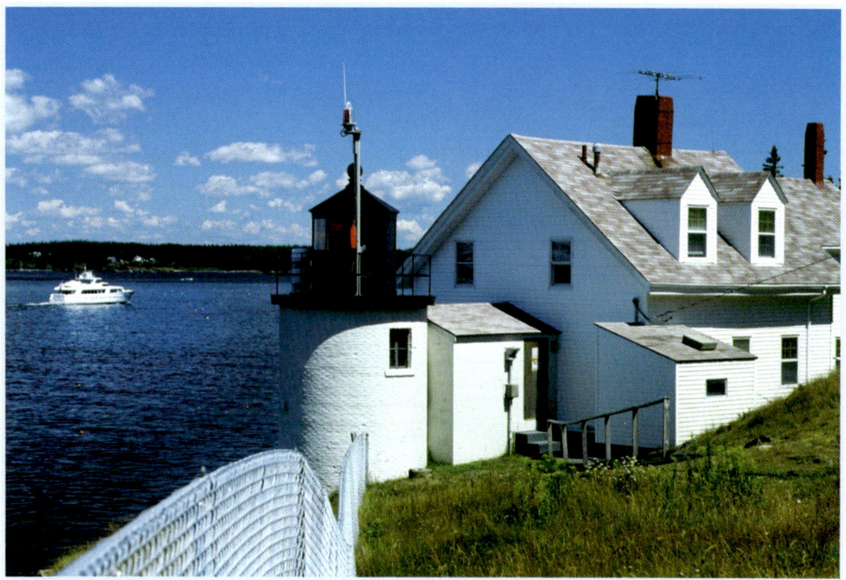

Browns Head Light was a favorite station for keepers and their families.

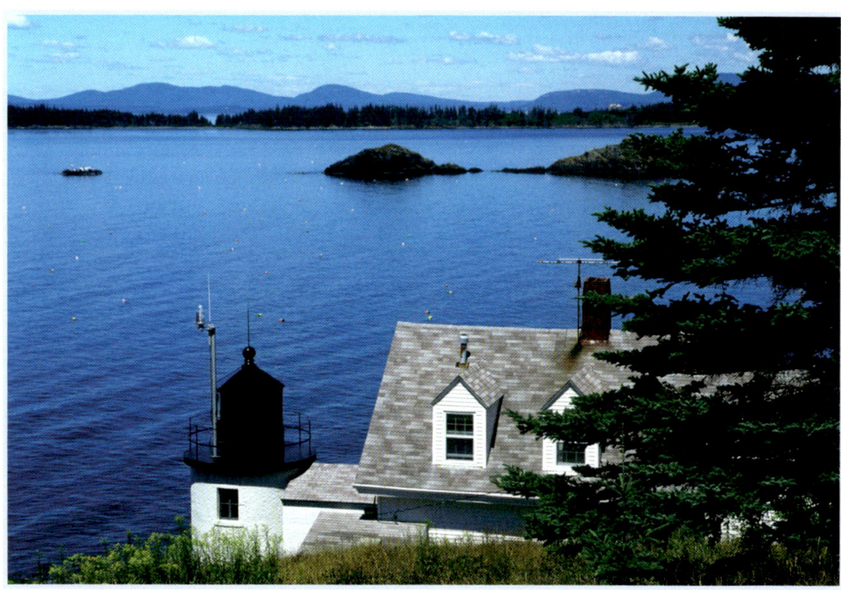

Browns Head Light on Vinalhaven Island.

For the next century, it was one of Maine's largest quarrying centers. The quarries are closed now, but the area still contains one of the largest lobster beds in the world.

Brown's Head Lighthouse helped guide ships through the western entrance to Fox Islands Thorofare. Originally constructed of rubble, the current lighthouse tower was reconstructed of bricks and mortar on a ledge foundation. Its location was often requested by keepers, as it was an ideal place to raise a family. Where many lighthouses had multiple keepers to deal with the amount of work needed, Brown's Head was always a one-keeper family station. The first lighthouse keeper was David Wooster, who served until his death in 1841 at the age of sixty-one. Benjamin Eldridge Burgess, raised on Matinicus Island, became keeper in 1867 and retired in 1905, thirty-seven years later, at the age of eighty. He had raised seven children and brought up three grandchildren between two wives, as his first died in her early years. Tragedy continued to follow him, as three daughters died in a four-year period. He was a thoughtful and neat man, well-liked by the locals. In 1987, Browns Head Light was among the last lighthouses in Maine to be automated. Today the town manager lives at the station.

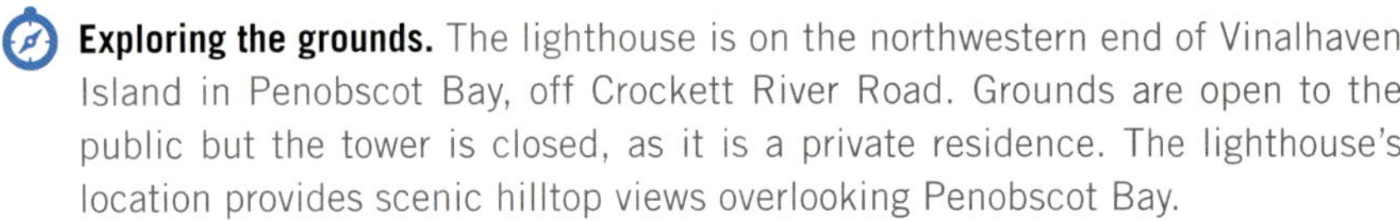

Exploring the grounds. The lighthouse is on the northwestern end of Vinalhaven Island in Penobscot Bay, off Crockett River Road. Grounds are open to the public but the tower is closed, as it is a private residence. The lighthouse's location provides scenic hilltop views overlooking Penobscot Bay.

Directions. The Maine State Ferry that departs from Rockland will bring you to Vinalhaven Ferry Terminal in about an hour and a half, and you can drive or bike the six miles to the lighthouse. Turn right out of the parking lot, then left before Key Bank. Continue on and bear right at the fork by the water's edge (yield sign) past the swimming quarries. Bear left at the fork with the "No Open Fires" sign and follow exactly four miles, where you'll find a dirt road on the left (look for a group of mailboxes at the intersection of Crockett River Road). Follow the dirt road past a cemetery on the right and take the next right on a dirt road to the parking lot in front of the lighthouse.

Grindle Point Lighthouse

Islesboro (1851) • Latitude: 44° 16' 56" N • Longitude: 68° 56' 34" W

Grindle Point Lighthouse overlooks the entrance to Gilkey Harbor, named for an early settler, John Gilkey, who came to Islesboro in 1772. His house became a landmark for passing mariners. The light is fifty-four feet above average high water. It was built in 1851 and replaced in 1874. The tower alone stands thirty-two feet tall and is constructed in a unique pyramidal shape. The first keeper was Rufus Dunning, who stayed until 1853. Captain Francis Grindle, who had gone to sea at a young age and achieved the title of master mariner, succeeded him. The captain died in 1857 at the age of seventy-three.

Nelson Gilkey, who also had side jobs as a postmaster and town clerk, was keeper from 1861 to 1869. His older brother, Avery, became keeper in 1872, but was not as dedicated as his brother. He was removed a year later for showing a lack of interest in his duties during a routine inspection.

The deed to the lighthouse property came under scrutiny in 1889. The boundaries were agreed upon in 1892, and a wire fence was constructed around the property.

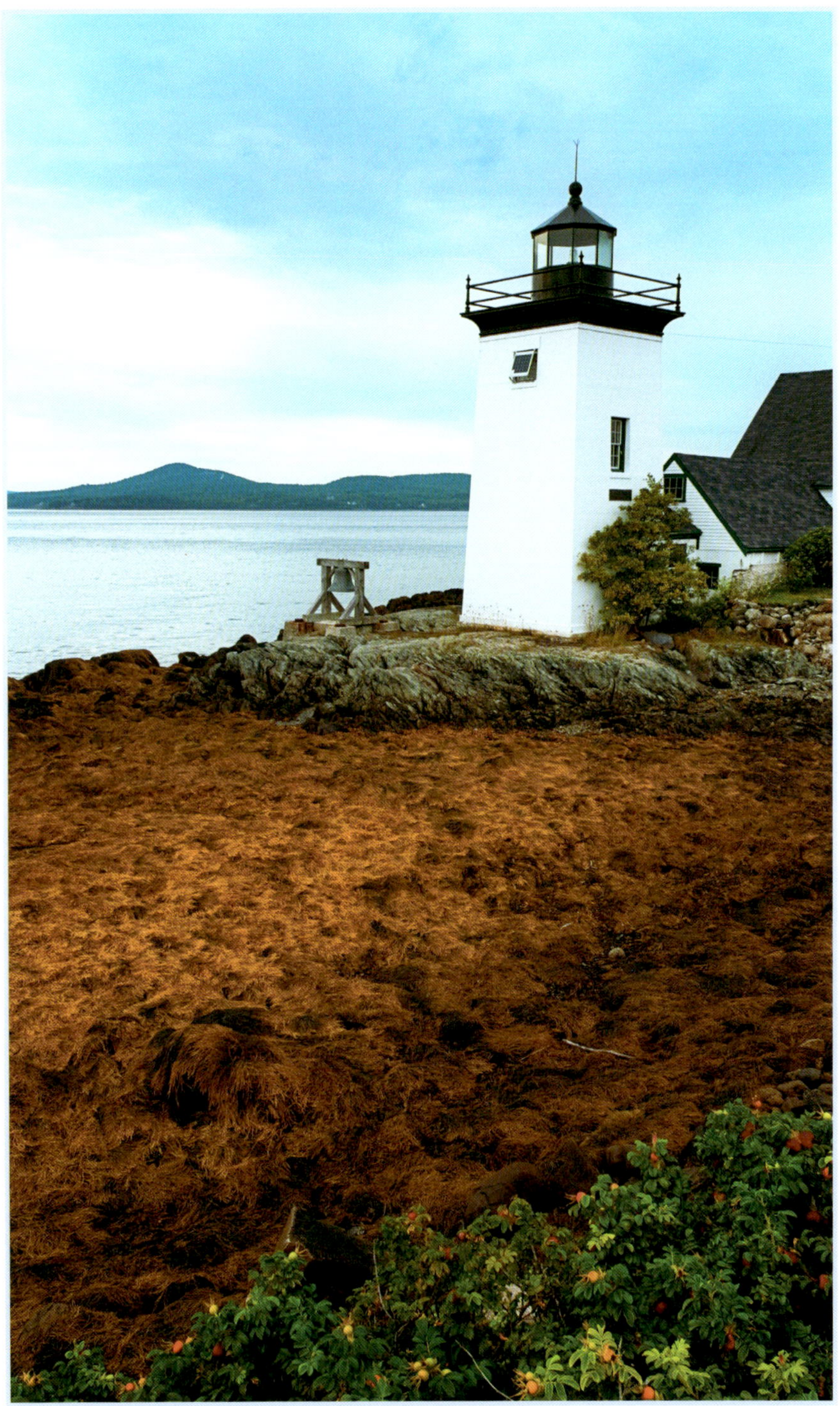

Grindle Point Light is next to the ferry dock in Gilkey Harbor.

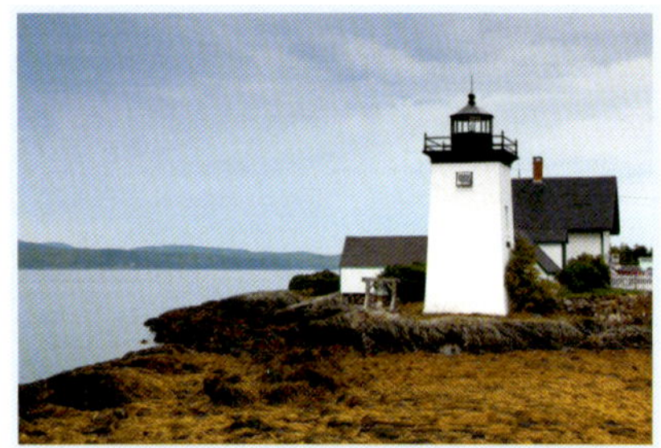
Grindle Point Lighthouse at low tide on Islesboro Island.

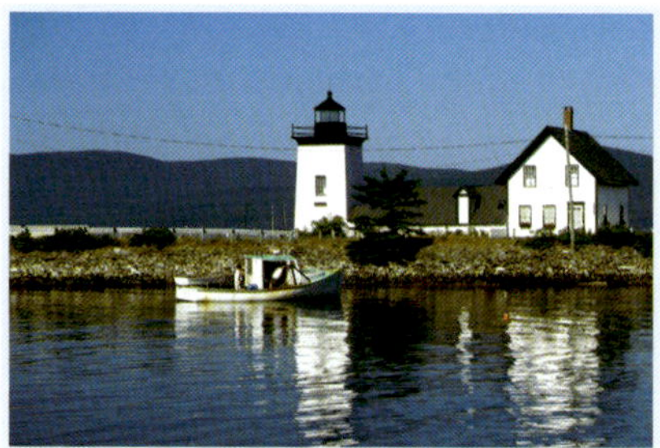
Grindle Point Light is still used by the lobstering community.

Keeper James Hall, previously at Matinicus Rock, was killed in 1916 from a rock-blasting accident at Grindle Point.

The light was deactivated in 1934 and replaced with a nearby skeleton tower. The keeper's house was converted to the Sailor's Memorial Museum in the late 1930s. Current museum volunteers have reported that things move by themselves during the night, and some tell of having seen an old, bearded man who disappears into the lighthouse wall. Many believe it is the early keeper, Captain Frances Grindle.

 **Exploring the grounds.** The ferry from Lincolnville Beach, in the small artist town of Lincolnville, allows you to bring a car or bike on the island. There is also a beach nearby. You'll find the lighthouse at the boat landing dock on Islesboro Island. It is privately owned, but the grounds are open to the public. The Sailor's Memorial Museum next to the lighthouse is open during the summer.

Fort Point Lighthouse

Stockton Springs (1836) • Latitude: 44° 28' 02" N • Longitude: 68° 48' 42" W

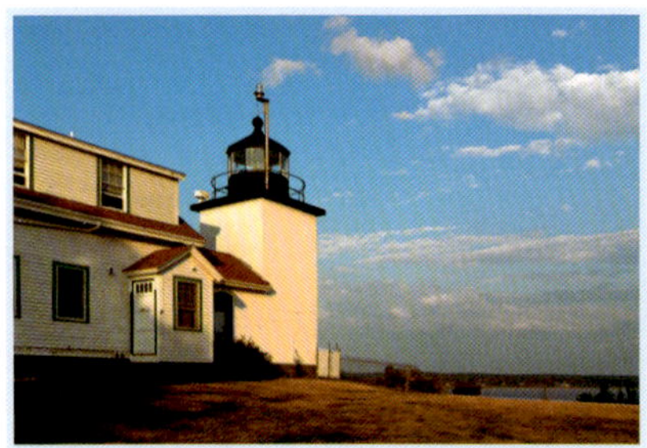
Fort Point Lighthouse guides traffic along the Penobscot River.

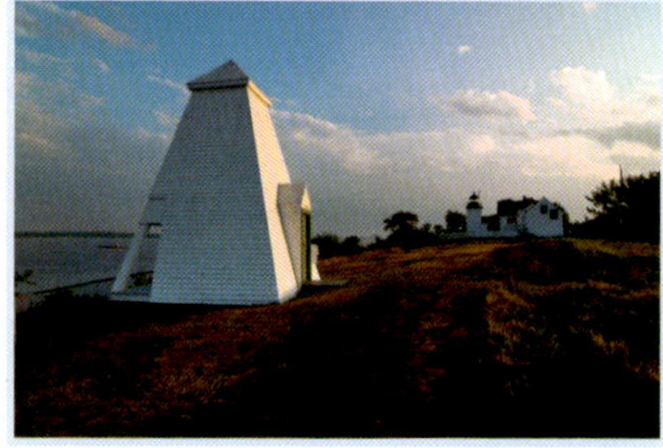
The pyramid-shaped bell tower is one of the few left in Maine.

A famous land and sea battle of disastrous proportions was fought here on August 14, 1799. Under the command of Colonel Paul Revere and Commodore Dudley Saltonstall, forty-three American ships were sunk and scattered all over this area of Penobscot Bay, and 1,000 soldiers fled from a smaller force of British ships and troops.

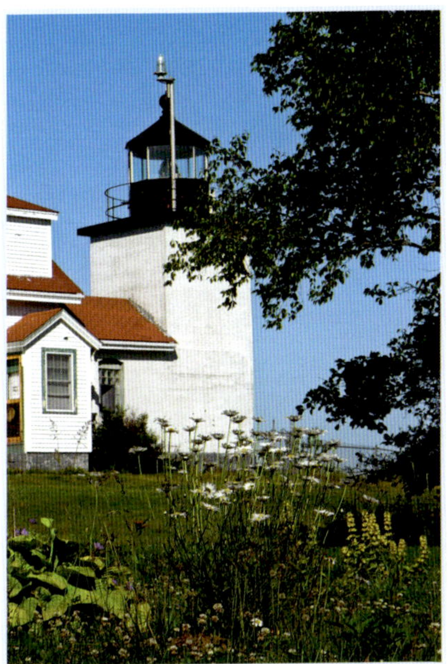

Fort Point Light is inside Fort Point State Park.

Fort Point Lighthouse's granite tower was built under President Andrew Jackson, and its first keeper was William Clewly, who owned the land and deeded it to the government. The poorly constructed lighthouse was rebuilt in 1857 and stands eighty-eight feet above the sea. The unique bell tower is one of the few left in Maine and is listed in the National Register of Historic Places. The original fog bell house still exists. The outside of the lighthouse is square, with a brick interior lining and circular stairs—the only one of its kind in Maine. The story goes that during construction of the square tower, a spiral staircase in good condition was found nearby, and the government carpenter adapted the plans to use it.

The luxury Fort Point Hotel was constructed near the lighthouse in 1872 to bring wealthy tourists to the area. The hotel had such luxuries as running water, gaslights, stables, a bowling alley, and two dance pavilions. The hope was that it would rival Bar Harbor, but it was unsuccessful and mysteriously burned to the ground four years later. The light was automated in 1988. Because of its desirable location, the lighthouse had only four lucky keepers stationed there from the 1880s into the 1930s. The Coast Guard leased it to the Maine State Bureau of Parks and Land in 1989, and it has since served as housing for the park supervisor. The deed was transferred to the state in 1998 under the Maine Lights Program.

Exploring the grounds. The lighthouse is on the western side entrance of the Penobscot River, off Fort Point Road inside Fort Point State Park. Lighthouse buildings and tower are a private residence, but the grounds are open to the public. A state park employee and his family occupy the keeper's dwelling all year, and you can walk the lighthouse grounds and photograph the unique fog bell house. The caretakers sometimes give tours in the summer. Visitors can picnic at Fort Point State Park and walk along the short trails there.

Directions. From Route 1 in Camden, go north through Belfast and Searsport. North of Searsport, turn right at the Stockton Springs sign. Take East Cape Road to Fort Point Road, turn left at the park's entrance, and continue to the parking area. If the park gate is closed, continue on Fort Point road to the "Y" intersection and bear left at a large dirt parking lot, proceeding past the entrance to Fort Point State Park. Take the next left and continue for about a mile to a small dirt parking lot. Those coming by boat can tie up at a 200-foot pier at Stockton Springs.

Dice Head Lighthouse

Castine (1828) • Latitude: 44° 22' 57" N • Longitude: 68° 49' 07" W

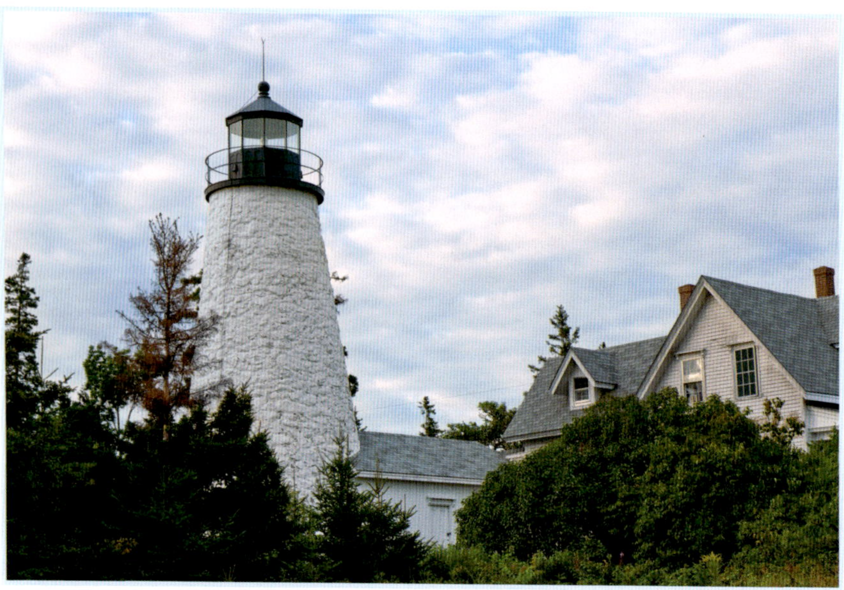

Dice Head Light in historic Castine.

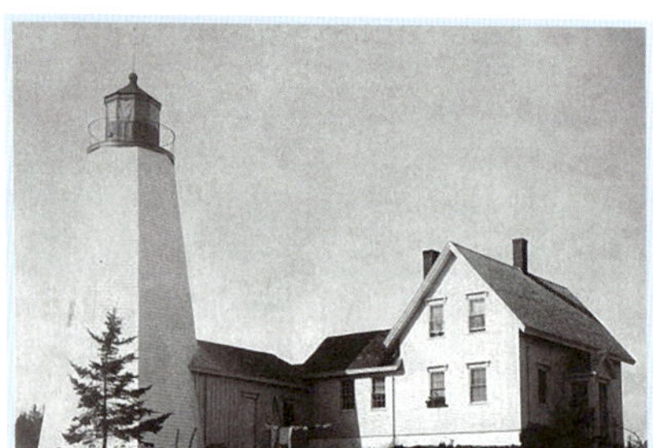

Vintage image with wooden tower. *Courtesy US Coast Guard.*

Castine was first settled in 1614 by French fur traders. Because of its strategic location, wars broke out occasionally, and it was occupied over the next sixty years at different times by the flags of the English of Plymouth Colony, France, and the Dutch. In 1676, Baron de St. Castine took possession and the town prospered, thanks to his marriage to the daughter of local Indian chief Madockawando.

During the Revolution, Paul Revere led his patriots on an unsuccessful attack on the British at Fort George. In the War of 1812, the British took over the US-built Fort Madison and controlled the area until the end of the war.

Many opulent nineteenth-century sea captains' homes are in Castine, as clipper ships left from here to embark on foreign trade. By the mid-1800s, Castine was the nation's second most prosperous town per capita, thanks to its six shipyards and lumber trade.

Dice Head Lighthouse guided Penobscot River mariners heading into the main lumber port of Bangor. The Dyce family sold the land to the government, and the name of the lighthouse evolved into Dice Head. Jacob Sherbourne, a former ship captain, was the beacon's first keeper.

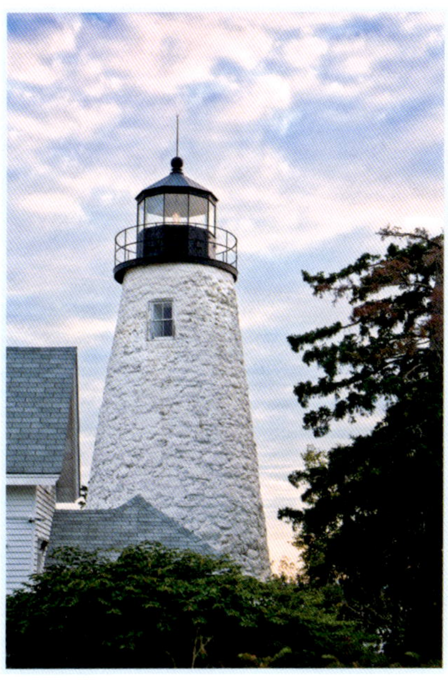

Sunset over Dice Head Lighthouse tower.

When Edward T. Spurling was appointed keeper in 1911, his six children were able to walk to school and attend classes with other children for the first time. Before that, his assignments had been at the remote Avery Rock and Franklin Island lights, where the children were home schooled. Spurling retired in 1930 and enjoyed life at Castine. When shipping decreased, a skeleton tower replaced it in 1935. Castine has maintained the keeper's house and property since 1937, and the lighthouse was also turned over to the town in 1956. In 1998, the lighthouse was renovated, but in 1999 a fire burned the roof and damaged the tower. The town repaired it, but in 2007 a microburst destroyed the 1935 skeletal tower. In October that same year, the Coast guard announced it would install a new optic in the tower to bring the lighthouse back to life after seventy-two years of inactivity.

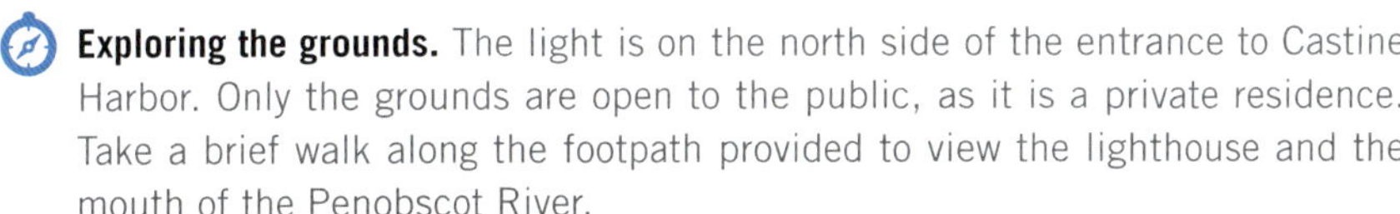

Exploring the grounds. The light is on the north side of the entrance to Castine Harbor. Only the grounds are open to the public, as it is a private residence. Take a brief walk along the footpath provided to view the lighthouse and the mouth of the Penobscot River.

Directions. From Route 1 in Orland, take Route 175 south to Route 166, past Fort George and the Maine Maritime Academy, to Battle Avenue. Park on the side of the road where you see the light.

Pumpkin Island Lighthouse

Little Deer Isle (1855) • Latitude: 44° 18' 33" N • Longitude: 68° 44' 33" W

Pumpkin Island Lighthouse had one of the earliest Fresnel lenses in Maine incorporated into its construction. It stands twenty-eight feet high with a black lantern. Its first keeper was John Chester Tibbetts, who owned the property and sold the island to the government. He stayed at the lighthouse until 1861, and then ran a local store, served as postmaster, and also served as deacon of a local church in Brooklin.

The popularity of powerboats kept keeper Charles Newman busy in the 1920s. Once he towed the disabled powerboat *Ark* to the station and helped repair its engine. In 1922, he rescued two women and two children adrift in their disabled powerboat, and in 1923, he put out a fire on another powerboat. He requested a

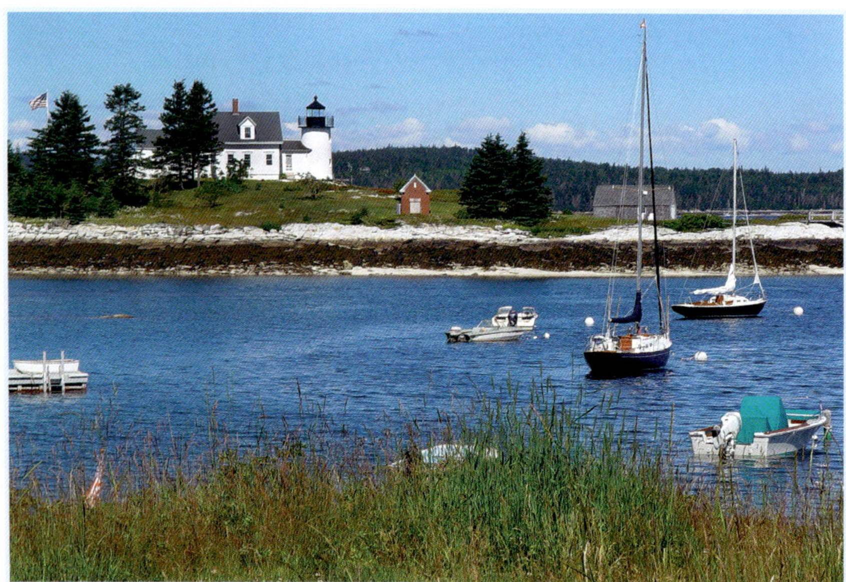

Pumpkin Island Light lies in a scenic fishing community.

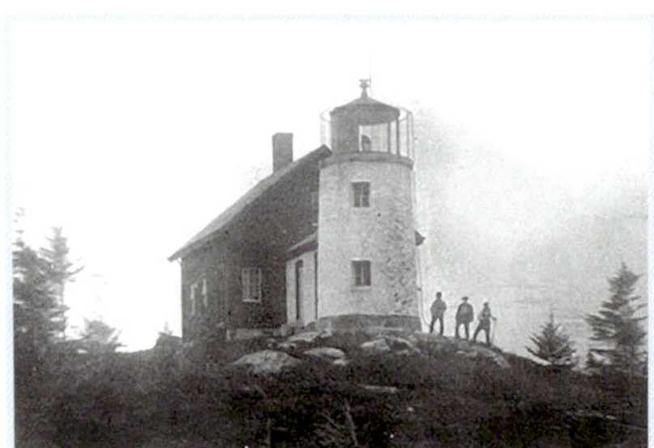

Vintage image. *Courtesy US Coast Guard.*

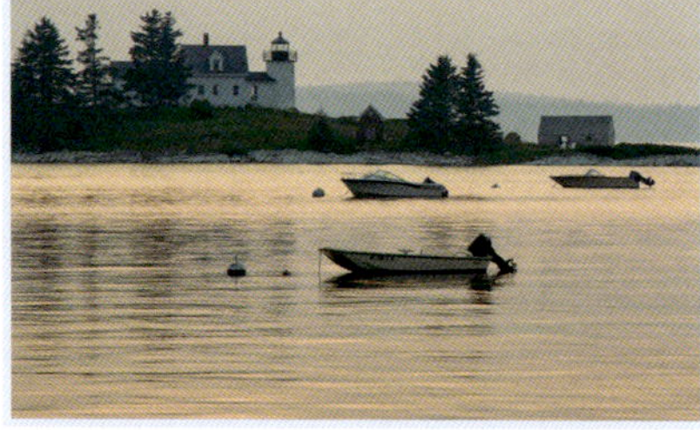

Pumpkin Island Lighthouse at dusk.

telephone to call for help in emergencies. This was prompted by an incident in 1922, when the bay froze and he fell into a hole in the ice and nearly froze to death. He had to put the telephone in at his own expense, but was happy to be connected.

Pumpkin Island's One-Legged Keeper. Amputee Charles Babson tended the beacon with one good leg from 1870 to 1902. During the Civil War at the battle of Fredericksburg, he had been shot and his leg was amputated. During his recuperation, he was mistakenly pronounced dead when he failed to move one day, and word went out to his family. Hours later, a nurse noticed one of his fingers moving and revived him. Meanwhile, his brother, William, was on his way to Rhode Island to retrieve Babson's body for burial. When he arrived and learned that his brother was alive, he started happily on his journey back to Brooklin. Unfortunately, William contracted pneumonia along the way and died weeks later.

Babson purchased land near the lighthouse and built a dining hall and a few tourist cottages, which became quite popular. The summer colony flourished along with the gentle keeper's popularity.

Directions. The lighthouse is a private residence off Route 15 on the northwestern entrance to Eggemoggin Reach. Good views of the lighthouse can be found at a turn-off spot before the road to the light. From Route 1 in Orland, take Route 175 south to Route 15. From Route 15, cross the Deer Island suspension bridge and turn right after the visitor station on Eggemoggin Road. Continue for almost three miles to the end. You'll find a turn-off spot where you are not allowed to go any farther (at the sign for the private path), but where you can still get a close view of the lighthouse.

Eagle Island Lighthouse

Deer Isle (1839) • Latitude: 44° 13' 04" N • Longitude: 68° 46' 04" W

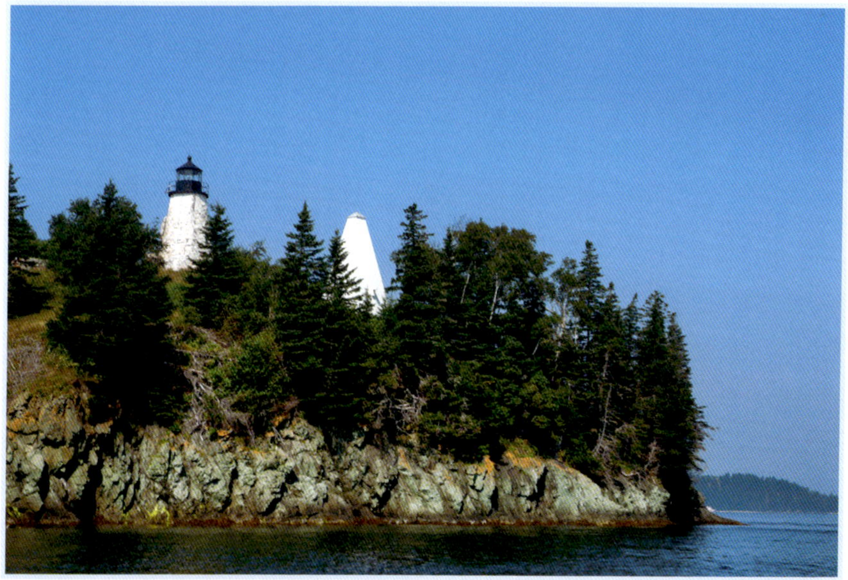

Eagle Island Lighthouse on Deer Isle.

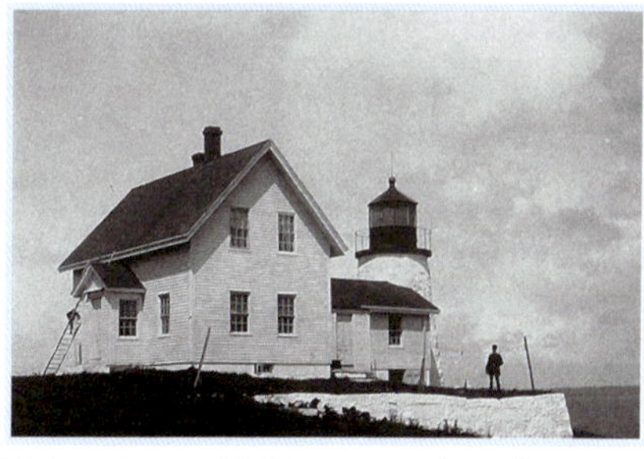

Vintage image 1856 construction. *Courtesy of US Coast Guard.*

On the east end of the island, Eagle Island Lighthouse guided vessels toward the Penobscot River and on to Bangor, America's leading lumber port in the nineteenth century. Its first keeper was John Spear, who had to supply his own boat. In 1857, with lumber supplies easily accessible, a wooden dwelling framed in hemlock and covered with clapboard pine replaced the original stone keeper's dwelling.

From 1883 to 1913, there were only two generations of keepers at the light. Keeper John Ball, and then his son Howard, tended the light until Howard died in 1913 from pneumonia while helping guide a fishing vessel to safety during a storm.

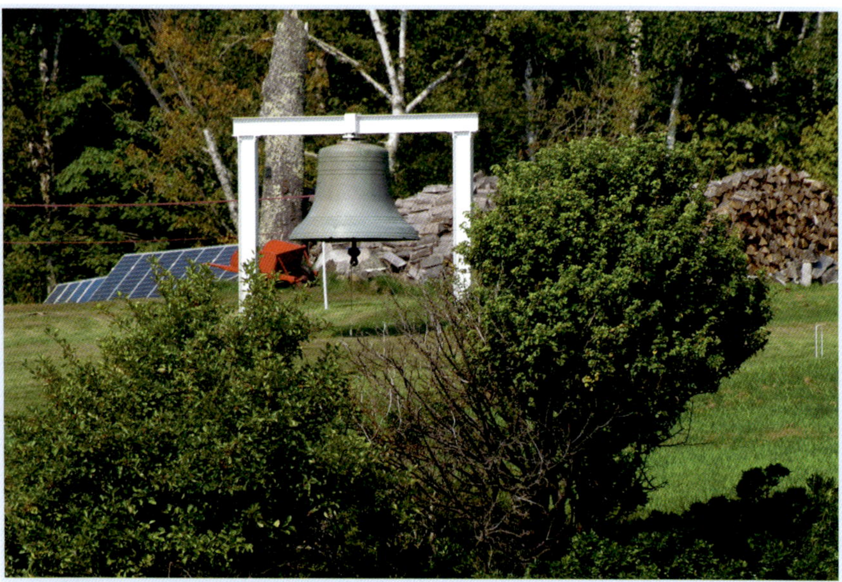

The fog bell was salvaged and placed on nearby Spruce Head Island.

The light was automated in 1959, and by 1964 all buildings except the tower were razed, leaving only the foundations behind, against fierce opposition from the locals.

When trying to remove the giant 4,200-pound fog bell, the Coast Guard demolition crew lost control and the bell slid down the cliff into the ocean. The crew didn't bother to retrieve the bell, and it was later hauled out by a local lobsterman. He towed it to nearby Great Spruce Head Island, where it still remains today.

Deer Island Thorofare (Mark Island) Lighthouse

Stonington (1857) • Latitude: 44° 08' 03" N • Longitude: 68° 42' 08" W

With a growing fishing industry and prosperous granite quarrying in the area, Deer Island Thorofare became a busy waterway in the nineteenth century. The lighthouse helped mariners negotiate the waters near Stonington along the western approach to the Thorofare. Thomas Small was appointed the lighthouse's first keeper, and he worked there until he was injured in a fall from a ship's rigging. He and his wife had fourteen energetic children.

Keeper Allan Holt was known for his many rescues of stranded boats on Mark Island, which included motorboats, lobster boats, and the steamer *Minnehah*. He is also credited with helping to float the stranded schooner *Sarah and Lucy* when it ran aground on nearby Andrews Island.

In February 1935, keeper Elmer E.Conary had an apparent heart attack and needed to be transported to the mainland. A tugboat was sent out to navigate through the frozen ice floes. It became stuck in Stonington Harbor, leaving no choice but to have Conary transported by lifeboat through the harbor. Conary and his

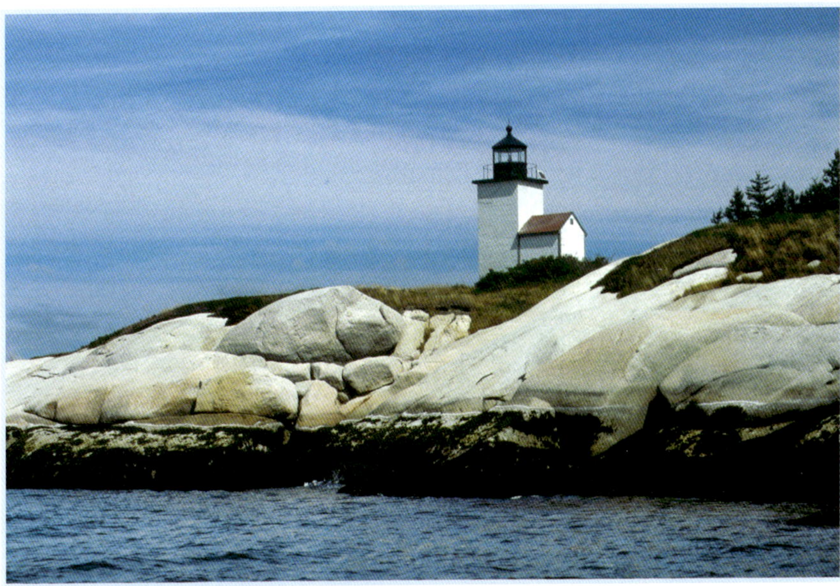

Deer Island Thorofare (Mark Island) Light.

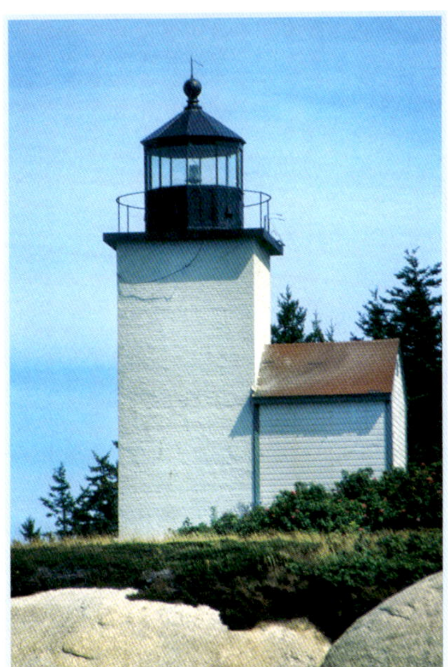

Only the lighthouse tower remains, and is still in use.

wife, Gertrude, were also known for equally splitting work and household duties, which in addition to the lighthouse tasks, involved growing potatoes and canning wild strawberries for their food supply.

In the summer of 1946, keeper Ralph Stanley Andrews slipped while boarding a dinghy from a motorboat and became temporarily paralyzed from the waist down. His wife and stepmother cared for the light until a relief keeper arrived at the station three days later. Eleven days after the incident, the keeper was able to return to his duties on crutches.

On September 10, 1958, a battery charger in the basement of the dwelling exploded, causing a fire that spread quickly. Firefighters from Stonington and members of the Coast Guard cutter *Laurel* managed to save the brick light tower, but the dwelling was a total loss. Since marine traffic had decreased, the Coast Guard decided to automate the station rather than rebuild the dwelling.

Isle au Haut Lighthouse

Isle au Haut (1907) • Latitude: 44° 03' 54" N • Longitude: 68° 39' 06" W

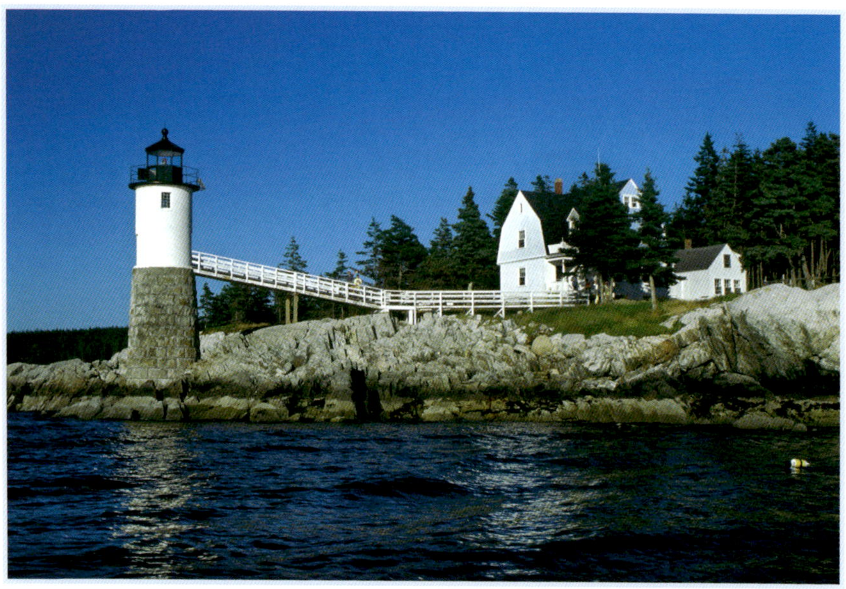

Isle au Haut Lighthouse lies near part of the island that is Acadia National Park.

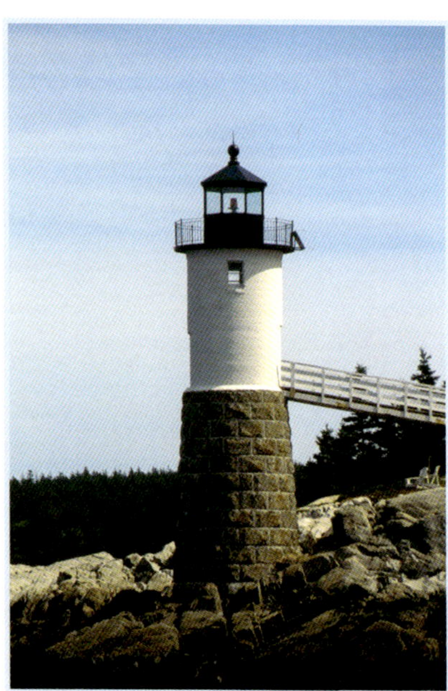

Isle au Haut Lighthouse station promotes conservation efforts and technologies.

Isle au Haut is still rustic, with only about fifty year-round residents, and most houses don't have electricity. It was the nation's last community to stop using crank-style telephones.

Isle au Haut Lighthouse guided mariners away from the rocky shoreline along the island, most of which is part of the Acadia National Park system, and was the final cylindrical brick light tower constructed in Maine. Land for the station on Robinson Point was purchased from Charles E. Robinson, and the light was called Robinson Point Lighthouse, although today it is more widely known as Isle au Haut Lighthouse. Robinson's Point leads into a shelter between Isle au Haut and Kimball Island where boats can find refuge during a storm. The Victorian keeper's house sits atop a rocky ledge connected to the lighthouse by a walkway and is popular today as a bed and breakfast. The first keeper was Frank Holbrook, previously stationed at Matinicus Rock. He stayed until 1922 and was replaced by the only other keeper, Harry Smith, who stayed on until it was automated in 1933. At that point, long-time resident Charles Robinson repurchased the station. For the next fifty years, generations of the Robinson family would spend their summers at the lighthouse. In 1986, Jeff and Judi Burke purchased the property, minus the tower. Judi was the daughter of a former Coast Guard keeper at Highland Light (Cape Cod Light), in Massachusetts. The Burkes converted the keeper's house into the Keeper's House Inn, and Jeff wrote a book that chronicled their remarkable efforts to make the place comfortable for visitors. They stayed for over twenty years and sold the property to Dr. Marshall Chapman, an associate professor of geology at Morehead State University. The keeper's house and lighthouse were then converted to a self-sustaining property. To quote from Chapman's website, "The property is an ecologist's dream. Powered by state of the art photovoltaics and a 30-kilowatt generator, fed by unlimited crystal-clear water drawn from the sea by the magic of a reverse osmosis system, and a garden-setting sewage treatment system using peat bogs and flower beds. This alternative yet historic home allows you to live with respect for the rest of the world." Chapman asked the Burkes to stay on as consultants, and they agreed.

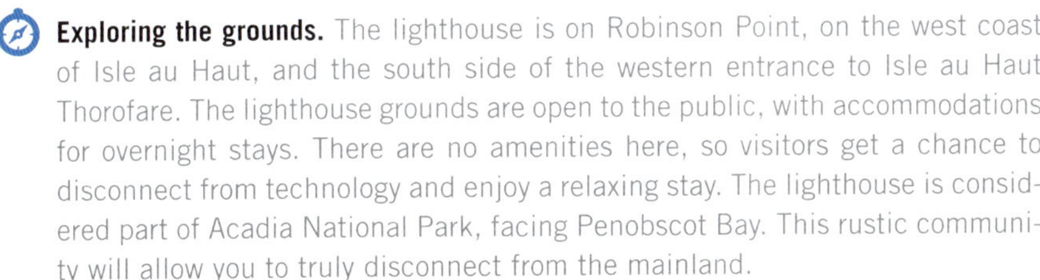

Exploring the grounds. The lighthouse is on Robinson Point, on the west coast of Isle au Haut, and the south side of the western entrance to Isle au Haut Thorofare. The lighthouse grounds are open to the public, with accommodations for overnight stays. There are no amenities here, so visitors get a chance to disconnect from technology and enjoy a relaxing stay. The lighthouse is considered part of Acadia National Park, facing Penobscot Bay. This rustic community will allow you to truly disconnect from the mainland.

Directions to the Isle au Haut Ferry at Stonington, and the Lighthouse. Isle au Haut is accessible by the Isle au Haut Ferry (mail boat) from Stonington (no cars are allowed on the ferry or the island). The mail boat journey takes about forty minutes. To get to the dock at Stonington for the trip to Isle au Haut, take I-295 north and I-95 to Augusta, then pick up Route 3 to Belfast. Take Route 1 & 3 east through Bucksport to Orland, and then follow Route 15 south to Stonington. I- 95 to Bangor then 395 to Brewer, and then Route 15 south to Stonington, where you'll find the mail boat dock. When you reach the landing dock on Isle au Haut, the lighthouse is about a mile hike along the shoreline with clear views.

Attractions along Mid-Coast Maine and Islands in Penobscot Bay

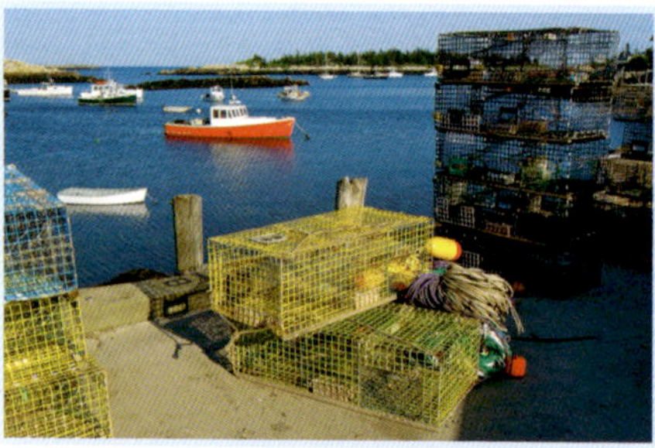

Maine's Island communities have been lobstering and fishing for generations.

Most visitors will find that exploring Maine's island communities is a unique, soulful experience that local fishermen and artists have enjoyed for generations. Its mainland coastal communities have a friendly connection with their island neighbors, as they share resources. Many of these islands haven't changed in decades and allow visitors to reconnect with a simpler lifestyle. Route 1 acts as a ribbon between predominantly rural communities, where much of the attraction is the scenery and wildlife.

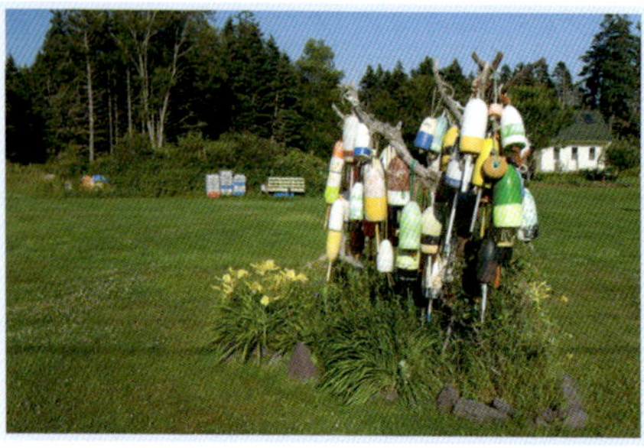

Matinicus islanders decorate their properties with buoys and fish nets.

Maine State Ferry Service out of Rockland ferries passengers to Matinicus Island a few times a month. As a result of the irregular ferry schedule and the island's remote location twenty-two miles from the mainland, there are few tourists here. There are a couple of "inns," which are typically private homes available to rent. There are no amenities, and little has changed here since the 1950s. As you walk around you'll find lobster buoys and fishnets used for all kinds of decorations on islanders' properties. The island is about two miles long, and about a mile wide. There are no paved roads, and the residents are very friendly. The cold, clear waters around this island have the greatest lobster beds in the world.

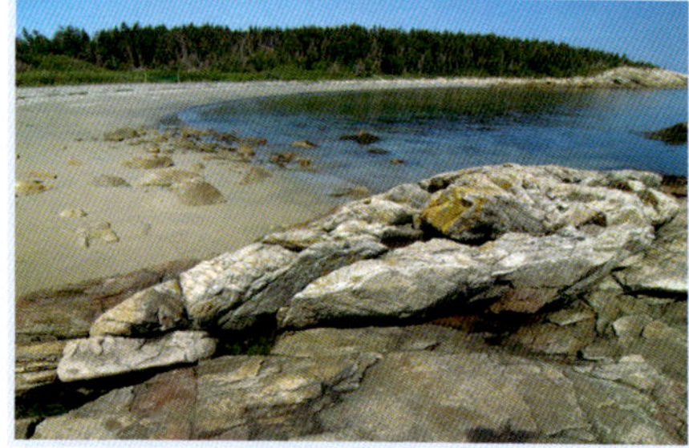

Beaches on Matinicus Island are quiet and the water is very cold.

There are two fairly large beaches on Matinicus Island: Markey Beach and South Sandy Beach. These are unusually sandy beaches nestled between rock formations that jut out into the ocean. It's like having your own private beach, though the water is very cold, even in the summer. You'll find plenty of hiking trails, isolated sandy and pebble beaches, coves, rocky bluffs, open fields, and woodlands, along with many species of birds. Many islanders sell lobsters, flowers, vegetables, grilled food, and music CDs from their homes. There are no restaurants, but the home-based Eva's Bakery has great pastries. In addition to a one-room schoolhouse for island children grades one through eight, there is a tiny post office, church, and phone service.

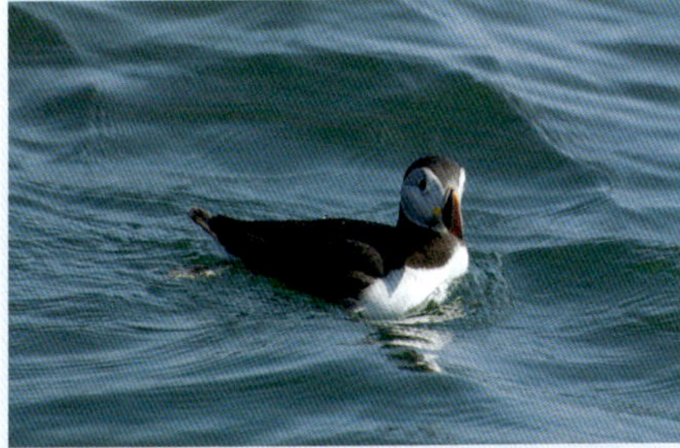

Matinicus Rocks Island protects a puffin colony.

Matinicus Rock, five miles from Manticus Island, is a bird sanctuary, particularly for a puffin colony that nests there from June to July. It is also where the famous lighthouse resides. Public boats are only allowed to circle the island. **Matinicus Excursions** out of Rockland provides nature tours to Matinicus Rock, Matinicus Island, and the surrounding islands on their lighthouse tours.

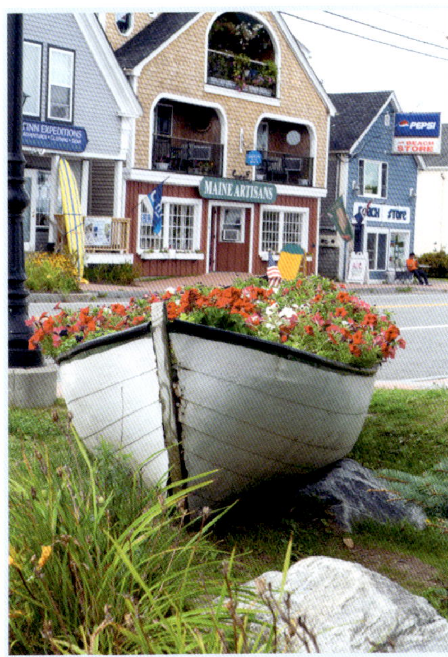

Coastal towns like Lincolnville are home to many artisans.

Vinalhaven Island is a fishing community with lots of small beaches and clear, spring-fed quarries (Booth's and Lawson's Quarries). About fifteen miles from the mainland, it is Maine's largest year-round island. Hike and picnic along Lane's Island Preserve, and explore town parks like Armbrust Hill, Grimes Park, Narrows Park, Isle au Haut Mountain, Tip Toe Mountain, and Arey's Neck Woods.

The auto ferry from Lincolnville Beach in the small artist town of Lincolnville takes you to the thirteen-mile long picturesque island of Islesboro, where you can enjoy a public beach, Grindle Point Lighthouse, and the Sailor's Memorial Museum next door. Step back in time and enjoy ice cream at Dark Harbor Store in the fishing village of Dark Harbor. The island also has some of the best sailing conditions around. Those seeking a rustic camping experience can kayak or canoe out of Islesboro Island's Gilkey Harbor to nearby **Warren Island State Park**. There are only ten campsites (with no amenities), so call ahead for reservations.

Quick stop! Perry's Nut House (founded 1927) is all about having fun while you're grabbing your favorite peanuts, jams, trinkets, gifts, or fudge. You'll be greeted by a giant stuffed gorilla and lots of crazy animals and amusements.

In Belfast on Route 1, you'll find great waterfront views along the harbor in historic Heritage Park. Here you'll also find interactive street art, galleries, boutiques, restaurants, and historic homes. Take in a show at the **Cold Comfort Theater** or take a two-hour **lobster boat tour** with Belfast Bay Company aboard the *Clara K.*, a traditional wooden lobster boat. For those who love sailing, the schooner *Timberwind*, first launched in 1931, provides a two-hour tour and a sunset tour out of Belfast Harbor.

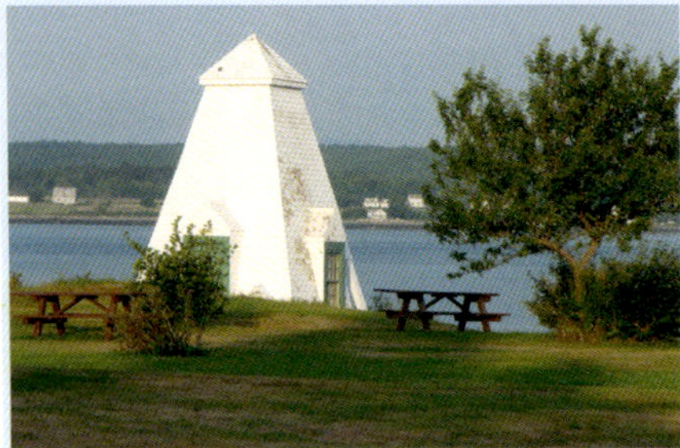

Fort Point State Park has great views by the lighthouse and pyramidal fog bell house.

Coast to Islands Sailing Charters provides dinner, yoga, and Sail and Hike cruises out of Thompson's Wharf in Belfast aboard the *Miss Nina*, a sixty-one-foot wooden pilothouse ketch sailboat. The Sail and Hike Cruise will take you to Fort Point State Park, where you may be provided a guided tour of Fort Point Lighthouse.

Fort Point Lighthouse lies within the old seaport artist community of Searsport, home of the **Penobscot Marine Museum**. This is Maine's oldest maritime museum with a series of buildings, including one that resembles a typical sea captain's residence. Relax at Fort Point State Park, which is part of the lighthouse grounds, and walk along some of the short trails there. Lighthouse tours inside the distinct tower are provided by the caretakers during the summer months. You can also tour the nearby ruins of Fort Pownall, a French fort built in 1759 during the French and Indian Wars.

Heading up Route 1 along the coast and following the Penobscot River, you'll come upon two amazing architectural structures, the **Penobscot Narrows Bridge and Observatory**, and **Fort Knox**, one of the best-preserved fortifications on the New England seacoast. Fort Knox was established in 1844 to protect the Penobscot River valley. The bridge is the same design as the Zakim Bridge in Boston and sits 135 feet above the river. At the bridge, take a one-minute ride on the fastest elevator in northern New England to the top of the tallest public bridge-observatory in the world. The observatory, at the top of one of the bridge towers, is a dizzying 420 feet high!

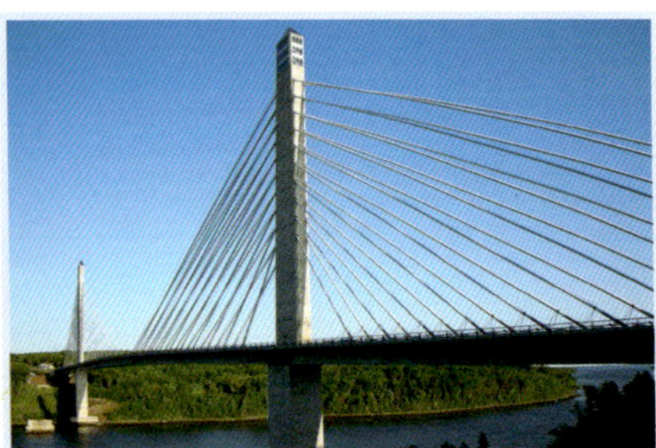

Penobscot Narrows Bridge and Observatory Tower rises 420 feet high.

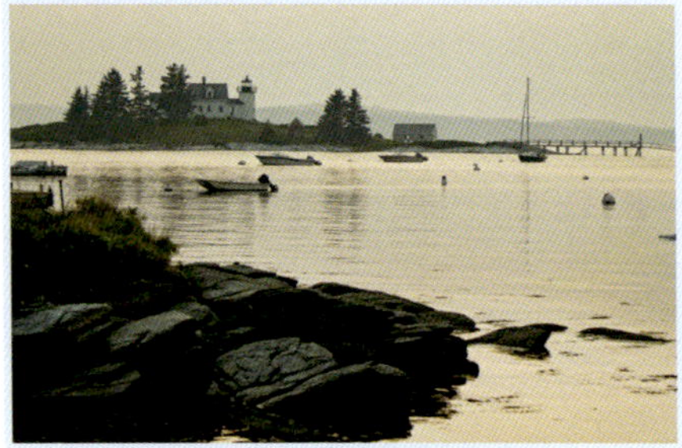

Little Deer Isle at dusk with Pumpkin Island Lighthouse in the background.

Heading down Route 175 to Route 166 off Route 1, Castine is one of the oldest towns in America, a quiet seaside village where you can tour the ruins of Fort George and Fort Madison or visit art galleries. More than 100 historic markers can be found in this town. Take a walk and enjoy its colorful eighteenth and nineteenth architecture or tour some of the historic museums operated by the **Castine Historical Society**, headquartered at the Abbott School, a restored schoolhouse. The Wilson Museum has exhibits of ancient farming and home equipment, and you can find an old blacksmith shop nearby. Castine's Maine Maritime Academy allows visitors to explore the *State of Maine*, a 500-foot naval research ship, when it is docked.

At Dice Head Lighthouse, take a brief walk along the public footpath. The Bagaduce River Watershed is ideal for kayaking and canoeing. Wadsworth Cove and Backshore Beach are also good places to relax.

Pumpkin Island Lighthouse is near Little Deer Isle, where visitors will find little has changed over the last fifty years. There are numerous fishing villages all around this area of islands with lobstering and fishing as the main industry. Because of its quaint untouched beauty, many artists and photographers live in or frequent this area. Causeway Beach is open to the public for free.

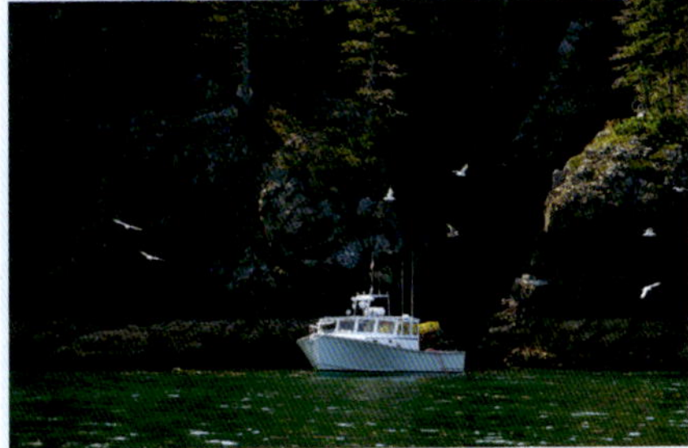

Lobster boat near island cliffs.

Part of Deer Isle, the town of Sunset is quite remote and there are lots of places to bike and hike without worrying about traffic. It is also a great launching point from which to explore the area's many small islands by kayak or canoe. Bridges also connect some of these islands. Excursion trips around the islands are offered via the **Eagle Island Mail Boat** (Sunset Bay Company) from the town of Sunset. The boat will pass by the Eagle Island Lighthouse en route to delivering mail to several islands in the area. The ride is about two hours and they are happy to give you time to take pictures of the lighthouse. To learn the art of lobster trap hauling or simply take a leisurely sunset or scenic tour, book a ride with **Penobscot Lobster Tours**.

Quick stop! Check out **Nervous Nellie's Jams and Jellies**. Not only can you get great-tasting jams, you can also pick up gift items such as a glass pot buoy, pottery, Nervous Nellie storybooks, and birdhouses. While you're there, explore the art sculptures made of industrial scrap, wood, and all kinds of materials by owner Peter Beerits.

Stonington is known as one of the most quiet, unspoiled fishing villages in Maine, and its most beautiful location offers a haven for artists and their galleries. It lies on Deer Isle and is easily accessible by a bridge from the mainland. The 100-year-old **Stonington Opera House** provides films, music, and theater year-round, including the Deer Isle Jazz Festival in early August. There are three large conservation areas with trails through mossy forests and along the shoreline maintained by the Island Heritage Trust. These include the Settlement Quarry off Oceanville Road, Crockett Cove

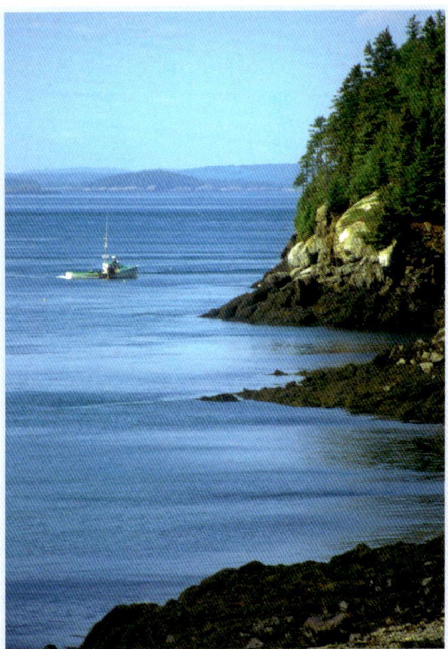

Isle au Haut shoreline in Acadia National Park.

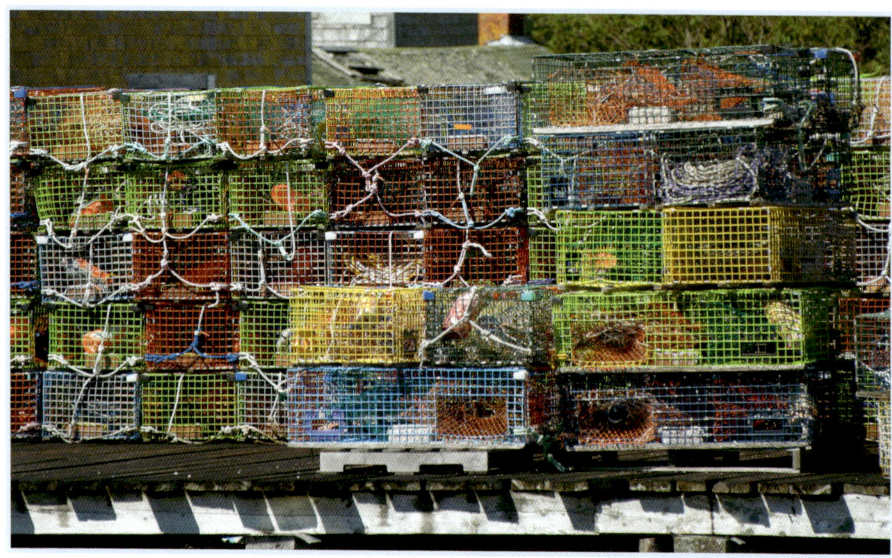

Lobstering is a dominant industry around the islands.

Woods off Route 15A, and Holt Mill Pond Reserve off Airport Road. You can also visit the Wreck Island Preserve and other island preserves that lie between Deer Isle and Isle au Haut.

Lighthouse Trail Weekend, sponsored by the Deer Isle Chamber, takes place mid-September and features tours to eight lighthouses. The **Isle au Haut Mail Boat** provides the main boat tour, along with daily cruises to Isle au Haut Island year-round. One Sunday a month, the mail boat offers a four-hour tour of six lighthouses.

About half of Isle au Haut is federal parkland under **Acadia National Park**, with plenty of trails and picturesque scenic views of this very rustic area. The other half is privately owned, supporting summer residents and a year-round fishing community. To camp in the Acadia Park, reservations must be made in advance. There are seventeen miles of hiking and biking trails on this island, along with nature preserves, but bring your own supplies, as there are few amenities here. If you are looking for a true rustic experience, to get away from modern civilization, this is the place.

Contacts for Mid-Coast Maine Attractions in Penobscot Bay

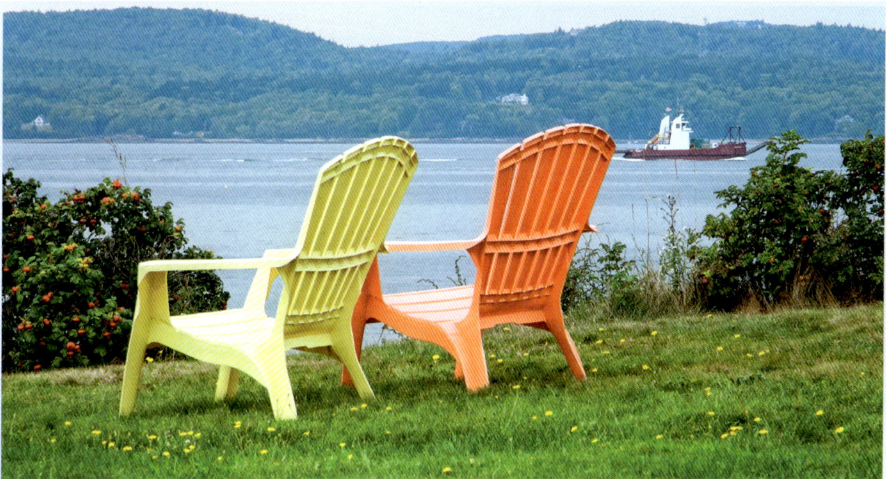
Relaxing on Islesboro Island.

Vinalhaven Chamber, Vinalhaven
vinalhaven.org

Warren Island State Park, Lincolnville
(207) 287-3824
maine.gov/doc/parks

Beacon Preservation, North Haven
(203) 400-9565
beaconpreservation.org

Lobster Boat Tour, Belfast
(207) 323-1443
belfastbaycompany.com

Schooner Timberwind, Belfast
(207) 619-0654
mainedaysail.com

Coast to Islands Sailing, Belfast
(207) 505-1618
sailingmissnina.com

Cold Comfort Theater, Belfast
(207) 930-7244
coldcomforttheater.com

Perry's Nut House, Belfast
(888) 673-7797
perrysnuthouse.com

Penobscot Museum, Searsport
(207) 548-2529
penobscotmarinemuseum.org

Observatory and Fort Knox, Prospect
(207) 469-6553
maine.gov/mdot/pnbo

Castine Historical Society, Castine
(207) 326-4118
castinehistoricalsociety.org

Lighthouse Trail Weekend, Deer Isle
(207) 348-6124
deerisle.com

Nervous Nellie's Jam, Deer Isle
(800) 777-6845
nervousnellies.com

Penobscot Tours, Deer Isle
(207) 348-3004
penobscotlobsterboattours.com

Stonington Opera House, Stonington
(207) 367-2788
operahousearts.org

Eagle Island Mail Boat, Sunset
(207) 701-9316
eagleislandrentals.com

Isle au Haut Mail Boat, Stonington
(207) 376-5193
isleauhaut.com

Isle au Haut Keeper's House, Isle au Haut
(207) 335-2990
keepershouse.com

Isle au Haut Acadia Park Camping, Isle au Haut
(207) 288-3338

Lighthouse Cruises and Ferries to Islands in Penobscot Bay

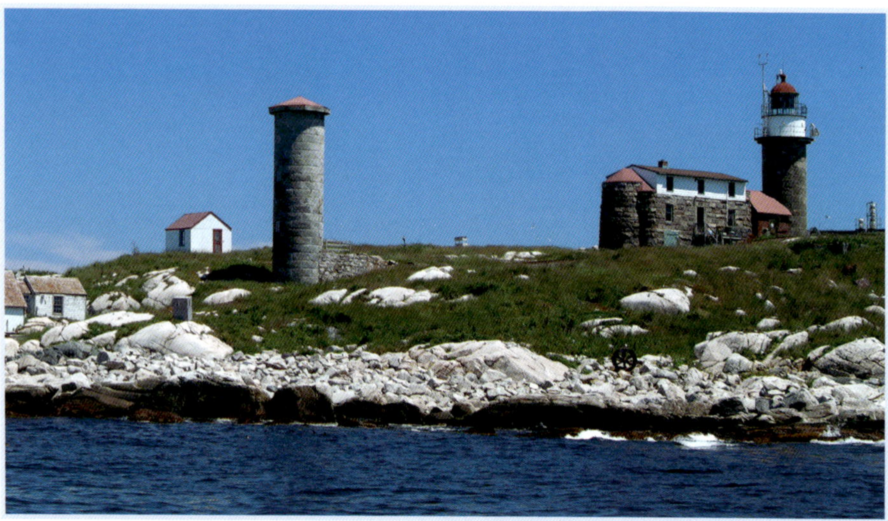

Matinicus Rocks Lighthouse is five miles from Matinicus Island.

Matinicus Excursions

Water taxi from the mainland at Rockland, chartered lighthouse trips, and other trips around Matinicus Rock involving bird watching, seals, and other marine life. You can get great views of Matinicus Rock Light from the boat.

- Matinicus
- (207) 691-9030
- matinicusexcursions.com
- **Lighthouses:** Owl's Head, Rockland Breakwater, Rockland Harbor, Heron Neck, Matinicus Rock, Saddleback Ledge, Isle au Haut, Goose Rocks, Browns Head

Maine State Ferry Service

- Islesboro Terminal, Islesboro
- (207) 734-6935

Ferry from Lincolnville to Islesboro

- Lincolnville
- (207) 789-5611
- **Lighthouse:** Grindle Point

Old Quarry Ocean Adventures

Beside puffin, natural history, sunset, and eco-cruises, they offer annual lighthouse cruises on East Penobscot Bay, Blue Hill Bay, and East Coast Bay, which includes Matinicus Rock. Cruises are seven and eight hours long, weather permitting.

- 130 Settlement Road, Stonington
- (207) 367-8977
- oldquarry.com
- **Lighthouses:** Isle au Haut, Saddleback Ledge, Browns Head, Goose Rocks, Eagle Island, Pumpkin Island, Matinicus Rocks (possible), Deer Isle Thorofare (Mark Island), Burnt Coat, Mount Desert Rock, Great Duck, Bass Harbor, Baker Island, Bear Island, and Blue Hill Bay

Guided Island Tours

- Capt. Walt Reed, Deer Isle
- (207) 348-6789
- guidedislandtours.com
- **Lighthouses:** Saddelback Ledge, Deer Isle Thorofare (Mark Island), Eagle Island

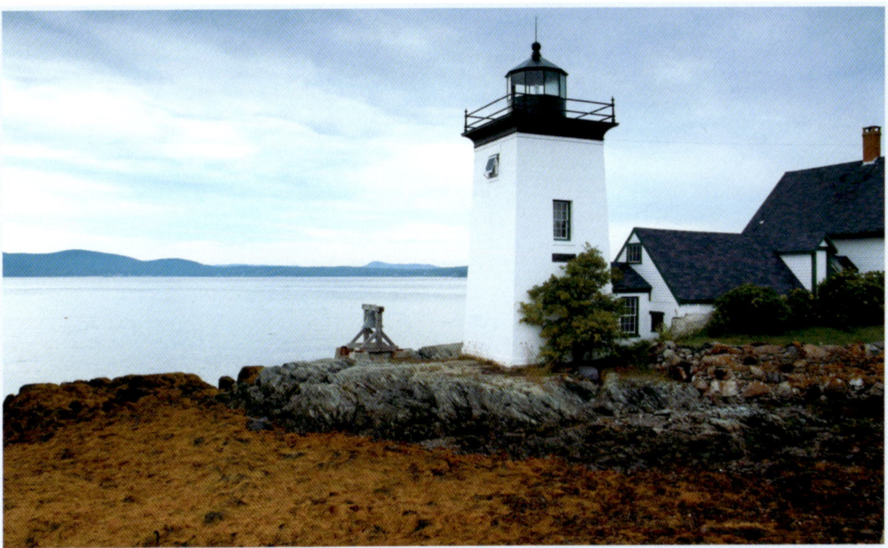

Grindle Point light on Islesboro Island at ferry dock.

Eagle Island Mail Boat

Leaves from Sylvester's Cove in Deer Isle and passes close by the Eagle Island Lighthouse six days a week during the summer.

Sunset Bay Company, Eagle Island, Sunset

(207) 348-9316

Lighthouses: Eagle Island

Sea Venture Custom Boat Tours

Personalized, specific chartered boat tours you can enjoy with a minimum of passengers. Lighthouse cruises last three to six hours and cover twenty to sixty miles.

Capt. Winston Shaw, Bar Harbor

(207) 288-3355

svboattours.com

Lighthouses: Pond Island, Petit Manan, Prospect Harbor, Mark Island, Egg Rock, Baker Island, Bear Island, Bass Harbor Head, Great Duck, Burnt Coat Harbor, Blue Hill Bay, Pumpkin Island

Isle au Haut Boat Company

Sea Breeze Avenue, Stonington

(207) 367-6516 or Fax: (207) 367-6503

isleauhaut.com

Lighthouse: Isle au Haut

Waterfront Directions

Most wharfs and town landings are right off Route 1.

Thompson's Wharf in Belfast

From Route 1 north, turn right on Northport Avenue, then left on Church Street.

Castine Harbor

From Route 1 north in Bucksport, turn right on Route 166 south. After about fifteen miles, bear right on Sea Street.

Stonington Public Landing

From Route 1 north, turn right onto Route 15 north, then right onto Route 199 south. Turn left onto Route 175 south, and continue onto Route 176, then continue as Route 176 becomes Route 15 south. At the end of Route 15 south, in Stonington, turn left on Seabreeze Avenue, then take a sharp right onto Colwells Lane.

Deer Isle

From Route 1 in Bucksport, take Route 15 (Front Ridge Road). Turn right on Route 199 south (North Penobscot Road), then left on Route 175 south. Merge onto Route 15 south, and continue for about eighteen miles.

Scenic Flights

Penobscot Island Air

Charters a variety of lighthouse viewing flights.

Knox County Regional Airport, Owls Head

(207) 596-7500 or (207) 542-4944

penobscotislandair.net

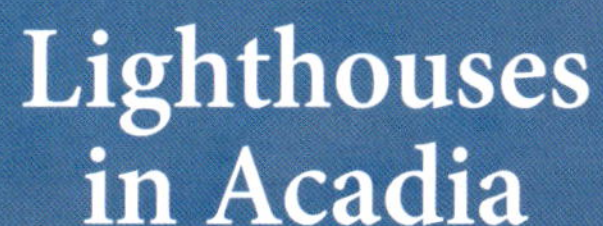

Lighthouses in Acadia

Tremont, Bar Harbor, Mount Desert Island, and surrounding islands

Mount Desert Island became an international tourist attraction in the nineteenth century as a main component of the Acadia National Park system. There are many islands in this area, including the Cranberry Islands, Baker's Island, Bear Island, Swan's Island, Great Duck Island, Egg Rock, and Mount Desert Rock. A series of lighthouses were built on and around Mount Desert Island to accommodate the influx of international and American tourists from the sea and guide mariners through Blue Hill Bay, Frenchman Bay, and Somes Sound. The term Down East (Downeast to Mainers) refers to the area from Acadia National Park and Bar Harbor to Lubec at the Canadian Border. Years ago, sailors hauling cargo to northeastern New England observed that the prevailing winds came from the southwest, pushing their schooners downwind in an easterly direction—hence the term Down East.

Bass Harbor Lighthouse is one of the most photographed beacons in New England.

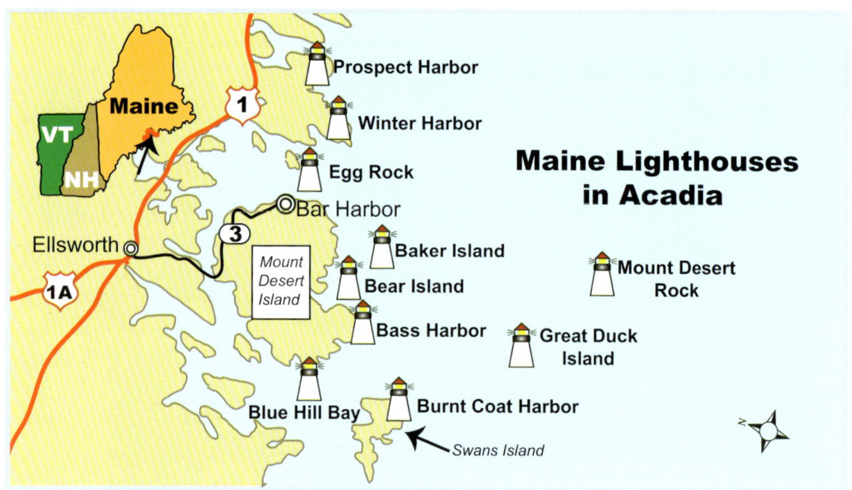

Map of lighthouses in Acadia.

Blue Hill Bay Lighthouse

Brooklin (1857) • Latitude: 44° 14' 56" N • Longitude: 68° 29' 55" W

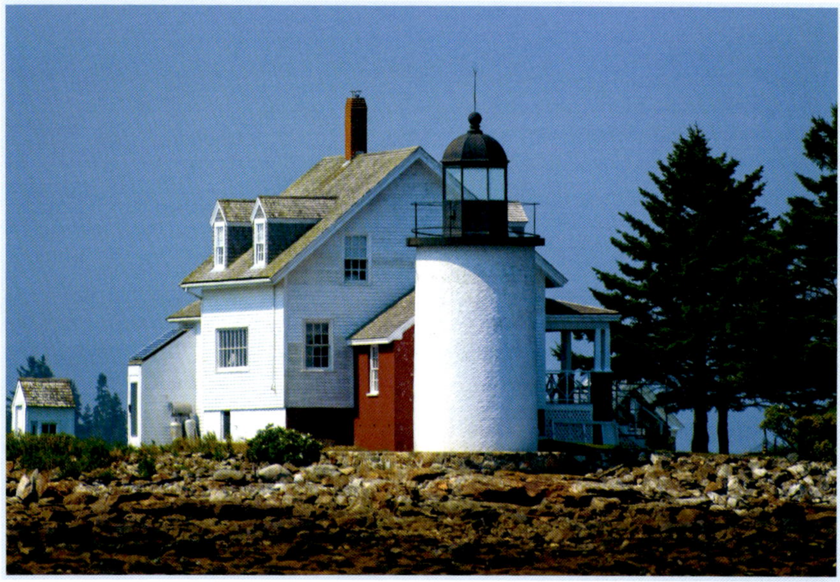

Blue Hill Bay Lighthouse.

With the increasing lumber trade from Ellsworth, a lighthouse was built on a low-lying strip of land called Green Island to guide mariners between Penobscot Bay and Blue Hill Bay. Blue Hill Bay Lighthouse, sometimes referred to as Sand Island Light or Eggemoggin Light, had the luxury of a rather fancy keeper's quarters with an attached barn, boathouse, outhouse, oil house, and a huge rain-collecting

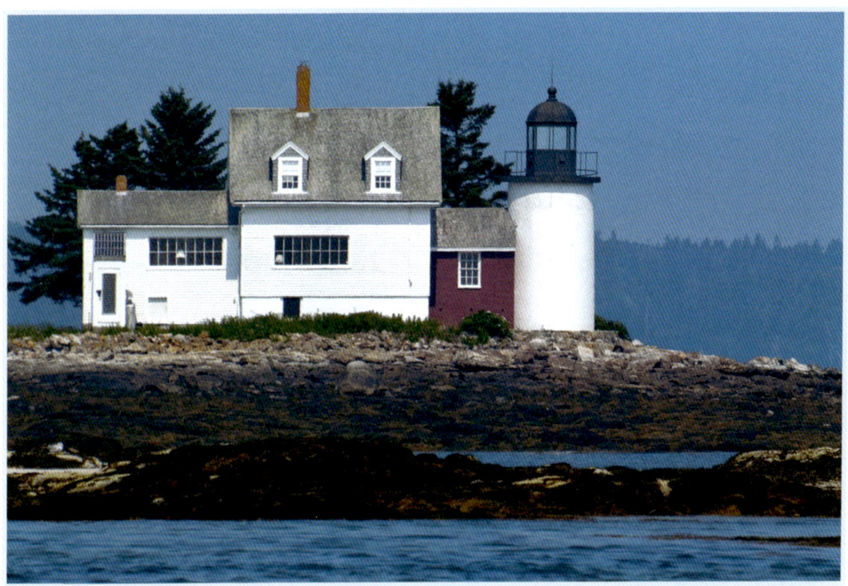

At low tide, the keepers' cows would be walked between islands to graze.

cistern for fresh water. As the island was rocky with little vegetation, keepers would use neighboring islands to graze sheep and cows during the warm months. In the 1890s, the five children of keeper Roscoe Lopaus were schooled by a teacher who also boarded on the island.

In the early 1920s, Keeper Roscoe Chandler's two teenage children tended his farm in nearby Monroe on the mainland. They would walk their cow from Monroe to the light station during low tide so it could be milked at the house. They would stop at a local farm along the way and swap some of the cow's milk for lodging and a meal. When Chandler developed a bad case of ulcers and required lots of fresh milk, two cows were purchased and brought to nearby Flye Island. The cows could be walked between the two islands during low tide. Sometimes during thunderstorms, they would try to swim from Flye Island to the lighthouse station. A family member had to go out in a boat to steer the animals back to the island to graze.

One foggy day, keeper Chandler heard four blows on a whistle nearby, which indicated a vessel in trouble. A skipper had made a turn too soon and was not in imminent danger, but simply lost. Chandler shouted directions to the ship and the vessel went on its way. The side-wheeler *J. T. Morse* was a familiar sight at the Blue Hill Bay Lighthouse, as it provided daily passenger and freight service between Rockland and Bar Harbor, and sometimes dropped off supplies for the keepers. There were no phones on the island in the 1920s, so when the keeper was needed on shore, a designated local on the mainland would hang a black suit or dress outside the house as a signal.

Bass Harbor Lighthouse

Tremont, Mount Desert Island (1858) • Latitude: 44° 13' 19" N • Longitude: 68° 20' 14" W

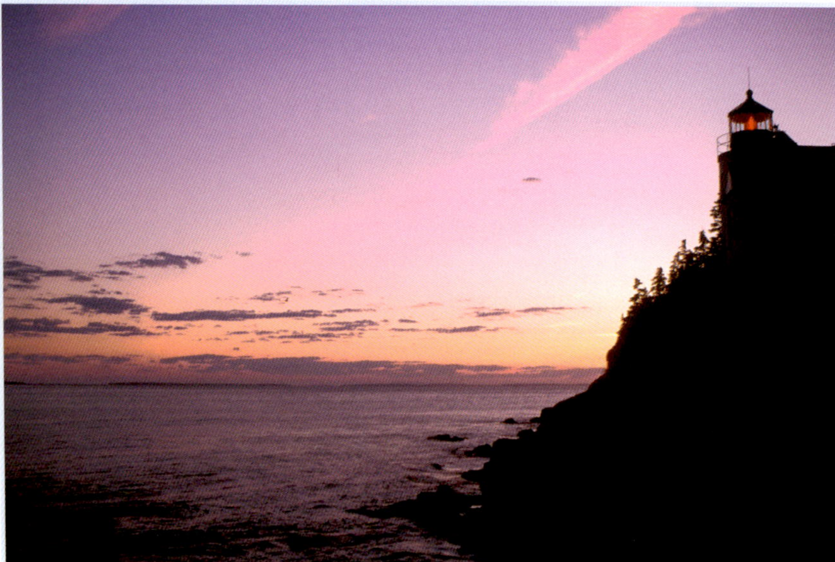

Bass Harbor Lighthouse at sunset.

The lighthouse guided mariners through the treacherous Bass Harbor Bar and into Blue Hill Bay. The station originally had a hand-rung fog bell, which was replaced in 1898 by a 4,000-pound fog bell with a striking type of machinery. It still exists next to the lighthouse, along with the original oil house. Around this same time a boathouse and slip were added, as it was difficult to land boats on the rocky shoreline. The lighthouse stands fifty-six feet above water and is now automated.

Bass Harbor Light's first keeper was John Thurston. His grandson, Charles, was born at the lighthouse to Thurston's son Solomon and daughter-in-law Mary. When Charles was three years old he nearly fell from the lighthouse window. Little boys wore one-piece "dresses" in those days, and this saved his life. A family member grabbed his garment and pulled him back from the edge just in time. Bass Harbor Light has always been a family station with only a single keeper needed.

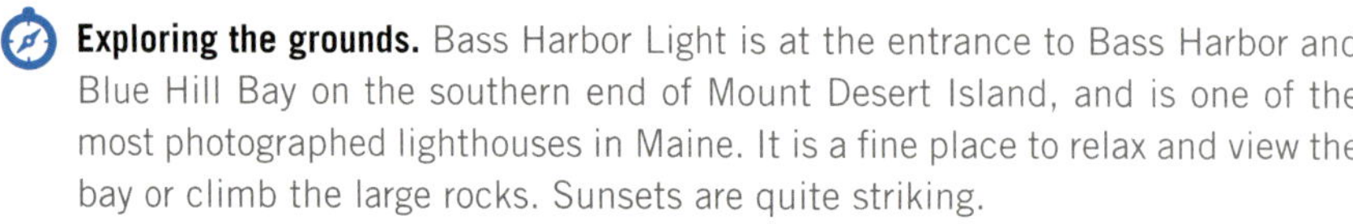

Exploring the grounds. Bass Harbor Light is at the entrance to Bass Harbor and Blue Hill Bay on the southern end of Mount Desert Island, and is one of the most photographed lighthouses in Maine. It is a fine place to relax and view the bay or climb the large rocks. Sunsets are quite striking.

Directions. From Route 1 in Ellsworth, take Route 3 onto Mount Desert Island (Acadia National Park). Bear right on Route 102 and follow south, bearing right on Route 102A to the parking lot by the lighthouse.

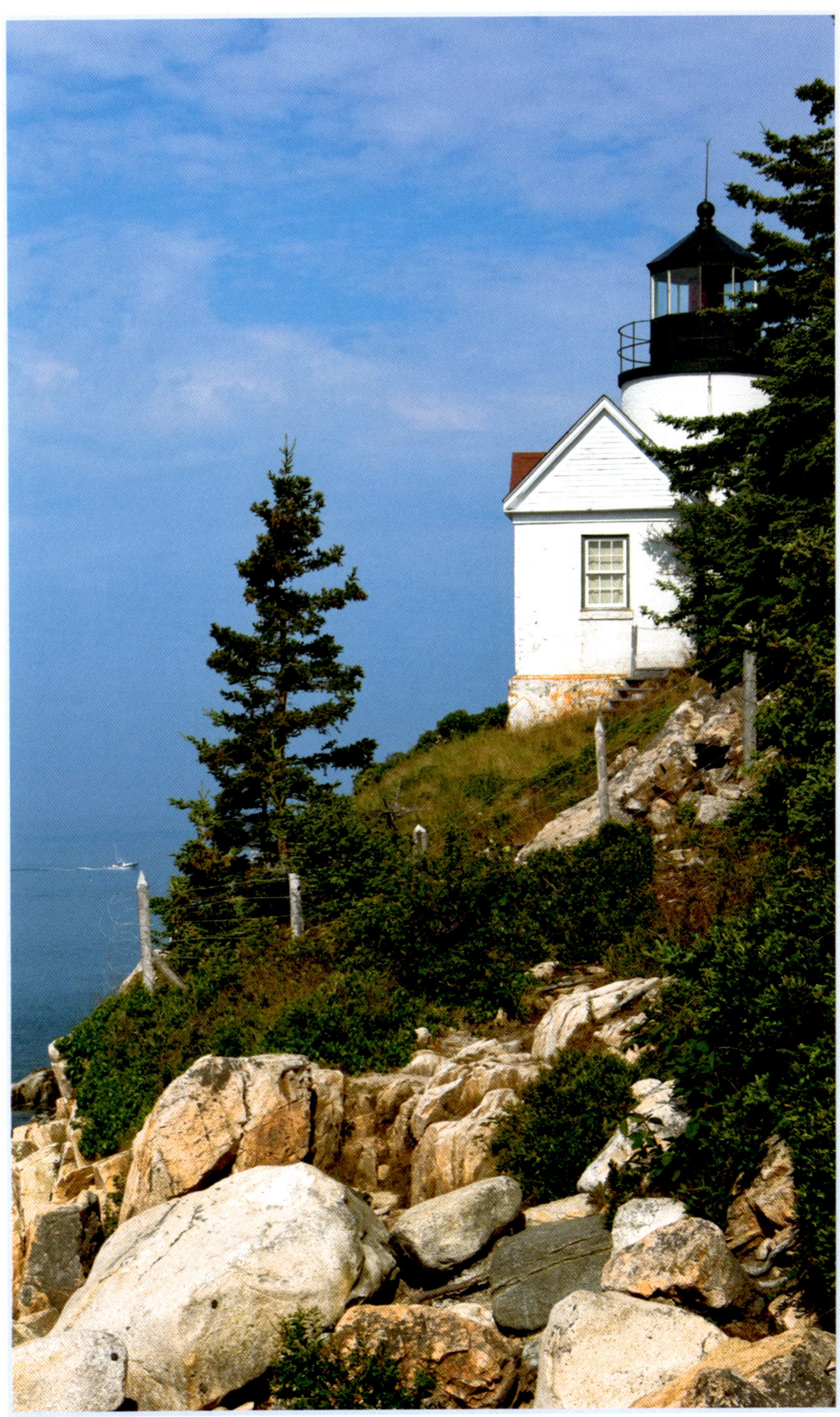

Bass Harbor Lighthouse is the only lighthouse on the shore of Mount Desert Island.

Burnt Coat Harbor (Hockamock Head) Lighthouse

Swan's Island (1839) • Latitude: 44° 08' 03" N • Longitude: 68° 26' 50" W

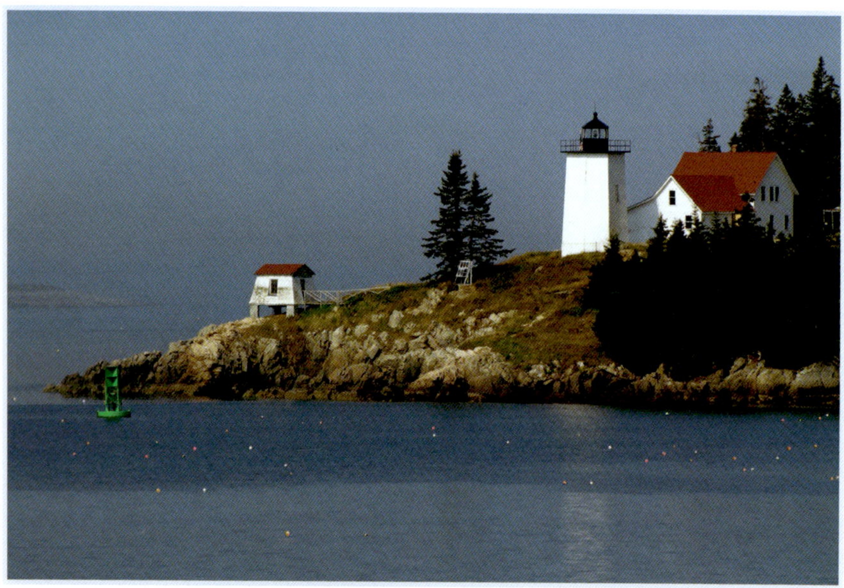

Fog starts to burn off at Burnt Coat Harbor Lighthouse.

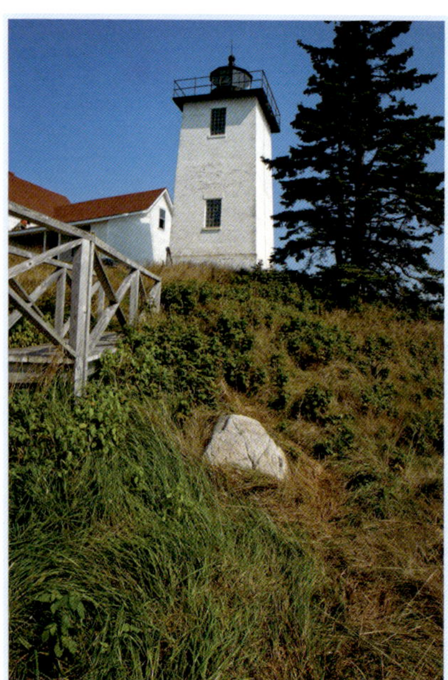

Burnt Coat Harbor Lighthouse is also referred to as Hockamock Head.

Swan's Island was first explored by Samuel de Champlain in 1604 and was frequented by the local Indians for fishing and hunting. The name came from James Swan, who bought the island and had participated in the Boston Tea Party that helped to start the American Revolution.

In the nineteenth century, the island was involved in the lobstering, fishing, and granite quarrying industries. Two range light lighthouses were established atop Hockamock Head, a large rocky hill along the shoreline. The range lights proved confusing to many mariners, and were considered responsible for at least one shipwreck annually.

In 1884, the Coast Guard granted residents' requests and discontinued one of the lights, leaving the current thirty-three-foot white square tower.

In the early 1900s, during a fierce storm, a schooner filled with coal broke apart on a nearby ledge. The crew survived the ordeal and many local residents salvaged the coal for fuel the following winter.

In 1982, the Coast Guard tried to save money by applying a clear sealant over the peeling exterior of the lighthouse. When locals complained that the lighthouse was blending into the landscape, the Coast Guard painted it white.

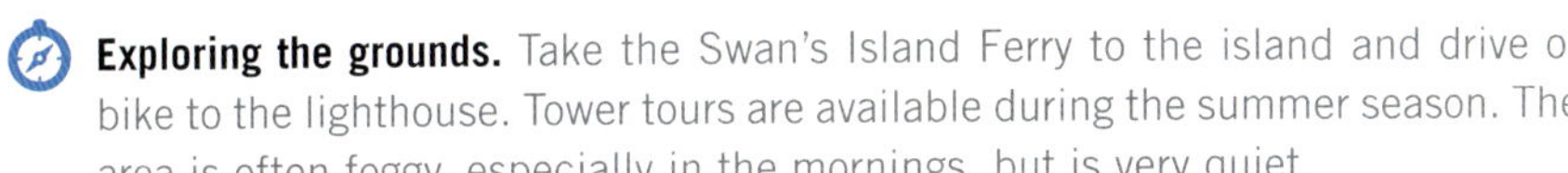

Exploring the grounds. Take the Swan's Island Ferry to the island and drive or bike to the lighthouse. Tower tours are available during the summer season. The area is often foggy, especially in the mornings, but is very quiet.

Directions. Turn right out of the Swan's Island ferry landing, and then turn right again at the T intersection nearly a mile later. Continue for another mile until you come to a fork and bear right. Continue for another two-and-a-half miles past the tiny village of Minturn into the town of Swan's Island, which the locals call "the Harbor." Stay on the main road and bear left to continue nearly five miles along a narrow road that follows the shoreline to a small parking area next to the lighthouse.

Bear Island Lighthouse

Northeast Harbor (1839) • Latitude: 44° 16' 59" N • Longitude: 68° 16' 10" W

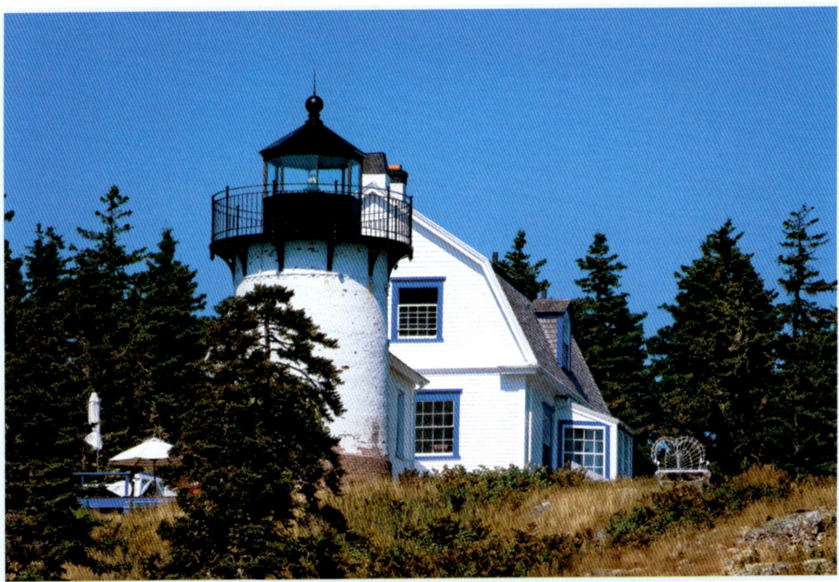

Bear Island Light had a keeper who served three non-consecutive terms when presidents of his political affiliation were in power.

Bear Island is part of the Cranberry Islands. Its lighthouse guided mariners into Northeast Harbor from Somes Sound, and was always a family station with a single

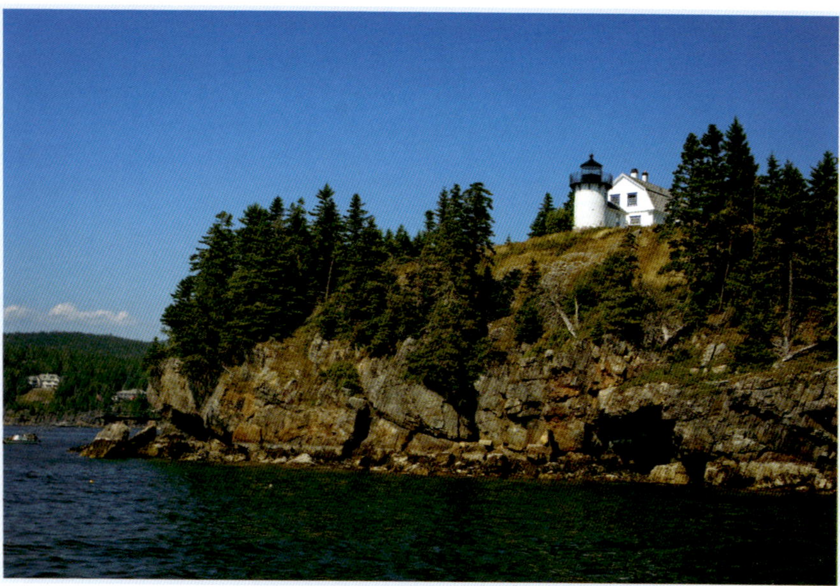

Bear Island Light sits atop jagged rocks.

keeper. Although John Bowan was the first documented keeper, it is believed that William Moore, who originally owned and deeded the land to the government, was the first keeper for a brief time. Bowen was removed twice when new presidential administrations came into power, and served three different terms as a result. In the early 1840s, the government questioned the need for continuing the lighthouse but decided to keep it active at the community's request. A Captain Doyle claimed that without the light, he would have lost his vessel with valuable cargo during a voyage from Eastport. Fire damaged the buildings in 1852, but by 1854 the damage had been repaired, and in 1859, the lighthouse was completely rebuilt. For several years during this period the island established a buoy depot for maintaining navigational aids and for buoy tenders to refuel.

Elmo J. Turner, keeper for several years in the 1930s, had a cow and chickens on the island. One day, the cow had to be taken to the mainland on the dory and got very seasick on the way back. In the late 1950s, Terry and Nancy Stanley lived at the lighthouse. Terry gained a local reputation for his elaborately carved wooden birds and fish.

Great Duck Island Lighthouse

Frenchboro (1890) • Latitude: 44° 08' 30" N • Longitude: 68° 14' 42" W

This remote island got its name from a pond in the center of the island that attracted huge crowds of ducks each spring. The lighthouse had three keeper's dwellings next to the lighthouse. This proved quite helpful for keeper Nathan Reed, who had seventeen children. At one time, a small school was established to educate the large number of keepers' children on the island, the only one of its kind.

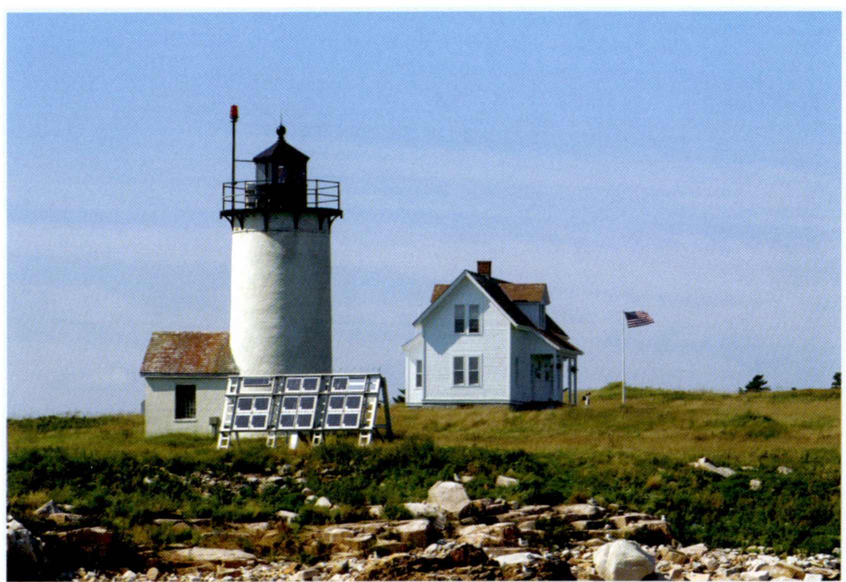

Great Duck Island Light once had three keeper's dwellings. One keeper had seventeen children.

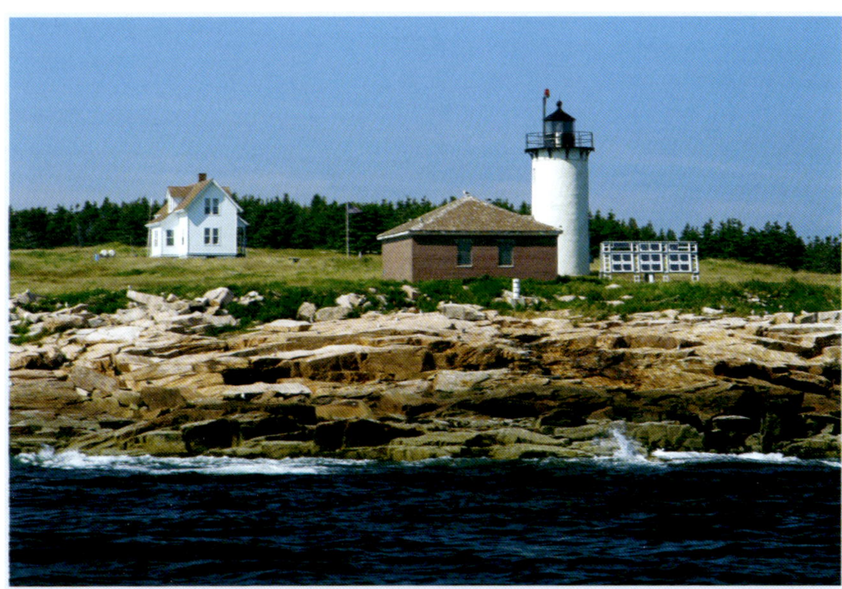

Great Duck Island had a famous dog named Seaboy who was saved by the keeper's daughter.

In early February 1955, a newly appointed Coast Guardsman to the lighthouse, Richard Swartz, found his pregnant wife going into an early labor. The seas were rough, and the local tugboat was docked on the other side of the island. Richard and his wife walked an hour and a half in deep snow to get to the boat. She was taken to the hospital on the mainland and gave birth to a baby boy.

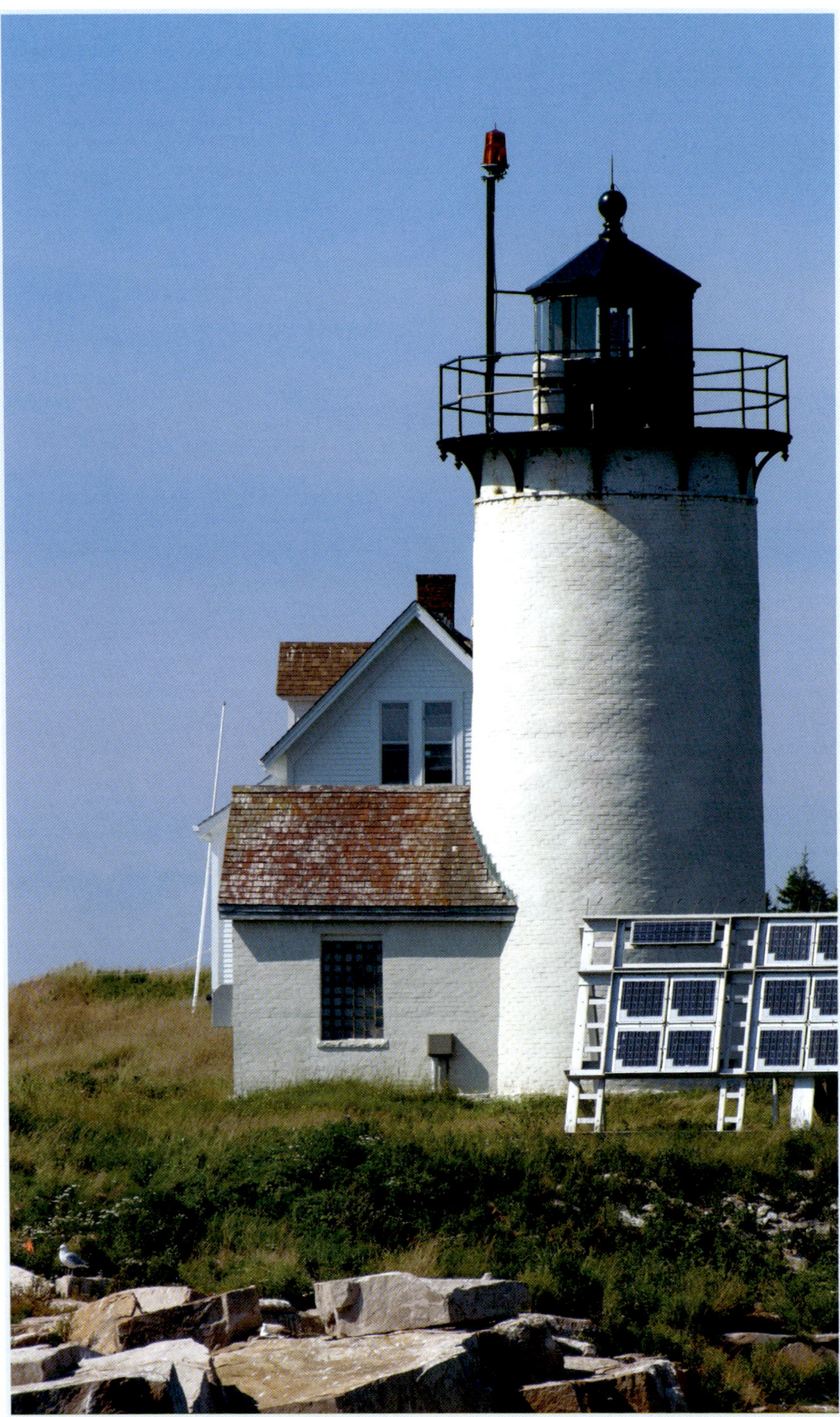

The story of Seaboy became the basis for the children's book *Captain's Castaway*.

The current lighthouse is southeast of Mount Desert Rock Light and stands sixty-seven feet above the water. It was automated in 1986. It is estimated that Great Duck Island supports of over one-fifth of Maine's nesting seabird population.

Keeper's Daughter Adopts Dog. Sometime around 1920, a fishing vessel wrecked near Great Duck Island in fog, with a large dog aboard. As the ship started to sink, the crew made haste onto a lifeboat and started to pull away. The dog leaped from the wreck and swam toward the lifeboat. As the crew tried to pull him into the crowded boat, his weight made the boat tip into the water, which scared one of the crew enough to push the dog away with an oar, injuring him. The crew watched the poor animal sink into the water and presumed he had drowned.

When the lifeboat reached Great Duck Island, the lighthouse keeper and his wife gave the crew warm clothes and food, and the grateful crew headed for the mainland.

The following day, the keeper's daughter was playing along the rocky shoreline when she noticed a dog washed up on the shore. The poor animal was covered in blood and barely alive. She quickly ran to get her parents to help her. The keeper and his wife ran down to the shore, wrapped the helpless animal in warm blankets, and brought it to the house, where they nursed it back to health. As the crew had departed days earlier, the dog was adopted and named Seaboy.

The keeper's daughter became very fond of her new best friend and the two became inseparable. She held tea parties with Seaboy, dressed him in clothes, and read to him. The dog would not leave her side and slept by her bed each night. Two years later, a stranger came to the lighthouse and told the keeper that he was the captain of the crew that had wrecked near the lighthouse. He heard the animal had survived and had come to retrieve the dog.

The little girl was beside herself when her parents reluctantly told her to give up the dog to its rightful owner. As Seaboy was led onto the fisherman's dory, she sobbed uncontrollably and could not bear to watch as the boat rowed away. All of a sudden, Seaboy leaped out of the boat and started the long swim back to shore. The family watched in disbelief as he reached the shore and ran to the girl's side. The fisherman did not try to reclaim the dog, and Seaboy lived on the island the rest of his life. News of the story spread and later became the basis for a popular children's book called *Captain's Castaway*.

Baker Island Lighthouse

Cranberry Island (1828) • Latitude: 44° 14' 29" N • Longitude: 68° 11' 56" W

Baker Island is one of the five Cranberry Islands in Frenchman Bay. The lighthouse guided mariners away from the sandbar and treacherous ledges nearby. The Gilley family owned the island in the early 1800s, and their son William became the first keeper in 1828. He was removed over twenty years later for political reasons. The keepers who came after Gilley were harassed by his sons. Legal battles ensued between the Gilleys and the government, with the family claiming the island was theirs. Finally the government was granted rights to the station and grounds, and the Gilley family was allowed to own and occupy the rest of the island.

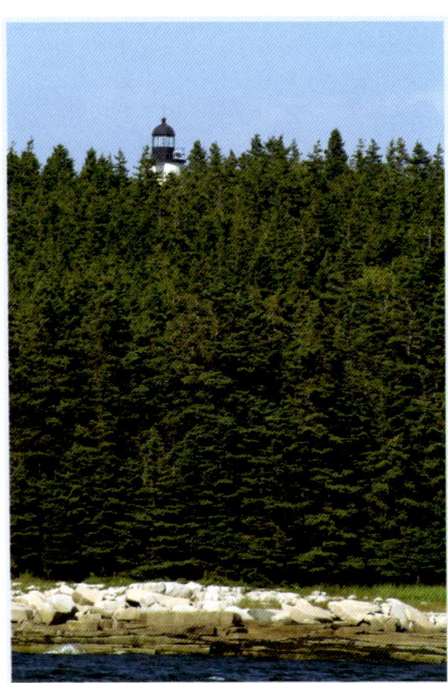
Baker Island Lighthouse is slowly being engulfed by trees.

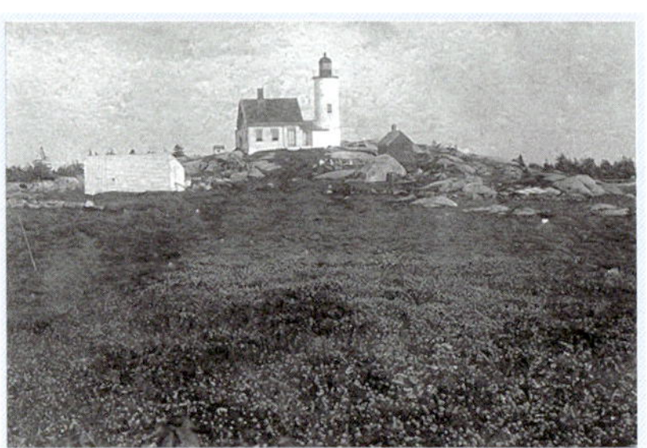
Vintage image. *Courtesy US Coast Guard.*

During a storm in November 1932, keeper Joseph Muise's wife went into labor. The assistant was on shore leave, so Muise enlisted the help of a lifesaving crew on a neighboring island to take his wife ashore, as he could not leave his post. As they were heading for Northeast Harbor about ten miles away, her labor pains became more frequent, and the men found themselves delivering a baby two miles from the mainland, donating their jackets to keep it warm. Both mother and daughter reached the mainland in good health.

The lighthouse was deactivated in 1955 and then reactivated in 1957 as an automated light. It was refurbished in 1989 and is now solar powered. In the early 1990s, the Coast Guard announced it was going to deactivate the lighthouse because the surrounding trees were obscuring its view. Local mariners petitioned to leave it alone, and the Coast Guard granted their request. The park service offers trips to the island and hikes to the lighthouse in the summer season.

Mount Desert Rock Lighthouse

Mount Desert Rock (1829) • Latitude: 43° 58' 06" N • Longitude: 68° 07' 42" W

Twenty-six miles from the mainland and a mere 600 yards long and 200 yards wide, Mount Desert Rock Lighthouse is the most isolated lighthouse in New England. In 1857, a fifty-eight-foot conical granite tower replaced the original wooden tower. Each spring, the keepers would bring in new soil and plant flower and vegetable gardens, replacing the soil that washed away in fall and winter storms.

In December 1902, the tugboat *Astral*, which was towing a barge, ran aground on Mount Desert Rock. Keeper Fred Robbins and his assistant threw a line to the tug and pulled seventeen of the eighteen crew members to safety; the eighteenth crew member had died of exposure. The barge that was being towed drifted to Rockland with several crewmen aboard, and was later rescued, with the crewmen safe. The keeper described ice several inches thick in the tug's pilothouse windows that had built up even before the incident occurred.

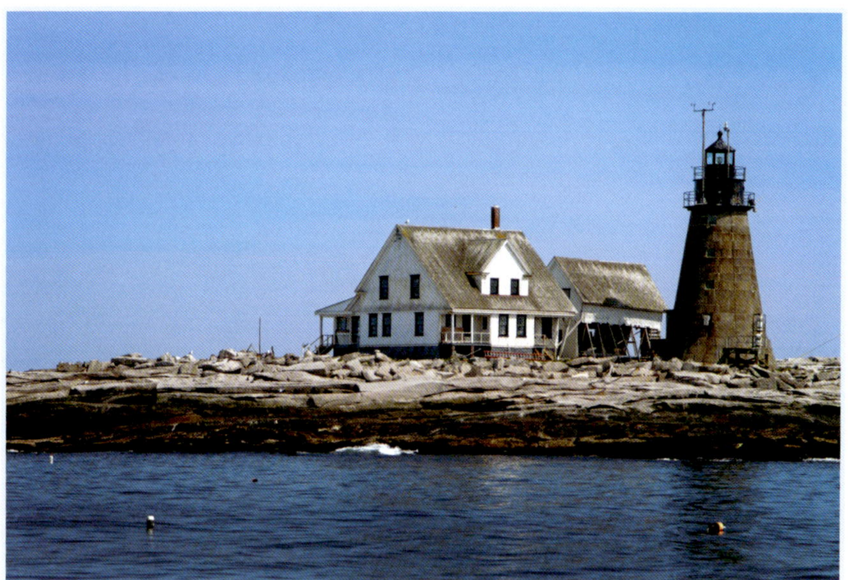

Mount Desert Rock Lighthouse is on a remote, protected island for nesting birds.

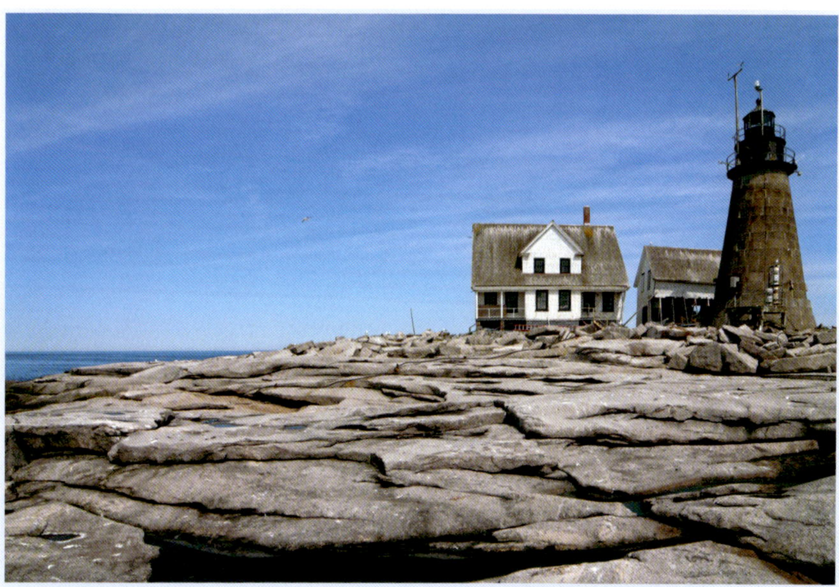

Mount Desert Rock Lighthouse is constantly battered by storms.

Lighthouse historian Edward Rowe Snow wrote that the island "seemed a part of another world." Snow was the "Flying Santa" who took over the duties of the original Flying Santa, Captain William H. Wincapaw.

In October 6, 1962, Hurricane Daisy swept away the walkway, fuel tanks, and other structures, while the three Coast Guardsmen stationed there spent the terrifying night in the swaying tower and survived. After the storm they found a four-ton boulder on top of the boathouse near the lighthouse.

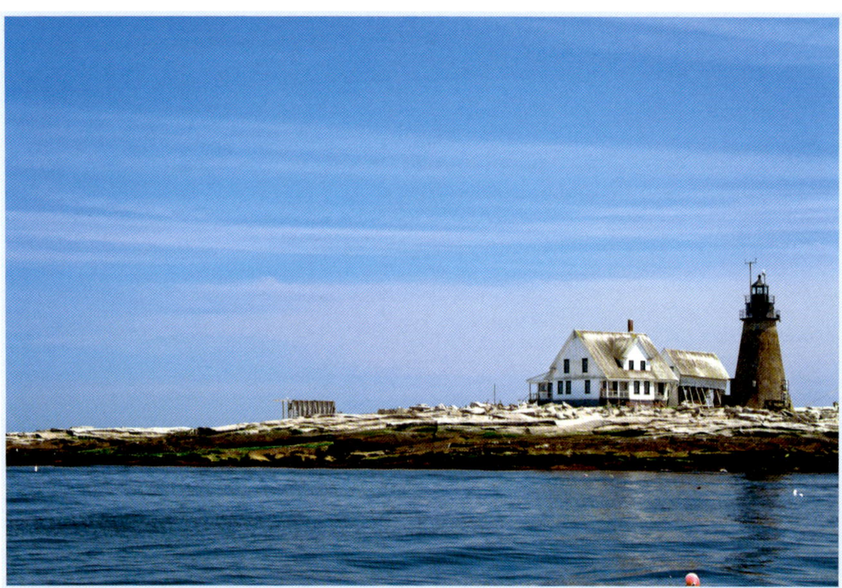

Mount Desert Rock Light is Maine's most remote beacon twenty-six miles from the mainland.

In the early 1970s a helicopter pad was built and was later washed away in a violent storm. In the late 1970s the lighthouse was leased as a whale-watching station to Bar Harbor's College of the Atlantic. In 1985 a new lantern was installed and the college helped to restore the lighthouse over the years. Today the station's engine room contains survival gear for any shipwrecked or lost mariners who find themselves on this isolated island. It is part of seven island wildlife refuges for nesting birds and is off-limits to the public.

Miracle Near Mount Desert Rock Lighthouse. In the early 1880s, the schooner *Helen and Mary* was carrying a load of granite from Halifax, Nova Scotia, when it started to storm. The first mate, Nelson White, tried to convince Captain Parker to take shelter in Jonesport Harbor, but the captain was eager to make his destination and receive payment for the cargo he was carrying. The captain's wife, who was also Nelson White's sister, accompanied the crew with their baby girl.

As the weather worsened, the captain realized his mistake and shouted orders to shorten the sails as wind gusts started to tip the vessel into the sea. As water filled the schooner, the captain's wife, baby, and crew members were quickly put into the first of two boats. Captain Parker and White tried to drop the second boat into the water, but it was too late. The vessel started to sink beneath the waves, sucking both men underwater. White managed to reach the surface and climbed atop a large piece of floating wreckage. He watched in horror as the first boat capsized and he could not locate any survivors near it. He agonized over the fact that all passengers and crew, including his sister, baby niece, and brother in law, had perished.

A short time later, the seas were starting to calm when he noticed a small bundle of heavy oilskin floating in the water. Lifting it out, he found his sister's infant daughter wrapped inside, barely wet. Ecstatic that she had survived such an ordeal,

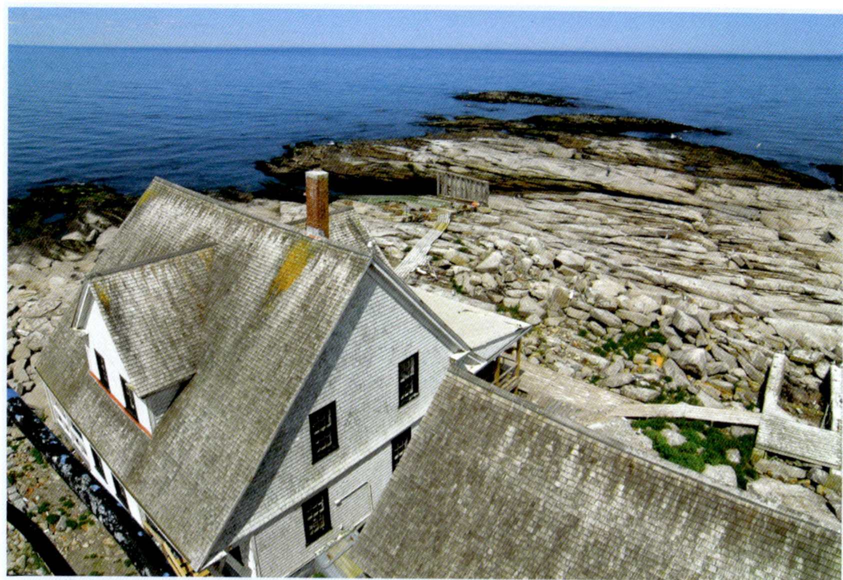

Mount Desert Island view from lighthouse tower.

he tied her close to his chest for warmth, secured himself to the deck load of wreckage, and collapsed in exhaustion. Hours went by and the weather cleared as the two survivors drifted in the seas.

By the early afternoon the following day, White was sighted by the lighthouse buoy tender *Iris* and was quickly brought aboard and given warm blankets and food. Both he and the infant recovered and were brought to Prospect Harbor Lighthouse for medical treatment. Everyone else on the *Helen and Mary* perished near Mount Desert Rock.

Little is known about what became of the miracle baby, but many believe that White raised her in honor of his sister and brother-in-law.

Egg Rock Lighthouse

Winter Harbor (1875) • Latitude: 44° 21' 12" N • Longitude: 68° 08' 18" W

This area of the Maine coast experiences a great deal of fog and pounding storms. On March 25, 1876, a storm flooded the keeper's dwelling, smashed its windows, and swept away a fuel shed. Less than year later, another storm washed away the bell tower. In October 1894, while Lewis F. Sawyer was keeper, the fishing schooner *Amy Hamsen,* coming up from Boston, struck a ledge about a half-mile southwest of the lighthouse. Before the schooner sank, its eighteen crewmen escaped and rowed ashore to Bar Harbor. On Christmas Eve 1899, the fishing boat *Julia* ran aground on Egg Rock during a storm and broke apart, drowning the two fishermen on board.

After a nor'easter flooded the lighthouse in February 1908, giant, thirty-ton boulders were displaced on the grounds. And on October of 1929, the schooner

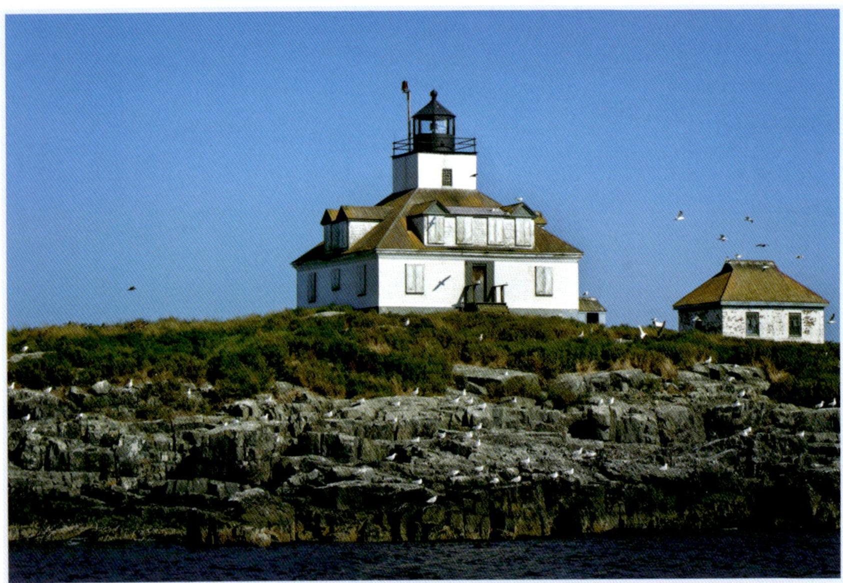

Egg Rock Lighthouse and island are part of a bird sanctuary.

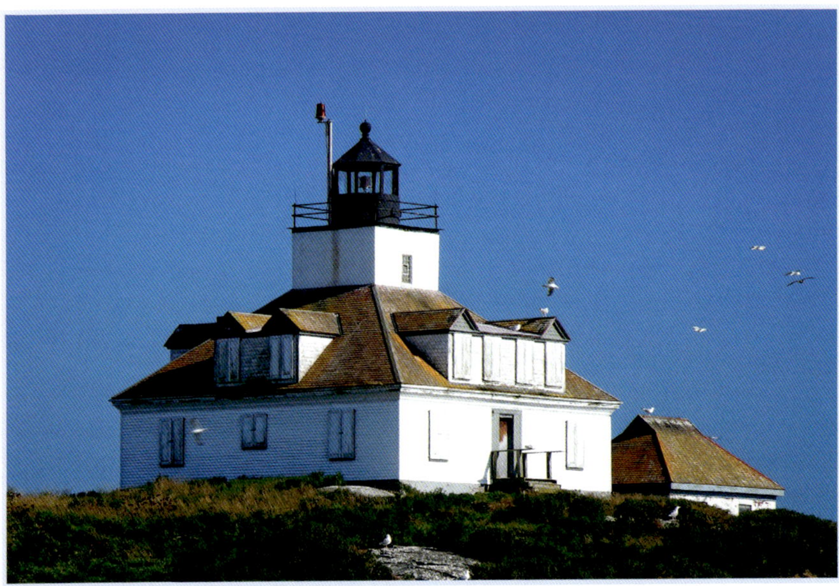

Egg Rock Light.

Lillian Louise became stranded on the rocks, but keeper Augustus Hamor and assistant J. B. Pinkham saved the crew.

Clinton L. "Buster" Dalzell arrived at Egg Rock as assistant keeper in 1933. In February 1935, he left for the mainland to pick up batteries for the motor of a boat he had just built. The seas were rough, and when he did not return, keeper J. B. Pinkham telephoned the place he was to pick up the batteries and learned that

Dalzell had never arrived. The police and Coast Guard started a search and Pinkham headed out in his own boat. He found Dalzell's overturned boat more than a mile from the lighthouse. The search continued for weeks until a fishing trawler recovered Dalzell's body. His third child was born three weeks later.

In 1998, the lighthouse was turned over to the US Fish and Wildlife Service under the Maine Lights Program. It is part of the Maine Coastal Islands National Wildlife Refuge.

Winter Harbor Lighthouse

Winter Harbor (1857) • Latitude: 44° 21' 40" N • Longitude: 68° 05' 13" W

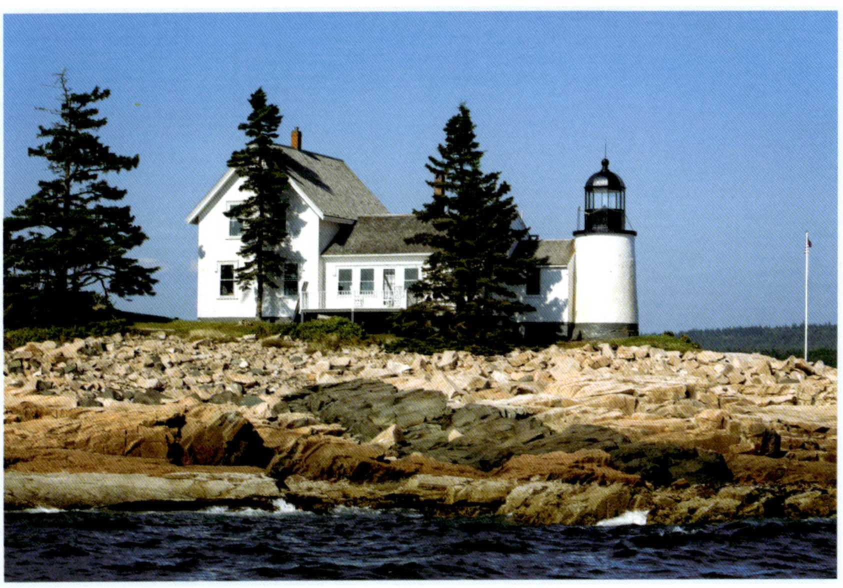

Winter Harbor Lighthouse guided mariners around its rocky shore.

Winter Harbor is a small, picturesque harbor that sheltered mariners from approaching storms. Just a mile from shore, its lighthouse was considered a good posting for keepers and their families. The first keeper of the lighthouse was Frederick Gerrish. Richard H. Higgins was keeper from 1866 to 1868. On November 2, 1868, while the forty-two-year old Higgins was leaving the island in his dory, he lost an oar, was washed away in heavy seas, and drowned. The last keeper was Captain Lester "Cap" Leighton. His one-year-old grandson, Chan, was visiting the lighthouse when his mother stepped out of the station's boat at the island, slipped, and "dunked" them both in the water. No one was hurt, and the keeper commented that his grandson was officially christened. Maine author Bernice Richmond lived here for a time. Her classic books, *Our Island Lighthouse* and *Winter Harbor*, were based on her experiences at the lighthouse.

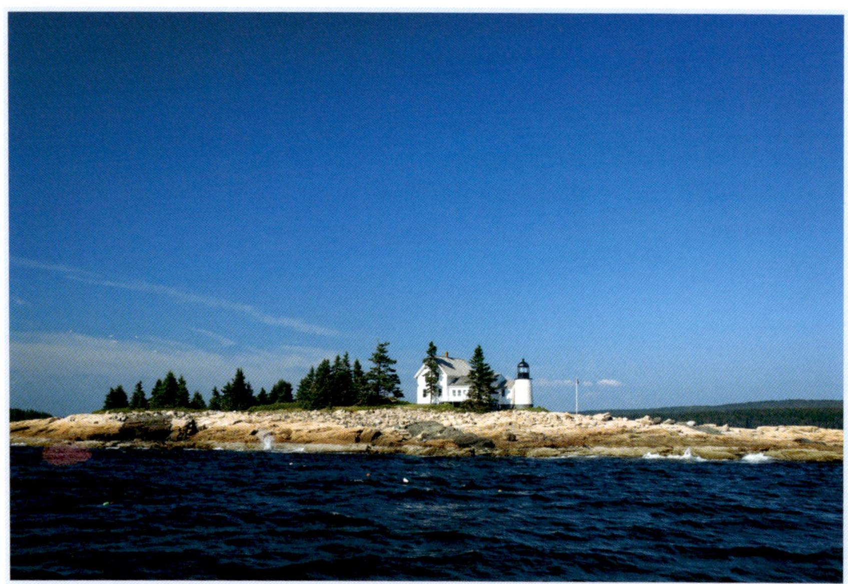

Winter Harbor Light was the home of various authors in recent years.

Directions for a distant view. From Route 1 in West Goldsboro, head south on Route 186 through Winter Harbor. Enter Acadia National Park and head toward Schoodic Point. The beacon can be viewed from the western side of the Schoodic Peninsula. Some of the better viewing spots are from the off-road lookouts a mile south of the park entrance.

Prospect Harbor Lighthouse

Prospect Harbor (1850) • Latitude: 44° 24' 12" N • Longitude: 68° 00' 48" W

Prospect Harbor has been a busy fishing harbor since the mid-1800s. Its granite lighthouse was built in 1850 and then deactivated between 1859 through 1870 when harbor use decreased. It was reactivated in 1870 and rebuilt of wood in 1891. The lighthouse still guides lobster and sardine fishermen to and from their homes.

The lighthouse was automated in 1934, but keeper John Workman was allowed to stay at the station until 1953. Today, as the lighthouse and grounds belong to the US Navy, the keeper's house is available for overnight stays for active and retired military families. The lighthouse and grounds are off-limits to tourists for security reasons.

The American Lighthouse Foundation helped to save the historic beacon from imminent collapse in 2004.

Those who've stayed at the keeper's quarters often notice paranormal activity. It seems that a small statue of a sea captain, out of reach on a high ledge at the top of the stairs, is consistently moved—facing the stairs one time, the sea another time. Some guests have claimed to see a ghost-like figure at night.

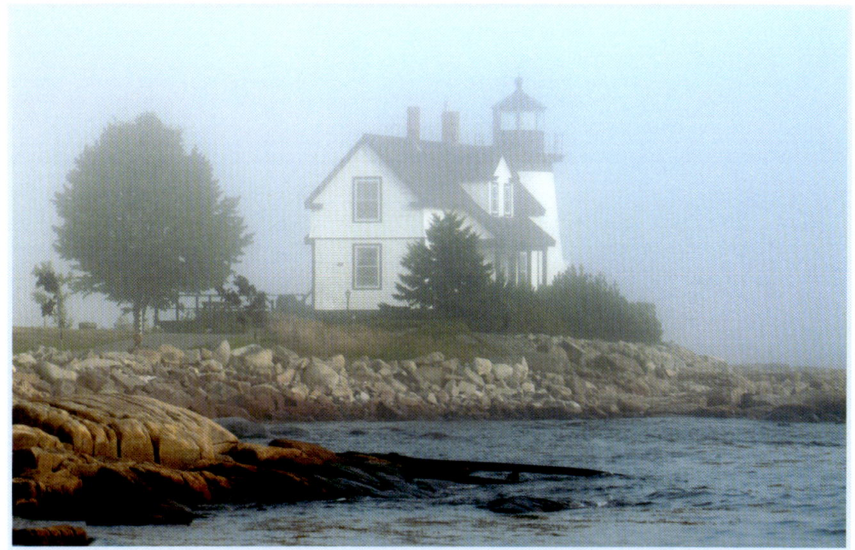

Prospect Harbor Lighthouse guides mariners through one of Maine's foggiest areas.

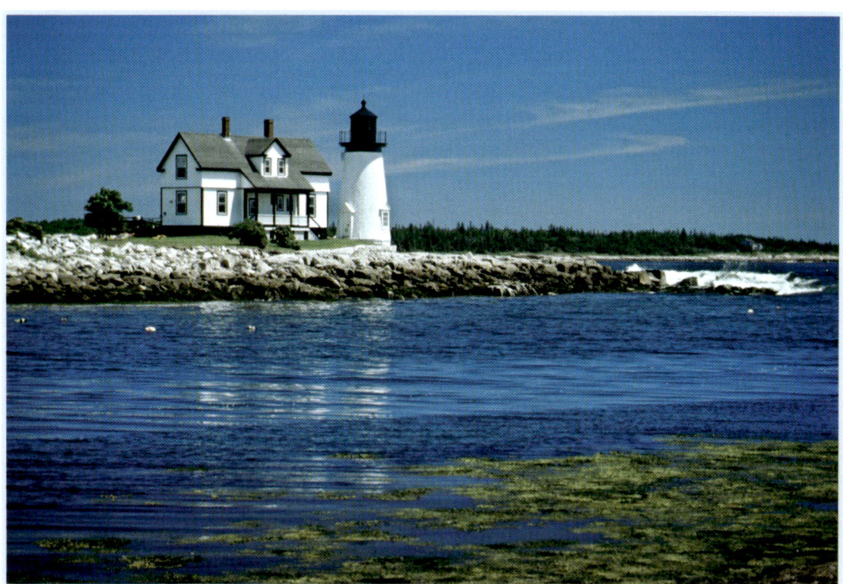

Prospect Harbor Light can be viewed from across the river.

Directions. From US Route 1 take Route 186 to Prospect Harbor. Turn right on 195, then bear right at the fork onto Lighthouse Point Road. You can view the light off from the shoreline outside the gates. Another view is from Winter Harbor on Route 186 at Prospect Harbor, near the grounds of Stinson Canning Company, where you can get samples of canned fish. Another view is from Lighthouse Point Road leading to the restricted Navy station. Drive past a sign that reads "Detachment Alpha" to where Route 195 bears left toward Corea.

Coastal Attractions in Acadia

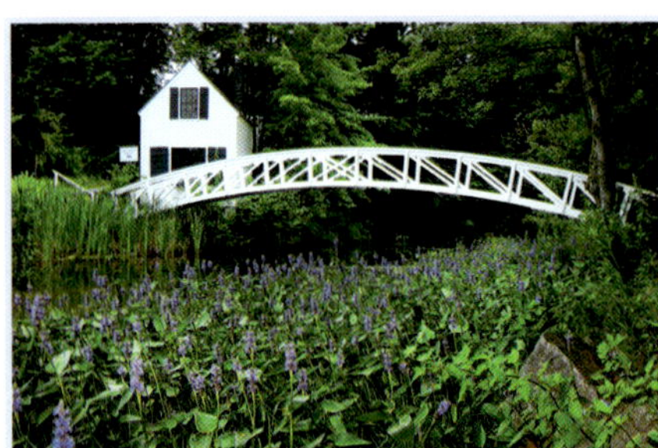

Somes Sound Bridge, on the western side, is Acadia's most photographed bridge.

Acadia National Park was the first park established east of the Mississippi River and is still a major tourist attraction. Boats for all kinds of excursions leave out of the resort town of Bar Harbor, where you'll find lots of specialty shops and restaurants. Outside Bar Harbor, visitors can explore the park's interior and coastline.

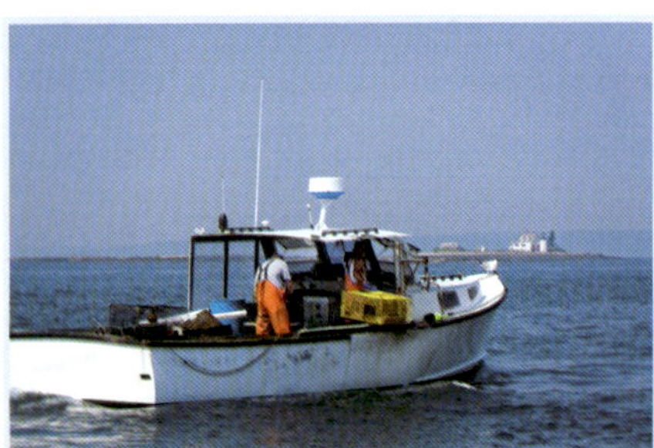

Lobster boat in Blue Hill Bay near the lighthouse.

Off Route 1 heading toward Mount Desert Island and Acadia National Park, numerous roads lead down to the many peninsulas with timeless fishing villages and harbors. Lobstering and fishing are still the main occupations in this region. Brooklin is a tiny, remote village with a general store and friendly people. The famous Brooklin Boat Yard is known for high-quality craftsmanship and restoration. In Brooklin, you can go to Naskeag Point dock and purchase live lobsters right off the boats in early afternoon. You may even be able to catch a ride out to Blue Hill Light with one of these fine folk. There is also a free public beach at the pier.

Where Route 1 intersects with Route 3 in Ellsworth, the **Downeast Scenic Railroad** offers two trips per day on Saturdays and Sundays through the season. The round-trip tour travels from Ellsworth on the historic Calais Branch Line to Ellsworth Falls and then to Washington Junction and back to Ellsworth. Taking Route 3 off Route 1, and following down Route 102 on the western side of the island, you'll find the quieter

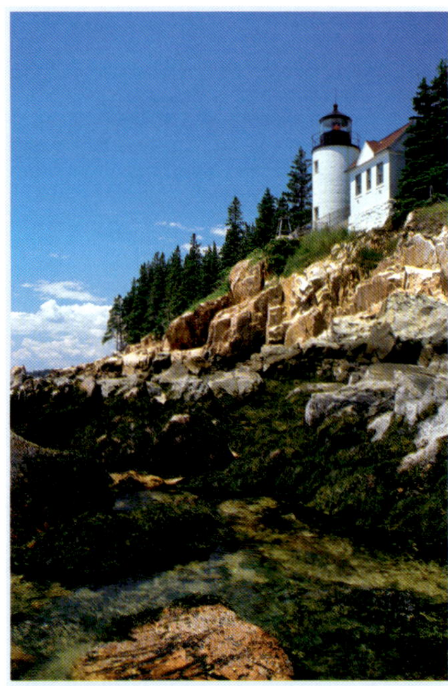

Bass Harbor Light is one of Maine's most picturesque beacons.

side of Mount Desert Island. The famous curved footbridge, named the Somes Sound Bridge, greets you as you drive into these quaint fishing communities. Somesville is the oldest settlement on Mount Desert Island.

Bass Harbor, in Tremont, is a vacationer's paradise. Near the lighthouse, the Ship Harbor Nature Trail is an easy hike with great views around the harbor. In Tremont, you'll find **Timber Tina's Great Maine Lumberjack Show**, in which men and women compete in pole climbing, chopping and sawing wood, ax throwing, log rolling, and the like.

Quick stop! On Frenchboro Island, an old working fishing village, you'll find the real deal in a lobster shack at **Lunt's Dockside Deli**, on the fisherman's wharf.

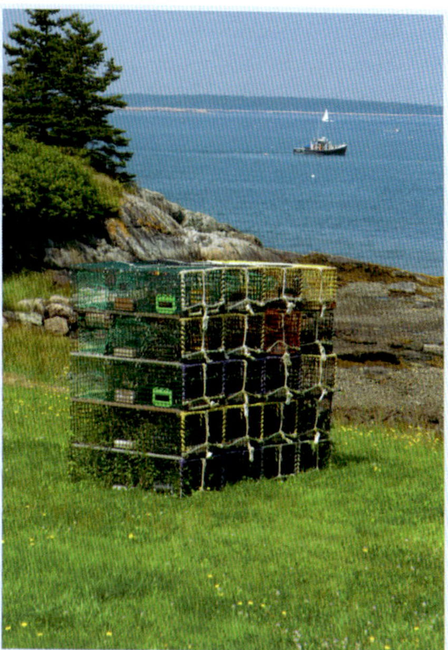

Swan's Island is a quiet fishing and lobstering community.

Island Cruises offers wildlife tours and lobster trap hauling around Bass Harbor, and cruises to some of the outer islands including the offshore fishing village of Frenchboro. One option is the Morning Lunch Cruise out to Frenchboro. The island, named Long Island, hasn't changed over the years and is a great place to relax and disconnect. The **Maine State Ferry** offers no-frills rides from Bass Harbor to Frenchboro and nearby Swan's Island.

Swan's Island is a small, quiet island of about 370 year-round residents who wave a friendly hello. You can stay overnight at Jeanie's Place B&B or the Harbor Watch Motel. There are two places to eat: the Island Bake Shop, which is like going to someone's house for breakfast or lunch, and the Boat House Restaurant, which also has excellent food. There is a quarry filled with fresh, deep water (Quarry Pond) to jump in on a hot day, like Tom Sawyer. You'll also find a general store and Fine Sand Beach on the island. You can take the Swan's Island Ferry in Bass Harbor to get to Swan's Island and drive or bike to Burnt Coat Harbor Light. Tower tours are available during the summer.

Acadia Park Service offers a narrated cruise and natural history walk to Baker Island aboard the Islesford ferry from Northeast Harbor. Park rangers offer all kinds of nature tours and cruises out of Northeast Harbor and Bar Harbor.

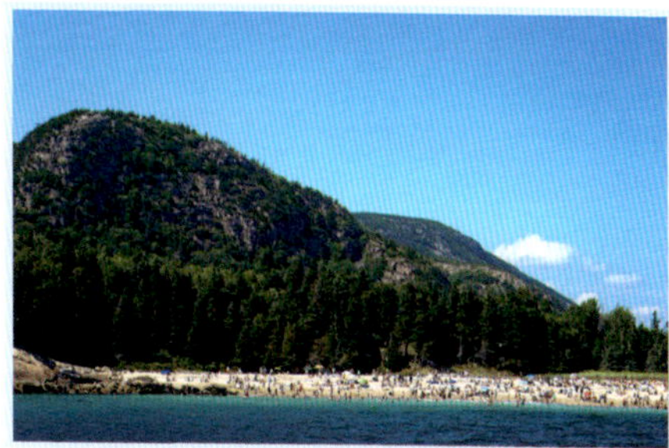

Beehive Hill overlooks Sand Beach.

Acadia National Park's twenty-seven-mile Park Loop Road begins at the Hulls Cove Visitor Center and offers access to Sand Beach for ocean swimming. The Beehive, a dominant geological feature, towers 520 feet over Sand Beach. Beehive Trail is rated as "strenuous" and is approximately a mile long. Hiking is through woods and exposed cliffs but the views are worth the trek. Echo Lake Beach offers warmer, freshwater swimming on the west side of the island.

Great Meadow Loop is an easy two-mile hike that connects Bar Harbor to Acadia National Park. Take a walk around the Wild Gardens of Acadia, with over 300 native plant species organized into display areas between well-groomed paths. It's open year-round at the Sieur de Monts Spring and Nature Center, two miles south of Bar Harbor, connected by the Great Meadow Loop, or right off Route 3 for those arriving by car. The Nature Center shows visitors the unique diversity of natural resources that make up Acadia and how they are studied and protected.

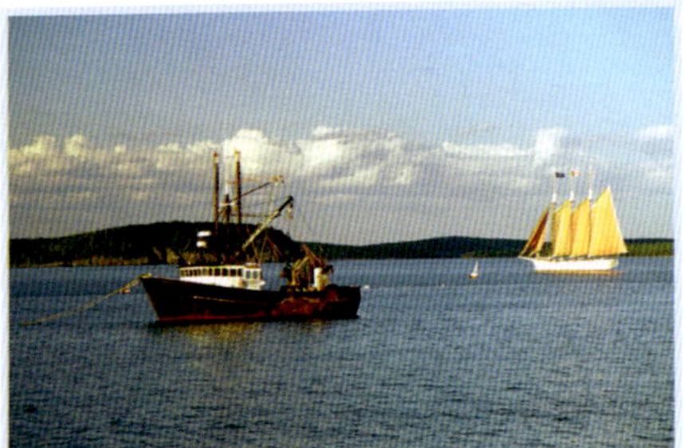

Schooner and fishing trawler embody the region's industries.

Northeast Harbor provides a unique opportunity to take the **Beal and Bunker Mail Boat and Ferry** out to the Cranberry Islands and nearby Sutton Island. It is also referred to as the Islesford ferry, as Islesford is a small harbor town on Little Cranberry Island. On these islands, strange go-cart-like vehicles may pass you, as there is little need for the usual safety rules. Most of these island communities are self-supporting and watch out for one another. The Islesford Historical Museum on Little Cranbury Island, which can be reached by mail boat or some of the tour boats, provides exhibits that tell the story of the Cranberry Islands and its people through ship models, navigation aids, photographs, and tools. Hitching a ride on these mail boats is very inexpensive. You can also take nature cruises and a cruise that passes Bear Island Lighthouse on the **Sea Princess**.

In Northeast Harbor, **Asticou Azalea Garden** is part of the Land and Garden preserve offering places to hike. Nearby, **Thuyta Gardens and Lodge** is a semi-formal English design in a floral and wooded area that overlooks Northeast Harbor.

For fishing adventures, **Acadia Deep Sea Fishing Tours** takes visitors out of Southwest Harbor, sometimes as far as Mount Desert Rock Light (weather permitting). They also haul up a lobster trap for visitors to see. You can take the **Cranberry Cove Ferry** out to the Cranberry Islands from the harbor as well. Consider sailing around Acadia National Park on the oldest Friendship Sloop, *Alice E.*, originally a working sailing lobster boat built in 1899. Charter a cruise out of either Northeast Harbor or Southeast Harbor with **Sail Acadia**. They also provide chartered cruises around Bear Island Light, the Cranberry Islands, and along the narrow channel out to the granite cliffs in Somes Sound, the only "fjord" on the East Coast. **Downeast Sailing Adventures** provides intimate, two-hour sailing adventures for up to six people aboard the *Friendship Sloop Surprise*, or sail with up to thirty passengers aboard the *Schooner Rachel B. Jackson* to the Cranberry Islands. They also provide a lobster boat tour on a traditional Downeast wooden lobster boat, the *Hurricane*, and a water taxi to nearby islands. There is an oceanarium near the dock where you can learn more about lobsters.

On Mount Desert Island, explore Thunder Hole, Otter Cliffs, Jordan Pond, and Cadillac Mountain, to name a few attractions.

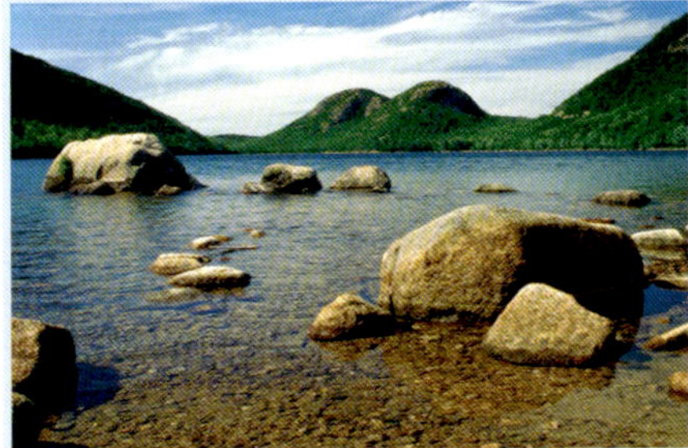

Freshwater Jordan Pond with Bubble Mountains in background.

Thunder Hole is a cavern formation just below the water, and when waves come in, a thunderous sound is created when water is forced out sometimes forty feet high. Drive, bike, or hike to the top of Cadillac Mountain (1,530 feet), the highest point in the region, and enjoy views of the islands jutting out of Bar Harbor. Visitors are allowed to sleep on top of the mountain and watch the sunrise as it reaches the harbor. One of the most spectacular sights is Otter Cliffs, at 110 feet, one of the highest headlands on the East Coast. Jordan Pond is a favorite attraction, not only for the trail that surrounds the pond and the Bubble Mountains in the background, but also for the **Jordan Pond House Restaurant**. The restaurant provides traditional tea & popovers reminiscent of the late 1800s, along with traditional menu items like soups, salads, sandwiches, and desserts.

Another favorite hiking trail, the Precipice Trail, on the east face of Champlain Mountain, is the most challenging hiking trail in the park with an exposed, almost vertical 1,000-foot climb.

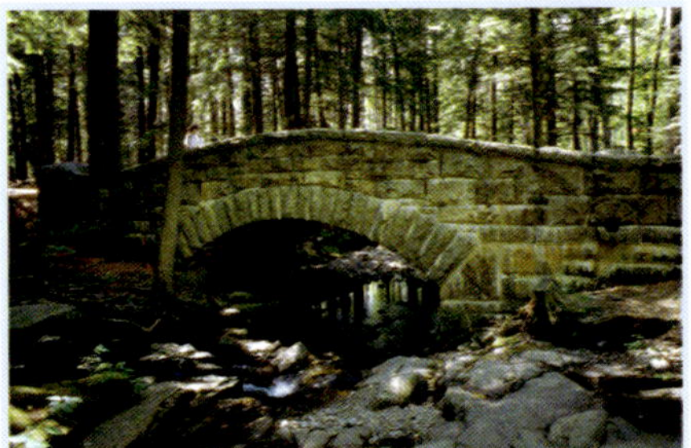

Carriage bridge in wooded area for bicyclists and hikers.

Between 1913 and 1940, John D. Rockefeller Jr. financed and directed the construction of fifty-seven miles of carriage roads and stone archway bridges throughout Mount Desert Island for hikers, bikers, horse riders, and horse-drawn carriages. Many roads have crushed rock surfaces and wind through the heart of the park. If you park at Eagle Lake or Jordan Pond, you can find wide trails along these roads. Eagle Lake is the largest freshwater lake in the park. To get a glimpse of earlier times, take a horse-drawn carriage ride from **Wildwood Stables**, an authorized vendor accessed from Park Loop Road. For people who want to bring their own horses for riding on the carriage roads, a horse camp is provided, and visitors can rent a stable. There are 120 miles of hiking trails and paths ranging from very easy to strenuous.

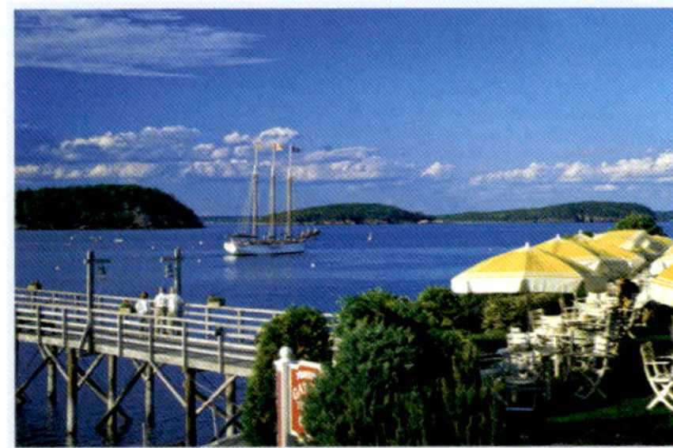

Relaxing at Bar Harbor.

Bar Harbor Whale Watch Company offers daily maritime tours, as does **Sea Venture Custom Boat Tours**. **Downeast Windjammer Cruises** provides two-hour sailing cruises on the two-masted schooner *Halie & Matthew*, which replicates a nineteenth-century fishing schooner, and the ninety-one-foot *Bailey Louise Todd*, a wooden hackmatuck schooner inspired by the era's Mississippi freight schooners. Sailing excursions are also provided on the large

151-foot four-masted schooner *Margaret Todd*. The company also offers an intimate sail for up to six people among the islands of Frenchman's Bay aboard *Chrissy*, a Maine lobster sloop built in 1910. Ferry service is available from Bar Harbor to various islands and harbors.

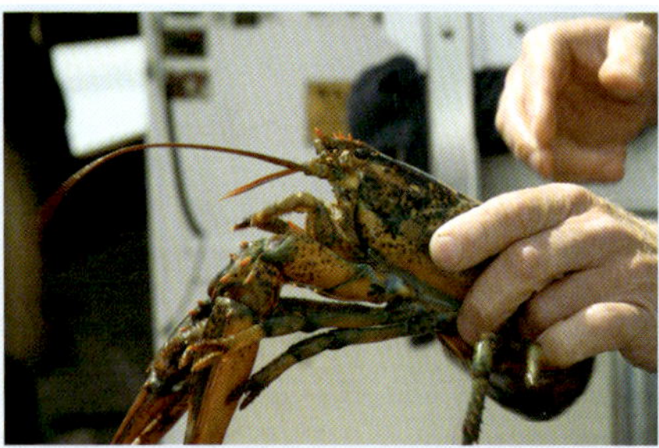

Lobsterboat demonstration.

Bar Harbor has many interesting museums, including the **Abbe Museum**, which shares the history and culture of Maine's native people, collectively known as the Wabanaki (Penobscot, Passamaquoddy, Micmac, and Maliseet). The **Acadia Nature Center** features natural history exhibits, and the **Door Museum of Natural History** has exhibits of Maine animal and marine life. For a unique marine experience, visit the **Lobster Hatchery**, part of the Mount Desert Oceanarium that hatches lobsters for return to the ocean. There you'll find mother lobsters, little lobsters up to two weeks old, and lobsters being released, and you can even see the beating hearts of baby lobsters. Also check out the **Lulu Lobster Boat Ride**.

For kayakers, **National Park Sea Kayak Tours** provides ecological sea kayak tours on the quiet western side of Acadia. Buses also travel from Bar Harbor to the other side of the island. **Coastal Kayaking Tours** runs tours on both the east and west sides of Mount Desert Island, with a quiet tour outside Bar Harbor in Frenchman Bay around the Porcupine Islands. Both companies provide half and full day tours, and sunset tours.

Among the many specialty shops and restaurants, Bar Harbor has its share of micro breweries that sell award-winning beer and ale. Walk it off on the nearly mile-long Shore Path beginning at the town pier next to Agamont Park. Trolley service is available with **Oli's Trolley** for one-hour and two-hour park tours. **Acadia National Park Tours** provides two-hour and three-hour bus tours out of Bar Harbor.

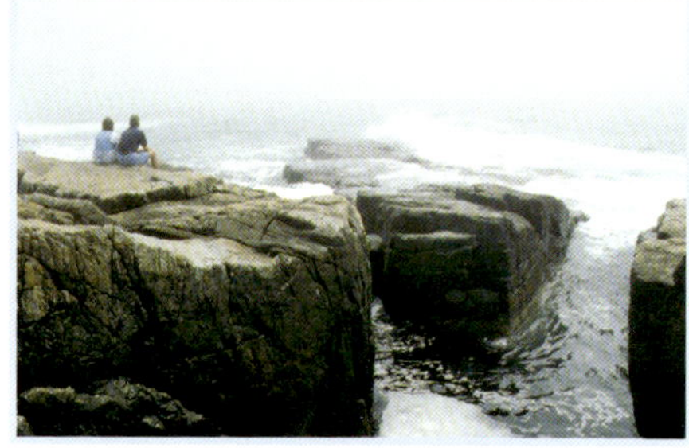

Watching the surf at Schoodic Point.

The Park Loop extends outside Mount Desert Island north to the Schoodic Peninsula. From the ferry pier, take the Island Explorer free shuttle bus to Schoodic Point, Winter Harbor, Birch Harbor, and Prospect Harbor. Winter Harbor is a classic Down East fishing village where lobstermen and scallop draggers thrive, as the harbor rarely freezes over in the winter.

As you head north out of Bar Harbor toward the peninsula, a dirt road on your left leads 440 feet up to Schoodic Head, a large hill that overlooks Frenchman Bay on one side and Dyer Bay on the other. The views are absolutely breathtaking, and it is so quiet you can hear the continuous roar of the surf. Here, as you continue south on the park's one-way loop road, you'll find an incredible display of surf smashing against a nearly 400-foot headland of rock formations. Heading back from Schoodic Peninsula, if you look carefully, there are

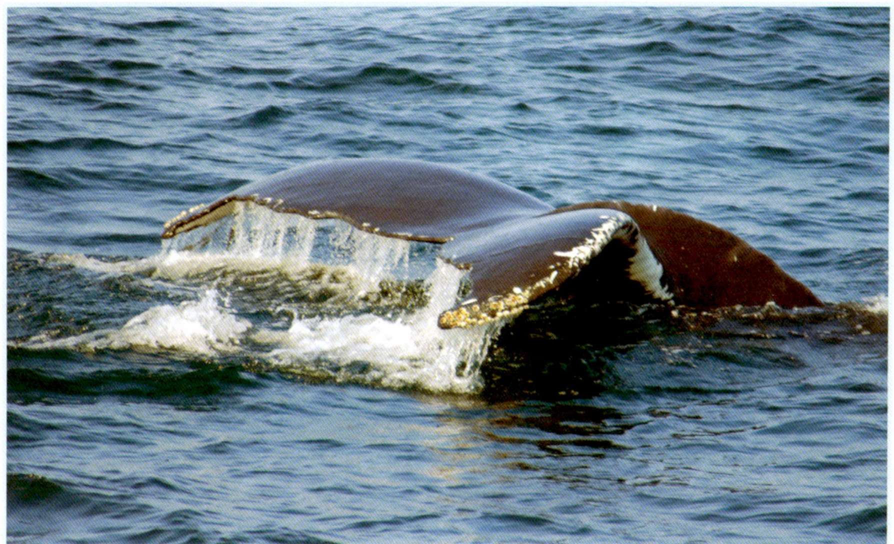

Lots of whale-watching tours leave out of Bar Harbor.

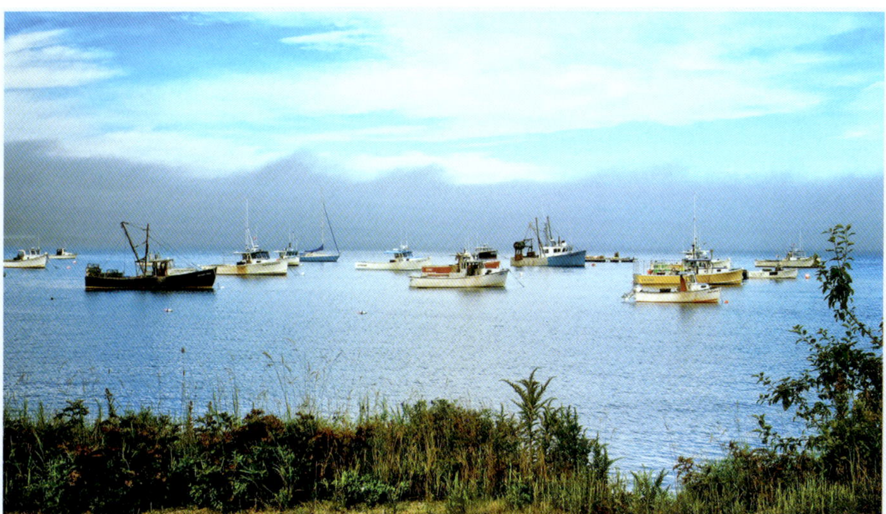

Prospect Harbor as fog starts to lift.

places along the road where you can pull over and hike along the shore. Near the Blueberry Hill sign is an intersection where you can pull over when the road rises and find this trail. When you reach the top of the hill you'll find another awe-inspiring view of the bay, its islands, and a distant view of Petit Manan Lighthouse; bring your binoculars.

Outside of Schoodic Point, Prospect Harbor is a quaint fishing village where you can enjoy some nice walks and view Prospect Harbor light purple lupine flowers are abundant in the summer.

Contacts for Attractions in Coastal Acadia

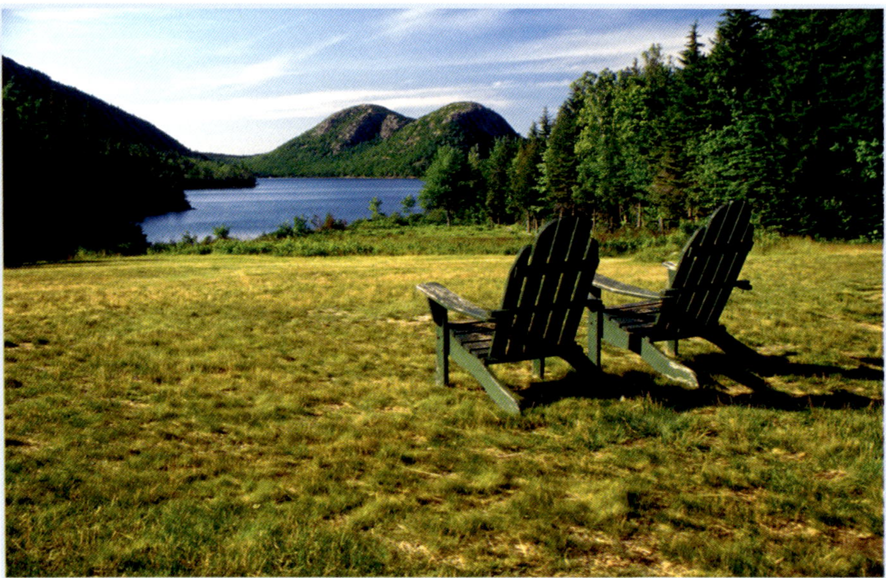

Acadia chairs overlooking Jordan Pond and Bubble Mountains.

Downeast Scenic Railroad, Ellsworth
(866) 449-7245
downeastscenicrail.org

Isle au Haut Keeper's House, Isle au Haut
(207) 335-2990
keepershouse.com

Acadia Park Service, Acadia
(207) 288-3338
nps.gov/acad/

Lumberjack Show, Trenton
(207) 667-0067
mainelumberjack.com

Island Cruises, Bass Harbor
(207) 244-5785
bassharborcruises.com

Maine State Ferry, Bass Harbor
(207) 244-3254
maine.gov/mdot/ferry/

Lunt's Dockside Deli, Frenchboro
(207) 334-2902
luntsdeli.com

Cranberry Cove Ferry, Southwest Harbor
(207) 244-5882
cranberryisles.com

Acadia Deep Sea Fishing, Southwest Harbor
(207) 244-5385
acadiafishingtours.com

Downeast Sailing Adventures, Southwest Harbor
(207) 288-2216
downeastsail.com

Cranberry Isles Mail Boat, Northeast Harbor
(207) 244-3575
cranberryisles.com

Islesford Historical Museum, Islesford
(207) 288-3388
islesfordhistoricalmuseum.info

Sea Princess Cruises, Northeast Harbor
(207) 276-5352
barharborcruises.com

Asticou Azalea Garden, Northeast Harbor
(207) 276-3727
gardenpreserve.org

Sail Acadia, Northeast Harbor
(207) 266-5210
sailacadia.com

Wildwood Stables, Houlton
(877) 276-3622
carriagesofacadia.com

Bar Harbor Info, Bar Harbor
(800) 345-4617
barharborinfo.com

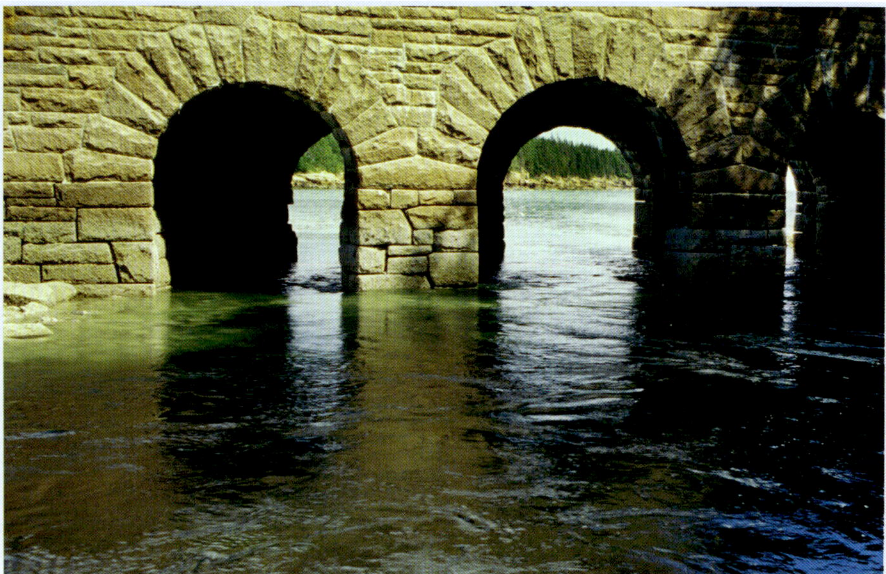

Old carriage bridges cover many miles over rivers in Acadia National Park.

Abbe Museum, Bar Harbor
(207) 288-3519
abbemuseum.org

Door Museum of Natural History, Bar Harbor
(207) 288-5015
coamuseum.org

Acadia Nature Center, Bar Harbor
(207) 288-3003
nps.gov/acad/

Bar Harbor Whale Watch, Bar Harbor
(207) 288-2386
barharborwhales.com

Lulu Lobster Boat Ride, Bar Harbor
(207) 963-2341
lululobsterboat.com

Baker Island Hike, Bar Harbor
(207) 288-2386
barharborwhales.com

Lobster Hatchery, Bar Harbor
(207) 244-7330
theoceanarium.com

National Park Kayak Tours, Bar Harbor
(800) 347-0940
acadiakayak.com

Coastal Kayaking Tours, Bar Harbor
(800) 526-8615
acadiafun.com

Bar Harbor Campground, Bar Harbor
(207) 288-5185
thebarharborcampground.com

Oli's Trolley, Bar Harbor
(207) 288-9899
olistrolley.com

Acadia National Park Tours, Bar Harbor
(207) 288-0300
acadiatours.com

Bar Harbor Ferry, Bar Harbor
(207) 546-2927
downeastwindjammer.com

Downeast Cruises, Bar Harbor
(207) 288-4585
downeastwindjammer.com

Schoodic Area, Winter Harbor
acadia-schoodic.org

Lighthouse Cruises around Acadia

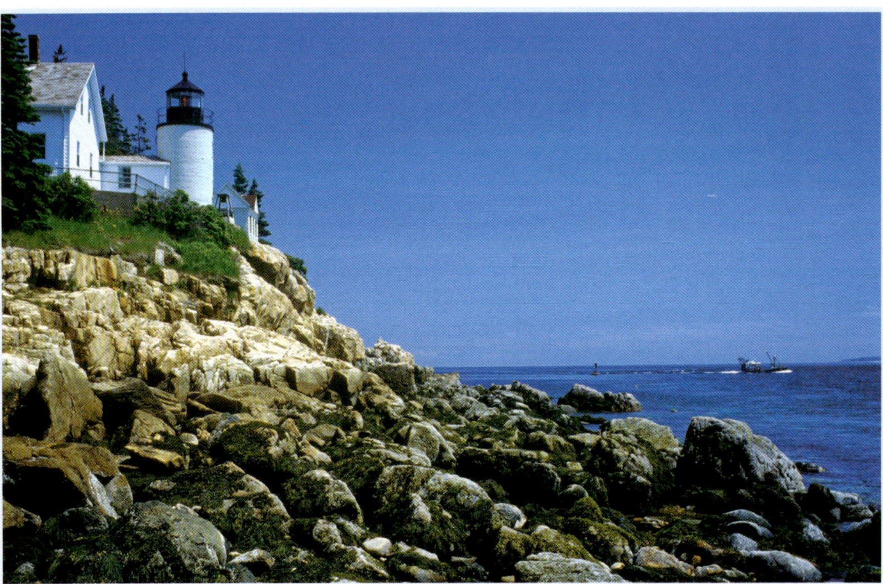

Bass Harbor Light is the most popular beacon in the Acadia region.

Isle au Haut Boat Company

Daily service to Isle au Haut.

Sea Breeze Avenue, Stonington

(207) 367-6516

isleauhaut.com

Lighthouse: Isle au Haut

Acadia Deep Sea Fishing Tours

Deep-sea fishing tours out of Southwest Harbor; sometimes goes out as far as Mount Desert Rock Light (weather permitting).

182 Clark Point Road, Southwest Harbor, ME 04679

(207) 244-5385

acadiafishingtours.com

Lighthouse: Mount Desert Rock

Sea Princess Cruises

Narrated wildlife cruises.

20 Sea Street, Northeast Harbor

(207) 276-5352

barharborcruises.com

Lighthouses: Bear Island and Bass Harbor

Sail Acadia

(*Allice E.)* 11 Apple Lane, Southwest Harbor

(*Helen Brooks*) 41 Harbor Drive, Northeast Harbor

(207) 266-5210

sailacadia.com

Lighthouse: Bear Island

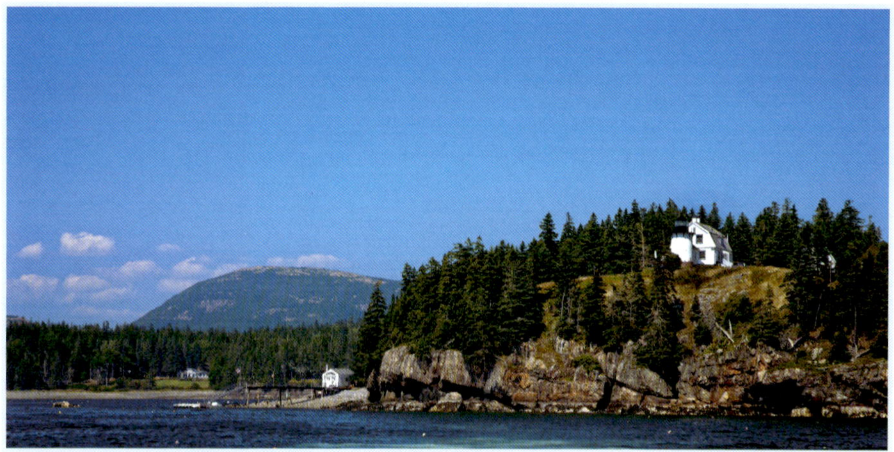

Cranberry Islands cruises often pass Bear Island Light.

Bar Harbor Whale Watch Company

Lighthouse tour to Baker Island allows you to walk to the lighthouse. There is also the Lighthouse and National Park Tour that visits up to five lighthouses.

1 West Street, Bar Harbor

(207) 288-2386 or (888) WHALES-4

barharborwhales.com

Lighthouses: Baker Island, Bear Island, Great Duck Island, Egg Rock, Winter Harbor

The Swan's Island Ferry

Maine Ferry Service.

118 Ferry Road, Swan's Island

(207) 526-4273 or (800) 491-4883

swansisland.org/ferry.htm

Island Cruises

Little Island Way, Bass Harbor, Maine

(207) 244-5785

bassharborcruises.com

Lighthouses: Bass Harbor

Bar Harbor Ferry

Tours and ferry service along Mount Desert Island from Bar Harbor to Little Cranberry Island to Southwest Harbor.

(207) 288-2984 or (207) 546-2927

downeastwindjammer.com/

Islesford Ferry

Ellsworth

(207) 276-3717 or (207) 422-6815

islesford.com

Lighthouses: Bear Island, Baker Island

Sea Venture Custom Boat Tours

Chartered boat tours for a small number of passengers.

Capt. Winston Shaw, Bar Harbor, Maine

(207) 412-0222

svboattours.com

Lighthouses: Pond Island, Petit Manan, Prospect Harbor, Mark Island, Egg Rock, Baker Island, Bear Island, Bass Harbor Head, Great Duck, Burnt Coat Harbor, Blue Hill Bay, Pumpkin Island

Acadian Nature Cruises

1 West Street, Bar Harbor, Maine

(888) 533-9253 or (207) 288-2386

acadiannaturecruises.com

Lighthouse: Egg Rock

Waterfront Directions

Southwest Harbor
Follow Route 3 to Route 102 and continue until you reach Main Street. Turn left on Seawall Road, Route 102A, and then left on Ocean House Road and right on Shore Road.

Northeast Harbor
From Route 3, stay straight to take Route 102/198. Turn left on Sound Drive, Route 3/198 and follow it to the harbor. Use Harbor Drive toward marina.

Bar Harbor
Follow Route 3 east for ten miles. Once you cross the causeway to Mount Desert Island, follow Route 3 to the left at the stoplight. In about ten miles, turn left onto West Street; the first street on your left is Bar Harbor.

Scenic Flights

Acadia Air Tours
Flights from a biplane or glider. Lighthouse tour includes Schoodic Peninsula, Winter Harbor, Cranberry Islands, Southwest Harbor, Bass Harbor, and seven lighthouses.

Bar Harbor Airport, Trenton

(207) 667-7627

acadia.net

Island Soaring

(207) 667-SOAR

islandsoaring.net

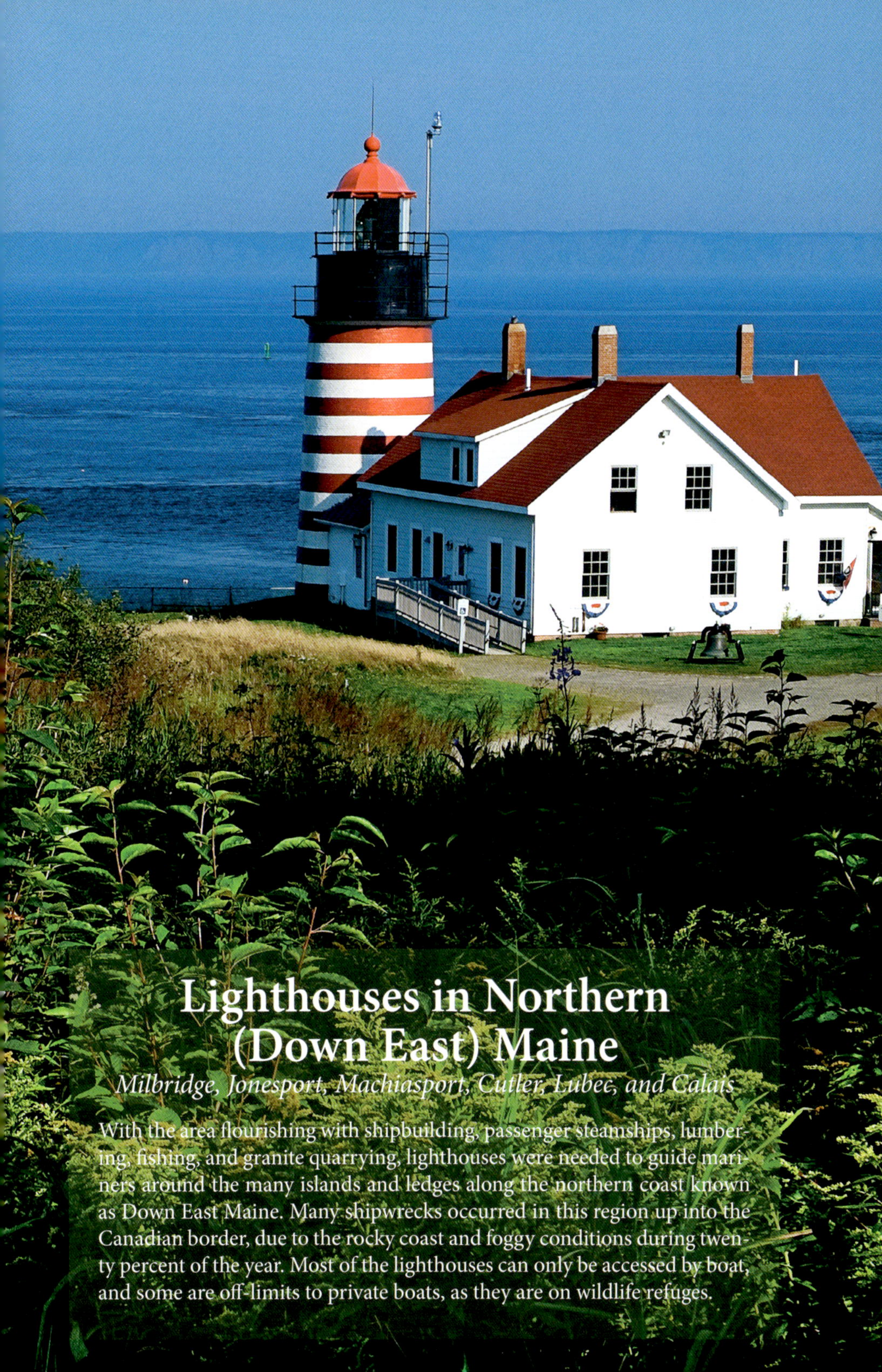

Lighthouses in Northern (Down East) Maine

Milbridge, Jonesport, Machiasport, Cutler, Lubec, and Calais

With the area flourishing with shipbuilding, passenger steamships, lumbering, fishing, and granite quarrying, lighthouses were needed to guide mariners around the many islands and ledges along the northern coast known as Down East Maine. Many shipwrecks occurred in this region up into the Canadian border, due to the rocky coast and foggy conditions during twenty percent of the year. Most of the lighthouses can only be accessed by boat, and some are off-limits to private boats, as they are on wildlife refuges.

West Quoddy Head Lighthouse lies in the easternmost corner of the United States.

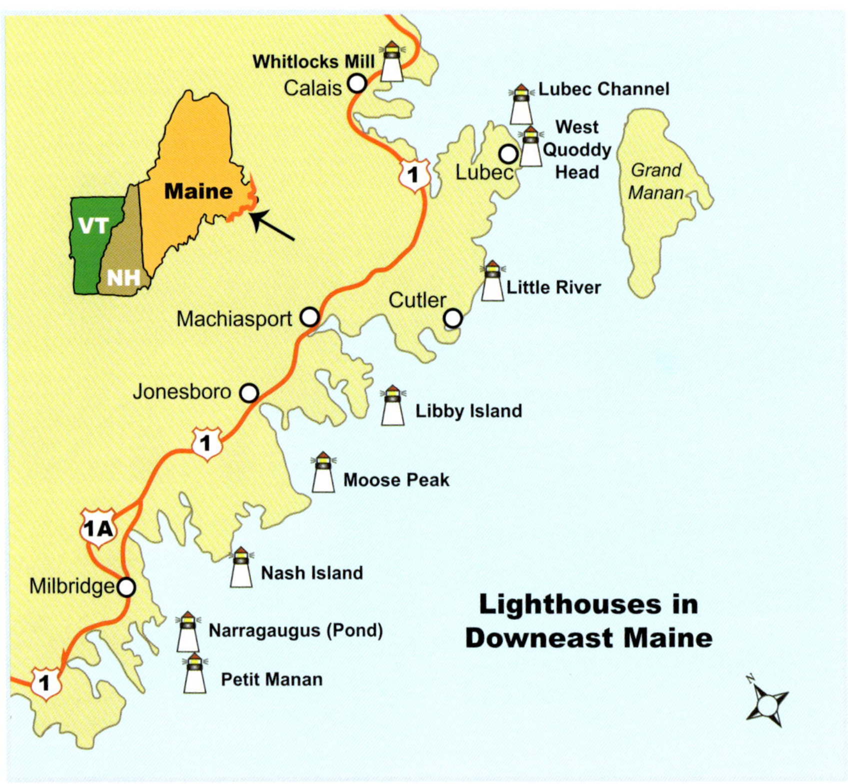

Lighthouses in northern (Down East) Maine.

Petit Manan Lighthouse

Corea (1817) • Latitude: 44° 22' 03" N • Longitude: 67° 51' 52" W

Petit Manan Lighthouse helped mariners navigate around a treacherous bar between Petit Manan Island and Petit Manan Point on the shore in this extremely foggy area outside the Mount Desert (Acadia) region. The current tower is Maine's second tallest (the tallest is on Boon Island). The first keeper, Robert Leighton, was fired because an inspector found the lighthouse dirty during a surprise visit that occurred when the keeper left his wife to look after the lighthouse while he went ashore to gather supplies. The lighthouse tower was rebuilt numerous times as a result of storm damage in the 1800s, and many keepers' logs recorded strange accumulations of dead birds in the lantern room and around the tower.

A one-room schoolhouse was built for the children of the keepers. When Lilla Cole arrived as a teacher in 1915, the keeper told her that his wife was about to give birth and asked for her help, as the doctor had not yet arrived. The surprised teacher ended up helping to deliver the couple's eighth child. When the doctor finally arrived, he congratulated Cole, thinking she was a nurse summoned to assist.

In December 1916, keeper Eugene C. Ingalls set out for Moose Peak Lighthouse in his boat. The beacon was some miles away and the keeper was looking forward

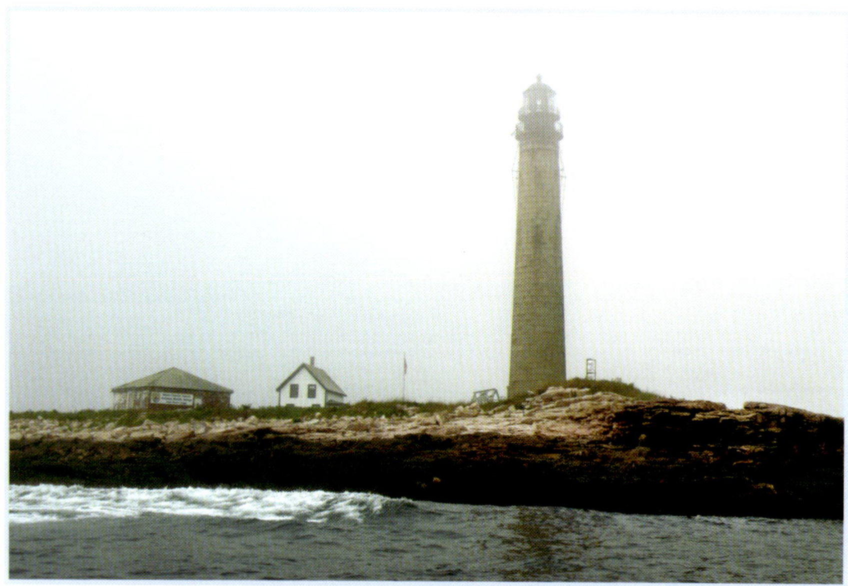

Petite Manan Lighthouse is Maine's second tallest beacon.

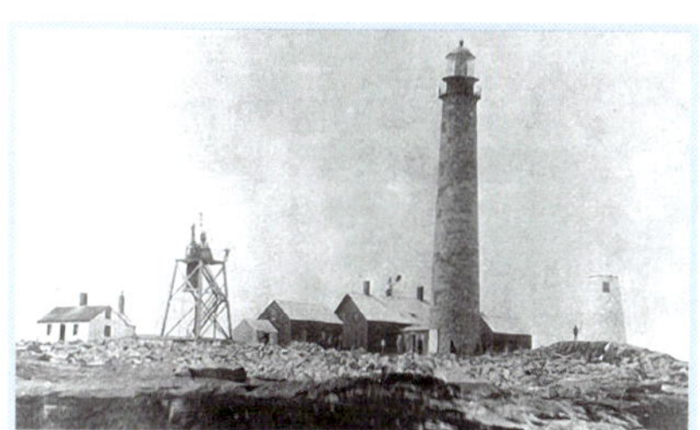

Early 1800s construction. *Courtesy US Coast Guard.*

to visiting his wife, who was visiting her father, the keeper of Moose Peak. Unfortunately, he disappeared in a storm and his body was never recovered.

During a severe winter storm in 1934, keeper Edward Pettegrow caught a distress signal from a lobsterman. A rescue was impossible, and a day and a half later, the lobsterman was feared lost, but the keepers caught sight of his boat from the lantern room and sent out a signal for help. Local seamen quickly rescued him. He was barely alive from hyperthermia, but the lucky man somehow managed to recover.

Petit Manan became the second brightest light in Maine following its conversion to electricity in 1938. The Coast Guard took over the station in 1939, turning it into a "stag" station of only men. The light was automated in 1972 and became part of the Petit Manan Wildlife Refuge, now part of the Maine Coastal Islands National Wildlife Refuge. Restoration efforts on the lighthouse and structures have been ongoing since the early 1990s.

Narragaugus (Pond Island) Lighthouse

Milbridge (1853) • Latitude: 44° 27' 19" N • Longitude: 67° 50' 00" W

Narragaugus (Pond Island) Lighthouse guided ships, carrying predominantly lumber, coming from the Narragaugus River into the harbor by Milbridge. Joseph

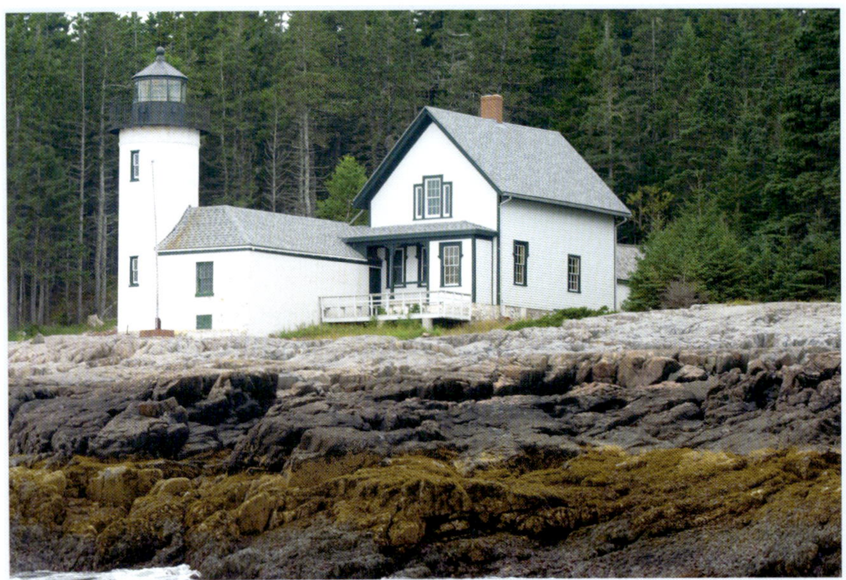

Narragaugus (Pond Island) Lighthouse is a half-mile from shore.

Brown served as the first keeper and was replaced in 1855 by Wyman Collins. Keepers had to walk a half-mile from shore to reach the lighthouse. Most of the keepers only stayed on for a few years, until William C. Gott arrived in 1893 and stayed until 1915.

Elizabeth Hitchcock was a local girl who loved to visit the Gott family at the lighthouse. On one visit, Gott was fishing near the lighthouse when Elizabeth spotted the inspector's boat approaching. Knowing the keeper was on the other side of the small island, she grabbed his uniform, and ran to inform him of the surprise inspection. Keeper Gott came out of the woods in full uniform just as the inspector landed.

On August 4, 1929, when the schooner *Valdare* shipwrecked on the Petit Manan Bar, the keepers of Petit Manan Lighthouse found that the crew and officers had made it safely to nearby Narragaugus Lighthouse in a rowboat, where they were cared for by keeper Charles Tracey for nearly two weeks. He and the keepers at Petit Manan received a letter of thanks from the British Counsel after the crew made it back to Nova Scotia.

The house has been the scene of paranormal activity. In the 1970s, two college boys, friends of the Dameron family at the lighthouse, came to help with repairs and were staying in a downstairs bedroom. They were awakened by the voice of a woman speaking angrily in a foreign language, and the only woman in the house was the owner Nancy Dameron, who only spoke English. The following night, one of the young men heard a loud noise next to him, as if a weight had fallen near his pillow, but could see nothing. Both boys got up and proclaimed that they were only there to help repair the house not to hurt it. During the rest of their stay, the room remained quiet.

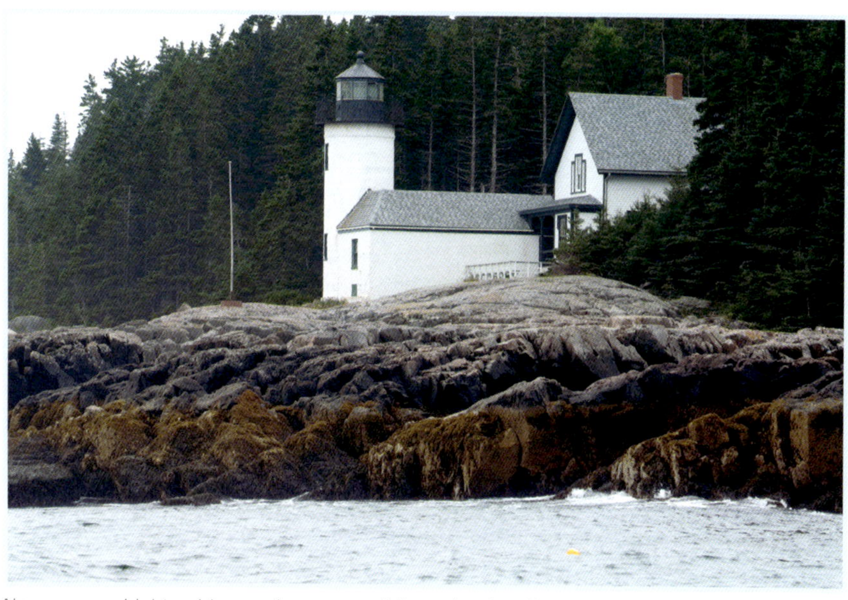

Narragaugus Light guides mariners around its rocky shoreline and nearby ledges.

Nash Island Lighthouse

Addison (1838) • Latitude: 44° 27' 50" N • Longitude: 67° 44' 45" W

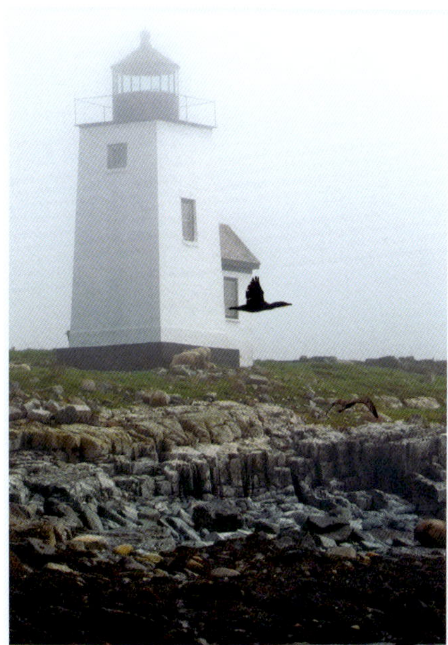

Nash Island Light is still used to graze sheep, and is usually in fog.

Many of the islands that had dotted Maine's coastline were used for pasturing sheep, and each spring there would be a shearing ritual. Today this practice has all but vanished, but there is still a pair of islands, Big and Little Nash Islands off Addison, where volunteers congregate each spring to keep the tradition alive.

John Purington was appointed keeper of the lighthouse on Little Nash Island in 1916. He and his wife Ellen raised nine children on the islands, and it was their daughter Jenney who helped to maintain the shearing tradition, as they kept sheep all during their tenure. After keeper Purlington retired in 1935, Jenny and her husband spent the next few years purchasing land that wasn't government-owned on Big and Little Nash Islands and kept her sheep there until she died in 2004, at the age of ninety-one. She even piloted her own lobster boats for over seventy

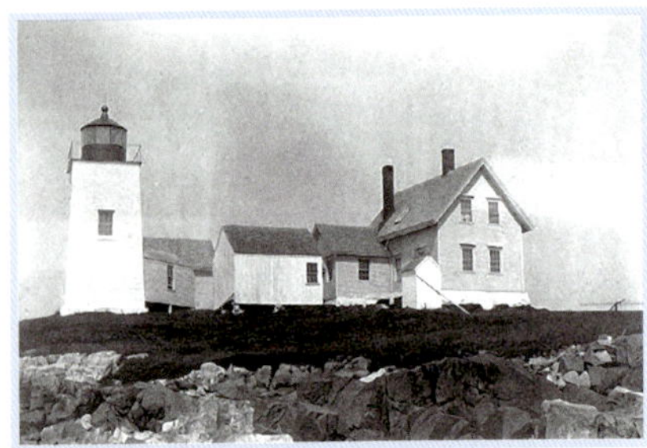

Vintage image with buildings. *Courtesy US Coast Guard.*

years. She inspired the continued preservation of the lighthouse and island.

With eleven children on the island including those of the assistant keeper, a small schoolhouse was built and a teacher was brought over from the mainland. When the children reached high school age, they attended high school on the mainland in Jonesport.

Keeper Allen Holt received a special commendation from Washington after rescuing the crew of a fishing schooner during a fierce storm. During his tenure on the island, his children were given the task of counting bird nests for the Audubon Society. Today Nash Island is a US Fish and Wildlife Service area for migratory birds and is maintained by the Friends of Nash Island Light.

Moose Peak Lighthouse

Jonesport (1825) • Latitude: 44° 28' 26" N • Longitude: 67° 31' 54" W

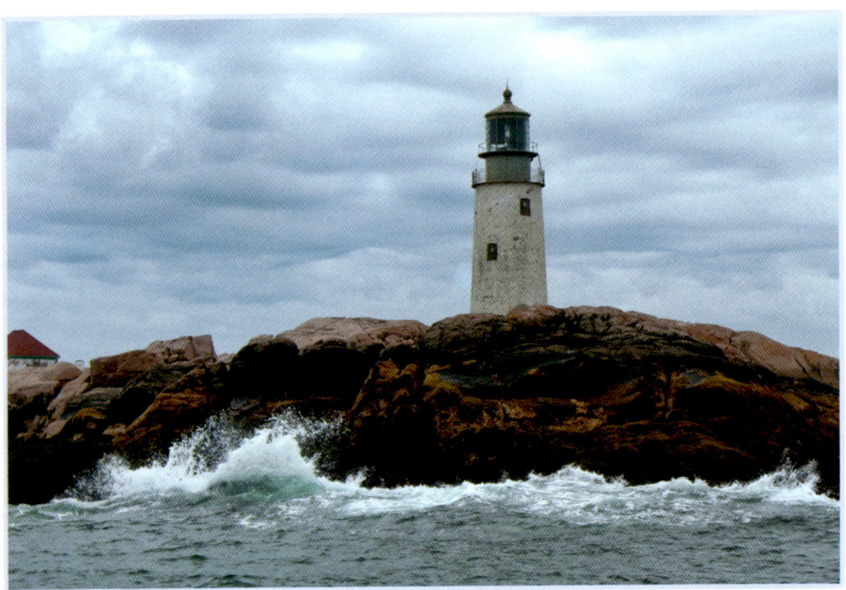

Moose Peak Lighthouse in Jonesport, Maine.

Mistake Island is one of the foggiest locations in Maine, prompting the need for Moose Peak Lighthouse, sometimes referred to as Mistake Island Light. The first keeper was Alexander Milliken, who filed a petition in 1831 "praying" for an outhouse. It is not known whether he received the much-needed outhouse. Milliken was the longest-serving keeper and retired in 1849.

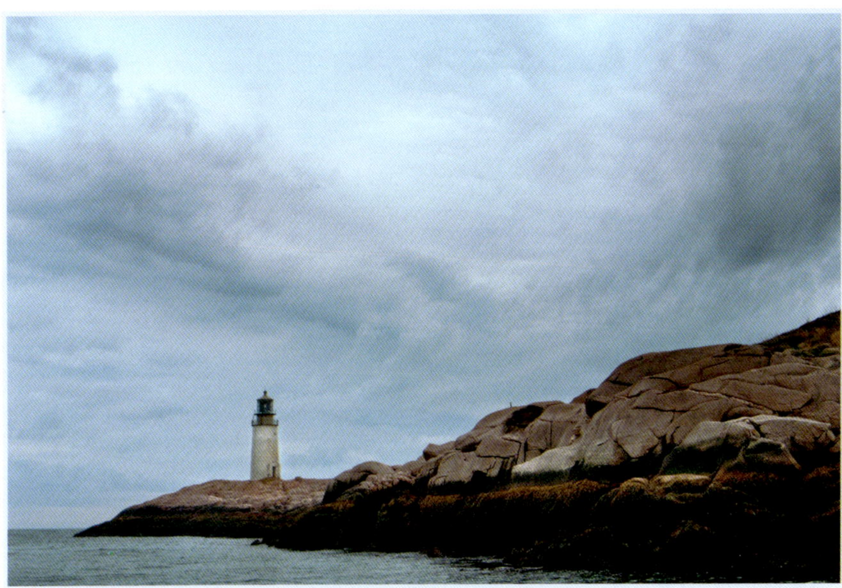

Moose Peak Light is in Maine's stormy and foggy region.

On November 26, 1896, keeper Charles R. Dobbins and his son rescued the crew of the Nova Scotian schooner *Ashton*. The Canadian government rewarded Dobbins for "humane and gallant services" with a gold watch, but the keeper could not accept the gift until an act of Congress was finally passed on March 28, 1900, authorizing him to do so.

Records indicate that the lighthouse is in fog at least twenty percent of the time. A powerful foghorn signal house with a diaphragm foghorn was erected in 1912. Fog was so bad for a number of days in 1916 that the loud blasts of the horn were heard for 181 hours straight. Between 1918 and 1934, Moose Peak Light logged more hours of dense fog than any other lighthouse in Maine, averaging about 1,600 hours per year.

In May of 1920, keeper Henry Kay and his assistant Maurice Beal, were approaching the island during heavy seas when a rogue wave knocked them out of their boat. They shouted for help, and second assistant Harry E. Freeman ran to the shore while keeper Ray's wife and children looked on. Freeman pulled Beal to safety, but the keeper was not as lucky. He tried to get back in the dory, and was thrown into the raging waters as the boat capsized. The outgoing tide pulled Kay away from the island in front of his family, and he disappeared beneath the waves.

The lighthouse was automated in 1972 but couldn't be sold for private property, as the sewerage system did not meet EPA standards and was too expensive to build.

In 1982, the military blew up the keeper's quarters as part of a training exercise. Instead of imploding, it exploded, causing damage to the lighthouse and nearby helicopter pad (oops!). The lighthouse was converted to solar power in 1999, and today the Nature Conservancy manages Mistake Island.

Libby Island Lighthouse

Machiasport (1823) • Latitude: 44° 34' 06" N • Longitude: 67° 22' 00" W

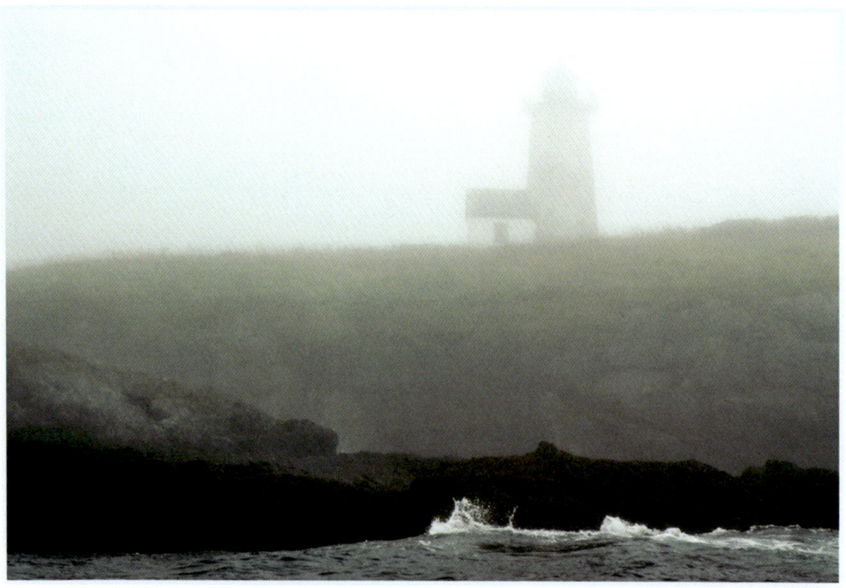

Libby Island Lighthouse engulfed in fog.

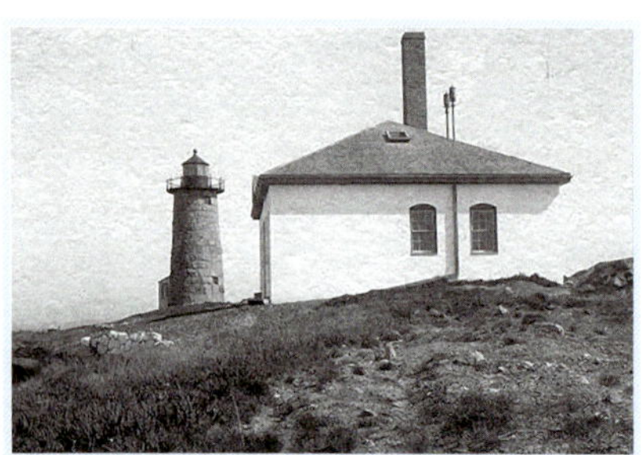

Vintage image. *Courtesy US Coast Guard*

The first naval battle of the American Revolution occurred near Libby Island. Although locals built a wooden lighthouse around 1817, the tower, set up by government funding, was built in 1823. John McKellar was its first keeper.

Because of the dense fog, Libby Island Lighthouse had to have two keepers on site, one responsible solely for the fog bell. In 1890, the fog bell sounded for over 2,200 hours. In 1878, the schooner *Caledonia* ran into ledges near the island, and only two passengers were saved.

Libby Island is actually two islands connected by a sand bar. During a fierce September storm in 1892, the keepers were able to rescue all crew members of the ship *Princeport,* which had run aground onto the bar. The ship was breaking apart, and all would have perished if not for the quick response of the lighthouse staff.

In dense fog in 1906, the schooner *Ella G. Ellis* was heading from New York City to New Brunswick, Canada, when the vessel wrecked near Libby Island. All crew members drowned as the ship broke apart immediately, and only the captain survived as he clung to the roof of the ship's cabin and drifted ashore with the incoming tide.

With two keepers and their families, there were up to twenty people on the island. They lived not only on fish and lobster, but at times had a cow and chickens. Libby Island and its neighboring islands were also abundant with berries.

The lighthouse was automated in 1974. In 1998, it was turned over to the US Fish and Wildlife Service, and in 2000, the tower was overhauled and the light was converted to solar power.

Little River Lighthouse

Cutler (1847) • Latitude: 44° 39' 03" N • Longitude: 67° 11' 32" W

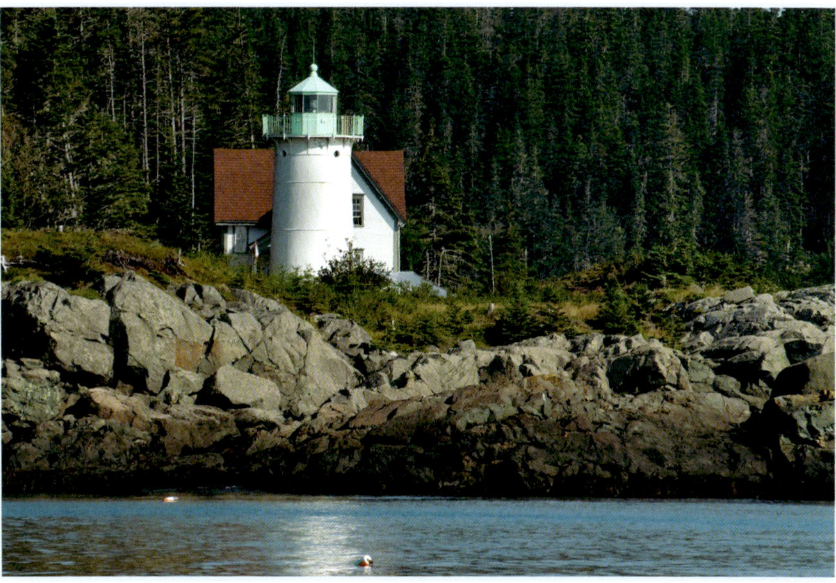

Little River Lighthouse outside Cutler Harbor, Maine.

Little River Lighthouse was originally a stone tower attached to a keeper's granite house. Its first keeper was Zebediah Tucker. In 1876 the stone tower was replaced with a cast iron tower, which is standing today. The granite keeper's house was replaced in 1888 with a wooden Victorian-style building, which is also still standing. Going to school meant a boat ride every morning and afternoon for the keeper's children, as their father ferried them to the mainland and back. When the weather was bad, they would stay with assigned families on shore until the keeper could retrieve them. As Cutler became a popular summer resort, passenger steamers wanted to add Little River Harbor as a stopping place, but they insisted that a more powerful steam fog signal be added to the station.

Keeper Lucius Davis provided food and shelter for a schooner's crew after it beached near the lighthouse on November 21, 1875, and he helped out a badly frostbitten crew that wrecked on January 28, 1881. The crew of a fishing schooner barely survived in December 1884, after being caught in a gale. On July 21, 1889, the crew of the Spanish steamer *Eduardo* didn't hear either Little River's fog bell or

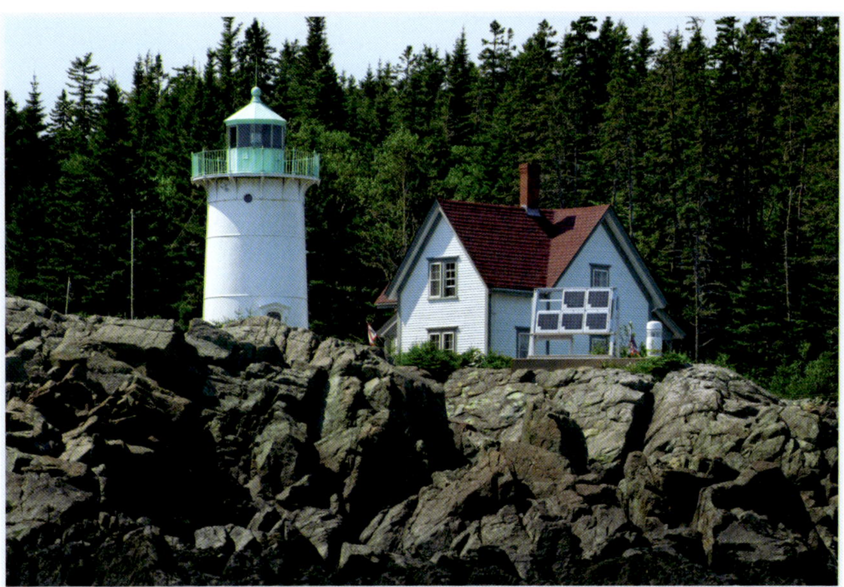

Visitors can make reservations to stay overnight at Little River Light.

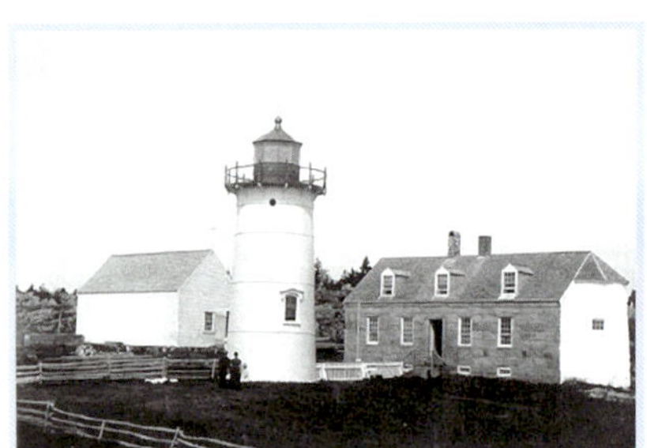

Vintage image 1876 construction. *Courtesy US Coast Guard.*

a nearby whistling buoy and struck the island at low tide on July 21, 1889, during a dense fog. The crew members survived, but the ship was a total loss. The lighthouse board determined that the wreck of the *Eduardo* and others would not have occurred if a stronger steam-driven fog signal had been installed. What is strange is that the board recommended a stronger fog signal each year for over fifteen years, but it was never built.

In December of 1897, the schooner *Julia A Warr* left Calais Maine for Fall River, Massachusetts, and sank in a storm with all six of her crew aboard. Two bodies found washed ashore near Little River Lighthouse were believed to be from the ill-fated schooner, and were buried near the boathouse. Plans were made to create a marker and fence around the site.

One keeper in the early 1900s, Neil Corbet, was quite a fiddler and would play at Saturday night dances. He tended Little River Lighthouse with his family for seventeen years. In 1975, a skeletal tower replaced the lighthouse tower. In 2000, the American Lighthouse Foundation took over some of the restoration efforts of the lighthouse and surrounding structures with the help of the Coast Guard, and in 2001 the lighthouse was relit with much fanfare. Restoration continues, funded partly by income from overnight visitors.

Lubec Channel Lighthouse

Lubec (1890) • Latitude: 44° 50' 31" N • Longitude: 67° 58' 36" W

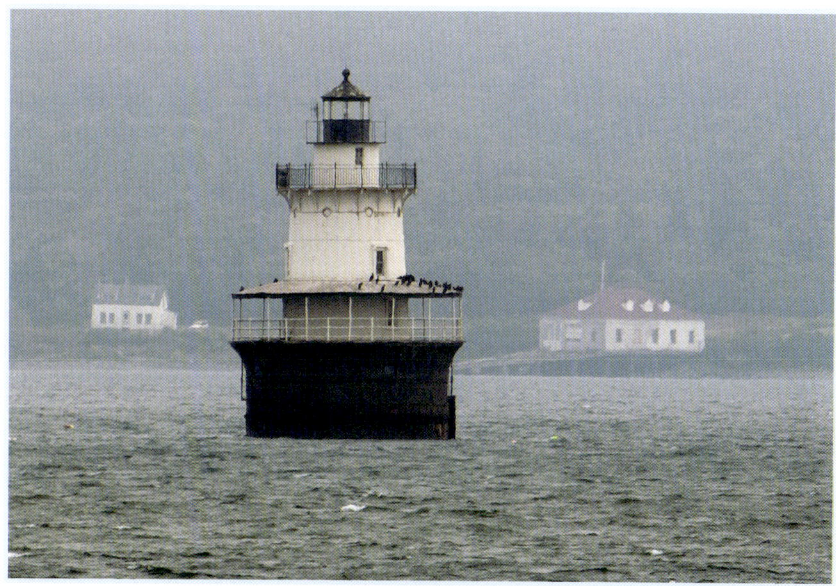

Lubec Channel Light is a fifty-three-foot sparkplug beacon with five floors.

Lubec Channel Lighthouse accommodated shipping in Lubec Channel from twenty sardine packing plants and other fishing industries, especially night traffic at the entrance to the Lubec Narrows Channel. Its first keeper was Frederick W. Morong, and its last keeper was Earl Ashby in 1939. The fifty-three-foot tower's spark plug design had five levels, two of which were keepers' living quarters. In 1939, the Grand Manan Ferry captain found the last assistant keeper, Nathaniel Alley, overcome by fumes from a coal stove. He was taken to Lubec for medical attention but later died.

Loring Myers was a steamboat captain who had lost his wife and three children to illness. He remarried and became keeper from 1898 to 1923. He also moonlighted as an entrepreneur and owned a sardine plant. In 1904, the keeper was credited with inventing a special type of lifeboat that was especially buoyant and watertight and could carry up to fifteen people. It was highly praised, but the steamship lines never adopted it because it was too expensive.

In 1989, the lighthouse was going to be discontinued, but local residents were able to save the lighthouse by mounting a "Save the Sparkplug" campaign that included handing out automobile spark plugs. The lighthouse had been setting at an angle for many years, and in 1992, as part of restoration efforts, the base was rebuilt to straighten out the tower. The lighthouse was repainted in 2001 and today is privately owned.

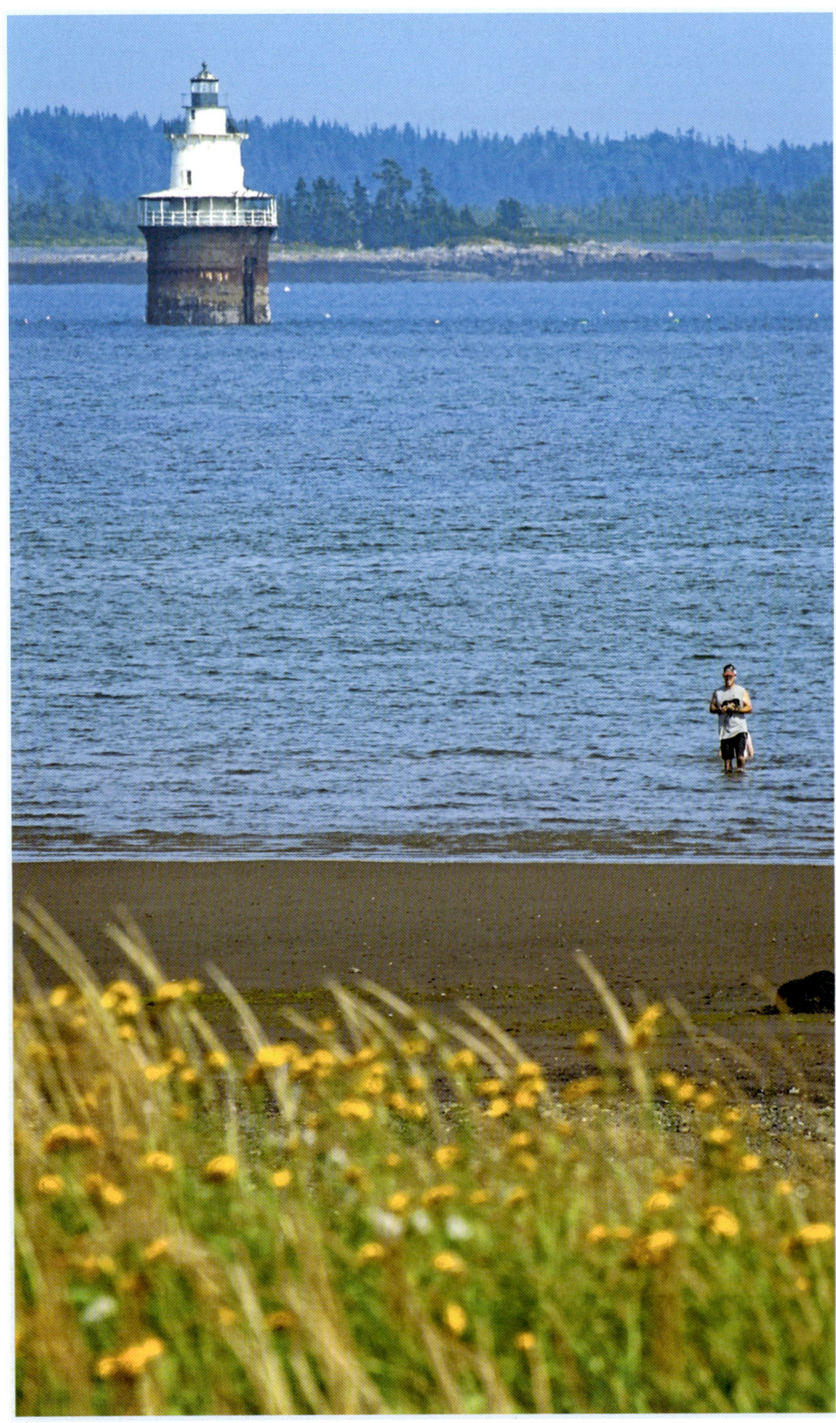

Lubec Channel Lighthouse view from shore.

 **Directions for a distant view of Lubec Channel Light.** To see the lighthouse from Highway 1 north in Whiting, continue east on Highway 189 for just under ten miles toward Lubec. Before reaching Lubec, turn south on Boot Cove Road, where you can get a distant view of the lighthouse in the channel.

West Quoddy Head Lighthouse

Lubec (1808) • Latitude: 44° 48' 55" N • Longitude: 66° 57' 04" W

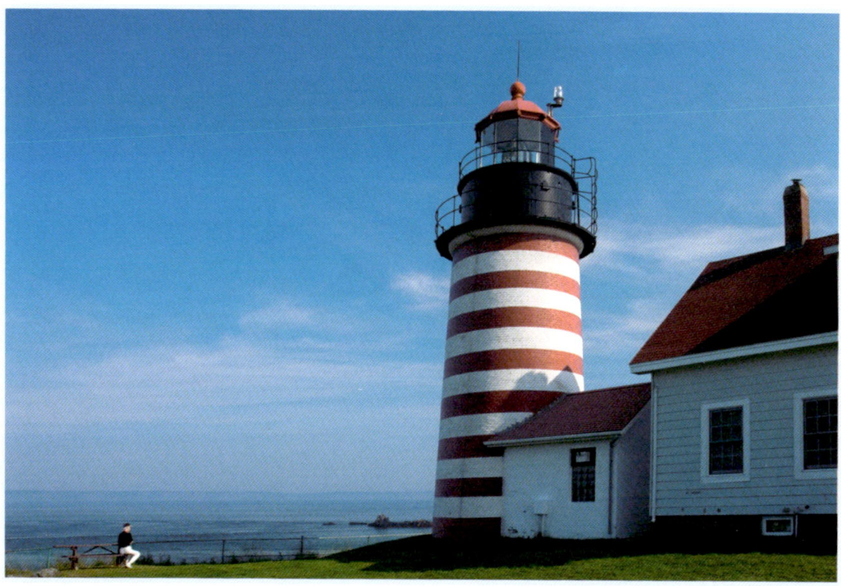

West Quoddy Head Lighthouse.

West Quoddy Head Lighthouse, on forty-foot-high cliffs overlooking Quoddy Narrows near the Bay of Fundy, stands on the easternmost point of the United States, although it is west of East Quoddy Head Light (also referred to as Head Harbor Light) a few miles away on Canada's Campobello Island. It is one of the oldest lighthouses in Maine, with Thomas Dexter as its first keeper.

To warn ships of the frequent fog banks that formed off the Bay of Fundy, a 500-pound fog bell was installed in 1820, one of the nation's first fog bells. When mariners had problems hearing the bell in time to avoid the rocks, the station tried a high-pitched bell, then a 1,500-pound deeper-sounding bell, and then a fourteen-foot triangular steel bar. None proved satisfactory. Today West Quoddy Head has a powerful foghorn activated by a robotic fog-sensing device.

West Quoddy Head Lighthouse was rebuilt in 1831, and in 1857 the tower was reconstructed as it appears today, rising eight-five feet above the water. Its distinctive red-and-white stripes offer daytime mariners better visibility, especially in winter months.

In thick fog on September 22, 1915, the three-masted schooner *Lanie Cobb* was heading to Calais from New York with a cargo of coal when it ran aground near the

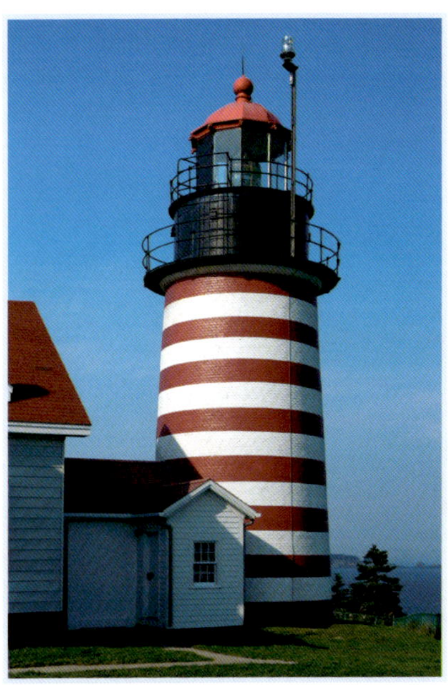

West Quoddy Head Light is also referred to as the "Candy Cane Lighthouse."

lighthouse and broke in two. The crew members were immediately rescued without any fatalities.

In 1929, keeper Ephraim N. Johnson received word that a ship had run aground about a mile from the station. He and assistant Eugene Larrabee ran down to the shoreline, along with locals who had heard the news. The two-masted vessel could be seen wedged on a rocky ledge not far from the shoreline. They were able to get a line to the wreck, allowing the crewmen to climb over to the rocks one at a time. As soon as everyone was safely onshore, the wreck slid off the rocks and sank below the waves within minutes.

The keepers' children had a two-mile walk to school in Lubec. In the 1920s, the children of keeper Arthur Robie Marston found lumber washed ashore and built a play hut in the woods. The structure was still standing into the 1990s.

Howard "Bob" Gray was the last civilian keeper (and first Coast Guard keeper) from 1934 to 1952; his father was also a keeper at other Maine stations. During WWII, Gray's daughters, Dorothy and Carolyn, along with a couple of friends, came upon what appeared to be a bomb at a beach nearby. They put the device in the back seat of Carolyn's old Chevy and drove home over a bumpy road to show their father. The surprised and anxious keeper immediately notified Washington. Inspectors determined that the device was a German-made decoy.

 **Exploring the grounds.** The lighthouse overlooks Quoddy Narrows at Quoddy Head State Park, off Route 189 from Route 1. The tower is closed, but visitors are welcome to enjoy the lighthouse grounds and explore the visitor center and museum run by the West Quoddy Head Light Keepers Association. The lighthouse is part of Quoddy State Park with miles of nature trails over scenic coastal terrain. The US Coast Guard buildings by the lighthouse, the keeper's cottage, cabin, and station house, have been restored and are available for overnight stays. The views at West Quoddy Head Light are spectacular, with Canada's Grand Manan Island in front of you as you stand on the cliff.

 **Directions.** From Route 1, take Route 189 at Whiting and head toward Lubec near the Canadian border. After about ten miles, turn right at the lighthouse sign on the road to Quoddy Head State Park. Follow this road for about five miles to the parking lot by the lighthouse.

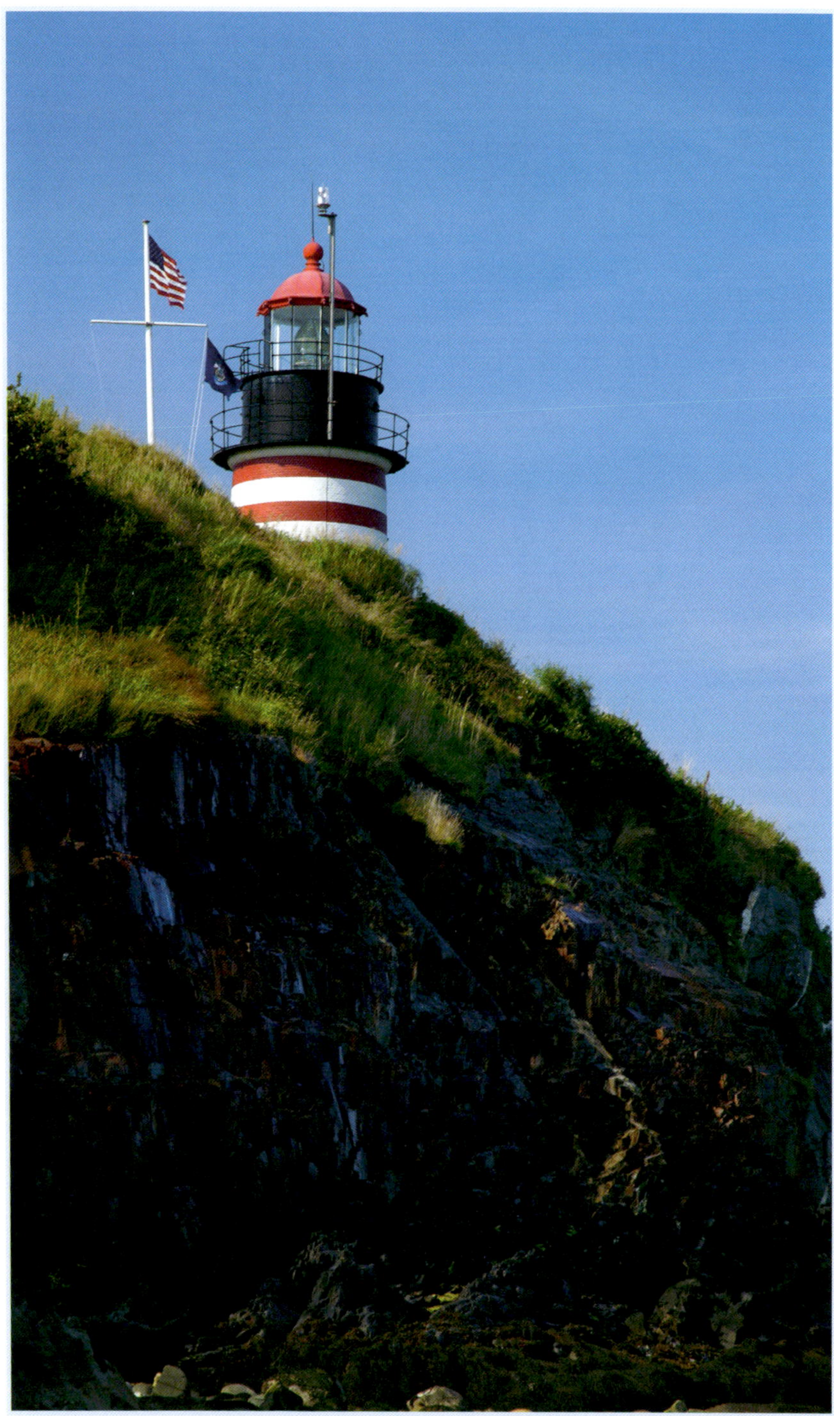

View of lighthouse tower over shoreline cliffs.

Whitlocks Mill Lighthouse

Calais (1910) • Latitude: 45° 09' 46" N • Longitude: 67° 13' 39" W

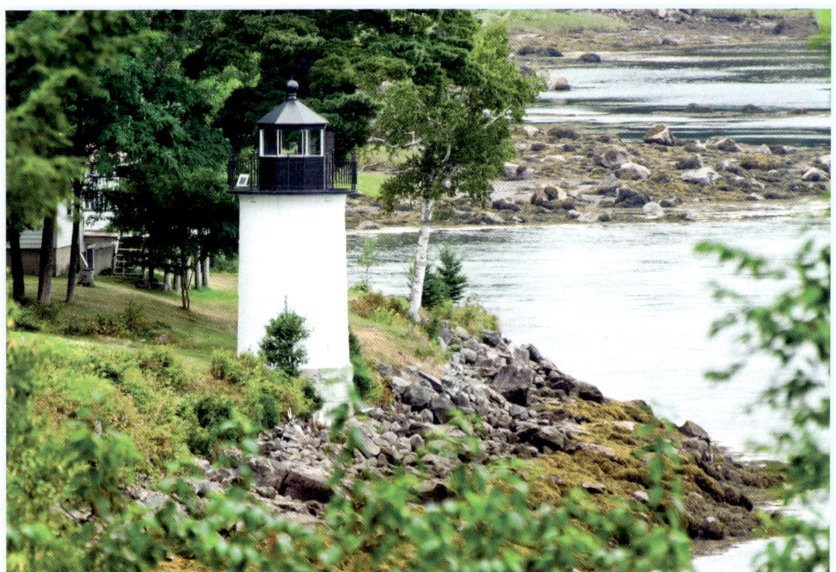

Whitlocks Mill Lighthouse is New England's northernmost lighthouse.

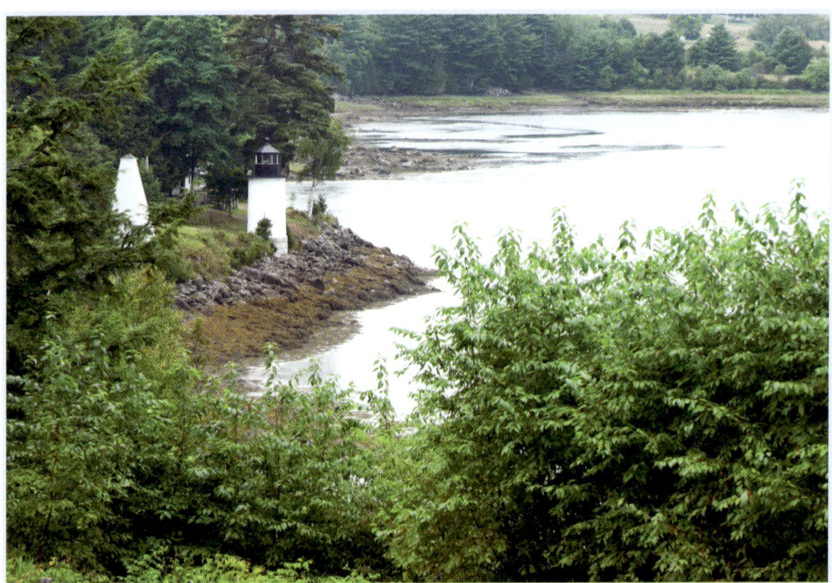

Whitlocks Mill Light protects mariners around a bend in the St. Croix River.

Calais was an important lumbering port in the late nineteenth century. In 1892, a lantern on a tree operated by local miller Colin Whitlock was used to guide mariners entering the St. Croix River. As Whitlock had a tendency for excessive drinking in the evenings, his wife was usually the one who tended the light at night. Whitlocks Mill Lighthouse was established in 1910 and is one of Maine's youngest lighthouses. Its location makes it the northernmost lighthouse in New England. Its first keeper was Frank Jellison, who stayed on for ten years until 1920.

Keeper Jasper Cheney was transferred from the remote foggy station of Libby Island Light to the Whitlocks Mill Light in 1949. Previously, his family was living onshore, as Libby Island was a stag station of only men. The new appointment allowed him to have his family with him at the station, on the mainland. They spent much time planting flowers and decorating the station and grounds for visitors to enjoy.

The interior is distinctively lined with white ceramic-faced brick. The quarters are now a private home, but the lighthouse is still operational.

Directions for a distant view. The lighthouse is on the south bank of the St. Croix River. It is a private residence and is well-guarded by grumpy dogs. There is a turnout nearby where you can get a fine view of the lighthouse. About three miles east of Calais on Route 1, you can see the lighthouse from the St. Croix River View Rest Area on Route 1 in Calais from the south.

Coastal Attractions in Northern (Down East) Maine

Milbridge, Machiasport, Cutler, Lubec, and Calais

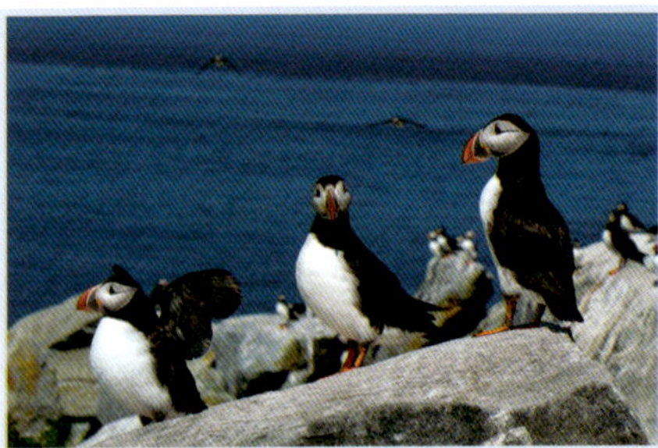

Close-up view of puffins on Machias Seal Island.

The term Down East (Downeast to Mainers) refers to the coastal region of Acadia National Park, heading north to the easternmost town of Lubec, and then up the St. Croix River by Calais, bordering Canada. Route 1 follows the shoreline in many places, and also has its share of roads that branch off to more rural fishing villages and small towns. Corea is a small fishing village about seven miles from the entrance to Schoodic Peninsula, the only area of Acadia National Park on the mainland. The rocky peninsula gives visitors a real sense of the ocean's fury.

There are many islands in this region, some which are protected as wildlife refuges part of the year, but many are open to the public for kayaking, canoeing, and hiking. Cruises that offer puffin-watching pass by Petit Manan Light, as it has become one of the sanctuaries of these and other nesting birds.

Milbridge offers seventy-five miles of coastline with spectacular views of the Narraguagus River and the Gulf of Maine. Milbridge was once a shipbuilding town and has a museum of local history. The **Petit Manan National Wildlife Sanctuary** is an island less than a half-hour from Milbridge, with its nesting area serving over 300 species of birds. Take a picnic down to McClellan Park and enjoy the ocean views, or stroll along the river through Riverside Park, or go fishing.

The Maine Historic Preservation Commission lists twenty-eight prehistoric archaeological sites along the Addison coastline. You may have an opportunity to visit some of these sites by getting their permission. **Pleasant River Boat Tours** provides nature cruises along the Pleasant River Estuary and out to nearby islands, which include views of Nash Island Light. On their puffin cruise, you'll also view Petit Manan Light and Pond Island Light.

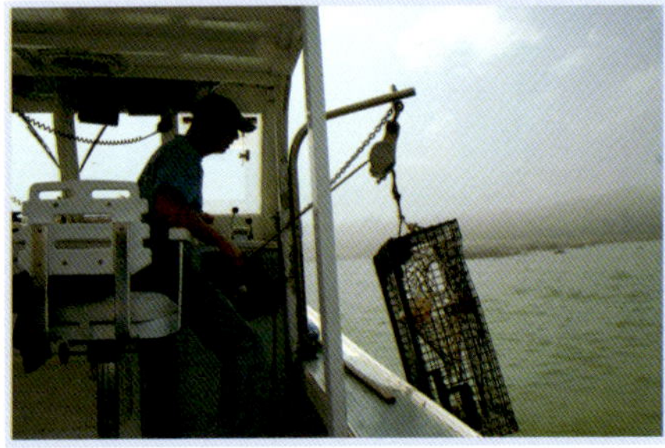

Hauling lobster traps.

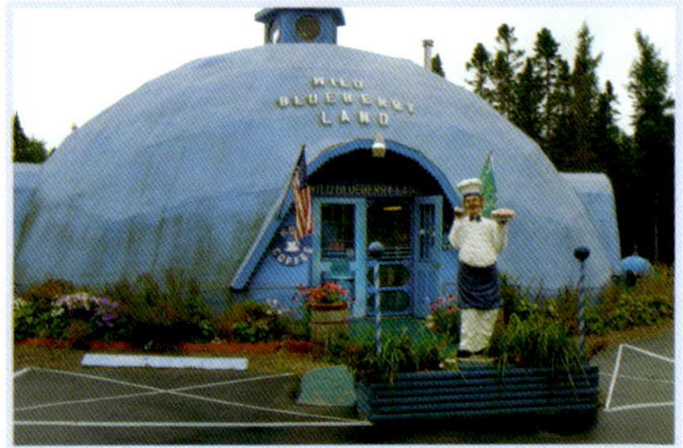

The largest "blueberry" at Wild Blueberry Land bakery and gift shop.

Quick stop! At the Corner of Route 1 and Route 187, you'll find Wild Blueberry Land, the **world's largest "blueberry" building** with a great bakery and organic grown food at reasonable prices. You're in Maine's true blueberry region and this landmark is a must-stop. There's even a nine-hole mini golf course and all kinds of photo ops.

Jonesport is a small fishing village along the heart of the rugged Down East coast. Samuel de Champlain anchored here in the early 1600s while mapping the area for the French King, Henri IV. There is an old quarry dock on Head Harbor Island nearby where you'll see huge, stacked pink-granite blocks. The area is full of islands that invite exploration by boat or kayak. Kayak to and hike through the wilderness at **Great Wass Island Preserve**.

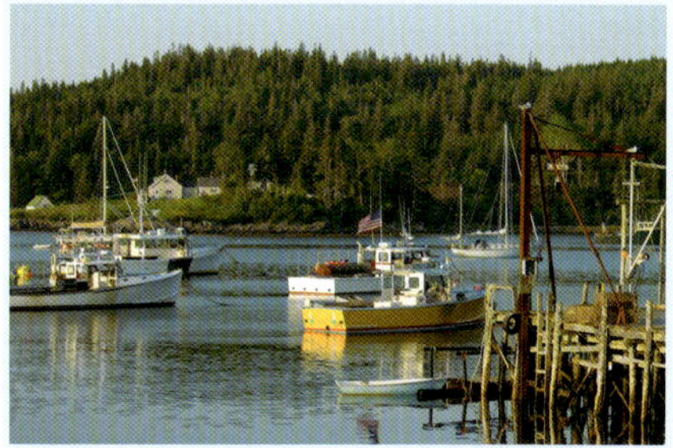

Cutler Harbor is the northernmost harbor in Maine.

In the scenic area of Machias, check out Jasper Beach in nearby Machiasport with its unique multicolored pebbles. It creates a picturesque coastline, and is often called the "Best Wilderness Beach in the Northeast." In mid-August, visit the annual **Blueberry Festival** in Machias, which has become a huge event in this region. A few miles away, relax on the white sand beach at Rogue Bluffs State Park or, at nearby Cobscook Bay, a favorite for boaters and sea kayakers. **Sunrise Canoe and Kayak** gives kayak tours along Machias Bay, along with a whitewater wilderness trip and multi-day kayak and canoe tours along the St. Croix River. **Tours of historic downtown Machias** are offered during the summer.

Cutler is a classic Down East fishing community. Sail from its picturesque harbor to Machias Seal Island and Grand Manan Island six miles offshore. It still has an active fishing fleet and is the last harbor before entering Canada. The **Cross Island National Refuge** consists of six offshore islands ten miles southeast of Machias in Machias Bay. It encompasses 1,700 acres in the town of Cutler and can be explored on your own by boat or kayak. You'll find all kinds of wildlife, including white-tailed deer, bald eagles, ospreys, and songbirds.

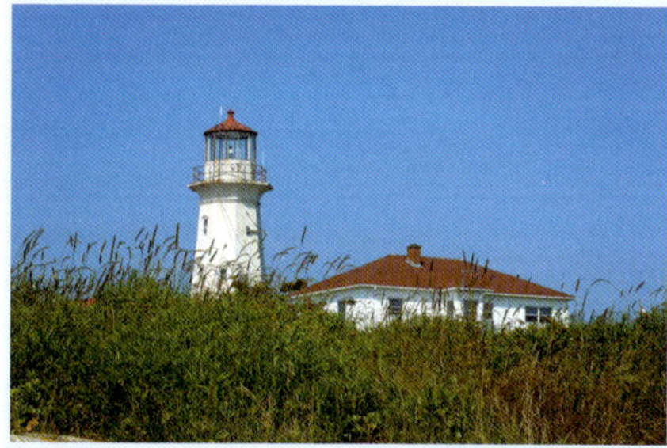

Machias Seal Island Lighthouse is operated by Canadian keepers and is not automated.

The **Bold Coast Charter Company** passes Little River Lighthouse heading to Machias Seal Island. They can also set up a charter to land on Little River Island to tour the lighthouse and keeper's dwelling. When you take the Bold Coast Charter trip to Machias Seal Island, you'll find the largest puffin colony on the coast. It is also the only place where visitors are allowed to step onto the island to view puffins up close. You'll also find **Machias Seal Island Lighthouse**, which is technically a Canadian lighthouse tended by Canadian keepers, the result of a treaty made between the two countries hundreds of years ago. You get

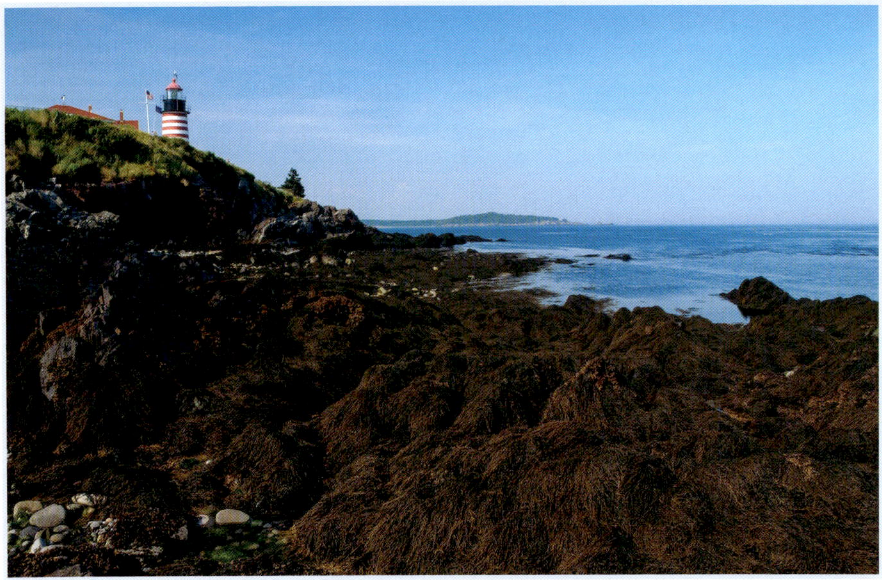

Exploring the shoreline around Quoddy Head Light during low tide.

to meet these great folks on the island.

Friends of Little River Lighthouse offer a few open house tours of the lighthouse in the summer, usually set up by the American Lighthouse Foundation, and you can stay overnight at the lighthouse. Bold Coast Charters may provide chartered tours to land on the island of Little River Light. Arrangements can be made to tour the interior of the lighthouse and the keeper's home. Tours of Libby Island Light may also be possible.

Lubec is on the banks of the St. Croix River near the United States and Canadian border. This former shipbuilding and sardine-packing town is the first town in the US to see the sunrise. It has no shopping malls, fast food restaurants, or stoplights, only rugged natural beauty. The community consists of artists, a few specialty shops, and fishermen.

Quoddy State Park has miles of nature trails over scenic coastal terrain. Some parts of the park have patches of arctic tundra, which you would typically find much farther north. In early summer, purple lupine flowers are everywhere and biking is a great way to go exploring. Whales have been spotted from the shore and there are bald eagle nests nearby.

The Quoddy Loop trail system includes trails across the Canadian border to Campobello Island. Lubec also offers three main conservation areas for hiking: Boot Head Preserve, Hamilton Cove Preserve, and Western Head Preserve between Cutler and Lubec. There are plenty of tours in the Lubec area and over the border featuring whale watching, deep-sea fishing, wildlife, and lighthouses. **Tours of Lubec and Cobstock** provide tours of historic aspects of Lubec and the area, natural history and wildlife tours. They also provide tours of the Tide Mill Organic Farm, which has been in operation since 1765, and the intertidal shore. For island hopping, take the **Eastport Ferry** between Eastport on Moose Island and Lubec. The island is part of the scenic Shackford Head State Park. For those interested in whale watching, **Bay Cruises at the Wharf** will take you out.

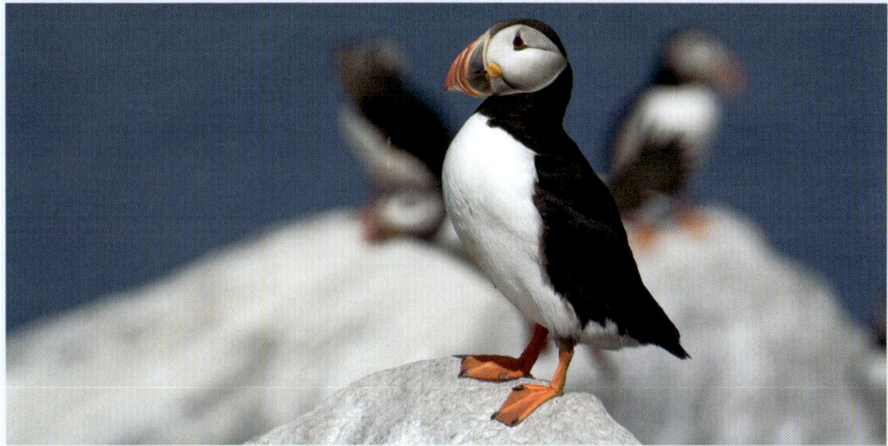

Puffins can be viewed up close on Machias Seal Island.

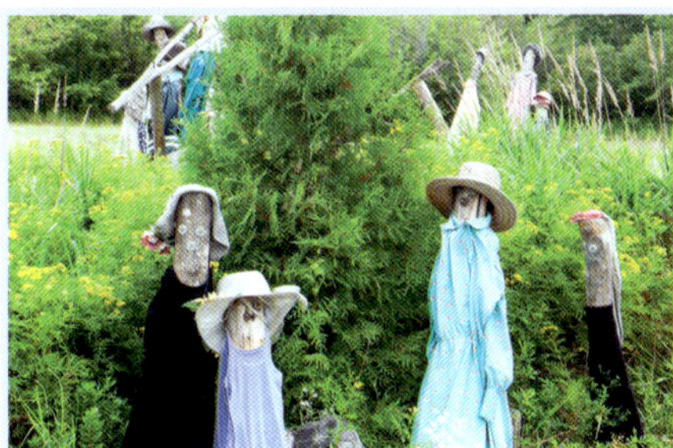

Dressed up log people are a popular sight enroute to Calais.

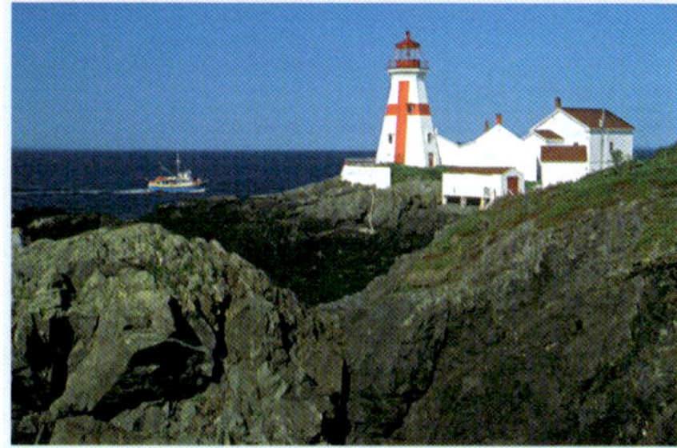

East Quoddy Head Lighthouse with its distinctive red cross.

 **Quick stop!** Traveling up Route 1 from Lubec toward Calais, you'll find an odd site where someone has decorated sticks and logs to create a colony of **"Log People."** You can appreciate the amount of work that went into this creation.

Calais is primarily a shopping area and enjoys a warm relationship with its sister town St. Steven, over the Canadian border, where even holidays are mutually celebrated. It is the eighth busiest port of entry into the United States. Visit the **Downeast Heritage Museum** or take a hike in the **Moosehorn National Wildlife Refuge**.

If you have time, cross the border into Canada and explore Roosevelt Park on Campobello Island. There you'll find Mulholland Point Lighthouse and plenty of walking trails. After passing Roosevelt's cottage fifteen miles away, you'll see stunning views of East Quoddy Head Lighthouse, also known as Head Harbor Light, with a giant red cross painted on its tower. If you time it right, at low tide you can walk over to the lighthouse, but when the tide starts to come in, get off the island, as the tide rises quickly. High tides average twenty-five feet and can run as high as fifty feet. **Downeast Charter Boat Tours** offers tours to Lubec and Campobello Island lighthouses and the "Old Sow" whirlpool, the largest whirlpool in the Western Hemisphere, created from a strong tidal turbulence.

Contacts for Coastal Attractions in Northern (Down East) Maine

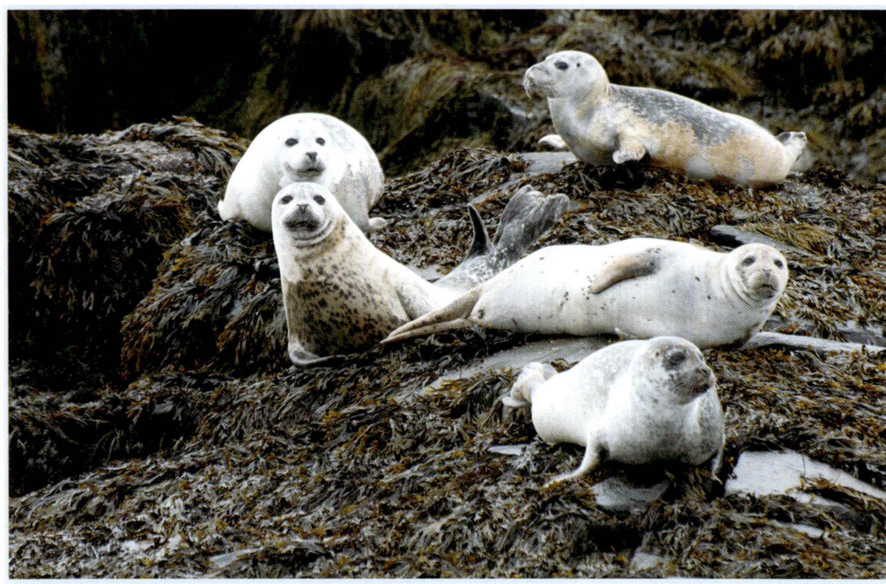

Seals basking on seaweed-covered rocks in low tide.

Great Wass Island Preserve, Jonesport
(207) 287-8044

Coastal Cruises & Dive, Jonesport
(207) 598-7473
cruisedowneast.com

Coastal Islands, Milbridge
(207) 594-0600
fws.gov/refuge/maine_coastal_is-lands

Cross Island Wildlife Refuge, Milbridge
(207) 546 2124 or (207) 594-0600

Petit Manan Refuge, Milbridge
(207) 546-2124
fws.gov/northeast/petitmanan

Robertson Sea Tours, Milbridge
(207) 483-6110
robertsonseatours.com

Wild Blueberry Land, Columbia Falls
(207) 483-2583
wildblueberryland.com

Pleasant River Boat Tours, Addison
(207) 483-6567
pleasantriverboattours.com

Blueberry Festival, Machias
(207) 255-6665
machiasblueberry.com

Sunrise Canoe and Kayak, Machias
(207) 255-3375
sunrisecanoeandkayak.com

Machias History Tours, Machias
(207) 255-4402
machiaschamber.org

Little River Light Overnight, Cutler
(877) 276-4682
littleriverlight.org

Puffins and Machias Seal Island, Cutler
(207) 259-4484
boldcoast.com

Tours of Lubec & Cobstock, Lubec
(207) 733-2997
toursoflubecandcobscook.com

Quoddy Loop Hiking, Lubec
(207) 853-2922

West Head Quoddy Visitor Center, Lubec
(207) 733-2180
westquoddy.com

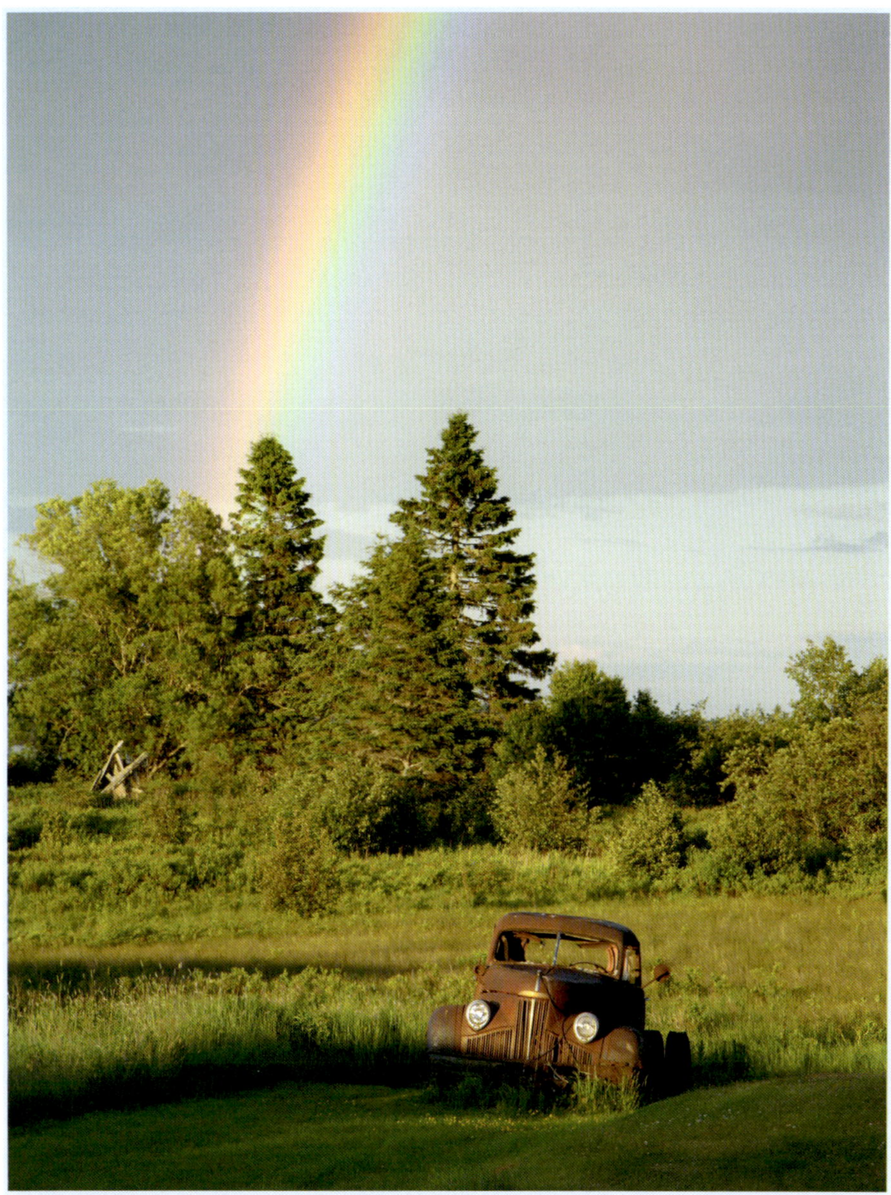

Rainbow over field in rural northern Maine.

Quoddy Light Overnight, Lubec
(877) 535-4714
quoddyvacation.com

Eastport Ferry, Lubec
(207) 288-4585
downeastwindjammer.com

Downeast Charters, Lubec
(207) 733-2009
downeastcharterboattours.com

Bay Cruises at the Wharf, Lubec
(207) 733-4400
theinnatthewharf.com

Campobello Island, New Brunswick, Canada
campobello.com

Moosehorn National Wildlife Refuge, Charlotte
(207) 454-7161

Lighthouse Cruises in Northern Maine

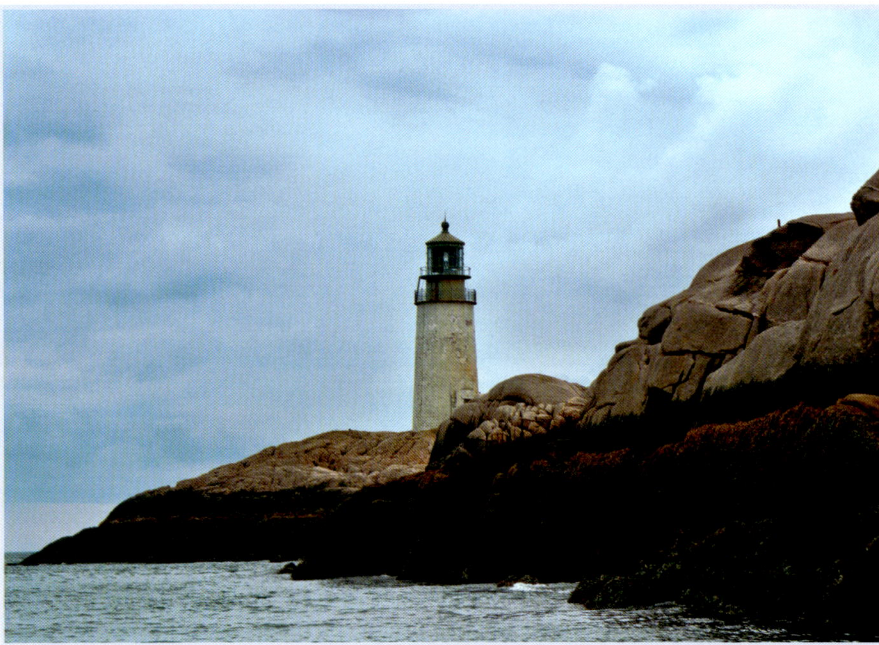

Moose Peak Lighthouse.

Robertson Sea Tours

Lighthouse cruises and nature trips along the shores of Down East Maine and Schoodic Peninsula area aboard a classic Down East lobster boat.

- Captain Jamie Robertson, Millbridge
- (207) 483-6110 or (207) 461-7439
- robertsonseatours.com
- **Lighthouses:** Pond Island, Nash Island, Petit Manan

Pleasant River Boat Tours

Nature cruises along the Pleasant River Estuary and out to nearby islands.

- 80 Water Street, Addison
- 598-6993 or (207) 483-6567
- pleasantrivertours.com
- **Lighthouses:** Pond Island, Nash Island, Petit Manan

Coastal Cruises and Dive Downeast

Lighthouse and nature cruises; diving excursions along the islands around Moose Peak and Libby Island lighthouses, and to the wreckage of the Crabtree Ledge Lighthouse, which was toppled by ice in 1950.

- 117 Kelley Point Road, Jonesport
- Laura Fish: (207) 598-7473
- cruisedowneast.com
- **Lighthouses:** Moose Peak, Libby Island, wreckage of Crabtree Ledge Light.

Bold Coast Charter Company

Puffin trips to Machias Seal Island and tours on the island of Little River Light. As the puffins are an endangered species, the trip to Machias Seal Island where they are nesting (also where Canadian-owned Machias Seal Island Lighthouse is located) is the only place visitors are allowed to view and photograph these animals up close, inside small shacks called blinds.

- Captain Andrew Patterson, Cutler
- (207) 259-4484
- boldcoast.com
- **Lighthouses:** Little River, Libby Island, Machias Seal Island (Canada)

Bay Cruises at the Wharf

Located on the Inn at the Waterfront, they offer whale watching and lighthouse tours.

- 69 Johnson Street, Lubec
- (207) 733-4400 or (239) 571-0208 (cell)
- theinnonthewharf.com
- **Lighthouses:** West Quoddy Head, Lubec Channel

Downeast Charter Boat Tours

Whale watching on a twenty-five-foot Northern Bay lobster yacht and may pass by the Lubec lighthouses.

- 31 Johnson Street, Lubec, ME 04652
- (207) 733-2009
- downeastcharterboattours.com
- **Lighthouses:** West Quoddy Head, Lubec Channel

Waterfront Directions

Milbridge

From Route 1 north, drive straight through to the town of Milbridge. Turn right at the realty sign and cross the bridges, then take the first right on Bayview Street.

Addision

From Route 1 north, turn right on Route 1A out of Milbridge. Merge onto Route 1 and turn right onto Abittoir Road, then merge onto Water Street.

Machias

From Route 1 north, turn right on Route 1A out of Milbridge. Merge onto Route 1 and turn right on Willow Street, then right on Water Street. Turn right on Route 191 south, and then take a slight right onto Simpson Wharf Road.

Cutler Harbor

From Route 1 north, turn right onto Route 1A out of Milbridge. Merge onto Route 1 and turn right onto Willow Street, then right onto Water Street. Turn right onto Route 191 south and follow to the end at Cutler Harbor.

The Inn on the Wharf, Lubec

From Route 1 north, turn right onto Route 189 into Lubec. Follow as it merges onto Main Street, turn left on Monument Street, then turn right onto Johnson Street.

Lighthouse Organizations in Maine

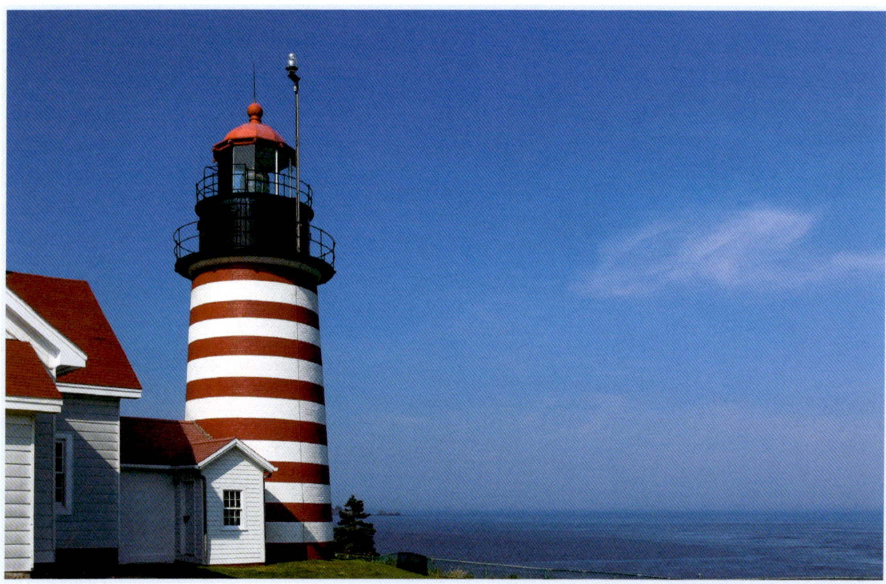

West Quoddy Head Lighthouse overlooking the Bay of Fundy.

Boon Island, York
American Lighthouse Foundation
(207) 594-4174

Brown's Head, Vinalhaven
Vinalhaven Historical Society
(207) 863-4410

Burnt Coat Harbor, Swan's Island
Town of Swans Island
(207) 526-4279

Burnt Island, Boothbay
Maine Marine Resources
(207) 633-9500

Cape Elizabeth, Cape Elizabeth
American Lighthouse Foundation
(207) 594-4174

Cuckolds, Southport
Inn at Cuckolds Lighthouse
(855) 212-5252

Curtis Island, Camden
Town of Camden
(207) 236-3353

Deer Island Thorofare, Deer Isle
Island Heritage Trust
(207) 348-2455

Dice Head, Castine
Town of Castine
(207) 326-4502

Eagle Island, Deer Isle
Eagle Light Caretakers

Egg Rock, Winter Harbor
Maine Coastal Islands Wildlife Refuge
(207) 546-2124

Fort Point, Stockton Springs
Fort Point State Park
(207) 941-4014

Goat Island, Cape Porpoise
Kennebunkport Conservation Trust
(207) 967-3465

Goose Rocks, Vinalhaven
Beacon Preservation, Inc.
(203) 400-9565

Great Duck Island, Frenchboro
College of the Atlantic
coa.edu

Grindle Point, Isleboro
Town of Isleboro
(207) 734-2253

Isle au Haut, Isle au Haut
The Keeper's House Inn
(207) 335-2990

Ladies Delight, Winthrop
Cobbosseecontee Yacht Club
cycmaine.org

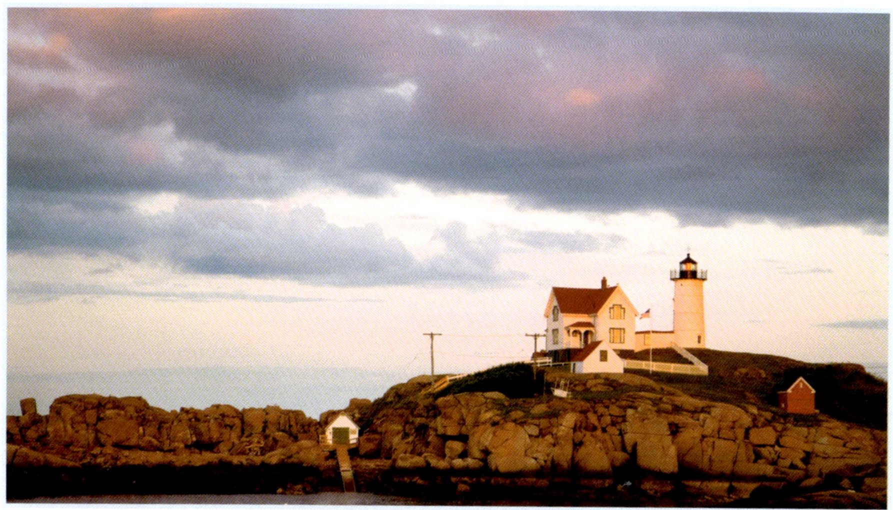

Sunset over Cape Neddick (Nubble) Light.

Little River, Cutler
Friends of Little River Lighthouse
littleriverlight.org

Many Lighthouses, East Machias
Lighthouse Digest Magazine
(207) 259-2121

Many Lighthouses, Rockland
American Lighthouse Foundation
(207) 594-4174

Marshall Point, Port Clyde
Marshall Point Lighthouse Museum
(207) 372-6450

Monhegan, Monhegan Island
Monhegan Museum
(207) 596-7003

Mount Desert Rock, Mount Desert Rock
College of the Atlantic
coa.edu

Nash Island, Addison
Friends of Nash Island Light
(207) 483-6102

Nubble (Cape Neddick), York
Friends of Nubble Light
nubblelight.org

Owls Head, Rockland
Friends of Rockland Harbor Lights
(207) 594-4174

Pemaquid, Bristol
Friends of Pemaquid Point Lighthouse
(207) 677-2492

Perkins Island, Georgetown
American Lighthouse Foundation
(207) 594-4174

Petit Manan, Corea
Petit Manan National Wildlife Refuge
(207) 594-0600

Portland Breakwater, South Portland
City of South Portland
(207) 767-3200

Portland Head, Cape Elizabeth
Museum at Portland Head Light
(207) 799-2661

Ram Island, Boothbay Harbor
Ram Island Preservation Society
(207) 633-4727

Rockland Breakwater, Rockland
Friends Rockland Breakwater Light
(207) 542-7574

Saddleback Ledge, Vinalhaven
Vinalhaven Historical Society
(207) 863-4410

Seguin Island, Georgetown
Friends of Seguin Island
(207) 443-4808

Spring Point Ledge, South Portland
Spring Point Ledge Light Trust
207) 699-2676

Squirrel Point, Arrowsic
Citizens for Squirrel Point
squirrelpoint.org

Two Bush, Milbridge
Maine Coastal Wildlife Refuge
(207) 546-2124

West Quoddy Head, Lubec
Quoddy Head Light Keepers
(207) 733-2180

Whaleback, Kittery
Friends of Portsmouth Harbor Light
(603) 534-0537

Whitehead, Brunswick
Whitehead Light Station Organization
(207) 200-7957

Wood Island, Biddeford
Friends of Wood Island Light
woodislandlighthouse.org

Maps of Maine Lighthouses

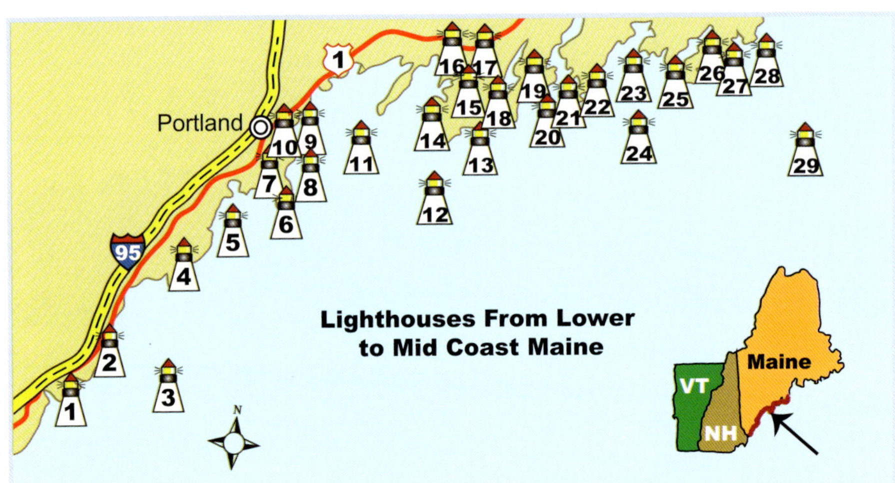

Map of lighthouses from the lower to mid-coast of Maine: **(1)** Whaleback, **(2)** Boon Island, **(3)** Nubble (Cape Neddick), **(4)** Goat Island (Cape Porpoise), **(5)** Wood Island, **(6)** Cape Elizabeth, **(7)** Portland Head Lighthouse, **(8)** Ram Island Ledge, **(9)** Spring Point Ledge, **(10)** Portland Breakwater (Bug Light), **(11)** Halfway Rock, **(12)** Seguin Island, **(13)** Pond Island, **(14)** Perkins Island, **(15)** Squirrel Point, **(16)** Doubling Point, **(17)** Doubling Point Range Lights (Kennebec River Range Lights), **(18)** Burnt Island, **(19)** Hendricks Head, **(20)** Cuckolds, **(21)** Ram Island, **(22)** Pemaquid Point, **(23)** Franklin Island, **(24)** Monhegan Island, **(25)** Marshall Point, **(26)** Tenants Harbor, **(27)** Whitehead, **(28)** Two Bush Island, **(29)** Matinicus Rock

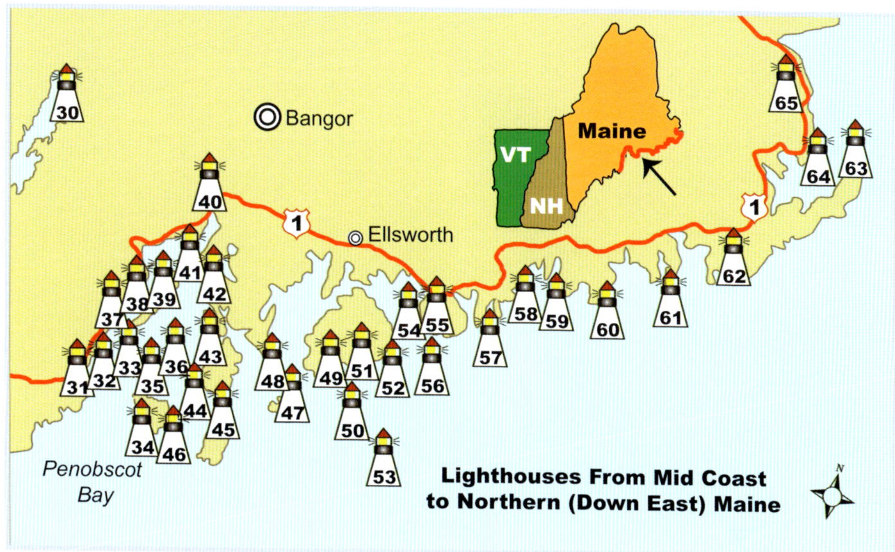

Map of lighthouses from mid-coast to northern (Down East) Maine: (30) Cobbossee (Ladies Delight), **(31)** Rockland Harbor Southwest, **(32)** Owl's Head, **(33)** Rockland Breakwater, **(34)** Brown's Head, **(35)** Goose Rocks, **(36)** Eagle Island, **(37)** Indian Island, **(38)** Curtis Island, **(39)** Browns Head, **(37)** Goose Rocks, **(38)** Eagle Island, **(39)** Grindle Point, **(40)** Fort Point, **(41)** Dice Head, **(42)** Pumpkin Island, **(43)** Deer Island Thorofare (Mark Island), **(44)** Saddleback Ledge, **(45)** Isle au Haut, **(46)** Heron Neck, **(47)** Burnt Coat Harbor, **(48)** Blue Hill Bay, **(49)** Bass Harbor Head, **(50)** Baker Island **(51)** Bear Island, **(52)** Egg Rock, **(53)** Mount Desert Rock, **(54)** Winter Harbor, **(55)** Prospect Harbor, **(56)** Great Duck Island, **(57)** Petite Manan, **(58)** Narragaugus (Pond Island), **(59)** Nash Island Light, **(60)** Moose Peak, **(61)** Libby Island, **(62)** Little River, **(63)** West Quoddy Head, **(64)** Lubec Channel, **(65)** Whitlocks Mill.

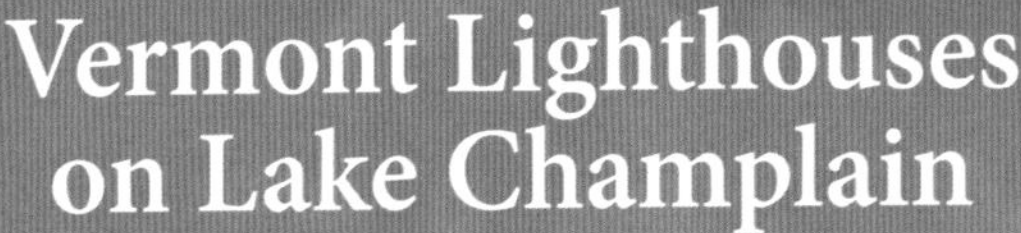

Vermont Lighthouses on Lake Champlain

Shelburne, Burlington, Saint Albans, Isle La Motte, and Alburg.

There are over 300 wrecks on Lake Champlain, varying from Revolutionary War ships to modern airplanes and powerboats. With the completion of the Champlain Canal in 1823, which connected the Hudson River and Lake Champlain, Burlington became the third largest port for lumber and quarried stone coming mainly from Vermont's interior and Canada. Ten lighthouses were originally established along Lake Champlain. The Burlington waterfront was built because of the increasing commercial traffic on Lake Champlain. With this expansion came the need for a breakwater to protect mariners from the constant weather changes and storms. Canal boats brought in most of the stones used to build the breakwater. These boats helped to make the connection with the Hudson River leading into New York City, which in turn helped Burlington develop as a world trade port. Juniper Island was the first lighthouse built on the lake about three miles from the mainland, and the breakwater created at Burlington had three beacons positioned at one point. Today it has two beacons, one at each end.

Colchester Reef was built to protect mariners from the reef seven miles out from shore. It was disassembled piece-by-piece and reassembled years ago as part of the massive outdoor Shelburne Museum exhibition, where it exists today.

Near the Canadian border, two lighthouses were built to guide mariners around a dangerous channel and between large islands. One is on the Isle La Motte. The other is on Windmill Point, the site of the first European settlement in Vermont.

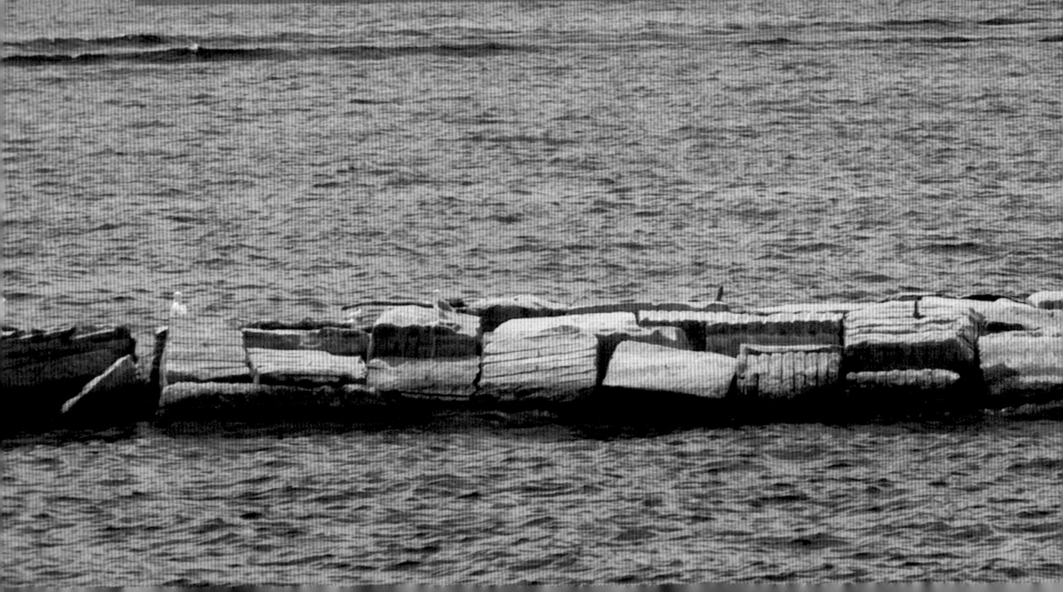

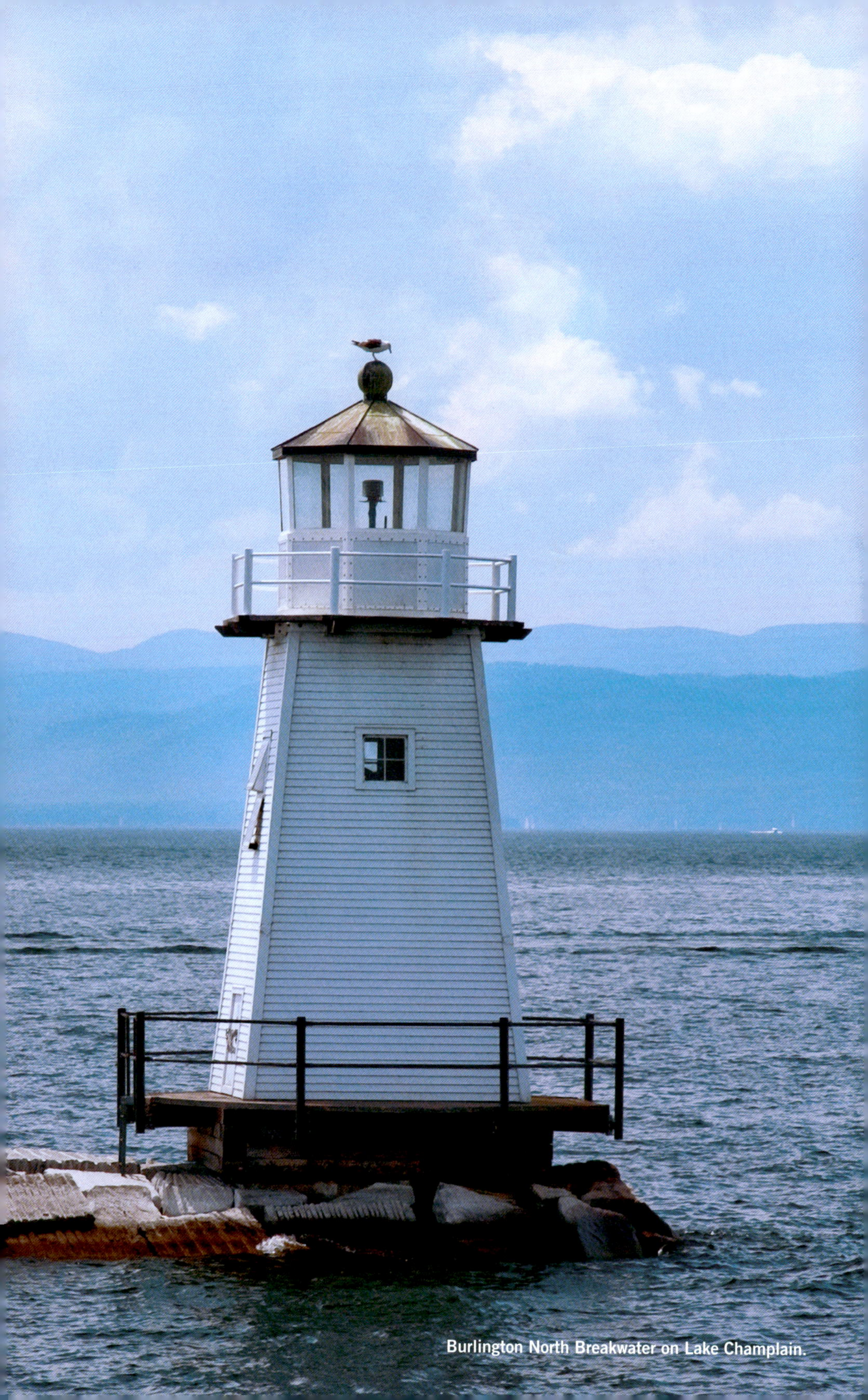

Burlington North Breakwater on Lake Champlain.

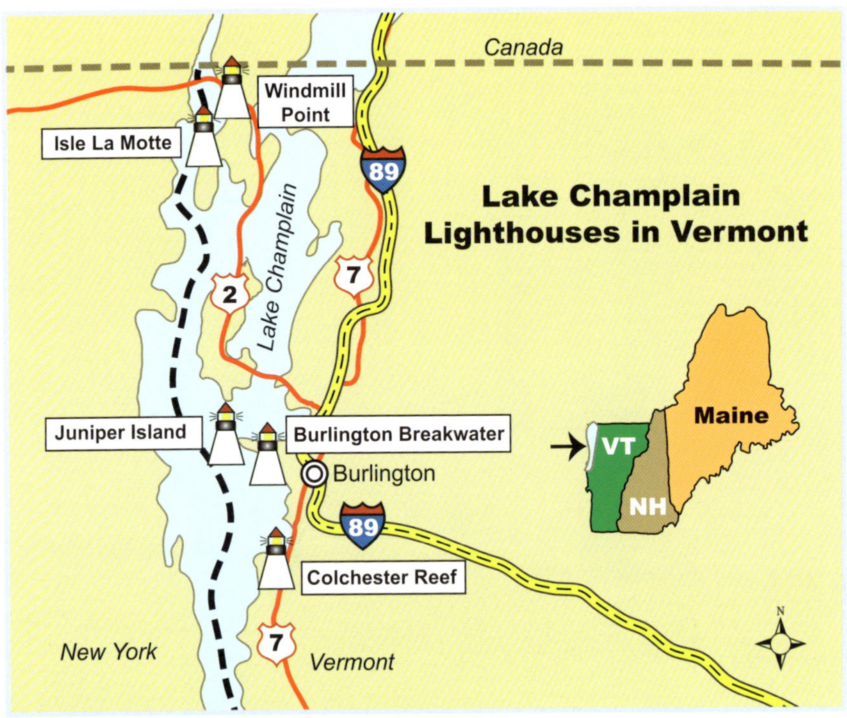

Map of Vermont's Lake Champlain lighthouses.

Colchester Reef Lighthouse

Shelburne (1871) • Latitude: 44° 33' 32" N • Longitude: 73° 20' 00" W

In 1869, the Lighthouse Service ran a national competition for the design of Colchester Reef Lighthouse, and the winner was Albert Dow, an engineering graduate from the University of Vermont. Colchester Reef Lighthouse was completed in 1871, but ran into foundation problems as a result of constant pounding from storms and ice jams. At first, supplies were brought to the lighthouse once a year without much input from the lighthouse keeper. The first keeper, Herman Malaney, received over nine tons of coal each year, more than he could use. The local ice fishermen looked forward to receiving a bag of coal from keeper Malaney each winter to heat their shanties.

On January 29, 1888, keeper Walter Button's pregnant wife, Harriet, went into labor. Button rang the lighthouse bell for a doctor, but the ice was too thin to cross and too thick for the doctor and his assistant to get a boat out to the lighthouse, a mile out on the frozen lake. The doctor and his assistant decided to risk their lives by walking across the lake to the lighthouse. When they were about half a mile out, the large ice floe they were standing on broke apart and sent them drifting northward. This caused the doctor and his assistant to jump from ice floe to ice flow to get safely to the mainland. They "landed" about four miles from their starting point. Luckily, a healthy baby girl was born at the lighthouse without medical assistance. Later that spring, keeper Button found a pair of squirrels on the rocks by the light-

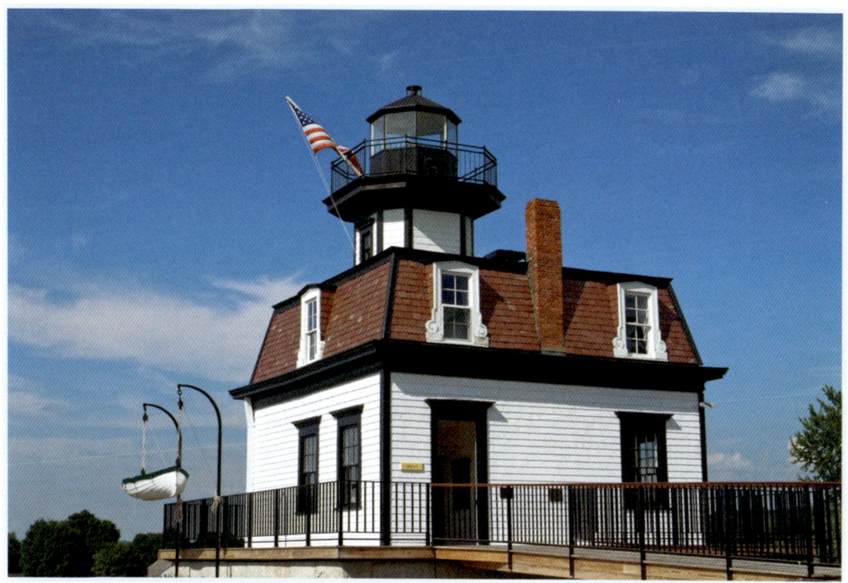

Colchester Reef Lighthouse in Shelburne, Vermont.

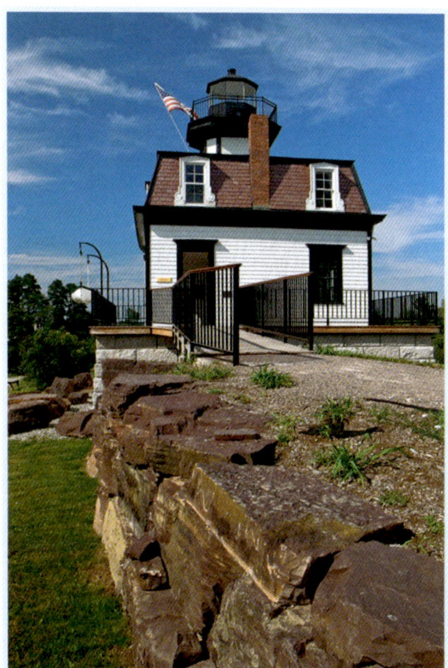

The reconstructed Colchester Reef Lighthouse is displayed at the outdoor Shelburne Museum.

house, which became tame enough to be the family's pets.

When William Howard was keeper at Colchester Reef Light, he grew weary of the solitary existence and wanted to move closer to civilization. Fortuitously, he met August Lorenz, a keeper from New York City, who longed for a quiet existence, and the two swapped locations. Lorenz became Colchester Reef's keeper in 1909 and enjoyed the solitude, even though he often dealt with extreme temperatures. Once he was nearly encased in ice from the freezing spray while rowing supplies to the lighthouse. He also had to contend with dangerous ice floes that bombarded the lighthouse foundation. One ice flow tore a large hole in the kitchen. Lorenz stayed at the lighthouse for nearly twenty-two years, until he was forced to retire in 1931 at age seventy. The lighthouse was also retired in 1933 and fell into disrepair over the years. In the early 1950s, it was sold at auction for $50, with the owners planning to use the lumber to build a house on shore. Electra Webb, a wealthy collector of New England artifacts and memorabilia who later founded the Shelburne Museum, heard about the plans and purchased the lighthouse from the

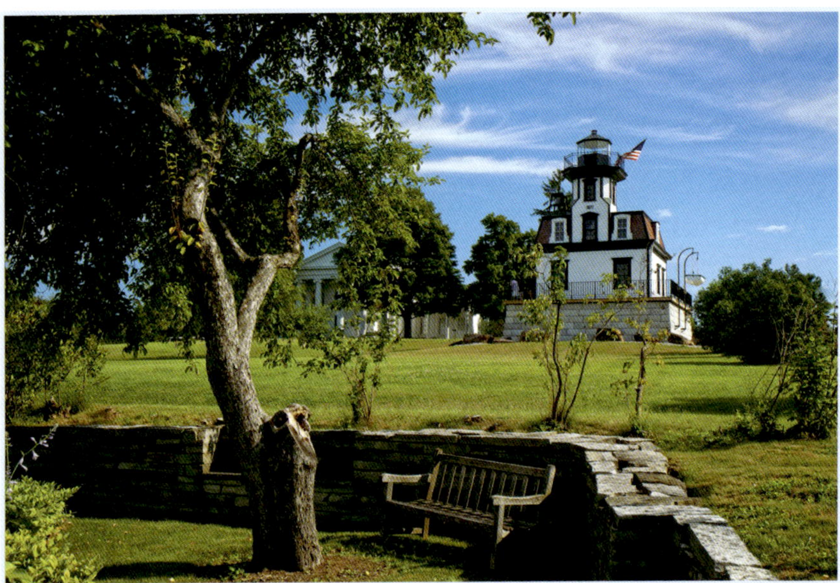

The Shelburne Museum grounds contain thirty-seven reconstructed buildings.

new owners for $1,300. Webb then had the lighthouse painstakingly disassembled and labeled piece-by-piece, then reconstructed to its original glory on the grounds of the current Shelburne Museum.

Exploring the grounds at Shelburne Museum. Visiting the Shelburne Museum, often referred to as "New England's Smithsonian" is an all-day affair that includes touring thirty-seven buildings and the grounds. Many of the nineteenth-century buildings have been painstakingly disassembled, labeled, and reconstructed on the new site. The lighthouse is not activated, but you can go inside the beacon and up into the tower.

Directions. From Burlington take Route 7 south for seven miles to Shelburne center. Continue on Route 7 one more mile and you'll see the Shelburne Museum on the right.

Burlington Breakwater Lighthouses (North and South)

Burlington (1854) • Latitude: 44° 28' 50" N • Longitude: 73° 13' 48" W

With the completion of the Champlain Canal, which connected the Hudson River and Lake Champlain, a breakwater was needed to protect mariners from the constant weather changes in Burlington's busy port. A 1,000-foot breakwater was completed in 1854 and extended as the waterfront grew. By the late 1800s, the breakwater was nearly 4,200 feet long. Wooden lighthouses on opposite ends of the breakwater were moved and rebuilt as the breakwater was extended, and a third beacon was placed

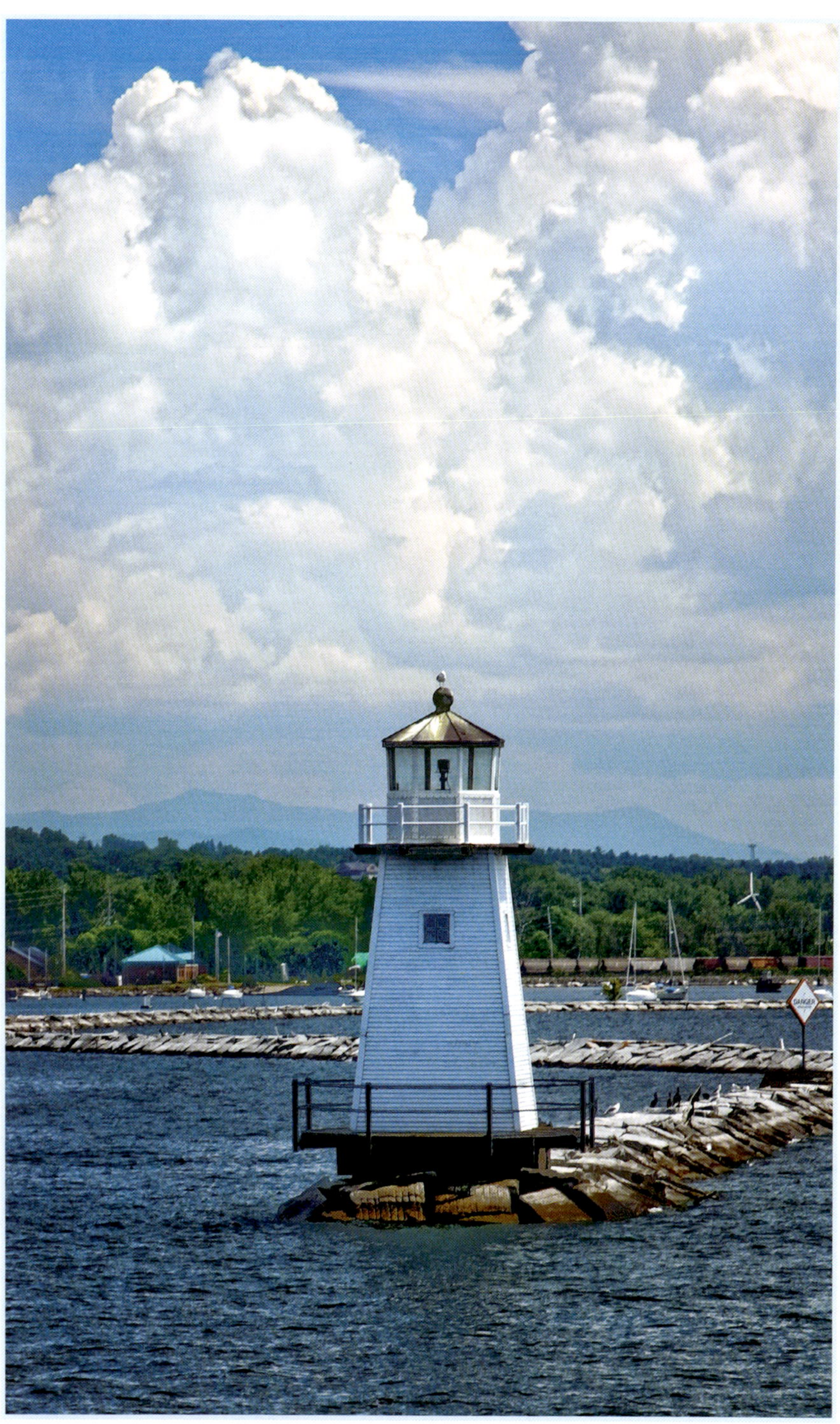

Burlington North Light at the end of the breakwater.

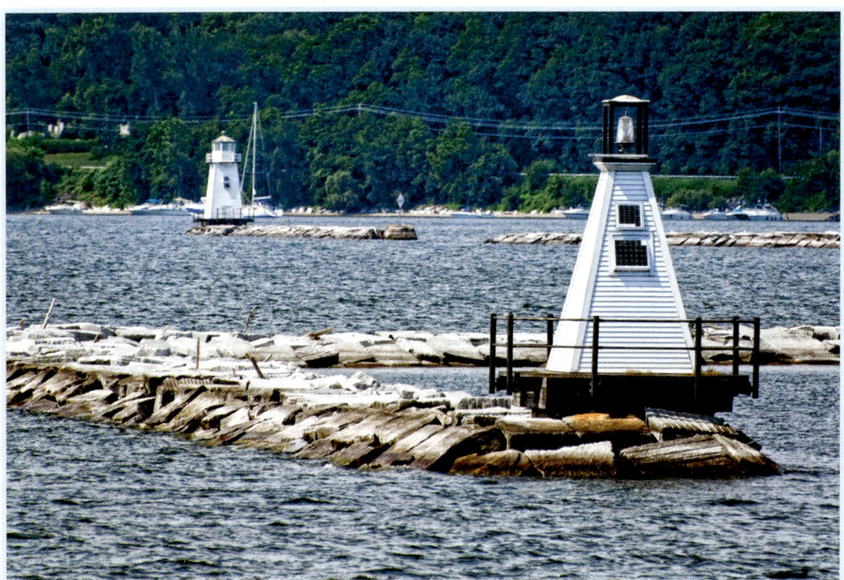

Burlington Breakwater South and North Lights.

in the middle around 1890. Over the years, the wooden structures succumbed to the elements. In 1870, the northern lighthouse burned to the ground, and in 1876 a storm knocked over the southern light.

In 1875, a keeper's dwelling was built on the breakwater, only a mile from the waterfront, but the keepers preferred to live in the city with their families and row out to the small lighthouses. The keeper's house was unoccupied for nearly ten years before it was auctioned off and moved ashore. Today it is a private residence near the waterfront.

The north and middle wooden lights were rebuilt with steel in 1925, and the south light was replaced with steel in 1950. After years of ugly skeletal towers, the north and south towers were rebuilt to their original design from old photos with funding help from Senator Patrick Leahy, and the breakwater was reconstructed. In 2003, the north and south lights were reactivated.

The Rescue of the General Butler. The *General Butler* was named after General Benjamin Butler, a Civil War hero. She was an eighty-eight-foot canal or cargo boat built in 1862 and was designed to sail through the Lake Champlain canal system. Captain William Montgomery was the third owner and lived in Isle La Motte in northern Vermont. On December 9, 1876, the *General Butler* was heading to Burlington from Fisk Quarry on the Isle La Motte with thirty tons of marble and stone. On board was a crewman, a quarryman seeking medical treatment for his injured eye, and two teenage girls—the captain's daughter, Cora, and her friend.

As the *General Butler* sailed toward Burlington, a storm hit them full force near Burlington Harbor. The rigging started to break apart, and the steering mechanism broke, causing it to be tossed around the thrashing waters near the Burlington breakwater. Captain Montgomery dropped anchor so he could try to jury-rig the

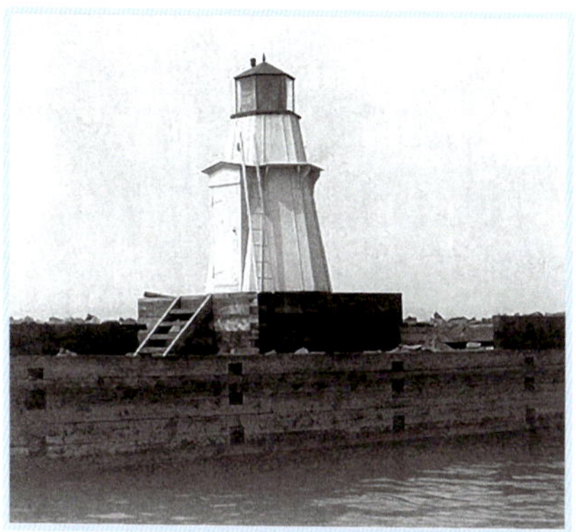

Early wooden construction of Burlington North Light. *Courtesy US Coast Guard.*

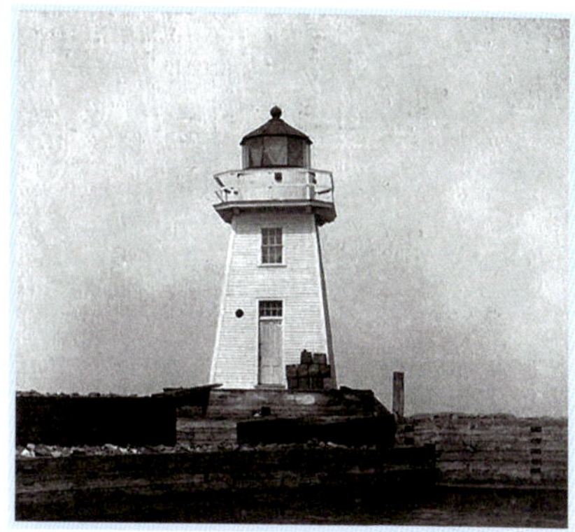

Burlington South Light's early wood construction. *Courtesy US Coast Guard.*

tiller bar to the steering post and steer the vessel into the harbor. He failed, and was forced to cut the anchor line as it started dragging across the sandy bottom. Montgomery sent out a distress signal as a crowd of onlookers watched from the waterfront.

As huge waves pushed the vessel onto the jagged breakwater, Captain Montgomery knew that the ship was about to sink with her heavy load and convinced the passengers to jump ship. One by one he helped them off onto the breakwater before jumping off himself. A few minutes later the *General Butler* slipped off the breakwater and sank. She came to rest forty feet deep on the sandy bottom of the lake, about seventy yards west of the southern end of the breakwater.

The five survivors were now in another perilous position, as they were being drenched by waves washing over the breakwater. They were about a mile out in the breakwater, which was not connected to the shore.

Keeper James Wakefield heard the distress call and arrived with his son. He knew they would freeze to death if help did not come quickly. He ran back to his house and grabbed their fourteen-foot lighthouse boat and made the daunting trip out to the breakwater. The captain of the vessel grabbed his daughter and her friend and placed them first into the strong arms of the keeper. Then one by one, as the boat rose on the waves close to the rocks, the three remaining crew jumped into Wakefield's little boat.

Wakefield and his son pulled the boat through the violent waters, bringing it safely ashore to a welcoming crowd. The survivors were given medical treatment and dry clothes at Wakefield's house.

The Burlington Breakwater South Lighthouse, near where the wreck occurred, was inoperable from a previous storm and was awaiting repairs. Without the light, the keeper used his knowledge of the area to maneuver the boat to the survivors, and Wakefield and his son became the heroes of Burlington. The *General Butler* can easily be viewed by divers and on shipwreck excursions with the Lake Champlain Museum. The wreck of the *General Butler* became the first shipwreck in the Vermont Underwater Historic Preserve program. The hull is still intact, and none of the interior has collapsed. The cargo hatches that were carrying the marble are easily viewable.

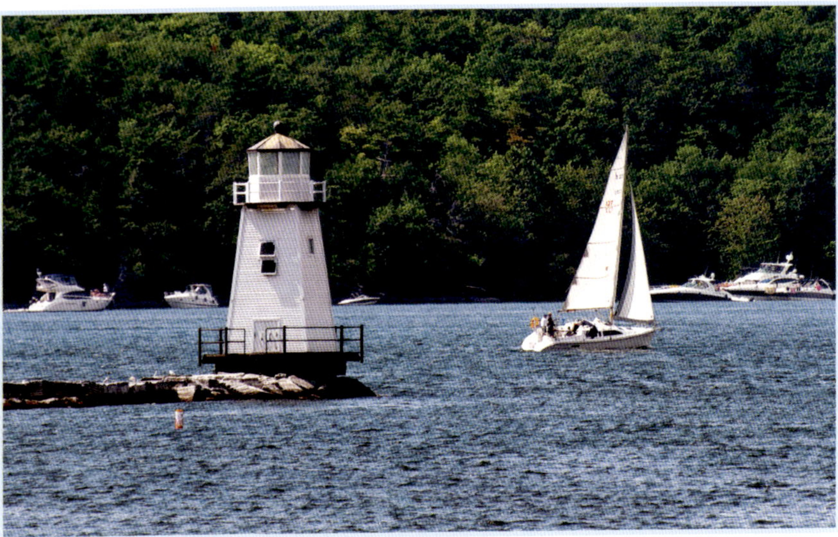

Sailing around Burlington Breakwater North Light.

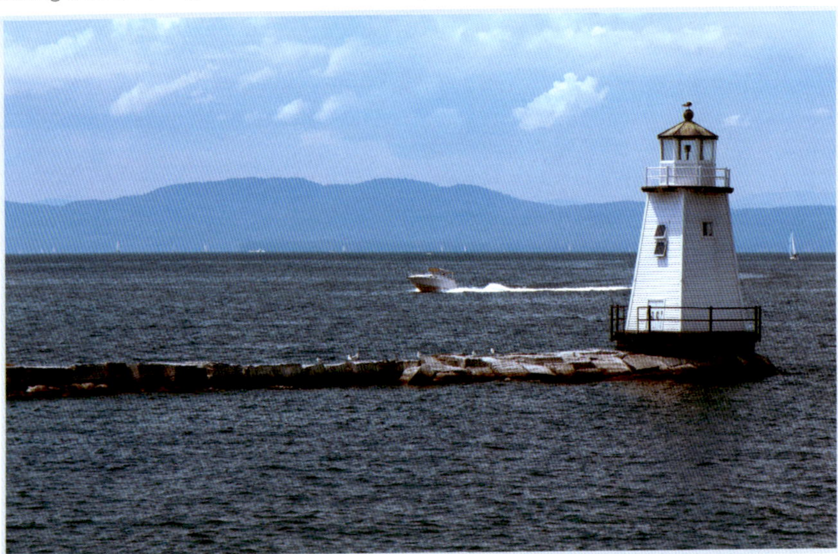

Burlington Breakwater North Light.

Directions. To see the north light, take Main Street in downtown Burlington to the waterfront. As you park, you'll see the lighthouse. You can also take Lake Street over the railroad tracks. The path to the public fishing pier is a good place to view the lighthouse.

To see the south light, from the waterfront facing the water, follow the railroad tracks on the left along the shore. Or, take Battery Street and stay right onto Maple Street, and then turn left on Valley Lane, which will bring you to the treatment facility where the lighthouse is at the end of the breakwater.

Juniper Island Lighthouse

Burlington (1826) • Latitude: 44° 27' 04" N • Longitude: 73° 16' 36" W

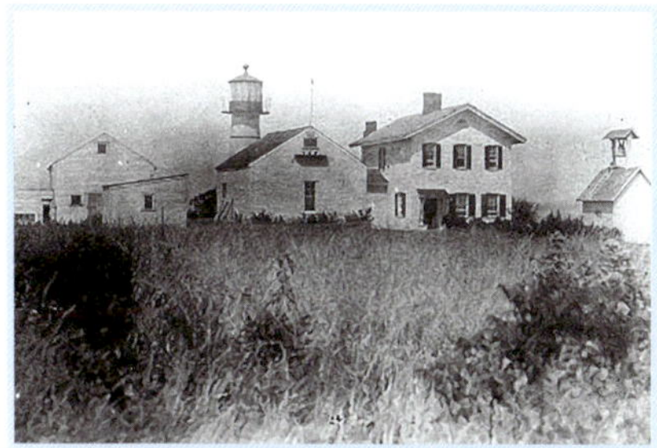

Vintage image. *Courtesy US Coast Guard.*

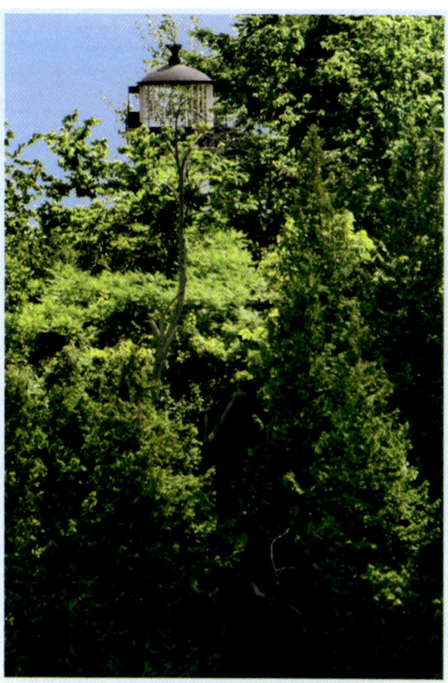

View from the water shows Juniper Island Lighthouse is gradually being engulfed by trees.

Juniper Island Lighthouse was the first to be built on Lake Champlain. It replaced a light that was mounted on a pole, maintained by a local commercial shipping company to help mariners around the island. The original lighthouse was poorly constructed and fell into disrepair a few years later. In 1846, the new tower was built with cast iron rings stacked together, similar to Monomoy lighthouse's on the Cape in Massachusetts. The fog bell was positioned atop a wooden shed and rung by a clock-type mechanical device.

A fierce gale in July 1890 destroyed boats and took several lives. In 1918, strong winds carried away thirty feet of the station's dock. A new concrete dock was erected in 1922. In 1954, a tall skeletal tower nearby that dwarfs the lighthouse tower replaced the original light.

The island was sold to Senator Fred Fayette in 1956. The keeper's house was destroyed by a careless camper's fire in 1962. Fayette's eleven children inherited the island after his death and helped to restore the keeper's house in 2001. Much of the effort was done voluntarily by family and friends using nearly 18,000 bricks from the original dwelling. Future plans involve reconstruction of the tower. The lighthouse is difficult to see from the water, as the surrounding trees consume it, and the property is off-limits to the public.

Isle La Motte Lighthouse

Isle La Motte (1856) • Latitude: 44° 54' 19" N • Longitude: 73° 20' 39" W

In the mid-1600s, the first French outpost on Lake Champlain's Vermont side was built on Isle La Motte. During the War of 1812, it was the site of the largest battle fought on Lake Champlain, known as the Battle of Plattsburgh, and was a major American victory.

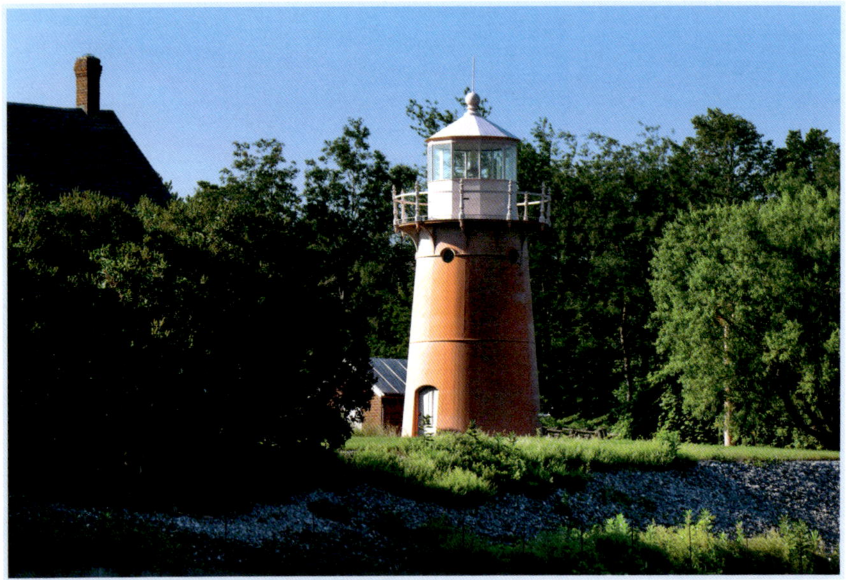

Isle La Motte Light is a few miles from the Canadian border.

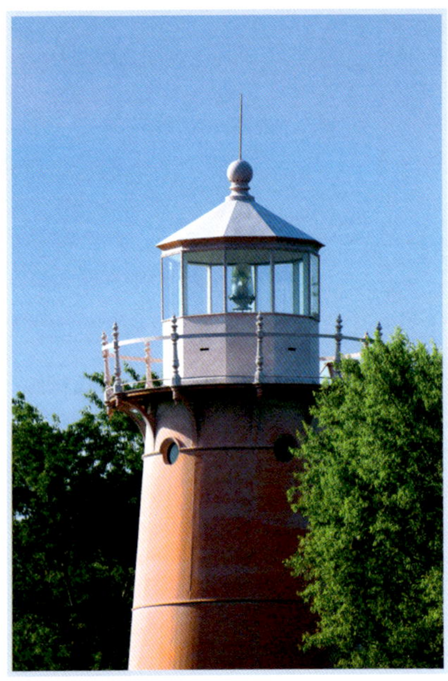

Isle La Motte Lighthouse tower.

With the completion of the Champlain Canal in 1823, shipping companies began placing navigational aids around the channels and islands of Lake Champlain. In 1829, a lantern was hung from a large pine tree on the island's northern point. The light was later moved to the attic window of a nearby stone house, which is still a private residence today.

The US government realized the need for more permanent structures with on-site keepers along Lake Champlain. In 1856, the makeshift light was replaced with a light on a pyramidal limestone tower tended by a local farmer. The problem was that on stormy nights, the light would simply blow out, as the farmer still had to travel some distance to the lighthouse.

A permanent lighthouse and keeper's dwelling was finally built in 1881. Wilbur Hill was its first and only keeper. Hill received awards for having the best-kept station in the district. He stayed on for forty-eight years while also tending his 100-acre farm nearby.

The light was replaced by a skeletal tower in 1933 and sold in 1949 to the Clark family, whose son would purchase nearby Windmill Point light in the early 1960s.

In 2001, the Coast Guard deemed it more cost-effective to replace the light on the tower than to maintain the deteriorating skeletal tower, and the tower was relit in 2002 with over 300 people at the ceremony.

Windmill Point Lighthouse

Alburg (1858) • Latitude: 44° 54' 53" N • Longitude: 73° 20' 30" W

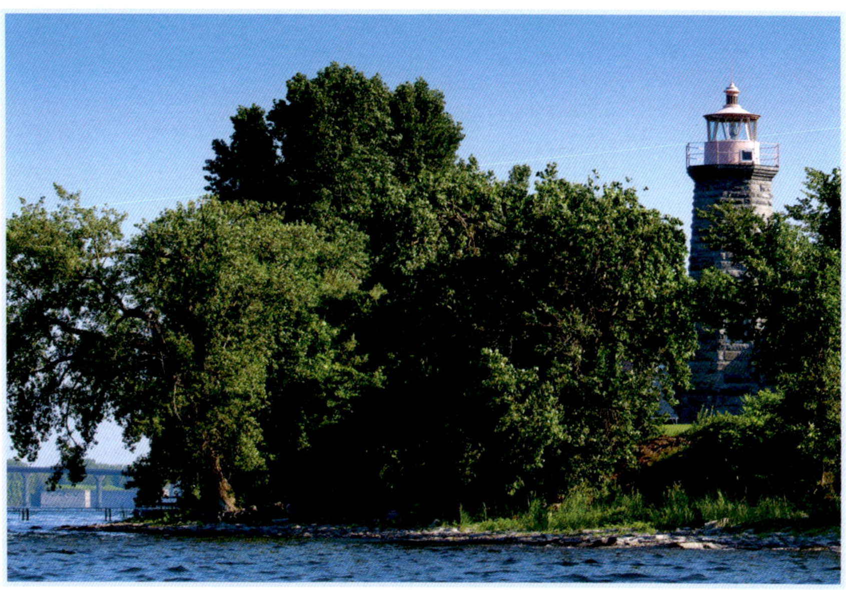

Windmill Point Light is Vermont's northernmost beacon.

The French once occupied the place where the current lighthouse stands and constructed a stone windmill there. The area also played a part in the Revolutionary War in September 1776, where General Benedict Arnold (a colonial at the time) anchored his fleet prior to the Battle of Valcour Island. Although his fleet suffered a loss, it delayed the British invasion long enough over the winter to allow the army to gain strength and defeat the British at Saratoga. Later, in the same area, the British ship *Thunderer*, carrying sick and wounded soldiers from the Battle of Saratoga, sank off the point in the shallow waters.

A lantern on a post was used as early as 1830. Finally in 1858, a proper lighthouse was built to help guide mariners around the northern portion of Lake Champlain. Together with the Isle La Motte Light, it forms a rough line marking the channel through the center of the lake. Windmill Point is the most northern lighthouse on Lake Champlain, a mere two miles from the Canadian border. It marks the entrance to the Richelieu River, and was one of ten lighthouses originally established along Lake Champlain.

In 1931, a skeletal tower replaced the tower, and the Customs Service used the lighthouse property to catch rum runners during the Prohibition. In 1963, a local man named Lockwood "Lucky" Clark was walking around the property with his

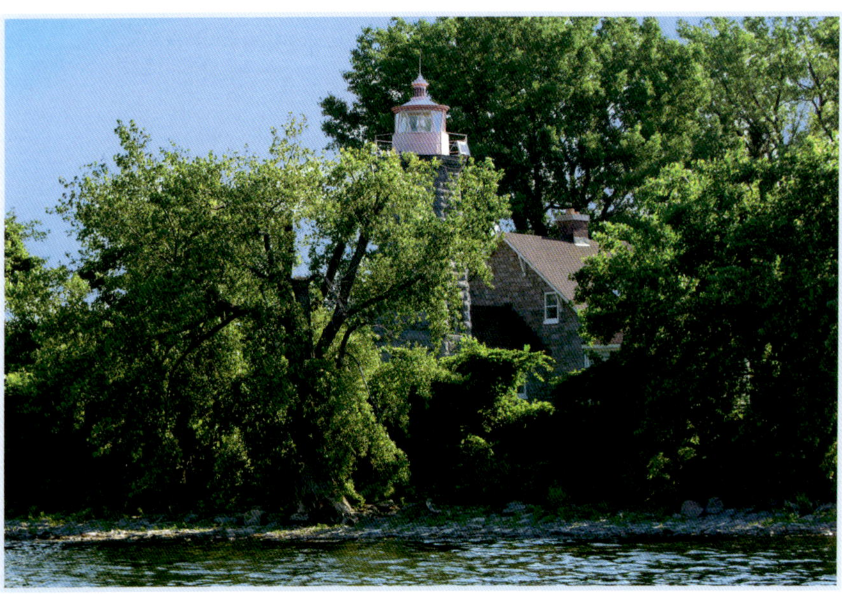

The lighthouse and adjoining keeper's building are made of local quarried stone.

bride-to-be when the owner came out and asked if he wanted to buy the property. Clark's father had already purchased the Isle La Motte lighthouse, and he decided to purchase Windmill Point to keep the neighboring lighthouses in the family.

In 2001, a Coast Guardsman petitioned that it would be more cost-effective to replace the light on the tower than to maintain the deteriorating skeletal tower. The lighthouse was relit in 2002, thanks to the Clarks' nearly 400 hours of work to ready the structure.

Through the centuries, northern Lake Champlain folklore describes a Loch Ness monster-type creature nicknamed Champ that lives in the area. There have been numerous sightings by visitors and locals alike, but nothing has ever been found.

Coastal Attractions on Lake Champlain near Vermont Lighthouses

Shelburne, Burlington, Saint Albans, and Isle La Motte

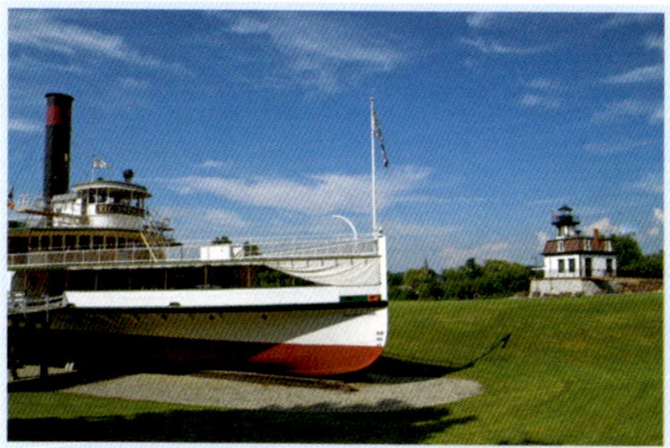

The steamer *Ticonderoga* and Colchester Reef Light are two of thirty-seven structures at the Shelburne Museum.

Lake Champlain Maritime Museum is on Basin Harbor, off Route 7 in Vergennes heading north toward Burlington. The museum leads tours out to one of the wrecks, which you can view with their remote underwater camera. Most visitors explore the *Champlain II*, across from Basin Harbor, or the *General Butler* in Burlington. You can actually "dive" to explore the wrecks if you are a certified diver. The museum also has a replica 1862-class canal schooner *Lois McClure* and a replica 1776 gunboat *Philadelphia II*.

The **Shelburne Museum** is a massive outdoor complex of thirty-seven buildings and other structures, mostly from the nineteenth century. Here visitors will find Colchester Reef lighthouse and the famous paddle wheel steamer *Ticonderoga*, America's last remaining side-paddle-wheel passenger steamer from the first half of the twentieth century. These buildings, including Colchester Reef Lighthouse and the *Ticonderoga*, have been painstakingly disassembled and reconstructed.

Stop at the **National Museum of the Morgan Horse** or check out **Shelburne Farms**, an interactive, 1,400-acre working farm for families and children. Take a factory tour of the country's largest manufacturer of handmade teddy bears at the **Vermont Teddy Bear Company**.

Enjoy wine tasting at **Shelburne Vineyard Winery**, or walk the nearly six acres of wildflower gardens at **Vermont Wildflower Farm**.

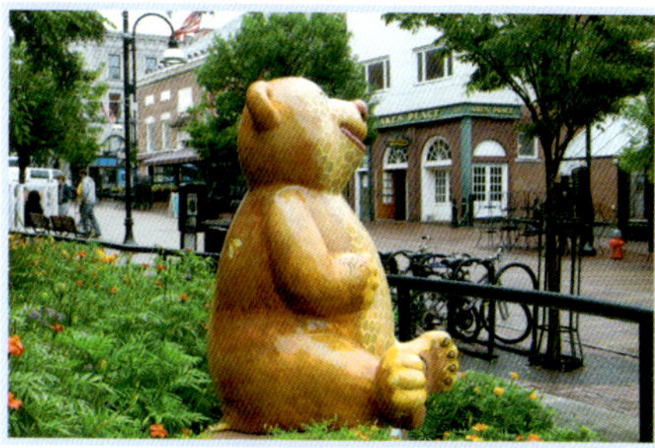

Church Street in Burlington is outlined with sculpted teddy bears promoting the Vermont Teddy Bear Company.

Burlington is Vermont's largest city and a college town with much to offer, especially along the **Church Street Marketplace**. You'll also find hiking and biking trails inside the city and along Waterfront Park, where you can view the Burlington Breakwater Lighthouses from the shore, walk along the boardwalk, or take boats out on the harbor and Lake Champlain. The **Waterfront Bike Path** is an eight-mile route along the lake. For picnicking and swimming, North Beach is off the Burlington Bike Path.

The Island Line Trail leads cyclists from Burlington to the Champlain Islands along the old Rutland Railroad. The **Horsford Gardens and Nursery** has heirloom plants dating to the 1800s. For the best chocolates, take a factory tour and taste gourmet goodies from **Lake Champlain Chocolates**.

 **Quick stop!** In Burlington's Battery Park, don't miss the twenty-four-foot-tall sculpture of **Chief Grey Lock**, an Abenaki tribal warrior from the early 1700s. Wood sculptor Peter Toth's "Whispering Giants" series honors Native Indian chiefs in each US state and the provinces of Canada with huge sculptures, using only basic wood cutting tools.

Explore seventy species of animals at the **ECHO Lake Aquarium** and Science Center, learn about Vermont's Revolutionary War hero at the **Ethan Allan Museum**, or visit the **Dakin Farm** for free food samples, special meats and exhibits, and demos on making maple syrup.

For those who enjoy the arts, **Firehouse Center for the Visual Arts** features five floors of contemporary art, and the **Flynn Center in Burlington** is one of the largest historic performing arts centers in New England.

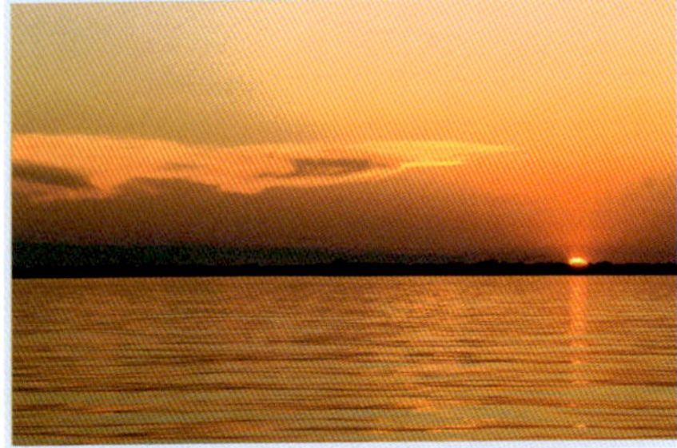

Sunset from the Vermont side of Lake Champlain.

 **Quick stop!** Scotland has its Loch Ness monster, and Lake Champlain has its Champ. On King Street by the Burlington Dock at the end of Perkins Pier, is a **granite monument erected to Champ**, with the inscription "Dedicated to Champ, Belua Aquatica Champlainiensis, and those people in Vermont who have sighted Champ, and are in search of Champ." The state has designated Champ an officially protected species.

Heading north, you'll find rural communities and picturesque views of farmland, forests, and wetlands. There are many biking and hiking trails that are also used in the winter by cross-country skiers and snowmobilers. There are also many islands in this area, and you can drive to the largest ones. Ten parks in the islands offer hiking, biking, canoeing, kayaking, performances, and educational programs. At North Hero island, enjoy a swim and quiet beach at **Knight Point State Park**.

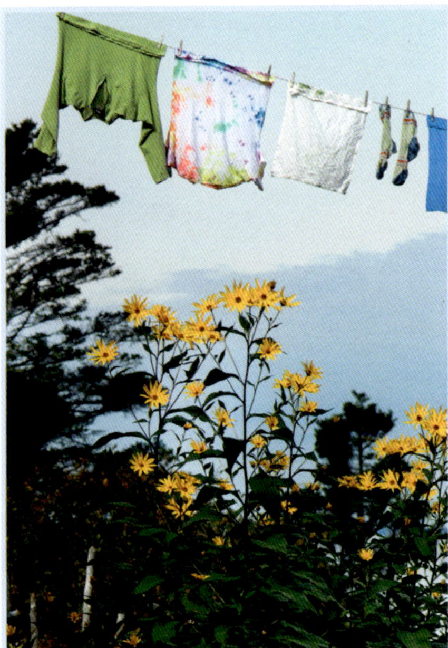

Many Vermonters disconnect from technology in rural island and farm communities.

The fourteen-mile-long Grand Isle is the largest island on Lake Champlain. Its town of South Hero is the home of the Hyde Log Cabin, built around 1783 by one of the island's pioneer settlers, and is one of the oldest cabins in the United States. **Grand Isle State Park** in South Hero offers camping adventures, boating, fishing, kayaking, and nature walks. Keeler Bay in South Hero has limestone rock formations millions of years old. The **South Hero Land Trust** protects much of the area from commercial development. The organization hosts many farm-market and other events. Farther north, Saint Albans also has a system of well-groomed trails for bikers, hikers, and skiers.

Isle La Motte is the northernmost island of Lake Champlain. It has relatively flat terrain for biking on the ten-mile Isle La Motte Ramble, and you can rent kayaks. Stop by a schoolhouse-turned-museum and the **Isle La Motte Library** made of local limestone.

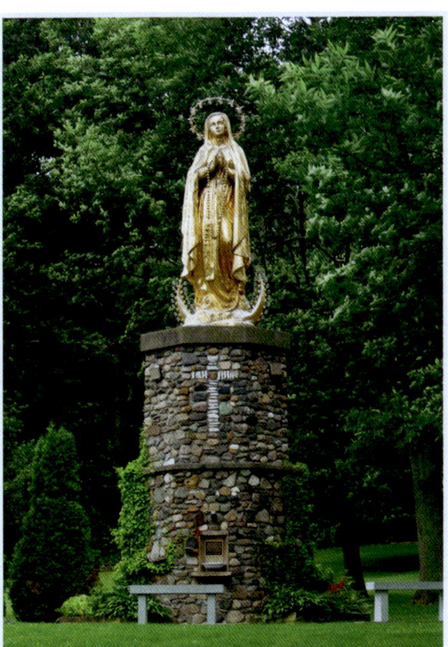

Saint Anne's Shrine and grounds mark Vermont's first celebrated mass.

Saint Anne's Shrine marks the spot where the first known mass in Vermont was celebrated. **Fisk Farm** hosts cultural heritage programs with arts and musical performances. Isle La Motte also contains a remarkable natural phenomenon known as the Chazy Fossil Reef. Part of the Fisk Quarry Preserve, it is the oldest exposed tilted reef in the world, where the bedrock of the southern third of the island displays primitive fossil remnants from over 480 million years ago.

Back on the mainland coast, the Central Vermont Rail Trail in St. Albans offers twenty-seven miles of remote Vermont scenery for those who enjoy horseback riding, mountain biking, hiking, cross-country skiing, and snowmobiling. The St. Albans Rail Trail also provides a nice long bike ride along the Lamoile River. The Missisquoi Valley Rail Trail in St. Albans is a twenty-six-mile bike trail between the towns of St. Albans and Richford through farms, forests, and wetlands.

The **Missisquoi National Refuge**, north of Swanton, is loaded with many species of migratory birds, especially waterfowl, from northern Lake Champlain. The Alburg Recreational Rail Trail offers nearly four miles of gravel pathway along the shores of Lake Champlain for birding, cross-country skiing, horseback riding, and mountain biking. The Flat and Fertile Vermont trail is a fourteen-mile mile trail near Swanton.

Alburg Dunes State Park has one of the longest beaches on Lake Champlain. You'll find quiet places to golf at the **Alburg Golf Links** on the nearby mainland.

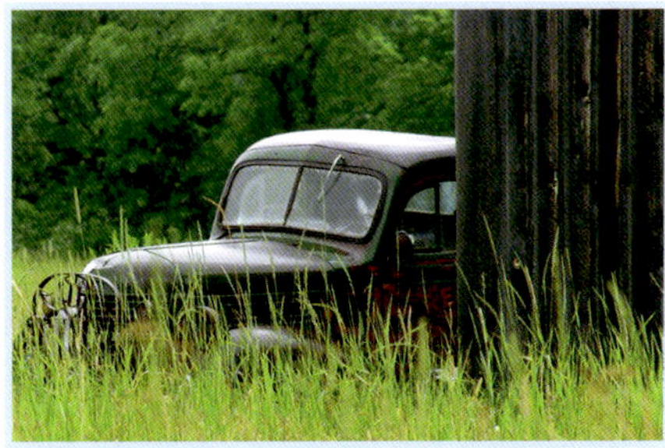

Old car and barn in rural northern Vermont.

Contacts for Attractions on Coastal Lake Champlain in Vermont

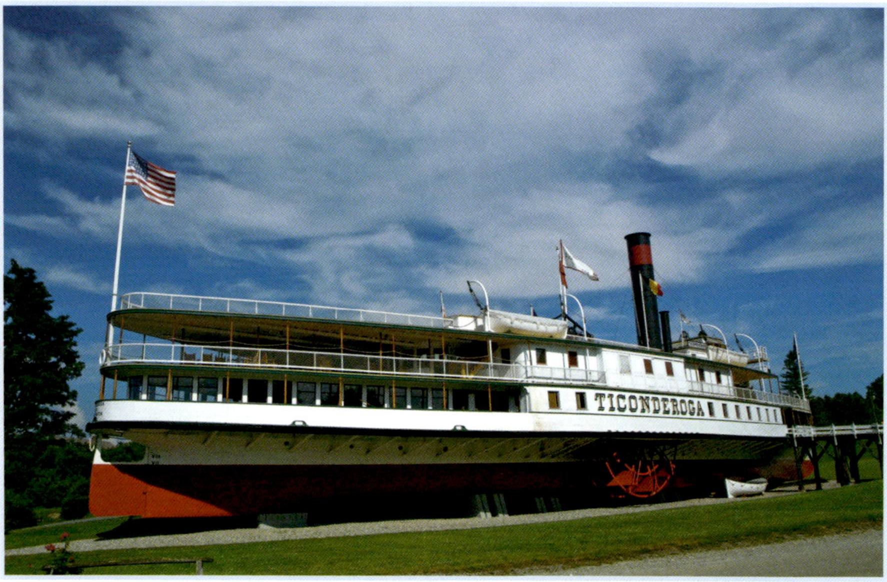

The original reconstructed paddle wheel steamer *Ticonderoga* at the Shelburne Museum.

Lake Champlain Maritime Museum, Vergennes
(802) 475-2022
lcmm.org

Shelburne Museum, Shelburne
(802) 985-3346
shelburnemuseum.org

Museum Morgan Horse, Middlebury
(802) 388-1639
morganhorse.com

Shelburne Farms, Shelburne
(802) 985-8686
shelburnefarms.org

Vermont Teddy Bear, Shelburne
(802) 985-3001
vermontteddybear.com

Shelburne Vineyard Winery, Shelburne
(802) 985-8222
shelburnevineyard.com

Vermont Wildflower Farm, Charlotte
(802) 425-3641
vermontwildflowerfarm.com

Horsford Gardens and Nursery, Charlotte
(802) 425-2811
horsfordnursery.com

Church Street Marketplace, Burlington
(802) 863-1648
churchstmarketplace.com

Burlington's Waterfront Bike Path, Burlington
btvbikepath.com

ECHO Lake Aquarium, Burlington
(802) 864-1848
echovermont.org

Whistling Man Schooner Company, Burlington
(802) 598-6504
whistlingman.com

Ethan Allan Museum, Burlington
(802) 865-4556
ethanallenhomestead.org

Dakin Farm, South Burlington
(800) 993-2546
dakinfarm.com

Firehouse Center Visual Arts, Burlington
(802) 865-7166
burlingtoncityarts.org

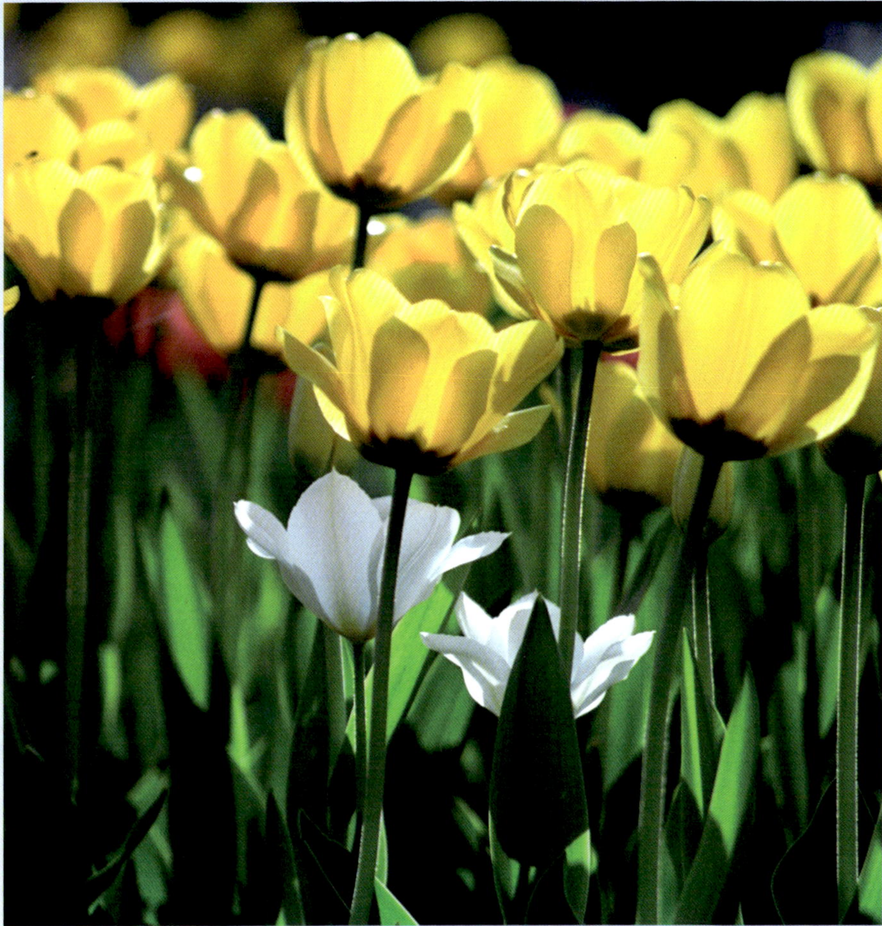

Tulips in Vermont.

Flynn Center in Burlington, Burlington
(802) 652-4500
flynncenter.org

Lake Champlain Chocolates, Burlington
(800) 465-5909
lakechamplainchocolates.com

Spirit of Ethan Allen III, Burlington
(802) 862-8300
soea.com

Lake Champlain Cruises, Burlington
(802) 864-9669
lakechamplaincruises.com

Grand Isle Park, Grand Isle
(802) 372-4300
vtstateparks.com/htm/grandisle.htm

South Hero Land Trust, South Hero
(802) 372-3786
shlt.org

Knight Point Park, North Hero
(802) 372-8389
vtfpr.org/parks/htm/knightpoint.htm
Isle La Motte Library, Isle La Motte
islelamotte.org/library

Fisk Farm, Isle La Motte
(802) 928-3364
fiskfarm.com

Saint Anne's Shrine, Isle La Motte
(802) 928-3362
saintannesshrine.org

Missisquoi National Refuge, Swanton
(802) 868-4781
friendsofmissisquoi.org/

Alburg Dunes State Park, Alburg
(802) 796-4170
vtstateparks.com/htm/alburg.htm

Alburg Golf Links, Alburg
(802) 796-3586
alburggolflinks.com

Lake Champlain Boat Tours and Ferries

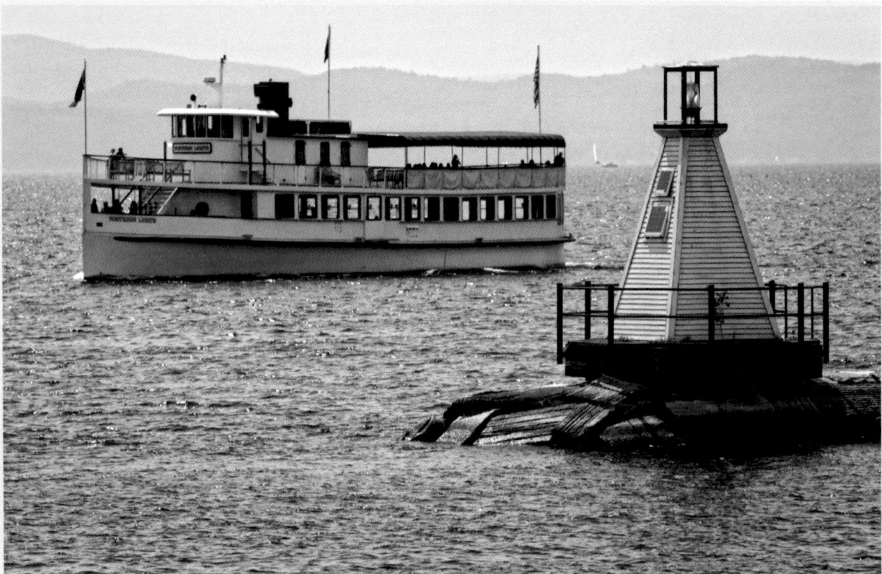

Tour boat passes Burlington Breakwater South Light.

Spirit of Ethan Allan III

Dinner and event cruises. Lighthouses are best viewed on the Scenic Narrated Cruise.

- 348 Flynn Ave., Burlington
- 802-862-8300
- soea.com
- **Lighthouses:** Juniper Island, Burlington North Breakwater, Burlington South Breakwater

Lake Champlain Cruises

Lunch and dinner cruises around the lake.

- 1 King Street, Burlington
- (802) 864-9669
- lakechamplaincruises.com
- **Lighthouses:** Burlington North Breakwater, Burlington South Breakwater

Lake Champlain Ferries

Ferry service from Burlington, Grand Isle, or Charlotte, heading across the lake to New York ports in Plattsburg, Port Kent, and Essex.

- 1 King Street, Burlington
- (802) 864-6830
- ferries.com
- **Lighthouses:** Burlington North Breakwater, Burlington South Breakwater

Whistling Man Schooner Company

Lake Champlain sailing cruises daily aboard the forty-foot *Friend Ship*, a Friendship fishing sloop.

- 1 College Street
- (802) 598-6504
- whistlingman.com
- **Lighthouses:** Burlington North Breakwater, Burlington South Breakwater

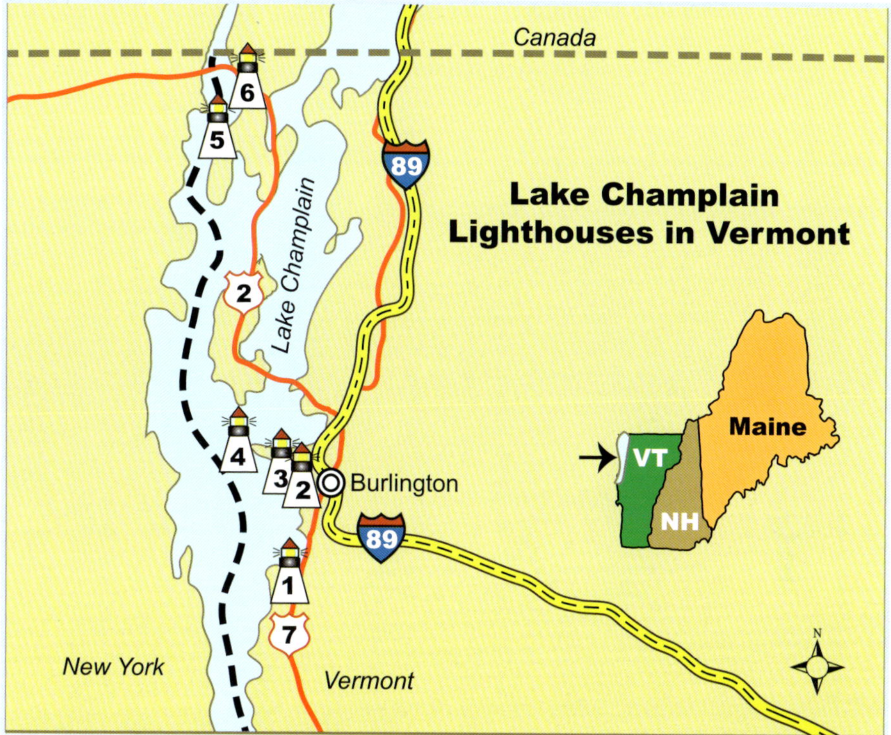

Map of Vermont's Lake Champlain lighthouses: **(1)** Colchester Reef, **(2)** Burlington Breakwater South, **(3)** Burlington Breakwater North, **(4)** Juniper Island, **(5)** Isle La Motte, **(6)** Windmill Point

Appendix A

Glossary of Mariner Terms

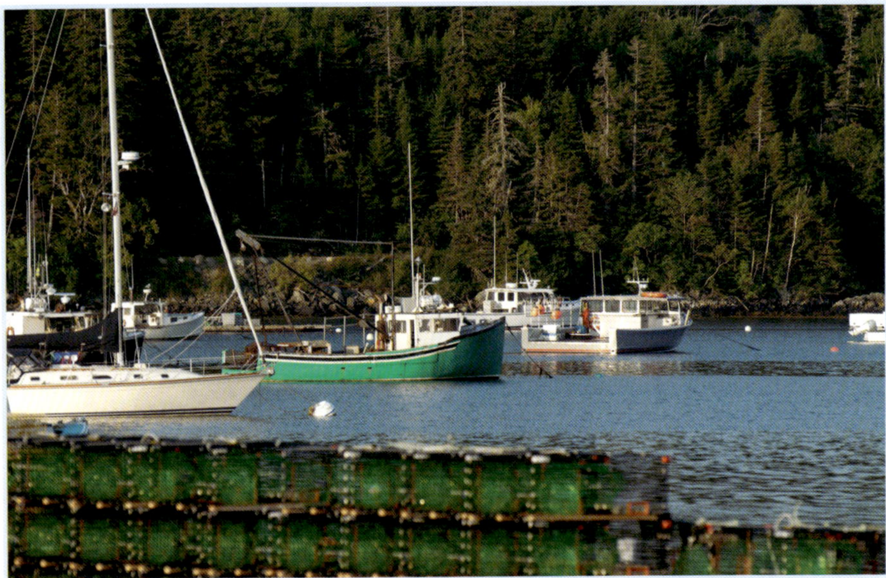

Sailing and lobster boats in Cutler Harbor in northern Maine.

Barque (also bark) is a vessel with at least three masts, and square sails.

Bow is the front section of a ship.

Bowsprit is a long, extended pole or spar in the front of the sailing ship.

Breeches buoy was a device used in rescues, which looked like a life preserver with canvas pants attached to catch the survivor so he or she could be towed ashore.

Breakwater is a rock structure that extends out in a harbor, acting as a barrier to protect it from the force of waves.

Brig is a two-masted, square-sail rigged ship.

Captain is a person in command of a ship. Captain may also be referred as the chief officer of a lifesaving station.

Congressional Gold Medal is an award bestowed by the United States Congress and is the highest civilian award.

Cutter is the same as a sloop, except that the mast is moved toward the front (aft) and another forestay is added on which to raise another sail (called the staysail). Typically a cutter is also full keeled so it tracks well but has a slower top speed.

First mate, also referred to as first officer, is a merchant ship's officer whose rank is just below captain.

Jetty is a wharf or pier that projects into the water to protect a harbor or shoreline from rising tides and strong currents.

Keeper, also called captain, is in charge of all lighthouse duties or lifesaving station training.

Ketch and yawl sailing vessels are both double-masted with the higher main mast toward the front and the shorter mizzen mast in the back. If the mizzenmast is behind the rudderpost the vessel is said to be a yawl. If the mast is ahead of the rudderpost she is said to be a ketch. Ketches and yawls are great for long-distance heavy weather sailing.

Knots are a unit measuring exactly 1,852 meters. It is how the speed of a boat is measured in units of distance for a certain amount of time.

Lifesaving stations were located between lighthouses and housed trained rescue crews.

Listed (list) occurs when a ship is tilted to one side.

Lyle gun is a cannon-like gun used to fire a line as far as 800 yards to a wreck for rescue.

Nor'easter is a storm that travels to the northeast from the south and the winds come from the northeast, producing high winds and a lot of precipitation.

Pilothouse (or pilot-house) is a glass-enclosed room on the highest or largest control deck and is controlled by the ship's pilot.

Port is the left side of a ship.

Revenue Cutter Service, established after the Civil War, was responsible for saving many lives from shipwrecks. Later it coordinated its efforts with lighthouses and lifesaving stations.

Schooner is a sailing ship with two or more masts, with the foremast shorter than the others. These large vessels are popular for today's sailing cruises.

Second mate is the third officer in command of a ship, and is a licensed member of the deck department of a merchant ship.

Seine fishing is fishing with a large net that hangs in the water with weights along the bottom edge. Boats equipped for seine fishing are called seiners.

Skiff is a small, flat-bottomed boat with a square stern.

Sloop is a single-masted sailboat in which the mast is positioned in the first third of the vessel. The sloop is easy to sail, points well to windward, and goes fast. It is a good boat for racing or cruising with a small crew.

Starboard is the right side of a ship.

Steamboat, or steamship, sometimes called a steamer, is a ship in which the primary method of propulsion is steam power, typically driven by either propellers or paddle wheels.

Stern is the rear section of a ship.

Surfman was a trained rescuer with a lifesaving station.

Tall ships do not use modern materials such as aluminum and steel and have more complex rigging as a result. The term tall ship came into widespread use in the mid-twentieth century with the advent of tall ship races.

Thwart is a seat where the rowers were to be placed in a lifeboat.

Tugs or tugboats are vessels that guide ships into ports or harbors.

United States Lifesaving Service was a government agency that grew out of private, local humanitarian efforts to save the lives of shipwrecked mariners and passengers.

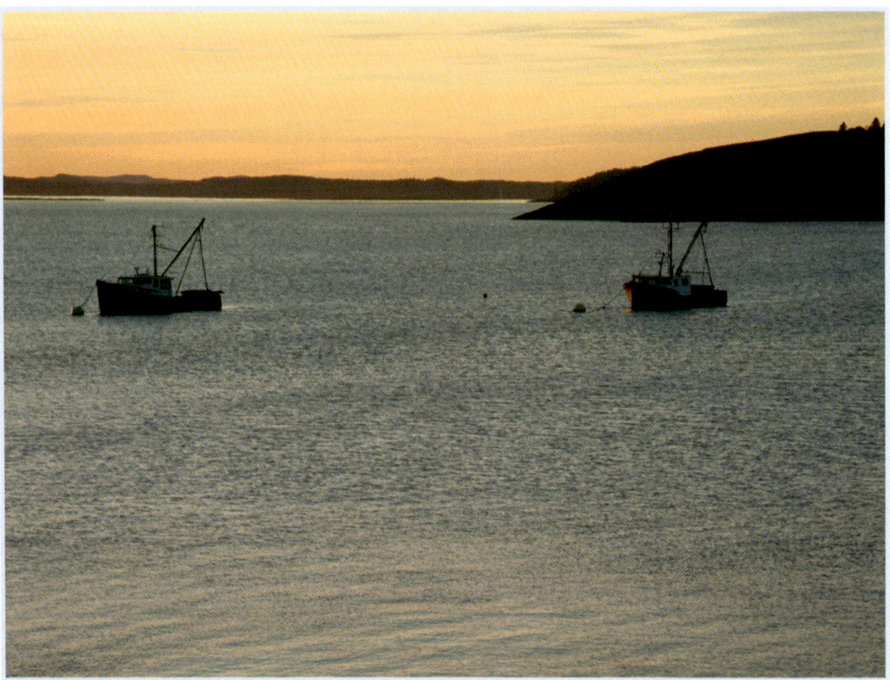

Fishing boats docked in Lubec Harbor in Maine.

Windjammer is a large sailing ship with an iron or steel hull built to carry cargo in the nineteenth and early twentieth centuries. Windjammers were the grandest of merchant sailing ships, with between three and five large masts and square sails, giving them a characteristic profile.

Wreckers are employed to unload enough cargo on a wrecked vessel to allow it to float off the sandbar, ledge, or shoal that grounded it, hopefully with most of the cargo intact.

Appendix B

Cruises on Windjammers, Tall Ships, Schooners, and Sloops

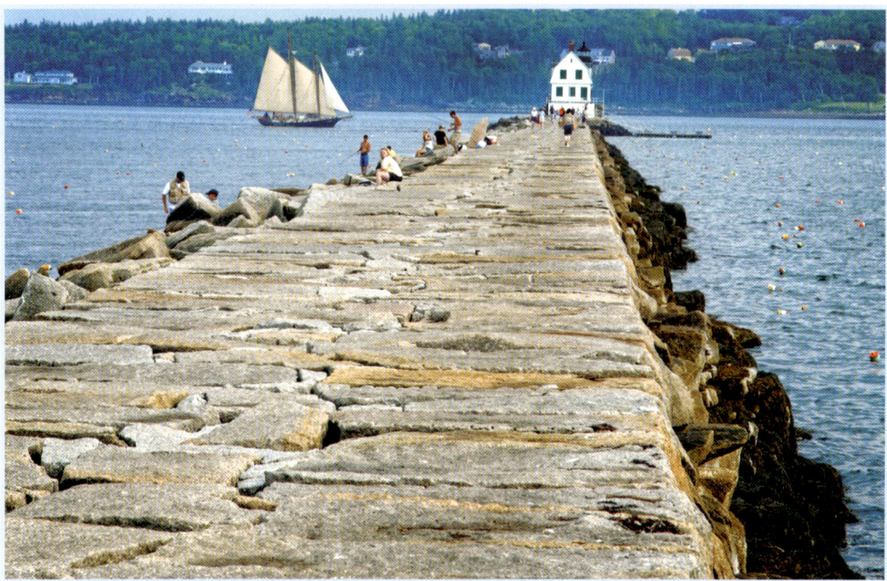

Schooner passes Rockland Breakwater Light in Maine.

These schooner, windjammer, and other sailing cruises often pass by lighthouses up and down the New England coast as part of sailing charters, narrated wildlife and historic tours, and other types of excursions. The predominant sailing regions in northern New England lie between Rockland and Camden, and on the Penobscot Bay region in Maine, but you can also find sailing opportunities in the western Acadia region and on Lake Champlain in Vermont.

Maine

Silverlining Sailing Cruises, Ogunquit
(207) 646-9800
silverliningsailing.com

The Gift Sailing Cruises, Ogunquit
(207) 646-3758
sailthegift.com

Cricket Sailing Cruises, Ogunquit
(207) 646-5227
cricketsailing.com

Schooner Eleanor, Kennebunkport
(207) 967-8809
schoonereleanor.com

Pineapple Ketch Sailing, Kennebunkport
(207) 468-7262
pineappleketch.com

Schooner Wendameen, Portland
(207) 766-2500
portlandschooner.com

Schooner Bagheera, Portland
(207) 766-2500
portlandschooner.co

Maine Sailing Adventures, Portland
(207) 749-9169
mainesailingadventures.net

Sloop Marisa III, Yarmouth
(207) 615-6917
gosailingcascobay.com

Schooner Alert, Bailey Island
(207) 833-5531
seaescapecottages.com

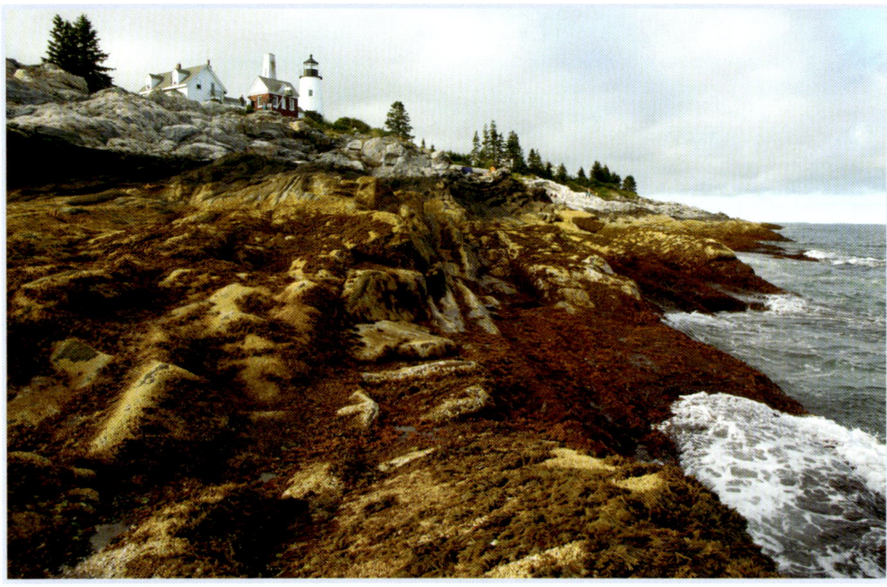

Unique shoreline around Maine's Pemaquid Point Light.

Schooner Eastwind Sailing, Boothbay
(207) 633-6598
schoonereastwind.com

Schooner Lazy Jack, Boothbay
(207) 633-3444
schoonerlazyjackcruises.com

Sloop Sarah Mead, Boothbay
(207) 380-5460
sailmuscongus.com

Sloop Bay Lady, Boothbay
(207) 633-2284
balmydaycruises.com

Bufflehead Sailing Charters, Rockland
(207) 691-5407
sailrockland.com

Morning in Maine, Rockland
(207) 594-1844
amorninginmaine.com

Schooner Isaac H. Evans, Rockland
(877) 238-1325
isaacevans.com

Schooner Victory Chimes, Rockland
(800) 745-5651
victorychimes.com

Schooner J. & E. Riggin, Rockland
(800) 869-0604
mainewindjammer.com

Schooner American Eagle, Rockland
(207) 594-8007
schooneramericaneagle.com

Schooner Stephen Taber, Rockland
(207) 594-4723
stephentaber.com

Schooner Bowditch, Rockland
(800) 999-7352
stephentaber.com

Schooner Heron, Rockport
(207) 236-8605
sailheron.com

Schooner Grace Bailey, Camden
(207) 236-2938
mainewindjammercruises.com

Schooner Mercentile, Camden
(800) 736-7981
mainewindjammercruises.com

Schooner Olad, Camden
(207) 236-2323
maineschooners.com

Schooner Angelique, Camden
(800) 282-9989
sailangelique.com

Schooner Mary Day, Camden
(800) 992-2218
schoonermaryday.com

Schooner Surprise, Camden
(207) 236-4687
camdenmainesailing.com

Liberation Charters, Camden
(207) 542-1908
liberationcharters.com

Camden Sailing Charters, Camden
(207) 691-6541
camdensailingcharters.com

Schooner Lewis R. French, Camden
(800) 469-4635
schoonerfrench.com

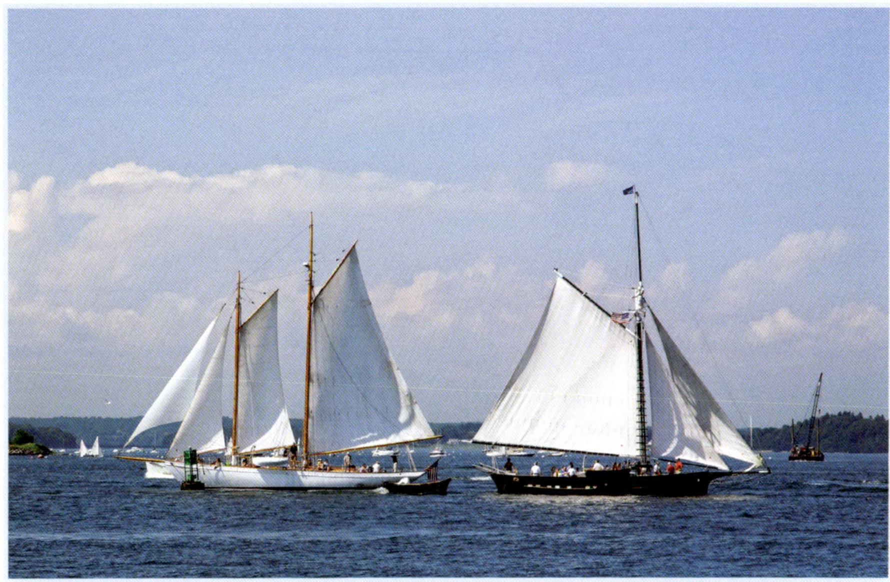

Sailing vessels greeting one another.

Schooner Appledore, Camden
(207) 236-8353
appledore2.com

Schooner Heritage, Camden
(207) 594-8007
schoonerheritage.com

Maine Windjammer Association, Camden
(800) 807-WIND
sailmainecoast.com

Coast to Islands Sailing, Belfast
(207) 505-1618
sailingmissnina.com

Schooner Timberwind, Belfast
(207) 619-0654
mainedaysail.com

Schooner Natalie Todd, Bar Harbor
(207) 288-4585
downeastwindjammer.com

Schooner Margaret Todd, Bar Harbor
(207) 288-4585
downeastwindjammer.com

Downeast Windjammer, Bar Harbor
(207) 288-4585
downeastwindjammer.com

Downeast Sailing Adventures, Southwest Harbor
(207) 288-2216
downeastsail.com

Schooner Rachel B. Jackson, Southwest Harbor
(207) 288-2216
downeastsail.com

Sloop Surprise, Southwest Harbor
(207) 288-2216
downeastsail.com

Sloop Alice E, Northeast Harbor
(207) 266-5210
sailacadia.com

Sail Acadia, Northeast Harbor
(207) 266-5210
sailacadia.com

Vermont

Schooner Whistling Man, Burlington
(802) 598-6504
whistlingman.com

Appendix C
Lighthouses Where You Can Spend the Night

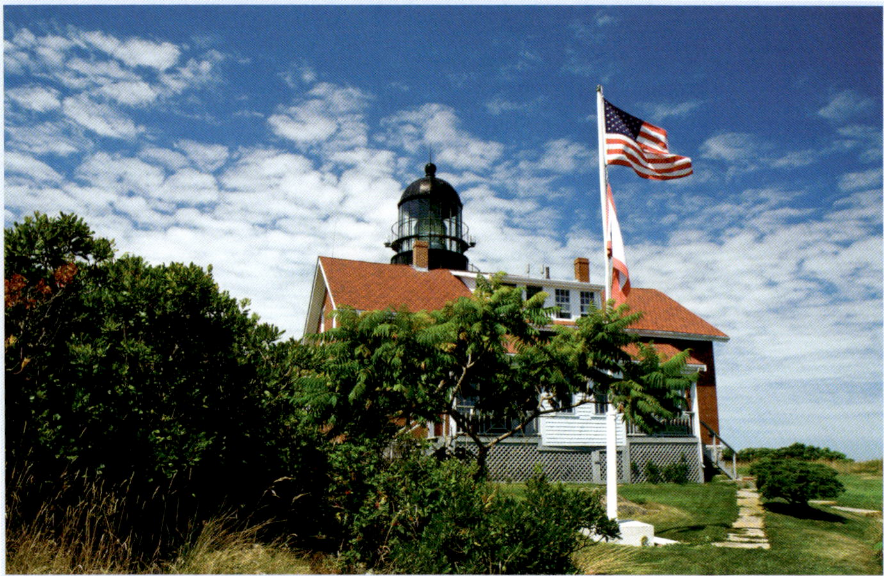

Seguin Island Lighthouse provides overnight lodging at the lighthouse and camping nearby.

Overnight accommodations at lighthouses range from the rustic to let guests experience how the early keepers lived, to renovated, elegant rooms with all the amenities; to green environments that use today's conservation technologies.

Seguin Island Light (Maine)

This mysterious and powerful lighthouse is two-and-a-half miles from the mouth of the Kennebec River. Its rustic accommodations are open to members of the Friends of Seguin Island (the membership payment is the lodging fee). Guests take the ferry Fish 'N Trips/Seguin Island Ferry to the island and hike up a steep hill to the lighthouse. The guest quarters includes two upstairs bedrooms (downstairs is the museum and gift shop); one bedroom has two twin beds; the other has one twin and one double bed. There are minimal amenities and cooking is limited to the charcoal grill provided. There is a private bath on the second floor with hot and cold running water and a composting toilet and a shower (or use the outhouse). Sheets, blankets, and pillows are provided. Camping is also allowed. Friends of Seguin Island Light Station, (207) 443-4808, seguinisland.org.

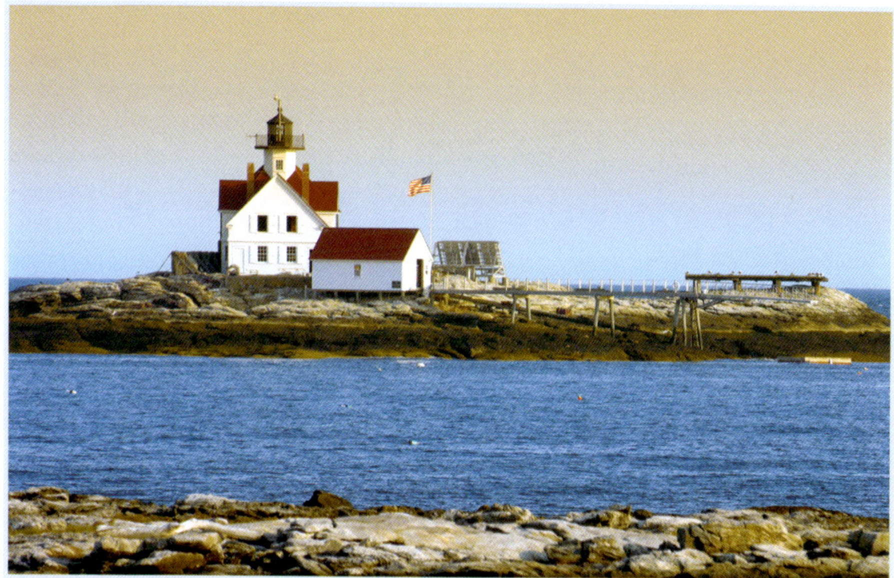

Maine's Cuckolds Light has been converted to luxurious rooms for rent.

Cuckolds / Inn at Cuckolds (Maine)

Cuckolds Lighthouse has been elegantly remodeled to include an East Suite and West Suite, with accommodations for two guests in each suite. Rent the entire island for a little peace and quiet. Inn at Cuckolds, (855) 212-5252, innatcuckoldslighthouse.com.

Whitehead Light (Maine)

The entire facility is available to rent for up to six nights, and the station is available for weekend rentals. Transportation is provided to and from the island, along with meals, on the Whitehead Light Station boat. Whitehead Light Station Organization, (207) 200-7957, whiteheadlightstation.org.

Goose Rocks Light (Maine)

Goose Rocks can accommodate up to six guests (two bedrooms and one bunk room) for an all-day or overnight visit with a minimum contribution towards its ongoing maintenance and restoration efforts. Access to Goose Rocks includes real risks, and a safe and enjoyable visit depends on guests' ability to climb a vertical ladder (from a boat) to the catwalk, as keepers did years ago. Visitors are responsible for their own provisions. Pickup is at the North Haven Town Dock (next to the ferry docking station at the terminal). Beacon Preservation, (203) 952-8100 (October through May) or (207) 867-4747 (June through September). beaconpreservation.org.

Isle au Haut (Robinson Point) Light (Maine)

The property contains a seven-room main house with four bedrooms and two baths, a four-room house with one bedroom and one bath, and two small heated cabins. All have been transformed with early-twentieth-century charm. The buildings are powered by photovoltaics and a generator. Evenings are illuminated by the glow of gaslights, candles, and kerosene lanterns. No telephones or Wi-Fi. Includes three gourmet meals prepared on-site by the chef. Keeper's House Inn, Dr. Marshall Chapman, Innkeeper, (207) 335-2990, keepershouse.com.

Little River Light (Maine)

In the unspoiled fishing village of Cutler, Maine, this station has been restored by the Friends of Little River Lighthouse, a chapter of the American Lighthouse Foundation. Friends of Little River Lighthouse meet guests at the public boat ramp in Cutler and take them on a twelve-minute boat ride to the island. Elegant rooms include the Keeper's Room, Oceanside Room, and Woods View Room. Friends of Little River Lighthouse, (877) 276-4682, littleriverlight.org/overnight-stays.

West Quoddy Head Light (Maine)

Guests choose from the Station House, Keepers Cottage, Cabin, and four units in the Lodge, or rent the entire seven-unit complex. Accommodations have fully equipped kitchens, private bathrooms, washers and dryers, linens, Wi-Fi, telephone,and DirecTV. Contemporary furniture is blended with antiques for traditional Down East comfort and Coast Guard polish. West Quoddy Head Light Keepers Association, (877) 535-4714, quoddyvacation.com.

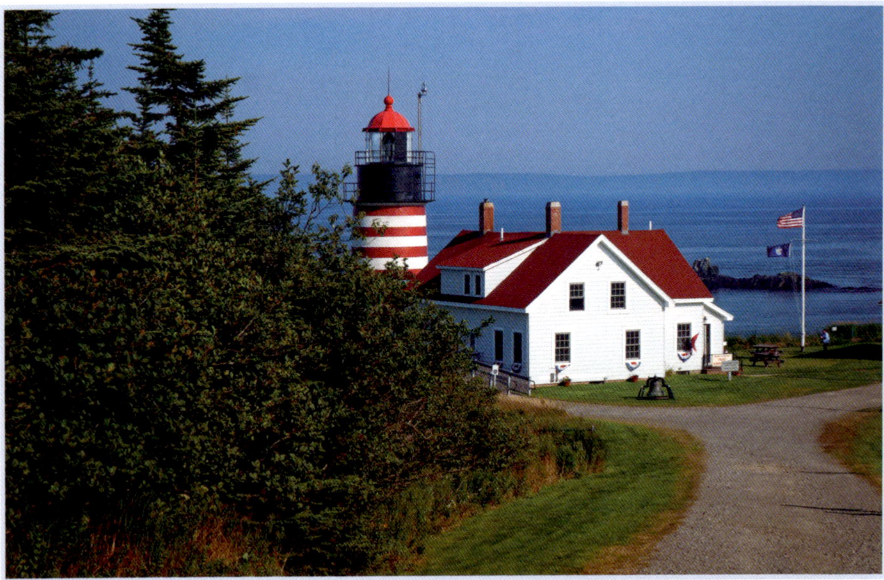

West Quoddy Head Light offers the keeper's cottage and other restored buildings for overnight stays.

Appendix D
Haunted Lighthouses

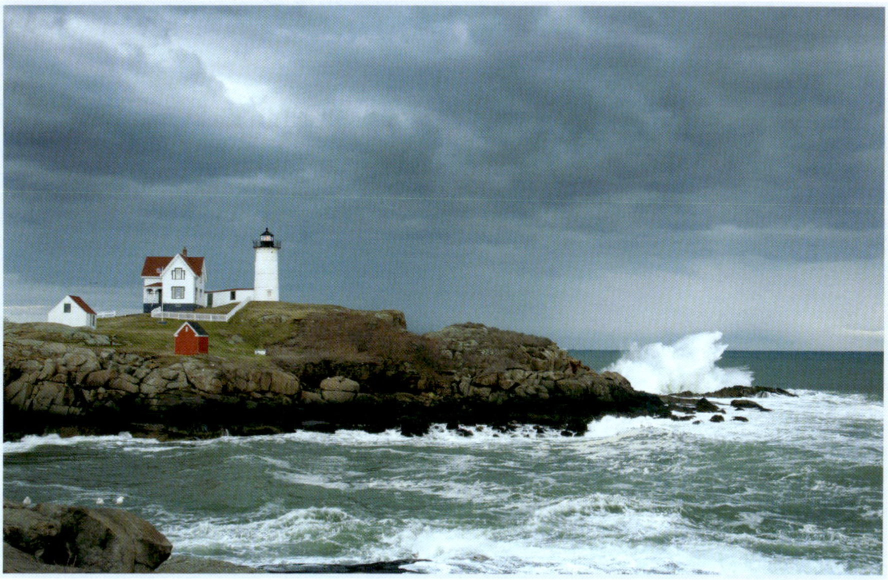
The area around Nubble Lighthouse is believed to be haunted by the ghost ship *Isadore*.

New England is filled with tales of ghosts. Many of these controversial stories were passed down over many years and are part of the folklore that surrounds this rugged coastline. Many lighthouses were built in isolated areas that sometimes were too much for the keepers or their wives, and suicides occurred, which sometimes resulted in ghost sightings afterward. Some keepers also became victims of foul play or were killed in storms or tragic accidents. Some keepers were so dedicated to their lighthouse stations that their ghosts were seen returning to make sure the lighthouse was well maintained. Many of these paranormal activities have been described by respected townsfolk, mariners, officers, or the keepers themselves.

White Island (Isles of Shoals) Light (New Hampshire)

Blackbeard's wife appears as a tall woman wrapped in a dark sea cloak with long flowing blonde hair. She has been seen on the rocks gazing out into the waters as if looking for her husband. Screeching, human-like sounds have also been heard from White Island, but many believe it is from the snowy white owls that frequent the area.

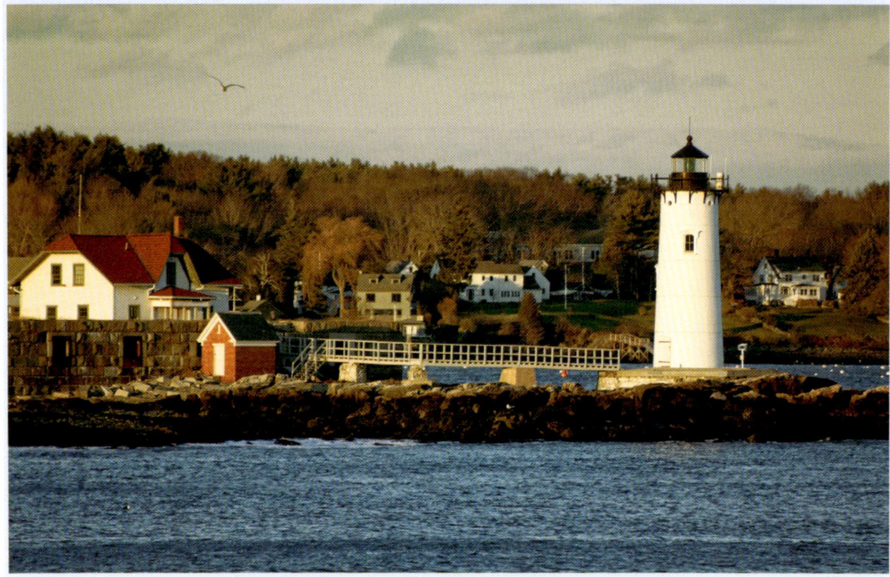

Portsmouth Harbor Light is haunted by a humorous keeper and those who may have perished during storms.

Portsmouth Harbor Light (New Hampshire)

Keeper Joshua Card supposedly retired after a stroke, but some have written that he retired against his will at age eighty-six. His ghost has been seen and heard for many years by Coast Guard staff and tourists. Members of the show *Ghost Hunters* documented footsteps on the lighthouse stairs, knocking, and strange noises in the keeper's quarters.

The ghost of keeper Joshua Card seems to enjoy the attention. He is said to visit the lighthouse on some nights, making sure the light is tended to, and helping to guide mariners home.

Boon Island Light (Maine)

In the mid-1800s a young keeper came to the distant lighthouse with his new bride. During a winter storm a few months later, he went out to check the tower, slipped on the icy rocks and drowned in the freezing waters while his wife watched in horror (see full story in the Boon Island Lighthouse entry).

Over the years, mariners and keepers have seen a ghostly figure of a young, sad-faced woman shrouded in white on the rocks at dusk, and moaning and screeching sounds have been heard. Some keepers claimed to have heard knocking on the door, and when they opened the door, they saw a faint apparition of a woman dressed in white heading to the tower. Sometimes when keepers would bring their cat or dog to Boon Island, the animals would refuse to go in the lighthouse tower. Some dogs barked constantly and seemed to be chasing something around the island.

In the 1970s, a Coast Guard keeper and crewman were fishing near the island and didn't make it back before dark to turn on the light on. Although no one was home, the light was glowing brightly by the time the keepers returned.

Nubble (Cape Neddick) Light (Maine)

The wreck of the *Isadore* on Thanksgiving night in 1842 resulted in the death of all fourteen aboard (see Nubble Light entry for full story). The *Isadore* still seems to appear as a phantom ship patrolling the bays near Cape Neddick (Nubble) Light. Since the day it perished, many mariners claimed to have seen the ship, and hotel guests in the shoreline inns of York, not knowing the story, have reported seeing a phantom ship.

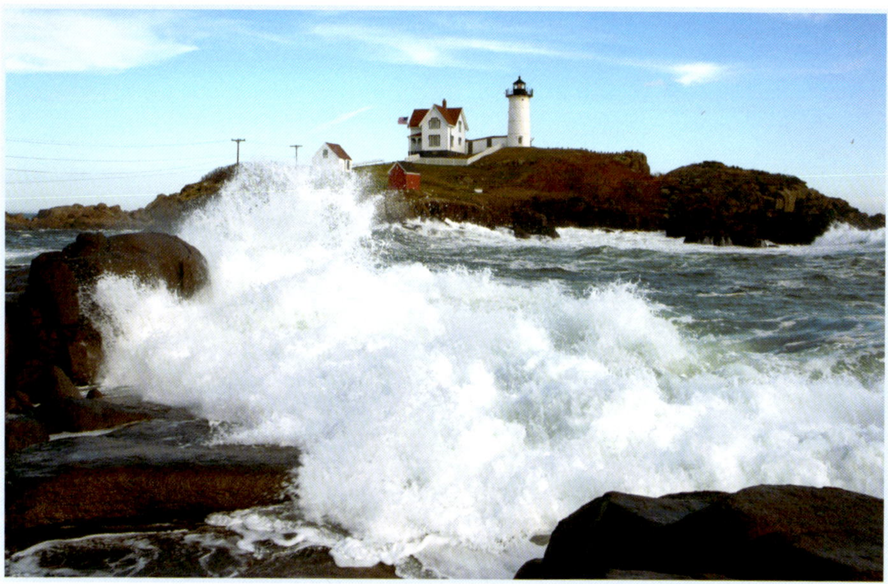

Crashing waves at Maine's Cape Neddick (Nubble) Light.

Goat Island (Cape Porpoise) Light (Maine)

Richard "Dick" Curtis started serving as caretaker on Goat Island in 1994, and was known for his sense of humor. One day in 2002, Curtis took his boat out with his dog and three other dogs he was caring for. He apparently got caught in some rough waves, fell overboard, and drowned. Two of the dogs were never found. Scott Dombrowski, who replaced Curtis as caretaker, shares the belief with many locals that Curtis's ghost remains on the island. According to the caretaker, after Curtis's death, items have gone missing and turned up on the kitchen table. The foghorn would go off without reason, even in broad daylight, and still went off when the power was disconnected. The horn finally stopped after the whole unit was replaced. One cold day, Dombrowski sat in front of an old electric heater that hadn't worked for years and asked the spirit of Curtis for some heat. All of a sudden the heater switched on. During a lighthouse tour, Dombrowski overheard one woman mentioning that the area was haunted. She later pulled the caretaker aside to let him know that Curtis was all right and was going to stay at the beacon, and that "one of the missing dogs had made it."

Wood Island Light (Maine)

One of the best-known Maine lighthouse legends involves a murder-suicide at Wood Island Lighthouse (see Wood Island Light entry). Since the incident, strange events have been reported. Moans are heard coming from the chicken coop, and locked doors have been mysteriously opened. Dark shadows have been observed near the lighthouse walkway and at the top of the tower, and strange voices have also been heard. There have also been sightings of a woman, believed to be the murdered man's wife.

In 1905, keeper Charles Burke, believing he was seeing and hearing ghosts, was so distraught that he left his post unattended and stayed overnight in a boarding house on the mainland. The next day, he jumped from a third-floor window to his death.

Cape Elizabeth Light, (Maine)

In January 1934, sixty-five-year-old keeper Joseph H. Upton went to fix an auxiliary light at the east tower. Hours later, when he failed to return, his wife discovered him unconscious with a fractured skull. He had fallen down the stairs to the base of the tower, and later died. Some claim to have seen the ghost of an older man in a lighthouse uniform near the tower or the driveway.

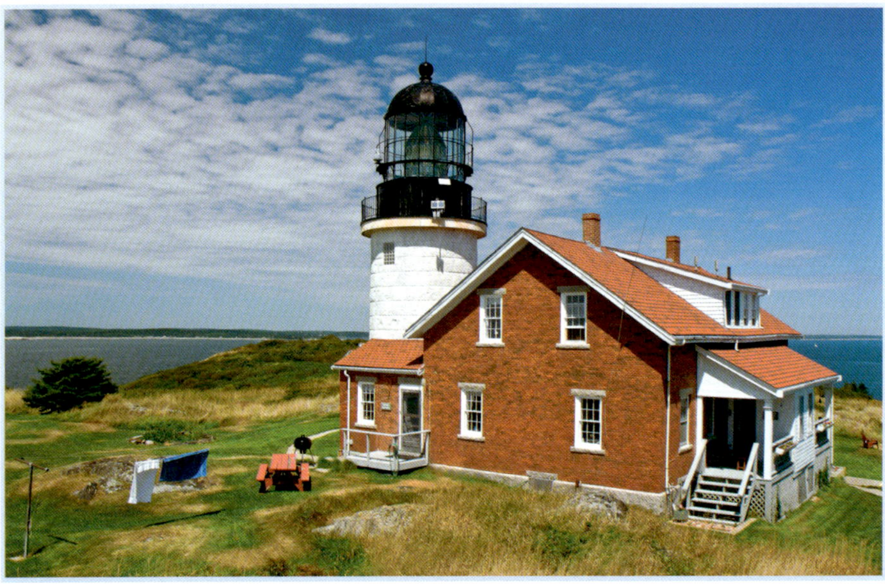

Seguin Light is the most haunted lighthouse in Maine.

Seguin Island Light (Maine)

Seguin Island Lighthouse is considered the most haunted lighthouse on the East Coast. Seguin Island Light's first keeper, Major (Count) John Polereczky, died penniless on the island. Some say his ghost has haunted the keepers who came after him. There have been sightings of a ghost named "Old Captain" climbing the staircase of the tower.

After the lighthouse was automated in 1985, the supervisor in charge of moving the furniture reported that the Old Captain ghost awoke him in the middle of the night, dressed in oilskins and shaking his bed. The Old Captain asked him not to take the furniture away and to leave his home alone. Convinced he was simply in a deep dream, the supervisor moved the furniture. The next day, the furniture was being lowered to the water in a boat when the cable snapped and the contents smashed on the rocks.

Over the years, caretakers have reported items moved around inside the house or seeing things tossed from shelves onto the floor, mysterious cold spots, tools disappearing and reappearing at random, and doors opening and closing. If furniture is moved, it is mysteriously in its original spot the following day. Some have reported hearing coughing.

Many mariners have claimed to hear an old Scot Joplin tune played by a piano over the waters on foggy weather, believed to be from the ghost of a woman who was murdered by her husband who went crazy when she kept playing the same tune all winter long.

There have also been sightings of a young girl running in the house, believed to be a keeper's daughter who died at the lighthouse.

Hendricks Head Light (Maine)

In late November, Charlie Pinkham, the keeper and a volunteer firefighter in the town, gathered a search party to look for a well-dressed woman from out of town who had asked where the shoreline was just before nightfall, and disappeared. The search party found her body about a week later on December 6, 1931, washed ashore near Hendricks Head Lighthouse with a clothing iron tied to her wrist. Detectives later discovered her bag was left at the Fullerton hotel, where she signed in as Louise Meade. No one claimed her body, and she was buried in an old cemetery on the road to Hendricks Head.

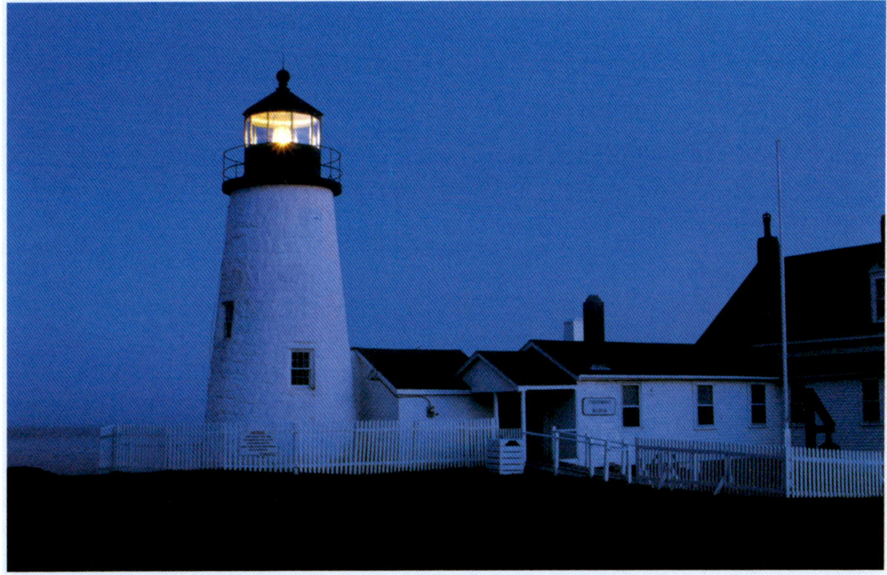

Pemaquid Point Light is haunted by a woman who stays by the fireplace and may have drowned.

Her ghost has been seen at twilight near Hendricks Head Lighthouse, and so she has become known as the "Lady of the Dusk." Numerous times, a black limousine has been seen driving down the Hendricks Head road and parking near the spot where her body washed ashore. Some say it comes during the first week of December that marks the anniversary of the death of this woman, known only as Louise Meade

Pemaquid Light (Maine)

A woman in a red shawl has been seen near the fireplace of the keeper's house. The entity appears wet and shivering, wearing period clothes, and distressed. There is no historical documentation of anyone passing away in the lighthouse; however, many wrecks occurred here. There have also been reports of lights suddenly switching on, and unexplained noises such as doors slamming.

Ram Island Light (Maine)

In the years before the lighthouse was built, a lobsterman and three fisherman took it upon themselves to tend a series of homemade lanterns for mariners. When the fourth man stopped tending the lantern, there were many stories of ghosts being seen on the island for years afterwards. The form of a ghostly "white woman" is said to have saved many lives by appearing with a light to warn ships of danger. Some reported seeing her in a burning boat or on a nearby reef, and even accompanied by lightning. But all described her as a glowing form frantically waving them off the rocks in the area. One captain reported hearing a fog whistle that saved him during a blizzard, even though there was never such an aid on Ram Island.

Owls Head Light (Maine)

There seems to be two paranormal presences at Owls Head Light. One, known as the "Little Lady," is often found in or near the kitchen, in one of the bedrooms, or looking out a window. Sometimes doors close or slam and dinnerware moves, but witnesses describe her as peaceful. In the late 1980s, the wife of the last Coast Guard keeper, Malcom Rouse, saw an outline of a woman dressed in white through the kitchen window. On numerous occasions, their son also described a short woman in white sitting in a chair in his room.

The other presence is believed to be the ghost of a previous lighthouse keeper—a very conscientious one, as he is reported to keep the thermostats turned down and the brass polished. The theory is that the spirits of some dedicated keepers, many of them former ship's captains, remain at the lighthouse when they die. At Owls Head Light, there have been many instances of mysterious footprints made by large workman's boots appearing after a rain or snowfall. The prints would usually lead in only one direction, up the ramp, up the stairs, and to the tower where the brass would be found polished and the lens cleaned.

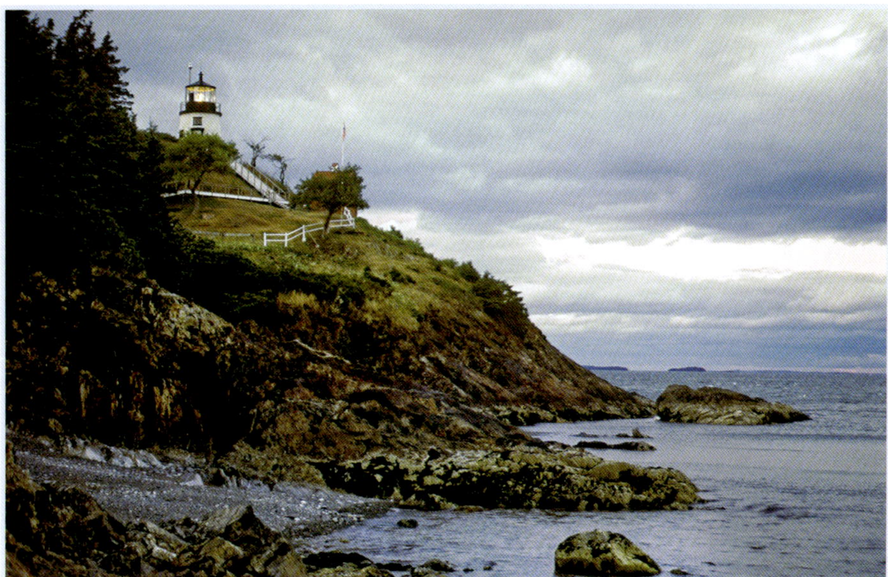

Owls Head is considered haunted by a conscientious keeper.

In the mid-1980s Andy Germann was a Coast Guard keeper at Owls Head Light with his wife Denise. The lighthouse was being renovated, and one night, after going to bed, Andy decided to go outside to make sure some construction materials were safely secured. As he left the bedroom he saw a faint cloud of smoke hovering in front of him and then pass through him. Although thinking it rather odd, he proceeded to check on the materials. Moments later, his wife Denise, felt someone getting back into bed and believed it was her husband. "How'd you make out outside?" she asked. When she received no reply, she turned over and observed a moving indentation in the bed next to her, but no one was there. She then demanded that it go away so she could get some sleep; the movement stopped, and she fell back to sleep. She and her husband compared their experiences in the morning.

Gerard Graham was in charge of the station in the late 1980s with his wife Debbie and their young daughter Claire. They didn't believe the ghost stories and gave Claire the small upstairs bedroom, while they slept in the room next door. During the years the Grahams lived at the station, little Claire had an imaginary friend she described as an "old sea captain." She said he had a beard and wore a blue coat and seaman's cap, though her parents were sure that no such person existed.

One night, Claire came into her parent's room and yelled out "Fog's rolling in! Time to put the foghorn on!" Gerard and Debbie were shocked as they had never heard her use that language before. They went outside and found fog was indeed rolling in, and turned on the foghorn to warn local mariners. Whatever the entity, the Grahams were not afraid of it, and their daughter seemed to enjoy the company of the "old captain." The presence seemed to be quite fond of the little girl as well.

Matinicus Rock Light (Maine)

The story goes that an assistant lighthouse keeper at Matinicus Rock climbed into one of the disabled towers, strung a rope around his neck, and hung himself. His death was discovered a few days later when the residents of Matinicus Island noticed the light wasn't lit.

There is no documentation that this incident occurred. However, Coast Guardsmen have reported a shadowy figure lurking around the north tower and incidences of breaking dishes, chairs turned over, and supplies thrown into disarray. Someone finally stopped the haunting by locking the door to the tower. One day, however, a crewman had to fetch something from the tower and opened the door, which resulted in more mysterious incidents. The light did not work routinely, machinery malfunctioned, and the foghorn developed a strange sound. The tower is now kept locked. As long as the door stays locked, the lighthouse operates smoothy.

Narragaugus (Pond Island) Light (Maine)

In the 1970s, two college boys, friends of the Dameron family living at the lighthouse, were spending nights in a downstairs bedroom while helping to renovate the house. One night, they were awakened by the voice of a woman speaking angrily in a foreign language. The following night, one of the young men heard a loud noise next to him, as if a weight had fallen near his pillow. The boys got up and proclaimed that they were only there to help repair the house, not to hurt it. The room was quiet for the rest of their stay.

Selected Bibliography

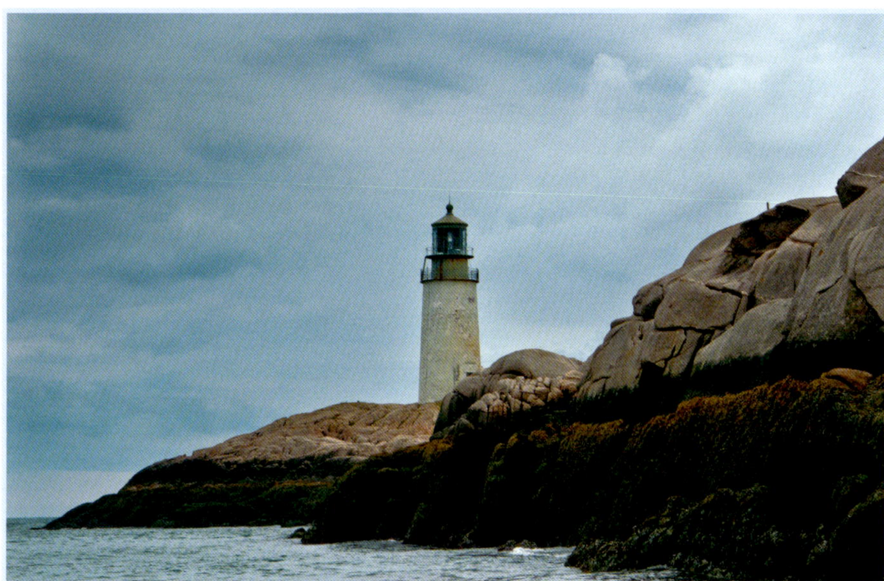

Moose Peak Lighthouse after a storm in Maine.

"American Lighthouse Foundation." American Lighthouse Foundation. http://www.lighthousefoundation.org/.

Bachand, Robert G. *Northeast Lights: Lighthouses and Lightships, Rhode Island to Cape May, New Jersey*. Norwalk, CT: Sea Sports Publications, 1989.

Cahill, Robert Ellis. *Lighthouse Mysteries of the North Atlantic*. Salem, MA: Old Saltbox Pub. House, 1998.

Cann, Donald, John Galluzzo, and Gayle Kadlik. *Isles of Shoals*. Charleston, SC: Arcadia Publishing, 2007.

"CG Continues Flying Santa Tradition." Coast Guard News. http://www.military.com/news/article/coast-guard-news/cg-continues-flying-santa-tradition.html.

"City of Salisbury (1938) - Graves Light Station." *Graves Light Station*. Web.

Claflin, James. *Lighthouses and Life Saving along the Maine and New Hampshire Coast*. Charleston, SC: Arcadia, 1999.

Clark, Sue. "Christmas Memories of the Flying Santa." Lighthouse News | News, Features, Opinions and More About Lighthouses Worldwide. December 24, 2008. http://lighthouse-news.com/2008/12/24/christmas-memories-of-the-flying-santa/.

"Coast Guard Lighthouses." US Coast Guard Home Page. http://www.uscg.mil/history/weblighthouses/LHCT.asp.

Cook, David E. *The Light Keepers of Lake Champlain*. Mayfield, NY: DreamChase Features, 2009.

Costopoulos, Nina. *Lighthouse Ghosts and Legends*. Birmingham, Ala.: Crane Hill Publishers, 2003.

Cutter, William Richard. *New England Families, Genealogical and Memorial: A Record of the Achievements of Her People in the Making of Commonwealths and the Founding of a Nation*. Salem, MA. Higginson Book, 2004. Google E-Books.

De, Wire Elinor. *The Lightkeepers' Menagerie: Stories of Animals at Lighthouses*. Sarasota, FL: Pineapple Press, 2007.

D'Entremont, Jeremy. *New England Lighthouses: A Virtual Guide*. http://www.newenglandlighthouses.net/.

D'Entremont, Jeremy. "Cape Elizabeth Lighthouse History." New England Lighthouses: A Virtual Guide - Photos, History, Tours, Cruises, Coastal Accommodations and More. http://lighthouse.cc/capeelizabeth/history.html.

D'Entremont, Jeremy. *Great Shipwrecks of the Maine Coast*. Beverly, MA: Commonwealth Editions, 2010.

D'Entremont, Jeremy. "Matinicus Rock Lighthouse History." New England Lighthouses: A Virtual Guide - Photos, History, Tours, Cruises, Coastal Accommodations and More. http://www.lighthouse.cc/matinicusrock/history.html.

D'Entremont, Jeremy. *The Lighthouse Handbook*. Kennebunkport, Me.: Cider Mill Press Book Publishers, 2008.

Downs, John W. "Sprays of Salt: Reminiscences of a Native Shoaler By John W. Downs." WHAT'S NEW? - -SeacoastNH.com. http://www.seacoastnh.com/smuttynose/downs3.html.

Downs, John William, and Gayle Patch Kadlik. *Sprays of Salt: Reminiscences of a Native Shoaler*. Portsmouth, NH: Peter E. Randall, 1997.

The Friends of Seguin Home Page. http://www.seguinisland.org/index.htm.

"Frozen in Ice - Maine Office of Tourism." Home - Maine Office of Tourism. http://www.visitmaine.com/attractions/sightseeing_tours/lighthouse/tales_legends/frozen_in_ice/

Haunted Lighthouses - Legends and Lore. http://www.hauntedlights.com/haunted2.html.

"History of U.S. Lightships." PalletMaster's Work Shop. http://www.palletmastersworkshop.com/lightship.html.

Holland, F. Ross. *America's Lighthouses: An Illustrated History*. New York: Dover, 1988.

Johnson, Tim. "VPR News: History Under the Waves: The General Butler." Vermont Public Radio: Home of VPR News and VPR Classical, and Vermont's NPR News Source. Accessed February 14, 2011. http://www.vpr.net/news_detail/85417/.

Knapp, Lewis G. *Stratford and the Sea*. Charleston, SC: Arcadia, 2002. Print.

Kobbe, Gustav. "Life in a Lighthouse."*In Century Magazine*, 365-74. Vol. 47.

Lanigan-Schmidt, Therese. *Ghostly Beacons: Haunted Lighthouses of North America*. Atglen, PA: Whitford Press, 2000.

"Lighthouse Digest - America's Lighthouse News & History Magazine." Lighthouse Digest - America's Lighthouse News & History Magazine. http://lighthousedigest.com/.

"Legendary Lighthouses." PBS: Public Broadcasting Service. http://www.pbs.org/legendarylighthouses.

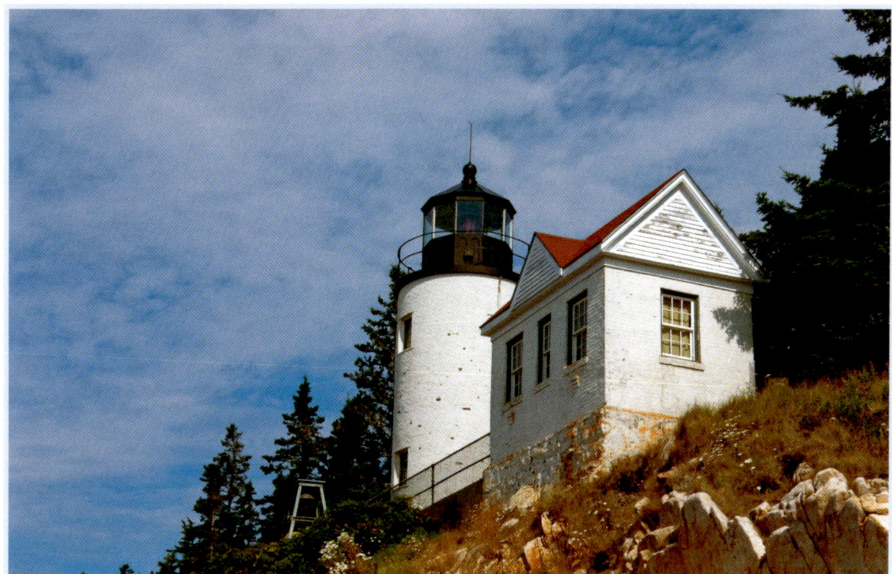

Bass Harbor Lighthouse in the Acadia region of Maine.

Lighthouse Friends. http://lighthousefriends.com/.

"Lighthouse Keepers in the Nineteenth Century." US National Park Service - Experience Your America. http://www.nps.gov/history/maritime/keep/keephero.htm.

Loubat, Joseph Florimond. *The Medallic History of the United States of America, 1776-1876.* New Milford: Connectiout, 1967.

Morrison, John H. *History of American Steam Navigation.* New York: Argosy-Antiquarian, 1967.

Noble, Dennis L. *Lighthouses & Keepers: The U.S. Lighthouse Service and Its Legacy.* Annapolis, MD: Naval Institute Press, 2004.

Noble, Dennis L. *Rescued by the U.S. Coast Guard: Great Acts of Heroism since 1878.* Annapolis, MD: Naval Institute Press, 2005. Google.

"Portland Head Lighthouse History." New England Lighthouses: A Virtual Guide - Photos, History, Tours, Cruises, Coastal Accommodations and More. http://lighthouse.cc/portlandhead/history.html.

"Rescue of Keeper's Daughter." Friends of Wood Island Light. http://www.woodislandlighthouse.org/xHistory/Rescue/index.html.

"RoadsideAmerica.com." Roadside America. http://www.roadsideamerica.com/.

Roberts, Bruce, Cheryl Shelton-Roberts, and Ray Jones. *American Lighthouses: A Comprehensive Guide to Exploring Our National Coastal Treasures.* Guilford, CT: Globe Pequot, 2012. Google.

"Sailor' the Famous Wood Island Light Fog Dog." Old News from Southern Maine. http://www.someoldnews.com/?p=485.

"Seguin Island Lighthouse, near Popham Beach, Maine." New England Lighthouses: A Virtual Guide - Photos, History, Tours, Cruises, Coastal Accommodations and More. http://www.lighthouse.cc/seguin/.

"Shipwrecks of Lake Champlain: Sailing Canal Boat General Butler." Lake Champlain Maritime Museum Home Page. http://www.lcmm.org/shipwrecks_history/uhp/general_butler.htm.

Snow, Edward Rowe. *Adventures, Blizzards, and Coastal Calamities*. New York: Dodd, Mead, 1978.

Snow, Edward Rowe. *The Lighthouses of New England*. Beverly, MA: Commonwealth Editions, 2002.

Snow, Edward Rowe. *Women of the Sea; [stories]*. New York: Dodd, Mead, 1962.

Strout, John. "Portland Head Light: A Strout Tradition." The Lighthouse Depot. May 1997. http://www.lighthousedepot.com/lite_digest.asp?action=get_article&sk=170.

Tague, Brian. "History of the Flying Santa." Friends of Flying Santa. http://www.flyingsanta.com/.

Theroux, Joseph P. "Flying Santa: Edward Rowe Snow and the Romance of History." *Historic Nantucket* 57 (Winter 2008): 18.

"United States Coast Guard Awards - Marcus Hanna." U.S. Coast Guard Home Page. http://www.uscg.mil/history/awards/28JAN1885.asp.

"US Lifesaving Service History." U.S. Coast Guard Home Page. http://www.uscg.mil/tcyorktown/Ops/NMLBS/Surf/surf1.asp.

"USCG: Frequently Asked Questions." U.S. Coast Guard Home Page. http://www.uscg.mil/history/people/Maria_Bray.asp.

Vaughan, Marcia K., and Bill Farnsworth. *Abbie Against the Storm: tTe True Story of a Young Heroine and a Lighthouse*. Portland, Or. Beyond Words Pub., 1999.

"Wood Island Lighthouse, Maine at Lighthousefriends.com." Lighthouse Friends. http://www.lighthousefriends.com/light.asp?ID=549.

"The Wreck of the General Butler, State of Vermont's Underwater Historic Preserve." Victory Sports Dive Shop - Colchester Vermont. http://victorysports.net/charters/genbutler.htm.

Other Schiffer Books on Related Subjects

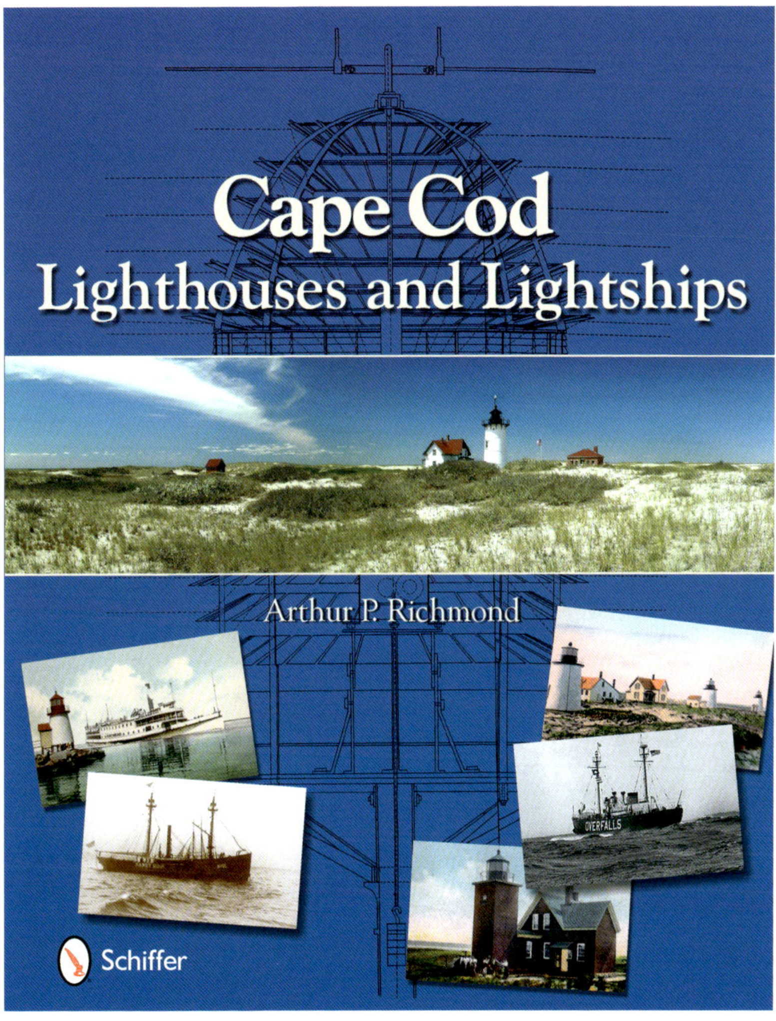

Cape Cod Lighthouses and Lightships
Arthur P. Richmond
ISBN 978-0-7643-3545-7

Other Schiffer Books by Allan Wood

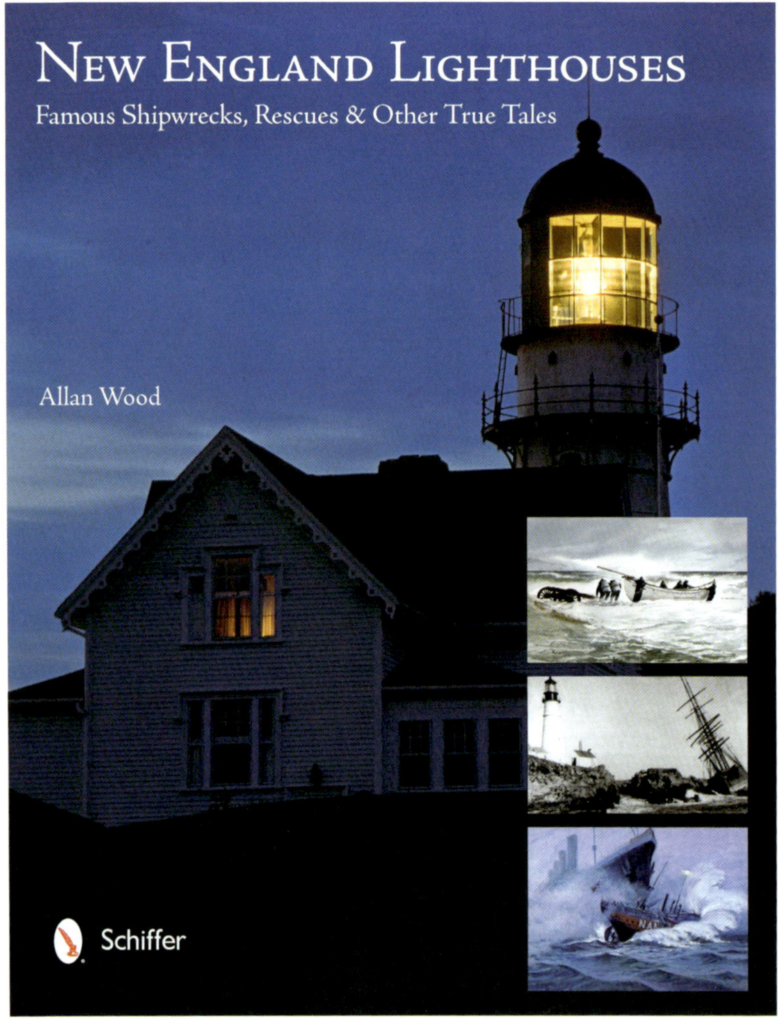

New England Lighthouses:
Famous Shipwrecks, Rescues, and Other Tales
ISBN 978-0-7643-4078-9

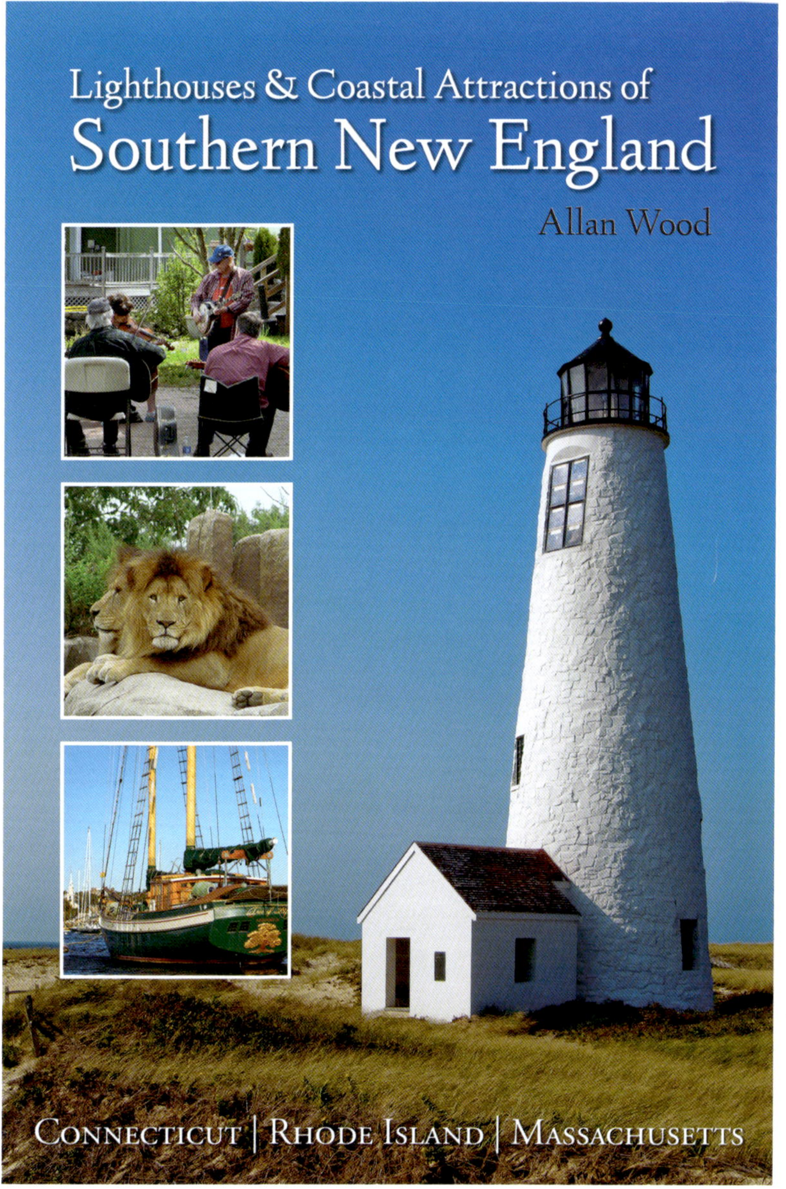

Lighthouses and Coastal Attractions of Southern New England: Connecticut, Rhode Island, and Massachusets

ISBN 978-0-7643-5245-4

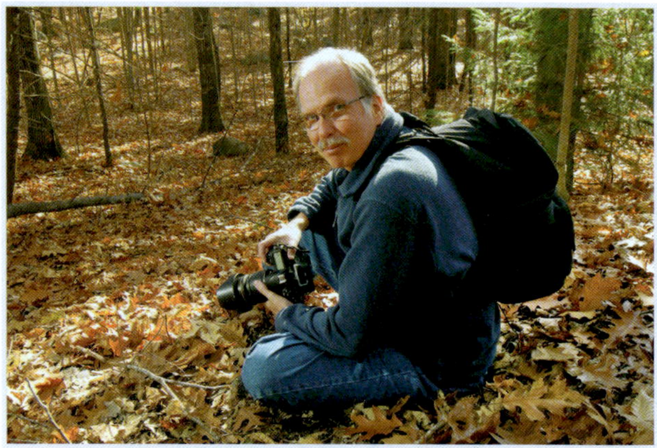

About the author

Allan Wood has been a college educator in business, photography, and digital media for many years. He has always had a passion for researching and photographing New England's lighthouses, has published many images, and lives near New Hampshire's seacoast with his family.